The Italian Yearbook of International Law

The Italian Yearbook of International Law

VOLUME 27

The titles published in this series are listed at *brill.com/iyil*

The Italian Yearbook of International Law Volume XXVII (2017)

BRILL
NIJHOFF

LEIDEN | BOSTON

Typeface for the Latin, Greek, and Cyrillic scripts: "Brill". See and download: brill.com/brill-typeface.

ISSN 0391-5107
E-ISSN 2211-6133
ISBN 978-90-04-39179-6 (hardback)

Editorial assistance for this volume has been provided by Anna Riddell. Manuscripts, books for review and correspondence may be sent to THE ITALIAN YEARBOOK OF INTERNATIONAL LAW - Prof. Daniele Amoroso, Dipartimento di Giurisprudenza, University of Cagliari, Via Nicolodi 102, 09123 Cagliari (Italy) and/or by e-mail to italianyearbook@gmail.com.

Each article submitted with a view to publication in the IYIL is subject to peer-review by two anonymous referees.

CONTENTS

NOTES AND COMMENTS

PRACTICE OF INTERNATIONAL COURTS AND TRIBUNALS

ITALIAN PRACTICE RELATING TO INTERNATIONAL LAW

TREATY PRACTICE
(edited by *Marina Mancini*)

LEGISLATION
(edited by *Pia Acconci*)

BIBLIOGRAPHIES

LARISSA VAN DEN HERIK (ed.), *Research Handbook on UN Sanctions and International Law*, Cheltenham, Edward Elgar Publishing, 2017 *(Natalino Ronzitti)*; OONA A. HATHAWAY and SCOTT J. SHAPIRO, *The Internationalists. How a Radical Plan to Outlaw War Remade the World*, New York, Simon & Shuster, 2017 – PHILIPPE SANDS, *East West Street. On the Origins of "Genocide" and "Crimes against Humanity"*, London, Orion, 2016 *(Giorgio Sacerdoti)*; ZENO CRESPI REGHIZZI, *L'intervento "come non parte" nel processo davanti alla Corte internazionale di giustizia*, Milano, Giuffrè, 2017 *(Giorgio Sacerdoti)*; GIOVANNI ZARRA, *Parallel Proceedings in Investment Arbitration*, Den Haag and Torino, Eleven International Publishing and Giappichelli, 2017 *(Lorenzo Gradoni)*; LAURENT MANDERIEUX and MICHELE VELLANO (eds.), *Éthique globale, bonne gouvernance et droit international économique*, Torino, Giappichelli, 2017 *(Federico Lenzerini)*; ANTHEA ROBERTS, *Is International Law International?*, Oxford, Oxford University Press, 2017 *(Alessandra Asteriti)*; PAOLO PALCHETTI (ed.), *L'incidenza del diritto non scritto sul diritto internazionale ed europeo*, Napoli, Editoriale Scientifica, 2016 *(Pierfrancesco Rossi)*; ALEXANDER PROELSS (ed.), AMBER ROSE MAGGIO, EIKE BILTZA and OLIVER DAUM (assistant eds.), *United Nations Convention on the Law of the Sea: A Commentary*, München, Oxford and Baden-Baden, C. H. Beck/Hart/Nomos, 2017 *(Roberto Virzo)*.

LIST OF ABBREVIATIONS

Periodicals[*]

AFDI	Annuaire Français de Droit International
AJIL	American Journal of International Law
ASIL	American Society of International Law Proceedings
AVR	Archiv des Völkerrecht
BISD	GATT – Basic Instruments and Selected Documents
BYIL	British Yearbook of International Law
CI	La Comunità Internazionale
CML Rep.	Common Market Law Reports
CML Rev.	Common Market Law Review
Columbia JTL	Columbia Journal of Transnational Law
Cornell ILJ	Cornell International Law Journal
CS	Comunicazioni e Studi
CYIL	Canadian Yearbook of International Law
DCI	Diritto del Commercio Internazionale
DCSI	Diritto Comunitario e degli Scambi Internazionali
DPCE	Diritto Pubblico Comparato ed Europeo
DUDI	Diritti Umani e Diritto Internazionale
DUE	Il Diritto dell'Unione Europea
EC Bull.	Bulletin of the European Communities
ECLR	European Competition Law Review
ECR	European Court Reports
EdD	Enciclopedia del Diritto
EG	Enciclopedia Giuridica (Treccani)
EHRR	European Human Rights Reports
EJIL	European Journal of International Law
EL Rev.	European Law Review
ETS	European Treaty Series
Foro It.	Foro Italiano
Giur. Cost.	Giurisprudenza Costituzionale
Giur. It.	Giurisprudenza Italiana
GU	Gazzetta Ufficiale della Repubblica Italiana
GYIL	German Yearbook of International Law
Harvard ILJ	Harvard International Law Journal
HRLJ	Human Rights Law Journal

---

[*] The present list covers only the most frequently cited periodicals.

ICJ Pleadings	International Court of Justice, Pleadings, Oral Arguments, Documents
ICJ Reports	International Court of Justice, Reports of Judgments, Advisory Opinions and Orders
ICLQ	International and Comparative Law Quarterly
IJCP	International Journal of Cultural Property
ILDC	International Law in Domestic Courts
ILM	International Legal Materials
ILR	International Law Reports
Int. Lawyer	International Lawyer
Int. Org.	International Organization
IRRC	International Review of the Red Cross
IYIL	Italian Yearbook of International Law
JDI	Journal du Droit International
JICJ	Journal of International Criminal Justice
JIEL	Journal of International Economic Law
JWT	Journal of World Trade
Leiden JIL	Leiden Journal of International Law
Max Planck UNYB	Max Planck Yearbook of United Nations Law
NILR	Netherlands International Law Review
NYIL	Netherlands Yearbook of International Law
OIDU	Ordine Internazionale e Diritti Umani
OJ EC	Official Journal of the European Communities
OJ EU	Official Journal of the European Union
PCIJ Series	Permanent Court of International Justice, Series
QIL	Questions of International Law
RBDI	Revue Belge de Droit International
RCADI	Recueil des Cours de l'Académie de Droit International de La Haye/Collected Courses of the Hague Academy of International Law
RCGI	Rivista della Cooperazione Giuridica Internazionale
RDI	Rivista di Diritto Internazionale
RDIPP	Rivista di Diritto Internazionale Privato e Processuale
RECIEL	Review of European Community and International Environmental Law
RGA	Rivista Giuridica dell'Ambiente
RGDIP	Revue Générale de Droit International Public
RIDPC	Rivista Italiana di Diritto Pubblico Comunitario
RMUE	Revue du Marché Unique Européen
RTDH	Revue Trimestrielle des Droits de l'Homme
Schw. ZIER	Schweizerische Zeitschrift für Internationales und Europäisches Recht
Texas ILJ	Texas International Law Journal
UNTS	United Nations Treaty Series
Yale JIL	Yale Journal of International Law

YEL	Yearbook of European Law
YIEL	Yearbook of International Environmental Law
YIHL	Yearbook of International Humanitarian Law
YILC/ACDI	Yearbook of the International Law Commission/ Annuaire de la Commission du droit international
ZAÖRV	Zeitschrift für Ausländisches Öffentliches Recht und Völkerrecht

Italian legal acts

Law	Legge (Act of Parliament)
DL	Decreto Legge (Decree-Law) (Decree adopted by the Government in case of extreme urgency which has the same, albeit provisional, effect of a Law, and which must be approved by the Parliament within 60 days. On the contrary, it looses its legal effect)
D.Lgs.	Decreto Legislativo (Legislative Decree) (Decree adopted by the Government upon delegation by the Parliament)
DPR	Decreto del Presidente della Repubblica (Decree of the President of the Republic)
DPCM	Decreto Presidente del Consiglio dei Ministri (Decree of the President of the Council of Ministers or Prime Minister)
DM	Decreto Ministeriale (Ministerial Decree)
Reg.	Regolamento (Administrative Regulation)

ITALIAN COURTS

Tribunale	Court of First Instance
Corte d'Appello	Court of Appeals
Corte di Cassazione	Court of Cassation
TAR	Regional Administrative Tribunal
Consiglio di Stato	Council of State (Supreme Administrative Court)
Corte Costituzionale	Constitutional Court

Symposium
SANCTIONS AND RESTRICTIVE MEASURES
IN INTERNATIONAL LAW

AUTONOMOUS AND COLLECTIVE SANCTIONS IN THE INTERNATIONAL LEGAL ORDER

NIGEL D. WHITE[*]

Abstract

The UK government is currently proposing the enactment of a "Sanctions Act" upon the UK's withdrawal from the EU in 2019, embodying a right to impose "autonomous sanctions" against other states and non-state actors, on the basis that the UK will no longer be able to benefit from the EU's collective sanctioning competence. The spotlight is again on the nature and purposes of sanctions in international law. The article addresses the legal framework applicable to sanctions by, first of all, showing that the nature of sanctions is different in the international legal order to how it is conceived in domestic legal orders in that sanctions are primarily imposed in response to threats to or breaches of the peace and, in so doing, the analysis will distinguish sanctions from countermeasures and other non-forcible measures. It then proceeds to demonstrate that the values of peace and security that underpin sanctions are essentially normative and should be seen as part of the international legal order and enforceable through sanctions alongside other fundamental norms of international law. Whether viewed as responses to breaches of international law or not, the analysis shows that sanctions are collective measures exclusively within the competence of international organizations. Having established the conceptual and legal frameworks for understanding sanctions, the article considers sanctions imposed against states and non-state actors, and explores whether the move towards targeted sanctions is a form of collective response to violations of international law. The article finishes by considering that, in contrast to countermeasures and other measures of self-help, collective sanctions are inherently lawful, but can only be legally justified as measures adopted out of a necessity to prevent major ruptures to peace and international law.

Keywords: autonomous sanctions; collective sanctions; countermeasures; collective countermeasures; United Nations; Security Council; European Union; United States

1. INTRODUCTION

Sanctions are embedded in international relations but their status in international law is often controversial. In this context it is worth considering the UK

---

[*] Of the Board of Editors.

government's response to its consultation of 2017 on the "future legal framework for imposing and implementing sanctions", which would follow from the UK's withdrawal from the EU in 2019, and consequent inability to help shape, or rely on, the EU's sanctioning powers. The UK government states that the "UK needs to be able to impose and implement sanctions in order to comply with our obligations under the […] UN Charter and to support our wider foreign policy and national goals. Many of our current sanctions regimes are established via powers in the European Communities Act 1972 (ECA) so we will need new legal powers to replace those once the ECA is repealed".[1] In the White Paper of April 2017 that shaped the consultation, the government stated that "when the UK withdraws from the EU we will need new legal powers that are compliant with our domestic legal system"; these powers "will enable us to preserve and update UN sanctions, and to impose autonomous UK sanctions in coordination with our allies and partners".[2]

The idea that powers belonging to the EU as an international organization with separate legal personality could be straightforwardly claimed by the UK as a non-EU member state, in the form of a proposed "Sanctions Act",[3] does not withstand scrutiny unless there is a separate international, and not merely national, legal basis for such "autonomous" sanctioning powers. It is interesting that the UK did not feel the need to claim an international legal basis for autonomous sanctions (i.e. those imposed outside of the UN Charter or the EU Treaties), when the doctrine of countermeasures might have provided an obvious, though problematic, legal basis. The UK's failure to put forward an international legal basis might be due to the fact that it views sanctions as something much broader than temporary and proportionate non-forcible measures taken in response to a violation of international law (countermeasures). It certainly suggested this by depicting sanctions as "an important foreign policy and national security tool", which "can be used to coerce a change in behaviour, to constrain behaviour by limiting access to resources, or to communicate a clear political message".[4]

It follows that the UK government views sanctions as distinct from countermeasures and other non-forcible measures of self-help by linking sanctions to its foreign policy and security and not just as responses to violations of the UK's international legal rights by another state. This article shows that while the UN and EU have autonomous sanctioning powers, individual states do not possess

---

[1] HM Government, "Public consultation on the United Kingdom's future legal framework for imposing and implementing sanctions: Government response", August 2017, para I.1, available at: <https://assets.publishing.service.gov.uk/government/uploads/system/uploads/attachment_data/file/635101/consultation-uk-future-legal-framework-sanctions-government-response.pdf>.

[2] HM Government, "Public consultation on the United Kingdom's future legal framework for imposing and implementing sanctions", April 2017, p. 7, available at: <https://assets.publishing.service.gov.uk/government/uploads/system/uploads/attachment_data/file/609986/Public_consultation_on_the_UK_s_future_legal_framework_for_imposing_and_implementing_sanctions__Print_pdf_version_.pdf>.

[3] "Public consultation", *cit. supra* note 1, para I.2.

[4] "Public consultation", *cit. supra* note 2, p. 6.

them beyond limited rights of self-help most clearly embodied in the doctrine of countermeasures taken in response to breaches of their international rights by other states. However, in asserting a wider autonomous sanctioning right, the UK will be joining the US in this regard as advocates of unilateral sanctions.

The article addresses the legal framework applicable to sanctions by, first of all, showing that the nature of sanctions is different in the international legal order to how it is conceived in domestic legal orders in that sanctions are primarily imposed in response to threats to or breaches of the peace and, in so doing, the analysis will distinguish sanctions from countermeasures. It then proceeds to demonstrate that the values of peace and security that underpin sanctions are essentially normative and should be seen as part of the international legal order and enforceable through sanctions alongside other fundamental norms of international law. Whether viewed exclusively as responses to breaches of international law or not, the analysis shows that sanctions are collective measures exclusively within the competence of international organizations. Having set up the conceptual and legal frameworks for understanding sanctions, the article considers sanctions imposed against states and non-state actors, and explores whether the move towards targeted sanctions is a form of collective response to violations of international law. The article finishes by considering that, in contrast to countermeasures, collective sanctions are inherently lawful, but can only be legally justified as measures adopted out of necessity to prevent major ruptures to peace and international law.

2. INTERNATIONAL LAW AND SANCTIONS

Sanctions were defined by the Royal Institute of International Affairs in 1938 as "measures taken in support of law" that "are applied with and by the general authority, not by any individual".[5] This definition went further and stated that "with the substitution of the word 'state' for the word 'individual' this is true [...]] of the sanctions of international, as well as national, law".[6] The key feature is that sanctions are imposed by a central authority, a feature that is given even greater emphasis in this definition than the events that trigger the sanctions themselves. However, this is not without objection since it has already been seen that the UK, along with the US,[7] argues that measures taken by individual states without any authorization from the UN or regional organization, can constitute "autonomous sanctions". This, as shall be seen, is a term which is used in a broader sense than "countermeasures", which are responses to breaches of a state's interna-

---

[5] GRANT and BARKER, *Parry and Grant Encyclopaedic Dictionary of International Law*, 3rd ed., Oxford, 2009, p. 539.

[6] *Ibid.*

[7] DAMROSCH, "Enforcing International Law through Non-Forcible Measures", RCADI, Vol. 269, 1997, p. 9 ff., pp. 99-101; LOWENFELD, "Unilateral versus Collective Sanctions: An American's Perception" , in GOWLLAND-DEBBAS (ed.), *United Nations Sanctions and International Law*, The Hague, 2001, p. 95 ff.

tional rights by other states in the form of temporary and proportionate counter-breaches. It is also a term that overlaps with but remains distinct from acts of "retorsion", which are unfriendly acts of "discourtesy or unfriendliness" that are not inconsistent with the initiating state's existing obligations, and are not necessarily taken in response to breaches by the target state though they often will be.[8] Non-forcible measures are thus a disputed aspect of international law even though there is a great deal of practice of them by states as well as international organizations.

Even before an understanding of "sanctions" in international law can be achieved, there is an extensive, if rather inconclusive, jurisprudential debate as to whether sanctions are a central part of any legal system or, indeed, a definition of law. Without undertaking an exhaustive philosophical exposition it is worth contrasting some of these views because the debates shed light on whether sanctions are viewed as an element of law or as responses to its breach. Nineteenth century English legal positivism depicted law as the command of a sovereign backed by a sanction,[9] thereby making the sanction element not only a method of enforcement but an essential element of the law. Indeed, because of its lack of "command", "sovereign" as well as "sanction", Austin was of the view that international law was not law "properly so-called" and instead dismissively equated it with the laws of fashion in this regard.[10]

In contrast, twentieth century positivism as portrayed by Hart did not regard sanctions as central to the concept of law, dismissing theories of law as "coercive orders" that meet "at the outset with the objection that there are varieties of law found in all systems which, in three principal respects, do not fit this description", for example those conferring powers upon legal persons.[11] Indeed, for Hart, international law is the paradigmatic set of laws that lack a centralized enforcement or sanctioning element.[12] Schachter reinforced this view by pointing to UN practice that for much of the Cold War concentrated on lawmaking without much regard to compliance, enforcement or sanctions.[13] Others such as Brierly and Kunz agree that the international legal system is a primitive one in which highly decentralized sanctions do exist, but argue that their application was left to the legal persons in that system, namely sovereign states.[14] It can be seen that, as well as disagreement about the centrality of sanctions to an understanding of law, there is a division between those jurists who see centralization in some shape or form as being integral to sanctions, while others see them being directly imposed by states.

---

[8] RUYS, "Sanctions, Retorsions and Countermeasures", in VAN DEN HERIK (ed.), *Research Handbook on UN Sanctions and International Law,* Cheltenham, 2017, p. 19 ff., p. 24.

[9] PENNER, *McCoubrey and White's Textbook on Jurisprudence*, 4th ed., Oxford, 2008, p. 37.

[10] AUSTIN, *The Province of Jurisprudence Determined*, London, 1832, lecture 1.

[11] HART, *The Concept of Law*, 3rd ed., Oxford, 2012, p. 48.

[12] *Ibid.,* pp. 216-220.

[13] SCHACHTER, "United Nations Law", AJIL, 1994, p. 1 ff., pp. 9-10.

[14] BRIERLY, "Sanctions", Transactions of the Grotius Society, 1932, p. 68 ff.; KUNZ, "Sanctions in International Law", AJIL, 1960, p. 324 ff.

However, it is true to say that modern international law, especially after the Cold War, has witnessed both an increased institutional sanctions usage, and a clarification of the law concerning unilateral non-forcible measures. There is a growing understanding of the distinction between collective sanctions and unilateral countermeasures; the former being deployed for the "public" enforcement of community based norms, while the latter are used for the "private" enforcement of bilateral norms. Unilateral victim state responses to breaches of legal duties owed by another state are seen as non-forcible reprisals or, to use the modern term, countermeasures; whereas sanctions are a collective power given by groups of states to international organizations, namely the UN and regional organizations. In this vein, Abi-Saab defined sanctions as "coercive measures taken in execution of a decision of a competent social organ, i.e. an organ legally empowered to act in the name of the society or community that is governed by the legal system". Sanctions are distinct from "coercive measures taken individually by States or group of States outside a determination and a decision by a legally competent social organ". Such reprisals, countermeasures and acts of retorsion "are manifestations of 'self-help' or 'private justice', and their legality is confined to the very narrow limits within which 'remnants' of 'self-help' are still admitted in contemporary international law".[15]

Despite the post-1945 proliferation of international organizations, the ILC's Articles on the Responsibility of States for Internationally Wrongful Acts of 2001 did not include sanctions in its system of secondary rules, only countermeasures as a bilateral means of law enforcement in a decentralized system,[16] where an injured state "may seek to vindicate their rights and to restore the legal relationship" with the responsible state, a relationship that "has been ruptured by" an unlawful act.[17] As noted by Alland, "countermeasures are a mechanism of private justice", which produce "contradictions inherent in a self-assessed (i.e. auto-interpreted or auto-appreciated) decentralized policing of an international *ordre public*".[18] Provost is even more explicit in depicting the weaknesses of such a system when he writes that "the right of states unilaterally to assess a breach by another state and to validate what would otherwise be an illegal act has the potential of significantly destabilizing international relations".[19] The depiction of states' use of countermeasures as a form of policing, albeit of a potentially destabilizing kind, of an international *ordre public* is blurring countermeasures which are an auto-interpretive mechanism of law enforcement of bilateral rights and duties, with sanctions which are a collective response to threats to the public order, peace and stability of states. It is

---

[15] ABI-SAAB, "The Concept of Sanction in International Law", in GOWLLAND-DEBBAS (ed.), *cit. supra* note 7, p. 32 ff., p. 38. See further ZOLLER, *Peacetime Unilateral Remedies: An Analysis of Countermeasures*, Dobbs Ferry, NY, 1984, p. 106.

[16] Articles on Responsibility of States for Internationally Wrongful Acts (ARSIWA), 2001, Arts. 49-54.

[17] CRAWFORD, *The International Law Commission's Articles on State Responsibility*, Cambridge, 2002, p. 281.

[18] ALLAND, "The Definition of Countermeasures", in CRAWFORD, PELLET and OLLESON (eds.), *The Law of International Responsibility*, Oxford, 2010, p. 1127 ff., pp. 1223-1235.

[19] PROVOST, *State Responsibility in International Law*, Aldershot, 2002, p. xv.

worthwhile hypothesizing about why the ILC did not include the notion of sanctions within its secondary rules on state responsibility by suggesting that sanctions were beyond the ILC's remit given their more fundamental role as measures for preserving peace and security, and not just as secondary responses to breaches of the primary rules of international law.[20]

The distinction between "public" sanctions and "private" countermeasures is relatively straightforward to make when considering the paradigmatic instances of each. However, the concept of countermeasures as depicted by the ILC is very narrow and does not capture the range of state practice on unilateral non-forcible measures and other forms of economic coercion.[21] Bederman suggests that "the central conceptual mission" of the ILC's Articles on countermeasures was "the search for a polite international society".[22] He contends further that the Articles on countermeasures represent a "profound impulse toward social engineering for international relations [...] imagining a time in international life when unilateral and horizontal means of enforcement through robust self-help will be a thing of the past".[23] The narrow clarity of the ILC's Articles on countermeasures leaves a great deal of practice on non-forcible forms of coercion unregulated by international law.[24]

Despite Hart's view that international law epitomises a diffused reactive legal system,[25] the evidence is that there has been greater centralization of sanctions in the international legal order than the pure customary system depicted by Hart, and that sanctions adopted by those centralized organs are both lawful and legitimate. Moreover, such sanctions are the only clear forms of lawful non-forcible measures designed to enforce community norms. Private justice is left in the hands of states that want to respond to a breach of a bilateral legal relationship with another state; these responses are seen as acts of self-help, not autonomous sanctions. The problem is that there is a grey area in between collective sanctions and unilateral countermeasures, where states make a range of claims to be able to take non-forcible measures, which are either depicted as "collective countermeasures" or "autonomous sanctions" taken by states in response to what each participating state perceives as a breach of community norms or, indeed, threat to national interests. The use of the term "collective" in connection with "countermeasures" should not disguise the fact that such measures are not institutional and may well be adopted by each sanctioning state independently of any other. In fact the term "autonomous sanctions" more fairly embodies the type of power being claimed by states as a right exercised independently from any international organization.

---

[20] CRAWFORD, *cit. supra* note 7, p. 168, p. 282, preferring the term "measures" to "sanctions".

[21] ELAGAB, *The Legality of Non-Forcible Counter-Measures in International Law*, Oxford, 1988, pp. 212-213.

[22] BEDERMAN, "Counterintuiting Countermeasures", AJIL, 2002, p. 817 ff., p. 819.

[23] *Ibid.*, p. 831.

[24] RUYS, *cit. supra* note 8, p. 24.

[25] HART, *cit. supra* note 11, p. 213.

3. Sanctions: Enforcing Peace or Law?

According to Kelsen "law is, by its very nature, a coercive order".[26] For Kelsen sanctions are integral to law in that law specifies the proscribed behaviour and also the response to such behaviour.[27] Kelsen was clear that the same conception applies to a legal order providing for collective security when he wrote that "a social order guaranteeing collective security is by its very nature a legal order, and a legal order is a system of norms providing for sanctions".[28] While this appears to be more difficult to sustain at the international level where the sanction element of any law is often unspecified or unused, Kelsen's analysis of sanctions is a normative one meaning that sanctions ought to be imposed not that they will be.

Even in theories such as Hart's, in which sanctions are not viewed as primary rules themselves, they are seen as a form of punishment or response to breaches of those rules, responses that become more centralized as the legal system develops from a primitive set of primary rules.[29] In Hart's words: "most systems have, after some delay, seen the advantages of further centralization of social pressure; and have partially prohibited the use of physical punishments or violent self-help by private individuals". Instead, legal systems have "supplemented the primary rules of obligation by further secondary rules, specifying [...] the penalties for violation", including an "exclusive power" conferred on officials of the system to impose penalties. "These secondary rules provide the centralized official 'sanctions' of the system".[30]

The issue of whether sanctions are primary rules of international law or secondary rules of responsibility where they would sit alongside countermeasures remains under-analysed, but certainly for Kelsen a sanction is part of the law not simply a consequence of its breach. Furthermore, according to Kelsen, and implicitly for most commentators, sanctions are "coercive reactions against an actual violation of the law", or alternatively, against suspected or expected violations.[31] This formulation does allow for some anticipatory sanctions, but the triggers remain actual or potential violations of the law. In contrast, it is clear that in the international legal order, especially in its collective security component, "sanctions" are not confined to actual or potential violations of international law, rather the primary triggers are actual or threatened ruptures of the peace. In this way they reinforce the basic pre-conditions necessary for any legal order to exist. Kelsen accepts that legal systems generally recognise the legitimacy of coercive

---

[26] KELSEN, *The Law of the United Nations*, New York, 1950, p. 706. ID. , *Principles of International Law*, New York, 1966, p. 22.

[27] KELSEN, "The Pure Theory of Law, Its Method and Fundamental Concepts", Law Quarterly Review, 1934, p. 474 ff., pp. 484-485.

[28] KELSEN, *Collective Security under International Law*, Washington DC, 1957, p. 101.

[29] HART, *cit. supra* note 11, pp. 91-99.

[30] *Ibid.*, pp. 97-98.

[31] KELSEN, *cit. supra* note 28, p. 102.

measures that have no relation to actual or potential violations of the law but, nevertheless, remain necessary to maintain or restore peace and security.

However, the examples given by Kelsen show that this is the exception rather than the rule within national legal orders; his examples of when sanctions may be imposed for reasons of necessity include the forcible destruction of buildings to prevent the spread of fire, or the forcible internment of people suffering infectious diseases in order to prevent an epidemic from spreading.[32] Arguably, in the international order, these sorts of exceptions are the norm so that sanctions are imposed by the UN Security Council to address threats to the peace,[33] whether or not those threats entails actual or possible violations of the law.[34] A different way of looking at it would be to see sanctions being directed at shoring up the basic conditions of peace and security necessary for a legal order to survive, thereby making sanctions part of the legal order. Kelsen does not go quite this far, but accepts that "by declaring the conduct of a state to be a threat to, or breach of, the peace, the Security Council may create new law", imposing an "obligation to refrain from this conduct".[35]

For Gowlland-Debbas, however, sanctions are an aspect of the "creation of international institutional responses to violations of […] core norms". She argues that although Chapter VII measures imposed by the Security Council were not intended to be restricted to cases of non-compliance with international law, the practice of the Council has moved considerably towards using its powers to address the responsibility of states for breaches of core norms of international law.[36] In a sense this anticipates the arguments for a Responsibility to Protect in international law emerging in 2001 with the proposition that when a state has failed to protect its population from the commission of core crimes then a responsibility lies with the Security Council to take measures, a proposition that remains *de lege ferenda*.[37] While it is argued in this article that sanctions against states remain primarily designed to tackle threats to or breaches of international peace and security, and only secondarily law, the development of sanctions against non-state actors is indicative of a trend towards punishment for violations of the law, given that this development has occurred against the background in international law and institutions of a move towards addressing individual responsibility for core crimes. Nonetheless, sanctions against non-state actors remain a mixture of enforcing peace and law but their primary purpose is the former.[38]

---

[32] *Ibid.*

[33] Charter of the United Nations, 24 October 1945, 1 UNTS XVI, Art. 39.

[34] KUNZ, *cit. supra* note 14, p. 329.

[35] KELSEN, *cit. supra* note 26, p. 736.

[36] GOWLLAND-DEBBAS, "UN Sanctions and International Law: An Overview", in GOWLLAND-DEBBAS (ed.), *cit. supra* note 7, p. 1 ff., pp. 7-9; GOWLLAND-DEBBAS, "Security Council Enforcement Action and Issues of State Responsibility", ICLQ, 1994, p. 55 ff.

[37] FOCARELLI, "The Responsibility to Protect Doctrine and Humanitarian Intervention: Too Many Ambiguities for a Working Doctrine", Journal of Conflict & Security Law, 2008, p. 191 ff.

[38] WHITE, "Sanctions against Non-State Actors", in RONZITTI (ed.), *Coercive Diplomacy, Sanctions and International Law*, Leiden, 2016, p. 127 ff., pp. 135-138.

Arguably the norms of the international *ordre public* are not only *jus cogens* norms, but are also those supporting the normative concepts of "peace" and "security", where both non-forcible and forcible sanctions are essential components of those norms. If then "peace" and "security" are considered fundamental norms of the international legal order underpinning those proscribing "aggression", "genocide" and "crimes against humanity", then the role and functions of sanctions in their enforcement can be considered as intra-legal issues. This contrasts with the orthodoxy where sanctions taken for the purposes of securing peace and security are seen in part as extra-legal, embodied in the statement by Kelsen that the purpose of enforcement "is not to maintain or restore law, but to maintain or restore peace, which is not necessarily identical with the law".[39] However, although it is common to see discussion of "peace" and "security" as international norms in international relations discourse,[40] they are not seen in this way in international law where states are protected from "aggression" or "uses of force" as peremptory norms, narrower concepts than "threats to or breaches of peace and security". The latter norms are protected to some extent by the Security Council,[41] but are traditionally seen as coming within that's organ's political discretion rather than its legal obligations,[42] despite that organ having "primary responsibility for the maintenance of international peace and security", with ensuing "duties".[43]

One obvious objection to the inclusion of the norms of "peace" and "security" in the hierarchy of international law is their apparent subjectivity.[44] The debates about what is a "threat to the peace", even a "breach of the peace" within the meaning of Article 39, are well known,[45] but the fact is that the Security Council in determining that a threat exists and then imposing sanctions on a target state or individual, has both determined the law and enforced it.[46] Despite its unappealing nature, at least to believers in objective laws,[47] this form of constructivist intersubjective agreement arguably enables international law to develop to achieve new understandings of security in an ever-changing world.[48]

In order to ensure the survival of the planet, more specifically the system of international relations based on nation-states, states and other key actors take measures to establish the basic conditions for the control of violence. Without

---

[39] KELSEN, *cit. supra* note 26, p. 294.

[40] FOOT and WALTER, "Global Norms and Major State Behaviour: The Case of China and the United States", European Journal of International Relations, 2012, p. 1 ff., p. 6.

[41] UN Charter, Art. 39.

[42] KELSEN, *cit. supra* note 26, 733.

[43] UN Charter, Art. 24(1).

[44] BUZAN, WAEVER, and DE WILDE, *Security: A New Framework for Analysis*, Boulder, 1998, pp. 23-26.

[45] KRISCH, "Article 39", in SIMMA (ed.), *The Charter of the United Nations: A Commentary*, 3rd ed., Oxford, 2012, p. 1272 ff., pp. 1278-1294.

[46] ORAKHELASHVILI, *Collective Security*, Oxford, 2011, p. 189.

[47] KOSKENNIEMI, *The Gentle Civilizer of Nations: The Rise and Fall of International Law 1870-1960*, Cambridge, 2001, p. 188.

[48] HURD, *International Organizations: Politics, Law and Practice*, 2nd ed., Cambridge, 2011, p. 24.

controlling and containing violence in international relations it would not be possible to establish a viable international political and legal order. Overall, the aim of collective measures such as sanctions is to reduce the levels of violence between states, and increasingly within states and against civilian populations (the achievement of peace); by addressing existential threats to states, peoples and groups (the achievement of security).

Historically, peace has been equated to the absence of wars; and security was viewed as the security of states from aggression by other states;[49] and international laws and structures have reflected this. However, as international laws and institutions have been strengthened in response to major ruptures of international peace, especially at the end of major conflicts with the creation first of the League of Nations and then the UN, there has been a deepening of the international consensus on what is meant by peace and security,[50] to cover sustainable peace within and between states, and the security of groups and individuals as well as states.[51] Having said that, it is true to say that international law remains based on state-security, reflected in fundamental inter-state compacts, and has been reinforced by a continued state-based monopoly on the means of using force.[52] However, changes in the understanding of state sovereignty mean that it is no longer absolute, rather it is qualified by a responsibility towards civilian populations leading to debates as to where responsibility to protect the population falls when the home government fails to act to stop core crimes being committed.[53]

The problem remains that measures taken to enforce the peace and security between states or within states are not seen as measures to enforce the law and, therefore, are kept distinct from our inherent notion that sanctions are taken to do just that.[54] However, a reconceptualization of "peace" and "security" as normative concepts that are actually fundamental principles of the international legal order would make the framing of sanctions, the analysis of them, and issues of their compliance with other laws, principally one of law.[55] This has the advantage

---

[49] ROTHWELL, SCOTT and HEMMINGS, "The Search for 'Antarctic Security'", in HEMMINGS, ROTHWELL and SCOTT (eds.), *Antarctic Security in the Twenty-First Century,* London, 2012, p. 1 ff., p. 3.

[50] NASU, "Law and Policy for Antarctic Security: An Analytical Framework", in HEMMINGS, ROTHWELL and SCOTT (eds.), *cit. supra* note 49, p. 18 ff., p. 24.

[51] Note by the President of the Security Council, The Responsibility of the Security Council in the Maintenance of International Peace and Security, 31 January 1992, UN Doc. S/23500, OXIO 127; FALK, *On Humane Governance: Toward a New Global Politics*, London, 1995, p. 147; HAMPSON, "Human Security", in WILLIAMS (ed.), *Security Studies: An Introduction*, London, 2008, p. 229 ff., p. 231.

[52] WEBER, "Excerpts from Politics as a Vocation", in LEMERT (ed.), *Social Theory: The Multicultural and Classic Readings*, Boulder, 1999, p. 111; KRAHMANN, "Private Security Companies and the State Monopoly on Violence: A Case of Norm Change?", PRIF-Reports No. 88, 2009, p. 2, available at: <https://www.hsfk.de/fileadmin/HSFK/hsfk_downloads/prif88_02.pdf>.

[53] 2005 World Summit Outcome, UN Doc. A/RES/60/1 (2005), paras. 138-139.

[54] FARRALL, *United Nations Sanctions and the Rule of Law*, Cambridge, 2007, p. 7.

[55] TSAGOURIAS and WHITE, *Collective Security: Theory, Law and Practice,* Cambridge, 2013, pp. 32-37.

of being able to judge the institutions adopting sanctions by standards of law rather than solely by reference to standards of effectiveness and impact. As long as "peace" and "security" remain outside mainstream international law there will be a tension and confusion between the political discretion at the heart of sanctions and understanding that sanctions are essentially legal-coercive means to ensure that laws are complied with and the basic conditions of peace and security necessary for the continued existence of the legal order are maintained.

4. SANCTIONING AUTHORITIES

Thus far, the understanding of sanctions is of non-forcible measures imposed by centralized authorities in response to breaches of peace, security and, increasingly law, while countermeasures and other acts of non-forcible self-help are imposed by a state in responses to breaches of law suffered at the hands of another state. Collective countermeasures blur this distinction to some extent in that they represent non-forcible attempts by non-victim states to enforce self-defined community norms outside of the institutional collective security regime and the bilateral mechanisms of normal countermeasure.[56]

In theory, sanctions imposed by organizations and countermeasures imposed by states are distinct.[57] However, if a collective right to take countermeasures is recognized, whereby states are permitted to take measures against a state in breach of obligations owed *erga omnes* i.e. to the whole international community, the line between countermeasures and sanctions appears less clear. Nevertheless, the concepts of collective sanctions and collective countermeasures are not the same, given that countermeasures, whether unilateral or collective, are rights of states to respond to violations of international law and signify temporary non-fulfilment of obligations owed by the victim state(s) to the responsible state; while sanctions are powers exercised by competent organizations that can go above and beyond suspending any existing obligations of states and, moreover, are not currently conceived primarily as punishments for violations of international law, but responses to threats to international public order. It follows that a sanctions regime could, like proportionate countermeasures, merely lead to the suspension of trade and arms agreements with a state; but it could go further and terminate those agreements and outlaw any further agreements on trade, arms or others areas such as technology and finance and, furthermore, could oblige all member states to adopt such measures.

The type of sanctions just described can only be applied lawfully by a few international actors, namely the UN Security Council under Chapter VII of the

---

[56] KATSELLI-PROUKAKI, *The Problem of Enforcement in International Law: Countermeasures, the Non-Injured State and the Idea of International Community,* London, 2010, pp. 90-209; DAWIDOWICZ, *Third Party Countermeasures in International Law,* Cambridge, 2017, pp. 3-5.

[57] ZOLLER, *Peacetime Unilateral Remedies: An Analysis of Countermeasures,* New York, 1984, p. 106.

UN Charter, and regional organizations as identified under Chapter VIII of the UN Charter and empowered by their own constituent treaties. As such, sanctions are clearly the result of a significant attribution of powers by the member states to those organizations. The limited range of institutional actors with sanctioning competence is not only due to the hierarchy contained in the UN Charter, whereby regional organizations are limited in their enforcement powers by the authority of the UN Security Council, but also by the obligation on member states to give priority to obligations arising from the UN Charter over those arising from other treaties including regional ones.[58]

This explains which organizations have competence but it does not explain why states do not have such. That lack is because only the UN and competent regional organizations have the power to impose *collective* measures that bind all member states to impose non-forcible measures against a target state. No single state has the power to bind other states to act in this way, although they may try to enmesh other states and actors by including an extraterritorial element in unilateral non-forcible measures imposed on a target state. For instance, under the US Helms-Burton Act 1996 penalties for breach of the Cuban embargo (emplaced under Presidential Executive Order since 1962),[59] for example importing into the US any goods of Cuban origin, in whole or in part, were increased.[60] Specifically, Title III of the Act granted US citizens a remedy in domestic courts against anyone "trafficking" in property that was US-owned before its seizure by the Cuban government in the early 1960s. This was one of the so-called extra-territorial effects of Helms-Burton objected to by the UK and EU amongst others as a breach of international laws limiting jurisdiction.[61]

Such over-reach is not an issue for most competent international organizations. Member states have not simply given the organization in question the right to take measures that each of them has individually, but have collectively given the organization a power to take measures against a target state that will require each member to adjust its diplomatic, financial, economic or sporting relations with the targeted state or non-state actor. No state has the power or right to ensure collective sanctions are taken under international law, although they have the right to take individual non-forcible countermeasures in response to violations of their rights by other states.[62]

---

[58] UN Charter, Arts. 53 and 103.

[59] Proclamation 3347 – Embargo on All Trade with Cuba, 3 February 1962, in which the President, acting under the Foreign Assistance Act 1961, prohibited "the importation into the United States of all goods of Cuban origin and all goods imported from or through Cuba".

[60] Cuban Liberty and Democratic Solidarity (Libertad) Act of 1996 (Helms-Burton Act), 110 Stat. 785, Section 110(a).

[61] UK Protection of Trading Interests Acts 1980, applied by The Extraterritorial US Legislation (Sanctions against Cuba, Iran and Libya) (Protection of Trading Interests) Order 1996, SI 3171, to trade with Cuba; Council Regulation (EC) Regulation 2271/96, 22 November 1996. Both remain in force, though there has been little enforcement.

[62] But see MORRISON, "The Role of Regional Organizations in the Enforcement of International Law", in DELBRUCK (ed.), *The Allocation of Law Enforcement Authority in the*

The UN Security Council is expressly empowered to impose non-forcible measures, including the "complete or partial interruption of economic relations and of rail, sea, air, postal, telegraphic, radio, and other means of communication, and the severance of diplomatic relations", in response to threats to the peace, breaches of the peace and acts of aggression.[63] This power is granted to the organization, specifically the Security Council, by the founding states to use against a member state and to oblige other members to so act,[64] although the almost universal nature of the UN has meant that the Council tends to imposes the obligations created by its non-forcible measures on all states, an extension that could be said to develop the obligation on the UN to ensure that non-member states act in accordance with the UN's principles "as far as may be necessary for the maintenance of international peace and security".[65] Nonetheless, this falls short of imposing obligation on non-member states meaning that the UN's extension of its sanctions' obligations to "all states" is problematic, as non-member states have not consented to the adoption of such measures. Arguments that the UN Charter is the constitution of the international community may help overcome this limitation but they have not been fully developed or explained.[66]

Examples of regional organizations with sanctioning competence include the Organization of American States (OAS) which, in response to any "fact or situation that might endanger the peace of America",[67] is empowered through its Organ of Consultation to take the following non-forcible measures against member states: "recall of chiefs of diplomatic missions; breaking of diplomatic relations; breaking of consular relations; partial or complete interruption of economic relations or of rail, sea, air, postal, telegraphic, telephonic, and radiotelephonic or radiotelegraphic communications [...]".[68] The African Union (AU), which replaced the Organisation of African Unity (OAU) in 2000, provides that "any Member State that fails to comply with the decisions and policies of the Union may be subjected to [...] sanctions, such as the denial of transport and communications links with other Member States, and other measures of a political and economic nature to be determined by the Assembly".[69] The EU's sanctioning competence, however, is external facing and targeted at non-member states although they only bind EU member states.[70] Given that these external measures

International System, Berlin, 1995, p. 39 ff., pp. 46-7, where he states that organizations cannot possess more powers than member states.

[63] UN Charter, Arts. 39 and 41.

[64] *Ibid.*, Art. 25.

[65] *Ibid.*, Art. 2(6).

[66] FASSBENDER, *The United Nations Charter and the Constitution of the International Community*, Leiden, 2009, p. 78.

[67] Charter of the Organisation of American States, 30 April 1948, entered into force 13 December 1951, Art. 29.

[68] Inter-American Treaty of Reciprocal Assistance (Rio Treaty), 2 September 1947, Art. 8.

[69] Constitutive Act of the African Union, 1 July 2000, Art. 23(2).

[70] Treaty on European Union, 7 February 1992, Art. 29; Treaty on the Functioning of the European Union, 13 December 2007, Art. 215. See GESTRI, "Sanctions Imposed by the

do not bind the target state but only EU member states, the lack of consent (to be bound) by the target state is not a legally insurmountable problem. However, assuming that a collective sanctioning power belongs to an organization for the purpose of controlling its membership, then the legal basis claimed for the EU's external measures is that they are a form of collective countermeasures.[71] If the EU's external non-forcible measures extend beyond the doctrine of countermeasures the legal ground becomes more unstable in that they would represent steps towards claiming autonomous sanctioning powers by a regional organization.

Chapter VIII of the UN Charter governs relations between the UN and regional organizations. Under this framework regional organizations have autonomy in matters of peace and security "as are appropriate for regional action", as long as they act consistently with the purposes and principles of the UN Charter. Furthermore, disputes between states within the region should be subject to peaceful settlement attempts by the regional organization before any reference to the UN Security Council.[72] As regards "enforcement action" by organizations for the purposes of collective or regional security, Article 53 of the Charter empowers the Security Council to utilize regional organizations for enforcement action taken under its authority, but clearly stipulates that "no enforcement action shall be taken" by regional organizations "without the authorization" of the UN Security Council. The ambiguity in the meaning of "enforcement action" is whether it covers both economic and military measures.[73]

Placing sanctions in the hands of central organs of a legal order is certainly the norm in modern domestic legal orders, but this has not been fully realized in the international legal order. For a start, sanctions are primarily adopted in response to threats to international public order, not breaches of international law.[74] Furthermore, while the use of military force by states is ruled out by the UN Charter except in the exercise of the right of self-defence or under the authority of the Security Council,[75] there is no equivalent clear prohibition on states deploying autonomous non-forcible measures.[76] It follows that while many domestic legal orders have ruled out self-help, this has not happened in the international legal order at least in the case of non-forcible measures. Nonetheless, the supremacy of the Security Council should not be underestimated, given that it is empowered to adopt sanctions that oblige member states to take such measures against the target state, group or individuals in order to address threats to the peace.[77] Finally, there is the aforementioned requirement that regional enforcement action needs authorization from the Security Council.[78] The intention was

---

European Union: Legal and Institutional Aspects", in RONZITTI (ed.), *cit. supra* note 8, p. 70 ff, p. 100.

[71] GESTRI, *cit. supra* note 70, p. 99.
[72] UN Charter, Art. 52.
[73] WALTER, "Article 53", in SIMMA (ed.), *cit. supra* note 45, p. 1478 ff., p. 1481.
[74] TSAGOURIAS and WHITE, *cit. supra* note 55, p. 224.
[75] UN Charter, Arts. 2(4), 42, 51 and 53.
[76] ELAGAB, *cit. supra* note 21.
[77] UN Charter, Arts. 25, 39 and 41.
[78] *Ibid.*, Art. 53.

to create supranational competence in the Security Council to oblige all member states (thereby having almost universal effect) to take non-forcible enforcement action, a competence not possessed by any other organization or actor,[79] although regional organizations have carved out an autonomy to impose sanctions on their own membership by dint of consent (in the treaty) and practice. The EU's extra-regional application of sanctions is exceptional in this regard and can either be put down to a form of collective countermeasures or, most controversially, as a form of autonomous sanctions if they extend beyond the limitations upon countermeasures.

Gestri states that with over thirty sanctions programmes in place, often imposed autonomously from the UN Security Council, the EU has become a "key player in the sanctions game", and despite its claim to always act in full conformity with international law, the "EU can be regarded as a trailblazer by the advocates of the controversial doctrine of collective countermeasures in reaction to *erga omnes* obligations, having on numerous occasions adopted sanctions without being individually affected by the breach of international law allegedly committed by the target state".[80] Furthermore, Gestri points to the pulling power of the EU on third states to bring their conduct vis a vis the target state into line with the EU's,[81] and the broadening jurisdictional scope of EU sanctions in spite of its criticisms of the extraterritorial extension of sanction regimes by the United States.[82] Collective countermeasures taken in response to violation of fundamental international laws remain controversial but, on a spectrum of legality, a reasonable argument can be made in their favour. In contrast, if sanctions going beyond countermeasures were to be imposed by the EU, it would become an even more controversial trailblazer for an autonomous external sanctioning power for regional organizations.

Institutional powers and practice on sanctions is difficult to reconcile with orthodox views of international law, where the state is the principal actor on the international stage with the most complete set of international rights and duties. Consequently, there have been attempts to rationalize the sanctioning power of organization by characterizing it as the collective application of rights belonging to states.[83] However, the cat was let out of the bag so to speak as soon the founding states adopted the UN Charter in 1945, placing sanctioning power in the hands of a separate corporate entity – the UN Security Council.

---

[79] SCHREUER, "Comments", in DELBRUCK (ed.), *cit. supra* note 62, p. 82.

[80] GESTRI, *cit. supra* note 70, p. 99.

[81] *Ibid.*

[82] *Ibid.*, p. 79

[83] DOPAGNE, "Sanctions and Countermeasures by International Organizations", in COLLINS and WHITE (eds.), *International Organizations and the Idea of Autonomy: Institutional Independence in the International Legal Order*, London, 2011, p. 178 ff.

5. MOVING THE TARGET BUT NOT THE PURPOSE

Centralized institutional competence has been shown to have immense potential to impact upon states and other actors, although it remains incumbent
on member states to carry out their obligations under the Charter or under regional treaties. If states do not fulfil their obligations, sanctions remain symbolic.
However, increasingly effective supervision and enforcement of sanctions has
raised concerns about the legal parameters of such measures. Whether viewed as
integral to law or a consequence of law's breach, collective sanctions are not unlawful per se, unlike countermeasures by states the wrongfulness of which is only
precluded if they are taken in response to a prior breach of international law.[84]

So far we have seen that collective sanctions in the international legal order
are imposed in response to, or to prevent, threats to or breaches of the peace
which, at least in orthodox thinking, are not concepts embodied in law. However,
given that sanctions are imposed to protect extra-legal values that ensure basic
conditions of stability in the international order, it can be contended that they are
primordially lawful actions. This section explores the move from general to targeted sanctions in order to ascertain whether a change in target has been accompanied by a change in purpose, namely from enforcing peace to enforcing law.

The rare instances of UN collective sanctions imposed during the Cold War
had the appearance of community responses to violations of basic international
laws respecting human rights and self-determination specifically by white racist
regimes against the black majorities in Rhodesia and South Africa. However, a
close reading of the applicable resolutions indicates that the measures were taken
to tackle threats to international peace and security. The Security Council was
careful to base its determinations of threats to the peace on a combination of the
nature of the regimes, and the impact that those regimes' policies had on peace for
the region, with evidence that internal violent struggles for freedom were spreading to neighbouring countries. This is clearly encapsulated in Resolution 418
(1977) imposing a mandatory arms embargo against South Africa in 1977, when
the Security Council, "having regard to the policies and acts of the South African
Government", determined that "the acquisition by South Africa of arms and related *matériel* constitutes a threat to the maintenance of international peace and
security". Other resolutions adopted the typology of simply determining that the
situation in Southern Rhodesia was a threat to international peace and security,[85]
thereby not linking the determination to anything other than peace and security.

The more recent turn to targeted sanctions imposed against non-state actors and
regime elites are often explained as humane responses to concerns about the devastating effects of general sanctions imposed on Iraq to force it to withdraw from
Kuwait following its aggressive occupation of that country in 1990,[86] and instead

---

[84] ARSIWA, Art. 22.
[85] UN Doc. S/RES/232 (1966).
[86] UN Doc. S/RES/661 (1990).

to target those individual violators of international standards and law.[87] In fact, targeted sanctions were first imposed in the early 1990s against non-state actors who were in control of territory. In other words the rationale was similar to those sanctions imposed against states in terms of imposing measures against a territory and those groups exercising control over it in order to force them towards peace.

The early post-Cold War instances of sanctions against non-state actors were imposed against those holding power but who had not attained full status as state actors; measures in the 1990s were imposed against rebel groups with *de facto* belligerent status (e.g. UNITA in Angola and the Bosnian Serbs), or against *de facto* governments (e.g. the Taliban in Afghanistan). The measures against UNITA rebels were designed to force that armed group to accept the Peace Accords that it had previously signed but had breached through its continued military actions in Angola, thereby constituting a threat to international peace and security.[88] UN collective sanctions taken against the Bosnian Serbs in the 1990s, the party to the conflict seen as acting most often in violation of international humanitarian law,[89] remain measures aimed at restoring peace and security. While certain other non-forcible measures were taken on the basis that the violations of international law themselves constituted threats to the peace, particularly the creation of the ICTY,[90] non-forcible sanctions were imposed upon the Bosnian Serb leadership for refusing to settle peacefully and for continued fighting. In other words, they were designed to tackle the threat to the peace caused by the Bosnian Serbs' continued aggression and failure to accept various peace plans.[91] Furthermore, the non-forcible measures taken by the UN Security Council to tackle violations of international law (viz. the establishment of the ICTY) were not targeted at the Bosnian Serbs leadership per se but at individual violators of international criminal law (including individuals from other armed groups as well as emerging states). That aspect of the threat arising from the violence in Bosnia and consisting of violations of international law was addressed by the creation of an international criminal tribunal with powers of punishment, while the continuing conflict and refusal by the Bosnian Serbs to settle peacefully were addressed by a variety of non-forcible and forcible measures imposed by the Security Council.

Even historically the first UN sanctions regime was imposed against the illegitimate white racist regime in Rhodesia in the late 1960s, a *de facto* government, though the measures imposed were not targeted and had a wider impact on the population.[92] The first "generation" of smart sanctions against non-state actors in the 1990s were pragmatically driven measures against those in control of territories even though they had not achieved recognition as legitimate leaders of states. A

---

[87] Report of the Secretary-General's High-Level Panel on Threats, Challenges and Change, A More Secure World: Our Shared Responsibility, UN Doc. A/59/565 (2004), para. 179.

[88] UN Doc. S/RES/864 (1993).

[89] Final Report of the Commission of Experts Established Pursuant to Security Council Resolution 780 (1992), UN Doc. S/1994/674.

[90] UN Doc. S/RES/827 (1993). See also Appeals Chamber, *Prosecutor v. Tadic*, Case No. IT-94-1-IT, Judgment of 10 August 1995, para. 19.

[91] UN Doc. S/RES/942 (1994).

[92] UN Doc. S/RES 232 (1966).

clear departure from measures analogous to sanctions against states was only taken with the extension of the Taliban sanctions regime, imposed in 1999, to Al-Qaida in 2000 and, in so doing, removing the link between Al-Qaida and the territory of Afghanistan,[93] followed in 2011 by the complete separation of the two regimes.[94]

A contrast can be made with EU sanctions which, because of the narrower consensus necessary to take decisions to impose measures and broader agreement on the values to be protected or promoted, show a faster and deeper trend towards sanctions directed at regime elites (for example, in Zimbabwe and Russia),[95] and to a lesser extent non-state actors such as terrorist groups.[96] For instance, targeted EU sanctions were initially imposed in 2002 by the Council against individuals in Zimbabwe on the basis of its assessment that the "Government of Zimbabwe continues to engage in serious violations of human rights and of the freedom of opinion, of association and of peaceful assembly". It decided that "for as long as the violations occur the Council deems it necessary to introduce restrictive measures against the Government of Zimbabwe and those who bear a wide responsibility for such violations".[97]

The EU's measures are framed as a response to violations of international human rights standards occurring in Zimbabwe and, therefore, fit the prescription for collective countermeasures. In contrast, in the case of measures imposed by the US on Zimbabwe, in an Executive Order of 2003, the President "determined that the actions and policies of certain members of the Government of Zimbabwe and other persons to undermine Zimbabwe's democratic processes or institutions contributing to the deliberate breakdown in the rule of law in Zimbabwe, to politically motivated violence and intimidation in that country, and to political and economic instability in the southern African region, constitute an unusual and extraordinary threat to the foreign policy of the United States", and declared "a national emergency to deal with that threat".[98] That formula of an executive Presidential Order, finding of a threat to the foreign policy and national security

---

[93] UN Doc. S/RES/1267 (1999); UN Doc. S/RES/1333 (2000); FARRALL, *cit. supra* note 54, p. 131.

[94] UN Doc. S/RES/1988 (2011); UN Doc. S/RES/1989 (2011).

[95] See, for example, EU targeted sanctions against regime individuals in Zimbabwe (Council Decision 2011/101/CFSP of 15 February 2011, OJ L 42, p. 6), and Syria (Council Decision 2013/255/CFSP of 1 June 2013, OJ L 147, p. 14). Targeted sanctions were imposed against certain Russian individuals responsible for actions which undermined or threatened the territorial integrity, sovereignty and independence of Ukraine following intervention in Ukraine (Council Decision 2014/145/CFSP of 17 March 2014, OJ L 78, p. 16).

[96] Measures against Al Qaida in Common Position 2002/402/CFSP of 29 May 2002, OJ L 139, p. 4; measures against individuals and entities associated with Al Qaida in Council Regulation (EC) No 881/2000 of 29 May 2002, OJ L 139, p. 9. See also Common Position 2001/931/CFSP of 28 December 2001, OJ L 344, p. 93; Council Regulation (EC) No 2580/2001 of 28 December 2001, OJ L 344, freezing funds and economic resources of certain persons, groups and entities with a view to combating terrorism.

[97] Restrictive measures against Zimbabwe in Common Position 2002/145/CFSP of 21 February 2002, OJ L 50/1.

[98] Executive Order 13288 – Blocking Property of Persons Undermining Democratic Processes or Institutions in Zimbabwe, 10 March 2003, 68 FR 11457.

of the United States and declaring a national emergency to deal with the threat, has been used on a number of occasions by the US to tackle a variety of perceived threats by imposing targeted autonomous sanctions against individuals and other non-state actors.[99] Less frequently, more normative based determinations of violations of human rights have been used by Congress to pass legislation imposing targeted sanctions.[100] The Presidential executive power to impose sanctions, derived from the International Emergency Economic Powers Act (IEEPA) originally adopted in 1977,[101] has been criticized on the grounds that "experience with IEEPA raises concerns that it may be used casually for spurious national emergencies".[102] The language of the Presidential executive order on Zimbabwe also demonstrates that executive security powers are being invoked to tackle threats arising out of denial of democratic rights. The autonomous sanctioning right claimed by the United States is not just problematic under US constitutional law but, as the above analysis shows, is also unsupported in international law.

The analysis above demonstrates that the overriding purpose of general or targeted sanctions remains to change the behaviour of states or individuals either directly (to stop them for example from committing terrorist acts), or indirectly (to stop states or non-state actors supporting them). It follows that it is important to discern whether the sanctions are aimed at changing the behaviour that constitutes a threat to peace and security, or the behaviour that constitutes unlawful acts.[103] The intended deterrent aspect of sanctions as punishment is to prevent future breaches of law, whereas the deterrent effects of sanctions to tackle threats to the peace is the immediate end of the behaviour that comprises the threat. Of course the dichotomy of what is a threat to the peace or what is a breach of the law is not always easy to maintain and criminal behaviour, particularly at the international level, can be a (part of) a wider threat to international peace. For instance, when imposing targeted measures against non-state actors in the Central African Republic (CAR) the UN Security Council, acting under a general determination that the violence there constituted a threat to regional peace and stability, imposed measures against individuals who were involved in planning, directing, or committing acts that violated international human rights law or international humanitarian law;[104] as well as against individuals "engaging in or providing support for acts that undermine the peace, stability or security of the CAR, including acts that threaten or violate transitional agreements, or that

---

[99] See for example: Executive Order 13611 – Blocking Property of Persons Threatening the Peace, Security, or Stability of Yemen, 16 May 2012, 77 FR 29533; Executive Order 13338 – Blocking Property of Certain Persons and Prohibiting the Export of Certain Goods to Syria, 13 May 2004, 69 FR 26751; Executive Order 13067 – Blocking Sudanese Government Property and Prohibiting Transactions With Sudan, 5 November 1997, 62 FR 59989.

[100] Venezuela Defense of Human Rights and Civil Society Act of 2014, 128 Stat. 3011, S.2142.

[101] 50 U.S.C. 35 (1982), Sections 1701-1702.

[102] CARTER, "International Economic Sanctions: Improving the Haphazard U.S. Legal Regime", California Law Review, 1987, p. 1159 ff., p. 1238.

[103] WHITE, cit. supra note 38, p. 136.

[104] UN Doc. S/RES/2134 (2014), para. 37(b).

threaten or impede the political transition process, including a transition toward free and fair democratic elections, or that fuel violence".[105] This suggests that targeted sanctions are designed with a dual purpose in mind, to tackle breaches of the law as well as threats to the peace.

Nonetheless, the overriding purpose and design of sanctions remains to tackle threats to the peace. Cutting off the arms supply of an armed group, for example, is a sanction designed to reduce the danger to peace and security that group represents. Seizing the assets of members of that group, especially of those who have committed such alarming levels of violence as to constitute breaches of international law, may seem more like punishment for their unlawful acts, but it too is aimed at restricting their impact on peace, given that the members' fortunes and those of the group will be intimately connected, and cutting off individual's access to money will restrict their impact on peace. Restricting access to money and weapons will also help reduce violations of international humanitarian law committed by armed groups but this is a consequence of reducing the threat to peace and security by means of sanctions. Seen in this way, imposing measures against individuals who have committed violations of international law is primarily an attempt to stop the occurrence of violence, not to punish individuals for violations of the law resulting from that violence. If targeted sanctions are viewed as sanctions taken to punish the guilty, guilt has not been determined by any judicial procedure but by a political body. It may be sometimes that the resolutions of the Security Council appear to come close to this but the argument here is that such resolutions are best read through the lens of the Council's primary responsibility for peace and security.[106]

The predominance of sanctions adopted to preserve or restore peace and security is explicable because of the higher levels of violence within the international legal order justifying institutional competence to deal with what might be called the pre-legal *conditio sine qua non* – that there is sufficient peace and security to preserve, or upon which to build, a legal order; what Hart might call the minimum content of natural law – self-evident conditions and norms of public order.[107] Just as an infectious disease might temporarily justify the exercise of emergency executive power at the national level, at the international level the equivalent of infectious diseases or rampant fires in the form of threats to international peace caused by civil wars, protracted internal violence, refugee flows, natural disasters, famine, climate change, arms proliferation, and yes infectious diseases, none of which are breaches of international law per se, are unfortunately prevalent within the international legal order.

The trend in UN Security Council targeted sanctions practice is to move towards widening the concept of "threat to the peace", to enable to be taken to tackle the threat including measures directed at deterring or stopping the violence by non-state actors, with specific focus on those responsible for violations of human rights law and humanitarian law. Assets freezes, travel bans and other

---

[105] UN Doc. S/RES/2196 (2015), para. 11.
[106] UN Charter, Art. 24(1).
[107] HART, *cit. supra* note 11, p. 188.

targeted measures have been imposed on individuals and groups either because they undermine the peace process or otherwise threaten the peace, but also if they threaten the human security of civilians, manifested in the commission of violations of international law. This is a reflection of a move towards not only securing peace within the state but also in establishing the security of individuals within it. Thus, although appearing to be a form of punishment for breaches of the law, they remain measures aimed at restoring peace and security but at the local level as well as state level. As well as the example mentioned above, whereby sanctions were taken on this basis against armed groups in the CAR, other examples can be found in Cote D'Ivoire,[108] Lebanon,[109] and Sudan.[110] However, in other instances, targeted measures are more narrowly directed at those regime elites and non-state actors who have threatened the peace; for example in Guinea-Bissau,[111] Iran,[112] North Korea,[113] Liberia,[114] Sierra Leone,[115] Somalia,[116] Eritrea,[117] South Sudan,[118] and Yemen.[119]

This review of UN, EU and US practice indicates a predominant trend towards targeted sanctions, but also that for the UN and US a primary concern to tackle peace and security and only indirectly violations of international law. Targeted UN sanctions have a clear constitutional basis in the UN Charter. US sanctions are legally problematic as they extend beyond unilateral or "collective" countermeasures or other forms of non-forcible measures of self-help and, thereby, constitute coercive measures in violation of the international legal principle of non-intervention.[120] The EU's move towards targeted sanctions against regime elites and non-state actors is largely premised on the enforcement of community norms and are, therefore, more readily justifiable as collec-

---

[108] For example, UN Doc. S/RES/1572 (2004), para. 9.

[109] For example, UN Doc. S/RES/1636 (2005), para. 3.

[110] For example, UN Doc. S/RES/1591 (2005), para. 3(c).

[111] UN Doc. S/RES/2048 (2012), para. 6.

[112] For example, UN Doc S/RES/1737 (2006), paras. 10 and 12.

[113] For example, UN Doc. S/RES/1718 (2006), para. 8(c).

[114] For example, UN Doc. S/RES/1343 (2001), paras. 2 and 5-7.

[115] For example, UN Doc. S/RES/1132 (1997), para. 5.

[116] For example, UN Doc. S/RES/1844 (2008), paras. 1 and 3.

[117] For example, UN Doc. S/RES/1907 (2009), para. 14.

[118] UN Doc S/RES/2206 (2015), para. 6.

[119] For example, UN Doc. S/RES/2140 (2014).

[120] Embodied, for example, in the Declaration on Principles of International Law concerning Friendly Relations and Cooperation among States in accordance with the Charter of the United Nations, UN Doc. A/RES/25/2625 (1970): "No State may use or encourage the use of economic, political or any other type of measures to coerce another State in order to obtain from it the subordination of the exercise of its sovereign rights and to secure from it advantages of any kind". See also Declaration on the Inadmissibility of Intervention in the Domestic Affairs of States and the Protection of their Independence and Sovereignty, UN Doc. A/RES/20/2131 (1965), para. 2. For analysis of "coercion" as the key component of unlawful intervention see JAMNEJAD and WOOD, "The Principle of Non-Intervention", LJIL, 2009, p. 345 ff., p. 371.

tive countermeasures, although that doctrine remains disputed in international law.[121]

6.   SANCTIONS AS VIOLATIONS OF INTERNATIONAL LAW

Countermeasures would be unlawful if they are not taken in response to actual breaches of international law, or if they are permanent or disproportionate, making them inherently destabilizing because such judgments are unlikely to be made by an independent court, rather than by the states themselves. Countermeasures and other forms of self-help may therefore be met by counter-countermeasures, as with Russia's response to the measures imposed on it by EU and other states for its intervention in Ukraine.[122] Although there is justification for imposing collective countermeasures against Russia for its breach of community norms prohibiting aggression, assuming that collective countermeasures are accepted as lawful, in other instances acts of self-help are clearly either spurious or disproportionate, thereby rendering them unlawful acts of coercion. A recent example of this involved Gulf States imposing an embargo on Qatar in June 2017 for allegedly supporting terrorism, including the demand that Qatar close the Al-Jazeera media network as well as desist in its support for Hamas, the Muslim Brotherhood, Hezbollah, and its relations with Turkey and Iran. These non-forcible measures of self-help taken by Saudi Arabia, the UAE, Bahrain and Egypt demonstrate the weaknesses of self-declared victim states acting as judge, jury and executioner.

Unilateral non-forcible measures of coercion are unlawful unless taken under a secondary rule of international law as countermeasures in response to a violation of a primary rule. On this basis there is no unilateral form of autonomous sanctioning power belonging to states. Collective sanctions are not inherently unlawful and, indeed, Kelsen's view is that they are an integral part of law so that a law consists of a proscription of behaviour and a punishment for misbehaviour. Furthermore, accepting the proposition discussed at the outset of this article, namely that sanctions are imposed by central authorities, the judgement is taken away from individual states and belongs to political organs of international organizations consisting of states but acting in a corporate manner, voting by majority, qualified majority, or unanimity, depending upon the voting rules specified in the constituent treaty.

The inherent legality of sanctions does not immunize decisions to impose them from international law. Sanctions can often be seen to be the cause of violations of international law. At the end of the Cold War before the advent of targeted sanctions, the concern within the UN was to learn from the leaky sanctions regimes against Rhodesia and South Africa of the 1960s and 70s. The move was

---

[121] The ILC's Articles did not accept their legality in 2001: see ARSIWA, Art. 54.

[122] KRAUSE, "Western Economic and Political Sanctions as Instruments of Strategic Competition with Russia – Opportunities and Risks", in RONZITTI (ed.), *cit. supra* note 38, p. 270 ff.

towards maximizing the effectiveness of general sanctions, with the result that their impact was not only devastating for the innocent, but provided opportunities for the guilty and their backers. In relation to the embargo against the extremely poor country of Haiti in response to the overthrow of the democratically elected government of President Aristide in 1993, the "wealthy elite and the military command were waxing rich off the contraband industry the economic sanctions spawned. The rest of the population, which had been deprived of its popularly elected government and whom we were supposed to be helping, was, without exaggeration, starving to death".[123]

The devastating impact of sanctions against Iraq was well-known and re-corded, when the UN Secretary-General's team headed by Marti Ahtisaari re-ported in March 1991 that the conditions in Iraq were "near apocalyptic", with scant medicines and humanitarian supplies getting through to those in need.[124] The Security Council responded by adopting the "oil-for-food" Resolution 706 (1991), which "served as the main source of sustenance for 60 percent of Iraq's estimated twenty-seven million people, reducing malnutrition amongst Iraqi chil-dren by 50 percent".[125] Despite the mitigating effects of the mis-managed and corrupted oil-for-food programme, the devastating impact of UN sanctions on the people of Iraq cannot be over-stated. The purpose of sanctions changed, from ending the Iraqi occupation of Kuwait, to forcing the regime to disarm. Both purposes were directed at forcing the Iraqi regime to change its behaviour and both concern different aspects of peace and security, and yet the sanctions had a direct effect on the Iraqi people. Sanctions did succeed in keeping the "revenue from Iraq's vast oil wealth out of the hands of Saddam Hussein", preventing the regime from rebuilding its military capabilities, thereby achieving peace and security aims.[126]

The oil-for-food programme in Iraq embodied the problem with general sanctions because the need for its creation recognized the inherently violative nature of such measures; they cause death and misery and the resulting attempts at mitigation can only slow that down. The emerging body of evidence about the impact of general sanctions led to criticism by human rights bodies. In a General Comment in 1997, the Committee on Economic, Social and Cultural Rights de-clared that "inhabitants of a given country do not forfeit their basic economic, social and cultural rights by virtue of any determination that their leaders have violated norms relating to international peace and security"; and warned that "lawlessness of one kind should not be met by lawlessness of another kind which

---

[123] REISMAN, "Assessing the Lawfulness of Nonmilitary Enforcement: The Case of Economic Sanctions", AJIL, 1996, p. 37 ff.

[124] CHESTERMAN, FRANCK and MALONE, *Law and Practice of the United Nations: Documents and Commentary*, 2nd ed., Oxford, 2016, p. 376.

[125] *Ibid.*, p. 354. VOLCKER, GOLDSTONE and PIETH, Independent Inquiry Committee into the United Nations Oil-for-Food Programme (Final Report), 7 September 2005, p. 179. See further MULLER and MULLER, "Sanctions of Mass Destruction", Foreign Affairs, 1999, p. 3 ff.

[126] CORTRIGHT, LOPEZ, and GERBER-STELLINGWORTH, "The Sanctions Era", in WEISS and DAWS (eds.), *The Oxford Handbook on the United Nations*, Oxford, 2007, pp. 208-9.

pays no heed to the fundamental rights that underlie and give legitimacy to any such collective action".[127] There was little doubt in the Committee's mind that sanctions caused "significant disruption in the distribution of food, pharmaceuticals and sanitation supplies, jeopardize the quality of food and the availability of clean drinking water, severely interfere with the functioning of basic health and education systems, and undermine the right to work".[128]

Despite the significant impact on the human rights of the peoples of Iraq, it has been argued that human rights *laws* are inapplicable to those sanctions given that, even if they bind the UN as an inter-governmental organization possessing international legal personality as a matter of customary law, there was no intention by the Security Council to violate those rights.[129] On the understanding that the Security Council did not intend to violate the rights of the Iraqi people, and, furthermore, that it is necessary to show intent to establish that it had violated international law in this regard,[130] it still should have foreseen the possibility and, therefore at the very least, it had obligations of due diligence to do all in its power to prevent human rights violations that are likely to result from its actions.[131]

The often-violative nature of unilateral sanctions that go beyond temporary and proportionate countermeasures is shown by the US embargo of Cuba first imposed 1962 in response to Cuba's nationalization of US property and businesses, but tightened considerably with the fall of the Soviet Union and the withdrawal of its support for Cuba in 1991 (meaning an immediate loss of 75-80% of Cuban trade),[132] by its incorporation in legislation in the form of the Torricelli and Helms-Burton Acts of 1992 and 1996 respectively.[133] This tightening of the embargo had dramatic effects on the health of the Cuban population. The government of the United States took cruel advantage of the removal of Soviet support to try and force regime change by a starving population. The effect on life expectancy, the reduction in weight of the average Cuban, the impact on new born babies were all detailed in a report by the independent and respected American Association for World Health (AAWH) in 1997.[134] For a period of 5-10 years after the demise of the Soviet Union, when the Cuban population was especially vulnerable, the US

---

[127] Committee on Economic, Social and Cultural Rights General Comment No 8 (1997) on the Relationship between Economic Sanctions and Respect for Economic, Social and Cultural Rights, 12 December 1997.

[128] *Ibid.* See also Committee on Economic, Social and Cultural Rights, General Comment No 12 (1999), The Right to Adequate Food (Article 11 of the Covenant), 12 May 1999, para. 37.

[129] O'CONNELL, "Debating the Law of Sanctions", EJIL, 2002, p. 63 ff., p. 73.

[130] BROWNLIE, *System of the Law of Nations: State Responsibility Part I*, Oxford, 1983, p. 40.

[131] International Law Association, Final Report of Committee on Accountability of International Organizations (2004), p. 15.

[132] GORDON, "Economic Sanctions as Negative Development", Journal of International Development, 2016, p. 474.

[133] LEONGRANDE, "Enemies Evermore: US Policy Towards Cuba After Helms-Burton", Journal of Latin American Studies, 1997, p. 211 ff.

[134] AAWH, *Denial of Food and Medicine: The Impact of the US Embargo on Health and Nutrition in Cuba*, Washington DC, 1997.

legislature chose to continue, indeed intensify, its sanctions against Cuba. That demonstrated sufficient intent to cause deliberate harm and damage to Cuba and to its people, over and above the US exercising its freedom to choose trade partners. Finishing off a weakened Cuban government would inevitably impact upon an even weaker Cuban population, a population who were not comforted by the stated purposes of the Helms-Burton Act to: "assist the Cuban people in regaining their freedom and prosperity"; ensure free and fair elections; protect the United States from Cuban terrorism; address the "theft" of US-owned property; and respond to Cuba's violation of human rights.[135]

One of the unaddressed aspects of when an organization or a state can be held legally responsible for violations of international law is causation – did the wrongful act (in the UN's continuation of sanctions against Iraq in the period 1991-2003, or by the continuation and tightening of the US embargo against Cuba in the period 1992-1996) cause damage to the Iraqi and Cuban peoples?[136] The decisions to continue the embargoes were clearly attributable to the UN and the United States but did the resulting measures cause the losses suffered by the Iraqi and Cuban populations? The evidence drawn from independent bodies, discussed above,[137] all clearly point to violations of the socio-economic rights of thousands of individuals in Iraq and Cuba as a result of the measures imposed as a result of decisions by the UN and US respectively.[138] This was deliberate damage inflicted on Iraq and Cuba, more specifically the populations of those countries, and was not sufficiently mitigated by any of humanitarian exceptions built into the embargoes.[139]

The fact that organizations and states imposing sanctions try to mitigate the effects of such measures on the ordinary people of the target state is indicative that they realize that such powers and rights should be exercised in ways that minimize human rights' violations. For instance, in the decision that imposed a comprehensive embargo against Iraq, the Security Council created an exception for payments and shipments of humanitarian foodstuffs and medical supplies;[140] but this did not mean that Iraq bought or distributed such supplies to its weakening citizens; hence the advent of the oil-for-food programme some years later. However, although the intention behind the humanitarian exception in sanctions resolutions is to reduce the impact of sanctions on the population, the evidence is

---

[135] Helms-Burton Act 1996, *cit. supra* note 60.

[136] STERN, "The Elements of an Internationally Wrongful Act", in CRAWFORD, PELLET and OLLESON (eds.), *cit. supra* note 18, p. 193 ff.

[137] See also UN Human Rights Council, Report Submitted by the Personal Representative of the High Commissioner for Human Rights on the Situation of Human Rights in Cuba, 26 January 2007, A/HRC/4/12, para. 7.

[138] GORDON, *Invisible War: The United States and the Iraq Sanctions*, Harvard, 2010, pp. 86-102; GORDON, *cit. supra* note 132, p. 474.

[139] For example, the prohibition of ships trading with Cuba from docking in the US meant that mixed cargoes containing medical supplies, for instance, would not be exported to Cuba: see Cuban government's statement in UN Secretary General's Report, UN Doc. A/71/91 (2016).

[140] UN Doc. S/RES/661 (1991).

that the powerful elites in the target country will take control of the supplies, and that such exceptions will encourage a black market in goods from which elites benefit, thereby strengthening their wealth and position and blunting the positive effects of humanitarian exceptions.

In striving to achieve security aims the UN's general sanctions against countries as a whole have proved too damaging to human rights and, thereby, have not achieved both peace and human rights. In what could perhaps be a developing duty of due diligence to ensure that human rights of the population are not violated, the Council has tried a number of routes including humanitarian exceptions and oil-for-food, but none have sufficiently mitigated the adverse effects of sanctions on the population. The use of lawfully imposed collective sanctions against a whole state seemed to have come to a natural and ugly end in 2003 when Saddam's regime was toppled. It is somewhat ironic that the main example of unlawful unilateral economic sanctions, the US embargo imposed and enforced against Cuba, continues despite overwhelming recognition of its illegality by the UN General Assembly.[141]

It is important, however, for the UN and regional organizations to have a range of non-forcible options in order to address threats to peace and security. In its search for an effective and legitimate non-forcible option, the UN has embraced the idea of "smart" or "targeted" sanctions emerging from the Stockholm Process,[142] comprising targeted and better designed measures aimed at achieving specific goals in relation to those political and military leaders responsible for the threat, and confining that threat, rather than exerting pressure on a whole country in the hope that this will lead to the regime conceding or collapsing.[143] Targeted measures are directed at changing the behaviour of those responsible for the threat and, therefore, have greater legitimacy than general sanctions that coerce the innocent into possibly risking everything to change the behaviour of those responsible.

While these new-style targeted sanctions have raised their own human rights concerns in terms of due process, rights to property, privacy and freedom of movement, they are quantitatively far fewer human rights violations when compared with the effects of punitive sanctions imposed against a state and, therefore, against the population of a state. Nonetheless, there is no doubt that effectively implemented targeted sanctions can have a profound effect on the lives of those targeted and their families. In the key UK judgment – the *Ahmed* case decided

---

[141] For example, UN Doc. A/RES/72/4 (2017), adopted by 191 votes to 2 (US and Israel). For the argument that unilateral embargoes may be lawful acts of retorsion see RUYS, *cit. supra* note 8, pp. 26-27. See statement by the International Court of Justice in *Military and Paramilitary Activities in and Against Nicaragua (Nicaragua v. United States of America)*, Judgment of 27 June 1986, ICJ Reports, 1986, p. 14 ff., para. 245. Without offering reasons, the Court found that a US trade embargo imposed on Nicaragua did not breach the customary international law principle of non-intervention.

[142] WALLENSTEEN, STAIBANO and ERIKSSON (eds.), *Making Targeted Sanctions Effective: Guidelines for the Implementation of UN Policy Options*, Uppsala, 2003, a report by Uppsala University presented by Sweden to Security Council: see UN Doc. S/4713 mtg (2003).

[143] CHESTERMAN, FRANCK and MALONE, *cit. supra* note 124, p. 343.

by the UK Supreme Court in 2010 – the Court was highly critical of the targeted sanctions regime in terms of its effects of such measures on the lives of individuals. Lord Hope described the impact of the executive orders on targeted individuals and their families as making them effectively "prisoners of the state".[144]

As with general sanctions, there is an on-going debate about the violative nature of targeted sanctions, especially of due process norms. However, the issue has not been resolved in favour of clear rights violations since the listing of individuals can be conceived as an executive or administrative process on the basis of perceived security threats, rather than a judicial one equivalent to a criminal conviction for breaches of core crimes even though the listing results in set of coercive measures, arguably de facto punishment, of those listed. Nevertheless, this has not stopped targeted individuals from claiming before domestic courts,[145] regional courts,[146] and in individual complaints to the Human Rights Committee.[147] While the temporary freezing of an individual's assets could be seen as a preventive administrative measure and, therefore, not subject to full due process protections, the fact that there is a degree of permanence in a number of listings means that there should be avenues for challenging such decisions. Temporary preventive targeted sanctions imposed by the UN Security Council in response to specific threats might enable states to modify their human rights obligations to the extent of suspending any conflict with their obligations arising under the UN Charter.[148] However, targeted sanctions imposed by states pursuant to the legislative resolutions of the Security Council, principally Resolution 1373 (2001),[149] do not fit the model of executive decisions necessitating the temporary trumping of human rights obligations. Furthermore, obligations arising from sanctions imposed by states unilaterally or by reason of a decision of a regional organization cannot claim to have primacy over human rights obligations owed by states.

Targeted sanctions may be adopted against regime and regime elites, and non-state actors such as those measures adopted in 1999 and 2000 against the Taliban and Al-Qaida. Criticism of their incompatibility with human rights norms by judicial bodies has led to the Security Council creating an Ombudsperson to consider requests for delisting and to make recommendations to the Security Council to that end. It is interesting to note that review by the Ombudsperson established by Security Council Resolution 1904 in 2009 only applies to those on the Al-Qaida Sanctions List as administered by the 1267 Committee and not to

---

[144] *Her Majesty's Treasury v. Mohammed Jabar Ahmed and Others,* [2010] UKSC 2, para. 4.

[145] For example, *Abdelrazik v. Canada (Minister of Foreign Affairs),* [2010] 1 FCR 267.

[146] Joined Cases. C-402/05 P and C-415/05 P, *Yassin Abdullah Kadi and Al Barakaat International Foundation v. Council and Commission,* ECR, 2008, I-06351, para. 334; European Court of Human Rights, *Nada v. Switzerland,* Application No. 10593/08, Judgment of 12 September 2012; European Court of Human Rights, *Case of Al-Dulimi and Montana Management Inc. v. Switzerland,* Application No. 5809/08, Judgment of 21 June 2016.

[147] *Nabil Sayadi and Patricia Vinck v. Belgium,* Communication No. 1472/2006, 29 December 2008, 16 IHHR 427.

[148] UN Charter, Art. 103.

[149] UN Doc. S/RES/1373 (2001).

any lists beyond that, including the Taliban list. This seemingly curious anomaly is probably explained by the overarching pragmatism of the Security Council on the matter of accountability for wrongly listing individuals; that complaints to international, regional and judicial bodies have derived largely from the 1267 list and the creation of the office of the Ombudsperson is a response to that development.[150]

The lack of remedies elsewhere in the UN system for wrongly listed individuals puts the creation of the Ombudsperson in perspective, but it also fits the apparent prevailing view in the Security Council that such measures are administrative ones taken in response to an international threat caused by the activities of international terrorist organizations and, therefore, any remedial measures should only be of a limited administrative nature. However, long-term listing arguably constitutes a form of punishment that raises issues of legal remedies based on violations of due process norms located in the international human rights obligations of states. The fact that those states are simultaneously under duties deriving from the UN Charter to carry out decisions of the Security Council is one of the pressing issues of international law that cannot be solved by the simple uncritical application of Article 103.[151]

The creation of more transparent listing procedures and, in particular, a non-judicial mechanism to review petitions at the UN level is no minor event, given the almost complete unaccountability of the Security Council for its actions in the past. However, the Ombudsperson is not only limited to those on the Al-Qaida list, but she cannot remove the listed individual given that the process consists of a dialogue with the petitioner, and then the presentation of arguments by the Ombudsperson to the 1267 Committee, which then decides whether or not to accept request. With the ultimate decision in the hands of the 1267 Committee, the very originator of the challenged sanctions, the latest development has not gone far enough in terms of providing a proper remedy at the international level.

7. CONCLUSION

It has been argued that accountability mechanisms tend to improve at the international level in response to crises,[152] even in the hard core of security matters dealt with by the Security Council, where it is likely that future improvements will be made to delisting mechanisms as the UN adjusts its sanctioning processes towards increased human rights compliance. Given that the Security Council has

---

[150] See criticism of the unevenness of access to remedies by the Ombudsperson, Kimberly Prost, in a briefing by her at the Security Council's Open Debate on "Working Methods of the Security Council" (UN Doc. S/2014/725) on the topic of: "Enhancing Due Process in Sanctions Regimes", 23 October 2014.

[151] LIIVOJA, "The Scope of the Supremacy Clause of the United Nations Charter", ICLQ, 2008, p. 583 ff., p. 612.

[152] MULGAN, "AWB and Oil for Food: Some Issue of Accountability", in FARRALL and RUBENSTEIN (eds.), *Sanctions, Accountability and Governance in a Globalised World*, Cambridge, 2009, p. 334 ff., p. 334.

now imposed targeted sanctions against a range of regime elites and non-state actors the demands for redress will inevitably increase. Collective sanctions, although lawful, have to be adjusted to fit within the broader international legal order.

Sanctions have changed over the decades: they have become more humane, they have become more common, but they remain exceptional to international law in the sense that they are largely imposed to enforce peace not law. Given the centrality of sanctions to any legal system there is clearly significant adjustments to be made to place sanctions within the parameters of international law, ensuring that they do not themselves violate fundamental norms. This is not to forget the Security Council's primary responsibility for peace and security or to argue that it should be solely an executive enforcer of international law. International law is not developed sufficiently to do that, nor is the UN itself based on a separation of powers.

What has been argued is that there is a need to conceptualize "peace" and "security" as normative concepts, accept their protection as public order norms in the international legal sphere, and work on their fit, their balance, and their position within the existing international legal fabric. Institutional practice on the nature and purposes of collective sanctions, reviewed above, is inconsistent; for example, collective sanctions taken in response to violations of existing core norms of the international legal order, as practised by the EU in particular, are not matched sufficiently by the UN Security Council at the universal level, due to the lack of consensus within the permanent membership as to when intervention in member states is justified.

The development of the idea of a "responsibility to protect" in cases of core crimes has helped to highlight inadequacy at the UN level, when at the very least non-forcible targeted measures should be imposed against those responsible for violating core crimes or for failing to prevent them.[153] A serious breach of international law, whether of norms protecting "peace", "security", "genocide", "crimes against humanity", extensive "war crimes", or "ethnic cleansing", has to be met with effective targeted sanctions in the majority of instances if international law is to raise itself above simply being a collection of primary rules proscribing behaviour, but not containing within those rules sanctions to counter such behaviour.

Collective sanctions imposed by legitimate centralized institutions, either universal or regional, are not only inherently lawful but are of a different order to the secondary rules of responsibility that permit states to apply inherently unlawful countermeasures in responses to breaches of their international rights by other states, a right that can easily be abused and become unbridled economic coercion as the enduring embargo of Cuba by the US demonstrates. It follows

---

[153] For example, non-forcible measures have not been imposed by the UN against the Syrian government, despite UN reports finding "crimes against humanity" have regularly been committed in Syria. The Security Council's non-forcible measures have been directed against ISIL and other terrorist groups, for example, in UN Doc. S/RES/2170 (2014); UN Doc. S/RES/2199 (2015); UN Doc. S/RES/2249 (2015).

there is no autonomous right belonging to states to impose sanctions beyond the limited forms of non-forcible self-help recognized primarily in the doctrine of countermeasures, despite extensive US practice and the suggestion from the UK government that it will also be claiming such rights on its departure from the EU in 2019.

Collective countermeasures, as responses to breaches of core crimes, are understandable responses to breaches of core international crimes and as such can be categorised as "public" responses to assaults on the international legal order, rather than the normal form of "private" countermeasures imposed in a strictly bilateral relationship.[154] However, given the inherent weaknesses in unilateral and subjective judgements by states as to when to impose such non-forcible measures, they can only ever be an unstable and, therefore, temporary stepping stone toward collective, centrally imposed, sanctions.

---

[154] See generally, DAVIDOWICZ, "Public Law Enforcement without Public Law Safeguards? An Analysis of State Practice on Third-Party Countermeasures and their Relationship to the UN Security Council", BYIL, 2006, p. 333 ff.

DEFINING ELEMENTS AND EMERGING LEGAL ISSUES
OF EU "SANCTIONS"

Leonardo Borlini[*] and Stefano Silingardi[**]

Abstract

With some 40 different types of restrictive measures in force, the European Union is undisputedly one of the major protagonists of today's sanction regimes. Measures such as selective trade embargos, asset freezes and travel bans have been adopted by the EU not only to implement Security Council mandated sanctions, but also in addition to (as with Iran and North Korea) or in the absence of UN action (as with Syria and Russia). Further, EU recent practice evidences that sanctions (Myanmar and Zimbabwe) have served the EU and its member states' own interests also with the view to promoting (the European construction of) values generally shared in international society. After outlining the legal discipline and the policy framework of EU restrictive measures, the present article analyses the legal issues emerging with respect to EU sanctions over the last four years. Among these, the 2017 ruling of the Grand Chamber of the Court of Justice of the EU in Rosneft, *Brexit and its consequences on the implementation/adoption of sanctions by the United Kingdom, and recent developments concerning the legal position of candidate countries which refused to align with the EU sanction adopted in reaction to the Ukraine crisis, are the most important.*

Keywords: European Union; sanctions; Common Foreign and Security Policy; judicial remedies; preliminary ruling; Brexit.

1. INTRODUCTION

In recent years, the European Union (EU) has made extensive use of sanctions as a foreign policy tool. According to the latest list of consolidated restrictive measures published by the European External Action Service (EEAS), there are 38 EU sanctions regimes in force.[1] But the number of sanctions regimes is growing steadily. On 13 November 2017 the Council of the EU adopted targeted and comprehen-

---

[*] Assistant Professor of International Law (Bocconi University), Ph.D. (Bocconi University), LL.M (Cantab.).

[**] Adjunct Professor of International Law (University of Modena and Reggio Emilia), Ph.D. (Bocconi University). This article is the outcome of a joint effort of both authors. However, Sections 3-5 and 8 are to be attributed to Stefano Silingardi, while Leonardo Borlini wrote Sections 2 and 6-7.

[1] See Service for Foreign Policy Instruments, Restrictive measures (sanctions) in force (updated 4 August 2017), available at: <http://ec.europa.eu/dgs/fpi/documents/Restrictive_measures-2017-08-04-clean_en.pdf>.

sive restrictive measures (including restrictions on admission, asset freezes, arms exports, equipment used for internal repression and telecommunications equipment) against Venezuela in view of the continuing deterioration of democracy, the rule of law and human rights in that country.[2] Further, on 26 February 2018, the Council announced that it might consider targeted measures against Cambodia if the "continu[ed] deterioration of democracy, respect of human rights and the rule of law" in that country failed to improve.[3] The same day, the Council called on the competent Maldivian institutions to "lift immediately the state of emergency and restore all constitutionally guaranteed rights", and concluded that, with no improvement of that state of affairs, it might consider targeted measures.[4]

Measures adopted by the EU to influence other subjects' conduct are manifold. Sanctions or "restrictive measures" (as they are known in EU parlance) have been adopted by the Union not only to implement the Security Council decisions decided under Chapter VII of the UN Charter, but also in addition to (as with Iran and North Korea)[5] or in the absence of UN action. The latter first occurred in the 1980s, with the adoption of sanctions against the Soviet Union (1980), Poland and Argentina (1982),[6] and is particularly significant as it shows the EU as an innovator in international relations where the Security Council is unable or unwilling to act (as in Syria[7] and

---

[2] See Council Decision (CFSP) 2017/2074 of 13 November 2017 concerning restrictive measures in view of the situation in Venezuela, OJ L 295, p. 60. See also Council Decision (CFSP) 2018/90 of 22 January 2018 amending Decision (CFSP) 2017/2074 concerning restrictive measures in view of the situation in Venezuela, OJ L 16I, p. 14. The list of natural persons subject to restrictive measures is included in Council implementing Regulation (EU) 2018/88 of 22 January 2018 implementing Regulation (EU) 2017/2063 concerning restrictive measures in view of the situation in Venezuela, OJ L 16 1/6, Annex.

[3] Council of the European Union, Council Conclusions, Cambodia (6416/18), 26 February 2018, paras. 3-4.

[4] Council of the European Union, Council Conclusions, The Maldives (6420/18), 26 February 2018, par. 4.

[5] Particularly, this holds true in respect of certain types of trade and transaction as well as travel bans and restrictions on admission. See *infra* Section 2.

[6] See BEAUCILLON, *Les mesures restrictives de l'Union européenne*, Bruxelles, 2013, p. 14 ff.

[7] On 27 May 2013, the Council of the EU adopted conclusions in which it condemned the violence and the continued widespread and systematic gross violations of human rights in Syria, the massacres committed by the Syrian armed forces and its militias, all instances of hostage taking of peacekeepers, and the atrocities committed by the Syrian regime. It expressed concern for military operations conducted by the regime and its supporters, as well as the rise of religiously or ethnically motivated violence. In view of the seriousness of the situation, on 31 May 2013, the Council of the EU adopted restrictive measures against Syria in numerous fields. See Council Decision 2013/255/CFSP of 31 May 2013 concerning restrictive measures against Syria, OJ L 147, p. 14. In view of the illegally removed goods belonging to Syria's cultural heritage, additional measures were introduced on 13 December 2013. See Council Decision 2013/760/CFSP of 13 December 2013 amending Decision 2013/255/CFSP concerning restrictive measures against Syria, OJ L 335, p. 50. On 12 December 2014, the Council of the EU further imposed a prohibition on export of items that were used by the Assad regime's air force which undertakes indiscriminate air attacks against the civilian population. See Council Decision 2014/901/CFSP of 12 December 2014 amending Decision 2013/255/CFSP concerning restrictive measures against Syria, OJ L 358, p. 28. Since 2014, in view of

Russia,[8] when the EU "autonomous sanctions" were surrogate for Security Council sanctions) or in situations which might not amount to threats to the peace but are nonetheless addressed by the EU (e.g. Myanmar,[9] Zimbabwe[10]). Measures against third States have also been taken by the EU on an autonomous basis to complement Security Council-mandated measures. Furthermore, outside the framework of the Common Foreign and Security Policy (CFSP), EU institutions undertake other sorts of actions designed to influence the conduct of third countries, such as the measures adopted in the context of commercial disputes or those consisting of the suspension or termination of bilateral agreements, of unilateral trade concessions or of cooperation with third countries.[11]

Focusing on EU restrictive measures *stricto sensu*, it is easy to note that they have unique features varying from their possible justifications, to the prospect of a complete system of legal remedies for individuals, and the role of member states in their implementation. Issues of general interest emerge from the EU practice also vis-à-vis candidate countries. Finally, the British exit from the Union poses unprecedented legal questions for restrictive measures. By focusing in particular on autonomous sanctions, the present article investigates the defining elements and emerging legal issues of EU sanctions in the light of recent practice and relevant case law.

---

the deteriorating situation in Syria, and the widespread and systematic violations of human rights and international humanitarian law, including the use of chemical weapons against the civilian population, the Council of the EU has repeatedly added names to the lists of persons and entities who are subject to restrictive measures.

[8] See Council Decision 2014/512/CFSP of 31 July 2014 concerning restrictive measures in view of Russia's actions destabilising the situation in Ukraine, OJ L 229, p. 13; and Council Decision 2014/659/CFSP of 8 September 2014 amending Decision 2014/512/CFSP concerning restrictive measures in view of Russia's actions destabilising the situation in Ukraine, OJ L 271, p. 54.

[9] See Council Decision 2013/184/CFSP of 22 April 2013 concerning restrictive measures against Myanmar/Burma and repealing Decision 2010/232/CFSP, OJ L 111, p. 75. Most recently, see also Council Conclusions, Myanmar/Burma (6418/18), 26 February 2018, paras. 1 and 12, where the Council also took stock of the situation in Myanmar/Burma, in particular in Rakhine State, and condemned the "ongoing widespread, systematic grave human rights violations committed by Myanmar/Burma military and security forces". It also invited the High Representative to make proposals for an extension to the existing arms embargo, as well as targeted sanctions to be imposed against senior military officers of the Myanmar armed forces (Tatmadaw) responsible for "serious and systematic human rights violations".

[10] Restrictive measures against Zimbabwe were first introduced on 18 February 2002 in relation to the escalation of violence and intimidation of political opponents and the harassment of the independent press. For measures in force, see Council Decision 2011/101/CFSP of 15 February 2011 concerning restrictive measures against Zimbabwe, OJ L 042, p. 6. See further WHITE, "Autonomous and Collective Sanctions in the International Legal Order", in this Volume.

[11] In effect, EU institutions generally maintain a distinction between "restrictive measures" strictly understood, adopted within the CFSP, and the above-mentioned actions, which are not addressed by this article. Needless to say though, they may be, and often are linked to or combined with, restrictive measures See CAMERON (ed.), *EU Sanctions: Law and Policy Issues Concerning Restrictive Measure*, Cambridge-Antwerp, 2013, p. 39.

2. JUSTIFICATIONS FOR AUTONOMOUS SANCTIONS

Autonomous sanctions are said not only to serve the EU and its member states' own interests but also to promote values shared by the international community. More specifically, such measures must be consistent with the objectives of the CFSP, as outlined in Article 21 of the Treaty on European Union (TEU): a) to safeguard its values, fundamental interests, security, independence and integrity; b) to consolidate and support democracy, the rule of law, human rights and the principles of international law; and c) to preserve peace, prevent conflicts and strengthen international security, in accordance with the purposes and principles of the United Nations Charter, with the principles of the Helsinki Final Act and with the aims of the Charter of Paris, including those relating to external borders.[12] The current formulation of Article 21 TEU confirms and codifies previous policy and guidance documents. From as early as 2004, by issuing the Basic Principles on the Use of Restrictive Measures (Sanctions),[13] the EU Council expressed in clear terms the EU's willingness to use restrictive measures as a key instrument of its foreign policy and, for the first time, designed a strategy for the use of sanctions.[14] As clarified by the 2012 Guidelines, "[i]n general terms, restrictive measures are imposed by the EU to *bring about a change in policy or activity by the target country, part of country, government, entities or individuals* […] Accordingly, the EU will repeal/adapt the restrictive measures as a function of *positive developments in light of its objectives*".[15] Such a statement and, particularly, the final indication of its teleological elements ("positive developments", "its objectives") reveals that, in the EU institutions' view, restrictive measures may be liberally deployed to pursue the EU's own goals and to promote its own founding values, such as democracy, rule of law and human rights.

In this respect, a rather delicate issue concerns EU autonomous sanctions when they are adopted vis-à-vis a target state accused of a breach of international law and the EU could not be regarded as being individually injured by the breach in question.[16] In such a case, the lawfulness of measures adopted by the EU could

---

[12] Consolidated version of the Treaty on European Union, OJ C 326, 26 October, 2012, p. 13, Article 21(2). See further DASHWOOD, "Article 47 TEU and the Relationships between First and Second Pillar Competences", in DASHWOOD and MARESCEAU (eds.), *Law and Practice of EU External Relations*, Cambridge, 2008, p. 99 ff.

[13] Council Document 10198/1/04 of 7 June 2014.

[14] See PORTELA, *European Union Sanctions and Foreign Policy: When and Why do they Work?*, London-New York, p. 28.

[15] See Guidelines on Implementation and Evaluation of Restrictive Measures (Doc. 11205/12), 15 June 2012, par. 4, emphasis added.

[16] For a fuller discussion on the issue of compatibility with international law of sanctions adopted *proprio motu* by the EU in the absence of a UN Security Council resolution, see PELLET, "Sanctions unilatérales et droit international – Unilateral Sanctions and International Law", in Annuaire de l'Institut de droit international – Séssion de Tallinn, 2015, p. 723 ff.; and GESTRI, "Sanctions Imposed by the European Union: Legal and Institutional Aspects", in RONZITTI (ed.), *Coercive Diplomacy, Sanctions and International Law*, Leiden, 2016, p. 70 ff., pp. 72-76 and the literature referred to therein. As the author remarks, "[i]n practice […] EU sanctions may fall into different categories". Alongside countermeasures adopted vis-à-vis

be established under international law only on the basis of the debated doctrine according to which states (and other entities), even if not directly affected, may take countermeasures in the presence of violations of *erga omnes* obligations.[17] It should be recalled that states have not consistently protested against the EU practice of autonomous restrictive measures, and a number of them (especially those which are partners of the European Neighbourhood Policy, but also candidate countries and other countries, such as, for instance, Switzerland) have expressly committed themselves to conform to such measures.[18] Recent practice provides first-hand evidence of the European tendency to universalise the regional,[19] also through the channel of sanctions: for example, the restrictive measures against Venezuela and Myanmar, and the conclusions on the possibility of adopting restrictive measures against the Maldivian and Cambodian institutions, all hint to the European perception of values generally shared in international society.[20] The nature of such measures and their possible uses were further emphasised by Advocate General (AG) Wahl in a 2016 non-binding European Court of Justice (ECJ) opinion in a case concerning a decision to deploy staff of an EU mission. The AG described them as being "akin to that of a penalty: restraining the ex-

---

violations of *erga omnes* obligations, the EU may adopt measures, qualified as "retorsion" under international law, that, even if designed to injure the target State, do not conflict with any international obligation such as the termination or suspensions of benefits unilaterally granted to third countries (development aid; technical assistance; cultural cooperation). Another example of this sort "is offered by the introduction of visa requirements for the entry into the EU of nationals of a given State or by the adoption of visa bans vis-à-vis certain individuals". A different situation arises when the restrictive measures adopted by the EU, "if considered *per se*, do conflict with international obligations deriving from customary of treaty law". In such a case, the sanctions adopted must be justified "under the law of the international responsibility of States (notably, pursuant to the rules on 'countermeasures') or under the law of treaties (notably, according to the principle *inademplenti non est adimplendum*)". A similar position is voiced also by DUPONT, "Unilateral European Sanctions as Countermeasures: The Case of EU Measures against Iran", in HAPPOLD (ed.), *Economic Sanctions and International Law*, Oxford, 2016, p. 37 ff., pp. 37-51.

[17] See further WHITE, *cit. supra* note 10, arguing that on a spectrum of legality, a reasonable argument can be made in favour of collective countermeasures taken in response to violation of fundamental international laws; "[i]n contrast, if sanctions going beyond countermeasures were to be imposed by the EU, it would become an even more controversial trailblazer for an autonomous external sanctioning power for regional organizations".

[18] By way of example, on 28 March, 2018, the Swiss Federal Council adopted sanctions against Venezuela in order to align itself with Council Decision (CFSP) 2017/2074, *cit. supra* note 2; and Council Decision (CFSP) 2018/90, *cit. supra* note 2. As a result, an arms and repressive goods embargo have been adopted, as well as targeted measures (asset freezes and travel restrictions) against 7 Venezuelan ministers/high-ranking officials. See "Verordnung über Massnahmen gegenüber Venezuela", available at: <https://www.admin.ch/opc/de/official-compilation/2018/1217.pdf>.

[19] On such general prospect see further KOSKENNIEMI, "International Law in Europe Between Tradition and Renewal", EJIL, 2005, p. 113 ff. See also WHITE, *cit. supra* note 10.

[20] See, e.g., Council Conclusions, Cambodia (6418/18), *cit. supra* note 9, para. 4, where the EU urged the Cambodian Government to "stop using the judiciary as a political tool to harass and intimidate political opponents, civil society, labour rights activists and human rights defenders".

ercise of certain rights which the target would otherwise enjoy. Their purpose is primarily to induce or force the author of the reprehensible conduct to stop or alter that conduct".[21]

3. LEGAL BASIS AND EU DECISION-MAKING FOR THE IMPOSITION OF SANCTIONS

It is the Council that, within the framework of the CFSP, imposes restrictive measures: acting under Article 29 TEU, and in accordance with the procedure envisaged in Articles 30 and 31 of the same treaty, the Council adopts a CFSP Decision.[22] The proposal for the adoption of that decision may come from EU member states or the High Representative of the Union for Foreign Affairs and Security Policy (HR), who can eventually act with the support of the EU Commission thus introducing a joint proposal. Thereafter the proposal is examined and discussed by the relevant Council groups – typically, the Council group responsible for relations with the third country concerned and, always, the Foreign Relations Counsellors Working Group (RELEX) and the Political and Security Committee (PSC).[23] Finally, the Committee of Permanent Representatives (COREPER II) refers the Common Position proposal to the Council for adoption. If intended to implement UN sanctions, the decision should be adopted "as quickly as possible. [...] The EU should aim to have the necessary implementing legislation in place without delay and within 30 days of the adoption of the UNSC Resolution at the latest".[24]

Given that in the field of CFSP the adoption of legislative acts is excluded (Article 31(1) TEU), a further distinction should be drawn: the Council decisions on sanctions, in order to be applicable vis-à-vis natural and legal persons, require further acts, which are implemented either by member states or the EU institutions, depending on the kind of sanctions envisaged and on the attribution of the competences between member states and the EU.[25] Certain measures foreseen in a decision, such as arms embargoes[26] or restrictions on the admission to the EU

---

[21] See Case C-455/14, *P.-H. v. Council of the European Union, European Commission*, Opinion of Advocate General Wahl, 7 April 2016, para. 77.

[22] On the procedural issues including rules on voting and abstention see further ECKES, "EU Restrictive Measures against Natural and Legal Persons: from Counterterrorist to Third Country Sanctions", CML Rev, 2014, p. 880 ff.; and GESTRI, *cit. supra* note 16, 82-83.

[23] Another important actor in this procedure is the European External Action Service (EEAS), which makes suggestions about what measures are advisable and whom to target with sanctions, presenting also drafts of the new legal bases to be negotiated in detail in RELEX.

[24] See Guidelines on implementation and evaluation of restrictive measures, *cit. supra* note 15, para. 38.

[25] GESTRI, *cit. supra* note 16, p. 83.

[26] The exception of arms embargoes is founded on Art. 346 TFEU, a provision on national security included in the Treaties since 1957. On the EU practice related to arms embargoes and on how consensus and national implementation requirements affect these measures, see further KRANZ, "European Union arms embargoes: the relationship between institutional design and norms", Cambridge Review of International Affairs, 2016, p. 970 ff.

territory of specifically listed third country nationals,[27] are implemented directly by the member states, without the need for any further EU-level act. By contrast, in another range of instances, the imposition of restrictive measures foreseen in a CFSP decision requires further EU legislation under the Treaty on the Functioning of European Union (TFEU). This is the case with decisions providing for the interruption or reduction, in part or completely, of economic and financial relations for which implementing legislation in the form of an EU Council regulation is required. In particular, Article 215 TFEU provides for two types of economic and financial sanctions: sanctions directed at states, normally falling under the EU Commercial policy,[28] and sanctions against natural or legal persons and groups or non-state entities, which affect the functioning of the internal market and the movement of capital. In terms of procedure, Article 215 provides a significant simplification compared to the previous EU Treaty, which was based on the joint application of Articles 301, 60 and the flexibility clause (Article 308 establishing the European Community) thus requiring a long two-step procedure that often resulted in notable delays, such as in the case of the 1998 sanctions against Serbia during the Kosovo crisis.[29] Under the Lisbon Treaty, the Council indeed decides, by a qualified majority on a joint proposal from the HR and the Commission, to adopt the measures necessary to implement such decision. As for the European Parliament, it is excluded from that procedure and should only be informed once the measures have been adopted.

Although Article 215 makes use of a formula ("necessary measures") that allows institutions to have recourse, in principle, to all types of legal acts envisaged by Article 288 TFEU, the EU legislative acts generally used in this field are regulations. As is well-known, regulations are, indeed, directly applicable in all EU member states. Moreover, they are binding in their entirety, are not required to be transposed into national law and, being part of EU law, take precedence over conflicting domestic legislation[30] so that, in principle, they represent the securest legal tool to ensure, without delay, uniformity in the application of restrictive measures.[31] Finally, when dealing with preventing and combating ter-

---

[27] On the role of member states in the implementation of such measures see *infra* Section 6.

[28] Case 124/95, *Centro-Com*, 14 January 1997.

[29] See Council Regulation (EC) No. 1294/1999 of 15 June 1999 concerning the freeze of funds and a ban on investment in relation to the Federal Republic of Yugoslavia, OJ L 153, p. 63; Council Regulation (EC) No. 1901/98 of 7 September 1998 concerning a ban on flights of Yugoslav carriers between the Federal Republic of Yugoslavia and the European Community, OJ L 248, p. 1. See BUCHET DE NEUILLY, "European Union's External Relations Fields: The Multipillar Issue of Economic Sanctions against Serbia", in KNODT and PRINCEN (eds.), *Understanding the European Union's external relations*, London, 2003, p. 92 ff.; and EECKHOUT, *Sanctions Policy*, Oxford, 2011, p. 505 ff.

[30] Case 6/64, *Flaminio Costa v. E.N.E.L.*, 15 July 1964.

[31] According to the Best Practices for the effective implementation of restrictive measures (Doc. 15530/16), 14 December 2016, para. 25, sanctions regulations require, however, that member states adopt legislation providing for penalties for breaching restrictive measures, and designate the competent authorities referred to in the regulations to implement measures at the national level. The point is discussed further *infra* Section 6.

rorism and related activities, it is Article 75 TFEU (replacing Article 60 of the previous EU Treaty) that applies. This article is placed within the EU's Area of Freedom, Security and Justice (Title V of TFEU), which is reflected in significant procedural differences. Pursuant to Article 75, the Council and the Parliament act through the ordinary legislative procedure (Article 294 TFEU), without a prior CFSP decision; further, implementation is made by a Council act on a proposal from the Commission and, once again, without involvement of the European Parliament.[32]

4. JURISDICTIONAL SCOPE OF APPLICATION AND TYPOLOGIES OF EU RESTRICTIVE MEASURES

Ratione personarum, EU restrictive measures align to the UN model, as they encompass both traditional *comprehensive* sanctions, directed at States, and *targeted* (or *smart*) sanctions, aimed at single individual or entities.[33] An issue of general interest emerging from the EU practice is the jurisdictional scope of application of restrictive measures. In fact, *ratione loci*, although by their very nature they are designed to have political effect in third countries, EU restrictive measures only apply within the jurisdiction of the EU. The EU Sanctions Guidelines expressly "condemn the extra-territorial application of national legislations imposing sanctions, notably in respect of natural and legal persons under the jurisdictions of EU member States"[34] and state that the EU "will refrain from adopting legislative instruments having extra-territorial application in breach of international law".[35] However, the practice shows that the jurisdictional scope of EU restrictive measures is fairly broad. According to the standard clause on jurisdiction envisaged by the EU Sanctions Guidelines, restrictive measures ap-

---

[32] See CREMONA, "EU external action in the JHA domain", in CREMONA, MONAR and POLI (eds.), *The External Dimension of the European Union's Area of Freedom, Security and Justice*, Brussels, 2011, p. 99. The choice for one of the two legal bases (Art. 215 or Art. 75 TFEU) also has implications for the geographical application of the measures. Whilst EU member states are not allowed to opt-out of measures adopted under Art. 215 TFEU, the UK and Denmark do have this option pursuant to Art. 75 TFEU. However, according to ECKES, "EU Counter-terrorist Sanctions against Individuals: Problems and Perils", European Foreign Affairs Review, 2012, p. 113 ff., p. 123, the UK tends to opt-in on it.

[33] As is well known, when the Security Council directs sanctions against individuals it has to use the member state as intermediaries. This is not so in the EU legal system, where acts of secondary legislation are directly applicable and binding in their entirety upon all member states, natural and legal persons. See, for instance, Council Decision 2011/782/CFSP of 1 December 2011 concerning restrictive measures against Syria and repealing Decision 2011/273/CFSP, OJ L 319/56, p. 56, which prohibits, *inter alia*, the sale of arms and related materiel of all types to Syria "by national of Member States" (Art. 1), and states that "all funds and economic resources belonging to, or owned, held or controlled by persons responsible for the violent repression against the civilian population in Syria, persons and entities benefiting from or supporting the regime, and persons and entities associated with them, as listed in Annexes I and II, shall be frozen".

[34] GESTRI, *cit. supra* note 16, p. 79.

[35] EU Sanctions Guidelines, *cit. supra* note 15, para. 52.

ply: within EU territory, including its airspace; to EU nationals, whether or not they are in the EU; to companies incorporated under the law of a member state, whether or not they are in the EU (this therefore includes branches of EU companies in third countries); to any business done in whole or in part within the EU; and on board aircrafts or vessels under the jurisdiction of a member state.[36] However, frequently sanctions policies do not apply to foreign-owned subsidiaries of sanctioned entities. In these cases – such as, for example, the sanctions imposed against Russia's leading financial institutions in 2014, which did not apply to the subsidiary banks those institutions owned within EU countries – the potential impact of the financial sanctions is, therefore, substantially weakened.[37]

Ratione materiae the types of EU restrictive measures do not perfectly match those of UN sanctions. On the one hand, the catalogue of EU restrictive measures is broader as it includes measures that are not covered by UN sanctions practice, such as, for example, the suspension or denunciation of trade agreements or of programmes of aid;[38] restrictions on the exports of telecommunications equipment, technology or software for monitoring and interception;[39] or the prohibition on importing, exporting, transferring or providing related brokering services for cultural property and other items of archaeological, historical, cultural, rare scientific and religious importance illegally removed from the targeted country.[40] On the other hand, the EU has decreed that further, and qualitatively different economic, financial or travel measures should be applied where the UN has already adopted its own set of sanctions. An interesting example is offered by Decision 2017/1860 of 16 October 2017,[41] under which the EU Council adopted a set of new measures to complement and reinforce UN sanctions in order to increase the

---

[36] *Ibid.*, para. 88.

[37] See EARLY, "Confronting the Implementation and Enforcement Challenges Involved in Imposing Economic Sanctions", in RONZITTI (ed.), *Coercive Diplomacy, cit. supra* note 16, p. 43 ff., p. 57.

[38] See European Council, Special Meeting (Doc. EUCO 147/14), 16 July 2014, par. 6, where, as a consequence of the EU's non-recognition of the illegal annexation of Crimea and Sevastopol by Russia, the European Council requested the European Investment Bank (EIB) to suspend the signature of new financing operations in the Russian Federation; and invited the Commission to re-assess, and eventually suspend, the implementation of EU-Russia bilateral and regional cooperation programmes (with the exception of projects dealing exclusively with cross-border cooperation and civil society). Finally, EU member states agreed to coordinate their positions within the European bank for Reconstruction and Development (EBRD) Board of Directors with a view to also suspending financing of new operations.

[39] Council Decision (CFSP) 2017/2074, *cit. supra* note 2, Art. 5; and Council Regulation (EU) 2017/2063 of 13 November 2017 concerning restrictive measures in view of the situation in Venezuela, OJ L 295, p. 21, Art. 6. See also Council Regulation (EU) No. 36/2012, of 18 January 2012 concerning restrictive measures in view of the situation in Syria and repealing Regulation (EU) No. 442/2011, OJ L 016, p. 1, Art. 4.

[40] See Council Regulation (EU) No. 36/2012, *cit. supra* note 39, Art. 11(c).

[41] Council Decision (CFSP) 2017/1860 of 16 October 2017 amending Decision (CFSP) 2016/849 concerning restrictive measures against the Democratic People's Republic of Korea, OJ L 265I, p. 8; and Council Regulation (EU) 2017/1858 of 16 October 2017 amending Regulation (EU) 2017/1509 concerning restrictive measures against the Democratic People's Republic of Korea, OJ L 265I, p. 1.

pressure on the Democratic People's Republic of Korea (DPRK) to comply with its obligations under international law. The new measures include: a) a total ban on EU investment in the DPRK in all sectors; b) a total ban on the sale of refined petroleum products and crude oil to the DPRK (subject to certain limitations under UN Security Council resolution 2375);[42] c) lowering the amount of personal remittances transferred to the DPRK from €15,000 to €5,000; and d) the decision not to renew work authorisations for DPRK nationals present on their territory, except for refugees and other persons benefitting from international protection.

A final remark on a very recent development of EU arms embargoes: when dual-use items or services related to military technology are concerned, they need to be listed in *ad hoc* regulations; in March 2018, acting under Directive 2009/43/EC ("Transfer Directive"), the EU attempted to provide interpretative guidelines for the term "specially designed for military use" (SDfMU). The guidance, directed to member states competent authorities and the defence industry alike, is intended to facilitate the assessment of whether a specific item is subject to control or not, while, at the same time promoting a unified approach across the EU.[43]

5. JUDICIAL REVIEW OF SANCTIONS AGAINST NATURAL OR LEGAL PERSONS BY THE EUROPEAN COURT OF JUSTICE

Before proceeding to the analysis of the implementation of EU sanctions and the role of member States, one final point should be discussed at the institutional level: i.e. the judicial review of sanctions performed by the ECJ. Although sanctions have been successfully challenged before other national and international (i.e. the European Court of Human Rights) jurisdictions on the ground that they hinder the fundamental rights of targeted persons, the EU is the legal order where judicial challenges have been quantitatively (i.e. in terms of numbers) and qualitatively (suffice it here to mention the impact of the judicial review of restrictive measures within the EU on the global system of economic sanctions) more significant. This is not the place to discuss the case-law which has nourished a huge body of literature in the last decade.[44] For the purposes of our analysis though, a recent judgment concerning the jurisdictional issue of the Court is of significance in that its final outcome is to strengthen the Court's power of judicial review of CFSP acts.

Article 275(2) TFEU introduced two exceptions (the "claw-backs") to the general rule whereby the Court of Justice has no jurisdiction in the field of

---

[42] See Security Council Resolution 2375 (2017), 11 September 2017, para. 14.

[43] The EU Commission has invited industry comments on the draft guidance via an online survey, available at: <https://ec.europa.eu/eusurvey/runner/Survey-Guideline-for-Specially-Designed-for-Military-Use-2018>.

[44] See further PANTALEO, "Sanctions Cases in the European Courts", in HAPPOLD (ed.), *cit. supra* note 16, p. 171 ff., and the literature referred to therein.

CFSP.[45] First, the Court may monitor compliance with Article 40 TEU (which replaces former Article 47 TEU). This provision establishes a mutual non-encroachment rule between the CFSP and the other EU competences.[46] According to the second exception the Court can rule on proceedings brought in accordance with the conditions laid down in the fourth paragraph of Article 263 TFEU, reviewing the legality of decisions providing for restrictive measures against natural or legal persons adopted by the Council in the field of CFSP.[47] According to those derogatory provisions, the Court of Justice has, therefore, not only jurisdiction over the executive regulation adopted on the basis of the CFSP act but also, contrary to the pre-Lisbon period, to review the legality of a CFSP act itself.[48] After the Judgment of 28 March 2017 in *Rosneft*,[49] this might happen not only by virtue of a literal interpretation of Article 275(2), to hear annulment proceedings of CFSP acts brought by private parties pursuant to Article 263(4) TFEU; but also in circumstances where the Court is seized, under the preliminary ruling procedure provided for in Article 267 TFEU, of a request by a national court or tribunal which has doubts as to the validity of such measures.[50] This case, referred to the Court by the High Court of Justice (England and Wales) in the United Kingdom, concerned Decision 2014/512 concerning restrictive measures in view of Russia's actions destabilising the situation in Ukraine, which was adopted under Article 29 TEU and implemented in the EU legal order by virtue of Regulation 833/2014.[51] First of all, in order to ascertain whether or not the question of jurisdiction was admissible[52] the Court observed

---

[45] See also Art. 24(1) TEU, which, *inter alia*, states that "[t]he Court of Justice of the European Union shall not have jurisdiction with respect to these provisions [i.e. CFSP], with the exception of its jurisdiction to monitor compliance with Article 40 of this Treaty and to review the legality of certain decisions as provided for by the second paragraph of Article 275 of the Treaty on the Functioning of the European Union".

[46] On the application of art. 40 TEU to CFSP decisions imposing sanctions, see BEAUCILLON, "Opening up the Horizon: the ECJ's New Take on Country Sanctions", CML Rev, 2018, p. 391 ff.

[47] See Consolidated version of the Treaty on the Functioning of the European Union, OJ C 326, 26 October 2012, p. 47, Art. 275(2).

[48] See BRKAN, "The Role of the European Court of Justice in the Field of Common Foreign and Security Policy After the Treaty of Lisbon: New Challenges for the Future", in CARDWELL (ed.), *EU External Relations Law and Policy in the Post-Lisbon Era*, The Hague, 2012, p. 110 ff. For earlier discussion, see BEBR, *Development of Judicial Control of the European Communities*, The Hague, 1981.

[49] See Case C-72/15, *PJSC Rosneft Oil Company v. Her Majesty's Treasury and Others*, 28 March 2017.

[50] The leading academic material on EU procedural law prior to the *Rosneft* case recognised that this is by no means a settled question and that the Court "may afford possibilities" in this area. See LENAERTS, MASELIS and GUTMAN, *EU Procedural Law* (edited by NOWAK), Oxford, 2014, p. 458.

[51] See Council Decision 2014/512/CFSP, *cit. supra* note 8, and Council Regulation (EU) No. 833/2014 of 31 July 2014 concerning restrictive measures in view of Russia's actions destabilising the situation in Ukraine, OJ L 229, p. 1.

[52] Most parties who submitted observations (the Council and the Commission, the UK, Czech, German, French, Polish and Estonian governments) were, indeed, in favour of the Court dismissing the case.

that if it were to examine, as a literal interpretation of Article 275(2) TFEU would suggest, solely the questions raised in the main proceedings in the light of Regulation No. 833/2014, that would be likely to provide an inadequate answer to the concerns of the referring court, as the *two acts were inextricably tied*.[53] Put differently, the Court argued that, having regard to how restrictive measures are imposed in the EU legal order, the assessment of the validity of Decision 2014/512 was of crucial importance in order to determine the scope of the resulting obligations, otherwise the potential invalidity of Regulation No. 833/2014 would have not had any effect on the obligation of member states to ensure that their national policies conformed to the restrictive measures established pursuant to Decision 2014/512. However, whilst it was undisputed that the Regulation, based on Article 215 TFEU, fell within the Court's jurisdiction, the justiciability of the Council Decision was much more controversial. The reasoning of the Court in answering positively was based upon two premises.

Firstly, the Court recalled that the EU is "a complete system of legal remedies",[54] and that requests for preliminary rulings which seek to ascertain the validity of a measure constitute, like actions for annulment, means for reviewing the legality of EU acts.[55] The Court thus argued that a breach of the principle of effective judicial protection – now established by Article 47 of the Charter of Fundamental Rights of the European Union – would occur if a national court or tribunal, with no jurisdiction to declare the invalidity of provisions contained in EU acts on which decisions or national measures are nonetheless based, was prevented from consulting the Court on that matter by means of a reference for a preliminary ruling.[56]

Secondly, the Court rejected a literal and restrictive interpretation of Article 275(2) TFEU, arguing that it is not the type of procedure (i.e. an action for annulment) that is covered by that provision, but rather the type of decisions the legality of which may be reviewed by the Court through any procedure institutionally designed with that aim.[57] To sum up, according to the Court, provided that, in those circumstances, it has jurisdiction *ratione materiae* to rule on the validity of EU restrictive measures against natural or legal persons, it would be inconsistent with the system of effective judicial protection established by the Treaties, as well as detrimental to the uniform application of EU law within the EU legal order, to interpret Article 275 TFEU as excluding the possibility for member states' courts and tribunals to refer questions to the Court on the validity of Council decisions prescribing the adoption of such measures. A reference for a preliminary ruling must however relate, in the Court's reasoning, to review either of the legality of the decision itself vis-à-vis Article 40 TEU or of the legality of restrictive measures against natural or legal persons.[58]

---

[53] *PJSC Rosneft Oil Company*, cit. *supra* note 49, para. 53.
[54] *Ibid.*, para. 66, citing Case 294/83, *Les Verts v. Parliament*, 23 April 1986, para. 23.
[55] *Ibid.*, para. 68, citing Case 314/85, *Foto-Frost*, 22 October 1987, para. 16.
[56] *Ibid.*, paras. 68-74.
[57] *Ibid.*, para. 70.
[58] *Ibid.*, ruling 1.

In the view of some authors, the scope of the Court's interpretative powers under Article 267 TFEU with regard to the CFSP rules, remains, despite this ruling, still largely unclear.[59] Others have suggested that the *Rosneft* judgment "squares the circle" of effective judicial review of restrictive measures, by extending general EU legal remedies to CFSP decisions on the basis of the principle of the rule of law.[60] It seems, however, undisputable that the *Rosneft* ruling added a further element to the unique character of the EU's experience towards sanctions in the international context. By validating the possibility of monitoring the legality of restrictive measures through the preliminary ruling procedure, not only did the Court encourage, from a bottom-up perspective, domestic courts to review the validity of such measures and apply for preliminary rulings before the ECJ (thus enabling them to play a far greater role in that area than they did previously),[61] but it also cemented a top-down approach which is intended to ensure that even in the CFSP area the core principle of effective judicial protection can not be evaded.

6. THE ROLE OF MEMBER STATES IN THE IMPLEMENTATION OF SANCTIONS

Another defining structural element of restrictive measures adopted by the EU is the role played by member states in their implementation. This is most evident at two distinct times: the adoption of additional acts by member states in order for the EU restrictive measures to be concretely applicable vis-à-vis natural and legal persons; and the day-to-day operation of the EU sanctions regimes.

Starting with the first, as mentioned above, the actual implementation of the restrictive measures imposed at EU level frequently requires further legislative or administrative action on the part of member states. This typically happens, *inter alia*, in respect of the determination of the so-called "secondary sanctions", that is to say penalties for violation of the restrictive measures.[62] In this regard, the regulations imposing restrictive measures regularly include a standard clause, which is also set out in the Sanctions Guideline,[63] referring to the duties of member states to "lay down the rules on penalties applicable to infringements of the provisions" of the relevant regulation; "take all the necessary measures to ensure that they are implemented", and provide penalties that "must be effective, proportionate and dissuasive".[64]

---

[59] See also WAHL and PRETE, "The Gatekeepers of Article 267 TFEU: On Jurisdiction and Admissibility of Reference for Preliminary Rulings", CML Rev, 2018, p. 520 ff.

[60] BEAUCILLON, *cit. supra* note 46, p. 393.

[61] *Ibid.*, p. 394.

[62] ECKES, *EU Counter-Terrorist Policies and Fundementak Rights: The Case of Individual Sanctions*, Oxford, 2009, pp. 54-56.

[63] Guidelines on implementation and evaluation of restrictive measures, *cit. supra* note 15, paras. 89-90.

[64] See, e.g., Council Regulation (EU) No. 692/2014 of 23 June 2014 concerning restrictions on the import into the Union of goods originating in Crimea or Sevastopol, in response to the illegal annexation of Crimea and Sevastopol, OJ L183, p. 9 ff.

In principle, by virtue of such a provision, member states can choose the legal nature of the penalty: in effect, penalties envisaged by member states range from measures of administrative or civil nature to criminal law penalties. Also the level of penalties remains within the discretion of each member state, which is only limited by the requirements concerning effectiveness, proportionality, and dissuasion.[65] Although this quasi-stereotypical formula was elaborated by the ECJ in its case law[66] and is now commonly used in EU legislation, the interpretation of the different requirements, being made pursuant to the case law discussed above, is not an easy task,[67] and has occasionally led to disputes. In particular, for criminal penalties, the legislative techniques used in the EU and its member states to criminalise the violations of sanctions have been challenged before both domestic judges and the European courts in the light of principle of legal certainty. [68] Furthermore, the delegation to the 28 (about to become 27) member states of the competence to lay down the rules on "secondary sanctions" could determine inconsistencies in the repression of violations.[69] The inconsistencies in member states' domestic legislations concerning secondary sanctions may favour non-compliance with, or circumvention of, restrictive sanctions decided at EU level. Looking at the possible solutions offered by the Lisbon Treaty, one has to conclude that attempts at "centralisation" are rather unlikely. First, even if it cannot be absolutely ruled out, a decision that, pursuant to Article 83(1) TFEU, identifies sanctions violations as an additional Euro-crime is rather unrealistic. By the same token, given the formulation of Article 83(2) TFEU, it does not seem that Article 215 TFEU can be included "among the areas for which ancillary criminal competence foreseen by the first provision could be exercised".[70]

Another defining element of the EU sanctions regimes is the member states' key involvement in their daily operation. As observed in the legal literature, "while the EU legislation sets EU sanctions policy, adopts sanctions programs and designated targets the day-to-day operation of the EU sanctions regime falls

---

[65] GESTRI, *cit. supra* note 16, pp. 88-89, to whom we refer for further considerations on the different techniques used in the member states.

[66] For instance, in Case 122/78, *SA Buitoni v. Fonds d'orientation et de régulation des marches agricoles*, ECR, 1979, 677, para. 16, in analysing sanctions for conduct affecting an EC interest, the ECJ opined that "they must not be disproportionate to the gravity of the infringement" and that the "penalty must not exceed what is appropriate and necessary to attain the objective sought". See also Case 68/88, *Commission v. Greece*, 21 September 1989, paras. 86-92.

[67] See the Joined Cases C-387/02, C-391/02 and C-403/02, *Berlusconi and Others*, Opinion of the Advocate General Kokott, 14 October 2004.

[68] See, *e.g.*, High Court of Justice, Queen's Bench Division, Divisional Court, *The Queen on the Application of PJSC Rosneft Oil Company v. Her Majesty's Treasury and Others*, 10 February 2015, [2015] EWHC 248 (Admin)

[69] ECKES, *cit. supra* note 62, pp. 55-56.

[70] GESTRI, *cit. supra* note 16, p. 91. Art. 83(2) refers to areas in which the ordinary or special legislative procedure is foreseen for the adoption of harmonisation measures, which is not the case of Art. 215 TFEU.

to the Member States".[71] This is because the EU is not endowed with enforcement agencies having general competence. Thus, it is up to member states to monitor the application of the restrictive measures by natural and legal persons and ensure the effective enforcement of the sanctions by the same subjects. National authorities are under the duty to report to the Commission on their monitoring and enforcing activities. Furthermore, the granting of exemptions, which is generally based on a case-by-case assessment, is also entrusted to member states.[72] It does not come as a surprise that the reliance on the national authorities of the separate member states for this other key aspect of the implementation of EU restrictive measures has raised concerns about possible inconsistencies in their concrete application.

To conclude on the point, divergences in the actual implementation of EU sanctions may indeed stem from unequal availability of financial resources in the different states, from different levels of expertise and professionalism of the authorities involved in the administration, but also from different positions in respect of the targeted entities or from an inclination to privilege the economic interests of domestic operators. At present, the only tool for "soft" coordination among member states in the implementation of EU sanctions consists of exchanging experience and developing best practices, which, in respect of the delegated competences at issue (monitoring and enforcement; granting of exemptions), is ensured by the Sanction Formation in RELEX. Finally, under EU law the full and proper implementation by member states of the EU legislation on restrictive measures should be guaranteed by the EU Commission ("the guardian of the Treaties") and, finally, the EU Courts. More specifically, while the infringement procedure against a member state which fails to adopt the necessary implementing rules in this matter, started by the Commission pursuant to Article 258 TFEU (or by another member state according to Article 259 TFEU) can be regarded as an *extrema ratio*, the same body plays a pivotal role in favouring the uniform implementation of sanctions through a relentless dialogue with national authorities and other stakeholders,[73] as well as through the practice of publishing guidance documents.[74]

7. PROSPECT ON SANCTIONS FOR THE UK AFTER BREXIT

Upon leaving the EU, the United Kingdom (UK) will pursue an independent foreign policy. However, the Foreign and Commonwealth Office (FCO) in a

---

[71] GOLUMBIC and RUFF, "Who Do I Call for an EU Sanctions Exemption?: Why the EU Economic Sanctions Regime Should Centralize Licensing", Georgetown Journal of International Law, 2013, p. 1007 ff., p. 1042.

[72] Guidelines on implementation and evaluation of restrictive measures, *cit. supra* note 15, para. 126.

[73] GESTRI, *cit. supra* note 16, pp. 94-5.

[74] See, *e.g.*, European Commission Notice of 25 September 2009, Commission Guidance note on the implementation of certain provisions of Regulation (EU) No 833/2014, C(2015) 6477 final.

recent report to the UK Parliament has observed that: "[w]e are seeking a close and cooperative relationship that goes beyond existing third country relationships with the EU".[75] In particular, the UK "will want to *continue to work closely together on sanctions*. There are several models this can take, from formal mechanisms for dialogue and information sharing, to more informal engagement, which is largely how the US works with the EU".[76]

The "sanctions' issue" will be dealt with according to the Sanctions and Anti-Money Laundering Bill (the Sanctions Bill), which was introduced in the House of Lords on 18 October 2017, and is, at the time of writing, before the House of Commons.[77] Considering that the European Communities Act (ECA) 1972, on which the UK's current implementation of UN and other multilateral sanctions regimes largely relies,[78] is due to be repealed by the European Union Withdrawal Bill 2017-19,[79] the Sanctions Bill will provide a new legal framework for imposing sanctions. This act, the first relating to Brexit that has been introduced in the Parliament, will provide, in particular, the UK with the necessary legal powers to continue to implement UN, EU and other international mandated sanctions,[80] and to introduce new measures which in practice may go beyond simply adopting UN and EU sanctions in their entirety.

---

[75] See FCO, "The future of UK diplomacy in Europe: Government response to the Committee's Second Report", 14 March 2018, available at: <https://publications.parliament.uk/pa/cm201719/cmselect/cmfaff/918/91802.htm>.

[76] *Ibid.*, emphasis added. On the introduction in the House of Lords of the Sanctions and Anti-Money Laundering Bill, see *infra* note 7, the Minister of State for Europe, Sir Alan Duncan, declared that: "[s]anctions are most effective when delivered by a coalition of countries acting together and we expect to continue working closely with our partners in the EU and the rest of the world to take decisive action when needed. This Bill will ensure we retain the powers we need to remain a responsible and reliable security partner"; available at: <https://www.gov.uk/government/news/new-sanctions-bill-introduced-in-house-of-lords>.

[77] See Sanctions and Anti-Money Laundering Bill [HL] 2017-19, Progress of the Bill, available at: <https://services.parliament.uk/bills/2017-19/sanctionsandantimoneylaundering.html>. See also WHITE, *cit. supra* note 10.

[78] Generally, UN-mandated sanctions as well as those adopted independently by the EU are usually applied in the UK by making Statutory Instruments (SIs or secondary legislation) using powers in the ECA 1972. In case sanctions decisions are accompanied by Council regulations using Art. 215 TFEU no SI is necessary. UK domestic powers are, in fact, limited to imposing sanctions in domestic counter-terrorism, through the Terrorist Asset-Freezing etc. Act 2010 (c. 38), and export control through the Export Control Act 2002 (c. 28). With regard to the Terrorist Asset Freezing Act (2010), it is worth noting that the Bill will repeal its Part 1 which sets out the current legal grounds on which the UK Government can impose terrorist-related sanctions.

[79] See European Union (Withdrawal) Bill 2017-19, Progress of the Bill, available at: <https://services.parliament.uk/bills/2017-19/europeanunionwithdrawal.html>.

[80] As for EU sanctions, the Withdrawal Bill will preserve (i.e. freeze) current sanctions regimes in effect on the Brexit date. Clause 8 of the Withdrawal Bill does empower ministers to make any regulation to prevent or remedy a breach of the UK's international obligations arising from withdrawal, but this would not provide a permanent legal basis for implementing sanctions. Without a new domestic legal framework, the UK would therefore not be able to add, amend or lift these sanctions regimes.

The Bill proposes the utilisation of similar prohibitions to those currently in place through EU legislation:[81] financial, immigration, trade, aircraft, shipping sanctions (Clauses 3-7) and other sanctions for purposes of UN obligations (Clause 8). As for the procedure for the adoption of regulations imposing sanctions, according to Clause 1 they may only be made by "an appropriate Minister" (defined as the Secretary of State or the Treasury): 1) to comply with a UN obligation, or with any other international obligations; or 2) for specific purposes, which include, *inter alia*, "to further the prevention of terrorism both in the UK and elsewhere; [...] to promote the resolution of armed conflicts or the protection of civilians in conflict zones; to promote compliance with international humanitarian and human rights law; [...] and to further a foreign policy objective".[82]

This part of the Bill has been openly and strongly criticised on the ground that it would give Ministers sweeping powers to legislate by regulation without sufficient Parliamentary control.[83] In order to address this criticism, a further requirement has been added by the Government in the latest version of the text: for regulations made for purposes other than compliance with a UN or other international obligation, the "appropriate Minister" must determine that there are "good reasons" to pursue the regulation's specific aim, and that the imposition of sanctions is "a reasonable course of action for that purpose" (Clause 2).[84]

The Bill has been also criticised where, dealing with regulations which authorise an "appropriate Minister" to designate persons by name, it sets out a need for "reasonable grounds to suspect" and for the minister concerned to decide that it is "appropriate" for sanctions to be applied (Clause 11). In the context of House of Lords debate, it was asked for an explicit reference to proportionality in that section of the Bill "since it is the legal test applied by UK courts and the ECJ".[85] At second reading, the Minister Lord Ahmad of Wimbledon, said that "where human rights are affected, a minister will always need to comply with the European Convention on Human Rights (ECHR) and Strasbourg case law, and that will include an assessment of proportionality". While expressing their gratitude for the Minister's confirmation that an assessment of proportionality will be required

---

[81] The most recent version of the text of the Bill, as amended in Public Bill Committee, 6 March 2018, is available at: <https://services.parliament.uk/bills/2017-19/sanctionsandanti-moneylaundering.html>.

[82] Note that, during the debate in the House of Lords held on 21 November 2017, Lady Northover proposed to leave out that last phrase wondering whether, for example, a person could be sanctioned for opposing Government policy like the invasion of Iraq in 2003; available at: <https://hansard.parliament.uk/Lords/2017-11-21/debates/E6CE0C5F-4B00-4A19-B104-8C30909958E5/SanctionsAndAnti-MoneyLaunderingBill(HL)#contribution-6365591D-C0FC-4F75-BE4F-EFACF77E9D13>.

[83] See further House of Common Library, Briefing Paper (CBP 8232), "The Sanctions and Anti-Money Laundering Bill 2017-2019", 15 February 2018, p. 30 ff., available at: <https://researchbriefings.parliament.uk/ResearchBriefing/Summary/CBP-8232#fullreport>.

[84] See also House of Lords, House of Commons, Joint Committee on Human Rights, Legislative Scrutiny: The Sanctions and Anti-Money Laundering Bill (HL Paper 87, HC 568), 1 March 2018, p. 4: "Inclusion of clause 2 mitigates our concerns about the broad powers given by clause 1 of the Bill".

[85] Briefing Paper (CBP 8232), *cit. supra* note 83, p. 44.

when making a designation affecting an individual's human rights, the Lords nevertheless recommended "that this important limitation on ministers' powers should be stated expressly on the face of the Bill".[86]

Due to limitations of space, we can only briefly comment on some further criticism raised in relation to the Sanctions Bill currently under discussion before the British Parliament. Although it provides for various powers of review by the appropriate Minister and the rights of designated individuals to request variation, revocation, or review of their designation, remarkably: Clause 21 reduces the frequency of reviews to a triennial review (while currently designations are reviewed annually);[87] Clause 34(2) removes the power of the courts to award damages unless the impugned decision was made in bad faith or negligence;[88] further, whilst, currently, under the Terrorist Asset-Freezing etc. Act 2010, an individual subject to an asset-freeze can exercise full rights of appeal, the Bill under discussion has regressed from this position by limiting the courts' powers to judicial review, which confines the court to assessing whether the decision was unlawful, unreasonable, or procedurally unfair, but does not allow it to conduct a full merits review.[89]

8. THE LEGAL POSITION OF CANDIDATE STATES

If we widen the gaze beyond the conventional sanctions sender-target polarity and observe the impact of sanctions on relations with third countries, it emerges that, since the beginning of the CFSP in the mid-1990s, the EU has asked third countries to publicly declare their support of sanctions.[90] In particular, when EU autonomous sanctions are adopted, EU institutions work "in order to enlist the support of the widest possible range of partners"[91] because, as noted in the EU Sanctions Guidelines "the effectiveness of restrictive measures is directly related to the adoption of similar measures by third countries".[92] Overall, the practice demonstrates that the EU often succeeds in aligning the conduct of a considerable number of countries with its own.[93] This holds true especially for candidate countries (Albania, Montenegro and, less consistently, the FYRM, Serbia and Turkey), potential candidates (Bosnia and Herzegovina and Kosovo) and members of the European Economic Area (EEA). As Gestri rightly notes, from a strictly legal viewpoint, third countries generally remain completely free

---

[86] *Ibid.*, p. 45.

[87] HL Paper 87, HC 568, *cit. supra* note 84, p. 16.

[88] *Ibid.*, p. 21.

[89] *Ibid.*, p. 19.

[90] See further HELLQUIST, "Either with Us or Against Us? Third Countries Alignment with EU Sanctions against Russia/Ukraine", Cambridge Review of International Affairs, p. 997 ff., pp. 1000-1007.

[91] Basic Principles on the Use of Restrictive Measures (Sanctions), *cit. supra* note 13, para. 4.

[92] Guidelines on implementation and evaluation of restrictive measures, *cit. supra* note 15, Annex 1, para. 21.

[93] HELLQUIST, *cit. supra* note 90, pp. 1003-1007.

to align with EU restrictive measures ("which are for them *res inter alios acta*"), or not.[94] Yet the case of candidate countries is worthy of further consideration. On the political level, they are generally expected by EU institutions to adhere to EU restrictive measures.[95] But are they under a legal obligation to do so?

A problem has recently arisen with the unwillingness of Serbia, the FYRM and Turkey to align with the EU sanctions in reaction to the Ukraine crisis.[96] Neither the official declarations rendered in 2014 by the EU Commissioner for Neighbouring Policy and Enlargement Negotiations, Johannes Hahn, nor the answers to a Parliamentary question by the HR, Federica Mogherini, on behalf of the Commission, on 20 February 2015, contain conclusive elements to assess the issue.[97] On the other hand, both Serbia and Turkey have openly contested the logic behind sanctions alignment. In particular, in an interview in the German weekly Die Zeit, Foreign Minister Cavusoglu underlined that Turkey is under no obligation to align with sanctions against Russia;[98] a position he reiterated by replying to a statement of HR Mogherini during an official visit to Ankara in December 2014, pointing to "a contradiction of the EU", where Turkey is asked to align while being "kept out of the decision mechanisms".[99]

Leaving aside the delicate political controversy, the legal position of candidate countries should be assessed vis-à-vis the different prisms of international and EU law. From the viewpoint of public international law, one could at best claim that, in the light of the principle of good faith, candidate countries having started accession negotiations (which is the case for both Serbia and Turkey),[100] are obliged not to intentionally undermine the CFSP.[101] On the other hand, as is well-known, under EU law, acceptance of the EU *acquis* is a pre-condition for accession and there is no doubt that a protracted failure, on the part of a candidate state, to conform to EU restrictive measures could end up blocking the accession process.

---

[94] GESTRI, *cit. supra* note 16, p. 77.

[95] Guidelines on implementation and evaluation of restrictive measures, *cit. supra* note 15, Annex 1, para. 22.

[96] HELLQUIST, *cit. supra* note 90, pp. 1009-1012.

[97] To this effect see also GESTRI, *cit. supra* note 16, pp. 78-79; HELLQUIST, *cit. supra* note 90, p. 1012.

[98] See "Türkei: Und Wie Helft Ihr?", Die Zeit, 2015, available at: <http://www.zeit. de/2015/07/tuerkei-aussenminister-pkk-islamischer-staat-ukraine-krise>.

[99] See "Turkey rebuffs EU criticism on waning foreign policy alignment", Newsweek/ Reuters, 9 December 2014, available at: <http://www.newsweek.com/turkey-rebuffs-eu-criti-cismwaning-foreign-policy-alignment-290393>.

[100] As to the FYRM, since October 2009, the Commission has recommended the opening of accession negotiations with the country, until 2015 when it made this conditional on continued implementation of the Pržino agreement and substantial progress in the implementation of the "Urgent Reform Priorities". See further: European Commission, "European Neighbourhood Policy And Enlargement Negotiations", available at: <https://ec.europa.eu/ neighbourhood-enlargement/node_en>.

[101] To this effect see authoritatively GESTRI, *cit. supra* note 16, p. 79. On the extension of the obligation to refrain from acts which would impair the object and purpose of an eventual agreement to the negotiations phase, see, *ex multis.*, BOISSON DE CHAZOURNES, LA ROSA and MBENGUE, "Article 18 (1969)", in KLEIN and CORTEN (eds.), *The Vienna Convention on the Law of Treaties: A Commentary*, Vol. 1, Oxford, 2011, p. 369 ff., p. 398.

9. CONCLUDING REMARKS

The foregoing analysis leads to a number of conclusions.

First, the assessment of the EU recent practice confirms, *inter alia*, that autonomous sanctions are ever more frequently made by the EU to complement UN Security Council mandated measures, and to substitute action by the same body when its members cannot agree on the imposition of restrictive measures. Second, it further evidences that the same sanctions have served the EU and its member states' own interests also with the view to promoting the European construction of values generally shared within international society. Thirdly, such a liberal use of restrictive measures on the part of EU institutions poses notable legal questions concerning their lawfulness. The lawfulness of each measure has to be carefully weighed against the law of treaties (according to the principle *inademplenti non est adimplendum*) or the law of the international responsibility of states and international organisations ("countermeasures"). Fourth, the concrete implementation of EU sanctions is mainly determined by the conduct of member states: this holds true especially for the adoption of administrative or legislative acts on the part of member states in order for restrictive measures to be concretely applicable vis-à-vis natural and legal persons, and for the day-to-day operation of the EU sanctions regimes. The delegation of such key aspects to the different member states' authorities may result in divergences in the actual implementation of EU sanctions and, hence also favour non-compliance with, or circumvention of, the same measures.

Finally, two cutting-edge developments deserve brief dedicated remarks. On Brexit: during the parliamentary debates, the UK draft legislation designed to regulate the issue of sanctions has been openly and strongly criticised on the ground of excessive power of the executive; concerns about the impairment of the principle of proportionality and attenuation of judicial review on the merits for individual sanctions. This signals that, although the UK is party to the ECHR and despite its long membership in the EU, its exit is perceived as potentially disruptive for the prerogatives of individuals affected by restrictive measures. As to the ruling of the Grand Chamber of the Court of Justice of the EU in *Rosneft*, its importance is self-evident. In the limited space of these closing notes, we would simply remark that, affirming its full jurisdiction to review sanctions also through the preliminary ruling procedure, the Court's judgment in *Rosneft* looks like a final say on the naïveté of doctrinal stances which still question the legitimacy of EU restrictive measures adopted in addition to, or in the absence of, UN sanctions under Article 41 of the Charter upon the ground that "the EU treaties do not provide a legal basis for EU's economic trade and financial measures of this kind".[102]

---

[102] ORAKHELASHVILI, "Sanctions and Fundamental Rights of States: The Case of EU Sanctions Against Iran and Syria", in HAPPOLD (ed.), *cit. supra* note 16, p. 13 ff., p. 33. In that perspective, it is worth mentioning the EU Court of Justice Case C-348/12, *Council v. Manufacturing Support & Procurement Kala Naft Co., Tehran*, 28 November 2013, para. 109, according to which Arts. 29 TEU and 215 TFEU *per se* give the Council the power to adopt "independent restrictive measures, distinct from the measures specifically recommended by the Security Council".

NATIONAL MARGIN OF APPRECIATION AS A STANDARD OF REVIEW FOR ECONOMIC SANCTIONS: IN SEARCH OF THE GOLDEN FLEECE?

Viktoriia Lapa*

Abstract

Recent economic sanctions imposed by the EU and US on Russia in relation to the Ukrainian conflict revived a discussion concerning the security exception clauses in international law. These clauses permit a particular state to take action aimed at protection of its national security that might be otherwise inconsistent with its substantive treaty obligations. Taking into account the ambiguity of such clauses, the question arises as to how to verify whether the adopted sanctions are indeed introduced with national security in mind and not to pursue pure protectionist aims. This article examines the national margin of appreciation from the perspective of its suitability as a standard of review for sanctions introduced under umbrella of the security exception provision of the General Agreement on Tariffs and Trade. Since this doctrine was developed in the case-law of the European Court of Human Rights both academics and practitioners alike are undecided as to its application in international trade and investment law disputes. In search of inspiration for an appropriate standard of review, the article briefly analyses recent Court of Justice of the European Union cases dealing with the security exception provisions. Drawing from the analysis of the relevant case-law of the international tribunals, the research points out that despite its frequent use by the European Court of Human Rights this doctrine remains vague, which, in turn, makes it hard to transplant to international economic law. The author concludes that the abstract contours of the national margin of appreciation doctrine, combined with diverging goals of the European Convention on Human Rights and world trade systems, make it unsuited for review of economic sanctions.

Keywords: economic sanctions; national margin of appreciation; GATT security exception provision; standard of review.

1. INTRODUCTION

States impose on each other different types of sanctions, including, but not limited to, travel-bans against specific persons, asset freezes and embargoes.

---

*PhD student in Legal Studies, International Law and Economics. Unless otherwise indicated, all websites were last accessed on 28 February 2018. The paper has benefitted greatly from discussions with and remarks of Professors Giorgio Sacerdoti and Gary N. Horlick. The author would also like to thank the researchers at Max Planck Institute for Comparative Public and International Law in Heidelberg for their meaningful comments. All errors are my own.

This research deals with economic sanctions, that is, trade-restrictive measures[1] introduced to coerce target countries into complying with their obligations under international agreements.[2] Economic sanctions have always been a tool of coercive diplomacy[3] and their use multilaterally under the auspices of the UN Security Council (UNSC)[4] and unilaterally by states under national legislation has increased recently. These are considered in light of the recent sanctions collaboratively imposed by the European Union (EU) and United States (US) on Russia in relation to the Ukrainian conflict.[5] Similar cases are the US sanctions against North Korea,[6] Russian sanctions against Turkey,[7] and the US sanctions against Iran[8] to name a few. In this regard, it is also worth mentioning counter-sanctions, like those brought by Russia against the EU and US.[9]

Since the imposition of trade-restrictive measures is contrary to the rules of the World Trade Organisation (WTO) and other obligations under international

---

[1] The terms "trade restrictive measures" and "economic sanctions" are used interchangeably.

[2] It is of note that some states may apply sanctions by recourse to their *erga omnes* obligations. For example, in the case of sanctions applied by Australia against Russia, Australia refers to "the Russian threat to the sovereignty and territorial integrity of Ukraine". The list of Australian sanctions is available at: <http://dfat.gov.au/international-relations/security/sanctions/sanctions-regimes/Pages/russia.aspx>. In other words, it may be claimed that Australia imposes sanctions within its *erga omnes* obligations against the act of aggression by Russia. For detailed discussion of *erga omnes* obligations see RAGAZZI, *The Concept of International Obligations Erga Omnes*, Oxford, 2000.

[3] Coercive diplomacy is the purposeful combination of threats and diplomacy aimed at "persuad[ing] an opponent to stop or undo his effort to alter a status quo situation that itself endangers the peace or [...] already involves naked military aggression": GEORGE, *Forceful Persuasion: Coercive Diplomacy as an Alternative to War* ,Washington DC, 1992, p. 11.

[4] Consolidated United Nations Security Council Sanctions is available at: <https://www.un.org/sc/suborg/en/sanctions/un-sc-consolidated-list>.

[5] For EU Sanctions, see Council Regulation (EU) No. 833/2014, available at: <http://eur-lex.europa.eu/legal-content/EN/TXT/?uri=celex:32014R0833>. For US Sanctions, see US President Executive Order (E.O.) 13660, 13661, 13662, 13685. The Ukraine/Russia-Related Sanctions are available at: <https://www.treasury.gov/resource-center/sanctions/Programs/pages/ukraine.aspx>.

[6] The US has imposed sanctions on North Korea to impede Pyongyang's development of missiles and nuclear weapons. The list of sanctions is available at: <https://www.treasury.gov/resource-center/sanctions/Programs/Pages/nkorea.aspx>.

[7] Russia imposed sanctions against Turkey following the shooting down of the Russian jet by Turkey on 24 November 2015. The sanctions were introduced by the Decree of the President of the Russian Federation of 28 November 2015, No. 538, "On the measures as to ensuring national security of the Russian Federation and defense of the citizens of the Russian Federation from the criminal or other illegal actions and on imposition of specific economic measures in relation to the Turkish Republic". Most of the economic measures were lifted on 31 May 2017.

[8] US sanctions against Iran are available at: <https://www.treasury.gov/resource-center/sanctions/Programs/Pages/iran.aspx>.

[9] Russia imposed a ban on agricultural products from the EU and other countries, that imposed sanctions on Russia by the Decree of the President of the Russian Federation "On imposition of special economic measures for the purposes of ensuring security of the Russian Federation", dated 06 August 2014, No. 560.

agreements, states resort to the security exception clauses to justify their sanctions if they are challenged before the international tribunals. In other words, "security exceptions" are the provisions that allow states to derogate from their treaty obligations to preserve their national security and/or to put pressure on other countries to stop aggressive actions. This article, in particular, tackles the exceptions that allow derogations from treaty obligations based on the security reasons that are found in trade cooperation agreements or free trade agreements or any other international economic agreements with the focus on the General Agreement on Tariffs and Trade (GATT) security exception. Given the ambiguity of such provisions, states could use them to justify the introduction of protectionist measures or countermeasures that may harm the economies of the target countries.[10] Taking into account the fact that there are no safeguards in place against the abuse of the security exception provisions, their invocation may lead to harmful systemic implications. It is clear that economic sanctions are contrary to the main principles of the world trade system like the most-favoured nation principle or the prohibition of quantitative restrictions. Therefore, the targeted countries have the right to challenge the application of sanctions in the WTO Dispute Settlement System. Following this line of thought the question arises as to how the review is to be conducted or, in other words, what the standard of review is. The absence of standards of review may lead to uncertainty and controversy as to the limits of sanctions. As Cann states, the

> [...] absence of standards perpetuated by a minority of nations poses an increasing threat to the stability of the international trade system. Poorer nations are concerned by the trend toward using economic sanctions for non-economic purposes.[11]

Taking into account the wide range of standards of review, from *de novo* review to total deference, it is beyond the scope of this article to grasp all of them. The author instead will address one possible standard of review based on the reasoning that since questions of national security require a lot of deference to states the standard of review should not be a strict one but provide some leeway. On its face, the national margin of appreciation appears to be the standard of review allowing the necessary room for manoeuvre to states. The main aim of this research therefore is to inspect the national margin of appreciation from the perspective of its suitability as a standard of review for sanctions introduced under umbrella of the security exception provision in GATT.

---

[10] There is also an opposing view on the abuse of security exceptions, described by Pelc by reference to the negotiation history of GATT Article XXI where the Chairman maintained that ultimately an abuse would be prevented by informal constraints: see PELC, *Making and Bending International Rules. The Design of Exceptions and Escape Clauses in Trade Law*, Cambridge, 2016, p. 100.

[11] CANN, "Creating Standards and Accountability for the Use of the WTO Security Exception: Reducing the Role of Power-Base Relations and Establishing a New Balance between Sovereignty and Multilateralism", Yale Journal of International Law, 2001, p. 413 ff., pp. 420-421.

To do so, the article first briefly overviews sanctions and the security exception provisions as a means to justify sanctions with particular focus on GATT
Article XXI. Then it proceeds to the justiciability of the GATT security exception
and concept of the standard of review. The article further reviews the national
margin of appreciation (NMA) and outlines its origin and content, as developed
by the European Court of Human Rights (ECtHR). To find inspiration for the
standard of review the article discusses the recent cases of the Court of Justice of
the European Union (CJEU) where sanctions have been justified by the security
exception provision. Then the use of the NMA outside the European Convention
on Human Rights (ECHR) is discussed. Having reviewed the cases where the
NMA has been applied beyond the ECHR, the research attempts to test whether
the NMA might be useful for review of economic sanctions. Finally, the article
draws tentative conclusions as to the suitability of the NMA as a standard of review for sanctions justified by the security exception clauses.

2. SANCTIONS AND SECURITY EXCEPTIONS

Economic sanctions, as defined by Lowenfeld, "are measures of an economic
– as contrasted with diplomatic or military – character taken by states to express
disapproval of the acts of the target state or to induce that state to change some
policy or practice or even its governmental structure."[12] Nephew differentiates
two broad categories of economic sanctions: trade-related sanctions and finance-
related sanctions.[13] In turn, the forms of different trade-related measures may
vary from restrictions on trade in certain products to complete trade bans between countries. To illustrate, the US sanctions against Russia dealt, *inter alia*,
with prohibitions on the export of goods, services and technology in certain areas along with sanctions on designated individuals and entities operating in the
Russian defence sector.[14]

Economic sanctions are widely used to attain different goals in international
relations. In this regard, Baldwin distinguishes "political" and "nonpolitical"
economic sanctions, where the "political" ones are used to influence another
state's human rights policy or other "political goals". In turn, "nonpolitical" refer
to those seeking to change another state's tariff policy or pursue other "economic
goals".[15] The line between these two sanction typologies is blurred, as often economic and political aspects are "inextricably intertwined".[16] Economic sanctions
can therefore pursue pure protectionist goals under the guise of being used for the
protection of national security. As put by Doraev, "political elites tend to forget

---

[12] LOWENFELD, *International Economic Law*, 2nd ed., New York, 2008, pp. 850-851.

[13] NEPHEW, *The Art of Sanctions*, New York, 2017, p. 47.

[14] The full list of the US sanctions against Ukraine is available at: <https://www.treasury.
gov/resource-center/sanctions/Programs/Pages/ukraine.aspx>

[15] BALDWIN, "Prologamena to Thinking about Economic Sanctions and Free Trade",
Chicago Journal of International Law, 2003, p. 271 ff., p. 271.

[16] *Ibid.*, p. 273.

that any economic sanction could be used not only to sue for peace, but rather to inflict economic suffering".[17]

Security exceptions are provisions that allow states to derogate from their obligations under international agreements and establish a framework under which the sanctions could be justified for the protection of national security. Therefore, the security exception provisions function like safety valves to justify sanctions aimed at the protection of national security. The practice of inserting the exception clauses into international agreements is common in international law since the flexibility is needed for international agreements to appeal to the greatest number of states. Hefler, when discussing flexibility in international agreements, classifies exceptions as formal collective flexibility mechanisms.[18] That is why the security exception provisions are also called derogations (since they allow obligations to be derogated from)[19] or non-precluded clauses (which allow states to take actions which are otherwise inconsistent with their treaty obligations).[20] They can be found in a variety of international economic agreements with the typical examples in multilateral trade agreements like GATT and General Agreement on Trade Services (GATS), free trade agreements and international investment agreements.[21]

The main thrust of this article is to concentrate on Article XXI of the GATT 1994 that might serve as a justification for economic sanctions. Article XXI reads:

> Nothing in this Agreement shall be construed
> (a) to require any contracting party to furnish any information the disclosure of which it considers contrary to its essential security interests; or

---

[17] DORAEV, "The 'Memory Effect' of Economic Sanctions Against Russia: Opposing Approaches to the Legality of Unilateral Sanctions Clash Again", University of Pennsylvania Journal of International Law, 2015, p. 335 ff., p. 418.

[18] HELFER, "Flexibility in International Agreements", in DUNOFF and POLLACK (eds.), *Interdisciplinary Perspectives on International Law and International Relations: The State of the Art*, Cambridge, p. 175 ff., p. 179.

[19] KURTZ, "Adjudging the Exceptional at International Law: Security, Public Order and Financial Crisis", Jean Monnet Working Paper 06/08, 2008, available at: <https://jeanmonnetprogram.org/paper/adjudging-the-exceptional-at-international-law-security-public-order-and-financial-crisis-2/>.

[20] BURKE-WHITE and VON STADEN, "Investment Protection in Extraordinary Times: The Interpretation of Non-Precluded Measure Provisions in Bilateral Investment Treaties", Virginia Journal of International Law, 2008, p. 307 ff.

[21] For example, the recent research reveals the rise of the security exception provisions in BITs, with the US being the most active user. See: SAUVANT, MEVELYN, LAMA and PETERSEN, "The Rise of Self-Judging Essential Security Interest Clauses in International Investment Agreements", Perspectives On Topical Foreign Direct Investment Issues, 2016, available at: <http://ccsi.columbia.edu/files/2016/10/No-188-Sauvant-Ong-Lama-and-Petersen-FOR-WEBSITE-FINAL.pdf>.

(b) to prevent any contracting party from taking any action which it considers necessary for the protection of its essential security interests

(i) relating to fissionable materials or the materials from which they are derived;

(ii) relating to the traffic in arms, ammunition and implements of war and to such traffic in other goods and materials as is carried on directly or indirectly for the purpose of supplying a military establishment;

(iii) taken in time of war or other emergency in international relations; or

(c) to prevent any contracting party from taking any action in pursuance of its obligations under the United Nations Charter for the maintenance of international peace and security.[22]

Hestermeyer distinguishes three separate parts of this provision: "an introductory sentence applicable to the whole provision ("nothing in this agreement shall be construed"), the security exceptions *stricto sensu* (lits a and b) and a paragraph on relationship with the UN Charter."[23]

Bhala mentions that Article XXI(b) is "the most important and controversial point of the exception".[24] Section (b)(iii) is of particular interest taking into account that it might justify economic sanctions for the protection of national security since it covers "war or other emergency in international relations" and most economic sanctions are adopted in this context. Most recent sanctions have been adopted by states independently from the UNSC and without reliance on the lit.c defence as a possible justification.[25] This trend is due to the ability of the Permanent Members of the UNSC to block the adoption of UNSC resolutions.[26] For example, the EU and US adopted their own sanctions against Russia notwithstanding the fact that there had been no UN sanctions against Russia.

---

[22] WTO, Analytical Index: GATT 1994, available at: <https://www.wto.org/english/res_e/booksp_e/analytic_index_e/gatt1994_08_e.htm#article21A>.

[23] HESTERMEYER, "Article XXI. Security Exceptions", in WOLFRUM, STOLL and HESTERMEYER (eds.), *WTO – Trade in Goods*, Leiden-Boston, 2011, p. 569 ff., p. 577.

[24] BHALA, "National Security and International Trade Law: What the GATT Says, and What the United States Does", University of Pennsylvania Journal of International Law, p. 263 ff., p. 267.

[25] For example, Russia and China blocked adoption of a draft resolution by the UNSC which would have established sanctions against Syria. See on this: "Russia, China block Security Council action on use of chemical weapons in Syria", UN News, 28 February 2017, available at: <https://news.un.org/en/story/2017/02/552362-russia-china-block-security-council-action-use-chemical-weapons-syria>.

[26] On proposals to reform the UNSC see GOULD and RABLEN, "Reform of the UN Security Council: Equity and Efficiency", Public Choice, 2017, p. 145 ff.; and on a need for institutional rebalancing of WTO and UN see YOO and AHN, "Security Exceptions in the WTO System: Bridge or Bottle-Neck for Trade and Security?", Journal of International Economic Law, 2016, p. 417 ff., p. 440.

In view of the ever-increasing reliance on sanctions, the security exception provision appears to be one of the points of consternation at the WTO.[27] The security exception is "awakening" at the Dispute Settlement Body (DSB) of the WTO: at the time of writing, three cases where the sanctions have been challenged were pending.[28] Apart from the above-mentioned cases, the security exception has been invoked by Russia in another WTO case, where Ukraine has challenged the Russian restrictions on traffic in transit of goods from Ukraine through the Russian Federation to third countries.[29] Since all the above-mentioned cases are still pending, it remains unclear how the Panel will deal with GATT Article XXI in the course of the examination. If the Panel has to interpret the security exception, the issue of the standard of review comes to the fore. Such standard should try to take into account the delicate balance between the state's sovereign right to protect itself in cases of threats to national security and the need to avoid potential abuse through the imposition of trade-barriers for purely commercial or political reasons.[30]

3. Justiciability of the WTO Security Exception

Before delving into the discussion of the standard of review, the question of the possibility of review as such should be addressed. Taking into account the wording "it considers", some scholars claim that it is up to the state to decide under which conditions to trigger security exceptions and that no other higher tribunal is competent to review the decision of the state. In other words, they claim that it is "self-judging".[31] Others are of the opinion that the completely self-judging provisions are a void legal instrument. To this end Judge Lauterpacht

---

[27] For example, see Russian Proposal on MC10 Ministerial Declaration asking to clarify on the meaning of the Security Exception, Part III – Russian Federation, WT/MIN(15)/W/14.

[28] *Ukraine – Measures Related to Trade in Goods and Services*, Request for consultations made by Russia on 19 May 2017, WT/DS525/1; *Russia – Importation and Transit of Certain Ukrainian products*, Request for consultations made by Ukraine on 13 October 2017, WT/DS532/1; *United Arab Emirates – Measures Relating to Trade in Goods and Services, and Trade-Related Aspects of Intellectual Property Rights*, Request for consultations made by Qatar on 31 July 2017, WT/DS 526/1. Moreover, the issue of the security exception was discussed at the Goods Council Meeting with regard to the US investigations under Section 232 of the US Trade Expansion Act of 1962. Although the latter situation is beyond the scope of this article, it should be mentioned that the Section 232 provision allows the adoption of tariffs and quotas as trade defensive measures for security reasons and if the US adopts such trade-restrictive measures, other WTO Members might challenge these measures at the WTO, while the US would likely refer to GATT Article XXI as a justification. See WTO, "National security cited in two trade concerns at Goods Council meeting", 30 June 2017, available at: <https://www.wto.org/english/news_e/news17_e/good_10jul17_e.htm>.

[29] *Russia – Measures Concerning Traffic in Transit*, Request for consultations, made by Ukraine on 14 September 2016, WT/DS512/1.

[30] WOODS, "The National Security Exception Part II", Woods Lafortune LLP, 17 April 2015, available at: <http://www.wl-tradelaw.com/the-national-security-exception-part-ii/>.

[31] AKANDE and WILLIAMS, "International Adjudication on National Security Issues: What Role for the WTO", Virginia Journal of International Law, 2003, p. 365 ff., p. 387.

claimed that such a provision is "[...] not a legal instrument. It is a declaration of a political principle and purpose".[32] This article posits that the GATT security exception is not self-judging since "it considers" is entailed not only in the GATT security exception, but also in other provisions, like Article 22.3(b) and 22.3(c) of the Dispute Settlement Understanding (DSU) ("if that party considers"). Notwithstanding "if that party considers" wording in Articles 22.3(b) and (c), the Arbitrators have a limited review.[33] Moreover, it is worth noting that the EU in its written submission in *Russia – Measures Concerning Traffic in Transit* states that "Article XXI of GATT 1994 is a justiciable provision and that its invocation by a defending party does not have the effect of excluding the jurisdiction of a panel".[34]

With this in mind, one has to understand what elements of GATT Article XXI(b)(iii) fall under review. Looking at the wording of "any action it considers", it follows that "it considers" is related to "any action". Thus, the state has the possibility to choose the action, i.e. the trade-restrictive measure, but it has been already established in the case-law that the "it considers" wording does not give a full discretion to states. An example occurred in *Djibouti v. France*[35] where France refused to provide some documents to Djibouti by reference to Article 2(c) of the Mutual Assistance Convention which states that the assistance in criminal proceedings "may be refused [...] *if the requested state considers* that the execution of the request is likely to prejudice its sovereignty, its security, its *ordre public* or other of its essential interests".[36] Notwithstanding the "it considers" wording, the International Court of Justice (ICJ) reviewed the actions of France which showed that "it considers" did not give full discretion to states. Thus the action should in principle be reviewable to avoid abuse. Indeed, in his speech during the negotiations of the GATT security exception, the US delegator stated that "[...] there was a great danger of having too wide an exception [...] that would permit anything under the sun".[37] Going further, there is the construct "for the protection of its essential security interest". Of course, states often claim that it is up to them to decide what constitutes their "essential security interest". However, the author submits that it is not solely within the power of the state to decide what is meant by essential security and that the core common denomina-

---

[32] As to the self-judging exception to a declaration under Art. 36(2) ICJ Statute (the so-called Optional Declaration), see *Certain Norwegian Loans* (*France v. Norway*), Separate Opinion of Judge Lauterpacht, ICJ Reports, 1957, p. 9 ff., pp. 44 and 48.

[33] *EC – Bananas III (Ecuador) – Article 22.6*, Decision by the arbitrators, 24 March 2000, WT/DS27/ARB/ECU, para. 52.

[34] EU Third Party Written Submission in *Russia – Measures Concerning Traffic in Transit case*, 8 November 2017, available at: <http://trade.ec.europa.eu/doclib/docs/2018/february/tradoc_156602.pdf>, para. 21.

[35] *Case Concerning Certain Questions on Mutual Assistance in Criminal Matters (Djibouti v. France)*, Judgment of 4 June 2008, ICJ Reports, 2008, p. 177 ff., para. 148.

[36] Mutual Assistance Convention between France and Djibouti, 27 September 1986, entered into force 1 August 1992, Art. 2(c).

[37] Economic and Social Council, Preparatory Committee of the U.N. Conference on Trade and Employment, Thirty-Third Meeting of Commission, UN Doc. E/PC/T/A/PV/33 (1947), Mr. Leddy on behalf of the United States, p. 20.

tor could be found. A parallel can be drawn with the concept of "public morals" which has a universal core and hence is easily reviewable. Similarly, "war or other emergency in international relations" is subject to review since there could be a common denominator as well.

Secondly, the issue arises as to the question of competence of the WTO Panel to review the cases dealing with national security issues.[38] Can the WTO adjudicate on the security issues of sovereign states?[39] Klonitskaya is adamant that the WTO should not engage in review of national security cases.[40] One could claim that national security is not for review by the WTO quasi-judicial body, however, as far as national security intertwines with trade-restrictive measures, the WTO member states have the right to challenge them under the DSU of the WTO. In turn, the Panels should pursue their obligations under Article 11 of DSU and make an objective assessment of the facts of the case.[41] The standard of review, as stated by Oesch, "might subtly balance out the delicate conflict over legal and political authority between panels and national authorities in trade and trade-related matters governed by the WTO agreements."[42]

4. STANDARD OF REVIEW

Before discussing the national margin of appreciation as a standard of review, it is useful to define the standard of review concept, and its nature and functions in relation to a review of the security exception. As a matter of procedure, the standard of review can be referred to as a scrutiny by international tribunals of measures adopted by states. It is used to decide whether the state overstepped its ability to use the security exception provision to justify trade-restrictive measures. As Ragni states:

> "[…] the issue of standard of review first comes into play in the application of derogation clauses, which are designed to preserve the exercise of a State's sovereignty in areas which are traditionally

---

[38] SCHLOEMANN and OHLHOFF, "'Constitutionalization' and Dispute Settlement in the WTO: National Security as an Issue of Competence", AJIL, 1999, p. 424 ff.

[39] It should be noted that in international investment law the security exception provision of the US-Argentina BIT has been reviewed by the ICSID tribunals. The wording of the security exception in the US-Argentina BIT differs from the security exception in GATT and its discussion goes beyond this article. For detailed review of the Argentinian cases see, for example, KURTZ, "Adjudging the Exceptional at International Investment Law: Security, Public Order and Financial Crisis", ICLQ, 2010, p. 325 ff.

[40] KLONITSKAYA, "Is the WTO the Right Forum to Hear National Security Issues?", Global Trade and Customs Journal, 2014, p. 508 ff.

[41] Article 11 DSU, dealing with functions of Panels.

[42] OESCH, Standards of Review in WTO Dispute Resolution, Oxford, 2003, p. 28.

considered as unsuitable for judicial assessment, such as in the case where security concerns are at issue".[43]

As to the nature of the standard of review, some scholars claim that it is a technical procedural concept that contains a number of requirements for the analysis of policies adopted by a country.[44] Other scholars point out that the standard of review is essentially "a matter of approach and a rhetorical device".[45] In this author's view, the standard of review should contain both elements: a technical concept and a rhetorical device. This composition stems from the fact that the rigid technical formula is of little use when dealing with security issues that require flexibility.

When it comes to the standard of review for WTO cases,[46] Jackson mentions that "the standard of review question has become something of a touchstone regarding the relationship of 'sovereignty' concepts to the GATT/WTO rule system".[47] In brief, guidelines on the standard of review (although without explicit reference to the term itself) in WTO agreements are addressed in Article 11 of the DSU and Article 17.6 of the Anti-Dumping Agreement.[48]

Lastly, it is worth mentioning the functions of the standard of review with regard to the review of the security exception provision. In essence, it can serve as a tool for WTO Panels to understand whether states invoking security exceptions have abused the concept and imposed sanctions pursuing a protectionist aim rather than for the protection of national security. There are alternative views that the "atmosphere" or informal constraints prevent the abuse of the security exceptions.[49] It seems that "atmosphere" refers to diplomacy as means to prevent the abuse of the invocation the security exception provision.

The impact of diplomacy on solving WTO disputes was discussed by Gray and Potter, who consider that disputes among the high-affinity states are "particu-

---

[43] RAGNI, "Standard of Review and the Margin of Appreciation before the International Court of Justice", in GRUSZCZYNSKI and WERNER (eds.), *Deference in International Courts and Tribunals: Standard of Review and Margin of Appreciation*, Oxford, 2014, p. 319 ff., p. 323..

[44] GUZMAN, "Determining the Appropriate Standard of Review in WTO Disputes", Cornell International Law Journal, 2009, p. 45 ff., p. 46.

[45] VADI and GRUSZCZYNSKI, "Standards of Review in International Investment Law and Arbitration: Multilevel Governance and the Commonweal", Journal of International Economic Law, 2013, p. 613 ff., p. 614.

[46] The standard of review in WTO law has been extensively discussed elsewhere, see OESCH, *cit. supra* note 42, or BOHANES and LOCKHART, "Standard of Review in WTO Law", in BETHLEHEM, MCRAE, NEUFELD and VAN DAMME (eds.), *The Oxford Handbook of International Trade Law*, Oxford, 2010, p. 379 ff., p. 382.

[47] CROLEY and JACKSON, "WTO Dispute Procedures, Standard of Review, and Deference to National Governments", AJIL, 1996, p. 193 ff., p. 194.

[48] It is a widely acknowledged fact that the ADA Art. 17.6 standard of review derived from the US *Chevron* doctrine, discussed by Croley and Jackson, *cit. supra* note 47, and also extensively discussed in VÁZQUEZ, "Judicial Review in the United States and in the WTO: Some Similarities and Differences", George Washington International Law Review, 2004, p. 587 ff.

[49] See PELC, *cit. supra* note 10, p. 100.

larly intractable and therefore might require an international arbiter to resolve".[50] Still, diplomacy might help resolve disputes between the countries with dissimilar policy preferences.[51] In the case of Russia and Ukraine, both of them adopted similar policies (i.e. sanctions against each other). The attempts to solve the conflict by diplomatic means, such as the Minsk Agreements, appear to have failed.[52] In such a situation a procedural instrument like a review by a third party might be of help. Since there is no established case-law on GATT Article XXI[53] and thus no standard of review developed in the case-law,[54] the following section examines the national margin of appreciation.

5. NATIONAL MARGIN OF APPRECIATION: ORIGIN AND CONTENT

At the outset, the difference between the terms "national margin of appreciation" and "margin of appreciation" should be clarified. El Boudouhi has rightly pointed out that the "margin of appreciation" is a concept similar to discretion or leeway and is available for any entity, judge or state when interpreting indeterminate norms and therefore refers to a margin of appreciation in a broader sense. The "national margin of appreciation", on the contrary, is a doctrine that allows for a discretion available to states before an international tribunal. Hence, a doctrine of the national margin of appreciation refers to the margin of appreciation *stricto sensu*.[55] Since this paper deals with the margin of appreciation which might be accorded by the WTO Panel to states under GATT Article XXI, the article will refer to the doctrine of the margin of appreciation and therefore the term "national margin of appreciation".[56] There is also another view by Cot, who differentiates between the margin of appreciation as a doctrine and as a standard of review. In his view, a standard of review implies a degree of review and a doctrine reflects the degree of flexibility in international law. If compared with El Boudouhi's view, it seems that Cot's margin of appreciation as a doctrine corresponds to El

---

[50] GRAY and POTTER, "Diplomacy and the Settlement of International Disputes", University of Pennsylvania Working Papers, 2017.

[51] *Ibid.*, p.10.

[52] The negotiations, established to bring peace to Ukraine, consisted of trilateral group: Russia, Ukraine and OSCE. Full text of the Minsk agreement is available at: <https://www.ft.com/content/21b8f98e-b2a5-11e4-b234-00144feab7de>.

[53] For an overview of Article XXI's record of use see PELC, *cit. supra* note 10, p. 101 ff.

[54] The standard of review for the self-judging clauses was discussed in SCHILL and BRIESE, "'If the State Considers': Self-Judging Clauses in International Dispute Settlement", Max Planck Yearbook of United Nations Law, 2009, p. 61 ff., p.108.

[55] EL BOUDOUHI, "A Comparative Approach of the National Margin of Appreciation Doctrine Before the ECtHR, Investment Tribunals and WTO Dispute Settlement Bodies", Robert Schuman Centre for Advanced Studies Research Paper No. RSCAS 2015/27, 2015, p. 1 ff., p. 1, available at: <http://cadmus.eui.eu/bitstream/handle/1814/35660/RSCAS2015_27.pdf?sequence=1&isAllowed=y>.

[56] COT, "Margin of Appreciation", Max Planck Encyclopedia of Public International Law, 2007, available at: <http://opil.ouplaw.com/view/10.1093/law:epil/9780199231690/law-9780199231690-e1438?rskey=YoxVF6&result=3&prd=EPIL>.

Boudouhi's notion of margin of appreciation as a concept. In turn, Cot's margin of appreciation as a standard of review corresponds to El Boudouhi's view of NMA as a doctrine where the Court gives flexibility for states. For example, the EU, in its third party written submission in *Russia – Measures Concerning Traffic in Transit*, submits that "Article XXI of GATT 1994, and in particular Article XXI(b) accords in one of the components of its wording a certain margin of discretion to the invoking Member [...]".[57] As has been seen, the EU refers to the margin of appreciation as leeway which is given to the member states when deciding what measures under Article XXI they can impose. This article submits that, on the contrary, the WTO Panel, when reviewing the measures imposed by a member state, should ascertain that margin of appreciation and therefore, apply a margin of appreciation *stricto sensu* to states.

To fully grasp the nature of the NMA, one should not lose sight of its origins. As argued by Hilf and Salomon "ancestry will regularly be able to provide guidance [...]".[58] It is a common knowledge that the concept has its origins in national legal systems.[59] For example, at national level the doctrine was used in French jurisprudence as *"marge d'appreciation"* as well as in administrative law in civil law countries.[60] At the supranational level, the national margin of appreciation was mainly developed and used by the ECtHR notwithstanding the fact that it is not mentioned anywhere in the ECHR. The ECHR could be considered as a native realm for the NMA. This article will not analyse its use by the ECtHR,[61] but its native area will be useful for a description of its content, as developed by the ECtHR.

Given the fact that the NMA has no basis in the legal norm[62] and was constructed through case-law, it has no clear definition. There are numerous descriptions of the concept, ranging from freedom to act and elbow room, to latitude that the government enjoy in applying treaties, to room for manoeuvre and area of discretion.[63]

---

[57] EU Third Party Written Submission, *cit. supra* note 34, para. 29.

[58] HILF and SALOMON, "Margin of Appreciation Revisited", in CREMONA et al. (eds.), *Reflections on the Constitualization of International Economic Law, Liber Amicorium for Ernst-Ulrich Petersmann*, Leiden, 2013, p. 37 ff., p. 49.

[59] For the common law discussion on judicial deference see CLAYTON, "Principles for Judicial Deference", Judicial Review, 2006, p. 109 ff.

[60] More on this in ARAI-TAKAHASHI, *The Margin of Appreciation Doctrine and the Principle of Proportionality in the Jurisprudence of the ECHR*, Antwerp, 2002.

[61] As to the national margin of appreciation by the ECtHR, see, for example, GREER, "The Margin of Appreciation: Interpretation and Discretion under the European Convention of Human Rights", Human Rights Files No.17, Council of Europe Publishing, July 2000; ARNARDÓTTIR, "Rethinking the Two Margins of Appreciation", European Constitutional Law Review, 2016, p. 27 ff.

[62] Although it is implemented in Article 1 of Protocol No. 15 of 24 June 2013, it is not ratified by all Members of the Council of Europe. The Protocol is available at: <https://www.echr. coe.int/Documents/Protocol_15_ENG.pdf>. As of 05 March 2018, 41 Members of the Council of Europe acceded/ratified the Protocol. The status is available at: <https://www.coe.int/en/web/conventions/full-list/-/conventions/treaty/213/signatures?p_auth=TL0w5vIR>.

[63] See HILF and SALOMON, *cit. supra* note 58, p.49.

The common point in all definitions of the NMA is the deference which is given to states by the Court. As Kratochvil clarifies "the Court, to a certain degree, defers to States in assessing, inter alia, whether the measure was proportionate, whether there was a pressing social need, whether the right balance was struck between competing interests, and whether the factual circumstances fall within a definition in the Convention".[64] Notwithstanding its broad nature, the doctrine has some distinguishable features. For example, it grants discretion to the domestic level that depends on the level of consensus among states, on the significance of the right at stake for society and the individual, and on the particular facts of the case.[65] Since the width of the NMA varies, the European consensus is used by the ECtHR to justify the width of the margin of appreciation.[66] Still, the ECtHR has never provided a definition of what it concretely understands as "consensus".[67]

There have been attempts to delineate the elements of the national margin of appreciation by scholars,[68] but despite this the contours are not clear enough. Even some ECtHR judges agree its nature is vague, acknowledging that the limits of the margin of appreciation are incapable of an abstract definition.[69] The margin of appreciation is thus "context-dependent" and its limits can be drawn only within a specific case.[70] The abstract shape of the NMA gives an opportunity for some scholars to claim that "it is not an independent standard of review but a variation of a unique 'reasonableness' – or proportionality – standard of review the application of which depends on the facts of each case".[71] Against this background Arato goes so far to claim that the margin of appreciation does not embody a particular standard of review. He claims that "[…] the margin of appreciation is essentially contentless. And indeed, as constructed by the ECtHR, the doctrine is contentless by design".[72] Along these lines the NMA, even applied in its "native"

---

[64] KRATOCHVIL, "The Inflation of the Margin of Appreciation by the European Court of Human Rights", Netherlands Quarterly of Human Rights, 2017, p. 324 ff., p. 330.

[65] GOLDMANN, "Soft Authority against Hard Cases of Racially Discriminating Speech: Why the CERD Committee Needs a Margin of Appreciation Doctrine", Goettingen Journal of International Law, 2016, p. 131 ff., p. 145.

[66] DZEHTSIAROU, "European Consensus: A Way of Reasoning", University College Dublin Law Research Paper, No. 11, 2009, available at: <https://ssrn.com/abstract=1411063>.

[67] REGAN, "'European Consensus': A Worthy Endeavor for The European Court of Human Rights?", Trinity College Law Review, 2011, p. 51 ff., p. 53.

[68] For discussion on content of the margin of appreciation, for example, see SAUL, "The European Court of Human Rights' Margin of Appreciation and the Processes of National Parliaments", Human Rights Law Review, 2015, p. 745 ff.

[69] For instance, BERNHARDT, "Thoughts on the Interpretation of Human-Rights Treaties", in MATSCHER, PETZOLD and WIARDA (eds.), *Protecting Human Rights: The European Dimension*, Koln, 1988, p. 65 ff.

[70] LAVENDER, "The Problem of the Margin of Appreciation", European Human Rights Law Review, 1997, p. 380 ff., p. 382.

[71] See EL BOUDOUHI, *cit. supra* note 55, p. 5.

[72] ARATO, "The Margin of Appreciation in International Investment Law", Virginia Journal of International Law, 2014, p. 545 ff., p. 558.

area has been criticised for being the "very cause" of incoherence of judgment.[73] In this regard Brauch even goes further by stating that the Court "must abandon the margin of appreciation" and use other tools, available under the Vienna Convention and failure to do so "will threaten the rule of law itself".[74]

The abstract nature of the NMA makes it hard to transplant to other areas of law. For example, Zarra points precisely to this problem by stating that authors, who support the use of the margin of appreciation outside of the ECHR context, never discuss the possibility of applying its features as technically developed by the ECtHR.[75]

The relevance of the NMA for review of the GATT security exception can be drawn from the fact that its use within the ECHR emerged in cases concerned with the possibility of derogating from some obligations under the ECHR in time of "public emergency threatening the life of nation" under Article 15 ECHR. This point holds true for GATT Article XXI as well: it can be invoked "in time of war or other emergency in international relations". Nonetheless, there are certain differences crucial for application of the NMA. To start with, Article 15 of the ECHR mentions the proportionality of the measures, i.e. that their extent be "strictly required by the exigencies of the situation". What is more, the ECHR imposes a general condition ("the compliance with other obligations under international law") and a general limit (i.e. non-violation of an untouchable core of individual rights, e.g.: right to life, except as a result of lawful acts of war; or the right not to be tortured).[76] Apart from that, the obligation to notify the Secretary General of the Council of Europe is also included in paragraph 3 of Article 15. In GATT Article XXI there is no requirement for the proportionality of the measures and no explicit limit to the measures. The notification requirement is mentioned in the Decision Concerning Article XXI of 1982 and not in GATT Article XXI itself; moreover, such notification provides only a partial obligation with regard to the notification – referring to the exception mentioned in Article XXI:a.[77] The upshot is that the ECHR contains more safeguards in the derogatory clause against its misuse. While using the NMA in the context of Article 15, its contours are therefore delimited by the provision itself. On the contrary, the NMA within the GATT security exception framework leads to confusion and unpredictability since there are no safeguards in the article itself.

---

[73] HUTCHINSON, "The Margin of Appreciation Doctrine in the European Court of Human Rights", ICLQ, 1999, p. 638 ff.

[74] BRAUCH, "The Margin of Appreciation and the Jurisprudence of the European Court of Human Rights: Threat to the Rule of Law", Columbia Journal of European Law, 2005, p. 150 ff.

[75] ZARRA, "Right to Regulate, Margin of Appreciation and Proportionality: Current Status in Investment Arbitration in Light of *Philip Morris v Uruguay*", Brazilian Journal of International Law, 2017, p. 94 ff., p. 113.

[76] FICHERA and HERLIN-KARNELL, "The Margin of Appreciation and Balancing in the Area of Freedom Security and Justice: A Proportionate Answer for a Europe of Rights?", European Public Law, 2013, p. 759 ff., p. 779.

[77] GATT, Decision Concerning GATT Article XXI of the General Agreement, 30 November 1982, L/5426.

The question of the difference between the derogatory clauses in the ECHR and WTO law boils down to the difference of the regimes as such. For example, in this regard El Boudouhi points out that the political and structural differences between the ECHR and the WTO as well as the investment dispute settlement systems preclude importing the NMA standard to the respective tribunals.[78]

6. POSSIBLE GUIDANCE FROM THE COURT OF JUSTICE OF THE EUROPEAN UNION?

As has already been mentioned, there is no adopted WTO case-law interpreting the security exception clause. There are however recent Court of Justice of the European Union (CJEU) judgments where a provision quite similar to the GATT security exception was considered. It bears noting that although comparisons between the EU and the WTO jurisprudence should be treated with caution, a comparison between the two systems can at least provide useful insights for scholarly discussion. Therefore, this section will briefly analyse some key points of the two recent CJEU judgments related to the security exception provisions.

In *Rosneft* case[79] one of the questions referred to the CJEU by the UK courts was the compatibility of the contested legal instruments with the EU-Russia Partnership Agreement.[80] The Court, however, stated that there was no need, in that case, to give a ruling on that question. It went further by claiming that "[…] even if the restrictive measures at issue in the main proceedings were not compatible with certain provisions of that agreement, Article 99 of that agreement permits their adoption".[81] Basically, the Court stated that the security exceptions clause was able to justify the sanctions.

In essence, Article 99(1)(d) of the EU-Russia Partnership Agreement reads as follows:

> Nothing in this Agreement shall prevent a Party from taking any measures:
> which it considers necessary for the protection of its essential security interests:
> […] (d) in the event of serious internal disturbances affecting the maintenance of law and order, in time of war or serious international tension constituting threat of war or in order to carry out obligations it has accepted for the purpose of maintaining peace and international security […]

---

[78] See EL BOUDOUHI, *cit. supra* note 55, p. 17.

[79] Case C-72/15, *PJSC Rosneft Oil Company v. Her Majesty's Treasury and Others*, 28 March 2017.

[80] Protocol Agreement to the Partnership and Cooperation establishing a partnership between the European Communities and their Member States, of the one part, and the Russian Federation, of the other part, 24 June 1994, entered into force 1 December 1997.

[81] *Rosneft*, *cit. supra* note 79, para. 110.

As we see, the wording of Article 99(1)(d) of the EU-Russia Partnership Agreement is different from the security exceptions clause enshrined in GATT Article XXI(iii)(b). For example, it contains the wording "international tension" instead of "time of war or other emergency in international relations". Moreover, this wording is less restrictive since it also provides for taking measures "in order to carry out obligations it has accepted for the purpose of maintaining peace and international security".

When reviewing the validity of the sanctions, the Court paid special attention to Article 99(1)(d) of the EU-Russia Partnership Agreement. In particular, as to the notions of "war" or "serious international tension constituting a threat to war" the Court stated that the provision does not require the war to directly affect the territory of the EU. Events which take place in a country bordering the EU are capable of justifying measures designed to protect essential EU security interests and to maintain peace and international security.[82] Then the Court proceeded to assess whether the trade-restrictive measures were necessary. While the Court was very vague in explaining the necessity test, it stated that "the Council has *a broad discretion* in areas which involve the making by that institution of political, economic and social choices, and in which it is called upon to undertake complex assessments".[83] It appears that the Court's deferential approach to the review of sanctions corresponds to the Council's broad margin of policy-making in the area of the EU's Common and Foreign Security Policy.[84] As the next step the Court stated that the aim of sanctions, i.e. promotion of the peace settlement in Ukraine, was consistent with the objective of maintaining peace and international security.[85] To sum up, the Court employed a deferential standard of review by use of the language "a broad discretion" although without a reference to the margin of appreciation as such.

The other recent case where EU sanctions have been challenged is *Kiselev v. Council*.[86] This case differs from *Rosneft* since it concerns the challenge of individual sanctions. The similarity with the *Rosneft* case, though, is that the CJEU touched upon the same Article 99 (1)(d) of the EU-Russia Partnership Agreement. What is interesting is that the Court interpreted this provision in a slightly different way. For example, the Court mentioned that the security exception may be invoked unilaterally and there is no requirement of one party to inform the other party beforehand, nor to consult it with reasons for its action.[87] With regard to the definition of "war" the Court went further in this case and stated that it may be considered that "the actions of the Russian Federation constitute 'war or serious international tension constituting threat of war' within the meaning of

---

[82] *Ibid.*, para. 112.
[83] *Ibid.*, para. 113. emphasis added
[84] KOUTRAKOS, "Judicial Review in the EU's Common Foreign and Security Policy", ICLQ, 2018, p.1 ff., p.19.
[85] *Rosneft, cit. supra* note 79, para. 115.
[86] Case T-262/15, *Kiselev D.K. v. Council of the European Union*, 15 June 2017.
[87] *Ibid.*, para. 32.

Article 99(1)(d) of the Partnership Agreement".[88] As to necessity, the Court was not as vague as in the *Rosneft* judgment, simply stating that the Council has broad discretion in this area. This time the Court stated that

> In view of the interest of the European Union and its Member States in having, as a neighbour, a stable Ukraine, it could be considered necessary to adopt restrictive measures in order to exert pressure on the Russian Federation to cease its activities undermining or threatening the territorial integrity, sovereignty or independence of Ukraine.[89]

Turning to the compatibility of the restrictive measures, the Court stated that they are compatible with the exemption in relation to security laid down in Article 99(1)(d) of the EU-Russia Partnership Agreement.

All in all, as can be seen, the CJEU, while touching upon the security exception, did not show explicitly what standard of review it applied. The Court simply reviewed whether the means employed by the Council corresponded to the aims stipulated in the documents that imposed trade-restrictive measures. Hence, the standard of review appears not to be well-defined in CJEU case-law either. Against this background, Pantaleo mentions that "in the EU legal order, different standards of judicial scrutiny of restrictive measures are simply not possible. The EU courts will review whether the reasons adduced by the Council are well founded and supported by evidence, including classified evidence".[90] Moreover, the above-mentioned cases reveal that the Court may intentionally be avoiding specifying any standard or remaining vague to "cover political flavour" behind the decision. In the case of the security exception provisions judges have to deal with two competing values: trade and security, so maybe they would prefer to avoid precise standards of review in order to make "the impression that there is any need to adjudicate competing values at all".[91]

With regard to the sanctions cases, the CJEU defends its sanctions policy since a lot of political elements are involved in the cases that concern the common foreign and security policy of the EU. Such position is also in line with the argument, posed by Alter, that the CJEU has a reputation for being less critical of European than it is of national legislative acts.[92] In many areas, the Court has adopted a more lenient standard of review towards the acts of Community institu-

---

[88] *Ibid.*, para. 33.

[89] *Ibid.*, para.33

[90] PANTALEO, "Sanctions Cases in the European Courts" in HAPPOLD and EDEN (eds.), *Economic Sanctions and International Law*, Oxford, 2016, p. 170 ff., p. 181.

[91] HOWSE, "Managing the Interface between International Trade and the Regulatory State: What Lessons Should (and Should Not) Be Drawn from the Jurisprudence of the United States Dormant Commerce Clause", in COTTIER, MAVROIDIS and BLATTER (eds.), *Barriers and the Principle of Non Discrimination in World Trade Law, Past, Present and Future*, Michigan, 2000, Vol. 2, p. 139 ff., p. 140.

[92] ALTER, *The New Terrain of International Law: Courts, Politics, Rights*, Princeton, 2014, p. 198.

tions than of member states.[93] The issue of the standard of review for sanctions in the CJEU case-law therefore also remains unexplored.

7.   NATIONAL MARGIN OF APPRECIATION BEYOND THE ECHR

Since the CJEU has not provided guidance as to the standard of review for the security exception, the application of NMA in the case-law beyond the ECHR will be analysed. As discussed above, the transplantation of the NMA from the ECHR to other areas of public international seems to be difficult, but nonetheless it has been referred to by other international courts.[94]

For example, in public international law the margin of appreciation doctrine was expressly invoked in front of the ICJ by Japan in its dispute with Australia.[95] In this case Japan claimed that it had competence to issue a special permit to kill, take and treat whales for the purpose of scientific research under Article VIII, para. 1, of the International Convention for the Regulation of Whaling (ICRW). Japan based its defence on the "margin of appreciation" and claimed that it provided to every state party to that Convention, the discretion to determine the meaning of the notion of "scientific research" and the activities related to that purpose. Conversely, Australia and New Zealand opposed the use of the margin of appreciation and stressed that the ICJ should avoid "importing" the doctrine of "margin of appreciation", and should "only rely on its own principles of interpretation and application. They suggested relying on the principles of the reasonableness, appropriateness and effectiveness".[96] The Court in its judgment did not use the "margin of appreciation" for review of the measures by Japan, but instead stated that "this standard of review is an objective one".[97] However, as mentioned by Cannizzaro it seems that the Court tacitly dismissed the margin of appreciation doctrine as having a general scope, but gave it a narrower role.[98]

---

[93] TRIDIMAS, "Proportionality in Community Law: Searching for the Appropriate Standard of Scrutiny", in ELLIS and EVELYN (eds.), *The Principle of Proportionality in the Laws of Europe*, Oxford, 1999, p. 65 ff., p. 66.

[94] Although most of the time the courts use the term "margin of appreciation" instead of "national margin of appreciation", from the substantive point of view they seem to discuss the "national margin of appreciation" as doctrine. The same applies to use of "margin of appreciation" by some scholars.

[95] *Whaling in the Antarctic* (*Australia v. Japan: New Zealand intervening*), Judgment of 31 March 2014, ICJ Reports, 2014, p. 226 ff.

[96] CHRISTAKIS, "The 'Margin of Appreciation' in the Use of Exemptions in International Law: Comparing the ICJ Whaling Judgment and the Case Law of the ECtHR", in FITZMAURICE and TAMADA (eds.), *Whaling in the Antarctic: Significance and Implications of the ICJ Judgment*, Leiden-Boston, 2016, pp. 139 ff.

[97] See *Whaling in the Antarctic case, cit. supra* note 95, paras. 67-68.

[98] In his article Cannizzaro develops an argument that the margin of appreciation might come as a part of assessment of proportionality: CANNIZZARO, "Proportionality and Margin of Appreciation in the Whaling Case: Reconciling Antithetical Doctrines?", EJIL, 2016, p. 106 ff., p. 109.

The NMA has not been widely used by WTO Panels, apart from episodic references by arbitrators in the *EC-Bananas* case where the arbitrators mentioned that the wording "if that party considers", leaves "a certain margin of appreciation to the complaining party concerned in arriving at conclusions in respect of an evaluation of certain factual elements [...]".[99] In essence, Panels or arbitrators refer to the margin of appreciation to say that the states have some discretion, and not as a standard of review. Recently, though, in international investment arbitration there has been an attempt to use the NMA as a standard of review.

In *Philip Morris v. Uruguay*, Philip Morris challenged the two tobacco-control measures enacted by the Uruguayan government for the purpose of protecting public health. Such measures consisted of a "single presentation" requirement[100] and an increase in the size of health warnings on cigarette packaging from 50 to 80% of the lower part of each of the main sides of a cigarette package.

The claimants argued, among other things, that the measures were unfair and inequitable. The tribunal upheld the legality of both measures. In rejecting the argument that the challenged measures were arbitrary, the majority of the tribunal considered that the "margin of appreciation" as developed in the jurisprudence of the ECtHR applied equally in disputes arising under BITs, and that tribunals *"should pay great deference to governmental judgments of national needs"*.[101]

However, Arbitrator Gary Born rejected the applicability of the margin of appreciation[102] in the BIT context and stated that the single presentation requirement breached the FET standard,[103] being arbitrary and irrational. In particular, he mentioned:

> The reasons that led to acceptance of the 'margin of appreciation' in the context of the ECHR are not necessarily transferable to other contexts, including specifically to a BIT between Switzerland and Uruguay. Rather, just as the meaning of Article 3(2)'s 'fair and equitable' treatment guarantee must be determined by interpretation of the BIT, so the standard of review and degree of deference to state regulatory and legislative judgments must be determined by interpretation of the BIT, not of the ECHR and decisions interpret-

---

[99] See *EC – Bananas III, cit. supra* note 33, para. 52.

[100] Meaning that tobacco manufacturers may not produce more than one variant of a single brand family of cigarettes.

[101] *Philip Morris Brands Sàrl, Philip Morris Products S.A. and Abal Hermanos S.A. v. Oriental Republic of Uruguay*, Case No. ARB/10/7, Award of 8 July 2016, para. 85 (emphasis added).

[102] However, Gary Born mentioned that there is only one award which appears to have adopted a "margin of appreciation" based upon ECtHR jurisprudence: *Continental Casualty Company v. Argentina*, where the was an express mention of the "public order" and "essential security interests". See para. 188 of the Concurring and Dissenting Opinion of Mr. Gary Born, Arbitrator, in *Philip Morris v. Uruguay*.

[103] Fair and equitable standard is intended to protect investors against serious instances of arbitrary, discriminatory or abusive conduct by host states.

ing that instrument international courts which have addressed the issue.[104]

Clearly, the opinions as to the use of the margin of appreciation differ among arbitrators and it comes as no surprise that scholars are also undecided as to this issue. While some scholars like Burke-White and von Staden support the use of the margin of appreciation "as the most appropriate standard for the resolution of public-law-type disputes,"[105] others call it "an aberration in international law" and claim that it has in fact diminished in importance in international law.[106] For example, Tallent claims that the use of NMA is inappropriate and "it would restrict a full review of state measures".[107] In line with this, Arato also argues that:

> [...] the import of the margin of appreciation into international investment law does active harm. Absent institutional centralization, the invocation of this open-ended doctrine tends to obstruct that process of dialogue essential to working out a more consistent approach to the standard of review over time.[108]

Zarra, while discussing the margin of appreciation in international investment law, calls recourse to it "inappropriate" and "useless" as the deference to states might be achieved by applying proportionality principle.[109] Along these lines, Follesdal, when discussing the margin of appreciation, seems not to encourage its use in trade and investment courts by saying that in these areas each state has more at risk. He even pointed out the fact that the doctrine first should be far more precisely defined to be adopted by other international courts and tribunals.[110] On the same note, Alvarez and Khamsi state that the problems of the margin of appreciation doctrine itself, the different goals of the investment regime and the ECHR regime and the risk of duplicating already-present forms of balancing are solid reasons to not import the margin of appreciation for the interpretation of Article XI of the US-Argentina BIT (the security exception provision).[111]

---

[104] See Concurring and Dissenting Opinion of Mr. Gary Born, *cit. supra* note 102, para. 185.

[105] BURKE-WHITE and VON STADEN, "The Need for Public Law Standards in Investor-State Arbitrations", in SCHILL (ed.), *International Investment and Comparative Public Law*, Oxford, 2010, p. 689 ff., p. 719.

[106] BJORGE, "Been There, Done That: The Margin of Appreciation and International Law", Cambridge Journal of International and Comparative Law, 2015, p. 181 ff., p. 181.

[107] TALLENT, "The Tractor in the Jungle: Why Investment Arbitration Tribunals Should Reject a Margin of Appreciation Doctrine", in LAIRD and WEILER (eds.), *Investment Treaty Arbitration and International Law*, Vol. 3, New York, 2010, p. 111 ff., p. 135.

[108] See ARATO, *cit .supra* note 72, p. 578.

[109] See ZARRA, *cit. supra* note 75, p. 108.

[110] FOLLESDAL, "Appreciating the Margin of Appreciation" in ETINSON (ed.), *Human Rights: Moral or Political*, Oxford, 2018, p. 269 ff.

[111] ALVAREZ and KHAMSI, "The Argentine Crisis and Foreign Investors: A Glimpse into the Heart of the Investment Regime", in SAUVANT (ed.), *Yearbook of International Investment Law and Policy 2008-2009*, New York, 2009, p. 379 ff.

Shany, on the contrary, supports the use of NMA and claims that the doctrine serves for those norms that are "intrinsically uncertain or consciously sacrifice legal certainty for pluralism (standard-type norms, discretionary norms and result-oriented norms)".[112] Against this background, the GATT security exception, by having the "it considers" wording, falls within the discretionary type of norms. It seems that combined, the vagueness of the NMA doctrine and the discretionary character of the security exception might bring even more confusion. Feingold develops this line of thought by arguing that "perhaps the reliance on the doctrine represents a politically motivated choice of action by a Commission and Court [...]".[113]

Coming back to the NMA as a standard of review for sanctions, it could be used: (i) to review the measures that the state has taken and their necessity (ii) to review whether the measures have been taken in time of "war" or "other emergency in international relations". The "margin of appreciation" of the state is wider in the first case with regard to the choice of the measures it can take and their necessity due to the "any measures it considers necessary" wording. The review of necessity, notwithstanding the wording "it considers" is still possible and some scholars claim that it could be exercised under the proportionality or good faith test.[114] There is also a view that "necessity" is a "self-judging" element, taking into account the difference between GATT Article XX and Article XXI.[115] In the second case the state has the discretion to decide whether it is a situation of "war or other emergency in international relations". In this regard the Panel has a wide margin for review since delineation of the situations of emergency and war could be defined at the international level any time by referring to the contemporary documents of the international organisations like the UN.[116] Nonetheless, the question of the substance of review remains open since the precise framework of the NMA is not established yet. Hence, it seems that the national margin of appreciation simply stands for the concept of deference in both cases. The misleading nature of NMA has been noticed by Möllenhoff, who noted that the "[...] reference to the margin of appreciation is often misleading [...] and it is necessary to uncover the underlying criteria which determine the ECtHR's assessment instead of focusing on the 'margin of appreciation' alone".[117]

To conclude, the NMA, while being flexible, remains very vague in terms of content and rather Europe-centered. Indeed, Mr. Born in *Philip Morris v Uruguay*, was on solid ground in suggesting that the rationales offered for the

---

[112] SHANY, "Toward the General Margin of Appreciation", EJIL, 2005, p. 907 ff., p. 939.

[113] FEINGOLD, "Doctrine of Margin of Appreciation and the European Convention on Human Rights", Notre Dame Law Review, 1977, p. 90 ff., p. 106.

[114] The proportionality along with other standards/principles of review in this regard was discussed by SCHILL and BRIESE, *cit. supra* note 54, p. 108.

[115] AKANDE and WILLIAMS, *cit. supra* note 31, p. 387.

[116] *Ibid.,* p. 400.

[117] MÖLLENHOFF, "Framing the 'Public Morals' Exception After EC – Seal Products With Insights from the ECtHR and the GATT National Security Exception", CTEI Working Paper, Geneva, 2015, p. 1 ff., p. 22, available at: <http://repository.graduateinstitute.ch/record/293785/files/CTEI-2015-07_Mollenhoff_EC-Seals-ECtHR.pdf>.

margin of appreciation as a term of European law are geographically and tempo-rally specific.[118] The vagueness of the NMA means it is of no use in clarifying the application of the security exception. The orientation of the ECtHR towards the European consensus complicates the use of NMA since there is no similar con-sensus within the WTO system. These traits combined make it hard to transpose this doctrine into other systems. That being said, it does not mean that the tribu-nals other than ECtHR do not recourse to the NMA. However, when they refer to the NMA, some tribunals[119] do so to state the deference that they give to the state. This approach is called by Vasani "bowing to the Queen" – i.e. providing undue deference simply because of the sovereign status of a state.[120] This doctrine needs further definition to be used in such sensitive areas as national security. Hilf and Salomon argue that "it would be desirable to find […] at least abstract rules on the use of margin of appreciation".[121] If such abstract contours of the NMA are found then its applicability as a standard of review for the sanctions cases might be brought up for discussion again.

8.   CONCLUDING REMARKS

To sum up, the security exception provisions due to their vague nature and the sensitive nature of national security can be used by states for protectionist measures. There is therefore a need for a mechanism to limit the deference to states. Subsequently, an accepted standard of review can serve as a tool for the courts to review the sanctions imposed by states.

The standards of review differ depending on their stringency: from the most lenient good faith standard to the strict *de novo* review. A well-defined frame-work between these two extremes is necessary, especially taking into account the gravity of the national security matters states refer to whenever invoking secu-rity exception clauses. In search for the standard of review this paper examined the national margin of appreciation as developed by the ECtHR. It appears that despite its frequent use by the ECtHR this doctrine remains vague. In search for standard of review the paper also briefly discussed the recent cases of the CJEU where the security exception provision has been interpreted. In the last part the author considered use of the NMA doctrine beyond the ECtHR by referring to some ICJ cases and ICSID awards. It appears that while in the *Philip Morris v. Uruguay* case before the ICSID the NMA was referred to as a possible standard of review, the opinions on its applicability have been divided. In addition, the CJEU, while adjudicating on sanctions-related cases, was rather imprecise in its argumentation.

---

[118] See Concurring and Dissenting Opinion of Mr. Born, *cit. supra* note 102, para. 85.
[119] *Ibid.*, para. 87.
[120] VASANI, "Bowing to the Queen: Rejecting the Margin of Appreciation Doctrine" in LAIRD and WEILER (eds.), *cit. supra* note 107, p. 137 ff., p. 138.
[121] See HILF and SALOMON, *cit. supra* note 58, p. 48.

Finally, the author considered the suitability of the NMA as a standard of review for the GATT security exception and came to the conclusion that at this stage the vagueness of the NMA doctrine precludes such an application. Notwithstanding the above, given the recent increased use of sanctions by states and the possible rise of cases interpreting security exception provisions, future research should address what other standards of review could solve this predicament.

THE PARLIAMENTARY ASSEMBLY OF THE COUNCIL OF EUROPE AND THE SANCTIONS AGAINST THE RUSSIAN FEDERATION IN RESPONSE TO THE CRISIS IN UKRAINE

Antonino Alì[*]

Abstract

The article examines the actions taken by the Parliamentary Assembly of the Council of Europe (PACE) against the delegation of the Russian Federation in response to the crisis in Ukraine. In 2014 the Assembly decided to suspend some of the rights of the Russian delegation and menaced to annul the credentials of the delegation if an effective effort was not made on the part of Russia to sort out the situation and to reverse the annexation. The adoption of sanctions against the Russian delegation raised several legal issues related to the very existence of a sanctioning power of the CoE and in particular of the Assembly. The question is whether the powers to "penalize" the parliamentary delegation have been exercised by PACE in conformity with the Statute. The Statute of the CoE does not attribute sanctioning powers to the Assembly in order to target the states which are in breach of Article 3 or international law more generally. This power falls firmly in the hands of the Committee of Ministers as a way to put pressure on, deter, and eventually punish a state which has seriously violated the core of the principles of the CoE system. PACE, in the exercise of its functions, may certainly contribute to activating procedures to monitor the activities of the member states, but the last word is in the hands of the Committee which may suspend the rights of representation of a state and request that the offending state withdraw from the Committee entirely. The Statute plainly does not attribute this power to PACE. In the absence of the jurisdiction of a Court to deal with the problems caused by the lack of harmonisation between the sanctions adopted by the Committee of Ministers and the ones introduced by the Parliamentary Assembly through some modifications of the Rules of Procedure, the recent call for a 4th Summit of Heads of State and Government of the CoE by the Assembly in order to "preserve and further strengthen this unparalleled pan-European project currently threatened by divisions and a weakening of member States' commitment" by "harmonising[...] the rules governing participation, representation and responsibilities of member States in both statutory organs, while fully respecting the autonomy of these bodies" should be welcomed.

Keywords: sanctions; credentials; Russian Federation; Ukraine; Parliamentary Assembly; Council of Europe.

---

[*] Associate Professor of International Law, Faculty of Law and School of International Studies, University of Trento.

1. INTRODUCTION

The European Union (EU), the United States (US) and other countries have adopted several measures against the Russian Federation in response to the events destabilising and threatening the territorial integrity, sovereignty and independence of Ukraine from 2014.[1] After a first set of diplomatic sanctions in response to Russian actions, further measures were adopted such as travel bans and asset freezes against natural and legal persons, sanctions on economic movements from Crimea and Sevastopol, on the sectorial cooperation and exchanges with Russia and some other measures in the field of economic cooperation. The sanctions were aimed at damaging Russian economic interests through the targeting of selected sectors and companies as well as targeting the Russian and philo-Russian Ukrainian civil and military leadership. These measures were adopted by States or by an international organisation, such as the EU, which has a competence in the field of foreign and security policy and international trade.

Quite surprisingly some measures were also adopted by the Council of Europe (CoE), the international organisation whose stated aim is to uphold human rights, democracy and the rule of law in Europe. These actions were taken by the Parliamentary Assembly (PACE), the deliberative organ of the Council of Europe, which possesses the duty to debate matters within its competence and present recommendations to the Committee of Ministers, the intergovernmental body of the CoE.[2] The Assembly decided to suspend several rights of the Russian delegation giving rise to a number of legal and institutional problems which this contribution will analyse.

2. THE RULES OF PROCEDURE, THE MONITORING COMMITTEE OF THE PARLIAMENTARY ASSEMBLY OF THE COUNCIL OF EUROPE AND THE CREDENTIALS PROCEDURE

PACE is composed of representatives of each member state, elected or appointed by national parliaments from among their members. The composition of delegations should reflect the political situation in their respective national parliaments. According to the same provision the term of office of representatives will date from the opening of the ordinary session following their appointment and will expire at the opening of the next ordinary session. The Parliamentary Assembly adopts its rules of procedure (RoP) and should determine *inter alia*:

---

[1] For a general overview of the sanctions, see the report of the European Parliamentary Research Service, "Sanctions over Ukraine: Impact on Russia", January 2018, available at: <http://www.europarl.europa.eu/RegData/etudes/BRIE/2018/614665/EPRS_BRI(2018) 614665_EN.pdf>.

[2] PACE is composed of 648 members of national parliaments (324 representatives and 324 substitute members) of the 47 CoE Member States, plus 30 Observers and 30 Partners for democracy. France, Germany, Italy, the Russian Federation, Turkey and the United Kingdom have the largest delegations (18+18).

the quorum, the manner of the election and terms of office of the President and other officers; the manner in which the agenda shall be drawn up and be communicated to representatives; the time and manner in which the names of representatives and their substitutes shall be notified (Rule 28 RoP).

Rule 6 governs the procedure for "Credentials", which in large international organisations such as the Council of Europe should serve as a proof that the individuals indicated by their respective States are what the organisation requires them to be. Typically, in international institutions the approval of credentials is considered a formality.[3] In the case of PACE, the credentials of the representatives are sent to the President of the Assembly by the President (Speaker) of the national parliament or the President (Speaker) of a national parliamentary chamber or any person delegated by them. The credentials must be transmitted not less than one week before the opening of the Session.[4] According to Rule 6.2 RoP, national delegations should be composed so as to ensure a fair representation of the political parties or groups in their parliaments and should include members of the under-represented sex.

Credentials shall be accompanied by a signed written statement by the individual members subscribing to the aims and basic principles of the CoE, mentioned in the Preamble, in Article 1(a) and in Article 3 of the Statute of the CoE. The credentials shall be submitted to the Assembly at the beginning of each ordinary session by the provisional President for ratification. The Assembly has the power to challenge both ratified and unratified credentials of the representatives and substitutes on procedural grounds (Rule 7) or of the national delegation on substantive grounds (Rule 8). For example, credentials challenged on procedural grounds may be referred for opinion to the Committee on Equality and Non-Discrimination, where credentials are questioned in relation to the representation of the sexes in the membership of the delegation concerned (Rule 7.2).

According to Rule 8, "[t]he credentials of the national delegation as a whole" may be challenged on the following substantive grounds:

> 8.2.a. serious violation of the basic principles of the Council of Europe mentioned in art. 3 of, and the Preamble to, the Statute;
> 8.2.b. persistent failure to honor obligations and commitments and lack of co-operation in the Assembly's monitoring procedure.

In response to a challenge or reconsideration of credentials, the Assembly may decide on:

> 10.1.a. ratification of the credentials, or confirmation of ratification of the credentials;
> 10.1.b. non-ratification of the credentials, or annulment of ratification of the credentials;

---

[3] On the credentials see SCHERMERS and BLOKKER, *International Institutional Law*, 5th ed., Boston-Leiden, 2011, pp. 200-202.

[4] The Parliamentary Assembly meets four times a year at plenary sessions.

> 10.1.c. ratification of the credentials, or confirmation of ratification of the credentials *together with depriving or suspending the exercise of some of the rights of participation or representation of members of the delegation concerned in the activities of the Assembly and its bodies.*[5]

The Parliamentary Assembly monitors the compliance by member states with their obligations to respect human rights and democratic standards. To ensure full compliance with the undertakings made by all member states is a fundamental task of the CoE and the Assembly decided to constitute a Monitoring Committee (MC) on the honouring of obligations and commitments by member states of the CoE.[6] The MC centralised the work that was distributed between several general committees with competences relating to member states' obligations and commitments[7] with the aim of reducing their workload.[8] The MC is responsible for verifying the fulfilment of the obligations assumed by the member states under the terms of the Statute of the CoE, the European Convention on Human Rights (ECHR) and all other CoE conventions to which they are parties, as well as the honouring of the commitments entered into by the authorities of member states upon their accession to the CoE.

According to the Resolution on the basis of which the Monitoring Committee was created, the Parliamentary Assembly "may *penalise* persistent failure to honour obligations and commitments accepted, and lack of co-operation in its monitoring process, by adopting a resolution and/or a recommendation, by the non-ratification of the credentials of a national parliamentary delegation at the beginning of its next ordinary session or by the annulment of ratified credentials in the course of the same ordinary session in accordance with Rule 6 of the Rules of Procedure".[9] Here one has to note that the term "penalise" was not meant to refer to a criminalisation of the conduct, rather it refers to the adoption of restrictive measures limiting the powers of the delegation (e.g. the rights to vote and to be a member of a committee).

Should the member state continue not to respect its commitments, the Assembly may address a recommendation to the Committee of Ministers requesting it to take the appropriate action in accordance with Articles 8 and 9 of the Statute of the CoE.[10]

---

[5] Rule 10 RoP (emphasis added).

[6] PACE Resolution 1115(1997), Setting up of an Assembly committee on the honouring of obligations and commitments by member states of the Council of Europe (Monitoring Committee), 29 January 1997.

[7] PACE Order 508 (1995), Honouring of obligations and commitments by member states of the Council of Europe, 26 April 1995.

[8] See LEACH, "The Parliamentary Assembly of the Council of Europe", in SCHMAHL and BREUER (eds.), *The Council of Europe. Its Law and Policies*, Oxford, 2017, p. 166 ff., p. 175.

[9] Resolution 1115(1997), *cit. supra* note 6, para. 12 (emphasis added).

[10] As will be explained more extensively later: see *infra* Section 4.

3. TWO MOTIONS FOR A RESOLUTION SUSPENDING THE RIGHTS OF THE RUSSIAN DELEGATION

Two different motions for a resolution were presented before the Parliamentary Assembly on March 2014 just after the US and the EU began adopting diplomatic and restrictive measures against Russia and the Ukrainian leadership.

The first one requested the Assembly to re-examine the ratified credentials of the Russian delegation. It was based on Rule 9.1.a RoP of the Assembly (Reconsideration of previously ratified credentials on substantive grounds)[11] according to which "[t]he Assembly may reconsider ratified credentials of a national delegation as a whole in the course of the same ordinary session [...]: on a motion for a resolution to annul ratification based on the grounds set out in Rule 8.2".[12]

The motion requested a condemnation without reservation of the violation of the territorial integrity and sovereignty of Ukraine by the armed forces of the Russian Federation in early March 2014 and expressed "its gravest concern that member of the upper House of the Russian Parliament unanimously authorised such action in advance". It also underlined that there had been a "serious violation of the basic principles of the Council of Europe" (Article 3 and the preamble of the Statute) and asked the Assembly for a reconsideration of the ratified credentials of the Russian delegation on substantive grounds.

Some days after the first, a second motion[13] was presented by 53 members on the basis of Article 9.1.a of the RoP of the Assembly. After recalling the importance of the "ideals and principles" of the COE, and "the binding procedures set up by the Assembly" to achieve a greater unity between its member states and to realise them, this group of members of the Assembly expressed their concern over "the persistent failure by the Russian Federation to honour its obligations and commitments". The motion underlined the need for a more extensive European construction after the conflict in Ukraine and qualified the actions of the Russian military forces as a violation of international law and, in particular, of the United Nations (UN) Charter, the OSCE Helsinki Final Act, the CoE Statute and the commitments made by Russia at the moment of accession.

This second motion, similarly to the first, put particular emphasis on the fact that the Russian actions were authorised by the Parliament of the Russian Federation. The whole Russian strategy was described as a grave threat to in-

---

[11] (Credentials of the Russian Delegation) – Motion for a resolution, Doc. 13456 of 21 March 2014, tabled by Mr Robert Walter and other members of the Assembly.

[12] Art. 8.2 reads: "The substantive grounds on which credentials may be challenged are: 8.2.a. serious violation of the basic principles of the Council of Europe mentioned in Article 3 of, and the Preamble to, the Statute; or 8.2.b. persistent failure to honour obligations and commitments and lack of co-operation in the Assembly's monitoring procedure". Art. 9.1.b allows the reconsideration of the credentials "on the basis of a report by the Monitoring Committee containing a text which recommends that the credentials be reconsidered".

[13] Suspension of the voting rights of the Russian delegation (Rule 9 of the Rules of Procedure of the Assembly), Doc. 13459 of 24 March 2014, motion for a resolution abled by Mr Michael Aastrup Jensen and others.

ternational security. In particular, the motion recalled the previous suspension in 2000 of the voting rights of the Russian delegation because of the conflict in Chechnya.[14] Therefore, the violation of the territorial integrity of Ukraine served as grounds to suspend the voting rights of the Russian delegation.

The first motion asked for a resolution reconsidering the ratified credentials on substantive grounds (the violation of founding principles of the CoE), the second one requested a "milder" suspension of the rights of the delegation.

On the basis of these two motions, the Parliamentary Assembly, after qualifying the actions of the Russian Federation a violation of international law, adopted Resolution 1990(2015) condemning the Russian Federation's actions with regard to Ukraine.[15] According to the Parliamentary Assembly the actions of the Russian Federation were in clear contradiction with the Preamble and Article 3 of the CoE Statute and the commitments undertaken by Russia upon its accession.[16]

The Assembly, after pointing out the rejection by the Russian Federation of any diplomatic efforts by the international community and the threat caused by the Russian actions, put particular emphasis on "the position taken by the members of both chambers of the Russian Parliament at different stages of the process of annexation, including the unanimous vote in the Council of the Federation authorising the use of military force in Ukraine, the approval of the constitutional amendments allowing for the annexation of Crimea and the ratification of the illegal treaty on unification" (paragraph 7). In other words, the CoE Assembly, triggered by the two motions, underlined the role of the Russian Parliament in the Ukraine actions. The parliamentary organ also pointed out the failure of the Russian Federation to implement the resolutions on the consequences of the war between Georgia and Russia[17] and expressed concern for the situation of the minorities in Crimea. The Assembly however expressed the view that the "suspension of the credentials" of the Russian delegation would have made a political dialogue impossible and that the Assembly could constitute a good forum for keeping the Russian delegation accountable.

---

[14] The ratified credentials of the Russian delegation were reconsidered and the Assembly deprived their rights to vote in the Assembly and its bodies. PACE Resolution 1241(2001) of 25 January 2001 decided to ratify the credentials and therefore the rights of the delegation were restored.

[15] PACE Resolution 1990(2014), Reconsideration on substantive grounds of the previously ratified credentials of the Russian delegation, adopted on 10 April 2014. The resolution was adopted by 145 votes to 21 with 22 abstentions. The Russian activities were considered also a violation of the memorandum signed between Russia, the US and the United Kingdom, and Ukraine, Belarus and Kazakhstan in 1994 on disarmament and on non-proliferation of nuclear weapons which would have undermined "the trust in other international instruments, in particular the agreements on disarmament and on non-proliferation of nuclear weapons".

[16] Opinion 193(1996), Application by Russia for membership of the Council of Europe.

[17] PACE Resolution 1633(2008), The consequences of the war between Georgia and Russia, 2 October 2008; PACE Resolution 1647(2009), Implementation of Resolution 1633 (2008) on the consequences of the war between Georgia and Russia, 29 January 2009; PACE Resolution 1683(2009), The war between Georgia and Russia: one year after, 29 September 2009.

Thus, the Parliamentary Assembly decided to "suspend some of the rights of the delegation" of the Russian Federation until the end of the 2014 session and reserved the right to annul the credentials of the Russian delegation if an effective effort was not made on the part of Russia to sort out the situation and to reverse the annexation.

The rights of the Russian delegation that were suspended were: voting rights, the right to be represented in the Bureau of the Assembly, the Presidential Committee and the Standing Committee, and the right to participate in election observation missions.[18] The Assembly considered that too strong an intervention on the credentials of the Russian delegation would have closed any kind of political dialogue. Therefore, the Assembly resolved to suspend "just" some of the rights of the delegation of the Russian Federation. Moreover, the Assembly reserved the right to annul the credentials of the Russian Federation if it did not de-escalate the situation and reverse the annexation of Crimea.

The reaction of the Russian delegation came quickly. On the basis of the "offer" in Resolution 1990 all contact with the Assembly were suspended, blocking any kind of dialogue on this point. Subsequently on 26 January 2015, the still unratified credentials of the Russian delegation were challenged on the basis of the violation of the Statute of the COE and the accession commitments. With Resolution 2034(2015) of 28 January 2015, the Assembly condemned, on the one hand, the illegal annexation of Crimea, the actions destabilising the eastern Ukraine and underlined the deterioration of the human rights situation in Crimea and in particular that of minorities (the Crimean Tatar community) and, on the other, resolved to ratify the credentials on the basis of some "clear signals" that the Duma wanted to start a dialogue with the Assembly. However, the Assembly decided to suspend for the duration of the 2015 session further rights of the Russian delegation and, in particular: "the right to be appointed rapporteur; the right to be a member of an ad hoc committee on observation of elections; the right to represent the Assembly in Council of Europe bodies as well as external institutions and organisations, both institutionally and on an occasional basis" and also confirmed the suspension of "the voting rights and the right to be represented in the Bureau of the Assembly, the Presidential Committee and the Standing Committee of the Russian delegation to the Assembly" (which had been suspended for the 2014 session).[19] These rights would have been reinstated if some progress towards the demands of the PACE had been made. At the same time, in paragraph 16 of Resolution 2034 the Assembly resolved to annul the credentials of the Russian delegation at its June 2015 part-session if no progress was made with regard to the implementation of the Minsk Protocol and the memorandum, demands and recommendations of the Resolution. In other words, a new set of sanctions were

---

[18] A sub-committee was created by the Monitoring Committee (Committee on the Honoring of obligations and commitments by member states of the CoE) to follow the situation.

[19] See paragraphs 14 and 15 of the PACE Resolution 2034(2015), Challenge, on substantive grounds, of the still unratified credentials of the delegation of the Russian Federation, 28 January 2015.

adopted against the Russian Federation (or rather, against the delegation of the Russian Federation) with the suspension of another "package" of rights.

After the parliamentary debate on 24 June 2015, and considering the lack of progress with regard to the requests made in Resolution 2034(2015) and the decision of the Russian delegation to suspend all official contact with the Assembly until the end of 2015 (including all visits on behalf of Assembly bodies), the Assembly "while noting the *sanctions* currently in place" resolved not to annul the ratified credentials.[20]

In Resolution 2063(2015) paragraph 7 PACE condemned the decision of the Russian authorities to release a blacklist of EU politicians barred from Russia (including a current and a former member of the Assembly and several members of the European Parliament).[21]

From 2015 the Russian delegation, as a measure to oppose the suspension of the rights, decided not to participate in the activities of PACE and ceased to cooperate with the monitoring procedure of the Assembly. From that moment, the Russian Federation has not submitted credentials to PACE. Furthermore, as announced on 30 June 2017, the Russian Federation decided to suspend payment of its contribution to the budget of the CoE for 2017 until full unconditional restoration of the rights of its delegation.

4. THE 'INTERNAL' SANCTIONING POWERS OF INTERGOVERNMENTAL ORGANS

The adoption of sanctions against the Russian delegation raises several legal issues related to the very existence of a sanctioning power of the CoE and in particular of the Assembly.

It is useful to note that in the context of the UN, for example, the Charter in Article 5 provides that "a Member of the United Nations against which preventive or enforcement action has been taken by the Security Council may be suspended from the exercise of the rights and privileges of membership by the General Assembly upon the recommendation of the Security Council" and that "the exercise of these rights and privileges may be restored by the Security Council". According to Article 6 of the UN Charter a Member "which has persistently violated the Principles contained in the Charter" maybe be expelled by the General Assembly upon a recommendation of the Security Council. According to a distinguished author the suspension of the rights of membership in the UN system was not intended as a sanction, although the same author noted that the "suspension of the exercise of the rights of membership could be an appropriate sanction against any violation of obligations of a Member".[22]

---

[20] See PACE Resolution 2063(2015), 24 June 2015, paragraph 9 (emphasis added).

[21] PACE Resolution 2063 (2015), Consideration of the annulment of the previously ratified credentials of the delegation of the Russian Federation (follow-up to paragraph 16 of Resolution 2034 (2015)), 24 June 2015.

[22] See KELSEN, "Sanctions in International Law under the Charter of the United Nations", Iowa Law Review, 1945-1946, p. 499 ff., pp. 505-506, according to whom the suspension

In the different framework of the EU, the Council under Article 7(2) of Treaty on European Union (TEU), acting by a qualified majority, may decide to suspend certain of the rights deriving from the application of the Treaties to the member states in case of a serious and persistent breach of the values referred to in Article 2 TEU (respect for human dignity, freedom, democracy, equality, the rule of law and respect for human rights, including the rights of persons belonging to minorities), including the voting rights of the representative of the government of that member state in the Council.[23] Suffice to say that in the EU system the EU parliament has a limited role also in the adoption of sanctions not only at the "internal" level (violations by EU member states)[24] but also at the "external" level (sanctions against third states or natural or legal persons).[25] It should be underlined that the latter are sanctions against third states, which by definition are not members of the organisation.

Turning to the CoE, the Statute in Article 8 includes a provision allowing the Committee of Ministers, the intergovernmental organ of the organisation, to sanction serious violations of the fundamental principles of the CoE by a member state:

> Any member of the Council of Europe which has seriously violated Article 3 may be suspended from its rights of representation and requested by the Committee of Ministers to withdraw under Article 7.

---

of the rights of membership "is an additional measure taken against a Member subjected to preventive or enforcement action. If the enforcement action (including a preventive enforcement action) is a sanction, suspension of the right of membership [...] maybe considered as an additional sanction". The same author candidly underlined that "[t]o ascertain whether a Member has violated its obligation under the Charter is to answer a legal question. Political bodies such as the Security Council and the General Assembly are certainly not the proper organs to fulfil this task. There was no sufficient reason not to confer it upon the International Court of Justice and to restrict the function of the Security Council and the Assembly, or of one of them, to apply for a decision of the Court and to act in conformity with". See, also, CHESTERMAN, JOHNSTONE and MALONE, *Law and Practice of the United Nations: Documents and Commentary*, 2nd ed., Oxford, 2016, p. 195 ff.; CONFORTI and FOCARELLI, *Le Nazioni Unite*, 10th ed., Milano, 2017, pp. 72-77; NESI, "Brevi note su diritto e politica all'ONU. Ammissione, accreditamento, rappresentanza e status di osservatore in Assemblea generale", in VELLANO (ed.), *Il futuro delle organizzazioni internazionali. Prospettive giuridiche (XIX Convegno SIDI – Courmayeur)*, Napoli, 2015, p. 601 ff.; MARCHISIO, *L'ONU. Il diritto delle Nazioni Unite*, 2nd ed., Bologna, 2012, pp. 102-106.

[23] See for all LENAERTS and VAN NUFFEL, *European Union Law*, 3rd ed., London, 2011, pp. 100-101; the procedure of Art. 7 of the Treaty on EU sets out ways for the EU to react with preventive measures when there is a risk of a serious breach of EU values (Art. 7(1)) or with sanctions when a serious and persistent breach of EU values has taken place (Art. 7(2)).

[24] The European Parliament should give its consent to the procedure under Art. 7 but the final decision is taken by the Council.

[25] The Council also imposes restrictive measures on the basis of a Common Foreign Security Policy decision adopted at unanimity and then implemented through separate Council regulations adopted on the basis of a joint proposal of the EU High Representative for Foreign Affairs and Security Policy and the European Commission (see Art. 215 of the TFEU). The limited power of the European Parliament was confirmed also by the Court of Justice in Case C-130/10, *European Parliament v. Council of the European Union*, 19 July 2012, para. 82.

> If such member does not comply with this request, the Committee may decide that it has ceased to be a member of the Council as from such date as the Committee may determine.[26]

Two elements are common to the examples given (UN, EU and CoE). The first is that the legal basis for the adoption of sanctions against a member of the organisation resides in the constitutive treaty (the "constitution") of the organisation which is the primary source of the powers of its organs. The second is that the procedure is substantially in the hands of the political organ which has an intergovernmental nature or, as in the UN system, is shared between the two intergovernmental bodies (i.e. the Security Council and the General Assembly). In other words, these powers were attributed by the High contracting parties to the organ in which their interest was best represented. It is worth noting that the powers of Article 8 of the Statute have never been used in the context of the CoE even though in some cases, like that of Greece during the dictatorship or of Russia in the second Chechen conflict, the situation was considered "a grave violation of Art. 3 of the Statute",[27] or a "clear contradiction" with the Statute of the CoE, in particular its preamble, and the obligations resulting from Article 3.[28]

5. THE CREATION OF A SYSTEM OF SANCTIONS BY THE PARLIAMENTARY ASSEMBLY OF THE COUNCIL OF EUROPE

It has been pointed out that "[b]ecause suspension and expulsion from the United Nations is very difficult, the credentials procedure has been used as a way of denying some states the right to participate – despite the fact the granting of credentials is meant to be a routine matter".[29]

At the same time in the CoE, because the decision to expel the state from the CoE under the aforementioned Article 8 is clearly a draconian measure that should be used only as last resort in the case of incompatibility of the state (an

---

[26] See KLEIN, "Membership and Observer Status", in SCHMAHL and BREUER (eds.), *cit. supra* note 6, p. 41 ff., pp. 67-72. According to Art. 7, "any member of the Council of Europe may withdraw by formally notifying the Secretary General of its intention to do so. Such withdrawal shall take effect at the end of the financial year in which it is notified, if the notification is given during the first nine months of that financial year. If the notification is given in the last three months of the financial years it shall take effect at the end of the next financial year".

[27] See PACE Resolution 1456(2000), Conflict in the Chechen Republic – Implementation by Russia of Recommendation 1444(2000), 6 April 2000, para. 25. MERILIN, "Gambling, Misunderstanding or Compromising? The Council of Europe and the War in Chechnya", in MALFLIET and PARMENTIER (eds.), *Russia and the Council of Europe: 10 Years After*, London, 2010, p. 143 ff.

[28] Resolution 1990, *cit. supra* note 15, para. 4: "As well as with the commitments undertaken by the Russian Federation upon accession and contained in Assembly Opinion 193(1996) on Russia's request for membership of the Council of Europe".

[29] CHESTERMAN, JOHNSTONE and MALONE, *cit. supra* note 22, pp. 225-232; FOX, "The Right to Political Participation in International Law", Yale JIL, 1992, p. 539 ff.; KLABBERS, *An Introduction to International Organizations Law*, 3rd ed., Cambridge, 2015.

irreconcilable conflict with the essence of the organisation), the credential procedure has been used (and modified) by the Assembly as a sanction on member states which are considered violators of the fundamental principles on the basis of which the CoE is founded.

The history of the modifications of the RoP proves that in the last twenty years a set of sanctions has been introduced by PACE as a way to exercise political control through procedural/legal means.

The first substantial modification was introduced just over twenty years ago in the challenge of credentials of national delegations in the course of an ordinary session (not limited to the opening of the ordinary session).[30] In other words the procedure could be activated any time during the activity of the Assembly.

Indeed in 1996 it was decided[31] to include a new paragraph 7 in Rule 6:

> Ratified credentials may be reconsidered in the course of the same ordinary session if a motion for a resolution[32] has been tabled with a view to annulling the ratification. Such a motion must state the reasons and shall be based:
> - on a serious violation of the basic principles of the Council of Europe mentioned in Article 3 and the preamble of the Statute; or
> - on paragraph 9 of Order No. 508 (1995).[33]

In 2000 there were 3 different procedures: the first served to challenge unratified credentials on procedural grounds (Rule 7), the second to challenge unratified credentials on substantive grounds (Rule 8), and the last for previously ratified credentials on substantive grounds (Rule 9).

In 2014 these three rules were merged into one (Rule 10). As underlined[34] in Section 2, the new system included a different solution constituted by the following alternatives: the non-ratification of the credentials, the annulment of the ratification of the credentials or the deprivation or suspension of the exercise of

---

[30] PACE Resolution 1081(1996), Challenge of credentials of national delegations in the course of an ordinary session, 22 April 1996.

[31] *Ibid.*, para. 3.

[32] Paragraphs 8 and 9 of the Resolution read: "8. The motion shall be referred to the Political Affairs Committee for report and to the Committee on Legal Affairs and Human Rights and the Committee on Rules of Procedure for opinion. The report including a draft text shall be submitted to the Assembly or the Standing Committee, if necessary under urgent procedure. 9. The draft text shall, if appropriate, justify annulling the ratification of credentials of a delegation and submit proposals with respect to the consequences such as: depriving the members of the delegation concerned of tabling official documents in the sense of Rule 23 of the Rules of Procedure, taking on duties and voting in the Assembly and its bodies, while maintaining those members' rights to attend and to speak at Assembly part-sessions and meetings of its bodies; or depriving the members of the delegation concerned of the exercise of the full rights of participation in the activities of the Assembly and its bodies."

[33] According to Order 508 (1995), *cit. supra* note 7, para. 9: "The Assembly may sanction persistent failure to honour commitments, and lack of co-operation in its monitoring process".

[34] See Rule 10, para. 2.

some of the rights of participation or representation of members of the delegation concerned in the activities of the Assembly and its bodies. In other words,
a structured system of *sanctions* against the delegation of a member state has
been progressively put in place using the power of the Assembly to adopt its own
rules of procedure. This phenomenon is confirmed by the frequent use of the
word "sanction" in the Resolutions adopted since 2014 concerning the Russian
Delegation.

This system has been modified since 1996, however the idea to use the credentials in an instrumental way is already there as has already been pointed out
with regards to Resolution 1115(1997) where the powers of PACE were described
in a structured way.[35]

PACE may sanction ("penalise")[36] the persistent failure to honour obligations
and commitments accepted, and lack of co-operation in its monitoring process,
with the non-ratification of the credentials of a parliamentary delegation at the
beginning of its next ordinary session (or by the annulment of ratified credentials
in the course of the same ordinary session).[37] In the case of a continuous infringement case PACE may recommend that the Committee of Ministers take the appropriate action in accordance with Articles 8 and 9 of the Statute of the CoE.[38]

6. AN (UNLAWFUL) SYSTEM OF SANCTIONS IN THE ABSENCE OF A LEGAL BASIS

The considerations discussed above raise the question of whether the powers
that have been exercised by the Assembly are in conformity with the Statute.[39]

The Statute of the CoE does not attribute sanctioning powers to the Assembly
(Consultative Assembly, according to the Statute) in order to target the states
which are in breach of Article 3 or international law more generally. This power
falls firmly in the hands of the Committee of Ministers as a way to put pressure
on, deter, and eventually punish a state which has seriously violated the core of
the principles of the CoE system.

PACE, in the exercise of its functions, may certainly contribute to activating
procedures to monitor the activities of the member states, but the last word is in
the hands of the Committee which may suspend the rights of representation of a
state and request that the offending state withdraw from the Committee entirely.
The Statute plainly does not attribute this power to PACE.

---

[35] See para. 2.

[36] See *supra* Section 1.

[37] See Resolution 1115(1997), *cit. supra* note 6, para. 12.

[38] As it has been explained more extensively above: see *supra* Section 4.

[39] Or even if the creation of such a system has been made *ultra vires*. Althought *stricto
sensu* the *ultra vires* notion should be reserved to acts or actions of international organisations
which are taken outside the scope of their competence and it is connected with the idea that
organisations have a limited power. See CANNIZZARO and PALCHETTI, "Ultra Vires Acts of
International Organizations", in KLABBERS and WALLENDAHL, *Research Handbook on the
Law of the International Organizations*, Cheltenham-Northampton, 2011, p. 365 ff.

In the above-mentioned case, since the rights of the delegation have been sus-pended, the Russian Federation has stopped paying its contributions to the CoE.[40] Ironically, this behaviour may be the basis for a "sanction" against the Russian Federation. Indeed, according to Article 9 of the Statute, "[t]he Committee of Ministers may suspend the right of representation on the Committee and on the Consultative Assembly of a member which has failed to fulfil its financial obliga-tion during such period as the obligation remains unfulfilled".

It seems difficult to argue that the Assembly has the power to suspend or reduce the rights of representation of a national delegation on the basis of the "self-adopted" rules of procedure on substantive grounds. This situation appears unlawful, because the procedure of presenting credentials was created for a com-pletely different purpose. A power has been attributed to PACE that has no legal basis in the founding treaty (the CoE Statute).

This situation seems to sit between the lack of competence of the organ to adopt such measures and an outright "misuse of powers", namely, the use of the annulment or non-ratification of the credentials for reasons other than those for which they could be annulled or non-ratified. In this regard, the practice of the challenge of the credentials by the PACE shows that there is a strong differ-ence between the use of the "sanctioning" power of the Assembly for procedural/ formal reasons from the ones based on substantive grounds. For example, at the opening of the PACE session in 2011, the still unratified credentials of the parlia-mentary delegations of Montenegro, San Marino and Serbia were challenged on procedural grounds (Rule 7 RoP), on the basis that they contained no female rep-resentative.[41] On this occasion, the Assembly decided to ratify the credentials of these parliamentary delegations, but it also decided to suspend the voting rights of their members in the Assembly and its bodies until the composition of their delegations was brought into conformity with the RoP.[42]

Another interesting case is that of Greece during the military junta between 1967 and 1974 where the Assembly, even in the absence of rules or procedure, decided not to recognise the credentials of the Greek delegates.[43] The Assembly first declared that the Greek regime was "in serious violation of the conditions for membership of the Council of Europe, as set out in Article 3 of the Statute" and that for that reason it "ought to draw the necessary conclusions and to consider its position under Article 7 of the Statute by virtue of which any Member of the

---

[40] See para. 3.

[41] Pursuant to Rule 6.2.a., "National delegations shall include the under-represented sex at least in the same percentage as is present in their parliaments and, at a very minimum, one member of the under-represented sex appointed as a representative". See Doc. 12488 of 25 January 2011, Challenge on procedural grounds of the still unratified credentials of the parlia-mentary delegations of Montenegro, San Marino and Serbia.

[42] PACE 1789(2011), Challenge on procedural grounds of the still unratified credentials of the parliamentary delegations of Montenegro, San Marino and Serbia, 27 January 2011.

[43] PACE Recommendation 547(1969), 30 January 1969. The Assembly recommended the Committee of Ministers "to take such action, within a specified period, as is appropriate, hav-ing regard to Articles 3, 7 and 8 of the Statute of the Council of Europe and to the resolutions of the Assembly cited above".

Council of Europe may withdraw". The Assembly then decided not to recognise the credentials of "any Greek delegate purporting to represent the Greek parliament until such time as the Assembly is satisfied that freedom of expression is restored and a free and representative parliament is elected in Greece".

In other words, the outcome of the contested act is at odds with the objectives for which the power was conferred. It is one thing to "sanction" the delegation because of its composition, for example the lack of some requirements implicit in the idea of an organ composed by "representatives of each member, elected by its parliament from among the members or appointed from among the members of that parliament". It is quite another thing to "penalise" a delegation because of the actions of the state they represent.

7. CONCLUSIONS

It seems that limiting the powers of the Russian delegation was a way to target the delegation and its members more than the behaviour of the state itself. As previously noted, in the motions that brought Resolution 1990(2014) and in the Resolution itself, the Assembly underlined the role the Federation Council of Russia had played in the use of armed forces in the territory of Ukraine and the subsequent annexation of Crimea and Sevastopol to the Russian Federation.

In 2004,[44] the same Assembly discussed the possibility of contesting the credentials of the parliamentary delegation of Serbia and Montenegro. This was due to the election of Slobodan Milošević, Vojislav Seselj and Nebojsa Pavkovic after they had been accused of serious violations of international humanitarian law before the International Criminal Tribunal for the former Yugoslavia. On this occasion, the Assembly noted "with regret" that, in their current wording, Rules 8 and 9 did not allow for challenging the credentials of individual members of a national delegation on substantial grounds. The "sanctions" adopted against the Russian delegation are certainly not "targeted sanctions" as conceived in the UN system or in the EU system. They look rather like a way to make the (whole) delegation internationally accountable for the violations of international law by the Russian Federation because of the active participation of the Russian Parliamentary organs in the crisis in Ukraine.[45]

While the situation in Ukraine appears as a violation of international law, at the same time the actions of the Committee of Ministers should be clearer. The lack of action of the Committee or maybe a desire to emulate the actions of the EU can be seen as potential triggers to the reaction of PACE.

In the absence of the jurisdiction of a Court to deal with the problems caused by the lack of harmonisation between the sanctions adopted by the Committee of Ministers and the Parliamentary Assembly, the recent call for a 4th Summit

---

[44] PACE Resolution 1370(2004), Contested credentials of the parliamentary delegation of Serbia and Montenegro, 27 April 2004.

[45] It may be questioned if these sanctions are *de facto* targeted.

of Heads of State and Government of the CoE by the Assembly[46] in order to "preserve and further strengthen this unparalleled pan-European project currently threatened by divisions and a weakening of member States' commitment" should be welcomed. In Resolution 2186(2017), PACE noted the "inconsistency in the composition of the two statutory organs, following the illegal annexation of Crimea by the Russian Federation and the Assembly's decision to apply, on these grounds, sanctions vis-à-vis the Russian parliamentary delegation" and underlined that for three consecutive years the Russian Federation has participated in the activities and been represented in the bodies of only one of the two statutory organs of the CoE and described the situation as "counterproductive". Therefore, the Assembly asked for a "harmonisation of the rules governing participation, representation and responsibilities of member States in both statutory organs, while fully respecting the autonomy of these bodies".[47]

---

[46] Resolution 2186(2017), Call for a Council of Europe summit to reaffirm European unity and to defend and promote democratic security in Europe, 11 October 2017. See CANNIZZARO and PALCHETTI, *cit. supra* note 39, p. 384, where the authors underline that, "absent indications to the contrary in the constituent treaty, control over the legality of the acts or conduct of an organ of the international organization may also be exercised, within the limits of their respective competences, by the organs of the international organization". *A fortiori* a summit between the two organs to discuss these issues would be a better option.

[47] See Recommendation 2113(2017), 11 October 2017.

ITALIAN PRACTICE IN THE IMPLEMENTATION OF INTERNATIONAL TARGETED SANCTIONS: ENHANCED PROTECTION OR ADDITIONAL COMPLEXITIES?

ELENA CARPANELLI*

Abstract

The proliferation of UN and EU targeted sanctions and their potential impact on individual rights and private interests require constantly monitoring how Member States implement such restrictive measures within their own domestic legal systems. This article focuses specifically on Italian practice in the implementation of UN and EU-mandated targeted sanctions. In so doing, it first dissects the relevant legal framework currently in place at the domestic level, taking into particular account the main novelties brought about by legislative decree (D. Lgs.) No. 90/2017. It then underscores some critical issues and shortcomings potentially stemming from its practical application. Finally, this article purports to examine the recent institution of a "domestic sanctions regime" and questions whether it might, in practice, end up rising additional grounds of concern, other then those already emerging from the implementation of UN and EU-mandated targeted sanctions, especially in terms of lack of adequate procedural guarantees for alleged human rights violations.

Keywords: UN Security Council; targeted sanctions; domestic implementation; national listing; procedural guarantees.

1. INTRODUCTION

Following the end of the Cold War and the consequent revival of the United Nations (UN) Security Council's powers, there has been a boost in the adoption of measures not involving the use of armed force as per Article 41 of the UN Charter.[1] These measures, mostly amounting to so-called "sanctions",[2] have taken a variety of forms – including arms embargoes, prohibitions on the import and export of goods, travel bans, asset freezes – and served an array of different

---

* Postdoctoral Research Fellow in Public International Law, Centre for Studies in European and International Affairs (CSEIA), University of Parma, Italy.

[1] Charter of the United Nations, 26 June 1945, entered into force 24 October 1945. Before the 1990s, the United Nations Security Council adopted resolutions imposing measures not involving the use of armed force only on two occasions: in the mid 1960s, when it imposed mandatory sanctions against Southern Rhodesia, and in the late 1970s, with the establishment of a mandatory arms embargo against South Africa.

[2] On the common use of this term to indicate multilateral measures imposed by States through international organizations see, *ex multis*, VERDIRAME, *UN and Human Rights: Who Guards the Guardians?*, Cambridge, 2011, p. 300.

purposes, ranging from conflict resolution to non-proliferation of weapons of mass destruction, to counterterrorism and human rights protection.[3] Moreover, this heterogeneous practice has evolved over time: originally structured principally as comprehensive economic and trade sanctions directed against States (such as against Iraq, the former Federal Republic of Yugoslavia and Haiti),[4] similar measures have, in fact, been subsequently crafted mostly as financial restrictions and travel bans targeting specific individuals or entities (either members of governmental structures or, more and more often, private individuals), with the view of preventing unintended harm to the civilian population.[5]

Remarkably, this reliance on sanctions has not occurred only at the universal level. Regional organizations have, in fact, increasingly relied on comprehensive and targeted sanctions also independently from – or to supplement – the adoption of UN Security Council's resolutions.[6] In the European context, for instance, sanctions have been resorted to as a policy tool driving the European Union (EU)'s intervention in preventing conflicts or responding to crisis.[7]

---

[3] For a comprehensive recent study on UN sanctions see, *inter alia*, VAN DEN HERIK (ed.), *Research Handbook on UN Sanctions and International Law*, Cheltenham-Northampton, 2017. On the topic see also PICCHIO FORLATI, *La sanzione nel diritto internazionale*, Padova, 1974.

[4] See, respectively, UN Security Council Resolutions 661 (1990) of 6 August 1990; 713 (1991) of 25 September 1991; and 841 (1993) of 16 June 1993.

[5] At the time of writing (February 2018), there are 14 UN-mandated ongoing sanction regimes, each one administered by a sanctions committee. All individuals and entities subject to sanctions measures imposed by the UN Security Council are inserted in the UN Sanctions List, available at: <https://www.un.org/sc/suborg/en/sanctions/un-sc-consolidated-list#composition list>. The most well known example of a list of individuals and entities subject to restrictive measures imposed by the UN Security Council is the one administered by the so-called "IISL (Da'esh)-Al Qaida Committee", established pursuant to UN Security Council Resolutions 1267 (1999) of 15 October 1999; 1989 (2011) of 17 June 2011; and 2253 (2015) of 17 December 2015.

[6] See, inter alia, GESTRI, "Sanctions Imposed by the European Union: Legal and Institutional Aspects", in RONZITTI (ed.), *Coercive Diplomacy, Sanctions and International Law*, Leiden, Boston, 2016, p. 70 ff.; SOSSAI, "UN Sanctions and Regional Organizations: An Analytical Framework", in VAN DEN HERIK, *cit. supra* note 3, p. 395 ff.

[7] See, e.g., the dedicated webpage of the European Union, available at: <http://ec.europa.eu/dgs/fpi/what-we-do/sanctions_en.htm>. These restrictive measures are grounded on decisions of the Council of the European Union, adopted within the framework of the Common Foreign and Security Policy, and have their legal basis in Art. 215 of the Treaty on the Functioning of the European Union (TFUE). On the issue potentially arising from EU "autonomous" sanctions see, inter alia, ORAKHELASHVILI, "The Impact of Unilateral EU Economic Sanctions on the UN Collective Security Framework: The Case of Iran and Syria", in MAROSSI and BASSET (eds.), *Economic Sanctions Under International Law*, The Hague, 2015, p. 3 ff. To date (February 2018), sanctions established "autonomously" at the EU level include restrictive measures against, for instance, Egypt, Libya, Bosnia-Herzegovina, the Russian Federation, Venezuela and Zimbabwe. Sanctions have been used for the same purposes also in other regional contexts. The African Union and the Economic Community of West African States, for example, have resorted to sanctions as a tool to cope with unconstitutional changes to governments. See, *inter alia*, CHARRON and PORTELA, "The UN, Regional Sanctions and Africa", International Affairs, 2015, p. 1369 ff., p. 1370.

As a consequence of the proliferation of these regimes, States have been called upon to abide by, and implement in their domestic legal systems,[8] an extensive and fragmented web of measures established at the international level. The process of implementation, however, often varies greatly from country to country, and even within the same State, different measures may intuitively be provided for, depending on the "type" of sanctions regime at stake. The implementation of international sanctions at the domestic level is indeed strictly linked to the traditional issue of the relationship between international and municipal law generally, and the incorporation of acts of international organizations in domestic legal systems more specifically.

In the absence of explicit provisions in the UN Charter concerning the implementation of UN Security Council's resolutions, States perform their obligation to respect the underpinning mandatory decisions, under Article 25 of the UN Charter, according to the requirements provided for in their domestic legal orders. Whilst this circumstance would create a divide between monist and dualist systems, entailing different implications based on the character of the norm as self or non-self-executing,[9] State practice has mostly shown a shared "understanding" in retaining UN Security Council resolutions imposing sanctions as triggering domestic legislative action.[10] Yet, a variety of approaches may in any case feature the legislative process intended to give effect domestically to UN-mandated sanctions, ranging from the enactment of "enabling legislation" (with *pro futuro* effects) to the adoption of *ad hoc* measures.[11]

If the sanctions regime is instead implemented through – or originates directly from – regional organizations, specific rules may then apply. Thus, EU regulations implementing UN sanctions are normally directly applicable in Member States and no further legislative action needs being undertaken domestically, unless specific matters fall outside the EU's competence *ratione materiae* or the relevant regulation requires "integrating" action in itself. This usually occurs, for instance, with respect to the determination of "secondary sanctions" (i.e. sanctions provided

---

[8] For a comparative study on the implementation of United Nations sanctions see, in particular, GOWLLAND-DEBBAS (ed.), *National Implementation of United Nations Sanctions. A Comparative Study*, The Hague-Leiden, 2004. On the risks of fragmentation underpinning national implementation of sanctions regimes see also PORTELA, "National Implementation of United Nations Sanctions. Towards Fragmentation", International Journal: Canada's Journal of Global Policy Analysis, 2009-2010, p. 13 ff. On more general issues related to domestic implementation see also, *ex multis*, CARISCH and RICKARD-MARTIN, "Implementation of United Nations Targeted Sanctions", in BIERSTEKER et al. (eds.), *Targeted Sanctions. The Impacts and Effectiveness of United Nations Action*, Cambridge, 2016, p. 150 ff., pp. 161-164.

[9] On the issue see, among many, VISMARA, "Il problema dell'efficacia diretta delle decisioni del Consiglio di Sicurezza", RDI, 2011, p. 1065 ff.

[10] See, *inter alia*, PAVONI, "UN Sanctions in EU and National Law: The Centro-Com Case", ICLQ, 1999, p. 582 ff., p. 584 (who highlights how the difference between monist and dualist systems would nonetheless have an impact on the outcome of judicial proceedings related to the possible conflicts arising out of the interplay among norms adopted at the universal, regional or domestic level).

[11] See, inter alia, CATALDI, "Sull'applicazione delle decisioni del Consiglio di sicurezza nel diritto interno", RDI, 1998, p. 1022 ff.

for in the case of a breach of restrictive measures) that EU Member States are under an obligation to establish.[12] Moreover, States' role does not usually end with the adoption of legislative measures; rather, it includes activities linked to their concrete application and enforcement. By way of example, competent national authorities are generally left to discretionally authorize exemptions provided for at the international level.[13]

Arguably, the way in which sanctions are implemented at the domestic level assumes increasing relevance at a time in which international restrictive measures mostly target individuals or entities and may encroach on individual rights and private interests, as highlighted by the extensive literature in the field.[14] In this context, in fact, the domestic level may even provide a sort of platform for

---

[12] See, for instance, Council Regulation (EC) No. 2580/2001 of 27 December 2001 on specific restrictive measures directed against certain persons and entities with a view to combating terrorism, OJ L 344 of 28 December 2001, Art. 9.

[13] *Ibid.*, Art. 5. But see, e.g., Case C-314/13, *Užsienio reikalų ministerija and Finansinių nusikaltimų tyrimo tarnyba v. Vladimir Peftiev and Others*, 12 June 2014 (*Peftiev* case), where the EU Court of Justice found that domestic authorities' discretion is not unlimited and should comply, *inter alia*, with the provisions of the EU Charter of Fundamental Rights.

[14] See, among many, CAMERON, "UN Targeted Sanctions, Legal Safeguards, and the European Convention on Human Rights", Nordic Journal of International Law, 2003, p. 159 ff.; ARCARI, "Sviluppi in tema di diritti di individui iscritti nelle liste dei Comitati delle sanzioni del Consiglio di sicurezza", RDI, 2007, p. 657 ff.; GESTRI, "Legal Remedies against Security Council Targeted Sanctions: *De Lege Lata* and *De Lege Ferenda* Options for Enhancing the Protection of the Individual", IYIL, 2007, p. 25 ff.; COUZIGOU, "La lutte du Conseil de Sécurité contre le terrorisme international et les droits de l'homme", RGDIP, 2008, p. 49 ff.; ECKES, *EU Counter-Terrorism Policies and Fundamental Rights: The Case of Individual Sanctions*, Oxford, 2009; MICHAELSEN, "Kadi and Al Barakaat v. Council of the European Union and Commission of the European Communities: The Incompatibility of the United Nations Security Council's 1267 Sanctions Regime with European Due Process Guarantees", Melbourne Journal of International Law, 2009, p. 329 ff.; WEEMA, "Kadi v. Council, Putting the United Nations in its Place", Tulane Journal of International and Comparative Law, 2009, p. 571 ff.; BAEHR-JONES, "Mission Possible: How Intelligence Evidence Rules Can Save UN Terrorist Sanctions", Harvard National Security Journal, 2011, p. 447 ff.; PANTALEO, "La protection des droits fondamentaux de la défense dans l'application des mesures ciblées. L'apport des juridictions à la gouvernance des problèmes sécuritaires", in ARCARI and BALMOND (eds.), *Global Governance and the Challenges to Collective Security*, Napoli, 2012, p. 149 ff.; FORWOOD, "Closed Evidence in Restrictive Measures Cases: A Comparative Perspective", in BRADLEY et al. (eds.), *Of Courts and Constitutions. Liber Amicorum in Honour of Nial Fennelly*, Oxford, Portland, 2014, p. 87 ff.; GENSER and BARTH, "Targeted Sanctions and Due Process of Law", in GENSER and STAGNO UGARTE (eds.), *The United Nations Security Council in the Age of Human Rights*, Cambridge, 2014, p. 195 ff.; HOLLENBERG, "The Security Council's 1267/1999 Targeted Sanctions Regime and the Use of Confidential Information: A Proposal for Decentralization of Review", Leiden JIL, 2015, p. 49 ff.; GARVEY, "Targeted Sanctions: Resolving the International Due Process Dilemma", Texas International Law Journal, 2016, p. 551 ff.; HOVELL, *The Power of Process. The Value of Due Process in Security Council Sanctions Decision-Making*, Oxford, 2016; LUGATO, *Sanctions and Individual Rights*, in RONZITTI (ed.), *cit. supra* note 6, p. 171 ff.; POST, "Security Council Sanctions and Fair Process", in VAN DEN HERIK (ed.), *cit. supra* note 3, p. 213 ff.

"remedial" actions vis-à-vis violations potentially stemming from international acts.[15]

Against this background, this contribution intends to focus specifically on Italian practice in the field of the implementation of international targeted sanctions. Whilst, in fact, this subject matter has already attracted much doctrinal attention,[16] recent normative developments impose to rethink once again about old and new problems in its application. To this end, the present contribution will analyse the relevant legal framework related to the implementation of international targeted sanctions in Italy (Section 2), especially in light of the main novelties introduced by *decreto legislativo* (legislative decree, or D. Lgs.) No. 90/2017 (Section 3), and will then focus on some of the most critical issues of application stemming from the normative picture currently in place (Sections 4 and 5). Some concluding remarks will follow (Section 6).

2. THE IMPLEMENTATION OF TARGETED SANCTIONS IN ITALY PRIOR TO THE ADOPTION OF LEGISLATIVE DECREE NO. 90/2017

From a theoretical standpoint, the issue of the implementation of international sanctions in Italy has not been treated differently than in any other country, inevitably revolving around the broader topic of the domestic implementation of acts of the organs of an international organization. Along this line, one of the most debated aspects has indeed concerned whether the law implementing the UN Charter could represent a sufficient ground for the automatic implementation within the Italian legal system of subsequent compelling acts issued by its organs (i.e., Security Council's mandatory decisions), thus relegating domestic authorities' intervention to cases where more legal clarity or specific integrations

---

[15] See, inter alia, CIAMPI, "Individual Remedies against Security Council Targeted Sanctions", IYIL, 2007, p. 55 ff.

[16] On the institutional and legal aspects of the implementation in Italy of targeted sanctions see, *inter alia*, CIAMPI, *Sanzioni del Consiglio di sicurezza e diritti umani*, Milano, 2007, pp. 439-451; DELLA MORTE, "L'application en Italie des sanctions ciblées du Conseil de Sécurité – Aspects institutionnels et problems juridictionelles", in RIDEAU et al. (eds.), *Sanctions ciblées et protections juridictionnelles des droits fondamentaux dans l'Union européenne. Equilibres et déséquilibres de la balance*, Bruxelles, 2010, p. 319 ff.; DI STASIO, *La lotta multilivello al terrorismo internazionale. Garanzia di sicurezza versus tutela dei diritti fondamentali*, Milano, 2010, pp. 596-602; SALERNO, "Il rispetto delle garanzie processuali nell'attuazione delle misure del Consiglio di sicurezza contro il terrorismo internazionale", in SALERNO (ed.), *Sanzioni 'individuali' del Consiglio di Sicurezza e garanzie processuali fondamentali*, Padova, 2010, p. 161 ff.; SACERDOTI and ACCONCI, "The Security Council's Assets Freeze against Gaddafi's Libya and and its Implementation in Italy", IYIL, 2011, p. 61 ff.; GUARINO JR., "Il quadro legislativo italiano e la lotta al terrorismo", in CADIN et al. (eds.), *Contrasto multilivello al terrorismo internazionale e rispetto dei diritti umani*, Torino, 2012, p. 119 ff. This contribution does not take into account the implementation of other sanctions, such as arms embargoes. On the topic see, however, MANCINI, "Sull'attuazione delle decisioni del Consiglio di Sicurezza nell'ordinamento italiano", RDI, 2000, p. 1027 ff.

are needed.[17] This doctrinal debate has, however, been somehow superseded by practice: UN Security Council resolutions, including those imposing sanctions, have been generally made effective in Italy through *ad hoc* measures pursuant to a mechanism comparable to the ordinary legislative procedure followed in the implementation of non-self-executing treaties;[18] this independently from their self or non-self-executing character.[19] Peculiar mechanisms involving some form of automatic application are instead in place only with respect to UN-mandated sanctions relating to arms embargoes – which are made directly applicable into the Italian legal system by Law No. 185/1990[20] – and with reference to specific domestic measures implementing international sanctions imposing embargoes towards foreign States, for which D. Lgs. No. 107/1995[21] provides the immediate termination or suspension of effects as soon as the international measure is revoked or suspended.

The fact that, nowadays, UN-mandated sanctions are mostly implemented at the EU level and, therefore, through regulations that are directly applicable in Italy, would, however, seemingly deprive, at least *prima facie*, the above-mentioned practice of any relevance. Yet, the growing role of the "EU layer" has not translated into a full disengagement of domestic authorities. As previously mentioned, in fact, domestic provisions, although playing a residual function, may still be needed in order to regulate matters that fall outside the scope of application of EU law. Moreover, national authorities may intervene with respect to UN measures that, even if already adopted at the universal level, have not been implemented yet at the EU level or that the EU has not implemented in full (and for which, theoretically, the Member State could be found in breach of its international obligation to abide by UN Security Council decisions). Finally, as also stated earlier, even when EU legislation is in place (either implementing UN-mandated sanctions or establishing autonomous restrictive measures), Member States may still be called upon to enact additional normative acts with an integrative function.[22]

---

[17] For an overview of this debate see, *inter alia*, CANNONE, *Trattato internazionale (Adattamento al)*, in *Enciclopedia del diritto, Annali*, Vol. 5, Milano, 2012, p. 1321 ff., p. 1332. On the topic see also again VISMARA, *cit. supra* note 9, where the main doctrinal arguments are extensively analysed.

[18] See, for an early example, *decreto legge* (decree law, or DL) No. 1007 of 3 October 1968, converted into Law No. 1188 of 19 November 1968, by which Italy implemented domestically UN Security Council Resolution 253 (1968) of 29 May 1968 imposing sanctions on Southern Rhodesia.

[19] See CIAMPI, *cit. supra* note 16, p. 439.

[20] Law No. 185 of 9 July 1990, as amended by D. Lgs. No. 105 of 22 June 2012. This Law prohibits the supply of arms to countries upon which a UN mandatory embargo is imposed.

[21] DL No. 107 of 7 April 1995, converted into Law No. 222 of 7 June 1995. For an analysis of the mechanism established by this legislative measure see, in particular, MANCINI, *cit. supra* note 16, pp. 1039-1045 and PIRRONE, "L'attuazione delle decisioni del Consiglio di sicurezza tra ordinamento nazionale e ordinamento comunitario", in *Studi di diritto internazionale in onore di Gaetano Arangio-Ruiz*, Vol. I, Napoli, 2004, p. 563 ff., pp. 574-575.

[22] For instance, in the aftermath of the adoption of EU legislation implementing UN Security Council Resolution 1333 (2000) of 19 December 2000, providing for sanctions against the

As far as targeted sanctions are concerned, Italian authorities have met most of these exigencies mainly through the adoption of D. Lgs. No. 109/2007 on "Measures to prevent, combat, and counter the financing of terrorism and the activities of countries which threaten international peace and security".[23] By means of this legislative decree, Italy has indeed adopted for the first time an organic and articulated regime for the implementation of most UN and EU targeted sanctions, thus replacing the fragmented and urgency-driven legislation that had characterized its previous action.[24] The decree has provided measures for implementing at the national level the freezing of funds and economic resources with the scope of countering terrorism or the activities of those States threatening international peace and security, in compliance with UN resolutions and EU decisions.[25] Comprehensive sanctions against foreign States – including arms embargoes – have instead been expressly excluded from the scope of application of the said instrument from the outset.[26]

By means of D. Lgs. No. 109/2007, the Financial Security Committee (hereinafter also Committee) has been placed at the core of the system of implementation of international sanctions.[27] The Committee – presided over by

---

Taliban, the Italian government issued DL No. 353 of 28 September 2001, later converted into Law No. 415 of 27 November 2001, which established sanctions for infringements of restrictive measures imposed by the relevant regulation (Council Regulation (EC) No. 467/2001 of 6 March 2001 prohibiting the export of certain goods and services to Afghanistan, strengthening the flight ban and extending the freeze of funds and other financial resources in respect of the Taliban of Afghanistan, and repealing Regulation (EC) No. 337/2000 of 14 February 2000, OJ L 67 of March 2001, pp. 1-23). In particular, the DL provided for the nullity of acts undertaken in breach of restrictive measures and for administrative fines. Neither the EU regulation nor the domestic law are still in force. On the topic see, *inter alia*, LANG, *Le Risoluzioni del Consiglio di sicurezza delle Nazioni Unite e l'Unione europea*, Milano, 2002, p. 118 ff.

[23] D. Lgs. No. 109 of 22 June 2007, entered into force on 10 August 2007. The D. Lgs. implements Directive 2005/60/EC of the European Parliament and the Council of 26 October 2005 on the prevention of the use of the financial system for the purpose of money laundering and terrorist financing, OJ L 309, 25 November 2005, pp. 15-36. The implementation of this Directive in the Italian system has occurred, however, also through D. Lgs. No. 231 of 21 November 2007, which details, *inter alia*, the obligations of financial operators to tackle money laundering and the financing of terrorism. D. Lgs. No. 109/2007 has been integrated and amended by means of subsequent legislative measures. See, e.g., D. Lgs. No. 54 of 11 May 2009, which expanded the scope of application of the decree to include also the implementation of freezing measures on funds or economic resources managed through a third party. See also D. Lgs. No. 141 of 13 August 2010 and D. Lgs. No. 169 of 19 September 2012.

[24] On the emergency approach of early domestic efforts in the implementation of UN targeted sanctions against suspected terrorists see again, *inter alia*, DELLA MORTE, *cit. supra* note 16, pp. 324-325. See also INGRAVALLO, "L'attuazione in Italia delle 'liste' antiterrorismo e la loro rilevanza nel processo penale", DUDI, 2008, p. 561 ff., p. 566.

[25] D. Lgs. No. 109/2007, Art. 2.

[26] *Ibid.*

[27] The Financial Security Committee had already been provisionally established by DL No. 369 of 12 October 2001, converted into Law No. 431 of 14 December 2001. This decree law, however, did not expressly entrusted the Committee with the authority to propose the designation of individuals to international authorities. Before the adoption of D. Lgs. No. 109/2007, this lacuna was, however, filled in by means of an internal regulation issued by the *Ministero dell'economia e delle finanze*, titled: Disposizioni in materia di formazione del-

the Director General of the Treasury – has indeed been upheld as the Italian authority in charge of the implementation of freezing measures established by UN or EU acts, as such competent, *inter alia*, for: proposing the enactment by the *Ministero dell'economia e delle finanze* (Ministry of Economy and Finances) of decrees implementing UN-mandated freezing measures, pending the adoption of implementing measures at the EU level;[28] collecting and transmitting pertinent information, including to other authorities entrusted with the practical enforcement of the measures; proposing to international bodies the designation or the cancellation of individuals or entities from the lists; reviewing requests of exemptions (to be, however, eventually approved by decree from the *Ministero dell'economia e delle finanze*).[29]

In accordance with the possibility of an intervention of Italian authorities pending the adoption of EU implementing legislation, D. Lgs. No. 109/2007 has moreover envisaged two different moments in which freezing measures could become effective: either the day of entry into force of the relevant EU legislation or the day after the publication in the Italian Official Journal of the national decree implementing the sanctioning measure.[30] Remarkably, whilst this double-track path could raise, at least *in abstracto*, potential issues in case of different standards of protection of individual rights[31] or, more generally, of inconsistencies between acts that alternate rapidly (for instance, when the subsequent EU legislation "supplements" UN-mandated sanctions), national authorities have, in practice, been reluctant to intervene autonomously pending the adoption of implementing EU legislation.

According to the procedure established by D. Lgs. No. 109/2007 the *Guardia di Finanza* (financial police) has been entrusted with the authority of enforcing the freezing measures,[32] while the *Agenzia del demanio* (the Italian institution in charge of public property) has been provided with the task of guarding and administratively controlling frozen funds or other economic resources[33]

---

le liste di soggetti da sottoporre alle misure di congelamento disposte dall'Unione europea per contrastare il terrorismo e il rilascio di autorizzazioni in deroga ai vincoli di congelamento, 14 February 2001, available at: <http://www.dt.mef.gov.it/export/sites/sitodt/modules/documenti_it/prevenzione_reati_finanziari/normativa/Regolamento-interno.pdf>. See, in particular, Art. 2(3). Moreover, Law No. 431/2001 only referred to the implementation of restrictive measures aimed at countering the financing of international terrorism (thus with the exclusion of restrictive measures against activities of States threatening international peace and security).

[28] D. Lgs. No. 109/2007, Art. 4.
[29] *Ibid.*, Art. 3.
[30] *Ibid.*, Art. 5(6).
[31] See again SALERNO, *cit. supra* note 16, p. 173.
[32] D. Lgs. No. 109/2007, Art. 11.
[33] Notably, with respect to some specific UN-mandated targeted sanctioning regimes, no assets or financial resources belonging to individual or entities enlisted have been frozen in Italy until recently: see, e.g., Annex to the note verbale dated 16 December 2016 from the Permanent Mission of Italy to the United Nations addressed to the Chair of the Committee established pursuant to Resolution 2127 (2013) concerning the Central African Republic, UN Doc. S/AC.O55/2016/3 (2016), and Annex to the note verbale dated 22 December 2016

until revocation, unless the same assets have also been subjected to seizure or confiscation measures adopted in the context of criminal or administrative proceedings. In the latter case, in fact, the above-mentioned tasks would rest with the authority ordering the seizure or confiscation.[34]

Furthermore, the recalled legislative measure has also provided for "secondary sanctions" by envisaging the voidness of acts put in place regardless of the restrictive measures,[35] as well as administrative fines in case of infringement of the same.[36] In this respect, the Italian legislator has therefore shown its proclivity in favour of the establishment of civil and administrative sanctions, rather than criminal penalties, thus avoiding *ex ante* any potential risk of incompatibility with the principles of legal certainty and *nulla poena sine lege certa*, which has been complained of with respect to the national implementation of certain sanctions regimes in other countries.[37]

One of the most important novelties introduced by the adoption of D. Lgs. No. 109/2007 has been, however, the provision of an ad hoc complaint procedure. Article 14, in fact, entrusted the *Tribunale amministrativo regionale (TAR) del Lazio* with the authority for receiving complaints related to the measures adopted on the ground of the said decree. Notably, this provision also set specific rules for when the decision of the case brought to the attention of the *TAR* would depend on the access to documents covered by investigative or State secrecy. In this case, the *TAR* could indeed suspend proceedings for up to two years. However, if and when the deadline expired with no progress in terms of disclosure, the *TAR* could fix a date by which the Committee should provide alternative documents to support the adoption of the challenged measure; otherwise, the *TAR* should decide on the basis of available documents.

Importantly, the legislative architecture provided for in D. Lgs. No. 109/2007 has been subsequently integrated by means of the decree of the *Ministero dell'economia e delle finanze* No. 203/2010, establishing specific rules on the functioning of the Financial Security Committee and on the restrictions of access to documents in its possession.[38] This decree has, *inter alia*, expressly prevented access to any documents, generated or detained by the Financial Security Committee, and relating to national security or defence, or to the correctness of

---

from the Permanent Mission of Italy to the United Nations addressed to the Chairs of the Committee established pursuant to Resolution 2206 (2015) concerning South Sudan, UN Doc. S/AC.57/2016/2 (2016). With respect to the implementation of Resolution 1373 (2001), see instead the report prepared by Italy and transmitted to the UN Counter-Terrorism Committee in 2004, UN Doc. S/2004/253 (2004). Subsequent reports are not public.

[34] D. Lgs. No. 109/2007, Art. 12. On this specific aspect see, *inter alia, Corte di Cassazione (Sez. I penale), Criminal proceedings against S. and A.G.,* 4 December 2008, No. 3718.

[35] D. Lgs. No. 109/2007, Art. 5(3).

[36] *Ibid.,* Art. 13.

[37] See, e.g., the facts at stake in Case C-72/15, *PJSC Rosneft Oil Company v. Her Majesty's Treasury and Others*, 28 March 2017, paras. 168-170 (*Rosneft* case), where the EU Court of Justice (Grand Chamber) eventually found that the vagueness of EU legislation does not impede Member States to provide for criminal penalties in case of infringement.

[38] Adopted on 20 October 2010.

international relations, which: summarize the work undertaken in the context of the Committee; contain exchanges of information among the authorities represented in the Committee or among the Committee and international bodies; consist of acts, studies, analysis, proposals and reports related to the Italian position and involvement with respect to the process of removal or designation of targeted individuals or entities, with the sole exception of that part of motivation of the final decision which is in the public domain; or which relate to the strategies for countering the financing of international terrorism or ongoing investigations.[39] In this respect, the *Ministero dell'economia e delle finanze* has thus made use of its authority pursuant to Article 24(2) of Law No. 241 of 7 August 1990 (as amended in 2005) to indicate documents covered by official secrecy. Additionally, the decree also upholds the so-called "originator control principle", by stating that, if a document in possession of the Committee concerns a foreign State or an international organization, the access to the same is dependent on the fact that the State or the international organization has provided its consent.[40]

Two elements deserve attention in this respect. First, the recalled provisions can significantly affect the complaint procedure provided for in Article 14 of D. Lgs. No. 109/2007. Indeed, the broad reach of official secrecy with respect to the Committee's documents makes it extremely likely that, in practice, proceedings brought against freezing measures could be suspended.[41] Second, doubts may arise with respect to the compatibility with Italy's obligations under international human rights law of the denial of access to documents grounded solely on the fact that the same are coming from other States or international organizations. Human rights monitoring bodies have, in fact, progressively inferred from the right to freedom of opinion and expression, which is upheld in international human rights instruments, a right of access to State-held information.[42] Whilst this right is not absolute, permissible restrictions – in accordance with the general structure of limitation clauses – are subjected to the condition to be established by law, in the interest of a legitimate aim envisaged in the relevant instruments, and be necessary in a democratic society. Against this background, it seems that the "origin" of the document, if not accompanied by other relevant elements,[43] may

---

[39] *Decreto ministeriale* (D.M.) No. 203/2010, Art. 14.

[40] *Ibid.*

[41] Notably, from an internal perspective, doubts have also been raised as to the compatibility, in practice, of these provisions with Art. 39(11) of Italian Law No. 124/2007 of 3 August 2007, pursuant to which State secrecy cannot cover information and documents related to terrorism. See, *inter alia*, INGRAVALLO, *cit. supra* note 24, p. 576.

[42] See, *inter alia*, MCDONAGH, "The Right to Information in International Human Rights Law", Human Rights Law Review, 2013, p. 25 ff.; O'FLAHERTY, "Freedom of Expression: Article 19 of the International Covenant on Civil and Political Rights and the Human Rights Committee's General Comment No. 34", Human Rights Law Review, 2012, p. 627 ff.; ZAYAS and AUREA, "Freedom of Opinion and Freedom of Expression: Some Reflections on General Comment No. 34 of the UN Human Rights Committee", NYLR, 2012, p. 425 ff.

[43] The list of legitimate aims for restrictions to the freedom of information contained in the main human rights instruments generally include (with some differences depending on the specific treaty at hand), *inter alia*, national security, public safety, the protection of health and morals, the protection of the rights and reputation of others.

hardly justify a restriction to the aforementioned right. Notably, this conclusion seems to have been recently upheld by the UN Special Rapporteur on the Promotion and Protection of the Right of Freedom of Opinion and Expression, who has stated that a lack of disclosure of information in possession of an international organization merely grounded on its "provenance" from Member States could not be considered a permissible restriction in light of current international human rights law.[44]

3. THE MAIN NOVELTIES INTRODUCED BY LEGISLATIVE DECREE NO. 90/2017

D. Lgs. No. 109/2007 has been profoundly amended by means of the recent adoption of D. Lgs. No. 90/2017, transposing EU Directive 2015/849[45] into the Italian legal system.[46]

First of all, by means of the aforesaid amendment, the scope of application of D. Lgs. No. 109/2007 has been extended to include also the implementation of measures aimed at countering the financing of programmes of proliferation of weapons of mass destruction.[47] From this point of view, the recent legislative action represents therefore a further step in the direction of setting an increasingly organic discipline for the implementation of UN and EU sanctions at the national level.

Additional amendments have aimed at clarifying key concepts, such as that of "economic resources", whose definition has been modified in order to include goods ("*beni*") and also resources only partially owned by the targeted persons or entities.[48] Moreover, the composition of the Financial Security Committee has also been partly modified, compared to its original structure, to also include among its members representatives of the custom agency and the *Ministero dello sviluppo economico* (Ministry of Economic Development).[49] On top of that, the amended

---

[44] UN Doc. A/72/350 (2017), para. 21.

[45] Directive (EU) 2015/849 of the European Parliament and of the Council of 20 May 2015 on the prevention of the use of the financial system for the purpose of money laundering or terrorist financing, amending Regulation (EU) No. 648/2012 of the European Parliament and of the Council repealing Directive 2005/60/EC of the European Parliament and the Council and Commission Directive 2006/70/EC, OJ L 141 of 5 June 2015, pp. 73-117.

[46] Adopted on 25 May 2017, entered into force 4 July 2017. See, in particular, Art. 6.

[47] See, in particular, Arts. 1 and 2 of D. Lgs. No. 109/2007, as amended by D. Lgs. No. 90/2017.

[48] *Ibid.*, Art. 1.

[49] Pursuant to Art. 3(3), as originally conceived, the Committee's members were appointed with a decree of the Minister of Economy and Finances, on the basis of designations made by the Minister of the Interior, the Minister of Justice, the Minister of Foreign Affairs, the Governor of the Bank of Italy, the Italy's Stock Exchange Commission and the supervisory authority for the insurance sector. The Committee also included representatives from the Ministry of Economy and Finances, the financial police (*Guardia di Finanza*), the *anti-mafia* investigation directorate, police forces (*Carabinieri*), and the national *anti-mafia* and anti-terrorism department. Moreover, when executing tasks relating to the management of frozen funds, the Committee was integrated by a representative of the *Agenzia del Demanio*.

decree provides that the President of the Committee may invite representatives of other entities or institutions to participate in the Committee's meetings, including representatives of the security and information services and, where necessary, members of professionals orders or private trade associations.[50]

As a matter of further novelty, D. Lgs. No. 90/2017 has introduced a time limit of six months, after which – unless it is expressly provided otherwise – the decree of the *Ministero dell'economia e delle finanze* implementing the freezing measures should expire.[51] However, the decree can be renewed for the same length of time and, in any case, automatically loses its effects once EU implementing legislation is published in the Official Journal of the EU.[52] Notably, by means of these provisions, the Italian legislator seemingly intervened to minimize the above-mentioned risk of incongruences that could potentially stem from the intersection and rapid alternation of implementing measures at different normative levels. Moreover, the provision of a precise time limit seems to be intended to counter the indeterminate duration of restrictive measures. Yet, the mechanism of renewal and the UN-mandate behind targeted sanctions arguably deprive the said time limit of any concrete relevance in this respect.

D. Lgs. No. 90/2017 has also enriched D. Lgs. No. 109/2007 with some brand-new provisions. Article 4-*bis*, for instance, provides that, pending the adoption of designating measures mandated by the UN Security Council, the Italian Ministry of Economy and Finances, on a proposal from the Financial Security Committee, may establish by decree, for a period of six months – renewable until the situation demands so –, freezing measures on funds or economic resources detained by individuals, groups or entities who committed or attempted to commit one or more acts for the purpose of terrorism (as defined by Italian criminal law), or meant to financing programmes of proliferation of mass destruction, or threatening international peace and security. Freezing measures may also be implemented at the request of another State, on the basis of the call to international cooperation in countering international terrorism upheld in UN Security Council Resolution 1373 (2001).[53] Remarkably, pursuant to the provision at stake, the decree envisaging national designation measures would produce effects from the moment of its adoption. This is, however, apparently in stark contrast with what is stated in the amended Article 5 of D. Lgs. No. 109/2007, according to which decrees ex Article 4-*bis* would start producing effects from the day after their publication in the *Gazzetta Ufficiale* (the Italian Official Journal). Worryingly, this incongruence may end up, in practice, adding further complexities to a scenario already made extremely intricate by the interplay of three different normative levels.

According to the last amendment occurred in 2017, the Committee is now composed of fifteen members, including one representative from the Ministry of Economic Development and one from the customs agency (see amended Arts. 3(2) and (3)).

  [50] See Art. 3(5) of D. Lgs. No. 109/2007, as amended by D. Lgs. No. 90/2017.

  [51] *Ibid.*, Art. 4(1).

  [52] *Ibid.*, Art. 4(2).

  [53] UN Security Council Resolution 1373 (2001) of 28 September 2001, paras. 1(c) and 3(c).

Articles from 4-*ter* to 4-*septies* mostly vest, instead, of "primary rank" provisions already envisaged in the above-recalled decree of the *Ministero dell'economia e delle finanze* No. 203/2010. Articles 4-*ter* and 4-*quarter* provide for the proactive participation of the Financial Security Committee in the designation of individuals or entities to be targeted by restrictive measures. According to the said provisions, the Committee can, in fact, propose to international bodies, through the *Ministero degli affari esteri* (Ministry of Foreign Affairs), the designation of individuals or entities and, to this end, take into account: the existence of elements suggesting their active participation in, or support to, terrorist activities; the pending proceedings or other judicial measures adopted against the to-be-designated person; the reasonable unlikeliness of mistakes concerning the identity of the person; the existence of parental or other relationships with individuals already on the lists; the adoption against the individual or entity of other restrictive measures established at the UN or EU level with the scope of countering the financing of terrorism or the activities of States that threaten international peace and security; any other relevant information in its possession. The Committee must take into account the same elements even when proposing the designation of individual or entities in the national list provided for in Article 4-*bis*. Article 4-*quater* further specifies the informative tasks of the police and the information that should be included in the proposal of designation.

Pursuant to Article 4-*sexies*, instead, the Committee, when suggesting the removal of individuals from the lists either to international bodies (through the *Ministero degli affari esteri*) or to the *Ministero dell'economia e delle finanze* (with respect to "autonomous" domestic sanctions), could take in due regard any acquittal decision issued in the context of criminal proceedings or any other element from which the involvement of the targeted individual in terrorist activities, in the financing of programmes of proliferation of weapons of mass destruction, or in activities threatening international peace and security, could be excluded.

In this respect, two elements are noteworthy. First, the continuous references to the (lack of) participation of individuals or entities in terrorist activities in the recalled provisions may, at least prima facie, lead to question over whether the Committee's involvement in the process of designation would also apply to situations in which targeted sanctions are provided for with respect to acts meant to finance programmes of proliferation of weapons of mass destruction. However, the "advisory" and "non-exhaustive" character of the indications contained in the said provisions eventually deprive this circumstance – most likely, a reflection of the origins and of the area of primary application of the norms at stake – of any legal relevance.

Second, it is evident from the above that the proposals of listing are mostly untied from the conviction or acquittal of the person in the context of criminal proceedings, and even from the very opening of a criminal investigation. Such circumstances are indeed only listed among the elements that the Committee could take into account when formulating a request of designation or removal. Yet, the possibility of imposing restrictive measures regardless of the existence of a conviction or criminal charges in the context of criminal proceedings is something that the Italian legal system has acknowledged and regulated for a long time with respect to organized crime. More worryingly, instead, it does not seem that the recalled provisions will provide much help in overcoming the issue linked to the lack of clear criteria on the ground of which restrictive measures of potentially indefinite duration are established. The listed elements, in fact, only provide some clarification as far as the proposals of designation or cancellation are concerned, but do not add anything with respect to the criteria on the basis of which the decision itself is undertaken. Whilst this is partly due to the fact that the decision is imposed from the outside, it nonetheless also applies to the newly introduced national mechanism of designation, in respect of which, as previously noted, Article 4-*bis* leaves broad discretion in determining which conduct may drive the listing or delisting decision (the only precise element being the implicit reference to Article 270-*sexies* of the Italian Criminal Code).

Notably, however, this seems to clash with the overall trend towards setting a mechanism more inclined to ensure the protection of the targeted individuals' rights. Most likely as a result of the developments which have occurred at the international level – where since 2006, the UN Security Council has engaged in the adoption of a series of measures meant to ensure fairer and clearer procedures of listing and delisting[54] – in fact, D.M. No. 203/2010 first and, most recently, D. Lgs. No. 90/2017, have introduced a periodic check of the lists and of the restrictive measures in place,[55] and a notification procedure meant to inform targeted individuals or entities of their insertion on, or removal from, the lists.[56] With respect to this last point, in particular, Article 4-*quinquies* establishes that the Committee should inform, through the financial police and according to the Italian rules on service of process, the targeted individual or entity of their designation, as well as of: the reasons motivating the decision, insofar as they are publicly available; the content of the restrictive measure and the applicable sanctions in case of breach of the related obligations; the procedure in place and the international and national authorities competent for receiving

---

[54] The main reference, in this respect, is the institution of the Focal point for delisting, established by means of UN Security Council Resolution 1730 (2006) of 19 December 2006, and of the Office of the Ombudsperson, established by UN Security Council Resolution 1904 (2009) of 17 December 2009. Arguably, these developments can be explained also as a result of the recognition, in the context of international judicial proceedings, that the system, as originally framed, did impinge on the fundamental rights of the targeted individuals. See, *inter alia*, EU Court of Justice, Joined Cases C-584/10 P, C-593/10 P and C-595/10 P, *European Commission and Others v. Yassin Abdullah Kadi*, Judgment of 18 July 2013; and Joined Cases C-402/05 P and C-415/05 P, *Yassin Abdullah Kadi and Al Barakaat International Foundation v. Council of the European Union and Commission of the European Communities*, Judgment of 3 September 2008. See also European Court of Human Rights, *Nada v. Switzerland*, Application No. 10593/08, Grand Chamber, Judgment of 12 September 2010 (*Nada* case).

[55] D.M. No. 203/2010, Art. 9. See also Art. 4-*quinquies* (4) of D. Lgs. No. 109/2007, as amended by D. Lgs. No. 90/2017.

[56] D.M. No. 203/2010, Art. 8. See also Arts. 4-*quinquies* and 4-*sexies*(5) of D. Lgs. No. 109/2007, as amended by D. Lgs. No. 90/2017.

a request of removal from the list or of authorization of exemptions, or before which presenting a complaint against the restrictive measures. In the same way, the person is notified of their removal from the list by the Committee through the financial police and according to the pertinent provisions on the service of process.

Article 4-*septies* further upholds the Committee's authority in authorizing exemptions from freezing measures. No indication whatsoever – apart from a generic reference to the compliance with international norms and procedures – is, however, provided for with respect to the substantive criteria based on which der-ogations should be authorized. Full discretion is also accorded to the Committee with respect to the operative mechanism for the authorization procedure.

Finally, D. Lgs. No. 90/2017 has introduced two other main elements of nov-elty with respect to the pre-existent legal framework. First of all, the Italian legis-lator has increased the maximum amount of administrative fines provided for in case of infringement of the restrictive measures[57] and even envisaged a specific procedure – implying the online publication of the sanctioning decree – in case of grave violations.[58] Second, the amended Article 14 of D. Lgs. No. 109/2007 – while confirming the mechanism of suspension of proceedings in case of claim of investigative or State secrecy – provides for the exclusive competence of the *Tribunale di Roma* with respect to the adjudication of complaints arising out of the sanctioning decrees adopted pursuant to the legislation at stake. Strikingly, the modified provision refers specifically to "sanctioning decrees", thus raising the question whether the complaint procedure envisaged therein also applies to other measures enforced according to D. Lgs. No. 109/2007, but not established by decree.[59] Such doubts are further strengthened by the illustrative report related to the scheme of D. Lgs. No. 90/2017.[60] According to it, in fact, the transfer of competence from the *TAR del Lazio* to the *Tribunale di Roma* was motivated by the need to adapt the normative framework to the most recent case law, which has upheld the competence of the ordinary judge with respect to administrative *pecuniary* sanctions.[61] Thus, it seems to emerge from the said illustrative docu-ment that the complaint procedure provided for in the amended Article 14 would only apply with respect to claims related to the application of "secondary sanc-tions", thus de facto excluding complaints arising out of the implementation of "primary sanctions".

---

[57] Art. 13 of D. Lgs. No. 109/2007, as amended by D. Lgs. No. 90/2017.

[58] *Ibid.*, Art. 13-*bis*. Moreover, by means of Arts. 13-*ter* and 13-*quater*, the Italian legislator has furthermore established the criteria and the procedure to be followed in establishing the amount of the sanction and in implementing it.

[59] The original text of Art. 14 used the generic word "*provvedimenti*" (i.e., measures).

[60] Available at: <http://documenti.camera.it/apps/nuovosito/attigoverno/Schedalavori/getTesto.ashx?file=0389_F001.pdf&leg=XVII>.

[61] *Ibid.*, p. 23.

4. ISSUES ARISING FROM THE APPLICATION OF SANCTIONS: WHAT DOMESTIC PROCEDURAL GUARANTEES FOR TARGETED INDIVIDUALS?

Against the normative framework just retraced, several potentially critical issues related to the domestic implementation of targeted sanctions stand out, some of which are linked to the procedural guarantees offered to those targeted by the restrictive measures.

As anticipated, the latest legislative amendments have ruled out from the scope of D. Lgs. No. 109/2007 any reference to an *ad hoc* judicial procedure before the *TAR del Lazio* by which targeted individuals or entities may contest freezing measures enforced against them. The Italian legislator has thus deprived the current legal discipline related to the implementation of international targeted sanctions at the national level of one of the most important novelties introduced by D. Lgs. No. 109/2007. This amendment is probably the result of a misreading of the pre-existing provision (arguably, by wrongly interpreting it as applying only to court cases related to secondary sanctions); however, whilst being highly questionable as such, it should not jeopardize the concrete possibility for targeted individuals to contest restrictive measures adopted against them before the *TAR del Lazio*. As it has been noted, in fact, D. Lgs. No. 109/2007 merely vested of legal certainty a solution that had already been upheld in practice.[62] It is thus likely that the competence of the *TAR* will continue being upheld by means of judicial practice. That notwithstanding, it is to be hoped that, in view of ensuring legal certainty and avoiding issues in application, Article 14 of D. Lgs. No. 109/2007 will soon be amended once again. Indeed, the current wording of the aforesaid provision could hypothetically also lead to a situation in which restrictive measures established by a decree of the *Ministero dell'economia e delle finanze*, pending EU implementing legislation, could be considered as falling within the scope of application of Article 14 and thus contested before the *Tribunale di Roma*, while identical measures stemming from implementing EU legislation would not (due to the lack of any "sanctioning decree").

The confusion deriving from the new text of Article 14 inevitably also involves the application of the suspension rule in case of secrecy claims. One could question, indeed, whether such a rule would stop applying to proceeding in which targeted sanctions are contested and could instead only be employed in "secondary sanctions" litigation. But even leaving this aspect aside, the way in which this rule has been conceived of and upheld in Article 14 raises concerns as to its compatibility with fair trial guarantees. Indeed, the fact that, in case of secrecy claims, the proceeding may be halted for up to two years and that – after the said term has expired – the competent judicial authority has merely the faculty (*"can"*) to fix a new deadline for the Committee's submission of alternative documents, questions whether its practical application may, in certain circumstances, lead to proceedings of unreasonable length, in breach of constitutional and international

---

[62] See again INGRAVALLO, *cit. supra* note 24, p. 575.

human rights provisions.[63] Regarding the assessment of the reasonable length, human rights monitoring bodies have found, *inter alia*, that one should take into account what it is at stake for the applicant in the dispute.[64] In this respect, the fact that the plaintiff would contest a restrictive measure adopted against him, most likely encroaching on his right to property, and usually without any previous judicial review, would arguably provide an attractive ground for challenging the compatibility of the measure with due process guarantees. Opposing arguments, however, could be grounded on the possibility to limit such guarantees under certain circumstances, such as when it is required by the need to protect national security (to which the invocation of State secrecy may be functional to), and on the Italian *Corte Costituzionale*'s upholding that State security is a fundamental aspect that prevails over any other.[65]

A further aspect of concern is instead linked to the practical reach of D. Lgs. No. 109/2007. Whilst targeted sanctions are currently mostly framed as financial measures – as such falling within the scope of application of D. Lgs. No. 109/2007 – the latter is indeed not all encompassing. As a matter of example, travel bans are still excluded from its reach, even after the 2017 legislative intervention.[66] This would translate, therefore, in the impossibility for individuals targeted by such restrictive measures[67] to rely on Article 14 of D. Lgs. No. 109/2007 – at least as originally construed – in order to allege breaches of their individual rights.[68]

---

[63] See Art. 111 of the Italian Constitution and, *inter alia*, Art. 6 of the Convention for the Protection of Human Rights and Fundamental Freedoms, 4 November 1950, entered into force 3 September 1953 (European Convention on Human Rights).

[64] See, *inter alia*, European Court of Human Rights, *Frydlender v. France*, Application No. 30979/96, Grand Chamber, Judgment of 27 June 2000, para. 43.

[65] See, *inter alia*, *Corte Costituzionale*, *President of the Council of Ministers v. Office of the Public Prosecutor at the* Tribunale di Milano, 11 March 2009, No. 106, commented by SCOVAZZI, "La Repubblica riconosce e garantisce i diritti inviolabili della segretezza delle relazioni tra servizi informativi italiani e stranieri?", RDI, 2009, p. 959 ff. The *Corte Costituzionale* confirmed, in practice, this approach also in its judgment in *President of the Council of Ministers v.* Corte di Cassazione *and* Corte d'Appello di Milano, 13 February 2014, No. 24, RDI, 2014, p. 582 ff.

[66] See DELLA MORTE, *cit. supra* note 16, p. 336.

[67] In this respect, Italy automatically implements UN-mandated travel restrictions by uploading the relevant lists in the national visa information system. Moreover, Italy may decide to refuse the issuance of visas when this is instrumental to the enforcement of other restrictions. As a matter of practical example, Italian authorities reported – among the actions undertaken to implement UN Security Council Resolution 2375 (2017) of 11 September 2017 – to have refused, in September 2017, the issuance of four short-term Schengen visas requested by individuals from the Democratic People's Republic of Korea, as their request was meant to discuss future cooperation in the textile industry. See Annex to the note verbale dated 12 December 2017 from the Permanent Mission of Italy to the United Nations addressed to the Chair of the Security Council Commission established pursuant to Resolution 1718 (2006), UN Doc. S/AC. 49/2017/141 (2017), p. 4.

[68] On the potential breach of the right to freedom of movement see, *inter alia*, LÓPEZ-JACOISTE, "The UN Collective Security System and its Relationship with Economic Sanctions and Human Rights", in VON BOGDANDY and WOLFRUM (eds.), Max Planck UNYB, 2010, p. 273 ff., pp. 322-325.

However, this different treatment may lose practical significance in light of the new formulation of Article 14.

Finally, one last aspect worth addressing is that of the likeliness that a review of constitutionality could take place at the domestic level with respect to those implementing measures allegedly encroaching on the fundamental substantive and procedural rights of targeted individuals. As far as EU-driven targeted sanctions are concerned, the said option could derive from the application of the doctrine of counter-limits (*controlimiti*), as already admitted in academic writings.[69] Arguably, this prospect may even be "strengthened" by the recent acknowledgment, made by the Italian *Corte Costituzionale* in an *obiter dictum*, that, in the case of a violation of the rights protected both by the Italian Constitution and EU law, the review of constitutionality by the same Court would take priority over the judicial review provided for at the EU level.[70] However, the entry into force of the Treaty of Lisbon[71] and the evolving case law of the EU Court of Justice[72] have filled some gaps that previously affected the possibility for individuals targeted by EU sanctions to be left with no protection vis-à-vis violations of their fundamental rights.

With respect to UN-mandated sanctions that are directly implemented at the international level, the above-mentioned possibility, while in theory admissible in light of Article 117(1) of the Italian Constitution, may instead be hindered by the reluctance to scrutinize UN Security Council resolutions.[73] However, even in this respect, it can be questioned whether the "audacious" stance underpinning the Italian *Corte Costituzionale*'s recent declaration of unconstitutionality of the provision of the Italian law giving execution to the UN Charter, which required domestic judicial authorities to comply with a judgment of the International Court of Justice in breach of the fundamental rights protected under the Constitution,[74] while coping with a partly different scenario, could still be indicative of a "change of course" in approach.

As has been noted in doctrine, the above issue is partly interlinked to that of the type of remedy, which may actually be provided at the domestic level to targeted individuals complaining that their substantive or procedural fundamental rights have been violated by international restrictive measures adopted against

---

[69] See, *inter alia*, CIAMPI, *cit. supra* note 16, p. 446.

[70] See *Corte Costituzionale*, *President of the Council of Ministers (intervening)*, 14 December 2017, No. 269, RDI, 2018, p. 283 ff., para. 5.2.

[71] The reference is mainly to the value of primary law that has been attributed to the EU Charter of Fundamental Rights.

[72] The EU Court of Justice has indeed repeatedly annulled restrictive measures on procedural grounds. The same Court, however, expressly acknowledged that the there are some EU acts in the field of the Common Foreign and Security Policy that may escape from its judicial review. See Opinion 2/13 of the Court (Full Court), 18 December 2014, para. 251.

[73] See again, *ex multis*, CIAMPI, *cit. supra* note 16, p. 447.

[74] See *Corte Costituzionale*, *Simoncini and ors v. Germany and President of the Council of Ministers of the Italian Republic (intervening)*, 22 October 2014, No. 238, IYIL, 2014, p. 1 ff., editorial by FRANCIONI and focus on the judgment with comments by PISILLO MAZZESCHI, BOTHE, CATALDI and PALCHETTI, ILDC 2237 (IT 2014), para. 4.

them. Given that the final decision on removal rests with international bodies,[75] commentators have found that, at least with respect to directly implemented UN-mandated sanctions,[76] the only effective domestic remedy would seemingly be the annulment of the national implementing measure, which, however, may be "impaired" by the international responsibility that would stem from it.[77]

Yet, even without reaching the above-considered scenarios, a recent order of the Italian *Consiglio di Stato* relating to a targeted sanction adopted at the EU level against a Russian oligarch has shown how, in certain cases, domestic judicial authorities may still intervene, in practice, in alleviating the impact of restrictive measures by balancing the interests at stake at the stage of their practical implementation. In the specific instance, the *Consiglio di Stato* ultimately authorized the temporary administration by the *Agenzia delle entrate* (the Italian revenue agency) of the frozen quota of a society, in order to avoid the complete paralysis of its activity.[78] While the case at hand raised issues in terms of the encroachment of the commercial interests of the society partly owned by the oligarch, other stakeholders and potential creditors, nothing prevents a similar "remedial" intervention of domestic judicial authorities even in cases in which UN-mandated sanctions and different individual rights are at stake. Remarkably, such an approach would moreover be fully consistent with the idea of the essential role that harmonious interpretation can play in avoiding possible (apparent) norm conflicts between UN Security Council resolutions and international human rights obligations, which the European Court of Human Rights has upheld, *inter alia*, in its judgments in the *Nada*[79] and *Al-Dulimi* cases.[80]

5.   NATIONAL LISTING: ADDING A THIRD "LEVEL" OF COMPLEXITY?

The amendments introduced by D. Lgs. No. 90/2017 to D. Lgs. No. 109/2007 also raise another set of concerns, which relate to the provision of autonomous national sanctions.[81]

---

[75] CIAMPI, *cit. supra* note 15, p. 75.

[76] As far as the EU acts in the field of the Common Foreign and Security Policy prescribing the adoption of restrictive measures are concerned, the decision on their validity belongs exclusively to the EU Court of Justice. See again *Rosneft* case, *cit. supra* note 37, para. 77.

[77] CIAMPI, *cit. supra* note 15, p. 76. Inevitably, different considerations would apply instead with respect to the newly introduced national listing process, for which nothing seems to prevent domestic judicial authorities from annulling the domestic measures and ordering the de-listing of the individual concerned.

[78] See *Consiglio di Stato (IV Sez.)*, *Aurora 31 s.r.l. v. Guardia di Finanza and ors.*, 5 May 2015, Order No. 01966.

[79] *Nada* case, *cit. supra* note 54, para. 197.

[80] *Al Dulimi and Montana Management Inc. v. Switzerland*, Application No. 5809/08, Grand Chamber, Judgment of 21 June 2016, para. 149.

[81] Remarkably, by means of this provision, the Italian legislator has implemented into the Italian legal system UN Security Council Resolution 1373 (2001), *cit. supra* note 53, which, as previously noted, generally requires UN Member States to freeze terrorists' assets to counter terrorist activities and their financing.

With respect to this type of sanctions, the Italian legislator has mainly upheld the same procedures and standards also applicable to international sanctions to be implemented at the national level. Thus, most of the provisions on designation, cancellation, exemptions and notification apply indifferently to measures adopted on the ground of international or national listing procedures. Arguably, however, this choice may lead to the extension to national autonomous sanctions of some of the criticisms related to the lack of human rights guarantees that has been already raised with respect to the international sanctions regime.[82] Moreover, if not accompanied, at a minimum, by *ad hoc* arrangements of the kind of those available at the UN or EU level, national restrictive measures may even give raise to additional concerns.

However, like UN and EU sanctions, restrictive measures established autonomously at the domestic level must also be consistent with human rights guarantees established – apart then in the national Constitution – in customary and treaty international rules binding on the State. In this respect, one could question, by way of example, whether the lack of a time limit with respect to the review of the position of those designated in the national sanctions list or the absence of a clear provision with respect to the right to bring a complaint against a designation measure in the current legislative framework do comply with due process guarantees.[83] Similar concerns also apply with respect to the potentially indefinite character of the sanctions. As already noted, in fact, whereas Article 4-*bis* of the amended D. Lgs. No. 109/2007 limits the length of the measure to six months, national authorities (i.e., the *Ministero dell'economia e delle finanze*, acting on the basis of the proposal of the Financial Security Committee) are left with broad discretion in renewing the same "until the situation so requires".

The risk thus exists that such a national mechanism[84] may end up turning into a sanctioning system which provides a weak protection to targeted individuals' rights, potentially in breach of international rules. Clearly, such a result strikingly defeats the very purpose of the introduction of national designating mechanisms, which should have the merit of unlashing the adoption of the relevant measures from international constraints and, thus, facilitating the application of domestic legal safeguards.

Rather, the inherent shortcomings of a system of national-based sanctions would most likely be the fragmented application of the same and, possibly, the potential "fragility" of the State-to-State architecture on which the adoption and enforcement of restrictive measures should inevitably be based. For instance,

---

[82] A similar issue has been recently raised also with respect to the UK Parliament Joint Committee of Human Rights on the UK Sanctions Bill. See "Legislative Scrutiny: The Sanctions and Anti-Money Laundering Bill", 1 March 2018, p. 4. See the contribution by WHITE and that by BORLINI and SILINGARDI in this volume.

[83] Established, *inter alia*, by the already recalled Art. 6 of the European Convention on Human Rights.

[84] According to the Italian legislator's illustrative report, this mechanism has been adopted with the scope of introducing more flexibility and overcoming the difficulties deriving from the existence of different listing criteria among UN Member States. See again the illustrative report, *cit. supra* note 60, p. 21.

Article 4-*bis*(2) of the amended D. Lgs. No. 109/2007 expressly provides that, when receiving a demand to adopt freezing measures by another State, the Italian authorities shall inform it about the final decision on the request. This provision thus vests national authorities with full discretion in deciding to implement the freezing measure coming from another State. Notably, however, this provision refers solely to bilateral requests submitted in the framework of the implementation of the aforementioned UN Security Council Resolution 1373 (2001), imposing a general obligation to freeze terrorists' funds. Nothing is said, instead, with respect to possible State-to-State requests of implementation of freezing measures aimed at countering the financing of programmes of proliferation of weapons of mass destructions or other activities threatening international peace or security. Only Article 3(11) of the amended D. Lgs. No. 109/2007 establishes that the Financial Security Committee may cooperate with bodies tasked with similar functions in other countries and may even lift official secrecy to this end. This type of provisions, however, hardly dispels the risk of a denial of implementation of State-to-State requests of adoption of freezing measures made on the ground of national designation.

The fact that the designation on the national list and the execution of the related restrictive measures are not subject to any meaningful judicial review also excludes from the outset the application of any envisaged mutual recognition mechanism among EU Member States with respect to freezing or confiscation orders issued in the context of criminal proceedings. Whilst the proposed EU Regulation on mutual recognition of freezing and confiscation orders,[85] if adopted, will indeed allow Member States to execute freezing measures adopted by other Member States without further formalities, a judicial decision or an act of validation by a judicial authority would be needed.[86] In this respect, it is thus regrettable that D. Lgs. No. 90/2017 has amended D. Lgs. No. 109/2007 so as to supress the reference to the President of the Financial Security Committee's duty to inform the competent prosecutor any time it decides to formulate a proposal of designation and a concrete risk existed that the to-be-frozen assets would meanwhile be dispelled, hidden, or used to finance terrorism.[87]

6. Concluding Remarks

D. Lgs. No. 90/2017, while significantly reforming the mechanism of implementation of targeted sanctions in the Italian legal system, seemingly missed the opportunity to reformulate the existing legislative framework so as to accommodate more incisive guarantees against possible human rights infringements. Whilst it is true, in fact, that some positive evolutions have been made – for instance by

---

[85] European Commission, Proposal for a Regulation of the European Parliament and the Council on the mutual recognition of freezing and confiscation orders, Doc. COM(2016) 819 final of 21 December 2016.

[86] *Ibid.*, Art. 2.

[87] See D. Lgs. No. 109/2007, Art. 3(10), before the amendments introduced by D. Lgs. No. 90/2017.

vesting with primary rank the provisions mandating the notification of the execution of freezing measures – most of the newly introduced discipline establishes vague procedures, entrusting governmental authorities with broad discretion and a wide margin of manoeuvre. Conversely, any intervention of the Italian legislator in the sense of a human rights-driven implementation of UN-mandated sanctions (e.g., by limiting executive authorities' discretion in the authorization of exemptions) would have been worthy of praise. Such a development would have indeed been consistent with the function that the European Court of Human Rights arguably has entrusted national authorities with in terms of minimization of the (apparent) conflicts between States' obligations to implement UN Security Council decisions and to comply with international human rights norms.

Moreover, the provision of an *ad hoc* judicial complaint procedure, which had already been upheld in existing legislation, is now inexplicably confusing. Nor the most recent legislative intervention has being able to overcome some preexisting issues, such as, for instance, the exclusion of travel bans from the scope of application of the organic discipline provided for in D. Lgs. No. 109/2007.

On top of the above, the low threshold of guarantees provided for in the amended decree has inevitably also pervaded the newly introduced national sanctions list, thus adding a further potential ground triggering State international responsibility for breach of international human rights norms.

Against this background, an important role rests on domestic judicial authorities, which may overcome at least some of the aforementioned shortcomings by means of a human rights-driven reading of the relevant provisions.

A CRITICAL OVERVIEW OF THE UNITED NATIONS ARCHITECTURE ON CHILDREN AND ARMED CONFLICT: WHAT ROLE FOR SANCTIONS?

Francesca Capone[*]

Abstract

The first comprehensive and systematic analysis of the impact of armed conflict on children has been submitted to the UN General Assembly in 1996. The UN has since adopted and implemented a large number of initiatives and resolutions, making up the basis for the enhancement of monitoring and accountability of all parties responsible for violations perpetrated against children. The efforts to quantify and monitor violations against children committed not only by States, but also by Armed Non-State Actors, are an important milestone in the attempt to improve the protection of children. Nonetheless, the current UN architecture on children and armed conflict presents a number of shortcomings, in particular the lack of effective enforcement mechanisms, which hinder its capability to increase the achievement of more concrete results. After presenting an overview of the UN architecture on children and armed conflict, lingering on its constitutive elements as well as on its current weaknesses, this article will question if and to what extent the imposition of sanctions against individuals and entities can enhance the comprehensive strategy to thwart the harmful impact of armed conflict on children and the long lasting consequences it has on durable peace, security, and development. Furthermore, the present article will identify possible ways forward to improve the current framework, by discussing, inter alia, *how the wealth of information gathered through the UN Monitoring and Reporting Mechanism could be used to feed into a more integrated information platform within the UN and also to strengthen accountability in international criminal tribunals.*

Keywords: UN Monitoring and Reporting Mechanism; Special Representative on Children and Armed Conflict; sanctions; child soldiers; Armed Non-State Actors

1. INTRODUCTION

The first comprehensive and systematic analysis of the impact of armed conflict on children has been submitted to the UN General Assembly in 1996.[1] The UN has since adopted and implemented a large number of initiatives and

---

[*] Research Fellow in Public International Law and Didactic Coordinator of the Master in Human Rights and Conflict Management, Scuola Superiore Sant'Anna, Pisa, Italy. E-mail: f.capone@santannapisa.it.
[1] MACHEL, The Impact of Armed Conflict on Children, UN Doc. A/51/306 (1996).

resolutions, making up the basis, together with the relevant international law provisions, for the enhancement of monitoring and accountability of all parties responsible for violations perpetrated against children. In a nutshell, the UN set of tools and mechanisms on children and armed conflict encompasses, besides the identification of six grave violations against children, the publication of the Secretary-General's Annual Report that includes an updated "list of shame" of conflicting parties; the Monitoring and Reporting Mechanism (MRM); the Special Representative on Children and Armed Conflict (SRCAC); and the UN Security Council (UN SC) Working Group on Children and Armed Conflict, which is the body in charge of reviewing reports and making recommendations that can trigger action by the Security Council and other actors. The existence of such an intricate system suggests that the widespread exposure of children and youth to conflict-related violence over the years has become an increasingly important issue for the UN. Yet, according to the United Nations Children's Fund (UNICEF), 2017 has been a devastating year for children affected by armed conflicts.[2] In particular, children came under attack in spaces where they should have been safe, e.g. in schools, homes, hospitals and on playgrounds and they were the deliberate target of several offences. The efforts to quantify and monitor violations against children committed not only by States, but also, and often foremost, by Armed Non-State Actors (ANSAs),[3] are an important milestone in the attempt to improve the protection of children.[4] Nonetheless, the current UN architecture on children and armed conflict presents a number of shortcomings, which hinder its capability to increase the achievement of concrete results. One of the most blatant deficiencies is the lack of effective enforcement mechanisms to deal with perpetrators unwilling to commit to halting violations against children or to fulfil the pledges already made. In order to fill this gap, the SRCAC has long been advocating for the adoption of sanctions by the Security Council and, at the same time, the Security Council in several resolutions has expressed its willingness to consider imposing targeted and gradual measures against parties to conflicts violating the rights of children.[5] Despite the declared intentions, the interplay between the UN architecture on children and armed conflict and the equally com-

---

[2] UNICEF, "Children under Attack in 2017", 28 December 2017, available at: <https://blogs.unicef.org/east-asia-pacific/children-attack-2017/>.

[3] See BELLAL, GIACCA and CASEY-MASLEN, "International Law and Armed Actors in Afghanistan", International Review of the Red Cross, 2011, p. 47 ff., p. 48; BILKOVA, "Treat Them as They Deserve?!: Three Approaches to Armed Opposition Groups Under Current International Law", Human Rights and International Legal Discourse, 2010, p. 111 ff.; ZEGVELD, Accountability of Armed Opposition Groups in International Law, Cambridge, 2003, pp. 59-92.

[4] See SOMER, "Engaging Armed Non-State Actors to Protect Children from the Effects of Armed Conflict: When the Stick Doesn't Cut the Mustard", Journal of Human Rights Practice, 2012, p. 106 ff.; THOMPSON, "Children and Armed Conflict", in GENSER and STAGNO UGARTE (eds.), The United Nations Security Council in the Age of Human Rights, New York, 2014, p. 98 ff.; CAPONE, Reparations for Child Victims of Armed Conflict: State of the Field and Current Challenges, Antwerp-Cambridge, 2017, pp. 92-103.

[5] UN Doc. S/RES/1539 (2004), para. 5(c); UN Doc. S/RES/1612 (2005), para. 9; UN Doc. S/RES/1882 (2009), para. 7(c); and UN Doc. S/RES/1998 (2011), para. 9(e).

plex UN sanctions regimes has been very limited so far, thus failing to fully explore and exploit the potential of a closer and better structured interaction.[6]

After presenting an overview of the UN architecture on children and armed conflict, lingering on its constitutive elements as well as on its current weaknesses, this article will question if and to what extent the imposition of sanctions against individuals and entities, can enhance the comprehensive strategy to thwart the harmful impact of armed conflict on children and the long lasting consequences it has on durable peace, security, and development. Furthermore, the present article will identify possible ways forward to improve the current framework, by discussing, *inter alia*, how the wealth of information gathered through the MRM could be used to feed into a more integrated information platform within the UN, also within the context of addressing accountability in international criminal tribunals.

2.   AN OVERVIEW OF THE UNITED NATIONS ARCHITECTURE ON CHILDREN AND ARMED CONFLICT AND ITS SHORTCOMINGS

As mentioned above, the alarming situation of children in armed conflict became a thematic issue on the UN agenda only after the submission of Machel's groundbreaking report. In the first place Machel's study led to the adoption by the UN General Assembly of Resolution 51/77 (1996) establishing the mandate of the Special Representative of the SRCAC. In line with the recommendations enshrined in the Machel's report, through the UN SC Resolution 1539 (2004), six grave violations against children have been identified due to their ability to be monitored and quantified, their egregious nature, and the severity of their consequences on the lives of children.[7] Such violations are: killing or maiming of children, recruitment or use of child soldiers, rape and other forms of sexual violence against children, abduction of children, attacks against schools and hospitals, and denial of humanitarian access to children.[8] The MRM, which represents one of the most innovative tools of the UN architecture on children and armed conflict, serves the purpose of gathering information concerning the six grave violations, the perpetrators, and the victims. As the coming paragraph is going to explain, the information collected through the MRM is used in UN reporting, including the Annual Report of the Secretary-General on Children and Armed Conflict (Annual Report),[9] country-specific reports of the Secretary-General, and reports of the SRCAC. These reports and the recommendations made by the Working

[6] See THOMPSON, *cit. supra* note 4, pp. 112-116.

[7] UN Doc. S/RES/1539 (2004), para. 1.

[8] Office of the Special Representative of the Secretary-General on Children and Armed Conflict (OSRSG-CAAC), "The Six Grave Violations Against Children During Armed Conflict: The Legal Foundation", Working Paper 1, October 2009, available at: <https://childrenandarmedconflict.un.org/publications/WorkingPaper-1_SixGraveViolationsLegalFoundation.pdf>.

[9] So far the Secretary-General has issued 16 Annual Reports on Children and Armed Conflict, the latest one was launched in August 2017 and covers the period from January to

Group on Children and Armed Conflict represent the basis to trigger further action by the Security Council as well as other actors, both at the national and international levels.[10]

As most of the countries mentioned in the annual reports are currently affected by non-international armed conflicts (NIACs) it follows that the six grave violations against children are not committed solely by States and their agents;[11] on the contrary, most of them are directly attributable to ANSAs. The creation of a MRM, which as mentioned above has the purpose to provide for the systematic gathering of accurate, timely and objective information on grave violations committed against children in armed conflict, stemmed especially from the necessity to find new ways to engage ANSAs in the promotion and protection of children's rights.[12] Once the MRM is activated in a given country, a task force is created. The task force responsible for collecting information on all six grave violations against children is chaired by the highest UN authority on the ground and composed of relevant UN agencies. The MRM task force is typically situated in the country's capital; however, locally based sub-task forces may also be established to ensure the effective implementation of the MRM throughout the conflict-affected areas of a given country.[13] Annual country reports are prepared by the task force, vetted by the Office of the Special Representative of the Secretary-General on Children and Armed Conflict (OSRSG-CAAC) as convener of the UN system on children and armed conflict, and finally submitted by the Secretary-General to the Security Council's Working Group. The Working Group reviews the reports of the Secretary-General and makes recommendations, presented as "conclusions", that suggest actions to be undertaken, by the UN SC and the international community at large, against the actors listed in the Secretary-General "name and shame" Annexes.[14] The reviewed information is then included in the Annual Report of the Secretary-General.

December 2016. See Annual Report of the Secretary-General on Children and Armed Conflict, UN Doc. A/72/361–S/2017/821 (2017).

[10] OSRSG-CAAC, UNICEF and United Nations Department of Peacekeeping Operations (DPKO), Field Manual, "Monitoring and Reporting Mechanism (MRM) on Grave Violations Against Children in situations of Armed Conflict", June 2014, pp. 47-50, available at: <https://childrenandarmedconflict.un.org/wp-content/uploads/2016/04/MRM_Field_5_June_2014.pdf>.

[11] On the distinction between international and non-international armed conflicts see generally FLECK, "The Law of Non-International Armed Conflict", in FLECK (ed.), *The Handbook of International Humanitarian Law*, Oxford, 2013, p. 605 ff., pp. 620–629.

[12] RYNGAERT and VAN DE MEULEBROUCKE, "Enhancing and Enforcing Compliance with International Humanitarian Law by Non-State Armed Groups: An Inquiry into some Mechanisms", Journal of Conflict & Security Law, 2012, p. 443 ff., pp. 459-461.

[13] Field Manual MRM, *supra* note 10, p. 4.

[14] In the Annexes to the Annual Report issued in 2017 there are 56 ANSAs, 51 listed in Annex I and 5 listed in Annex II, and 9 Government forces, all of them listed in Annex I. Annex I lists the parties that commit grave violations affecting children in situations of armed conflict on the agenda of the UN SC, Annex II instead focuses on the parties to armed conflicts not on the agenda of the Security Council. Both annexes in turn are divided in two parts, A and B; the first includes the listed parties that have not put in place measures during the reporting period to improve the protection of children, the second encompasses the listed parties that

Another crucial piece of the UN architecture on children and armed conflict involves the preparation and implementation of action plans, which are concrete time-bound and verifiable (by the MRM) commitments by a listed party to a conflict to halt recruitment and use of child soldiers, sexual violence, killing and maiming, abduction of children, and/or attacks on schools and hospitals. Such action plans could be characterized as "special agreements" under Common Article 3 of the Geneva Conventions,[15] pursuant to which children's protection in NIACs is strengthened.[16] Furthermore, the action plans are sometimes accompanied by ANSAs' unilateral declarations, through which the obligations undertaken are publicly acknowledged.[17] The completion of an action plan, and the subsequent cessation of violations, is the only officially defined way to be delisted from the Annexes to the Secretary-General's Annual Report,[18] although factual developments may lead to the same end result (e.g. if a party ceases to exist).[19] Up until now, 28 listed parties have signed 29 action plans, including 11 Government forces and 17 ANSAs. Of those, 11 parties have fully complied with their action plans and were subsequently delisted from the Annexes.[20]

It is important to stress that the action plan process is premised largely on parties agreeing voluntarily to end violations and to take specific steps in that regard.[21] Therefore, Security Council experts and advocates for the protection of children have recognized from the outset that relying on parties voluntarily to enter into action plans will often be insufficient and that stronger measures may be needed.[22] Furthermore, the action plans can be signed exclusively between

---

have put in place measures during the reporting period. See Annual Report 2017, *supra* note 9, pp. 38-41.

[15] SIVAKUMARAN, "Re-envisaging the International Law of Internal Armed Conflict", EJIL, 2011, p. 219 ff., p. 259.

[16] RYNGAERT and VAN DE MEULEBROUCKE, *cit. supra* note 12, p. 459.

[17] *Ibid.*

[18] In 2016, former UN Secretary-General Ban Ki-moon's decision to remove the Saudi Arabia-led coalition from the Annexes soon after it was listed for the grave violations of killing and maiming and attacks against schools and hospitals in Yemen, raised questions about the politicisation and the impartiality of the listing process. The decision of current Secretary-General António Guterres to list the Saudi Arabia-led coalition in 2017 has helped restore some trust in the listing mechanism. See Security Council Report, Monthly Forecast, "In Hindsight: Children and Armed Conflict", November 2017, p. 2, available at: <http://www.securitycouncilreport.org/atf/cf/%7B65BFCF9B-6D27-4E9C-8CD3-CF6E4FF96FF9%7D/2017_11_forecast.pdf>.

[19] If there is a delisting and formally the MRM ends, monitoring continues informally for at least one cycle of the Global Annual Report, to ensure there are no renewed violations, see Field Manual MRM, *supra* note 10, p. 61.

[20] Further information is available at: <https://childrenandarmedconflict.un.org/our-work/action-plans/>.

[21] NYLUND and HYLLESTED, "Protecting Children Affected by Armed Conflict: Accountability for Monitoring, Reporting, and Response", Journal of Human Rights Practice, 2010, p. 71 ff., p.84.

[22] KOLLER and ECKENFELS-GARCIA, "Using Targeted Sanctions to End Violations against Children in Armed Conflict", Boston University International Law Journal, 2015, p. 2 ff., p. 5.

the UN and the parties listed in the Annexes to the Annual Report, thus meaning that only five of the six grave violations identified can be the object of the
agreement. Denial of humanitarian access to children, which can have a severe
impact on hundreds of thousands of boys and girls,[23] is currently excluded despite the numerous episodes occurring in many of the countries included in the
Annual Report, thus creating a significant loophole in the existing framework.[24]
Moreover, in comparison with the other grave violations child recruitment is the
one that gets steadily prioritized and in fact it represents the focus of most of the
action plans signed so far.[25] A relevant example of the emphasis placed on child
soldiering is provided by the public awareness campaign, entitled "Children, not
soldiers", which was launched jointly by the OSRSG-CAAC with UNICEF in
2014.[26] Such prioritisation fails to take into account the fact that the law relevant
to child recruitment, despite some criticalities,[27] provides a detailed framework
whereas other crimes against children do not match the same level of legal sound-
ness and do not enjoy the same global attention.

Another important shortcoming is represented by the lack of focus on the
post-conflict dimension.[28] While few parties included in the Annexes to the
Annual Report to date have successfully completed the action plans signed with
the UN, a comprehensive response component is needed long after a State or
non-State actor is delisted. In the case of child soldiers, for example, the range
of initiatives that should be undertaken following the release of children associated with armed forces or groups include reintegration programmes as well as
capacity building on child rights and child protection issues.[29] In order to prevent
the risks of re-recruitment, stigmatisation and marginalisation, such actions need
to be implemented for a sufficient amount of time after the signing of peace
agreements, fulfilment of actions plans and the focused attention of the Security
Council. Similarly, the rehabilitation of children, both girls and boys,[30] affected

---

[23] See Field Manual MRM, *supra note* 10, p. 6.

[24] The recruitment and use of child soldiers was the first violation able to trigger the listing
of a party in the Secretary-General's Annual Report on Children and Armed Conflict. See UN
Doc. S/RES/1379 (2001), para. 16. Abduction of children was the last violation included in the
Annexes, see UN Doc. S/RES/2225 (2015), para. 3.

[25] Successful action plans focussing on child soldiering have been implemented, for example, in Myanmar, South Sudan and Uganda.

[26] More info about the campaign is available at: <https://childrenandarmedconflict.un.org/
children-not-soldiers/>.

[27] See CAPONE, *cit. supra* note 4, pp. 50-60; DRUMBL, *Reimagining Child Soldiers in
International Law and Policy*, Oxford, 2012, pp. 134-167; MCBRIDE, *The War Crime of Child
Soldier Recruitment*, The Hague, 2014, pp. 18-35.

[28] See NYLUND and HYLLESTED, *cit. supra* note 21, p. 91. On the importance of devel-
oping and implementing adequate rehabilitation and reintegration processes see CAPONE,
"'Worse' than Child Soldiers? A Critical Analysis of Foreign Children in the Ranks of ISIL",
International Criminal Law Review, 2017, p. 161 ff., pp. 180-185.

[29] DUTHIE and SPECHT, "DDR, Transitional justice, and the Reintegration of Former
Child Combatants", CUTTER PATEL, De GREIFF and WALDORF (eds.), *Disarming the Past:
Transitional Justice and Ex-Combatants*, New York, 2010, p. 193 ff.

[30] See VENTEVOGEL et al., "Child Mental Health, Psychosocial Well-Being and Resilience
in Afghanistan: A Review and Future Directions", in FERNANDO and FERRARI (eds.), *Handbook*

by conflict related sexual violence entails the promotion of their psychosocial well-being and recovery through a wide array of differentiated supportive activities that normalize life and enable positive social interaction.[31]

Another concern is triggered by the challenges posed by the multitude of actors that figure in present-day armed conflicts. The reports and actions that are part of the UN architecture on children and armed conflict in principle should be coordinated together, or at least in close consultation, with local Governments.[32] This necessity has emerged quite strongly from the outset, as highlighted in UN SC Resolution 1612 (2005) that established the actual MRM framework.[33] Often, however, Governments refuse dialogue with armed groups or would like to see only the violations perpetrated by ANSAs reported.[34] Furthermore, although ANSAs' engagement in this context serves a humanitarian objective and does not bestow any recognition or political legitimacy,[35] the fact that some non-State actors are regarded as "terrorist" further complicates the interaction with States and affects the protection of children's rights in the settings where these groups are active.[36]

It should also be noted that the current UN architecture on children and armed conflict, and especially the MRM, could play an important role in the context of addressing individual accountability before international criminal tribunals; in particular before the International Criminal Court (ICC), due to the fact that the UN SC has the option to refer a situation to the ICC,[37] and that all the six grave violations are criminalized under the Rome Statute.[38] Even though the standard of proof applied in a formal judicial setting is different from the evidentiary process of the MRM,[39] the documents emanating from the MRM can still be used to inform a criminal investigation. For example, as noted by some authors, in referring the Darfur situation to the ICC, the submission by the UN SC of the reports on children and armed conflict in Sudan could have prompted the Court to add charges based on crimes against children, but this option was

---

of Resilience in Children of War, Heidelberg, 2013, p. 51 ff., p. 68.

[31] KOSTELNY and WESSELLS, "Child Friendly Spaces: Promoting Children's Resiliency Amidst War", in FERNANDO and FERRARI (eds.), *cit. supra* note 30, p. 119 ff.; pp. 124-127.

[32] Field Manual MRM, *cit. supra* note 10, p. 4.

[33] UN Doc. S/RES/1612 (2005), para. 2(b), where the UN SC stated that "[…] this mechanism must operate with the participation of and in cooperation with national Governments and relevant United Nations and civil society actors, including at the country level".

[34] NYLUND and HYLLESTED, *cit. supra* note 21, p. 85.

[35] See TALMON, "Recognition of Opposition Groups as the Legitimate Representative of a People", Chinese Journal of International Law, 2013, p. 219 ff., pp. 230-237; see also JO, *Compliant Rebels: Rebel Groups and International Law in World Politics*, Cambridge, 2015, pp. 52-65.

[36] On the double standard adopted in particular with regard to children recruited by ANSAs labelled as "terrorist", see generally CAPONE, *cit. supra* note 28, pp. 171-176.

[37] Rome Statute of the International Criminal Court, 17 July 1998, entered into force 1 July 2002, Art. 13(b).

[38] See CAPONE, *cit. supra* note 4, pp. 159-160; see also OSRSG-CAAC Working Paper 1, *supra* note 8.

[39] Field Manual MRM, *supra* note 10, p. 48.

not even considered.[40] Furthermore, in the Working Group's conclusions, there is no reference to the need to foster a more structured interaction with the ICC and mention of the Court's work appear primarily as a corollary to "the responsibility of all Member States to comply with their respective obligations to end impunity and to investigate and prosecute those responsible for genocide, crimes against humanity, war crimes and other egregious crimes perpetrated against children".[41] There are a number of practices that could contribute to promoting a better cooperation between the UN architecture on children and armed conflict, in particular the Security Council's Working Group on Children and Armed Conflict, and the ICC, such as transmitting the Working Group's conclusions of relevant situations to the Office of the Prosecutor (OTP) of the ICC as a matter of course and scheduling regular briefings from the OTP to the Working Group.[42] Despite their feasibility and the compatibility with the respective mandates, those measures have not been implemented yet.

In addition to the issues briefly presented above, it is worth emphasizing that, as duly stressed by several commentators,[43] the main shortcoming of the current UN framework on children and armed conflict remains the lack of adequate enforcing mechanisms to deal with recalcitrant perpetrators. The next section will discuss to which degree increasing the adoption of sanctions could contribute to filling this gap as well as to overcoming some of the weaknesses of the exiting UN architecture on children and armed conflict.

3.1 STRENGTHENING THE SANCTIONS REGIME AGAINST INDIVIDUALS AND ENTITIES COMMITTING GRAVE VIOLATIONS AGAINST CHILDREN: THE RIGHT TOOL TO ENHANCE COMPLIANCE AND ACCOUNTABILITY?

As stated in UN SC Resolution 1612 (2005), the UN framework on children and armed conflict does not intend to replace the protection or rehabilitation role of national and local authorities, but rather aims at supporting and complementing these tasks.[44] Therefore, it is fundamental that States maintain their leadership in the response, accountability and prevention activities associated with the MRM and the other tools. However, States' predominant role in those areas does not exclude a more incisive approach by the actors involved in the UN architecture on children and armed conflict. Already in 2006, under the French Presidency, the Security Council's Working Group developed a "tool-kit" containing options involving either direct action by the Working Group or recommendations to the UN SC and other actors. The options listed in the tool-kit, described as indicative and non-limitative, were grouped into five types of measures. Those measures

---

[40] THOMPSON, *cit. supra* note 4, p. 117.
[41] UN Doc. S/RES/2225 (2015), tenth preambular paragraph.
[42] THOMPSON, *cit. supra* note 4, pp. 117-118.
[43] NYLUND and HYLLESTED, *cit. supra* note 21, pp. 89-90; CAPONE, *cit. supra* note 4, pp. 102-106.
[44] UN Doc. S/RES/1612 (2005), para. 2(c).

include also enhancing the role of the sanctions committees and providing information to the relevant justice mechanisms.[45] Nonetheless, the majority of recommendations made so far have been appeals to parties, letters to donors and, more recently, improving the children and armed conflict dimension of peacekeeping and political missions.[46] With regard in particular to the possibility to strengthening the role of sanctions, the tool-kit vaguely states that the Working Groups can recommend to the UN SC to "consider and forward *to the existing Sanctions Committees* [...] relevant information received by the Working Group and its conclusions thereon".[47] The Working Group, which in any case cannot recommend the creation of a new sanctions regime, until now has been very cautious in suggesting to impose sanctions against those engaged in violations against children's rights.[48] However, as already stressed, in several resolutions the Security Council itself has voiced the intention to consider imposing targeted and gradual measures against parties to conflicts violating the rights of children.[49] Moreover, also the Special Representative of the Secretary-General on Children and Armed Conflict has long been advocating for the adoption of sanctions by the Security Council to end impunity and halt children's victimisation.[50] Regrettably, and despite the apparent convergence of wills, this measure has not been enforced as often and systematically as expected. Among the reasons that have made the call for sanctions not as effective as hoped, one should take into account political considerations, which inform most of the UN SC actions or lack thereof, combined with the fact that the sanctions system established within the UN is extremely complex.[51]

---

[45] Options for Possible Actions by the CAAC Working Group of the Security Council, UN Doc. S/2006/724, paras. 1-5.

[46] THOMPSON, *cit. supra* note 4, p. 108.

[47] Options for Possible Actions, *cit. supra* note 45, para. 5 (emphasis added).

[48] See HAPPOLD, "UN Sanctions as Human Rights and Humanitarian Law Devices", in VAN DEN HERIK (ed.), *Research Handbook on Sanctions and International Law*, Cheltenham, 2017, p. 125 ff., p. 144. So far the Working Group has recommended the imposition of sanctions only in relation to the situations in the DRC, Côte d'Ivoire, Afghanistan, Iraq, and Somalia. See also KOLLER and ECKENFELS-GARCIA, *cit. supra* note 22, pp. 13-14.

[49] See *supra* note 5.

[50] Field Manual MRM, *cit. supra* note 10, p. 45.

[51] See CONFORTI and FOCARELLI, *The Law and Practice of the United Nations*, 5th ed., Leiden, 2016, p. 252. See, *inter alia*, DOXEY, "International Sanctions: A Framework for Analysis with Special Reference to the UN and Southern Africa", International Organization, 1972, p. 527 ff.; FARRALL, *United Nations Sanctions and the Rule of Law*, Cambridge, 2007, pp. 3-13; CIAMPI, "Security Council Targeted Sanctions and Human Rights", in FASSBENDER (ed.), *Securing Human Rights? Achievements and Challenges of the UN Security Council*, Oxford, 2011, p. 98 ff.; HAPPOLD and EDEN (eds.), *Economic Sanctions and International Law*, London, 2016; VAN DEN HERIK, "The Individualization and Formalization of UN Sanctions", in VAN DEN HERIK (ed.), *cit. supra* note 48, p. 1 ff. See BIERSTEKER, ECKERT and TOURINHO, "Designing United Nations Targeted Sanctions", August 2012, pp. 10-11, available at: <http://graduateinstitute.ch/files/live/sites/iheid/files/sites/internationalgovernance/shared/PSIG_images/Sanctions/Designing%20UN%20Targeted%20Sanctions.pdf>. See also Security Council Report, "Special Research Report on UN Sanctions", 25 November 2013, pp. 9-12, avail-

The sanctions committees that are currently dealing with violations against children have imposed three measures, namely, arms embargos, historically included in all UN sanctions regimes and capable of reducing the operational capacity of those engaged in violations against children, minimizing the impact of conflict on children, and encouraging peaceful dispute resolution;[52] and the two most narrowly tailored measures, i.e. travel bans and assets freeze that target specific individuals, groups, or entities.[53] Those types of sanctions can be adopted to coerce behavioural changes, to signal consequences for breaches of international norms, and/or stigmatize or isolate targets and activities that violate international law.[54] So far sanctions triggered by violations against children have been predominantly imposed on individual members of ANSAs. Notably, sanctions against individuals are likely to have an impact on the groups at large when the ANSAs are centrally and hierarchically organized under a leader who relies heavily on his freedom of movement, wealth, or global reputation and therefore will be affected by personalized sanctions.[55] If these conditions are not met, and the sanctions focus on individuals that do not play a prominent role in the group, their implementation will be ineffective and thus unable to achieve the desired results.[56]

3.1. The Establishment and Implementation of Sanctions Regimes for Violations against Children

In relation to violations committed against children in armed conflict, sanctions can be adopted only if two cumulative criteria are met, namely the existence of a sanctions committee already in place and the explicit mention of violations against children as a designation trigger.[57] Out of the 14 existing UN sanctions regimes, nine concern specifically countries in which operate State and non-State actors listed in the Annual Report on Children and Armed Conflict,[58] and one is a thematic regime with "a global reach" as it is applicable to any individual and entity associated with ISIL (Da'esh) and Al-Qaida, two terrorist organizations that appear in the Annual Report for crimes committed against children in Iraq, Syria, Libya (ISIL), and Yemen (ISIL and Al-Qaida). So far, only the sanctions committees dealing with the situations in Somalia/Eritrea, the Democratic Republic of Congo (DRC), South Sudan, Mali and the Central African Republic

---

able at: <http://www.securitycouncilreport.org/atf/cf/%7B65BFCF9B-6D27-4E9C-8CD3-CF6E4FF96FF9%7D/special_research_report_sanctions_2013.pdf>.

[52] KOLLER and ECKENFELS-GARCIA, cit. supra note 22, p. 18.

[53] HAPPOLD, cit. supra note 48, p. 141.

[54] KOLLER and ECKENFELS-GARCIA, cit. supra note 22, p. 21.

[55] Ibid., p. 22.

[56] In Côte d'Ivoire, for example, the sanctions initially applied were considered ineffective because they focused on "insignificant" individuals: ibid., p. 24.

[57] THOMPSON, cit. supra note 4, p. 116.

[58] The countries are Somalia, Iraq, DRC, Sudan, Libya, CAR, Yemen, South Sudan and Mali. See Annual Report 2017, cit. supra note 9.

(CAR) have explicitly incorporated violations against children as a designation criterion. More in detail, the Somalia/Eritrea Sanctions Committee,[59] the DRC Sanctions Committee,[60] the South Sudan Sanctions Committee,[61] the Mali Sanctions Committee,[62] and the CAR Sanctions Committee have all included the recruitment and use of child soldiers in their listing criteria.[63] Remarkably, in four cases, i.e. Somalia, South Sudan, DRC, and Mali, the UN SC extended the imposition of sanctions to actors, individuals and entities, responsible for violations of international law involving the targeting of civilians, also children and women, in situations of armed conflict, including killing and maiming, sexual and gender-based violence, attacks on schools and hospitals, abduction, and forced displacement.[64] In such instances the links with the Security Council's thematic work are clear and are referred to in the preambles to the various resolutions. Other committees, i.e. the Sudan Sanctions Committee, the Libya Sanctions Committee, the CAR Sanctions Committee and the Yemen Sanctions Committee, adopt a less specific language on those acting in breach of human rights and humanitarian law,[65] which has been generally interpreted to cover also violations against children.[66] Nonetheless, such a mild language strikes with the fact that CAR, Libya, and Sudan, appeared in the Annual Report issued in 2017 as situations, still on the agenda of the UN SC, where grave violations against children are widely perpetrated, despite the perpetrators' alleged commitment to the action plans already in place.[67] Moreover, obstructing the delivery, or access to, or distribution of, humanitarian assistance in Somalia, DRC, South Sudan, Mali, CAR and Yemen is identified as a listing criterion by the respective sanctions committees, even though none of them specifically mentions the impact of this violation on children.[68]

With regard to the implementation of sanctions against individuals and entities responsible for the commission of grave violations of children's rights,

---

[59] Only with regard to Somalia, UN Doc. S/RES/2002 (2011), para. 1(d). Notably, the sanctions regime initially established for Somalia was extended to Eritrea following the UN SC's determination that Eritrea was providing support to ANSAs working to destabilize Somalia. UN Doc. S/RES1907 (2009), para. 14.

[60] UN Doc. S/RES/1857 (2008), para. 12.

[61] UN Doc. S/RES/2206 (2015), para. 7(e).

[62] UN Doc. S/RES/2374 (2017), para. 8(g).

[63] UN Doc. S/RES/2399 (2018), para. 21(d).

[64] UN Doc. S/RES/2093 (2013), para. 43(e); UN Doc. S/RES/2206 (2015), para. 7(d); UN Doc. S/RES/2293 (2016), para. 7(e); UN Doc. S/RES/2374 (2017), para. 8(f).

[65] See UN Doc. S/RES/1591 (2005), para. 3(c); UN Doc. S/RES/2213 (2015), para. 11(a); UN Doc. S/RES/2399 (2018), paras. 21(b) and (c); and UN Doc. S/RES/2140 (2014), para. 18(c), referring to "[…] planning, directing, or committing acts that violate applicable international human rights law or international humanitarian law, or acts that constitute human rights abuse […]".

[66] See THOMPSON, cit. supra note 4, p. 113.

[67] Annual Report 2017, supra note 9, paras. 36-49, 104-110, and 155-167.

[68] See UN Doc. S/RES/2093, para. 43(c); UN Doc. S/RES/2293 (2016), para. 7(f); UN Doc. S/RES/2206 (2015), para. 7; UN Doc. S/RES/2374 (2017), para. 8(f); UN Doc. S/RES/2399 (2018), para. 21(f); and UN Doc. S/RES/2216 (2015), para. 19.

it is worth stressing that the explicit or implicit inclusion of crimes against children in the listing criteria does not automatically lead to the prompt imposition of targeted measures. In fact, the committees *could* designate individuals and entities on the basis of the specified criteria, but it is not guaranteed that they will actually decide to do so.[69] So far, sanctions, in the form of travel ban and assets freeze, against individual perpetrators of crimes against children have been imposed in a handful of cases, i.e. DRC,[70] Côte d'Ivoire,[71] and South Sudan.[72] Concerning sanctions against entities, the DRC Sanctions Committee has been the only committee to date that has added three armed groups, i.e. the M23, the Forces Démocratiques pour la Libération du Rwanda (FDLR), and the Allied Democratic Forces (ADF), to the sanctions list in response to the commission of several violations of international law, including recruiting and using child soldier, as well as killing, maiming, and sexually abusing women and children.[73]

It has been argued that not having violations against children in armed conflict as a clear designation criterion makes it less likely that perpetrators will be added to the sanctions list on those grounds, also in cases where the UN SC is perfectly aware of the fact that one or more of the six grave violations against children have been committed.[74] Even though the truth of this statement is hardly questionable, it is important to highlight that the recent efforts to extend the sanctions regimes and formalize the inclusion of violations against children amidst the possible trigger for designation have not brought substantial changes to the Security Council's approach, nor reinvigorated its actions in this area.

---

[69] KOLLER and ECKENFELS-GARCIA, *cit. supra* note 22, p. 8.

[70] The largest use of sanctions against perpetrators of children's rights violations has been made in relation to DRC, where 19 individuals have been listed on these grounds.

[71] The sanctions regime concerning Côte d'Ivoire, terminated pursuant to UN Doc. S/RES/2283 (2016), had one militia leader designated for the recruitment and use of child soldiers. Security Council, Press Statement, "Security Council Committee Concerning Côte d'Ivoire Issues List of Individuals Subject to Measures Imposed by Resolution 1572 (2004)", 7 February 2006, UN Doc. SC/8631, available at: <http://www.un.org/press/en/2006/sc8631.doc.htm>.

[72] See Security Council, Press Statement, "Security Council Sanctions Committee Concerning South Sudan Adds Six Individuals to Its Sanctions List", 1 July 2015, UN Doc. SC/11958, available at: <https://www.un.org/press/en/2015/sc11958.doc.htm>.

[73] Security Council, Press Statement, "Sanctions Committee Concerning Democratic Republic of Congo Adds Two Individuals, Two Entities to Sanctions List", 31 December 2012, UN Doc. SC/10876, available at: <https://www.un.org/press/en/2012/sc10876.doc.htm>; Security Council, Press Statement, "Security Council Committee Concerning Democratic Republic of Congo Updates List of Individuals and Entities Subject to Travel Ban, Assets Freeze", 1 July 2014, UN Doc. SC/11459, available at: <https://www.un.org/press/en/2014/sc11459.doc.htm>.

[74] THOMPSON, *cit. supra* note 4, p. 116.

3.2. The Effectiveness of the Threat and Use of Targeted Sanctions in Response to Violations against Children in Armed Conflict

The UN SC has threatened sanctions in the face of the continued failure of the parties on the Secretary-General's "name and shame" Annexes to sign or implement action plans, but up until now it has rarely made good on the threats. Thus, as emerged from the brief overview of the sanctions regimes established and implemented so far, their concrete impact on the situation of children in armed conflict has not been particularly remarkable, and yet their invocation as a potentially powerful tool to effectively increase pressure on the perpetrators mentioned in the Annual Report has not diminished, especially in light of the fact that the mere possibility of being sanctioned by the UN SC can result in moral disapprobation and reputational harm that both States and ANSAs may seek to avoid. Broadly speaking two overarching considerations can be made on how to foster the effectiveness of the Security Council's sanctions practice in the field of children in armed conflict. *In primis*, the UN SC should consider including violations against children as a designation criterion in all future country-specific sanctions regimes. In fact, even if violations against children are not yet reported in a given situation, adding these violations to the sanctions regimes' mandates helps to spread a strong message of zero-tolerance across the international community that may deter potential offenders.[75] With regard to the situations where no sanctions regime exists, the UN SC has the option either to promptly establish new country-specific regimes or to create a thematic sanctions mechanism, with the Working Group acting as the Sanctions Committee.[76] The latter option would have the benefit of being readily available to implement targeted measures on those who commit crimes against children as soon as a conflict breaks out and/or violations are reported, thus overcoming the political and practical hurdles that often accompany the establishment of a new sanctions regime.[77] Regrettably, the possibility to set up a thematic sanctions regime has been debated during the 2012 Security Council's Annual Open Debate on Children and Armed Conflict and, since two permanent members of the UN SC, i.e. China and the United States, have expressed their opposition to this proposal, it is unlikely that practical actions in this sense will ever be undertaken.[78]

Secondly, since the list provided under Article 41 of the UN Charter includes some examples of measures that can be deployed, but it is not exhaustive, the Security Council might order any other measure whose purpose is to provide a sanction and which does not involve the use of armed force.[79] Hence, in principle

---

[75] KOLLER and ECKENFELS-GARCIA, *cit. supra* note 22, pp. 28-29.

[76] THOMPSON, *cit. supra* note 4, p. 116.

[77] KOLLER and ECKENFELS-GARCIA, *cit. supra* note 22, p. 29.

[78] See Watchlist on Children and Armed Conflict, "Review of the 2012 Security Council Open Debate on Children and Armed Conflict", 19 September 2012, available at: <https://watchlist.org/wp-content/uploads/Watchlist-review-and-analysis-of-Open-Debate-2012.pdf>.

[79] CONFORTI and FOCARELLI, *cit. supra* note 51, p. 234. An example of measure ex Art. 41 not considered by the UN Charter and nonetheless ordered by the Security Council is the institution of international criminal tribunals.

nothing stops the UN SC from envisaging and adopting new measures, or a wider combination of the existing ones, intended to have a stronger impact on ending and/or preventing grave violations against children.

Looking more closely at the issues singled out in section 2 of the present article, it is possible to affirm that increasing the use of targeted sanctions can contribute to improving the overall efficiency of the UN architecture on children and armed conflict, at least with regard to three of the main shortcomings identified above. In the first place unlike the action plans, which outline commitments concerning the five grave violations that can act as a trigger for the listing of a party in the Annexes to the Secretary-General's Annual Report, sanctions can be imposed also to individuals and entities that obstruct the delivery, or access to, or distribution of, humanitarian assistance when this violation is included in the designation criteria. The sanctions committees that have a specific mandate to monitor the denial to humanitarian access could contribute to filling an important gap and at the same time diverting the international community's attention from the phenomenon of child soldiering, which so far has almost monopolized the efforts of the UN tools devoted to promote the protection of children affected by armed conflict.

Another significant crack in the current UN architecture on children and armed conflict is represented by its inability to foster compliance by ANSAs labelled as "terrorist". Terrorist groups like ISIL and Al-Qaida are duly listed in the "name and shame" Annexes, and their crimes widely described across the Annual Report on Children and Armed Conflict.[80] These groups' complete lack of engagement with Governments and UN actors on the ground clearly shows that voluntary pledges in those instances are not a viable option and need to be replaced by the adoption of coercive measures. Even though both the ISIL (Da'esh) and Al-Qaida Sanctions Committee, and the so-called 1988 Sanctions Committee dealing with individuals, groups, undertakings, and entities associated with the Taliban in Afghanistan,[81] impose sanctions on the basis of affiliation with the terrorist groups and not on the basis of particular violations, placing emphasis on children's victimisation could sharpen the cooperation among relevant stakeholders and actors in the field of counter-terrorism, thus addressing the risks that terrorism poses not only as a global security threat, but as a phenomenon with wide human rights and humanitarian law implications in all the settings where it manifests itself.

Finally, as stressed in the course of this contribution, compliance-monitoring tools like the ones established under the aegis of the UN framework on children in armed conflict lack accountability mechanisms that render the perpetrators'

---

[80] Annual Report, 2017, *supra* note 9, in particular paras. 21-31, 76-79, and 188.

[81] CAPONE, "Countering 'Foreign Terrorist Fighters': A Critical Appraisal of the Framework Established by the UN Security Council Resolutions", IYIL, 2016, p. 228 ff., pp. 245-249; VAN DEN HERIK, "Peripheral Hegemony in the Quest to Ensure Security Council Accountability for Its Individualized UN Sanctions Regimes", Journal of Conflict & Security Law, 2014, p. 427 ff., pp. 442-445; BIANCHI, "Security Council's Anti-Terror Resolutions and their Implementation by Member States", JICJ, 2006, p. 1044 ff., pp. 1048-1051.

responsibility operational.[82] This shortcoming can be addressed only by developing a stronger relationship between the UN SC, the Working Group, the sanctions committees, and international justice mechanisms, especially the ICC.[83] In addition to increasing the level of communication and exchange of information between the Working Group on Children and Armed Conflict and the OTP of the ICC,[84] strengthening the link between the Court and the existing sanctions committees would also be of crucial importance. Several commentators have highlighted the asymmetry that exists between the list of ICC indictees and the Consolidated Sanctions List.[85] In order to provide support for the ICC work and overcome the mismatch between those lists, the UN sanctions committees might use their power to list individuals that are subject to arrest warrants issued by the Court's Pre-Trial Chambers.[86] The listing could, and should, not be limited to the situations referred by the UN SC, but extended to all the situations in which the Court is acting. Since the OTP has pledged to place a special focus on prosecuting crimes against children and, whenever the evidence permits, it is committed to "seek to include charges for crimes directed specifically against children, as well as crimes that acutely or disproportionately affect children",[87] building on mutual synergies with the Security Council and the sanctions committees is likely to improve the effectiveness of actions with respect to crimes affecting children.

4. CONCLUSION

The history of international humanitarian law shows that States have consistently rejected any form of binding supervision of their conduct in armed conflict, especially in NIACs,[88] and that in most instances ANSAs that are parties to armed conflicts may lack either the will or capacity to enforce legal provisions, including those related to the protection of children. In this "far from ideal" scenario the establishment and development of a complex system for monitoring and reporting violations committed by both States and ANSAs has put under the spotlight the harm suffered by children, paving the way for a period of innovation, engagement and substantial efforts.[89] Nevertheless, many relevant problems remain. As discussed in the present article, the most important shortcoming of the current

---

[82] See RYNGAERT and VAN DE MEULEBROUCKE, *cit. supra* note 12, p. 461.

[83] THOMPSON, *cit. supra* note 4, p. 117.

[84] See *supra* section 2.

[85] THOMPSON, *cit. supra* note 4, p. 117.

[86] See RUIZ VERDUZCO, "The Relationship between the ICC and the United Nations Security Council", in STAHN (ed.), *The Law and Practice of the International Criminal Court*, Oxford, 2015, p. 30 ff., p. 61-64.

[87] ICC/OTP, "Policy on Children", November 2016, available at: <https://www.icc-cpi.int/iccdocs/otp/20161115_otp_icc_policy-on-children_eng.pdf>.

[88] PFANNER, "Various Mechanisms and Approaches for Implementing International Humanitarian Law and Protecting and Assisting War Victims", International Review of the Red Cross, 2009, p. 279 ff., p. 307.

[89] THOMPSON, *cit. supra* note 4, p 99.

framework is that the pledges made by the State and non-State actors that sign the action plans may not be worth much if they are not backed up by credible enforcement mechanisms. In order to fill this gap and enhance the consistency of the existing framework, the threat and use of sanctions has been widely and often invoked as a means to alter the behaviour of offenders of children's rights during war. However, so far the intention to implement sanctions has been declared in several instances by the Security Council, but not acted upon, raising legitimate questions as to whether the body that has fully supported the issue of children in armed conflict over many years will ever be inclined to consider new approaches and possible changes to sharpen the existing framework.

The growing involvement of the UN SC in the issue of conflict-affected children can arguably be seen as a natural component of its mandated function to maintain international peace and security, and is in line with the declared scope of the UN, which is "to save succeeding generations from the scourge of war".[90] Hence, due to the Security Council's engagement, on the one hand there is certainly a greater attention registered at the global level towards the situation of children in armed conflict, but on the other hand there are significant limits that derive primarily from the fact that the UN SC action (or inaction) is often politically motivated.[91] This means that the UN architecture on children and armed conflict and its tools are highly dependent on political considerations, as emerges, for example, from the overly cautious approach of the Working Group in the formulation of its recommendations,[92] the UN SC sparing deployment of targeted sanctions against perpetrators of grave violations against children, and the refusal to consider the possibility to set up a thematic sanctions committee to implement measures against individuals and entities responsible for the victimisation of children in armed conflict. Of course a more systematic and coherent use of sanctions by the UN SC could not redress and overcome all the shortcomings of the UN architecture on children and armed conflict as some of them, like the lack of focus on the post-conflict dimension, would require to rethink and expand the scope of the whole framework. Nonetheless, increasing and strengthening the effective use of sanctions could contribute to the development of a new and more comprehensive strategy towards parties, and in particular ANSAs, that have not responded to current forms of pressure.

---

[90] See the Preamble to the UN Charter. See NYLUND and HYLLESTED, cit. supra note 21, p. 75.

[91] Ibid., p. 86.

[92] See HAPPOLD, "Protecting Children in Armed Conflict: Harnessing the Security Council's 'Soft Power'", Israel Law Review, 2010, p. 360 ff., p. 370.

Focus
THE ILC'S WORK ON THE IDENTIFICATION
OF CUSTOMARY INTERNATIONAL LAW

THOUGHTS ON DOMESTIC ADJUDICATION
AND THE IDENTIFICATION AND FORMATION
OF CUSTOMARY INTERNATIONAL LAW

CAMERON MILES[*]

Abstract

Article 38(1)(d) of the ICJ Statute provides that "judicial decisions" may serve as a subsidiary means for the determination of customary international law. The absence of a qualifying adjective to the term "judicial decisions" confirms that, at least ex facie, there is no priority to be given to international over domestic judgments in this respect. And yet – as the International Law Commission's Draft Conclusions on Formation and Identification of Customary International Law confirms – the reality of international adjudication is one in which domestic judicial decisions are often side-lined. In this paper, I question the ILC's assertion that this is due to the relative expertise of international versus domestic courts, and instead posit a model based on the shifting architectonics of international adjudication. Two related developments are key: (1) the florescence of international adjudicative bodies in the post-1945 era, and (2) the tendency for international courts and tribunals to see domestic judicial decisions as evidence of state practice and opinio juris under Article 38(1)(b), rather than as subsidiary means for the determination of custom – that is, as factual rather than legal precedents.

Keywords: customary international law; domestic courts and tribunals; international courts and tribunals; International Law Commission; International Court of Justice

1. INTRODUCTION

The mid-19th century was a time of evolution for international law. Whilst the field as a whole was still little more than a rule-based extrusion of international diplomacy – what WE Hall accurately (and perhaps slightly cruelly) dubbed "a rough jurisprudence of nations"[1] – certain areas demonstrated capacity

---

[*] LLM, PhD (Cantab); Barrister, 3 Verulam Buildings, London. An earlier version of this paper was given as part of a panel on the ILC's work on customary international law at the 3rd biennial conference of the Italian branch of the International Law Association at LIUC Università Cattaneo in Milan on 17 November 2017. Many thanks to the Yearbook's editors, Professor Attila Tanzi, Dr. Eirik Bjorge, Mr. William Bateman, Ms. Arezou Farivar and my fellow panellists for their helpful comments on earlier drafts. The usual caveat applies.

[1] HALL, *A Treatise on International Law*, 8th ed., Oxford, 1924, p. 395.

for development. Chief amongst these was the (largely[2]) customary law of prize, being the system of rules that permitted belligerent states to seize maritime assets during time of war.[3] But it might surprise modern observers to learn that one of the driving forces behind the development of prize law during that time was a single British judge, Sir Walter Scott (later Lord Stowell), sitting in the High Court of Admiralty.[4]

Roughly a century and a half later, a very different picture presents itself. Outside of certain discrete sectors, the idea of a domestic judge having a profound impact on public international law – let alone being recognised as one the greatest international lawyers of his or her day, as Scott was[5] – seems, at best, a remote concept. This much is reflected in Draft Conclusions of the International Law Commission (ILC) on the formation and identification of customary international law,[6] with Draft Conclusion 13(2) reading:

> Regard may be had, *as appropriate*, to decisions of national courts concerning the existence and content of rules of customary international law, as a subsidiary means for the determination of such rules.

The inclusion by the ILC of the (mildly condescending) "as appropriate" tells the historically aware reader that something in the structure of international law has altered to diminish the role of domestic adjudication – formerly one of the laboratories of the law of nations – as a driving force for normative development.[7] The purpose of this article is to offer a few thoughts on what that something might have been in the context of customary international law[8] – with a

---

[2] But see Declaration of Paris concerning Maritime Law, 16 April 1856, entered into force 16 April 1856. Further: STOCKTON, "The Declaration of Paris", AJIL, 1920, p. 356 ff.

[3] Generally: KRASKA, "Prize Law", in WOLFRUM (ed.), *Max Planck Encyclopedia of Public International Law*, 2009, available at: <http://opil.ouplaw.com/home/EPIL>.

[4] BOURGUIGNON, *Sir William Scott, Lord Stowell: Judge of the High Court of Admiralty, 1798–1828*, Cambridge, 1978. The bulk of his more important judgments can be found in ROSCOE (ed.), *Reports of Prize Cases Determined in the High Court of Admiralty before the Lords Commissioners of Appeals in Prize Causes, and before the Judicial Committee of the Privy Council, from 1745 to 1859*, Vol. II, London, 1905. Ironically, Sir William was not the best lawyer in his family – his younger brother, John, became Lord Eldon, the celebrated equity judge and Lord Chancellor.

[5] BOURGUIGNON, *cit. supra* note 4, pp. 280–285. See also ZEIGLER, *The International Law of John Marshall: A Study of First Principles*, Chapel Hill, 1939, pp. 18–19.

[6] Set out with commentaries in ILC, Report on the work of the sixty-eighth session, UN Doc A/71/10 (2016), p. 79 (Draft Conclusions Commentary). See also the complementary memorandum prepared by the ILC Secretariat, Identification of customary international law: The role of decisions of national courts in the case law of international courts and tribunals of a universal character for the purpose of the determination of customary international law, UN Doc A/CN.4/691 (2016).

[7] For one measure of comparison, see BJORGE and MILES, "Introduction", in BJORGE and MILES (eds.), *Landmark Cases in Public International Law*, Oxford, 2017, p. 1 ff., pp. 1–3.

[8] Decisions of domestic courts are also of relevance to other sources of international law. They are considered state practice within the meaning of Art. 31(3)(b) of the Vienna

particular focus on certain structures of international adjudication that reflect the changing character of international law in the post-1945 era.

Put another way, the question to be answered is this: why do international courts and tribunals inevitably serve as the final arbiter of what is and is not customary international law when compared to their domestic counterparts?

2. THE FORMAL ROLE OF DOMESTIC COURTS IN THE IDENTIFICATION AND FORMATION OF CUSTOMARY INTERNATIONAL LAW

The question can only be explained when one looks at the *formal* role played by domestic courts in the identification and formation of customary international law. Within the positive law on the sources of international law, international courts do not have any *a priori* supremacy over their domestic counterparts. Article 38(1)(d) of the ICJ Statute is clear on the point, providing (in the relevant part) that:[9]

> The Court, whose function it is to decide in accordance with international law such disputes as are submitted to it, shall apply [...] judicial decisions and the teachings of the most highly qualified publicists of the various nations, as a subsidiary means for the determination of rules of law.

As Andenas and Leiss point out, the function of Article 38(1)(d) is to provide a basic communicative framework for "communitarian semantics" and "systematic institutional integration" in the development of international law.[10] Put another way, it creates something of a nervous system for the horizontally-organized network of international courts and tribunals that purport to apply international law in the resolution of contested issues – and their counterparts on the domestic legal plane.

Convention on the Law of Treaties, 23 May 1969, entered into force 27 January 1980. They may also serve as a source of general principles of law within the meaning of Art 38(1)(c) of the ICJ Statute: *Oil Platforms (Iran v. United States of America)*, Judgment of 6 November 2003, Separate Opinion of Judge Simma, ICJ Reports, 2003, p. 161 ff., paras. 66–74. The latter is subject to the admonition of Judge McNair in the *South West Africa* advisory opinion: *International Status of South West Africa*, Advisory Opinion of 11 July 1950, Separate Opinion of Sir Arnold McNair, ICJ Reports, 1950, p. 128 ff., p. 148.

[9] Art. 38(1)(d) is perhaps less well-understood than the other sub-paragraphs of Art. 38(1), but there are some significant discussions of the provision as it applies to judicial decisions: see e.g. NOLLKAEMPER, "The Role of Domestic Courts in the Case Law of the International Court of Justice", Chinese Journal of International Law, 2006, p. 301 ff.; THIRLWAY, *The Sources of International Law*, Oxford, 2014, pp. 120–126; ANDENAS and LEISS, "The Systematic Relevance of 'Judicial Decisions' in Article 38 of the ICJ Statute", ZaöRV, 2017, p. 1 ff. For a recent discussion of the application of Art. 38(1)(d) to "the teachings of the most-highly qualified publicists of the various nations", see SIVAKUMARAN, "The Influence of Teachings of Publicists on the Development of International Law", ICLQ, 2017, p. 1 ff.

[10] ANDENAS and LEISS, *cit. supra* note 9, pp. 8–16.

It is by now more or less agreed that Article 38(1)(d) applies to domestic judgments.[11] Within the provision, no jurisdictional adjective is appended to the words "judicial decisions". *Ex facie*, international and domestic judicial decisions carry equal weight as subsidiary means for the determination of rules of law – including custom. The text of Article 38(1)(d), moreover, must be viewed in light of its drafting by the 1920 Advisory Commission of Jurists, prior to its inclusion in the PCIJ Statute as Article 38(4).[12] At that time – with the (notably failed) exception of the Central American Court of Justice[13] – no international court or tribunal of plenary jurisdiction existed, such that there was no reliably expanding reservoir of judicial decisions, of a (more or less) guaranteed consistency and considering all aspects of international law from which to draw. As a consequence, the *ad hoc* international arbitral tribunals and claims commissions of the 19th and early 20th century had become accustomed to using the decisions of domestic courts as a subsidiary means for the determination of custom.[14] The utility of domestic decisions in this respect was made clear in the *Trail Smelter* case, where it was noted:

> No case of air pollution dealt with by an international tribunal has been brought to the attention of the Tribunal nor does the Tribunal know of any such case. The nearest analogy is that of water pollution. But, here also, no decision of an international tribunal has been cited or has been found. There are, however, as regards both air pollution and water pollution, certain decisions of the Supreme Court of the United States which may legitimately be taken as a guide in this field of international law, for it is legitimate to follow by analogy, in international cases, precedents established by that court or with other controversies concerning the quasi-sovereign rights of such States, where no contrary rule prevails in international law and no reason for rejecting such precedents can be adduced from the limitations of sovereignty inherent in the Constitution of the United States.[15]

Moreover, and notwithstanding their formal equality in Article 38(1)(d), domestic courts may be superior to their international counterparts in terms of

---

[11] *Ibid.*, 52.

[12] For a discussion of consideration of domestic judicial decisions by the 1920 Advisory Committee in the *travaux préparatoires* of Art. 38(1)(d), see ILC Secretariat, *cit. supra* note 6, paras. 7–14. See also ANDENAS and LEISS, *cit. supra* note 9, p. 19.

[13] Further: HUDSON, "The Central American Court of Justice", AJIL, 1932, p. 759 ff.; ALLAIN, *A Century of International Adjudication: The Rule of Law and Its Limits*, Berlin, 2003, pp. 67-92.

[14] See e.g. *Aroa Mines (Great Britain v. Venezuela)*, 1903, Reports of International Arbitral Awards, Vol. IX, 2006, p. 402 ff., pp. 413 and 436; *ER Kelley (United States of America v. United Mexican States)*, 8 October 1930, Reports of International Arbitral Awards, Vol. IV, 2006, p. 608 ff., pp. 612–613.

[15] *Trail Smelter Case (United States v. Canada)*, 16 April 1938 and 11 March 1941, Reports of International Arbitral Awards, Vol. III, 2006, p. 1905 ff., pp. 1963–1964.

their wider utility to customary international law. Article 38(1)(d) is of general application – that is, it applies equally to each of the formal sources of law that are listed in the provision. But in the text of Article 38, domestic courts make a repeat, albeit indirect, appearance when the discussion turns to customary international law in Article 38(1)(b). Acts of a state's judiciary are acts of the state itself[16] – and accordingly generate state practice and *opinio juris*[17] that may, in turn, harden into custom. International courts, as they are not formal lawmakers in the international system, cannot so contribute.[18] Put another way, both international and domestic courts can *identify* customary international law – but only domestic courts have a part to play in its *formation*.

3. DOMESTIC JUDGMENTS AND THE ILC'S DRAFT CONCLUSIONS ON THE FORMATION AND IDENTIFICATION OF CUSTOM

Confronted with the formalistic position set out above, an observer might well protest that, whatever the plain wording of Article 38(1)(d), the reality of international adjudication is rather different. It is this reality that has been acknowledged by the ILC in Draft Conclusion 13(2). Further explanation is given in the commentary to that provision, where it is said:

> Some caution is called for when seeking to rely on decisions of national courts as a subsidiary means for the determination of rules of customary international law. [...] [I]t has to be borne in mind that national courts operate within a particular legal system, which may incorporate international law only in a particular way and to a

---

[16] *Difference relating to Immunity from Legal Process of a Special Rapporteur of the Commission on Human Rights*, Advisory Opinion of 29 April 1999, ICJ Reports, 1999, p. 62 ff., para. 62.

[17] See e.g. *Nottebohm (Liechtenstein v. Guatemala)*, Judgment of 6 April 1955, ICJ Reports, 1955, p. 4 ff., p. 22; *Arrest Warrant of 11 April 2000 (Democratic Republic of the Congo v. Belgium)*, Judgment of 14 February 2002, ICJ Reports, 2002, p. 3 ff., paras. 56–58; *Jurisdictional Immunities of the State (Germany v. Italy; Greece intervening)*, Judgment of 3 February 2012, ICJ Reports, 2012, p. 99 ff., paras. 55, 64, 71–77 and 118.

[18] An international judicial decision – being the product of a mechanism by which the parties ask a third-party adjudicator to resolve some question of customary international law and then abide by the result – can arguably be conceived of as a source of state practice under Art. 38(1)(b). In this, the decision may be seen to play a similar role to a resolution of an international organization (e.g. the UN General Assembly), which may serve as an item of collective state practice and *opinio juris* that is subsequently seen as reflecting custom: THIRLWAY, *cit. supra* note 9, pp. 79–81; Draft Conclusions Commentary, *cit. supra* note 6, Art. 4, paras. 3–8. But this hypothesis is unavailing in the case of an international judicial decision, for three reasons: (1) compliance with the decision may be seen as a consequence of the binding force of the decision (see e.g. Art. 59 of the ICJ Statute) rather than agreement with the reasoning behind it (resulting in a failure of *opinio juris*); (2) even if (1) is not the case, it is formally state compliance with the underlying decision which is constitutive of state practice, not the decision itself; (3) in any event, the court or tribunal conceives of itself only as assessing *existing* practice as part of its adjudicative function, not generating *new* practice *sua sponte*.

limited extent. Unlike international courts, national courts may lack international law expertise and may have reached their decisions without the benefit of hearing argument by States.[19]

This stands in contrast to the treatment given to international courts and tribunals – and particularly the ICJ – in Draft Conclusion 13(1), which provides without qualification that:

> Decisions of international courts and tribunals, in particular of the International Court of Justice, concerning the existence and content of rules of customary international law, are a subsidiary means for the determination of such rules.

To the eyes of the international lawyer who practices not infrequently before domestic courts, this seems a little churlish. True it is, there are any number of domestic decisions that may be seen to get international law wrong. One need only point to decisions such as that of the Italian Court of Cassation in *Ferrini*,[20] which was overruled by the ICJ in *Jurisdictional Immunities* (to be returned to presently), or to the decision of the Ghanaian High Court[21] that prompted the *ARA Libertad* case[22] under Part XV of the UN Convention on the Law of the Sea,[23] to be reminded of this fact.

However, it is not as though the record of international courts and tribunals is entirely spotless – and the international case law contains its fair share of decisions that some observers may consider misguided. In *Tadić*, the International Criminal Tribunal for the former Yugoslavia (ICTY) attempted to recast the ICJ's *Nicaragua* test of "effective control" of non-state actors[24] for the purposes of attribution as one of "overall control" – a lesser standard.[25] A sharp corrective was

---

[19] Draft Conclusions Commentary, *cit. supra* note 6, Art. 13, para. 7.

[20] *Corte di Cassazione (Sezioni Unite Civili)*, *Ferrini v. Federal Republic of Germany*, 11 March 2004, No. 5044, ILR, Vol. 128, 2006, p. 658 ff. See also the subsequent decision of the Italian Constitutional Court rejecting the *Jurisdiction Immunities* judgment as unconstitutional: *Corte Costituzionale*, *Simoncioni, Alessi and Bergamini v. Federal Republic of Germany and Presidency of the Council of Ministers*, 22 October 2014, No. 238, IYIL, 2014, p. 1 ff., with comments by FRANCIONI, PISILLO, BOTHE, CATALDI, and PALCHETTI; CHECHI, IDLC 2237 (IT 2014). Further: TANZI, "Un Difficile Dialogo tra Corte Internazionale di Giustizia e Corte Costituzionale", CI, 2015, p. 13 ff.; PALCHETTI, "Judgment No 238/2014 of the Italian Constitutional Court: In Search of a Way Out", QIL, Zoom-out II, 2014, p. 44 ff.

[21] Set out in *Ghana v. High Court (Commercial Division) Accra, ex parte Attorney-General (NML Capital Ltd and Republic of Argentina, interested parties)*, Judgment of 20 June 2013, ILR, Vol. 156, 2014, p. 240 ff.

[22] *ARA Libertad (Argentina v. Ghana)*, Order of 15 December 2012, ITLOS Reports, 2012, p. 332 ff.

[23] United Nations Convention on the Law of the Sea, 10 December 1982, entered into force 16 November 1994.

[24] *Military and Paramilitary Activities in and against Nicaragua (Nicaragua v. United States of America)*, Judgment of 27 June 1986, ICJ Reports, 1986, p. 14 ff., paras. 115–116.

[25] *Prosecutor v. Tadić (Appeal Against Conviction)*, Judgment of 15 July 1999, ILR, Vol. 126, 2003, p. 61 ff., para. 131.

issued in the *Bosnian Genocide* case,[26] but the international community had to wait eight years to get clarity on the subject. The PCIJ's inelegant formulation of the so-called "*Lotus* principle"[27] – producing a kind of "crude atomism"[28] – persisted unchecked for decades until it was finally dragged from its pedestal in *Arrest Warrant*, never to be rehabilitated.[29] And in decisions such as in *Kadi*[30] and *Achmea*,[31] the CJEU may be seen to have prioritized the purity of the EU juridical order over the wider coherence of the international legal system that created it, to the ultimate detriment of both.

At the same time, there are decisions of domestic courts that have proved invaluable in our understanding of custom. It is difficult, for example, to conceive of the law on state secession – a subject of deep contemporary relevance – without the Supreme Court of Canada's masterful judgment in the *Quebec Secession Reference*.[32] Similarly, the judgment of Lord Denning MR, sitting in the Court of Appeal of England and Wales, in *Trendtex v. Central Bank of Nigeria*[33] ushered in (at least for common law legal systems[34]) the restrictive theory of state immunity that is now given full voice in Article 10 of the UN Convention on the Jurisdictional Immunity of States and Their Property.[35]

To put the matter more pithily, the institutional characteristics of domestic courts do not necessarily entail a greater possibility of legal error – nor do the in-

---

[26] *Application of the Convention on the Prevention and Punishment of the Crime of Genocide (Bosnia and Herzegovina v. Serbia and Montenegro*, Judgment of 26 February 2007, ICJ Reports, 2007, p. 43 ff., paras. 399–407. Further: CRAWFORD, *State Responsibility: The General Part*, Cambridge, 2013, pp. 146–156.

[27] *SS Lotus (France v. Turkey)*, Judgment of 7 September 1927, PCIJ Reports, Series A, No. 10, p. 1 ff., pp. 19–20.

[28] LOWE, *International Law*, Oxford, 2007, p. 241.

[29] *Arrest Warrant, cit. supra* note 17, Separate Opinion of Judges Higgins, Kooijmans and Buergenthal, paras. 49–52. On the decline of the *Lotus* principle, see further GUILFOYLE, "*SS Lotus (France v Turkey)* (1927)", in BJORGE and MILES (eds.), *Landmark Cases in Public International Law*, Oxford, 2017, p. 89 ff.

[30] Joined Cases C-402/05 P & C-415/05 P, *Kadi and Al Barakaat International Foundation v. Council and Commission*, ECR, 2008, I–6351. Further: DE BÚRKA, "The European Court of Justice and the International Legal Order After *Kadi*", Harvard ILJ, 2010, p. 1 ff.; cf. KOKOTT and SOBOTTA, "The *Kadi* Case – Constitutional Core Values and International Law – Finding the Balance", EJIL, 2012, p. 1015 ff.

[31] C-284/16, *Slovak Republic v. Achmea BV*, Judgment of 6 March 2018.

[32] *Reference Re Secession of Quebec* [1998] 2 SCR 217, paras. 109–146; MACNEIL, IDLC 187 (CA 1998).

[33] *Trendtex Trading Corporation v. Central Bank of Nigeria* [1977] QB 529, 555A–557G (CA); MURRAY, IDLC 1735 (UK 1977). See also *Rahimtoola v. Nizam of Hyderabad* [1958] AC 379, 422 (HL); *Thai-Europe Tapioca Service Ltd v. Government of Pakistan, Directorate of Agricultural Supplies* [1975] 1 WLR 1485, 1491 (CA).

[34] Civilian systems had proved rather more enlightened, with Italian and Belgian courts introducing the restrictive theory of state immunity in the early 20th century: see the cases referred to in Judgment No. 238/2014, *cit. supra* note 20, para. 3.3.

[35] United Nations Convention on Jurisdictional Immunities of States and Their Property, 2 December 2004, not yet in force. Further: WITTICH, "Article 10", in O'KEEFE and TAMS (eds.), *The United Nations Convention on Jurisdictional Immunity of States and Their Property*, Oxford, 2013, p. 167 ff.

stitutional characteristics of international courts entail a greater prospect of success. Indeed, the latter seems to have been implicitly acknowledged by the ILC in its commentary to Draft Conclusion 13, where it said:

> Decisions of [international] courts and tribunals on questions of international law, in particular those decisions in which the existence of rules of customary international law is considered and such rules are identified and applied, may offer valuable guidance for determining the existence or otherwise of rules of customary international law. *The value of such decisions varies greatly, however, depending both on the quality of the reasoning of such decisions (including the extent to which it is founded upon a close examination of evidence of an alleged general practice accepted as law) and on the reception of the decision by States and by other courts.* Other considerations might, depending on the circumstances, include the composition of the court or tribunal (and the particular expertise of its members); the size of the majority by which the decision was adopted; and the conditions under which the court or tribunal operates/conducts its work. [...][36]

The ILC's assertion that the precedential force of a judicial decision under Article 38(1)(d) is dependent on the quality of that decision's reasoning (with special regard to the decision's proper identification of state practice and *opinio juris*) creates problems for its prioritization of international over domestic adjudication. If the ILC's assertion that Article 38(1)(d) is primarily concerned with the quality of a decision's reasoning alone, then any notion of an *a priori* international supremacy must fail on its own terms. Reference may be made in this respect to Talmon's argument that the ICJ (the *ne plus ultra* of Article 38(1)(d), according to the ILC) has been known to derive customary international law from mere assertion, rather than a rigorous and predictable methodology – a thesis that, if true, diminishes the persuasiveness of the Court's decisions on the subject.[37]

From this, we see that the ILC has glibly drawn something of a false dichotomy in Draft Conclusion 13. And yet the ILC's ultimate premise is instinctively correct – decisions of international courts *do* carry greater weight in the identification of custom than do domestic courts. Why is this the case? I would like to suggest two answers based on the structure of international adjudication: one simple, and one slightly more complicated.

---

[36] Draft Conclusions Commentary, *cit. supra* note 6, Art. 13, para. 3 (emphasis added).
[37] TALMON, "Determining Customary International Law: The ICJ's Methodology between Induction, Deduction and Assertion", EJIL, 2015, p. 417 ff. See also CHIGARA, *The Legitimacy Deficit in Custom: A Deconstructionalist Critique*, Burlington, 2001, p. xix.

4. THE DUAL REALITY OF DOMESTIC JUDGMENTS

4.1. Development of international adjudication and international law

The first answer concerns the development of international law and international adjudication over the course of the 20th century, over the course of which it is fair to say the field was transformed into a modern legal discipline concerned with the practical application of the law.[38] Before 1945, international law-making processes were far more disparate than they are today. The primary engine of international law was not treaty, but custom.[39] The ILC did not exist, and codification efforts – such as the 1930 Hague Conference conducted under the auspices of the League of Nations – were sporadic and prone to failure.[40] The PCIJ was extant, but seised only rarely, and other international tribunals were invariably temporary in character, or boasted restricted jurisdictional mandates,[41] e.g. the inter-war Mixed Arbitral Tribunals.

By contrast, today there exists a constellation of international courts and tribunals of increasingly specialized jurisdiction building a similarly increasing corpus of case law.[42] This process began in 1945 with the inauguration of the ICJ as successor to the PCIJ, but accelerated dramatically with the fall of the Berlin Wall, when international adjudicative organs of specialized and compulsory jurisdiction (the International Tribunal for the Law of the Sea, the Dispute Settlement Body of the World Trade Organization, regional human rights and economic bodies, investor-state arbitration tribunals, etc.) began to emerge – a by-product of a moment of world history where the "old" way of doing things appeared to be disrupted, prompting a search for "new" strategies by political actors.[43] Whatever one may feel about the permanence of that moment,[44] the struc-

---

[38] SPIERMANN, "Twentieth Century Internationalism in Law", EJIL, 2007, p. 785 ff.

[39] CRAWFORD, "Chance, Order, Change: The Course of International Law", RCADI, Vol. 365, 2013, p. 9 ff., p. 90.

[40] ROSENNE (ed.), *League of Nations Conference on the Codification of International Law (1930)*, Vol. I, The Hague, 1975, p. xliii. The failure of the 1930 Hague Conference – in which the codifying impulse was placed in the political context of an international conference supported by governments – proved a powerful motivation for the development of the rather more insular and successful model of the ILC: CRAWFORD, "The Progressive Development of International Law: History, Theory and Practice", in ALLAND et al. (eds.) *Unity and Diversity of International Law: Essays in Honour of Professor Pierre-Marie Dupuy*, Leiden, 2014, p. 1 ff.

[41] O'CONNELL and VANDERZEE, "The History of International Adjudication", in ROMANO, ALTER and SHANY (eds.), *The Oxford Handbook of International Adjudication*, Oxford, 2015, p. 40 ff.

[42] KINGSBURY, "International Courts: Uneven Judicialisation in Global Order", in CRAWFORD and KOSKENNIEMI (eds.), *The Cambridge Companion to International Law*, Cambridge, 2012, p. 203 ff., pp. 205-211.

[43] ALTER, "The Multiplication of International Courts and Tribunals After the End of the Cold War", in ROMANO, ALTER and SHANY (eds.), *cit. supra* note 41, p. 63 ff.

[44] CRAWFORD, "The Current Political Discourse Concerning International Law", Modern Law Review, 2018, p. 1 ff.

ture of international adjudication that emerged from it remains – and a globalized legal profession and academy is on hand to disseminate its decisions widely.[45]

Further and in addition, international law itself has changed. The field has undergone a process of "widening and thickening",[46] growing from its essentially bilateral or transactional roots and becoming far more diverse, regulating areas such as the trade, investment, the environment, human rights, criminal law, etc.[47] Now that the pearl-clutching of the fragmentation debate (so-called) of the late 20th/early 21st century has abated,[48] we see a system in which states are increasingly willing to allocate swathes of inter-state (and even intra-state) relations to the province of law, conditioning sovereign autonomy thereby. In large part, however, the norms generated by this system will not ordinarily be subject to domestic legal processes – and even if they are, domestic courts may on occasion bar themselves from pronouncing on such matters through public law doctrines of non-justiciability, such as Crown and foreign act of state.[49]

A fortiori, given states' appetite for international adjudication and international law, the opportunities for a domestic court to pronounce on customary international law have diminished accordingly.[50] At the same time, given the optional jurisdiction of a great many international courts and tribunals (including the ICJ), and the limited capacity for others to determine the sheer volume of disputes that touch on international issues, a vacuum is created that domestic courts may be able to fill.[51] But as the ILC Secretariat has noted, the areas in which deci-

---

[45] SCHACHTER, "The Invisible College of International Lawyers", Northwestern University Law Review, 1977, p. 217 ff. This longstanding utopian view has recently been demonstrated to have its limits, at least in terms of the diversity of players involved in the game: ROBERTS, *Is International Law International?*, Oxford, 2017.

[46] HIGGINS, "A Babel of Judicial Voices: Ruminations from the Bench", ICLQ, 2006, p. 791 ff., p. 792.

[47] CRAWFORD, *cit. supra* note 39, p. 228. Further: GREENWOOD, "Unity and Diversity in International Law", in ANDENAS and BJORGE (eds.), *A Farewell to Fragmentation: Reassertion and Convergence in International Law*, Cambridge, 2017, p. 37 ff.

[48] KOSKENNIEMI, Fragmentation of International Law: Difficulties Arising from the Diversification and Expansion of International Law, UN Doc A/CN.4/L/682 (2014).

[49] In the UK, see most recently *Rahmatulluh v. Ministry of Defence* [2017] 2 WLR 287; *Belhaj v. Straw & Ors (United Nations Special Rapporteur & Ors intervening)* [2017] 2 WLR 456. Further: MALEK and MILES, "International Dimensions", in CLARRY (ed.), *The UK Supreme Court Yearbook, Vol 8: 2016–2017 Judicial Year*, London, 2017, p. 447 ff; SMITH, "Acts of State in *Belhaj* and *Rahmatullah*", Law Quarterly Review, 2018, p. 20 ff. On doctrines of non-justiciability in the civil law, see CRAWFORD, *Brownlie's Principles of Public International Law*, 8th ed., Oxford, 2012, pp. 103–110.

[50] This remains the case even when considering synchronizing concepts such as the incorporation of custom into domestic law, the utility of which – in the common law tradition at least – has always been more exaggerated than real: O'KEEFE, "The Doctrine of Incorporation Revisited", BYIL, 2008, p. 7 ff. See also *Tel-Oren v. Libyan Arab Republic*, 726 F.2d 744, 811 (DC Cir, 1984) (Bork J). For concepts of customary incorporation in the civil law, see CRAWFORD, *cit. supra* note 49, pp. 88–93.

[51] CONANT, "Whose Agents? The Interpretation of International Law in National Courts", in DUNOFF and POLLACK (eds.), *Interdisciplinary Perspectives on International Law and International Relations: The State of the Art*, Cambridge, 2013, p. 394 ff., p. 394. This is particularly the case in jurisdictions (such as the US and Australia) that are not part of a sophisti-

sions of domestic courts are considered relevant to custom are largely confined to areas concerning their own jurisdiction over states and their agents – enforcement jurisdiction, supervisory jurisdiction, state immunity, diplomatic immunity, etc.[52] In addition, when a domestic court is called upon to decide a contested point, specialist counsel are on hand to direct them towards the most recent international jurisprudence, guiding the court back towards the international *status quo* and reducing the scope for innovation or elaboration.[53] Thus, whereas previously the appellate courts of a small number of developed states were among the most authoritative judicial voices in international law, the present state of play is one in which international courts have a functional (if not formal) superiority to domestic courts. Gone, therefore, are the days of cases such as *R v. Keyn*, where an English court was able to produce a decision that shaped the juridical conception of the territorial sea in international law.[54]

4.2. Aggregation and refinement of customary norms

So the development of international law and its adjudication is one reason for the current dominance of international courts and tribunals in the identification of custom.[55] What is the other one? Put shortly, it concerns the way in which international and domestic legal adjudication differs as a process – and the ways in which questions of customary international law may find themselves intertwined with the case at bar. It is rare in domestic proceedings for questions of customary international law to dominate proceedings. For the most part, they occupy the periphery – an interesting sideshow, to be sure, but hardly the main game. Even *Trendtex v. Central Bank of Nigeria* – pronouncements on the competing theories of immunity aside – was at its core a rather pedestrian commercial dis-

---

cated international court system that interfaces directly with domestic law: WARD, "National and International Litigation: Partners or Competitors?", in KLEIN (ed.), *Litigating International Disputes: Weighing the Options*, Cambridge, 2014, p. 42 ff.

[52] ILC Secretariat, *cit. supra* note 6, para. 23. Further: *Jurisdictional Immunities, cit. supra* note 17, Separate Opinion of Judge Keith, para. 4.

[53] Though some decisions still slip the net: see e.g. *La Générale des Carrières et des Mines v. FG Hemisphere Associates LLC* [2013] 1 All ER 409 (PC); RISVAS, ILDC 2014 (UK 2012), where the Privy Council decided what was functionally a question on attribution and state responsibility by principal reference to the law of state immunity. This slightly curious choice can perhaps be chalked up to the fact that neither of the counsel appearing before the Privy Council had specialist experience in international law, leading them to argue the case by reference to the State Immunity Act 1974 (UK) out of sheer familiarity: O'KEEFE, "Decisions of British Courts during 2012 Involving Questions of Public International Law", BYIL, 2013, p. 202 ff., p. 236, note 134.

[54] *R v. Keyn ("The Franconia")* (1876) 2 Ex D 63. Despite the enduring significance of the decision, the case made no such determination as a matter of *ratio decidendi*, and it is irresponsible to suggests that it stands for any sort of concrete proposition: MILES, "The *Franconia* Sails On: Revisiting the Intellectual History of the Territorial Sea in the United States, Canada and Australia", Oxford University Commonwealth Law Journal, 2013, p. 347 ff.

[55] See also the remarks at *supra* note 18 on international judicial practice as a form of state practice under Art. 38(1)(b).

pute for non-payment of demurrage charges arising from congestion in the Port of Lagos.

Before international courts and tribunals, however, international law self-evidently plays a far more central and specialized role. Its interrogation is far more detailed. From that detail can emerge more persuasive analyses of issues that may be accorded greater weight under Article 38(1)(d). In that centrality lies a core reason for the functional primacy of international courts over domestic courts in the identification of custom. For example, it is difficult to think of a situation in which a domestic court would pronounce on the customary process by which maritime boundaries are delimited – although it is not difficult to think of one in the international context, and the *North Sea Continental Shelf* cases mean we do not have to.[56]

But a further reason for the relative dominance of international courts is the process by which a nascent rule of customary international law is subject to continual refinement by a variety of adjudicatory processes. Under this model, there may be a wide variety of customary pronouncements by domestic courts. Some of these may even engage in the kind of comparative analysis of state practice and *opinio juris* that Article 38(1)(d) requires if persuasive force is to be generated. But at a certain point in time, they are subject to international processes of aggregation that diminish their overall relevance as subsidiary means for the identification of custom.

A useful case study here is that of *Jones v. Saudi Arabia*, a decision of the UK House of Lords.[57] In that case, the claimants in two separate actions alleged that they had been systematically tortured whilst imprisoned in Saudi Arabia. On returning to the UK, they brought claims in tort against the Kingdom claiming damages for resulting psychological problems. Saudi Arabia promptly claimed immunity for itself and the various government officials alleged to have tortured the claimants directly under Section 1(1) of the State Immunity Act 1978 (UK). At first instance, the immunity was upheld and permission to serve out refused, but on appeal, the immunity of the Kingdom's officials was held not to apply on the basis that as torture constituted a crime under international law in respect of which states were required to ensure redress under Article 14(1) of the Convention against Torture,[58] it could

---

[56] *North Sea Continental Shelf (Federal Republic of Germany v. Denmark; Federal Republic of Germany v. Netherlands)*, Judgment of 20 February 1969, ICJ Reports, 1969, p. 3 ff. That is not to say, however, that domestic court decisions could not furnish factual material relevant to the process of delimitation (for example by repeatedly exercising jurisdiction over a contested maritime area) – merely that they are exceedingly unlikely to engage in the process of delimitation itself.

[57] *Jones v. Ministry of the Interior for the Kingdom of Saudi Arabia & Anor (Secretary of State for Constitutional Affairs & Ors intervening)* [2007] 1 AC 270 (HL); FURLONG, ILDC 521 (UK 2006). For the decision below, see *Jones v. Ministry of the Interior Al-Mamlaka Al-Arabiya AS Saudiya (the Kingdom of Saudi Arabia)* [2005] QB 699 (CA); RISVAS, ILDC 109 (UK 2004). Further: O'KEEFE, "Decisions of British Courts during 2006 Involving Questions of Public International Law", BYIL, 2007, p. 458 ff., pp. 499–520.

[58] United Nations Convention against Torture and Other Cruel, Inhuman or Degrading Treatment or Punishment, 4 February 1985, entered into force 26 June 1987.

not be treated as an official act in respect of which immunity *ratione materiae* could not be granted. It was further held that a blanket immunity for state officials alleged to have committed acts of torture would therefore be inappropriate and contrary to the claimants' right of access to justice under Article 6 of the European Convention on Human Rights.[59]

The House of Lords overturned the decision of the Court of Appeal, with substantial judgments given by Lord Bingham and Lord Hoffmann (with whom Lord Rodger, Lord Walker and Lord Carswell agreed). Both judgments dispelled the notion that despite the *jus cogens* character of the prohibition on torture, that (a) did not compel *ipso facto* the domestic availability of a claim in damages, and (b) render torture committed by state agents for a state purpose not a state act. Put another way, the argument that state immunity did not apply in cases where the underlying allegations concerned violations of *jus cogens* was rejected.

In reaching this conclusion, Lord Bingham engaged in an impressive analysis of state immunity, referring to (*inter alia*) case law and practice from the UK, US, Italy, Canada, European Court of Human Rights, ICTY and ICJ in denying the existence of a new customary exception to state immunity based on violations of *jus cogens*.[60] Furthermore, relying on Fox's treatise on state immunity,[61] Lord Bingham also pointed out that rejection of such an exception was well-grounded as a matter of logic. If state immunity is a procedural bar going to the jurisdiction of a domestic court, then the substantive norm underpinning the dispute is formally beyond the reach of the court until such time as jurisdiction is positively established.[62]

On the basis of this analysis, his Lordship said (approving the Kingdom's submissions):

> [T]here is no evidence that states have recognised or given effect to an international law obligation to exercise universal jurisdiction over claims arising from alleged breaches or peremptory norms of international law, nor is there any consensus of learned or judicial opinion that they should. This is significant, since these are sources of international law. But this lack of evidence is not neutral: since the rule on immunity is well understood and established, and no relevant exception is generally accepted, the rule prevails.[63]

In a similar vein, Lord Hoffmann said (with specific regard to the *Ferrini* case, where precisely the opposite conclusion was reached by Italy's Court of Cassation):

---

[59] Convention for the Protection of Human Rights and Fundamental Freedoms, 4 November 1950, entered into force 3 September 1953.

[60] *Jones v. Saudi Arabia, cit. supra* note 57, paras. 7–28.

[61] FOX, *The Law of State Immunity*, Oxford, 2002, 525.

[62] *Jones v. Saudi Arabia, cit. supra* note 57, para. 24.

[63] *Ibid.*, para. 27.

[If *Ferrini*] had been concerned with domestic law, [it] might have been seen by some as 'activist' but would have been well within the judicial function. As Professor Dworkin demonstrated in *Law's Empire* (1986), the ordering of competing principles according to the importance of the values which they embody is a basic technique of adjudication. But the same approach cannot be adopted in international law, which is based upon the common consent of nations. It is not for a national court to 'develop' international law by unilaterally adopting a version of that law which, however, desirable, forward-looking and reflective of values it may be, is simply not accepted by other states.[64]

For a time, *Jones v. Saudi Arabia* became one of the defining authorities on the procedural character of state immunity and its interaction with substantive norms. Even if its reasoning was disagreed with,[65] it was a lucid judgment that was of considerable utility in the identification of custom. But its reach was limited. No matter how impressive its analysis, it could only be the decision of a single appellate court, and there remained scope for argument in other jurisdictions (e.g. Italy). That was, until it was picked up by the ICJ in *Jurisdictional Immunities*, and its core ruling affirmed emphatically.[66]

This vindication was arguably the worst thing that could have happened to *Jones v. Saudi Arabia* as a legal precedent – that is, as a decision that derives its persuasive force through the quality of its reasoning.[67]

The *Jurisdictional Immunities* case, as noted, represented an escalation of the *Ferrini* decision to the international plane. *Ferrini* had concerned claims brought against Germany before the Italian courts in relation to violations of international humanitarian law committed by the Third Reich during the Second World War

---

[64] *Ibid.*, para. 63.

[65] See e.g. McGregor, "Torture and State Immunity: Deflecting Impunity, Distorting Sovereignty", EJIL, 2007, p. 903 ff.; Orakhelashvili, "State Immunity and the Hierarchy of Norms: Why the House of Lords Got It Wrong", EJIL 2007, p. 955 ff.

[66] Further: Sender and Wood, "*Jurisdictional Immunities of the State (Germany v Italy; Greece intervening)* (2012)", in Bjorge and Miles (eds,), *Landmark Cases in Public International Law*, Oxford, 2017, p. 564 ff.

[67] Self-evidently, international law lacks a formal doctrine of precedent in the sense of *stare decisis*. But that by no means prevents decisions from serving as precedents in the sense identified by Lord Wright, "Precedents", Cambridge Law Journal, 1943, p. 118 ff., p. 144: "Have we not had this before or something like it?". Put another way, the legitimacy of international judicial law making depends (at least in part) upon adjudicators at least making an effort to square their reasoning with past decisions: von Bogdandy and Venzke, "The Spell of Precedents: Lawmaking by International Courts and Tribunals", in Romano, Alter and Shany (eds.), *cit. supra* note 41, p. 503 ff., pp. 507–511. *A fortiori*, a concept of legal precedent serves an invaluable system-building function: Jacob, "Precedents: Lawmaking through International Adjudication", in von Bogdandy and Venzke (eds.), *International Judicial Lawmaking: On Public Authority and Democratic Legitimation in Global Governance*, Berlin, 2012, p. 35 ff., pp. 47–59. Further: Shahabuddeen, *Precedent in the World*, Cambridge, 1996.

and in respect of which the Court of Cassation had found that Germany was not immune on the basis that (*inter alia*) the underlying allegations constituted violations of *jus cogens*.[68] Following that decision in 2004, Germany commenced legal proceedings before the ICJ alleging breach of the customary law of state immunity in 2008.

By way of final judgment in 2012, the Court resolved the issue in Germany's favour. In so doing, it noted the same logical fallacy that formed the crux of Lord Bingham's reasoning – without acknowledging that it was traversing ground that had already been covered elsewhere.[69] It then turned to consider the question of the exception more directly, noting:

> To the extent it is argued that no rule which is not of the status of *jus cogens* may be applied if to do so would hinder the enforcement of a *jus cogens* rule, even in the absence of a direct conflict, the Court sees no basis for such a proposition. A *jus cogens* rule is one from which no derogation is permitted but the rules which determine the scope and extent of jurisdiction and when that jurisdiction may be exercised do not derogate from those substantive rules which possess *jus cogens* status, nor is there anything inherent in the concept of *jus cogens* which would require their modification or would displace their application.[70]

The Court then referred to its earlier practice in the context of Article 38(1) (d),[71] before turning to decisions of national courts that reached a similar result – but implicitly confining these within the ambit of Article 38(1)(b):

> In addition, this argument about the effect of *jus cogens* displacing the law of State immunity has been rejected by the national courts of the United Kingdom (*Jones* v. *Saudi Arabia*, House of Lords, [2007] 1 *AC* 270; *ILR*, Vol. 129, p. 629), Canada (*Bouzari* v. *Islamic Republic of Iran*, Court of Appeal of Ontario, *DLR*, 4th Series, Vol. 243, p. 406; *ILR*, Vol. 128, p. 586), Poland (*Natoniewski*, Supreme Court, *Polish Yearbook of International Law*, Vol. XXX, 2010, p. 299), Slovenia (case No. Up-13/99, Constitutional Court of Slovenia), New Zealand (*Fang* v. *Jiang*, High Court, [2007] *NZAR*, p. 420; *ILR*, Vol. 141, p. 702) and Greece (*Margellos*, Special Supreme Court, *ILR*, Vol. 129, p. 525). [...] It follows, therefore, that the judgments of the Italian courts which are the subject of

---

[68] *Ferrini v. Germany*, cit. supra note 20, pp. 669–674.

[69] *Jurisdictional Immunities*, cit. supra note 17, para. 82.

[70] *Ibid*, para. 95.

[71] *Ibid*, citing *Armed Activities on the Territory of the Congo (New Application: 2002) (Democratic Republic of the Congo v. Rwanda)*, Judgment of 3 February 2006, Jurisdiction and Admissibility, ICJ Reports, 2006, p. 6 ff., paras. 64 and 125, and *Arrest Warrant, cit. supra* note 17, paras. 58 and 78.

the present proceedings are the only decisions of national courts to have accepted the reasoning on which this part of Italy's second argument is based.[72]

Consequently, although it was addressed by the Court, at the level of strict form, *Jones v. Saudi Arabia* was exposed as a factual precedent – henceforth not to be not used as an authority for the *identification* of custom under Article 38(1)(d) of the ICJ Statute.[73] Instead, its future lay on the heap of decisions from other jurisdictions to demonstrate a settled pattern of behaviour combined with *opinio juris* – mere state practice under Article 38(1)(b). Put another way, the internal reasoning of *Jones v. Saudi Arabia* was irrelevant as far as the Court was concerned – the only thing that mattered was the result, to be placed on one side of the ledger or another as circumstances dictated.[74] Regardless of how heated the debate over the hierarchical ordering of procedural and substantive norms in international law may have been previously, the Court's decision became overnight the definitive *status quo*.[75] Put another way, in the wake of *Jurisdictional Immunities*, there was no longer any reason for scholars or practitioners of international law to refer to *Jones v. Saudi Arabia* as anything more than a second parallel citation.

In this, the supposed strength of a domestic judicial decision relative to that of an international court or tribunal – its ability to reflect state practice or *opinio juris* – is revealed to be a weakness. It is precisely *because* Article 38(1)(b) allows these decisions to be reduced to a positive or negative entry on the customary balance sheet that an international court or tribunal can avoid evaluation of their reasoning. By contrast, in cases where an international court or tribunal is confronted with another international decision on the same legal question, there is no available alternative – Article 38(1)(d) must be deployed and the earlier

---

[72] *Jurisdictional Immunities, cit. supra* note 17, para. 96. It is possible to read this passage as referring to decisions of national courts in the context of Art. 38(1)(d) – however, the subsequent reference by the Court to other state practice in the form of legislation would tend to indicate that these decisions were only considered relevant insofar as Art. 38(1)(b) was concerned: ILC Secretariat, *cit. supra* note 6, para. 26. See also the Court's analysis earlier expressly treating the same decisions as state practice in rejecting Italy's related argument that the gravity of an alleged violation of international law may affect the availability of immunity: *Jurisdictional Immunities, cit. supra* note 17, paras. 83–84.

[73] But see *Al-Malki & Anor v. Reyes (Secretary of State for Foreign and Commonwealth Affairs intervening)* [2017] 3 WLR 923, para. 40 (SC) in which Lord Sumption described the ICJ as having "endorsed the Appellate Committee's reasoning on this point". This is analysis is perhaps a little too optimistic – whilst the reasoning of *Jones v. Saudi Arabia* may have been adopted without attribution by the ICJ in *Jurisdictional Immunities*, the decision itself was treated as state practice only.

[74] The Court did elsewhere refer to the internal reasoning of *Jones v. Saudi Arabia*, but only to confirm that an item of state practice identified by Italy as pointing in the opposite direction – the House of Lords' decision in *R v. Bow Street Metropolitan Stipendiary Magistrate, Ex parte Pinochet Ugarte (No 3)* [2000] 1 AC 147; MURRAY, ILDC 1736 (UK 1999) – was not applicable: *Jurisdictional Immunities, cit. supra* note 17, para. 87.

[75] See e.g. TALMON, "*Jus Cogens* after *Germany v Italy*: Substantive and Procedural Rules Distinguished", Leiden JIL, 2012, p. 979 ff.

decision's reasoning interrogated. Thus, the ICJ in *Bosnian Genocide* could not reflexively affirm its reasoning on the question of attribution and "effective" control in *Nicaragua* in reflexive preference to the "overall" control test put forward by the ICTY in *Tadić v Prosecutor* "just because" the former was a decision of the Court and the latter was not – it was required by Article 38(1)(d) to forensically dismantle its rival's reasoning to ensure the legitimacy of its decision.

5. CONCLUSION

The shifting architectonics of international legal adjudication show the difficulties of maintaining unqualified propositions about the relative authority of international and domestic courts *vis-à-vis* international custom. As such, the ILC was perhaps too hasty to lionise the expertise of international bodies, and downplay the relevance of domestic courts. But it was not *entirely* wrong. International courts do necessarily carry greater weight under Article 38(1)(d) than do domestic courts. Now is the era of international dispute settlement, something that cannot be said of the international law of the 20th century. But there is also something to be said for the structure of international adjudication, and the process by which state practice is aggregated to create (or deny) a customary rule. Put another way, a conversation may start in Beijing, London, Paris, Rome or Washington, DC – but the final word, sooner or later, is uttered in The Hague.

THE STANDARDS FOR THE IDENTIFICATION
OF EXCEPTIONS TO CUSTOMARY LAW

Mariangela La Manna*

Abstract

This paper addresses some methodological concerns regarding the identification of customary rules. It presents a brief theory of the ascertainment of exceptions to customary rules and, more specifically, enquires whether the identification of an exception follows the same standards and the same evidentiary threshold as the identification of a brand new customary rule or not.

Keywords: customary international law; exception; ascertainment; fragmentation; change.

1. Introduction

This paper enquires whether exceptions to existing customary rules and new customary rules may be identified following to different standards or if the ascertainment technique is instead the same with reference to both cases. The focus of the enquiry will accordingly be on ascertainment standards and, thus, on the issue of the identification of customary rules.[1] It is difficult to think of the ascertainment of customary international law as a formal process at all, let alone a codified procedure, given the inherent informal and spontaneous character of this source

---

*Adjunct Professor of International and EU Law, Catholic University, Milano. This paper was presented during the 3rd Biennial Conference of the Italian branch of the International Law Association (ILA), which was held on 17th November 2017 at the Law School of the Carlo Cattaneo-LIUC University. The author wishes to thank Prof. Gabriella Venturini and Prof. Alberto Malatesta for organizing the event, as well as Prof. Attila Tanzi for the generous guidance and insight in the preparation of the final draft. Prof. Massimo Iovane, prof. Daniele Amoroso and the anonymous reviewer are also owed many thanks for help and suggestions. The author is extremely grateful to her fellow panelists for their counsel and support. All mistakes are the author's only.

[1] Though "formation" and "identification" of customary rules are based on the same elements, the former has a sociological component to it, while the latter only refers to the ascertainment by judges of the existence and the content of a customary rule. The distinction is subtle indeed. See Wood, First Report on the Formation and Evidence of Customary International Law, UN Doc. A/CN.4/663 (2013), as well as Id., Second Report on the Identification of Customary International Law, UN Doc. A/CN.4/672 (2014), para. 2. See also International Law Association, Committee on Formation of Customary (General) International Law, Final Report of the Committee. Statement of Principles Applicable to the Formation of General Customary International Law, Report of the Sixty-Ninth Conference Held in London 25-29th July 2000, ILA Reports of Conferences, Vol. 69, 2000.

of international law.[2] Besides, if the formation of customary international law is described as an informal process, the same may also be said with reference to its identification by national and international courts. Nonetheless, addressing this issue may be very useful, in order to understand if exceptions to customary rules are subject to the very same evidentiary demands as new customary rules or not and, thus, if international law is neutral as to stability and change of customary regimes.

To that end, some methodological indications will be looked for in the work of the International Law Commission (Section 2). Subsequently, the case-law of international instances dealing with new areas of international law will be addressed (Section 3). The relevant case-law of the International Court of Justice related to previously regulated regimes allegedly having their scope altered by the surfacing of exceptions will be considered eventually (Section 4). Finally, a tentative assessment will be performed (Section 5).

2. THE CONTRIBUTION OF THE ILC IN THE RECOGNITION OF STANDARDS FOR THE IDENTIFICATION OF EXCEPTIONS TO CUSTOMARY RULES

The issue of the existence of a specific standard with reference to the identification of exceptions to customary rules has not so far been explicitly addressed by the International Law Commission (ILC). However, some useful references may be found in the ILC's work on the issue of fragmentation.[3] The Study Group coordinated by prof. Koskenniemi, in fact, observed that the issue of a normative conflict,[4] absent a hierarchical relationship between the conflicting rules, may be addressed in terms of generality v. particularity, as well as settled by resorting to the *lex specialis* principle.[5] That may also apply to a conflict involving two non-treaty standards, i.e. two customary rules.[6] The relationship of a particular rule with a general one may either take the form of an application of the latter, i.e. an updating or a development thereof, or of an exception to it, i.e. a new norm setting aside the previous regime in a given case.[7]

The Study Group made sure to clarify that an exception does not produce a change in the law, but an occasional, punctual deviation from it, to be ascribed to

---

[2] See GRADONI, "La Commissione del diritto internazionale riflette sulla rilevazione della consuetudine", RDI, 2014, p. 667 ff.

[3] KOSKENNIEMI, Fragmentation of International Law: Difficulties Arising from the Diversification and Expansion of International Law. Report of the Study Group of the International Law Commission Finalized by Martti Koskenniemi, UN Doc. A/CN/.4/L.682 (2006), YILC, Vol. II, Part 2, p. 175 ff.

[4] *Ibid.*, paras. 21-26.

[5] *Ibid.*, paras. 46-55.

[6] "Though express practice is not abundant, it is hard to see why *lex specialis* – or at least the reasoning behind it – would not be applicable to the relations between general and special custom", *ibid.*, para. 84.

[7] *Ibid.*, paras. 88 and 103-107.

the existence of peculiar factual elements.[8] The methodological instruction to be taken from the Report on Fragmentation is that an exception may derogate from a general customary rule by virtue of the *lex specialis* principle. When performing such an assessment, however, judges are always called upon to consider the overall normative context, together with the nature and purposes of the general law.[9]

As for the current work in progress on customary international law, at first sight no indication seems to be drawn from the draft conclusions adopted by the ILC in 2016.[10] The Commission, in fact, upholds the traditional two-elements approach with reference to the formation and the identification both of customary rules and of exceptions to them, and makes no mention whatsoever of an allegedly differentiated identification standard. This may indeed lead to the conclusion that the ILC does not acknowledge any difference in the standard to be applied, but instead considers the two cases as being covered by the same ascertainment process. Nonetheless, some interesting elements may be obtained from the Special Rapporteur's Reports and the debate during the sessions. The problem of the identification of an exception to a customary rule is only implicitly addressed with reference to the weight to be accorded to State inaction.[11] This may be relevant to the issue at hand since, when inaction is concerned, it is not immediately clear whether a State is merely violating an existing customary rule, or is instead acting with a view to promoting the emergence of an exception to an existing custom.[12] This uncertainty may only be swept away by investigation into the *opinio juris*, which will clarify the motives for non-compliance with an existing customary rule, as already established by the Permanent Court of International Justice in one of its seminal judgments.[13] Inaction is now the object of Draft conclusion 10§3: "Failure to react over time to a practice may serve as

---

[8] *Ibid.*, para. 105.

[9] *Ibid.*, paras. 119-122.

[10] International Law Commission, Report of the work of the sixty-eight session – Identification of Customary International Law, UN Doc. A/71/10 (2016). An indirect reference to the peculiarities of exceptions to general rules seems to have been made in the latest Special Rapporteur's Report, with reference to Draft Conclusion 3 on assessment of evidence for the two constitutive elements. However, such a stance should not be over-emphasized, since the Special Rapporteur made no suggestion to amend Draft Conclusion 3. See WOOD, Fifth Report on Identification of Customary International Law, UN Doc. A/CN.4/717 (2018), paras. 31-34, especially para. 33.

[11] WOOD, Third Report on Identification of Customary International Law, UN Doc. A/CN.4/682 (2015), paras. 19-26.

[12] VISMARA, "Rilievi in tema di inaction e consuetudine internazionale alla luce dei recenti lavori della commissione del diritto internazionale", RDI, 2016, p. 1026 ff., pp. 1030-1031. See also *Case Concerning Military and Paramilitary Activities in and Against Nicaragua (Nicaragua v. USA)*, Judgment of 27 June 1986, ICJ Reports, 1986, p. 14 ff., para. 186.

[13] "Even if the rarity of the judicial decisions to be found among the reported cases were sufficient to prove in point of fact the circumstance alleged by the Agent for the French Government, it would merely show that States had often, in practice, abstained from instituting criminal proceedings, and not that they recognized themselves as being obliged to do so; for only if such abstention were based on their being conscious of having a duty to abstain would it be possible to speak of an international custom", *The Case of the S.S. "Lotus" (France v. Turkey)*, Judgment of 7 September 1927, PCIJ Reports, Series A, No. 10, p. 1 ff., p. 28.

evidence of acceptance as law (*opinio juris*), provided that States were in a position to react and the circumstances called for some reaction".[14]

In sum, the relevance given by the ILC to the formation of exceptions to customary rules is risible. With reference to the identification of exceptions, the ILC did not even bother considering an alleged differentiated procedure, which confirms the general applicability to new rules and exceptions to existing rules alike of the traditional two-elements method.

3. WHAT DOES IT TAKE TO ACKNOWLEDGE THE APPEARANCE OF A NEW CUSTOMARY REGIME: THE CASE-LAW OF THE ICTY

Finding an assessment of a customary norm in an unbeaten path is not an easy task. Today, in fact, the creation of a new regime may be described as a transformation of a previous one;[15] thus, it looks hard to admit that there are any gaps at all in the system.[16] The latest examples of brand new areas or areas not completely disciplined under international law may be international human rights law,[17] international criminal law,[18] international environmental law[19] and, to some extents, international humanitarian law.[20] Within these domains, courts have performed an ascertainment of one or more customary rules even before their forma-

---

[14] Report on the work of the sixty-eighth session, *cit. supra* note 10. See also ARAJARVI, "The Requisite Rigour in the Identification of Customary International Law. A look at the Reports of the Special Rapporteur of the International Law Commission", International Community Law Review, 2017, p. 9 ff., pp. 22-23.

[15] TANZI, *Introduzione al diritto internazionale contemporaneo*, 5th ed., Padova, 2016, pp. 102 and 187-204.

[16] KOSKENNIEMI, *cit. supra* note 3.

[17] WOUTERS and RYNGAERT, "Impact on the Process of Formation of Customary International Law", in KAMMINGA and SCHEININ (eds.), *The Impact of Human Rights Law on General International Law*, Oxford, 2009, p. 111 ff. See also WOOD, *cit. supra* note 1, para. 98.

[18] BAKER, "Customary International Law in the 21st Century: Old Challenges and New Debates", EJIL, 2010, p. 173 ff. See also SCHABAS, "Customary Law or 'Judge-Made' Law: Judicial Creativity at the UN Criminal tribunals", in DORIA et al. (eds.), *The Legal Regime of the International Criminal Court: Essays in Honour of Professor Igor Blishchenko*, Leiden-Boston, 2009, p. 77 ff.; FRULLI, "The Contribution of International Criminal Tribunals to the Development of International Law: The Prominence of Opinio Juris and the Moralization of Customary Law", The Law and Practice of International Courts and Tribunals, 2015, p. 80 ff., especially p. 89 ff.; KIRAKOSYAN, "Finding Custom: the ICJ and the International Criminal Courts and Tribunals Compared", in VAN DEN HERIK and STAHN (eds.), *The Diversification and Fragmentation of International Criminal Law*, Leiden-Boston, 2012, p. 149 ff.

[19] PALMER, "New Ways to Make International Environmental Law", AJIL, 1992, p. 259 ff.

[20] D'ASPREMONT, "An Autonomous Regime of Identification of Customary Humanitarian International Law: Do Not Say What You Do or Do Not Do What You Say?", in VAN STEENBERGH (ed.), *Droit international humanitaire: un régime spécial de droit international?*, Bruxelles, 2013, p. 67 ff.; MERON, "The Continuing Role of Custom in the Formation of International Humanitarian Law", AJIL, 1996, p. 238 ff.

tion was complete and their content crystallized.[21] Those branches have in fact been explored either through the identification of the subjective element of custom only, i.e. *opinio juris*, or by resorting to general principles and mere logical argumentation.[22] The core element of this approach is the absence of precedent,[23] which will lead to the appearance of a customary norm nearly *ex novo*. When there is no or scarce practice to be weighed, *opinio juris* – to be looked up for in treaties and declarations made by States within international fora (e.g. UNGA), adopted by large majorities, or even unanimously, multilateral agreements with very broad participation, and the like – will be sufficient.[24]

International criminal law (ICL) is probably the area where more often judges resorted to a more relaxed standard.[25] Within the vast *corpus* of the ICTY's case-law, the most innovative finding is the applicability of the grave breaches regime and, accordingly, of individual criminal responsibility to internal armed conflict, which was established in the seminal *Tadic* case.[26] This specific find-

---

[21] ROBERTS, "Traditional and Modern Approaches to Customary International Law: A Reconciliation", AJIL, 2001, p. 757 ff.

[22] On the different methods of ascertainment of sources of international law see CANNIZZARO, "Unità e pluralità dei metodi di accertamento del diritto consuetudinario", in PALCHETTI (ed.), *L'incidenza del diritto non scritto sul diritto internazionale ed europeo. XX Convegno SIDI di Macerata, 5-6 giugno 2015*, Napoli, 2016, p. 23 ff., p. 27, pointing out that deductive methodology can take two different forms: it is either based on the sole identification of *opinio juris* or it can be performed by resorting to mere logical argumentation; TALMON, "Determinining Customary International Law: The ICJ's Methodology between Induction, Deduction and Assertion", EJIL, 2015, p. 417 ff.

[23] AKEHURST, "Custom as a Source of International Law", BYIL, 1976, p. 1 ff., especially p. 15, where the author states that "the supposed requirement of time, like the supposed requirement of repetition, can usually be dispensed with if there are no precedents which can be cited against the alleged rule of customary international law". See also SHAW, *International Law*, 8th ed., Cambridge, 2017, pp. 66-68.

[24] See FRULLI, *cit. supra* note 18, pp. 90-91, pointing out that since the practice of international criminal law is very scant "heavy reliance on *opinio juris* was almost mandatory". The technique valuing *opinio juris* above State practice is described as the "sliding scale" argument, which implies that the presence of one of the constitutive elements of customary law is weighed against the presence of the other and that a more robust presence of the one may supplement for the scarcity or even the absence of the other. See KIRGIS, "Custom on a Sliding Scale", AJIL, 1987, p. 146 ff.

[25] CASSESE, *International Law*, 2nd ed., Oxford, 2005, pp. 160-161; ICTY, Trial Chamber, *Prosecutor v. Kupresic et al.*, Case No. IT-95-16-T, Judgment of 14 January 2000, para. 527. See also CONDORELLI, "Customary International Law: the Yesterday, Today, and Tomorrow of General International Law", in CASSESE (ed.), *Realizing Utopia. The Future of International Law*, Oxford, 2012, p. 147 ff., p. 150. See also HOFFMANN, "The Gentle Humanizer of Humanitarian law – Antonio Cassese and the Creation of the Customary Law of Non-International Armed Conflict", in STAHN and VAN DEN HERIK (eds.), *Future Perspectives on International Criminal Justice*, Leiden-Boston, 2010, p. 58 ff. The risible role played by State practice in those instances (as opposed to the paramount importance of ILC's documents and international case-law) is clearly acknowledged by IOVANE, "L'influence de la multiplication des juridictions internationales sur l'application du droit international", RCADI, Vol. 383, 2017-I, p. 233 ff., pp. 395-397.

[26] ICTY, Appeals Chamber, *Prosecutor v. Dusko Tadic*, Case No. IT-94-1, Decision on the Defence Motion for Interlocutory Appeal on Jurisdiction of 2 October 1995, paras. 76, 120.

ing is more than any other the product of a value-oriented approach, entirely focused on the arbitrariness of the applicability of the grave breaches regime to international armed conflicts only,[27] coupled with "elementary considerations of humanity and common sense"[28] as well as "substantive justice and equity".[29] However other important normative statements, entirely based on the desirability of a value-oriented set of customary rules, are to be found not only in the very same judgment, but throughout the case-law of the Tribunal.[30] The two *ad hoc* Tribunals were confronted with serious gaps in ICL and filled these gaps by simply declaring as customary some specific positions without much further inquiry as to State practice,[31] as well as by resorting to meta-juridical notions such as fairness, morality or justice, which has led some commentators to describe such a technique as a "*contrôle de justesse*".[32] Besides, even the notion of *opinio juris* cherished by the Tribunals is especially broad and flexible, including not only the sense of legal obligation and the belief in the legally binding nature of the practice, but also the "requirements of humanity and the dictates of public conscience".[33] The peculiar nature of the ascertainment mechanism resorted to by the Tribunals has been remarked by many commentators depicting ICL as a self-contained regime benefitting from a specific, very informal process for the ascertainment of the applicable law,[34] in some cases amounting to an actual law-making function exercise.[35] The resort to a different standard may accordingly be justified by referring to the peculiar features of this specific branch of international law.

---

[27] "Why protect civilians from belligerent violence, or ban rape, torture or the wanton destruction of hospital, churches, museums or private property, as well as proscribe weapons causing unnecessary suffering when two sovereign States are engaged in a war, and yet refrain from enacting the same bans or providing the same protection when armed violence has erupted 'only' within the territory of a sovereign State? If international law, while of course duly safeguarding the legitimate interests of States, must gradually turn to the protection of human beings, it is only natural that the aforementioned dichotomy should gradually lose its weight", *ibid.*, para. 97.

[28] *Ibid.*, para. 119.

[29] *Ibid.*, para. 135.

[30] See KIRAKOSYAN, *cit. supra* note 18, pp. 156-159.

[31] FRULLI, *cit. supra* note 18, p. 85.

[32] IOVANE, *cit. supra* note 25, pp. 428-435.

[33] *Kupresic* case, *cit. supra* note 25, para. 527: "principles of international humanitarian law may emerge through a customary process under the pressure of the demands of humanity or the dictates of public conscience, even where State practice is scant or inconsistent. The other element, in the form of opinio necessitatis, crystallizing as a result of the imperatives of humanity or public conscience, may turn out to be the decisive element heralding the emergence of a general rule or principle of humanitarian law". The spontaneous character of *opinio juris* had already been acknowledged by the Italian literature on the sources of international law. See AGO, *Scienza giuridica e diritto internazionale*, Milano,1950, pp. 86-108.

[34] BAKER, *cit. supra* note 18, p. 174.

[35] *Ibid.*, p. 184; see also SCHABAS, *cit. supra* note 18, p. 101 and WOOD, *cit. supra* note 1, para. 70.

4. THE IDENTIFICATION OF EXCEPTIONS TO CUSTOMARY RULES IN THE CASE-LAW OF THE INTERNATIONAL COURT OF JUSTICE

With reference to the methodology resorted to by the International Court of Justice (ICJ) in its case-law, it has been pointed out that the Court, notwithstanding its oft-proclaimed allegiance to the dualistic approach to the identification of customary international law, more and more often focuses instead on *opinio juris*.[36] This observation may certainly have some basis, since the Court may have indeed resorted to a more flexible approach, especially within the area of the non-use of force,[37] in cases such as *Nicaragua*[38] or in the Advisory Opinion on *Nuclear weapons*.[39] In these cases utmost relevance was, in fact, given to *opinio juris* as expressed in UNGA resolutions.

When concerned with the identification of an exception to customary international rules, however, the ICJ seems to have religiously resorted to the dualistic approach,[40] and, even more so, to have relied on practice especially. The role State practice plays in the ascertainment process of an alleged customary exception is especially relevant.[41] Some commentators acknowledge that when a change in the law is sought, the standard of proof is higher than usual and that a greater quantity of practice instances is, in fact, needed to overturn existing rules of customary law.[42] Being the formation of customary norms a process of claim and response,[43] the State claiming a deviation from the existing regime will need to gather the support of an adequate number of States.[44] The case-law of the ICJ does not seem to support this statement completely.

---

[36] CONDORELLI, *cit. supra* note 25, p. 150.

[37] As a general reference see CANNIZZARO, PALCHETTI (eds.), *Customary International Law on the Use of Force. A Methodological Approach*, Leiden-Boston, 2005.

[38] *Nicaragua* case, *cit. supra* note 12.

[39] *Legality of the Threat or Use of Nuclear Weapons*, Advisory Opinion of 8 July 1996, ICJ Reports, 1996, p. 226 ff.

[40] *North Sea Continental Shelf Cases (Federal Republic of Germany v. Denmark; Federal Republic of Germany v. the Netherlands)*, Judgment of 20 February 1969, ICJ Reports, 1969, p. 3 ff., paras. 70, 73-74 and 77.

[41] See ALVAREZ-JIMÉNEZ, "Methods for the Identification of Customary International Law in the International Court of Justice's Jurisprudence: 2000-2009", ICLQ, 2011, p. 681 ff.

[42] While commenting ICJ judgment in the *Continental shelf* case Akehurst claims that "the equidistance principle conflicted with what the Court regarded as the existing rule of customary law on the subject, and the amount of practice which is needed to establish a new rule which conflicts with the previously accepted rule is greater than the amount of practice needed to establish a new rule *in vacuo*", see AKEHURST, *cit. supra* note 23, p. 17. In that case Denmark and the Netherlands were trying not only to establish a new rule of customary law but also to overthrow the old customary regime. They claimed that the Federal Republic of Germany, not a party to 1958 Geneva Convention, was nonetheless bound under the principle of equidistance established under the convention, by virtue of the customary nature that the principle had since acquired.

[43] MENDELSON, "The Formation of Customary International Law", RCADI, Vol. 272, 1998-I, p. 155 ff., pp. 245-293.

[44] *Nicaragua* case, *cit. supra* note 12, paras. 207-208.

In the *Arrest Warrant* case[45] the Democratic Republic of Congo had laid a claim against Belgium for the adoption of an arrest warrant against a sitting Congolese Minister for international crimes. Belgium had resisted by claiming – among other things – the existence of an international crimes exception to the customary norm envisaging personal immunity for high-level sitting State agents. The Court enquired the rationale for the applicability of personal immunity to Ministers for Foreign Affairs and acknowledged that "immunities accorded to Ministers for Foreign Affairs are not granted for their personal benefit, but to ensure the effective performance of their functions on behalf of their respective States"[46] and that, accordingly "the functions of a Minister for Foreign Affairs are such that, throughout the duration of his or her office, he or she when abroad enjoys full immunity from criminal jurisdiction and inviolability"[47] This may lead one to conclude that the Court resorts to a deductive, logical technique.[48] Subsequently, the ICJ performed a very brief survey of State practice in order to ascertain the emergence of a customary exception to the customary norm on personal immunity and, having addressed the few instances of national legislation as well as national case-law available, coupled with the provisions in the Statutes of the *ad hoc* Tribunals, concluded that no exception to the customary rule according immunity to incumbent Ministers for Foreign Affairs could have been inferred from that practice.[49] It is quite safe to say, however, that the main focus of the Court's legal reasoning was not on the actual practice of States inasmuch as it was on the theoretical justifications for personal immunity. Even more so, the very careful formulation of the so-called "functionalist approach to personal immunity" reflects the structural principles of the international legal order as well as the horizontal, sovereignty-oriented asset of the international community. This did not leave much room for a thorough analysis of State practice and *opinio juris*.

Another very important example of the ascertainment of exceptions to customary rules performed by the ICJ is to be found in the *Jurisdictional Immunities of the State* case.[50] In this case Italy had been convened by Germany before the Court to answer for the conduct of its judiciary branch, which, by denying State immunity to Germany in a set of reparation cases for wrongful conducts performed

---

[45] *Case Concerning the Arrest Warrant of 11 April 2000 (Democratic Republic of the Congo v. Belgium)*, Judgment of 14th February 2002, ICJ Reports, 2002, p. 3 ff.

[46] *Ibid.*, para. 53.

[47] *Ibid.*, para. 54.

[48] CANNIZZARO, *cit. supra* note 22, pp. 32-33, TALMON, *cit. supra* note 22, pp. 418 and 425-426.

[49] *Arrest Warrant* case, *cit. supra* note 45, para. 58. *Contra* see *ibid.*, Dissenting Opinion of Judge Al-Khasawneh, para. 8, and Dissenting Opinion of Judge *ad hoc* Van den Wyngaert, paras. 24-28; SANDS, "International Law Transformed? From Pinochet to Congo…?", Leiden JIL, 2003, p. 37 ff., pp. 48-49; CASSESE, "When May Senior State Officials Be Tried for International Crimes? Some Comments on the *Congo v. Belgium* Case", EJIL, 2002, p. 853 ff., pp. 864-866; WIRTH, "Immunity for Core Crimes? The ICJ's Judgment in the *Congo v. Belgium* Case", EJIL, 2002, p. 877 ff., pp. 884-889.

[50] *Jurisdictional Immunities of the State (Germany v. Italy, Greece Intervening)*, Judgment of 3 February 2012, ICJ Reports, 2012, p. 99 ff.

by the German army in Italian territory during the Second World War,[51] had allegedly violated Germany's immunity under international law. It is certainly true that
State immunity has experienced several modifications of its scope throughout the
last century[52] and can no longer be considered as an absolute notion, since quite a
few exceptions emerged over time. In this case, however, Italy was invoking yet
another exception, not quite crystallized in State practice:[53] a particular version
of the so-called "territorial tort exception", in that the one formulated by Italy
implied that a State could not invoke its immunity from the civil jurisdiction of
the forum State for conducts of its armed forces amounting to gross violations of
human rights having occurred in the territory of the forum State.[54]

The applicable rules to the case were to be found in customary international
law, since no international convention was applicable with reference to the case at
hand.[55] Unlike the *Arrest Warrant* judgment, this judgment represents a vindication of the traditional method of custom identification since the Court proclaimed
its firm allegiance to the dualistic approach and adopted a "manifesto" listing the
instances of State practice and *opinio juris* to be considered.[56] These included
international treaties,[57] national legislation,[58] national decisions,[59] claims before
foreign courts[60] and statements made by States in relation to the work of the ILC.
It also looked for *opinio juris* by checking the assertions of the existence of such
an exception in the international legal order, acknowledgment by States of other
States' immunity and assertion by States of a right to exercise jurisdiction over

---

[51] *Ibid.*, paras. 27-29.

[52] CONFORTI (ed. by IOVANE), *Diritto internazionale*, 11th ed., Napoli, 2018, pp. 273-
278.

[53] To be fair, the Italian argument was very complex and also invoked a "forum of last
resort" exception, on which see McGREGOR, "State Immunity and Human Rights. Is there a
Future after *Germany v. Italy?*", JICJ, 2012, p. 1 ff. However, for length constraints the whole
argumentation cannot be addressed in full. Accordingly, only the Court's assessment of State
practice on the tort territorial exception will be considered here.

[54] More specifically, the scope of the exception invoked by the Italian defence was narrower as the ICJ was requested to determine if a State could be sued before national courts
for conducts allegedly amounting to international crimes performed by its armed forces in the
territory of the forum State during an armed conflict.

[55] *Jurisdictional Immunities*, *cit. supra* note 50, paras. 54-55 and 62.

[56] "In the present context, State practice of particular significance is to be found in the
judgments of national courts faced with the question whether a foreign State is immune, the
legislation of those States which have enacted statutes dealing with immunity, the claims to
immunity advanced by States before foreign courts and the statements made by States, first in
the course of the extensive study of the subject by the International Law Commission and then
in the context of the adoption of the United Nations Convention. *Opinio juris* in this context
is reflected in particular in the assertion by States claiming immunity that international law
accords them a right to such immunity from the jurisdiction of other States, in the acknowledgment, by States granting immunity, that international law imposes upon them an obligation to
do so; and, conversely, in the assertion by States in other cases of a right to exercise jurisdiction
over foreign States", *ibid.*, para. 55.

[57] *Ibid.*, paras. 65-69.

[58] *Ibid.*, paras. 70-72.

[59] *Ibid.*, paras. 73-77.

[60] *Ibid.*, paras. 72-73 and 76.

other States. In this process, however, State practice was especially valued, in a classic inductive fashion. The Court's practice evaluation was however criticized for being policy-oriented, if not biased.[61] Leaving the outcome of the practice recognition aside, which led the Court to conclude that no customary territorial tort exception to State immunity could be figured out for conducts as those to the case at hand,[62] the judgment has been noted to be very conservative with reference to the methodology resorted to, especially with reference to its purely quantitative analysis of State practice as well as for its very scarce consideration of *opinio juris*.[63] It seems very difficult to reconcile this judgment with the one in the *Arrest Warrant* case. It seems even more difficult to acknowledge a specific technique resorted to by the Court when charged with the identification of an exception to a customary rule.

5. CONCLUSION

The suggestion that a different standard may be involved in the identification of a brand new customary rule and an exception to it respectively may apparently be drawn from the judgment of the US Supreme Court in the *Schooner-Exchange v. Mc Faddon* case dating back to 1812.[64] The decision is very well known and has commonly been described as one of the milestones of the discipline of State immunity.[65] In a famous *dictum* the US Supreme Court provided a blueprint for the ascertainment of customary rules by stating that "[i]n exploring an unbeaten path with few, if any, aids from precedents or written law, the court has found it necessary to rely much on general principles, and on a train of reasoning, founded on cases in some degree analogous to this".[66] This implies that, absent a previous regime, the applicable rules to a case may be inferred by relying on general principles or just as well by resorting to analogy. At the same time, however, the

---

[61] See CIAMPI, "The International Court of Justice Between 'Reason of State' and Demands for Justice by Victims of Serious International Crimes", RDI, 2012, p. 374 ff., esp. pp. 381-388; PAVONI, "An American Anomaly? On the ICJ's Selective Reading of United States Practice in *Jurisdictional Immunities of the State*", IYIL, 2011, p. 143 ff.; BIANCHI, "Il tempio e i suoi sacerdoti. Considerazioni su retorica e diritto a margine del caso *Germania c. Italia*", DUDI, 2012, p. 293 ff.

[62] *Jurisdictional Immunities* case, *cit. supra* note 50, paras. 78-79.

[63] PISILLO MAZZESCHI, "Il rapporto fra norme di *ius cogens* e la regola sull'immunità degli Stati: alcune osservazioni critiche sulla sentenza della Corte internazionale di giustizia del 3 febbraio 2012", DUDI, 2012, p. 310 ff.

[64] United States Supreme Court, *Schooner Exchange v. McFaddon*, 11 US (7 Cranch) 116 (1812). See TANZI and GRADONI, "Immunità dello Stato e crimini internazionali tra consuetudine e bilanciamento: note critiche a margine della sentenza della Corte internazionale di giustizia del 3 febbraio 2012", CI, 2012, p. 203 ff.

[65] In that case the Court was called upon to ascertain whether France could be the object of a claim within the U.S. domestic legal order for the seizure of a ship. The former owners of the Schooner Exchange, a ship that had been seized by French forces while sailing from Baltimore to Spain, had laid a libel against France in order to obtain the restitution of the seized vessel.

[66] *Schooner Exchange* case, *cit. supra* note 64.

Court laid down the criteria to identify exceptions to existing rules, by stating that "[a]ll exceptions, therefore, to the full and complete power of a nation within its own territories must be traced up to the consent of the nation itself. They can flow from no other legitimate source. [...] This consent may be tested by common usage and by common opinion, growing out of that usage".[67]

The language will sound familiar to any international lawyer, since "common usage" and "common opinion" immediately recall the objective and subjective elements of customary international law. In short, in order to identify an exception to a well-established customary rule such as the one on territorial sovereignty the Court required the coexistence of the two constitutive elements of customary international law and implicitly rejected the possibility to resort to general principles and analogical argumentation.

However fascinating, this differentiated methodology has not been upheld in other instances. No specific mention of a peculiar ascertainment procedure to be applied with reference to exceptions only is to be found in the work of the ILC. Nor can any special or aggrieved evidentiary standard be found in the case-law of the ICJ. With few deviations, in fact, the Court more or less constantly stays true to its ascertainment methodology, based on the drafting of Article 38(1)(b) of the ICJ Statute. With reference to the "milder" test to be used when addressing an unbeaten path, based on general principles and analogy, it may be true that lower evidentiary standards were employed in some cases. A more flexible approach in the ascertainment of customary law was used in particularly sensitive areas, as international criminal law or international humanitarian law. However, far from resorting to general principles and analogy, the *ad hoc* Tribunals undertook a quasi-normative exercise. It is hard to deny that such an approach is to be explained by social needs. Postulating norms of international law without a convincing analysis of practice is, in fact, a clear symptom of the social urgency of creating norms of international law in selected areas, which may lead to a softening of the practice requirement. This may precisely be a characteristic of self-contained regimes and not of general customary rules.

In a normative system as fragmented as international law, however, it is good to have a common methodological frame of reference at least in so far as "general" customary rules are concerned. The application of the common identification standard also to exceptions to customary rules makes perfect sense, especially if one considers that a careful assessment of State practice and *opinio juris* may contribute to the legitimacy and legality of the new exception as well as to legal certainty.

---

[67] *Ibid.*

REMARKS ON THE ILC WORK ON THE IDENTIFICATION OF CUSTOMARY LAW AND HUMAN RIGHTS: CURBING "DROIT DE L'HOMMISME"?

LUDOVICA CHIUSSI[*]

Abstract

The specific features of human rights have sometimes been used to claim exception from the basic rules on the formation of customary international law. This article explores the International Law Commission (ILC) Work on the Identification of Customary Law, with particular regard to human rights. According to Draft Conclusion 3, evidence of practice and opinio juris must be carefully assessed according to the overall context and the relevant circumstances. The argument will be made that the Draft Conclusions provisionally adopted by the ILC Drafting Committee allow adequate flexibility to accommodate the "speciality" of human rights.

Keywords: International Law Commission, Customary international law, Codification, Human Rights Law, Droit de l'hommisme.

1. INTRODUCTION

About twenty years ago the Italian Yearbook of International Law published a contribution by Alain Pellet, entitled "'Human Rightism' and International Law".[1] In the words of Professor Pellet, "human rightism", or *droit de l'hommisme*, represents

> that 'posture' which consists in wanting at all costs to confer 'autonomy' (which, in my opinion, it does not possess) to a 'discipline' (which, in my opinion, does not exist as such): the protection of human rights.[2]

The present article addresses the work of the International Law Commission (ILC) on the "Identification of Customary International Law", with particular ref-

---

[*] Doctoral Research Fellow in Public International Law, University of Oslo and University of Bologna. This paper was presented at the 3rd Biennial Conference of the Italian Branch of the International Law Association, LIUC Università Carlo Cattaneo, 17 November 2017. The author is grateful to Professors Attila Tanzi and Gentian Zyberi for their helpful comments on an earlier version of the article. The usual disclaimer applies.

[1] PELLET, "'Human Rightism' and International Law", IYIL, 2000, p. 3 ff.

[2] *Ibid.*, p. 3.

erence to human rights.[3] It will proceed in two parts. First, it will discuss the issue of *"droit de l'hommisme"* which, as anticipated, refers to the tendency of human rights lawyers to rely on the speciality of their field to claim exceptions from general international law. Second, it will consider the position taken on human rights by the ILC Special Rapporteur on the Identification of Customary International Law, as well as the text of the ILC Draft Conclusions on the topic, as adopted by the Drafting Committee on second reading.[4] The argument will be made that the Draft Conclusions provisionally adopted by the ILC Drafting Committee allow adequate flexibility to accommodate the "speciality" of human rights, while avoiding exceptions to be taken to the extreme.

By way of introduction, I should like to spend few words on the role of custom in a body of international law, like that of human rights, highly dominated by treaties.[5] Customary rules have not vanished since the adoption of the human rights covenants, treaties and conventions over the last seventy years.[6] Custom remains the bedrock of international human rights law and of international law in general, providing a parallel source of obligations binding in their original capacity.[7] It may be resorted to between non-state parties to human rights treaties, it contributes to the protection of those rights not explicitly covered by the treaty and it overcomes the reservations to the latter. Together with general principles of law, custom provides the basic rules of interpretation, as well as the background of the secondary rules.[8]

---

[3] At its sixty-fourth session, in 2012, the ILC decided to include in its current programme of work the topic "Formation and Identification of Customary International Law", and to appoint Sir Michael Wood as special rapporteur. The reports and the Draft Conclusions of the ILC Drafting Committee are available at: <http://legal.un.org/ilc/guide/1_13.shtml>; see also GRADONI, "La Commissione di diritto internazionale riflette sulla rilevazione della consuetudine", RDI, 2014, p. 667 ff.; YEE, "Report on the ILC Project on 'Identification of Customary International Law'", Chinese Journal of International Law, 2015, p. 375 ff.

[4] ILC, Identification of Customary International Law, Text of the Draft Conclusions as Adopted by the Drafting Committee on Second Reading, UN Doc A/CN.4/L.908 (2018).

[5] On the relationship between customary international law and human rights see, among others, MERON, *Human Rights and Humanitarian Norms as Customary Law*, Oxford, 1989; WOUTERS and RYNGAERT, "Impact on the Process of the Formation of Customary International Law" in KAMMINGA and SCHEININ (eds.), *The Impact of Human Rights Law on General International Law*, Oxford, 2009, p. 111 ff.; DE SENA, "Prassi, consuetudine e principi nel campo dei diritti dell'uomo. Riflessioni internazionalistiche", Ragion pratica, 2014, p. 511 ff.; THIRLWAY, "Human Rights in Customary Law: An Attempt to Define Some of the Issues", Leiden JIL, 2015, p. 495 ff.; TASIOULAS, "Custom, Jus Cogens, and Human Rights" in BRADLEY (ed.), *Custom's Future: International Law in a Changing World*, Cambridge, 2016, p. 95 ff.; WOOD, "Customary International Law and Human Rights", Distinguished Lectures of the Academy of European Law, EUI Working Paper AEL 2016/03, available at: <http://cadmus.eui.eu/bitstream/handle/1814/44445/AEL_2016_03.pdf?sequence=1&isAllowed=y>; BESSON, "Sources of International Human Rights Law: How General is General International Law?", in BESSON and D'ASPREMONT (eds.), *The Oxford Handbook of the Sources of International Law*, Oxford, 2017, p. 837 ff.

[6] WOOD, "Customary International Law", *cit. supra* note 5, pp. 2-3.

[7] See CLAPHAM, *Human Rights Obligations of Non-State Actors*, Oxford, 2006, p. 85.

[8] WOOD, First Report on Formation and Evidence of Customary International Law, UN Doc. A/CN.4/663 (2013), para. 35: "Even in fields where there are widely accepted 'codifica-

2. "DROIT DE L'HOMMISME": EXCEPTIONS TAKEN TO THE EXTREME

Perhaps it is no coincidence that the expression "*droit de l'hommisme*", or "human rightism", was coined by Alain Pellet,[9] who has been the ILC Special Rapporteur on the issue of reservations to treaties.[10] The "speciality" of the then relatively young field of human rights soon became evident in many dimensions of treaty law.[11] The Human Rights Committee, which monitors the implementation of the UN International Covenant on Civil and Political Rights, observed:

> Although treaties that are mere exchanges of obligations between States allow them to reserve inter se application of rules of general international law, it is otherwise in human rights treaties, which are for the benefit of persons within their jurisdiction. Accordingly, provisions in the Covenant that represent customary international law [...] may not be the subject of reservations.[12]

Almost twenty years before, the European Court of Human Rights (ECtHR) recalled that the European Convention on Human Rights (ECHR)

> Unlike international treaties of the classic kind, [...] comprises more than mere reciprocal engagements between contracting States. It creates, over and above a network of mutual, bilateral undertakings, objective obligations which, in the words of the Preamble, benefit from a "collective enforcement".[13]

---

tion' conventions, the rules of customary international law continue to govern questions not regulated by the conventions and continue to apply in relations with and between non-parties. Rules of customary international law may also fill possible lacunae in treaties, and assist in their interpretation"; see also RIPHAGEN, Third Report on the Content, Forms and Degrees of International Responsibility (Part Two of the Draft Articles), UN Doc. A/CN.4/354 and Add. 1 and 2, p. 28; see GUZMAN, "Saving Customary International Law", Michigan Journal of International Law, 2005, p. 115 ff., pp. 119-120.

[9] PELLET, "La mise en oeuvre des normes relatives aux droits de l'homme" in DECAUX and TIERRY (eds.), *Droit international et droits de l'homme. La pratique juridique française dans le domaine de la protection internationale des droits de l'homme*, Paris, 1990, p. 126.

[10] ILC, Guide to Practice on Reservation to Treaties, YILC, 2011, Vol. II, Part 2. The reports of the Special Rapporteur on Reservation to Treaties are available at: <http://legal.un.org/ilc/guide/1_8.shtml>.

[11] See SIMMA, "Sources of International Human Rights Law: Human Rights Treaties", in BESSON and D'ASPREMONT (eds.), *cit. supra* note 5, p. 871 ff.

[12] UN Human Rights Committee, General Comment No. 24: Issues Relating to Reservations Made upon Ratification or Accession to the Covenant or the Optional Protocols thereto, or in Relation to Declarations under Article 41 of the Covenant, UN Doc. CCPR/C/21/Rev.1/Add.6 (1994), para. 8.

[13] *Ireland v. The United Kingdom*, Application No. 5310/71, Merits, Judgment of 18 January 1978, para. 239. For a similar approach, see Inter-American Court of Human Rights, *The Effect of Reservations on the Entry into Force of the American Convention (Arts 74 and 75)*, Advisory Opinion OC-2/82 of 24 September 1982, Series A No 2, 1982, pp. 14-16, paras. 29-33, and *Restrictions to the Death Penalty (Arts 4(2) and 4(4) of the American Convention*

Yet the peculiar features of human rights treaties have not precluded them from falling back on general international law.[14]

With particular regard to customary international law, the well-known bi-partite formula of Article 38(1)(b) of the Statute of the International Court of Justice requires for the customary law-making process the concurrent presence of practice and *opinio juris*.[15] It has been claimed, however, that such a traditional understanding of the customary law process would not suit the field of human rights.[16] According to this view, the values at stake would justify a departure from the traditional formula, allowing *opinio juris*, alone, to create the law.[17]

Apart from the literature, it may be noted that the International Tribunal on the Former Yugoslavia, in referring to the customary status of the Martens Clause, posited:

---

on Human Rights), Advisory Opinion OC-3/83 of 8 September 1983, Series A No 3, 1983, pp. 76-77, para. 50. See HIGGINS, "Human Rights: Some Questions of Integrity", Commonwealth Law Bulletin, 1989, p. 598 ff., p. 607: "Human rights treaties are not just an exchange of obligations between states where they can agree at will, in a web of bilateral relationships within a multilateral treaty, what bargains they find acceptable. Human rights [...] reflect rights inherent in human beings, not dependent upon grant by the State".

[14] See, among others, *McElhinney v. Ireland*, Application No. 31253/96, Judgment of 21 November 2001, para. 36: "[t]he Convention [...] cannot be interpreted in a vacuum. The Court must be mindful of the Convention's special character as a human rights treaty, and it must take the relevant rules of international law into account. The Convention should so far as possible be interpreted in harmony with other rules of international law of which it forms a part"; for a similar approach see *Bankovic v. Belgium and others*, Admissibility, Decision of 12 December 2001, p. 351, para. 57. Judge Bruno Simma warned against an over-dramatization of the inherent peculiarities of human rights law. "Human rights treaties do possess distinctive features [...]. On the other hand, these differences are not as profound as some observers among the human rights community appear to think. In particular, human rights treaties do not constitute 'self-contained regimes' decoupled from the general law of treaties and of State responsibility": see SIMMA, "How Distinctive are Treaties Representing Collective Interest? The Case of Human Rights Treaties", in GOWLLAND-DEBBAS (ed.), *Multilateral Treaty-Making*, The Hague/Boston/London, 2000, p. 83 ff., p. 87.

[15] ILC, Draft Conclusions, *cit. supra* note 4, Conclusion 2; *North Sea Continental Shelf (Federal Republic of Germany v. Netherlands; Federal Republic of Germany v. Denmark)*, Judgment of 20 February 1969, ICJ Reports, 1969, p. 3 ff., p. 44; *Continental Shelf (Libyan Arab Jamahiriya v. Malta)*, Judgment of 3 June 1985, ICJ Reports, 1985, p. 13 ff., p. 29, para. 27; see JENNING and WATTS, "Oppenheim's International Law", Vol. 1, 9th ed., London-New York, 2008, p. 25 ff.

[16] See SCHACHTER, "International Law in Theory and Practice", RCADI, Vol. 178, 1982-V, p. 1 ff., pp. 334-335; GUNNING, "Modernizing Customary International Law: The Challenge of Human Rights", Virginia Journal of International Law, 1991, p. 211 ff., p. 212.

[17] See LILLICH, "The Growing Importance of Customary International Human Rights Law", Georgia Journal of International and Comparative Law, 1995-1996, p. 8 ff; HENKIN, "Human Rights and State 'Sovereignty'", Georgia Journal of International and Comparative Law, 1995-1996, p. 31 ff., pp. 34-35; FLAUSS, "La protection des droits de l'homme et les sources du droit international", in *La protection des droits de l'homme et l'évolution du droit international*, Paris, 1998, p. 65; THIRLWAY, *cit. supra* note 5, pp. 495-500; WOUTERS and RYNGAERT, *cit. supra* note 5, p. 129; KAMMERHOFER, "Orthodox Generalists and Political Activists in International Legal Scholarship", in HAPPOLD (ed.), *International Law in a Multipolar World*, Abingdon, 2012, p. 138 ff., p. 147.

in the light of the way States and courts have implemented it, this Clause clearly shows that principles of international humanitarian law may emerge through a customary process under the pressure of the demands of humanity or the dictates of public conscience, even where State practice is scant or inconsistent. The other element, in the form of *opinio necessitatis*, crystallising as a result of the imperatives of humanity or public conscience, may turn out to be the decisive element heralding the emergence of a general rule or principle of humanitarian law.[18]

The issue of human rights in customary international law went unnoticed in the famous 2000 International Law Association (ILA) Report on Custom.[19] Eight years later, the ILA's Committee of International Human Rights Law and Practice published a report on the Impact of International Human Rights Law on General International Law.[20] Here, it was maintained that the techniques to identify customary rules differ depending on the subject matter. It should not be assumed that such techniques "are the same for commercial shipping as for warfare".[21]

There is no denying that in international law there is something different about human rights.[22] What calls for more legal analysis is the question in *what respect* human rights law deserves a different treatment in international law.[23] Human rights are "inward-targeted". Their impact on domestic systems has turned the *"domaine réservé"* inside out.[24] Unlike in other branches of interna-

---

[18] ICTY, Trial Chamber, *Kupreskic et al.*, Case No. IT-95-16-T, Judgment of 14 January 2000, paras. 525 and 528.

[19] ILA Committee on Formation of Customary (General) International Law, Final Report on the Formation of Customary (General) International Law, 2000, available at: <http://www.ila-hq.org/index.php/committees>. A reference to human rights was made when pointing out the increasing role of international organisations and multilateral treaty making in the formation of customary rules in the field of human rights, environment, maritime jurisdiction and state immunity, para. 3.

[20] ILA Committee on International Human Rights Law and Practice, Final Report on the Impact of International Human Rights Law on General International Law, Rio de Janeiro Conference, 2008.

[21] *Ibid.*, p. 6. For the purpose of the present article, formation and identification of customary international law are considered as part of the same phenomenon; see the statement of the Chairman of the Drafting Committee, 7 August 2014, p. 3, available at: <http://legal.un.org/ilc/>); for a different approach, see CANNIZZARO, "Unità e pluralità dei metodi di accertamento del diritto consuetudinario", in PALCHETTI (ed.), *L'incidenza del diritto non scritto sul diritto internazionale ed europeo*, Napoli, 2016, p. 23 ff.

[22] See CONFORTI, "The Specificity of Human Rights and International Law", in ULRICH et al. (eds.), *From Bilateralism to Community Interest: Essays in Honour of Bruno Simma*, Oxford, 2011, p. 433 ff.

[23] See ADDO, *The Legal Nature of International Human Rights*, Leiden/Boston, 2010, p. 512.

[24] SIMMA and PULKOVSKI, "Of Planets and the Universe: Self-contained Regimes in International Law", EJIL, 2006, p. 483 ff., p. 524.

tional law, reciprocity has little room in this field,[25] given the *erga omnes* nature of human rights obligations.[26] The suspension of fundamental rights cannot be the object of countermeasures.[27]

The problem arises when such specific features, which could very well be accommodated in general international law, are taken to the extreme, transforming human rights into "human rightism" and hampering the coherence of the system. Here Professor Pellet criticised the "human rightist" attitude according to which "the rules of general international law are sound, but totally unsuited to this branch of law".[28]

Even if one did not share the position of Professor Pellet, who equalised "human rightists" to activists disguised as lawyers, it is a matter of fact that human rights scholars have a certain tendency to cite each other as supporting authority, often avoiding properly grounding their arguments in public international law. Propositions *de lege ferenda* are sometimes presented as customary rules,[29] "blessing with the oil of custom any norm judged to be desirable *ad majorem gloriam* of human rights".[30] But the common opinion of scholars does not suffice to make the law.[31] And, in any case, human rights-oriented lawyers may have a better case by framing their mutual citations as "teachings of the most highly qualified publicists" under letter (d) of Article 38(1) of the ICJ Statute.

3. THE ONGOING ILC WORK ON THE IDENTIFICATION OF CUSTOMARY INTERNATIONAL LAW

In his First Report, the Special Rapporteur Sir Michael Wood raised the question whether "there are different approaches to the formation and evidence of customary international law in different fields, such as international human rights law", and "whether, and if so to what degree, different weight may be given to

---

[25] See PROVOST, "Reciprocity in Human Rights and Humanitarian Law", BYIL, 1994, p. 383 ff., p. 386

[26] UN Human Rights Committee, General Comment No. 31, The Nature of the General Legal Obligation Imposed on States Parties to the Covenant, UN Doc. CCPR/C/21/Rev.1/Add.13 (2004), para. 2. See also GAJA, "The Protection of General Interests in the International Community", RCADI, Vol. 364, 2013, p. 9 ff., p. 101.

[27] ILC, Articles on Responsibility of States for Internationally Wrongful Acts, UN Doc. A/56/10 (2001), Art. 50(1)(a).

[28] PELLET, "'Human Rightism' and International Law", *cit. supra* note 1, p. 3; see also SHEERAN, "The Relationship of International Human Rights Law and General International Law: Hermeneutic Constraint, or Pushing The Boundaries?", in SHEERAN and RODLEY (eds.), *Routledge Handbook of International Human Rights Law*, Abingdon, 2013, p. 79 ff.

[29] JENNINGS, "International Law Reform and Progressive Development", in HAFNER et al. (eds.), *Liber Amicorum Professor Ignaz Seid-Hohenveldern in Honour of his 80th Birthday*, The Hague/Boston, 1998, p. 325 ff., p. 334.

[30] PELLET, "'Human Rightism' and International Law", *cit. supra* note 1, p. 7.

[31] PETERSEN, "Customary Law without Custom? Rules, Principles, and the Role of State Practice in International Norm Creation", American University International Law Review, 2008, p. 275 ff., p. 301.

different materials depending on the field in question".[32] In his Second Report the Special Rapporteur raised the point anew, just to answer that "this is not the case",[33] and to add that any different approach would impair the systemic nature of international law.[34] The answer reminds one of the symptoms of fragmentation as described by the ILC Special Rapporteur on the topic, when "answers to legal questions become dependent on whom you ask, what rule-system is your focus on".[35]

Yet at the same time the Special Rapporteur Michael Wood left a door open to some flexibility, by conceding that "there may […] be a difference in application of the two-element approach in different fields (or, perhaps more precisely, with respect to different types of rules)".[36] The margin left by the Special Rapporteur reminds us that the wording of Article 38(1)(b) of the Statute of the ICJ falls short of indicating a specific methodology for the identification of such constituent elements.[37] So much so that the ICJ itself had to find its own way to identify custom, relying on the classical two-pronged criterion, to be assessed, more or less rigorously, deductively or inductively, according to the context.[38]

The laconic reference to human rights by the ILC Reports referred to above may not be particularly useful in finding one's own position between traditional views which seek to tame custom in hyper positivistic formulas and "human rightist ones" ones which try to overstretch Article 38(1)(b).[39] Yet, it is arguable that the ILC Draft Conclusions on the identification of customary international law may smooth the edge.

---

[32] WOOD, First Report, *cit supra* note 8, para. 19.

[33] WOOD, Second Report on Identification of Customary International Law, UN Doc. A/CN.4/672 (2014), para. 28.

[34] *Ibid.*

[35] KOSKENNIEMI, Fragmentation of International Law: Difficulties Arising from the Diversification and Expansion of International Law, Report of the Study Group of the International Law Commission, UN Doc. A/CN/.4/L.682 (2016), para. 483.

[36] WOOD, Second Report, *cit. supra* note 33, para. 28.

[37] PELLET, "Article 38", in ZIMMERMANN et al. (eds.), *The Statute of the International Court of Justice*, 2nd ed., Oxford, 2012, p. 731 ff., p. 749.

[38] See, among others, ROBERTS, "Traditional and Modern Approaches to Customary International Law: A Reconciliation", AJIL, 2001, p. 757 ff; ALVAREZ-JIMENEZ, "Methods for the Identification of Customary International Law in the International Court of Justice's Jurisprudence: 2000–2009", ICLQ, 2011, p. 681 ff; GOWLLAND-DEBBAS, "Reflections on a Decade of International Law: Dark Ages or *Renouveau*?", in ALLAND et al. (eds.), *Unité et diversité du droit international: Ecrits en l'honneur du professeur Pierre-Marie Dupuy*, Leiden-Boston, 2004, p. 42 ff.; WORSTER, "The Inductive and Deductive Methods in Customary International Law Analysis: Traditional and Modern Approaches", Georgetown Journal of International Law, p. 445 ff.; for a critical perspective on the ICJ methodology, see TALMON, "Determining Customary International Law: The ICJ's Methodology Between Induction, Deduction and Assertion", EJIL, 2015, p. 417 ff; GRADONI, "The International Court of Justice and the International Customary Law Game of Cards", in ANDENAS and BJORGE (eds.) A *Farewell to Fragmentation: Reassertion and Convergence in International Law*, Oxford, 2015, p. 371 ff.

[39] For an overview of advantages and disadvantages of traditional and modern views of customary law, see LEPARD, "Customary International Law as a Dynamic Process", in BRADLEY (ed.), *cit. supra* note 5, p. 62 ff.

Draft Conclusion 3 acknowledges that on a case-by-case basis assessment of evidence of the constitutive elements of custom, account must be given to the "overall context, the nature of the rule, and the particular circumstances in which the evidence is to be found".[40] It suggests that the type of evidence consulted (and consideration of its availability or otherwise) may be adjusted to the "overall context". Depending on such context, certain forms of practice and evidence of acceptance as law (*opinio juris*) may be of particular significance.[41] One may argue that the language of Draft Conclusion 3 allows for the appropriate flexibility in addressing the customary dimension of human rights law.

Part Five of the Draft Conclusions seems to offer additional flexibility. This Part, entitled "Significance of Certain Materials for the Identification of Customary International Law", identifies four elements that may be of assistance in ascertaining the existence of a custom; namely, treaties, resolutions of international organizations and intergovernmental conferences, decisions of courts and tribunals and teachings.[42]

Conduct in connection with treaties – intended as "all acts related to the negotiation and conclusion of treaties, as well as their implementation" – already falls within the forms of practice listed in Draft Conclusion 6. Similarly, Commentary to Draft Conclusion 11, which concerns the role of treaties in the identification of custom, emphasises that "the extent of participation in a treaty may be an important factor in determining whether it corresponds to customary international law; treaties that have obtained near universal acceptance may be seen as particularly indicative in this respect".[43] This does not imply that all the provisions contained in the widely ratified human rights treaties reflect obligations of a customary nature. But given the high record of ratifications that the major human rights treaties can boast, strong arguments could be made regarding the customary nature of the rights most widely protected in such treaty instruments.[44]

---

[40] Draft Conclusion 3; see also *Jurisdictional Immunities of the State case* (*Germany v. Italy*), Judgment of 3 February 2012, ICJ Reports, 2012, p. 99 ff., p. 123, para. 55.

[41] ILC, Draft Conclusions, *cit. supra* note 4, see Commentary to Draft Conclusion 3.

[42] *Ibid.*, Part Five.

[43] *Ibid.*, Commentary to Draft Conclusion 11. On the role of human rights treaties as evidence of customary international law, see D'AMATO, "The Concept of Human Rights in International Law", Columbia Law Review, 1982, p. 1129 ff; for a different view, see AKEHURST, "Custom as a Source of International Law", BYIL, 1974, p. 1 ff., p. 3.

[44] *Questions Relating to the Obligation to Prosecute or Extradite* (*Belgium v. Senegal*), Judgment of 20 July 2012, ICJ Reports, 2012, p. 422 ff., p. 457, para. 99: "the prohibition of torture is part of customary international law and it has become a peremptory norm (jus cogens). That prohibition is grounded in a widespread international practice and on the opinio juris of States. It appears in numerous international instruments of universal application (in particular the Universal Declaration of Human Rights of 1948, the 1949 Geneva Conventions for the protection of war victims; the International Covenant on Civil and Political Rights of 1966; General Assembly resolution 3452/30 of 9 December 1975 on the Protection of All Persons from Being Subjected to Torture and Other Cruel, Inhuman or Degrading Treatment or Punishment) and it has been introduced into the domestic law of almost all States".

As to resolutions of international organizations, their role as relevant material for the identification of custom is recognised by Draft Conclusion 12, with the caveat that a resolution cannot itself create customary international law and under the condition that "all due caution" is used and that "actual practice is not absent, different or inconsistent".[45] Very much in line with this rationale, it is arguable that resolutions in the field of human rights can provide a rich source of evidence, following the perceived normative value of the particular resolution and the circumstances surrounding its adoption.

With regard to courts and tribunals, their role in the formation and identification of customary rules is well known.[46] Within the approach of the Draft Conclusions, the role of domestic courts' decisions is primarily one of evidence of state practice and *opinio juris*.[47] International decisions, on the other hand, operate as subsidiary means for determining customary rules,[48] a role which is reinforced by the increasing tendency of international courts and tribunals to rely on their previous decisions, or on decisions of other international adjudicative bodies.[49] In the human rights context such material is to be complemented by the numerous decisions and recommendations of quasi-judicial human rights treaty bodies monitoring treaties of a quasi-universal scope.[50]

Having regard to the old-fashioned contribution of the teachings of the most highly qualified publicists under Article 38(1)(d) of the ICJ Statute, the general view is that one should not place too high expectations on their actual role nowadays.[51]

---

[45] ILC, Draft Conclusions, *cit. supra* note 4, Commentary to Draft Conclusion 12, paras. 6 and 8. *Military and Paramilitary Activities in and Against Nicaragua (Nicaragua v. United States of America)*, Judgment of 27 June 1986, ICJ Reports, 1986, p. 14 ff., para. 188: "opinio juris may, though with all due caution, be deduced from, inter alia, the attitude of the Parties and the attitude of States towards certain General Assembly resolutions [...]. The effect of consent to the text of such resolutions [...] may be understood as an acceptance of the validity of the rule or set of rules declared by the resolution by themselves". See also MERON, "Revival of Customary Humanitarian Law", AJIL, 2005, p. 817 ff., p. 819.

[46] See HIGGINS, "Human Rights in the International Court of Justice", Leiden JIL,. 2007, p. 745 ff.; SIMMA, "Human Rights Before the International Court of Justice: Community Interest Coming to Life", in TAMS and SLOAN (eds.), *The Development of International Law by the International Court of Justice*, Oxford, p. 301 ff.; CONFORTI (ed. by IOVANE), *Diritto internazionale*, 11th ed., Napoli, 2018, pp. 44 and 57-58.

[47] ILC, Draft Conclusions, *cit. supra* note 4, Draft Conclusions 6(2), 10 (2) and 13(2). The ILC envisages a minor role of domestic decisions as subsidiary means for the determination of custom; on this point, see MILES, "Thoughts on Domestic Adjudication and the Identification and Formation of Customary International Law", in this Volume.

[48] ILC, Draft Conclusions, *cit. supra* note 4, Draft Conclusion 13(1).

[49] See IOVANE, "L'influence de la multiplication des juridictions internationales sur l'application du droit international", RCADI, Vol. 383, 2017, p. 233 ff., pp. 396-397; ANDENAS and LEISS, "The Systematic Relevance of 'Judicial Decisions' in Article 38 of the ICJ Statute", ZAÖRV, 2017, p. 1 ff.; ALSHNER and CHARLOTIN, "The Growing Complexity of the International Court of Justice's Self-Citation Network", EJIL, 2018, p. 83 ff.

[50] See KANETAKE, "UN Human Rights Treaty Monitoring Bodies before Domestic Courts", ICLQ, 2017, p. 201 ff.

[51] See D'ASPREMONT, *Formalism and the Sources of International Law*, Oxford, 2011, p. 210.

Yet human rightists could make good use of Article (38)(1) (d) adding "legal shape" to their mutual and reiterated cross-quotation.[52]

In sum, the process of formation of customary international law in the field of human rights, not unlike in other fields, falls within a broader process where treaties, resolutions, court decisions and scholarly works constitute the raw material.[53] The lapidary terms of Article 38(1)(b) of the ICJ Statute should not lead to an overly simplistic reading of what turns out to be a complex process. Nor does this seems to have been the intention of the ILC work. Customary international law is not a monolithic landmass and the two constitutive elements belong to the same process.[54]

Admitting that in different branches of international law the weight put on practice and *opinio juris* may differ according to the "context" should not lead to unnecessary claims of exceptionalism on the part of human rights lawyers; nor does a logical attention to the specific "context" of any given custom imply that the uniform theory of customary law is to be replaced by sectorial theories of custom. Whilst the ICJ recognises that both practice and *opinio juris* lay at the core of the customary process, it does not expect that "for a rule to be established as customary, the corresponding practice must be in absolutely rigorous conformity with the rule".[55]

At the same time, the inherent flexibility of customary international law cannot go so far as to reject its essential nature as a general practice accepted as law. In each case, a careful process of legal analysis is required in order to ensure that only a rule of customary international law properly so called is identified.

4.   CONCLUDING REMARKS

International law governs today an increasing number of areas previously confined to the *domaine réservé*. Some of these areas, like that of human rights, are more receptive to change, contributing to the progressive development of

---

[52] On the role of scholars in developing international law, see SIMMA, "Scholars in the Construction and Critique of International Law", American Society of International Law Proceedings, 2000, p. 317 ff., p. 319; WOOD, "Teachings of the Most Highly Qualified Publicists (Art. 38(1) ICJ Statute)", Max Planck Encyclopedia of Public in International Law, 2010, available at: <http://opil.ouplaw.com/home/epil>, para. 16; SIVAKUMARAN, "The Influence of Teachings of Publicists on the Development of International Law", ICLQ, 2017, p. 1 ff.

[53] CASSESE and WELLER, *Change and Stability in International Law-Making*, Berlin-Boston, 1988, p. 13 ff.

[54] STERN, "Custom at the Heart of International Law", Duke Journal of Comparative & International Law, 2001, p. 89 ff.; see also JENNINGS, "General Course on Principles of International Law", RCADI, Vol. 121, 1967-II, p. 323 ff., p. 335. CONDORELLI, "Custom", in BEDJAOUI (ed.), *International Law: Achievements and Prospects*, Paris-Dordrecht-Boston-London, 1991, p. 179 ff., p. 188.

[55] *Military and Paramilitary Activities in and against Nicaragua, cit. supra* note 45, p. 14, para. 186.

international law.[56] This cannot but have an impact on the process of formation and on the identification of the customary nature of any given rule.[57] However, it is in the nature of general law to apply generally; if we allowed different rules to apply to the formation and identification of customary law in certain areas only, one would wonder what would be left of general international law.[58] Special care should be taken to avoid depriving human rights of the authority of general international law, which provides a common structure for its sub-systems and a basic legal platform for an often under-enforced field such as that of human rights.[59]

Professor Alain Pellet is right in pointing out that, when "human rightists" are upset by the results of treaty-making, which they find unduly slow, "they seek consolation in custom […] to 'harden' a law that is deemed excessively soft […].[60] Indeed, some, like Professor Jean d'Aspremont, regard custom as a tool for the expansionist agenda of international human rights law.[61] But by accepting that anything goes when it comes to human rights, 'human rightists' harm the cause that they intend to defend more than they serve it".[62] For the sake of the effectiveness of the human rights process, any departure from general international law should rest on solid legal grounds. This would also benefit the impact of human rights on general international law.[63] Rather than overstretching customary law, human rights lawyers could look for authority for their legal arguments by referring more to other sources of international law. Principles of law, being both a source of law and an interpretative technique, provide a powerful tool in that direction, though all too often neglected.[64]

---

[56] See PISILLO MAZZESCHI, "Human Rights and the Modernization of International Law", in LENZERINI and VRDOLJAK (eds.), *International Law for Common Goods: Normative Perspectives on Human Rights, Culture and Nature*, Oxford/Portland, 2014, p. 89 ff.

[57] See MÜLLERSON, "The Interplay of Objective and Subjective Elements in Customary Law", in WELLENS (ed.), *International Law: Theory and Practice Essays in Honour of Eric Suy*, The Hague/Boston/London, 1998, p. 161 ff.

[58] TREVES, "Customary International Law", Max Planck Encyclopedia of Public in International Law, 2006, available at: <http://opil.ouplaw.com/home/epil>, para. 3: "[t]he essential characteristic which customary international law rules have in common is the way they have come into existence and the way their existence may be determined".

[59] SIMMA and PULKOVSKI, *cit. supra* note 24, p. 512.

[60] PELLET, "'Human Rightism' and International Law", *cit. supra* note 1, p. 6.

[61] D'ASPREMONT, "Expansionism and the Sources of International Human Rights Law", Israel Yearbook on Human Rights, 2016, p. 223 ff., p. 234.

[62] PELLET, "'Human Rightism' and International Law", *cit. supra* note 1, p. 4.

[63] PRONTO, "'Human-Rightism' and the Development of General International Law", Leiden JIL, 2007, p. 753 ff.; see also CASSESE, *International Law*, 2nd ed., Oxford, 2005, pp. 296-297.

[64] SIMMA and ALSTON, "The Sources of Human Rights Law: Custom, Jus Cogens, and General Principles", Australian Yearbook of International Law, 1992, p. 82 ff.; WOUTERS and RYNGAERT, *cit. supra* note 5, pp. 120-122; ANDENAS and CHIUSSI, "Cohesion, Convergence and Coherence in International Law", in ANDENAS et al. (eds.), *General Principles and the Cohesion of International Law*, Leiden/Boston, forthcoming. Alain Pellet warns against the use of principles of law in the field of human rights, arguing that many human rights are far from being incorporated in all domestic legal systems, in PELLET, "'Human Rightism' and International Law", *cit. supra* note 1, p. 7. At the same time Pellet himself recognises that "[l]'existence juridique du droit au développement peut être déduite de multiples textes in-

In the meantime, one could avoid tarring any slightly different approach to the identification of customary human rights rules with the brush of "human rightism". Enough flexibility is envisaged by Draft Conclusion 3 to cover the peculiarities of the different fields of international law, and it seems that other "Grotian moments"[65] of international law have benefitted from more tolerance on the part of public international lawyers.

A final remark on the ILC work on the identification of customary law. According to Article 13 of the UN Charter, the ILC has a mandate to progressively develop and codify international law.[66] With regard to the topic in hand, the ILC was required to "describe the current state of international law on the formation and evidence of rules of customary international law, without prejudice to developments that might occur in the future".[67] The aim was "to secure a common understanding of the process of identifying customary international law among all those who are called upon to apply it – not least given the considerable differences of approach amongst writers".[68]

In this regard, the work of the ILC is meant to be a generally available legal kit for the ascertainment of customary rules by judges, practitioners and scholars. It seems no less appropriate in relation to a heavily value-loaded field of international law, such as human rights.

---

ternationaux, dont on peut inférer que le principe constitue le fondement commun de certains droits de l'homme" in PELLET, "Note sur quelques aspects juridiques de la notion de droit au développement", in FLORY and OTHERS (eds.), *La formation des normes en droit international du développement*, Paris/Algers, p. 71 ff.

[65] SCHARF, *Customary International Law in Times of Fundamental Change: Recognizing Grotian Moments*, Cambridge, 2013, p. 8: "[t]he Grotian Moment concept illuminates how and why customary international law can sometimes develop with surprising rapidity and limited state practice. The concept reflects the reality that in periods of fundamental change, whether by technological advances, the commission of new forms of crimes against humanity, or the development of new means of warfare or terrorism, rapidly developing customary international law may be necessary to keep up with the pace of developments".

[66] Art. 1(1) of the Statute of the International Law Commission, adopted by the General Assembly in resolution 174 (II) of 21 November 1947. On the relevance of the forms of codification, see TANZI, "A Relative Approach to the Tensions between Voluntaristic and Jusnaturalistic Trends in the Codification process", in BODEAU-LIVINEC (ed.), *Formes du droit international: réflexions sur le devenir des travaux de la Commission du droit international des Nations Unies*, Paris, forthcoming.

[67] WOOD, Fifth Report on Identification on Customary International Law, UN Doc. A/CN.4/717 (2018), para. 21.

[68] SENDER and WOOD, "Custom's Bright Future: The Continuing Importance of Customary International Law", in BRADLEY (ed.), *cit. supra* note 5, p. 360 ff., p. 366.

THE PERSISTENT OBJECTOR RULE IN THE WORK OF THE INTERNATIONAL LAW COMMISSION ON THE IDENTIFICATION OF CUSTOMARY INTERNATIONAL LAW

JAMES A. GREEN*

Abstract

The persistent objector rule is a well-known but controversial mechanism for a state to exempt itself from norms of customary international law. This article examines the rule with a specific focus on the work of the International Law Commission (ILC) on the Identification of Customary International Law, through a consideration of Conclusion 15 and the commentary to it that have been adopted, as well as the ILC plenary debates on the topic. The state usage and, indeed, very existence of the rule will be considered, given that this has been so controversial in the ILC and wider literature. The article further examines whether the rule rightly formed an aspect of the Commission's work, and looks at the terminology employed in Conclusion 15. Finally, it assesses the requirements for the operation of the persistent objector rule as expressed by the ILC, through comparison to the manner in which the criteria have been employed in state practice.

Keywords: persistent objector rule; persistent objection; customary international law; International Law Commission; ILC.

1. INTRODUCTION

This article examines the engagement by the International Law Commission ("ILC"), in the context of its work on the Identification of Customary International Law,[1] with the so-called "persistent objector rule". It evaluates the ILC's approach to, and understanding of, persistent objection, both in its debates on the topic and in the draft conclusions and commentaries that it has now adopted.

All international lawyers are familiar with the basic notion of the persistent objector rule: the broad concept is that where a state objects to a norm of customary international law persistently, and does so while that norm still is emerging, the state is said to gain an exemption from the norm when it crystallises into binding customary international law. The rule is a ubiquitous feature of mainstream international law scholarship[2] and has been endorsed in a number of decisions by

---

* Professor of Public International Law, University of Reading, United Kingdom.

[1] See International Law Commission, Analytical Guide to the Work of the International Law Commission: Identification of Customary International Law, available at: <http://legal.un.org/ilc/guide/1_13.shtml>.

[2] See, e.g., WOOD, Fourth Report on Identification of Customary International Law, Addendum, UN Doc. A/CN.4/695/Add.1 (2016), pp. 19-20.

international[3] and domestic[4] courts and tribunals. For some commentators, it is viewed as crucial for protecting the voluntarist notion that states are only bound by law to which they have consented to be bound by, on the basis that the rule allows states to *withhold* consent to customary international law.[5]

The persistent objector rule has formed an aspect of the ILC's recent work on the Identification of Customary International Law, and is set out in Conclusion 15 [previously 16] of the draft conclusions on the topic that were provisionally adopted by the Commission's drafting committee in 2015,[6] and then adopted by the ILC as a whole in 2016.[7] Conclusion 15 reads:

> *Persistent objector*
> 1. Where a State has objected to a rule of customary international law while that rule was in the process of formation, the rule is not opposable to the State concerned for so long as it maintains its objection.
> 2. The objection must be clearly expressed, made known to other States, and maintained persistently.

This adopted conclusion may be seen, at least in broad terms, as amounting to an endorsement by the ILC of the orthodox view of the persistent objector rule. However, the debates in the Commission on the Identification of Customary International Law reveal that there remain underlying controversies in relation to the rule, which are considered herein. Further, while Conclusion 15 presents a relatively orthodox picture of the rule, the commentary to it goes into more detail than most accounts of the rule. The requirements that the ILC has set out for the rule's operation therefore are tested in this article against the way in which the rule has developed in state practice (as well as in case law and scholarship).

The space constraints of an article of this kind mean that in-depth engagement with state practice and case law is impossible, but it should be noted that it

---

[3] See, e.g., *Fisheries case (United Kingdom v. Norway)*, Judgment of 18 December 1951, ICJ Reports, 1951, p. 116 ff., p. 131; Inter-American Commission on Human Rights, *Domingues v. United States*, Case 12.285, Merits, Report No. 62/02 of 22 October 2002; *BG Group Plc v. Republic of Argentina*, UNCITRAL tribunal, Final Award of 24 December 2007.

[4] See, e.g., United States Court of Appeals for the Ninth Circuit (United States), *Siderman de Blake v Republic of Argentina*, 22 May 1992, 965 F.2d 699 (9th Cir. 1992), p. 715; Bundesverfassungsgericht (Germany), *Philippine Embassy Bank Account Case*, 13 December 1977, 65 ILR 146, para. 6; Supreme Court of Appeal (South Africa), *S v Petane*, 3 November 1987, 1988 3 SA 51 (C), ILDC 1348 (ZA 1987), para. 64 A-B.

[5] See, e.g., STEINFELD, "Nuclear Objections: The Persistent Objector and the Legality of the Use of Nuclear Weapons", Brooklyn Law Review, 1996, p. 1635 ff., p. 1655. See also International Law Commission, Provisional Summary Record of the 3252nd Meeting, UN Doc. A/CN.4/SR.3252 (2015), p. 8 (WISNUMURTI).

[6] UN Doc. A/CN.4/L.869 (2015), p. 5.

[7] UN Doc. A/71/10 (2016), pp. 112-114.

draws on the findings of a major six year project on the rule previously conducted by the author.[8]

2. THE USAGE (AND VERY EXISTENCE) OF THE RULE

It was noted in the ILC's Report on the work done in its sixty-seventh session in 2015 that while "[s]everal members supported the inclusion of the [persistent objector] rule in the set of draft conclusions [...] some other members considered that it was a controversial theory not supported by sufficient State practice and jurisprudence [...]".[9] A review of the Commission's plenary debates both in 2015 and 2016 confirms that a substantial minority of members were sceptical about *very existence* of the persistent objector rule, or at least had significant concerns about its inclusion in the draft conclusions given that they felt it was insufficiently supported by state practice.[10]

This minority, but fundamental, critique of the persistent objector rule in the ILC is reflective of the wider academic literature. Despite the ubiquity of the rule in scholarship, as one ILC member rightly stressed in plenary debate,[11] plenty of writers doubt whether it exists *at all*[12] on the basis that it is never (or almost never) used. For example, Anthony D'Amato wrote in 2014 that "[t]he persistent objector rule *has never been* invoked in state practice".[13] In total contrast, another group of scholars have argued that there is in fact a notable amount of state usage of the rule.[14] Maurice Mendelson asserted in 1998, for example, that there was

---

[8] Published as GREEN, *The Persistent Objector Rule in International Law*, Oxford, 2016 (paperback edition, 2018).

[9] UN Doc. A/70/10 (2015), p. 46. See also International Law Commission, Provisional Summary Record of the 3340th Meeting, UN Doc. A/CN.4/SR.3340 (2016), p. 8 (TLADI).

[10] See, e.g., UN Doc. A/CN.4/SR.3252, *cit. supra* note 5, p. 4 (MURASE), pp. 8-9 (CAFLISCH), p. 16 (KAMTO); Provisional Summary Record of the 3253rd Meeting, UN Doc. A/CN.4/SR.3253 (2015), p. 9 (PETRIČ), p. 11 (VÁZQUEZ-BERMÚDEZ); Provisional Summary Record of the 3254th Meeting, UN Doc. A/CN.4/SR.3254 (2015), p. 8 (GÓMEZ-ROBLEDO); Provisional Summary Record of the 3302nd Meeting, UN Doc. A/CN.4/SR.3302 (2016), p. 9 (PARK).

[11] Provisional Summary Record of the 3288th Meeting, UN Doc. A/CN.4/SR.3288 (2015), p. 14 (CAFLISCH).

[12] See, e.g., DUMBERRY, "Incoherent and Ineffective: The Concept of Persistent Objector Revisited", ICLQ, 2010, p. 779 ff.; DUPUY, "A propos de l'opposabilité de la coutume générale: enquête brève sur 'l'objecteur persistant'", in *Le droit international au service de la paix, de la justice et du développement: Mélanges offerts à Michel Virally*, Paris, 1991, p. 257 ff.

[13] D'AMATO, "Groundwork for International Law", AJIL, 2014, p. 650 ff., p. 668 (emphasis added).

[14] See, e.g., International Law Association, Committee on Formation of Customary (General) International Law, Final Report of the Committee (2000), available at: <http://www.ila-hq.org/en/committees/index.cfm/cid/30>, pp. 27-28; COLSON, "How Persistent Must the Persistent Objector Be?", Washington Law Review, 1986, p. 957 ff., p. 969.

"quite a wealth of state practice in support of the persistent objector rule" and that scholars simply have not "looked hard enough" to find it.[15]

The reality falls somewhere between these two extremes of "no usage" and "significant usage". When one reviews state practice it is clear, at least in the view of the present author, that there has been more than enough invocation of the persistent objector rule by states, and recognition of the exempt status that it brings, to conclude that the rule exists, especially when one adds to this the numerous endorsements of the rule in case law and the majority (if far from universal) support for it in scholarly opinion.[16] D'Amato's claim that the rule "has never been invoked in state practice" is patently, demonstrably wrong. Indeed, not only is the persistent objector rule being used by states, it is being used with increasing regularity in the 21st century.[17] Nonetheless, it also is important not to overstate the amount of state usage of the persistent objector rule. The rule is used, and increasingly so, but it is undeniable – when one does "look hard enough" at practice – that it is still not used all that much.[18]

While deep-rooted disagreement persists amongst experts (including in the ILC), it is telling that states themselves widely accept the rule's existence,[19] even if they do not use it all that often. Indeed, this is something that is evident purely from the ILC's work on the Identification of Customary International Law topic. In the submissions made to the Commission by states on the subject, no state expressed any concern about including the rule in the draft conclusions – which might have been expected had there been any significant dissent on the matter – and some states explicitly endorsed it.[20] Switzerland, for example, stressed that

> [l]es notions d'objecteur persistant et d'objecteur subséquent ont été précisées à plusieurs reprises et de manière conjointe par les autorités suisses. Les autorités suisses n'ont cependant, à l'heure actuelle, jamais invoqué une objection persistante de la Suisse à la formation de la coutume.[21]

Thus, Switzerland went so far as explicitly accepting persistent objection even while stressing that it had, as yet, never used the rule itself.

---

[15] MENDELSON, "The Formation of Customary International Law", RCADI, Vol. 272, 1998, p. 155 ff., p. 238.

[16] See GREEN, *cit. supra* note 8, particularly pp. 33-56.

[17] See *ibid*, pp. 54-55; BRADLEY, "The Juvenile Death Penalty and International Law", Duke Law Journal, 2002-2003, p. 485 ff., p. 517. See also UN Doc. A/CN.4/SR.3253, *cit. supra* note 10, p. 12 (HUANG).

[18] See GREEN, *cit. supra* note 8, particularly p. 55 and pp. 63-65.

[19] UN Doc. A/71/10, *cit. supra* note 7, p. 113; UN Doc. A/CN.4/SR.3253, *cit. supra* note 10, p. 11 (VÁZQUEZ-BERMÚDEZ).

[20] See REINISCH, on behalf of the Permanent Mission of Austria to the United Nations in New York, 2016, p. 3, available at: <http://legal.un.org/docs/?path=../ilc/sessions/68/pdfs/english/icil_austria.pdf&lang=E>; "La pratique suisse relative à la détermination du droit international coutumier", Information submitted by Switzerland to the ILC, 2016, p. 57, available at: <http://legal.un.org/docs/?path=../ilc/sessions/68/pdfs/french/icil_switzerland.pdf&lang=F>.

[21] "La pratique suisse", *cit. supra* note 20.

States use the persistent objector rule and accept its use. Admittedly, the assertion in the ILC's adopted commentary to Conclusion 15 that "[t]he persistent objector rule is *quite frequently* invoked and recognized",[22] arguably goes slightly too far, in that it may indicate that the rule is used more than is actually the case. Nonetheless, crucially, Conclusion 15 and its commentary effectively, and correctly, reject the repeated claims that the rule is never (or hardly ever) used.

3. THE RULE AND THE IDENTIFICATION OF CUSTOM

Notwithstanding the conclusion in the previous section that the ILC rightly has found that the persistent objector rule exists and is used, one might question whether the rule should have been included as part of the Commission's adopted conclusions, or form an aspect of the programme of work on the Identification of Customary International Law topic.

The persistent objector rule is a "secondary rule"[23] of the international legal system,[24] in that it is a "rule about rules". However, it is not a "secondary rule *of recognition*",[25] in that it does not contribute to the *creation* or *determination of content* of substantive primary rules of customary international law. Instead, the persistent objector rule "concerns the scope of application of a customary international law rule or its 'opposability'".[26] On that basis, it was debated in the Commission whether the persistent objector rule fell outside of the scope of the ILC's work, given that it is focused on the *identification* of customary international law.[27] Some ILC members concluded that the rule is not, strictly speaking, relevant to the identification of custom, because it does not help to identify the content or existence of such rules.[28] Others, in contrast, took a broader view of the notion of "identification", arguing that it encompassed not just the identification of existence or content, but also the identification of the *legal effect* of customary rules,[29] something with which the persistent objector obviously is directly concerned.

The decision that that the persistent objector rule should be included in the Commission's programme of work (and the resulting draft conclusions) was largely reached on a pragmatic basis, notwithstanding whether or not the rule "technically" fell within the scope of the Commission's topic. Omitting the rule from the conclusions was seen as something that would make them less valuable as a practical tool

---

[22] UN Doc. A/71/10, *cit. supra* note 7, p. 113 (emphasis added).

[23] See HART, *The Concept of Law*, 2nd ed., Oxford, 1994, particularly pp. 79-99.

[24] STEIN, "The Approach of the Different Drummer: The Principle of the Persistent Objector in International Law", Harvard ILJ, 1985, p. 457 ff., p. 458.

[25] HART, *cit. supra* note 23, particularly pp. 94-99.

[26] YEE, "Report on the ILC Project on 'Identification of Customary International Law'", Chinese Journal of International Law, 2015, p. 375 ff., p. 381.

[27] See Statement of the Chairman of the Drafting Committee, Mr. Mathias Forteau (2015), p. 18.

[28] See, e.g., UN Doc. A/CN.4/SR.3252, *cit. supra* note 5, p. 4 (MURASE); UN Doc. A/CN.4/SR.3340, *cit. supra* note 9, p. 7 (MURASE).

[29] See, e.g., *ibid.*, p. 8 (NOLTE and WOOD).

for engaging with customary international law, and this in itself was considered sufficient to justify its inclusion.[30] As the Special Rapporteur, Sir Michael Wood, noted, the question of persistent objection "might well arise before judges who were asked to identify rules of customary international law. It would thus be useful to provide practitioners with guidelines on how the matter was to be evaluated [...]".[31]

This reasoning is hard to dispute. The absence of the persistent objector rule would have given readers of the draft conclusion an incomplete picture of how customary international law operates, as well as fuelling the incorrect claims that the rule does not exist. However, it may have been helpful for the practical value underpinning the rule's inclusion to have been made explicit in the commentary to Conclusion 15. The commentary instead adopted the rather vague wording proposed by Donald McRea,[32] that the rule is something that "not infrequently arises in connection with the identification of rules of customary international law".[33] That statement is correct, and neatly side-steps the question of whether the rule is about the "identification of custom" or not. Yet it lacks the clarity of an explicit assertion as to why the Commission felt the rule should be included, given that its relationship to the "identification of customary international law" can at least be questioned.

4. IS THE PERSISTENT OBJECTOR "RULE" A RULE?

Another way in which the continued controversy surrounding the concept of persistent objection manifested in the ILC was in relation to terminology. The persistent objector rule commonly is referred to as just that: a "rule". It therefore appears somewhat strange that the adopted text of Conclusion 15 refers not to the "persistent objector rule", but simply to "persistent objector".

The term "rule" was avoided because some members of the Commission were uncomfortable with labelling persistent objection in that way.[34] For example, some felt it was rather more nebulous than a "rule", and, as such, should be referred to as a "doctrine" or "concept".[35] Other members went further, indicating their underlying scepticism about the very notion of persistent objection, by instead terming it the persistent objector "theory".[36]

---

[30] See Summary Record of the 3280th Meeting, UN Doc. A/CN.4/SR.3280 (2015) p. 13 (Report of the Drafting Committee); Statement of the Chairman of the Drafting Committee, *cit. supra* note 27, pp. 18-19; UN Doc. A/CN.4/SR.3254, *cit. supra* note 10, p. 9 (SINGH), p. 14 (WOOD)

[31] *Ibid.*

[32] UN Doc. A/CN.4/SR.3340, *cit. supra* note 9, p. 8 (MCREA).

[33] UN Doc. A/71/10, *cit. supra* note 7, p. 112.

[34] See, e.g., UN Doc. A/CN.4/SR.3340, *cit. supra* note 9, p. 7 (PETRIČ, SABOIA and JACOBSSON).

[35] See, e.g., *ibid.*, p. 6 (PARK), p. 7 (ŠTURMA and McRAE).

[36] See, e.g., UN Doc. A/CN.4/SR.3252, *cit. supra* note 5, p. 8 (CAFLISCH); UN Doc. A/CN.4/SR.3254, *cit. supra* note 10, p. 8 (GÓMEZ-ROBLEDO). See also WOOD, Annex A. Formation and evidence of customary international law, UN Doc. A/66/10 (2011), p. 308.

Whether or not the process of persistent objection amounts to a "rule" of course depends as much on how one defines a "rule" in an international legal context – hardly a settled question – as it does on the content or mechanics of persistent objection. This is not the place to delve into philosophical constructions of what a "rule" is, but one might note that persistent objection has some of the features that have been associated with legal rules, at least by some.[37] In particular, it has a prescriptive and algorithmic structure (i.e., it has criteria that underpin its operation[38] and its application leads to a direct legal effect). As one member of the ILC stated, at least in the formulation in which it appears in Conclusion 15, the mechanism for persistent objection certainly seems to be presented as a "rule",[39] and, as was discussed above in Section 1, that formulation is broadly reflective of the way in which persistent objection commonly is framed in wider doctrine.

The terminology used in Conclusion 15 – while interesting – admittedly is perhaps a minor issue. It is telling that, while the term "rule" was omitted from Conclusion 15, the term "persistent objector *rule*" is used repeatedly in the adopted commentary to Conclusion 15. For those ILC members who supported the rule's inclusion in the draft conclusions, there presumably seemed little to be gained by insisting that it be made explicit that it is "a rule" in the conclusion itself, in the face of opposition from other members. The use of the open-ended term "persistent objector" is a neat solution, which allows readers to infuse it with their own preferred understanding. Had an alternative descriptor (such as "concept" or – worse – "theory") been adopted instead of "rule", it would have embedded significant uncertainties as to the rule's existence and nature in the draft conclusions.

What is important is that the *content* of the notion of persistent objection was endorsed in the adopted draft conclusions. As Georg Nolte stressed in plenary debate, the persistent objector rule "did not stop being a rule simply because the Commission did not describe it as one."[40] A spade is a spade, and – in this writer's view – the persistent objector rule is a rule, whether we call it one or not.

5. THE CRITERIA FOR THE OPERATION OF THE PERSISTENT OBJECTOR RULE

As the ILC correctly noted in its commentary to Conclusion 15, the persistent objector rule is subject to "stringent requirements".[41] The criteria for per-

---

[37] For discussion, see, e.g., ALEXANDER, "The Objectivity of Morality, Rules, and Law: A Conceptual Map", Alabama Law Review, 2013, p. 501 ff.; PERRY, "Hart on Social Rules and the Foundations of Law: Liberating the Internal Point of View", Fordham Law Review, 2006, p. 1171 ff.

[38] See *infra* Section 5.

[39] UN Doc. A/CN.4/SR.3340, *cit. supra* note 9, p. 8 (TLADI).

[40] UN Doc. A/CN.4/SR.3340, *cit. supra* note 9, pp. 7-8 (NOLTE). See also, *ibid.*, p. 8 (COMISSÁRIO AFONSO and TLADI).

[41] UN Doc. A/71/10, *cit. supra* note 7, p. 112 and p. 114. See also Statement of the Chairman of the Drafting Committee, *cit. supra* note 27, p. 20.

sistent objection are onerous,[42] as is appropriate for a rule that sanctifies exceptionalism.[43] They also involve a notable degree of flexibility and uncertainty. Of course, the basic aspects of the persistent objector rule – particularly the need to object persistently, and to do so before the norm being objected to has crystallised into binding law – are extremely familiar,[44] but there remains a lack of clarity as to exactly what is required for persistent objection, and how the criteria for its operation are to be applied in practice.

Despite such uncertainties, an examination of state practice and jurisprudence provides insights into the manner in which the rule is used and, thus, the necessary criteria for its use.[45] The present author conceptualises the requirements for persistent objection as five criteria. All of these five criteria have been reflected in the work of the ILC on the identification of customary international law to some extent, as well as all being present in wider scholarship. Having said this, these criteria are often framed in different ways: for example, sometimes they are combined or articulated through alterative terms. More notably, they are emphasised to different extents by different commentators, to the point that some of them are at times entirely overlooked.

5.1. Objection

It is perhaps inane to say that a state must "object" for it to be considered a persistent objector. However, it is important to note that not any objection will suffice. In particular, objection must be openly expressed, so that it is effectively communicated to other states. This is evident from a review of practice[46] and, perhaps rather obviously, stems from requirements of certainty and the need for other states to be able to rely on the dissenter's objections.[47] It therefore is pleasing that these elements of the required "quality" of objection, which are often overlooked in literature, have been made explicit in the ILC's outcomes, not only in the commentary to the draft conclusions,[48] but in text of Conclusion 15 itself, which, it will be recalled, states that "[t]he objection must be clearly expressed [and] made known to other States."[49]

---

[42] See, e.g., BÖLÜKBAŞI, *Turkey and Greece: The Aegean Disputes – A Unique Case in International Law*, London, 2004, p. 217; GUZMAN and HSIANG, "Some Ways that Theories on Customary International Law Fail: A Reply to László Blutman", EJIL, 2014, p. 553 ff., pp. 557-558.

[43] GREEN, *cit. supra* note 8, p. 278.

[44] *Ibid.*, p. 274.

[45] See *ibid.*, pp. 59-188.

[46] See, e.g., Permanent Court of Arbitration, *Chagos Marine Protected Area Arbitration* (*Mauritius v. United Kingdom*), Reply of the Republic of Mauritius, 18 November 2013, p. 124.

[47] GULDAHL, "The Role of Persistent Objection in International Humanitarian Law", Nordic Journal of International Law, 2008, p. 51 ff., p. 54.

[48] UN Doc. A/71/10, *cit. supra* note 7, p. 114.

[49] *Ibid.*, p. 112.

Beyond the need for objections to be open and clear, it is evident that no particular form of objection – in the sense of a particular formal pronouncement or issued document – is required,[50] and the ILC commentary again rightly notes this.[51] It also is clear that states can gain exemption through persistently objecting by way of statements alone: the objector need not necessarily practice what it is preaching.[52] This, too, correctly is confirmed by the commentary to Conclusion 15: "a clear verbal objection, either in written or oral form, as opposed to physical action, will suffice to preserve the legal position of the objecting State."[53] However, this passage potentially creates uncertainty as to whether a state can object *purely* through its physical actions/contrary practice. The use of the term "as opposed to physical action" could be read simply as a way of describing, by contrast, what was intended by "verbal objection"; alternatively, it could be read as suggesting that physical actions/contrary practice *cannot* amount to objection.

When one examines the way in which states have responded to the usage of the rule by other states, it is clear that physical acts have not been seen as sufficient if unaccompanied by explicit statements of objection (in whatever form).[54] However, contrary "deeds" can act as objection if *combined* with "words" (whether oral or written).[55] As phrased, the commentary could potentially be seen as suggesting that "acts of objection" may undermine accompanying explicit statements of objection, which is – for this writer – incorrect. It is unlikely that this was what was intended, but it would have been desirable for the Commission to more clearly highlight that, while physical acts of objection alone will not be sufficient (unlike statements of objection alone, which can be), they can contribute to a pattern of persistent objection if combined with statements.

5.2. Persistence

If a state wishes to rely on the persistent objector rule, as the rule's name would suggest, it must have objected *persistently*. State practice demonstrates that single or isolated objections will not suffice.[56] Voluntarist theory cannot explain this requirement of persistence: if the rule was only about consent, then one

---

[50] See BÖLÜKBAŞI, *cit. supra* note 42, p. 206 (discussing the wide range of forms that Turkey's objections to an extension of the territorial waters limit took).

[51] UN Doc. A/71/10, *cit. supra* note 7, p. 114.

[52] See, e.g., GREEN, *cit. supra* note 8, p. 80 (discussing the UK's persistent objections to the prohibition on belligerent reprisals against civilians).

[53] UN Doc. A/71/10, *cit. supra* note 7, p. 114.

[54] See, e.g., Court of Appeal (Hong Kong Special Administrative Region), *C et al. v Director of Immigration and Secretary for Security*, Judgment of 21 July 2011, CACV 132-137/2008, para. 72.

[55] See, e.g., United States District Court for the Eastern District of New York, *In Re: Agent Orange Product Liability Litigation*, Statement of Interest of the United States, 21 January 2005, pp. 4-13, available at: <http://www.state.gov/documents/organization/87322.pdf>.

[56] GREEN, *cit. supra* note 8, pp. 91-96.

clear statement of objection would presumably be enough.[57] However, the criterion is justified by more pragmatic, practical concerns: the need for persistence tests the will of the objector to ensure that the rule is not used frivolously and, at least to an extent, promotes clarity and certainty.[58]

In the view of this author, Conclusion 15 and its commentary accurately reflects the persistence requirement. In particular, it acknowledges that the requirement is notably difficult to apply, because precisely *how* persistent the objector must be – as with so many aspects of the operation of customary international law – is a context-specific question.[59] This is made explicit in the ILC commentary: "[a]ssessing whether this requirement has been met needs to be done in a pragmatic manner, bearing in mind the circumstances of each case."[60] This acts as a helpful reminder that dissenting states are best served by objecting as often as possible.

5.3. Consistency

As well as objecting persistently, a dissenting state must object *consistently*: indeed, the "persistent objector rule" should be called the "persistent and consistent objector rule". Consistency is not the same thing as persistence. While the term "persistence" denotes repetition, as well as a degree of steadfastness,[61] consistency requires a level of *uniformity* of objection, or what might be called "non-derogation" by the state from its dissenting stance. A state could "persistently" object to a newly forming rule (by regularly and repeatedly rejecting it), but in fact do so inconsistently (by accepting or affirming the rule on a minority of occasions, in the midst of its general policy of objecting persistently). It is evident that both persistence and consistency are required in practice.[62] The consistency requirement is commonly noted in the literature on the persistent objector rule,[63] but, unfortunately, the criterion often is unhelpfully amalgamated with the persistence requirement.[64]

It was therefore notable that Michael Wood's third report on the identification of custom topic explicitly asserted that "[a] State must maintain its objection

---

[57] MENDELSON, *cit. supra* note 15, p. 239.
[58] GREEN, *cit. supra* note 8, pp. 96-98.
[59] See, generally, COLSON, *cit. supra* note 14, p. 957 ff.
[60] UN Doc. A/71/10, *cit. supra* note 7, p. 114.
[61] GUZMAN, *cit. supra* note 8, p. 169.
[62] See, e.g., GREEN, *cit. supra* note 8, pp. 107-115.
[63] See, e.g., CRAWFORD, "Chance, Order, Change: The Course of International Law", RCADI, Vol. 365, 2013, p. 9 ff., p. 247; FIDLER, "Challenging the Classical Concept of Custom: Perspectives on the Future of Customary International Law", GYIL, 1996, p. 199 ff., p. 209; LAU, "Rethinking the Persistent Objector Doctrine in International Human Rights Law", Chicago Journal of International Law, 2005-2006, p. 495 ff., p. 498.
[64] See, e.g., GULDAHL, *cit. supra* note 47, p. 54; LEPARD, *Customary International Law: A New Theory with Practical Applications*, Cambridge, 2010, p. 239.

both persistently *and* consistently."[65] However, this welcome clarification in one of Special Rapporteur's background reports perhaps makes it all the more disappointing that the text of Conclusion 15, as ultimately adopted by the ILC, refers only to the need for objection to be "maintained persistently",[66] without any reference to consistency.

The Drafting Committee took the view that the term "persistently" in Conclusion 15 "meant that the State must maintain its objection both persistently and consistently."[67] This means that while the Commission reinforced the confused amalgamation of "persistence" and "consistency" in the literature by not including both in Conclusion 15, it at the same time did accept the need for both criteria. The decision not explicitly to affirm the consistency requirement in the draft conclusion therefore is regrettable for two reasons. First, because such merging of the criteria is a particular failing of much of the existing academic commentary (with this programme of work representing an opportunity for the Commission to remedy that fact), but also, secondly, because the ILC, at least as a whole, clearly took the (correct) view that persistence and consistency both are required for persistent objection (meaning that not only the circumstances but also the will to remedy this issue in the literature was present).[68]

It is, however, pleasing that the consistency requirement was confirmed in the adopted commentary to Conclusion 15,[69] reflecting the position set out in the Special Rapporteur's third report. The reasoning expressed by the drafting committee – that the word "persistence" in the draft conclusion itself in fact refers to the dual requirements of persistence and consistency – is also made clear in the commentary.[70]

In terms of understanding what the consistency criterion requires, the commentary to Conclusion 15 states that

> objection should be reiterated when the circumstances are such that a restatement is called for (that is, in circumstances where silence or inaction may reasonably lead to the conclusion that the State has given up its objection). This could be, for example, at a conference attended by the objecting State at which the rule is reaffirmed. States cannot, however, be expected to react on every occasion, especially where their position is already well known […] [S]uch repeated objections must be consistent overall, that is, without significant contradictions.[71]

---

[65] WOOD, Third Report on Identification of Customary International Law, UN Doc. A/CN.4/682 (2015), p. 66 (emphasis added).

[66] UN Doc. A/71/10, *cit. supra* note 7, p. 112.

[67] UN Doc. A/CN.4/SR.3280, *cit. supra* note 30, p. 13.

[68] See *ibid.*; UN Doc. A/CN.4/SR.3252, *cit. supra* note 5, p. 4 (MURASE); UN Doc. A/71/10, *cit. supra* note 7, p. 114.

[69] *Ibid.*

[70] *Ibid.*

[71] *Ibid.*

This accurately represents the manner in which the criterion is applied in practice. The requirement is onerous, with even one explicit statement that is contrary to the objection appearing to be terminal.[72] Similarly, even silence can be seen as inconsistent, when this occurs in circumstances where other states might reasonably expect the dissenter to have objected.[73] The ILC commentary also is correct that 100% consistency is not required in all circumstances,[74] albeit that, applying an ultra-critical eye, one might take issue with the final statement of the quote passage (that objection "must be consistent overall, that is, without significant contradictions"). That line may be somewhat misleading, because even "less significant" contradictions have been viewed as being unacceptable by states on occasion.[75]

Nonetheless, while it is a shame that the consistency requirement was not made explicit in Conclusion 15, the important distinction between, and requirement for both of, the persistence and consistency requirements is present in the outcomes of the ILC's work, and, further, it may be said that the way in which the requirement is applied in practice is well-reflected in the draft conclusion's commentary.

5.4. Timeliness

Persistent objection must be *timely*, in the sense that it must occur before the customary norm being objected to crystallises: as Conclusion 15 makes clear, objection must begin "while that rule [of customary international law] was in the process of formation".[76] There is no "subsequent objector" rule,[77] despite a small minority of writers who support this.[78] There are good policy reasons for this timeliness criterion, related to the maximisation of stability in the system and limiting exceptionalism,[79] and, again, the criterion can be identified in state practice.[80]

---

[72] See, e.g., PRICE, "Emerging Customary Norms and Anti-Personnel Landmines", in REUS-SMIT (ed.), *The Politics of International Law*, Cambridge, 2004, p. 106 ff., p. 124; GREEN, *cit. supra* note 8, pp. 118-120 (both discussing the position of Turkey in relation to antipersonnel landmines).

[73] *Ibid.*, pp. 112-130.

[74] See, e.g., *ibid.*, pp. 120-122 (discussing US objections to the prohibition on the use of herbicides in armed conflict).

[75] See, e.g., HAMPSON and SALAMA, "Working Paper on the Relationship between Human Rights Law and International Humanitarian Law", UN Doc. E/CN.4/Sub.2/2005/14 (2005), para. 70.

[76] UN Doc. A/71/10, *cit. supra* note 7, p. 112.

[77] This is made explicit in the ILC's commentary, *ibid.*, 113. See also ABASHEIKH, "The Validity of the Persistent Offender Rule in International Law", Coventry Law Journal, 2004, p. 40 ff., p. 46

[78] See, e.g., BRADLEY and GULATI, "Withdrawing from International Custom", Yale Law Journal, 2010, p. 202 ff.; HELFER, "Exiting Custom: Analogies to Treaty Withdrawals", Duke Journal of Comparative and International Law, 2010, p. 65 ff.

[79] GREEN, *cit. supra* note 8, pp. 145-153.

[80] *Ibid.*, pp. 138-143.

However, applying the timeliness criterion may be extremely difficult, given the uncertainties surrounding the point of crystallisation for any given norm of customary international law, which acts as the "end date" for effective persistent objection.[81] The ILC commentary acknowledges this uncertainty: "the line between objection and violation may not always be an easy one to draw [...]"[82] It perhaps is important to note that this is a symptom of wider uncertainty in customary international law generally (and, particularly, the point of "crystallisation" for any given rule), rather a particular flaw of the persistent objector rule itself. Nonetheless, the timeliness requirement is, like the other criteria for persistent objection, a notably onerous one. States must pay significant attention as to when they may need to begin objecting: even the most vigilant state may still find that its objections come too late. This, too, is acknowledged in the ILC commentary, which notes that the objector's "position will be more assured if it did so at the earliest possible moment".[83]

5.5. *Maintenance of Objection after Crystallisation*

Finally, objection must be (persistently and consistently) maintained *after* the custom has crystallised.[84] The timeliness requirement means objection must begin before the new norm of custom has formed, but it is very clear from practice that states also must continue to object post-crystallisation or they will lose the exempt status that they have acquired.[85]

Compared to some aspects of the persistent objector rule's operation, this need for "ongoing" objection is one of the elements that sometimes is overlooked in literature, but it is a crucial aspect of the rule in terms of returning exempt states to the legal orthodoxy where possible. Pleasingly, this requirement is clearly indicated, if implicit, in Conclusion 15: " [...] the rule is not opposable to the State concerned *for so long as it maintains its objection* [...] [and objection must be] *maintained* persistently".[86] Even more pleasingly, the requirement for ongoing objection post-crystallisation then is made entirely explicit in the commentary: "[t]he requirement that the objection be maintained persistently applies both before and after the rule of customary international law has emerged."[87]

---

[81] See CONFORTI, "Cours général de droit international public", RCADI, Vol. 212, 1988-V, p. 9 ff., p. 74.

[82] UN Doc. A/71/10, *cit. supra* note 7, p. 113.

[83] *Ibid.*

[84] See, e.g., HENCKAERTS and DOSWALD-BECK, *Customary International Humanitarian Law – Vol. I: Rules*, Cambridge, 2005, p. xlv.

[85] See, e.g., UNICEF, Legislative Reform to Support the Abandonment of Female Genital Mutilation/Cutting, 2010, p. 7, 21 and 46 (Mauritania's abandonment of its position on female genital mutilation), available at: <http://www.unicef.org/policyanalysis/files/UNICEF_-_LRI_Legislative_Reform_to_support_the_Abandonment_of_FGMC_August_2010.pdf>,

[86] UN Doc. A/71/10, *cit. supra* note 7, p. 112 (emphasis added).

[87] *Ibid.*, p. 114. See also UN Doc. A/CN.4/SR.3253, *cit. supra* note 10, p. 11 (VÁZQUEZ-BERMÚDEZ).

6. CONCLUSION

The work of the ILC on the wider Identification of Customary International Law topic reveals that there remain controversies about the place of the persistent objector rule in international law, including highlighting the endurance of the minority view that it *has no* such place. This article has argued that the rule does exist – for good or ill – and that the ultimate conclusion of the Commission to that effect, and the determination that it is an important aspect of the functioning of customary international law, is therefore welcome. When considering the way in which Conclusion 15, and particularly the commentary to it, set out the underpinning criteria for the rule's operation, it becomes apparent that, at least in broad terms, the ILC's work also has accurately reflected the way in which the rule is applied in practice and case law. Indeed, there are aspects of the rule's operation that are less often noted or less well-known in wider doctrine that the Commission has helpfully underlined. There are, unsurprisingly, aspects of the draft conclusions and commentaries in relation to persistent objection that the present author feels could have better reflected practice and/or brought more clarity to our understanding of the rule. However, despite notable divisions within the Commission, it should be applauded for the outcomes that it reached on this controversial secondary rule of the international legal system.

NOTES AND COMMENTS

SECESSION REVISITED: GENERAL FRAMEWORK AND LESSONS FROM THE REFERENDA IN CATALONIA AND KURDISTAN

ENRICO MILANO[*]

Abstract

The recent referenda held in Catalonia and Kurdish Iraq have reignited the debate over referenda, self-determination and unilateral secession and over the role of international law as a legal framework capable of governing and channelling those dramatic changes towards desired ends. The debate has been ever present in the Post Cold War period, considering that the number of states has increased from just over 150 to 196, with many of the new states emerging from non-consensual processes of separation. The present article assesses the general international legal framework applicable to secession, including the scope and content of principles such as territorial integrity, self-determination and uti possidetis *and tests whether and to what extent the two recent separatist claims in Catalonia and Kurdistan fit into that framework. The lessons drawn are that international law is increasingly relevant to the regulation of secession and yet the practice related to the referendum in Catalonia highlights international law's subsidiary regulatory function and the fact that, indeed, even in the twenty-first century, international law may, in some cases, remain neutral in secession attempts.*

Keywords: referenda; Catalonia and Kurdistan; secession and self-determination; territorial integrity; neutrality of international law.

1. INTRODUCTION

25 September 2017 and 1 October 2017 will be remembered as historical events in the quest for collective rights and the self-determination of Kurdistan and Catalonia respectively. In Kurdish Iraq, the Kurdish Regional Government organised a referendum, with ballots held both in the Kurdish Region and in the neighbouring areas under Kurdish control, where people were called to vote on the following question: "Do you want the Kurdistan Region and the Kurdistani areas outside the administration of the Region to become an independent state?". More than 3 million people participated, with 92.73% in favour of independence.[1] Five days later, in Catalonia, under an initiative promoted by the Catalan

---

[*] Professor of International Law, University of Verona.

[1] Unofficial English translation retrieved from Reuters, "Kurdistan supervisors begin counting votes in independence referendum", available at: <https://www.reuters.com/article/us-mideast-crisis-kurds-referendum-close/kurdistan-supervisors-begin-counting-votes-in-independence-referendum-idUSKCN1C02H3>. The original referendum question was drafted in four official languages, namely Kurdish, Arabic, Turkmen, and Assyrian. The results of the

regional institutions, more than 2 million Catalans went to vote (around 43% of Catalan voters), with 90.18% voting affirmatively to the question "Do you want Catalonia to become an independent state in the form of a republic?".[2] The two referenda were the result of two long processes of gradual development of separatist claims, each with its own distinctive features.

In the case of Kurdistan, Kurdish-controlled areas have been *de facto* independent from Baghdad since the US, the UK and France imposed a no-fly zone above the 36th parallel in 1991 and the Kurds gained fully-fledged constitutional autonomy with the Iraqi constitution of 2004. Since the referendum Iraq's central government has undertaken military action to retake control over large swathes of territory, including the city of Kirkuk, outside the Kurdish Region, but under the control of the Peshmerga.[3]

In the case of Catalonia, the referendum was the latest, and most dramatic act, in a political conflict within Spain that has escalated since Judgment No. 31 issued by the Spanish Constitution on 28 June 2010, in which the Court annulled several provisions of the Statute of Catalonia and opined that the term "Catalan nation" within the Statute should be interpreted as "nationality within the single Spanish Nation", without recognising for the Catalans the so-called "historical rights" that the Spanish constitution extends to the Basque population and to the population of Navarra.[4] Following the referendum, on 27 October 2017, the Catalan Parliament, absent the representatives of the political parties opposing independence, approved a declaration of independence, which in turn led to the intervention of the central government taking control of the Catalan institutions through the emergency procedure envisaged under Article 155 of the Spanish Constitution.[5]

While the purpose of the present article is not to examine all legal and political implications related to the separatist claims in Kurdish Iraq and Catalonia, and while it is important to stress from the outset that the holding of a referendum resulting in popular support for independence is neither a necessary, nor a suf-

---

Kurdistan independence referendum were retrieved from the website of the Kurdistan Regional Government, available at: <http://cabinet.gov.krd/a/d.aspx?s=040000&l=12&a=55861>.

[2] Unofficial English translation retrieved from the website of the Government of Catalonia, available at: <http://exteriors.gencat.cat/web/.content/00_ACTUALITAT/notes_context/Law-19_2017-on-the-Referendum-on-Self-determination.pdf>. The original referendum question was drafted in Catalan. Voting results are available at: <http://www.catalannews.com/politics/item/90-18-yes-vs-7-83-no>.

[3] "Iraqi forces complete Kirkuk province takeover after clashes with Kurds", Reuters, available at: <https://www.reuters.com/article/us-mideast-crisis-iraq-kurds-clash/iraqi-forces-complete-kirkuk-province-takeover-after-clashes-with-kurds-idUSKBN1CP0PT>.

[4] CREMA, "Le consultazioni popolari in Catalogna e nel Kurdistan iracheno", DUDI, 2018, p. 173 ff.

[5] "Spain's Constitutional Court cancels Catalonia declaration of independence", Reuters, available at: <https://www.reuters.com/article/spain-politics-catalonia-constitutionalc/spains-constitutional-court-cancels-catalonia-declaration-of-independence-idUSE8N1MF0A9>. The English translation of Art. 155 of the Spanish Constitution is retrievable from the website of the Spanish Government, available at: <http://www.lamoncloa.gob.es/lang/en/espana/leyfundamental/Paginas/titulo_octavo.aspx>.

ficient condition, to succeed in secession and acquire statehood under international law, the two events have reignited the debate over independence referenda, self-determination and unilateral secession and over the role of international law as a legal framework capable of regulating such phenomena, which are often associated with conflicts, including military conflicts, instability and human rights violations. The debate has not faded since the beginning of the 1990s, as new states have continued to emerge in the international arena, often through unilateral processes of separation. The present article will reassess the main doctrinal contributions to the understanding of the phenomenon of secession and will elaborate a more flexible and, at the same time, possibly more accurate analytical framework, which departs from established, normative theories of secession to describe the role of international law and its rules and principles in these phenomena. The main submission of the article is that international law lacks a coherent and general regulation of the phenomenon of secession and yet it is increasingly regulating the process and outcomes of unilateral separations with *ad hoc* solutions according to the subsidiary role it is called to play in each specific instance. The recent cases of Kurdistan and Catalonia, with their own distinctive features, confirm the need to adopt such an analytical framework.

2.   SECESSION BEYOND THE COLONIAL CONTEXT BETWEEN NEUTRALITY AND JURIDICAL PARADIGMS

The debate over secession and international law in the post-colonial context is not novel and it is very much related to the attempt to rejuvenate the reading and understanding of the principle of self-determination after the 1990s. The revival of the debate is not surprising: since the end of the Cold War, the number of states in the international community has steadily increased, from 151 in 1990 to 196 in 2018. This phenomenon is largely due to instances of non-consensual separation of part of the parent state, which can be qualified as secessions under international law; and to the gradual increase of political parties, organisations and territorial movements aimed at separating from the parent state and creating a sovereign and independent nation. The apparent paradox of this phenomenon is that, in an age characterised by globalisation, through "bottom-up" transfers of authority to supranational and international organisations and "top-down" empowerment of local institutions, civil society and private economic actors, the pull towards statehood is becoming stronger and stronger.[6] This trend could be considered to demonstrate the centrifugal force against existing state sovereignties, regardless of their democratic or dictatorial nature.

Whilst not seeking to provide an all-encompassing analysis of the impressive bulk of literature produced by international lawyers in the last 25 years, this

---

[6] KOHEN, "Introduction", in KOHEN (ed.), *Secession: International Law Perspectives*, Cambridge, 2006, p. 1 ff., p. 2.

article identifies the three doctrinal streams which have proved most influential in the current debate on secession.

According to "realist" conceptions of statehood, international law, as much as it does not regulate any process of state formation, is also neutral with regard to secession: it neither legitimises nor prohibits it.[7] The effects and consequences of secession, namely the eventual creation of a new state, the loss of sovereignty over a portion of its territory by the parent state and the ensuing succession of the putative state, are recognised by international law only when the separation is effective and irreversible and a new political and administrative organisation is capable of displaying full, uncontested powers over the territory and the resident population.[8] Before effectiveness is acquired, the relations between the separatist movement and the parent state are regulated by the latter's domestic law, with the exception of a few fundamental rules of international humanitarian law, whenever an armed conflict has broken out between government forces and the insurgents.[9] In other words, international law does not favour secession; on the other hand, it does not prohibit it by imposing rules protecting the parent state's sovereignty, such as the rules deriving from the principle of territorial integrity. The latter is applicable in the relations between and among states only, and as such, it does not prohibit non-state actors from striving to acquire statehood.[10]

The second doctrinal stream, which is normally associated with authors espousing a juridical notion of statehood under international law, maintains that international law is capable of regulating processes of state formation, and thus it is also capable of regulating secession and its outcomes. The first way that international law can regulate these processes is by authorising secession as an exercise of the right of self-determination: a) in the context of former colonial territories or territories under foreign occupation (the last example of the latter having been the secession of the Baltic Republics from the Soviet Union between 1990 and 1991);[11] b) in cases where the right of self-determination of a territorial unit is provided under the constitution of the parent state and the central government systematically hinders an internal exercise of self-determination (for

---

[7] ABI-SAAB, "Conclusion", *ibid.* in KOHEN (ed.), *cit. supra* note 6, p. 470 ff., pp. 473-476.

[8] GIOIA, "Kosovo's statehood and the role of recognition", IYIL, 2008, p. 3 ff., pp. 12-13. According to Thürer and Burri, "[i]nternational law remains neutral vis-à-vis secession and neither prohibits nor permits it. International law becomes important, however, when the facts have been consolidated and the new State has come into existence, in particular when it comes to matters of State recognition and succession": see THÜRER and BURRI, "Secession", in WOLFRUM (ed.), *Max Planck Encyclopedia of Public International Law*, June 2009, para. 42, available at: <http://opil.ouplaw.com/view/10.1093/law:epil/9780199231690/law-9780199231690-e1100?rskey=A0BJoT&result=1&prd=EPIL>).

[9] With regard to the rules of international humanitarian law applicable in armed conflicts involving government forces and insurgents, see CORTEN, "Are There Gaps in the International Law of Secession?", in KOHEN (ed.), *cit. supra* note 6, p. 231 ff., pp. 242-246.

[10] GIOIA, *cit. supra* note 8, pp. 23-27. Accordingly, HILPOLD, "What Role for Academic Writers in Interpreting International Law? – A Rejoinder to Orakhelashvili", Chinese Journal of International Law, 2009, p. 291 ff.

[11] STERIO, *The Right to Self-determination Under International Law: Selfistans, Secession, and the Rule of the Great Powers*, London, 2013, pp. 37-38.

example, as occurred in the dissolution of the Former Yugoslavia according to some authors);[12] and c) in cases in which the incorporation of a territory within a state is conditional to the enjoyment of fully-fledged autonomy within the state (such as the independence of Eritrea in 1993).[13] The second way international law becomes involved is by prohibiting secession when it is connected to grave violations of peremptory norms of international law, such as the prohibition of aggression (Turkish Republic of Northern Cyprus and Crimea) or the right of self-determination of peoples (South Rhodesia and the South African *bantustans*), or where the secessionist movement uses force inducing the UN Security Council to reaffirm the parent state's territorial integrity (Abkhazia and Kosovo during the 1990s).[14] According to these authors, there still remains a "grey area" outside the above scenarios, but its perimeter is gradually decreasing.[15] Finally, some authors have also maintained that under contemporary international law a so-called "right to remedial secession" has arisen, which is applicable in all scenarios in which a distinct ethnic, national or religious group, with a distinct territorial basis, is subject to gross and systematic discrimination and exclusion from participation in the political and institutional life of the parent state. In these circumstances, such a group, as a last resort, would be entitled to "externally" exercise its right to self-determination.[16]

A third doctrinal stream has developed a procedural paradigm of secession. According to these authors, international law does not legitimise or sanction states which have emerged as a result of a process of unilateral separation; nor is international law capable of invalidating a state, which has been formed as a direct consequence of a grave violation of one of its fundamental norms. And yet international law addresses and regulates the processes by which secession is produced, thus facilitating those putative states which comply with certain legal requirements, namely: the lack of support via external military intervention, the need to make all reasonable efforts to negotiate a compromise solution with the central government, respect for the *uti possidetis* principle and the clear manifestation of will by the local population in favour of secession; and increasingly discouraging those processes of secession which are not in compliance with the above requirements.[17]

---

[12] RAIC, *Statehood and the Law of Self-Determination*, The Hague, 2002, pp. 313-316.

[13] KOHEN, *cit. supra* note 6, p. 20.

[14] *Ibid.*, p. 19.

[15] *Ibid.*, pp. 19-20; CORTEN, *cit. supra* note 9, p. 254.

[16] MURSWIEK, "The Issue of a Right of Secession – Reconsidered", in TOMUSCHAT (ed.), *Modern Law of Self-Determination*, Leiden, 1993, p. 21 ff.; RAIC, *cit. supra* note 12, pp. 362-366. The original proponent of the thesis of remedial secession is BUCHHEIT, *Secession: the Legitimacy of Self-Determination*, Yale, 1978.

[17] TANCREDI, *La secessione nel diritto internazionale*, Padova, 2001; ID., "A Normative "Due Process", in KOHEN (ed.), *cit. supra* note 6, p. 184 ff.; ID., "Some Remarks on the Relationship between Secession and General International Law in the Light of the ICJ's Kosovo Advisory Opinion", in HILPOLD (ed.), *Kosovo and International Law. The ICJ's Advisory Opinion of 22 July 2010*, Leiden-Boston, 2012, p. 79 ff.; ID., "In Search of a Fair Balance between the Inviolability of Borders, Self-determination and Secession in International Law", in NICOLINI, MILANO and PALERMO (eds.), *Law, Territory and Conflict Resolution*, Leiden-

An analysis of state practice and manifestations of *opinio juris* since the 1990s is not conclusive; at best it can be concluded that the neutralist paradigm seems to be increasingly contradicted by the developments of recent state practice, which are instead supportive of both the substantive and procedural paradigms.

Before turning to state practice, we must underline that case law is limited and the two advisory opinions, rendered by the Canadian Supreme Court in 1998 in *Secession of Quebec* and by the International Court of Justice in 2010 in *Accordance With International Law of the Unilateral Declaration of Independence of Kosovo,* seem to point in different directions: on the one hand, we have a reasoned and extensive analysis of the international law applicable to cases of secession, yet presented by a domestic court (albeit the highest court in Canada); and on the other hand we have a laconic and narrow reading – heavily criticised in the literature – rendered by the main judicial organ of the United Nations.[18] The former opinion considerably limits the legal scope of the principle of effectiveness – with the eloquent metaphor of a squatter occupying a property;[19] and it reinforces both the procedural legal principles that may legitimise a secession process,[20] and those of a substantive nature which balance out

---

Boston, 2016, p. 90 ff. See also PALERMO, "Dichiarazione di indipendenza del Kosovo e potere costituente nella prospettiva della Corte internazionale di giustizia: dal pluralismo al formalismo", in GRADONI and MILANO (eds.), *Il parere della Corte internazionale di giustizia sulla dichiarazione di indipendenza del Kosovo – un'analisi critica*, Padova, 2011, p. 179 ff., pp. 194-195. According to Peters, "[…] even if secession as such is conformity with international law (or not regulated by it), *the process* is regulated. Use of force is prohibited, while peaceful and democratic procedures are prescribed. Any extraordinary allowance to secede has to be realized in the appropriate procedures, notably under recourse to a free and fair referendum on independence or after democratic elections, ideally under international supervision" (PETERS, "Does Kosovo Lie in the Lotus-Land of Freedom?", Leiden JIL, 2011, p. 95 ff., p. 107).

[18] Supreme Court of Canada, *Reference re Secession of Quebec*, (1998) 2 S.C.R. 217; *Accordance with International Law of the Unilateral Declaration of Independence in Respect of Kosovo*, Advisory Opinion of 22 July 2010, ICJ Reports, 2010, p. 403, para. 442.

[19] "The principle of effectivity operates very differently. It proclaims that an illegal act may eventually acquire legal status if, as a matter of empirical fact, it is recognized on the international plane. Our law has long recognized that through a combination of acquiescence and prescription, an illegal act may at some later point be accorded some form of legal status. In the law of property, for example, it is well known that a squatter on land may ultimately become the owner if the true owner sleeps on his or her right to repossess the land. In this way, a change in the factual circumstances may subsequently be reflected in a change in legal status. It is, however, quite another matter to suggest that a subsequent condonation of an initially illegal act retroactively creates a legal right to engage in the act in the first place. The broader contention is not supported by the international principle of effectivity or otherwise and must be rejected" (*Reference re Secession of Quebec, cit. supra* note 18, para. 146).

[20] "[O]ne of the legal norms which may be recognized by states in granting or withholding recognition of emergent states is the legitimacy of the process by which the de facto secession is, or was, being pursued. The process of recognition, once considered to be an exercise of pure sovereign discretion, has come to be associated with legal norms. See, e.g., European Community Declaration on the Guidelines on the Recognition of New States in Eastern Europe and in the Soviet Union, 31 I.L.M. 1486 (1992), at p. 1487. While national interest and perceived political advantage to the recognizing state obviously play an important role, foreign states may also take into account their view as to the existence of a right to self-determination on the part of the population of the putative state, and a counterpart domestic

the right of territorial integrity of the state and the right of self-determination of peoples.[21] The latter opinion, while avoiding taking a stance on the issue of state creation in Kosovo and on the legality of secession, and while conceding that unilateral declarations of independence produced in the context of grave violations of peremptory norms have been condemned by the international community, came to the conclusion that both general international law and the legal regime deriving from UN Security Council Resolution 1244 were not applicable to the declaration of independence issued in 2008; it also declared that the scope of application *ratione personae* of the principle of territorial integrity is limited to relations between states.[22]

If instead we take into consideration the practice of states and international organisations, as well as their manifestations of *opinio juris*, in the post-Cold War period, the "legalist" approach to secession is reinforced, both in a substantive, and in a procedural sense.

In particular, the reaffirmation of the principle of territorial integrity in different regional contexts seems to support the proposition that the principle plays a fundamental role in processes of secession, unless we are ready to maintain that it is essentially a political principle, unable to produce consequences at the level of international law, especially in terms of rights and obligations. While far from univocal (as the case of Kosovo demonstrates), state practice shows that external intervention in support of secession is considered contrary to international law, as it violates the territorial integrity of existing states. For instance, the practice related to the Russian-Georgian conflict of 2008, with Russia militarily intervening in support of Abkhazia and South Ossetia, is a clear example where the international community not only reaffirmed the right of states to have their territorial integrity protected from external military threats and actual use of force, but also against any form of external intervention in support of secession, including political recognition. The latter broad understanding of the principle of territorial

---

evaluation, namely, an examination of the legality of the secession according to the law of the state from which the territorial unit purports to have seceded. As we indicated in our answer to Question 1, an emergent state that has disregarded legitimate obligations arising out of its previous situation can potentially expect to be hindered by that disregard in achieving international recognition, at least with respect to the timing of that recognition. On the other hand, compliance by the seceding province with such legitimate obligations would weigh in favour of international recognition" (*ibid.*, para. 143).

[21] "The international law principle of self-determination has evolved within a framework of respect for the territorial integrity of existing states. The various international documents that support the existence of a people's right to self-determination also contain parallel statements supportive of the conclusion that the exercise of such a right must be sufficiently limited to prevent threats to an existing state's territorial integrity or the stability of relations between sovereign states" (*ibid.*, para. 127).

[22] *Accordance with International Law of the Unilateral Declaration of Independence in Respect of Kosovo*, cit. *supra* note 18, para. 80. See Corten, according to whom "[b]y insisting on the strictly inter-state character of the territorial-integrity principle, the Court refused to challenge the 'legal-neutrality' thesis" (CORTEN, "Territorial Integrity Narrowly Interpreted: Reasserting the Classical Inter-State Paradigm of International Law", Leiden JIL, 2011, p. 87 ff., p. 89). Accordingly, TANCREDI, "Some Remarks", cit. *supra* note 17, p. 86.

integrity is clear in the declaration issued by the Council of the European Union on 1 September 2008, following Russian recognition of the two republics:

> The European Council strongly condemns Russia's unilateral decision to recognise the independence of Abkhazia and South Ossetia. That decision is unacceptable and the European Council calls on other States not to recognise this proclaimed independence and asks the Commission to examine the practical consequences to be drawn. It recalls that a peaceful and lasting solution to the conflict in Georgia must be based on full respect for the principles of independence, sovereignty and territorial integrity recognised by international law, the Final Act of the Helsinki Conference on Security and Cooperation in Europe and United Nations Security Council resolutions.[23]

The EU Council's declaration condemns the Russian recognition, as a political act supporting the independence of South Ossetia and Abkhazia, not the use of force employed by Russia; it refers to territorial integrity as "recognised by international law"; it refers to the 1975 Helsinki Final Act, which upholds the principle of respect for internationally recognised borders.

Moreover, state practice and the practice of international organisations, in contexts as diverse as Georgia, Nagorno-Karabakh, Bosnia and Herzegovina, Cyprus, the Comoros Islands, Chechnya, Transnistria, FYROM, and Crimea on the one hand show a tendency to "internationalise" conflicts related to processes of secession, especially when those conflicts escalate into an armed conflict, hence contradicting the reserved domain principle, which is central in the neutralist paradigm. On the other hand, there is also a tendency to reaffirm the principle of territorial integrity as one of the principles to be safeguarded in the political process, often through arrangements of enhanced autonomy for the secessionist movement and yet in full respect of the internationally recognised borders of the parent state.[24] In other words, the principle of territorial integrity is opposed to those entities which acquire full subjectivity under international law as a result of effective territorial control – hence qualifying as insurgents – or due to the their recognition in international legal instruments – namely, treaties or legally binding UN Security Council resolutions. The key question is not so much whether the principle of territorial integrity implies a general prohibition of unilateral secession under international law – and the answer is certainly in the negative – ; nor whether it is relevant under a substantive perspective or procedural one – it is submitted that it is relevant under both perspectives – ; rather how international law paradigms are reflected in the practice of recent decades concerning the principle of territorial integrity.

---

[23] Conclusions of the Council of the European Union, 1 September 2008, para. 2, available at: <http://www.consilium.europa.eu/ueDocs/cms_Data/docs/pressData/en/ec/102545.pdf>.

[24] For a comprehensive analysis of state practice see CHRISTAKIS, *Le droit à l'autodétermination en dehors des situations de decolonization*, Paris, 1999, pp. 208-219.

From a procedural perspective, one may observe the recurrent invocation of the principles of democracy and self-determination and the application of the principle of *uti possidetis*. In this respect, practice is even more widespread. States and international organisations have supported and recognised secessionist processes of state creation, conditioning such support and recognition upon the objective determination of popular will, often through referenda, or through a presumption of popular support, and upon the respect of administrative boundaries previously drawn and transformed into international borders (*uti possidetis juris*).[25] The separation of Slovenia and Croatia (*ex post processo* qualified as dismemberment), the independence of the Baltic countries and of Eritrea and the more recent independence of South Sudan are all examples of practice pointing in that direction.[26] Once more, the key issue here is not so much whether the above standards are part of general international law, or whether they were applicable to the cases in point; rather that the international community has not evaluated processes of secession as mere factual processes. Much thinner, instead, is the practice supporting the emergence of a right of external self-determination in the post-colonial context, for instance in the form of a right to "remedial secession".[27]

The same trend can be detected in the manifestations of *opinio juris* by states. The approval of important multilateral instruments, such as the Final Declaration of the 1993 Vienna World Conference on Human Rights and the 1997 General Assembly resolution 51/55 on the violent dissolution of existing states confirm the existence of widespread *opinio juris* in the international community that the principle of territorial integrity is a principle of international law, which can be

---

[25] With regard to the practice related to the manifestation of popular will and *uti possidetis*, see TANCREDI, *La secessione nel diritto internazionale, cit. supra* note 17, pp. 682-713.

[26] See the statement issued by the EU and its Member States on 9 July 2011 after the referendum on independence held in South Sudan: "The EU has consistently supported the implementation of the 2005 Comprehensive Peace Agreement, culminating in the referendum on self-determination for South Sudan. *The Referendum was conducted peacefully and credibly and its outcome was a true reflection of the democratically expressed wishes of the people of South Sudan*. On this historic day, the EU and its Member States welcome the Republic of South Sudan as a new independent state" (Press release of the European Union on the independence of Sudan, 9 July 2011, available at: <http://www.consilium.europa.eu/uedocs/cms_data/docs/pressdata/EN/foraff/123591.pdf>; (emphasis added)). See also: European Community, Declaration on the Guidelines on the Recognition of New States in Eastern Europe and in the Soviet Union, ILM, 1992, p. 1485 ff., p. 1487; VIDMAR, *Democratic Statehood in International Law*, Oxford, 2013, pp. 74-77.

[27] A few authors have considered the independence of Croatia from the Former Yugoslavia as an exercise of the right to remedial secession (MURSWIEK, "The Issue of a Right of Secession – Reconsidered", in TOMUSCHAT (ed.), *Modern Law of Self Determination*, Dordrecht-Boston-London, 1993, p. 21 ff., pp. 32-33; RAIC, *cit. supra* note 12, pp. 362-366). The same argument was employed by certain delegations during the advisory proceedings on the declaration of independence of Kosovo before the ICJ (see *infra* Section 5). For an assessment see VIDMAR, "Remedial Secession in International Law: Theory and (Lack of) Practice", St. Antony's International Review, 2010, p. 37 ff.; DEL MAR, "The Myth of Remedial Secession", in FRENCH (ed.), *Statehood and Self-determination*, Cambridge, 2013, p. 79 ff.

opposed when self-determination is invoked to justify unilateral secession.[28] The 1995 Framework Convention on National Minorities and the 2007 UN General Assembly Declaration on the rights of indigenous peoples, which contribute to the emergence of collective human rights at the level of international law, do contain safeguard clauses with regard to the territorial integrity of existing states. This confirms the latter's status as a norm of general international law which is applicable in cases of attempted secessions, in particular when the seceding entities and subjects have already found international recognition in treaty law or general international law, as is the case with national minorities and indigenous people.[29] The advisory proceedings before the ICJ in the *Kosovo* case confirmed these trends in terms of the manifestation of *opinio juris*. Of the 42 states that participated in the proceedings before the Court, only nine supported the thesis of neutrality, whereas the others, with varying different approaches, held that processes of secession may be regulated by legal principles, such as self-determination, *uti possidetis* and territorial integrity even beyond the colonial context.

3. ABSENCE OF REGULATION AND THE CONTEXTUAL APPLICATION OF NORMS
    AND PRINCIPLES

What has been outlined above indicates that the juridical paradigms construing secession as a phenomenon which can be regulated by rules of international

---

[28] Vienna Declaration and Programme of Action, UN Doc. A/CONF.157/23 (1993), para. 2; UN General Assembly Res. 51/55 (1997), UN Doc. A/RES/51/55, on the violent dissolution of States, paras. 3 and 4, "[a]ffirms the need for strict compliance with the principle of the inviolability of international borders among States" and "[...] the need for strict compliance with the principle of the territorial integrity of any State". In this sense see CHRISTAKIS, *cit. supra* note 24, pp. 190-193. According to Odendahl the "'safeguard clause' [of the Vienna Declaration] does not prove that the principle of territorial integrity binds internal non-State actors. It does prove, however, that the principle of territorial integrity might be applicable in certain intra-State situations. It limits the right of peoples to self-determination derived from public international law" (ODENDAHL, "The Scope of Application of the Principle of Territorial Integrity", GYIL, 2010, p. 511 ff., p. 538).

[29] The 1995 Framework Convention on National Minorities in the preamble recalls "[...] the principles to be respected and the obligations which flow from them, in order to ensure, in the member States and such other States as may become Parties to the present instrument, the effective protection of national minorities and of the rights and freedoms of persons belonging to those minorities, within the rule of law, respecting the territorial integrity and national sovereignty of states"; at Article 21 it also provides for a safeguard clause according to which "[n]othing in the present framework Convention shall be interpreted as implying any right to engage in any activity or perform any act contrary to the fundamental principles of international law and in particular of the sovereign equality, territorial integrity and political independence of States". A similar safeguard clause can be found in the 2007 UN Declaration on the Rights of Indigenous People: "[n]othing in this Declaration may be interpreted as implying for any State, people, group or person any right to engage in any activity or to perform any act contrary to the Charter of the United Nations or construed as authorizing or encouraging any action which would dismember or impair, totally or in part, the territorial integrity or political unity of sovereign and independent States": see United Nations Declaration on the Rights of Indigenous Peoples, UN Doc. A/RES/61/295 (2007), Art. 46).

law have been reinforced in recent decades. In an increasingly globalised and interdependent international community, in which normative values are no longer built solely on states' sovereign rights, but are also aimed at protecting the values of humanity and of individuals, this seems logical. Today's international community is called upon to regulate processes of secession, given that it is often associated with instability, violence and conflict, which threaten basic human rights.

To be clear, international law still does not contain any general regime dealing with state creation. The only existing treaty regime can be found in the 1933 Montevideo Convention on the Rights and Duties of States – although this has only been ratified by 16 states – and the requirements of statehood under Article 1 are occasionally invoked by states and international organisations when recognising new states. The fact that this regime is not recent, that it is characterised by rather indeterminate normative elements, that it is increasingly invoked with caveats and that other criteria are jointly invoked, such as the representativeness of the new government, the respect for the principles of *uti possidetis* and prohibition of the use of force, show that the Montevideo criteria are not sufficient and necessary elements of statehood under customary international law, including in cases of secession.[30]

And yet international law does not provide for any express and/or specific regime concerning secession as such. The practice that has been analysed above shows a general disapproval of contemporary international law for processes of secession beyond the remaining, rare instances of former colonial territories still under colonial or foreign occupation, but it is hard to infer from that disapproval a general prohibition: practice has indeed shown some cases of separation, which may be qualified as secession, and the characterisation of these processes as violations of international has not been significant in terms of the numbers of states and international organisations involved.[31]

---

[30] According to Vidmar the presumption that the Montevideo criteria are reflective of customary international law is "[...] problematic. The norms of customary international law need to be precisely that – legal norms. Are the statehood criteria legal norms of a prescriptive quality? If they were, they would need to have (at least some of them) the following effects: (i) entities would become states by meeting the statehood criteria; (ii) entities that do not meet them would not become states; (iii) the recognition of entities that do not meet the statehood criteria would be prohibited; and (iv) the recognition of entities that meet the statehood criteria would be mandatory. None of the above is true in contemporary international law. It appears that they are, at best, policy guidelines rather than legal norms. Indeed, the fact that states grant recognition even where statehood criteria *are not* met and withhold it where they *are* met indicates that state practice does not accept that statehood would depend on the Montevideo criteria. These criteria do not produce any direct legal effects. To some degree, they can only influence the international practice of acceptance or non-acceptance of claims for independence" (VIDMAR, *cit. supra* note 26, p. 241).

[31] The absence of a general prohibition on secession is also shared by those authors with an extensive understanding of the principle of territorial integrity. See KOHEN, *cit. supra* note 6; CORTEN, *cit. supra* note 9. According to Christakis "[i]l s'agissait de savoir si le fameux principe du respect de l'intégrité territoriale d'un État avait ou non une dimension interne. Or [...] un grand nombre de juristes considère que ce principe ne s'applique que dans les relations interétatiques. Cette affirmation doit, selon nous, être quelque peu nuancée à la lumière de l'analyse des instruments internationaux dans ce domaine. Le principe du respect de l'intégrité

What we see "in action" is a "casuistic" and *sui generis* approach by the international community, in which the procedural requirements are increasingly applied and in which the various principles of international law – territorial integrity, obligation to negotiate, prohibition on the use of force, *uti possidetis*, self-determination – are invoked and mobilised, in order to regulate and even determine the outcomes of secessionist processes. In other words, the principles of general international law, which are also characterised by vagueness and indeterminacy, but also adaptability and flexibility, are applied to every case with *sui generis* and specific legal solutions and rules of conduct, which interact with the more traditional Montevideo criteria.[32] Namely, there is a deductive application of principles of general international law which have emerged in other contexts, that are capable of adapting and producing consequences in the context of post-colonial secessions. An example is the principle of self-determination, which emerged in the colonial context, and yet is recurrently invoked by separatist entities and those states supporting separation;[33] another is the *uti possidetis* principle, which emerged in the colonial context and was subsequently transposed into the dissolution processes of the former socialist republics;[34] one can think also of territorial integrity, which was originally associated with the prohibition on the use of force in international relations and the prohibition of armed aggression in accordance with Article 2, paragraph 4(4), of the UN Charter and subsequently applied to prevent and regulate secessionist processes.[35]

---

territoriale a une dimension interne dans le sens où il s'adresse souvent, dans plusieurs instruments, directement aux différent peuples, populations autochtones ou minorités. Mais ce principe ne va pas jusqu'à interdir la secession. Il a en fait pour but d'exclure la reconnaisance d'un droit de sécession, de restreindre l'étendue des droits reconnus par les différénts instruments et montrer, à la limite, la réprobation de la communauté interétatique vis-à-vis du phénomène de la sécession, en indiquant aux composantes des États (et surtout aux minorités nationales) qu'ils devraient 'réellement considérer que [leur] avenir réside dans l'État partie', pour reprendre la formulation du Comité pour l'elimination de la discrimation raciale à propos de la minorité albanaise de l'ERYM" (CHRISTAKIS, *cit. supra* note 24, p. 319). Crawford departs from the proposition that "secession is neither legal nor illegal in international law, but a legally neutral act the consequences of which are regulated by international law" (CRAWFORD, *The Creation of States in International Law*, 2nd ed., Oxford, 2006, p. 390). And yet, after having examined the post-1945 state practice concerning secession, he concludes that such practice has "normative significance" and that translates into a "strong international reluctance to support unilateral secession or separation" (*ibid.*, pp. 417-418).

[32] PERTILE, "Il parere sul Kosovo e l'autodeterminazione assente: quando la parsimonia non è una virtù", in GRADONI and MILANO (eds.), *cit. supra* note 17, p. 89 ff., pp. 120-121.

[33] *Ibid.* See also AMOROSO, "Whither the Principle of Self-Determination in the Post-Colonial Era? The Case for a Policy-Oriented Approach", ESIL Conference Paper Series, Conference Paper No. 9/2015, available at: <https://ssrn.com/abstract=2715694>.

[34] With regard to the principle of *uti possidetis* see, especially, NESI, *L'uti possidetis iuris nel diritto internazionale*, Padova, 1996; RATNER, "Drawing a Better Line: *Uti Possidetis* and the Borders of New States", AJIL, 1996, p. 590 ff.; SANCHEZ RODRIGUEZ, *L'uti possidetis et les effectivités dans les contentieux territoriaux et frontaliers*, RCADI, Vol. 263, 1997, p. 149 ff.

[35] CHRISTAKIS, *cit. supra* note 24, pp. 184-236.

As a result, we can affirm that international law does not construe "secession" as a coherent and unitary phenomenon, which is precisely defined and regulated by legal rules; but "secessions" are increasingly taken into consideration and international law may guide and condition them with *ad hoc* solutions.[36] In one of the few passages of the *Kosovo* advisory opinion in which the Court fully took into account the specific context of Kosovo's declaration of independence, the Court held:

> Several participants have invoked resolutions of the Security Council condemning particular declarations of independence: see, *inter alia*, Security Council resolutions 216 (1965) and 217 (1965), concerning Southern Rhodesia; Security Council resolution 541 (1983), concerning northern Cyprus; and Security Council resolution 787 (1992), concerning the Republika Srpska. The Court notes, however, that in all of those instances *the Security Council was making a determination as regards the concrete situation existing at the time that those declarations of independence were made*; the illegality attached to the declarations of independence thus stemmed not from the unilateral character of these declarations as such, but from the fact that they were, or would have been, connected with the unlawful use of force or other egregious violations of norms of general international law, in particular those of a peremptory character (*jus cogens*). In the context of Kosovo, the Security Council has never taken this position. The exceptional character of the resolutions enumerated above appears to the Court to confirm that no *general prohibition against unilateral declarations of independence* may be inferred from the practice of the Security Council.[37]

According to the Court, it is the specific context that shows the application of principles and rules of general international law with regard to declarations of independence ("in all of those instances the Security Council was making a determination as regards the concrete situation existing at the time that those declarations of independence were made"); and it is the deductive method which explains the application of those principles to those acts and the latter's qualification as illegal ("the illegality attached to the declarations of independence thus stemmed not from the unilateral character of these declarations as such, but from the fact that they were, or would have been, connected with the unlawful use of force or other egregious violations of norms of general international law, in particular those of a peremptory character").

---

[36] According to Kohen "in some cases international law prevents secession, in some cases it authorizes it, yet in some others – the remaining situations only – it neither permits nor interdicts secession" (KOHEN, *cit. supra* note 6, p. 19).

[37] *Accordance with International Law of the Unilateral Declaration of Independence in Respect of Kosovo*, *cit. supra* note 18, para. 81 (emphasis added).

If secession is not *per se* a phenomenon which is generally regulated by international law, but it is a phenomenon which may be regulated on *ad hoc* basis, also through the contextual application of principles of general international law, we must enquire whether international law is really capable of regulating and ordering these phenomena or whether it is simply a discursive tool that states and international organisations resort to in order to justify certain political choices.[38] If the latter is true, we would be looking at an international law which is subservient to effectiveness, especially political effectiveness. It is submitted that that is an oversimplification of the role that international law plays in processes of secession. International law is indeed binding, as those principles of general international law, to which states are generally committed, are applied by those subjects, mainly states, secessionist entities and international organisations, which are involved in the dispute and/or conflict, either as parties or "third" actors involved in the dispute settlement process, through their provision in formal instruments – namely agreements or resolutions of competent international organisations or unilateral acts – or through the affirmation of coherent positions, which are held over time, expressed in good faith and generate legitimate expectations in the counterparts and actors involved. It is evident that, especially in secession processes, which are characterised by conflicting claims to territorial integrity and self-determination, international law is not always capable of dictating solutions and outcomes and the instruments and norms guaranteeing those principles are often absent or inadequate; it is to be expected that in a situation of polarisation of positions on the final outcome (independence versus territorial integrity), international law will often regulate secession only in a procedural sense. But that is not tantamount to maintaining that international law is irrelevant and neutral with regard to secessions.

Two examples of practice well illustrate this point. During the conflict in the Former Yugoslavia, besides the declarations of independence issued by the federated republics, there were several declarations of independence which emanated from new entities, formed along ethnic lines, from within the territories of the federated republics, e.g. the Serb Republic of the Krajinas, the Republika Srpska and the Republic of Herzeg-Bosna in Bosnia and Herzegovina, and the Republic of Kosovo in Serbia. These attempted secessions, with the only exception of Kosovo, were to a large extent effective and yet they occurred in the context of the violent dissolution of the Former Yugoslavia, where the international community and the principal local actors eventually came to accept the application of a number of principles of general international law.

---

[38] According to Borgen "[i]nternational law, perhaps more than anything else, has become a consensual vocabulary and grammar for how states talk about international relations. The process of normative change is, in part, a language game in which meanings, definitions, and constructions are contested. How we define the substance of international law can change the community's interpretation of what constitutes international law" (BORGEN, "The Language of Law and the Practice of Politics: Great Powers and the Rhetoric of Self-Determination in the Cases of Kosovo and South Ossetia", Chicago Journal of International Law, 2009, p. 1 ff., p. 33).

The most important are those of *uti possidetis* and the inadmissibility of territorial changes brought about through the use of force. The Badinter Arbitration Committee, when called upon in its Opinion No. 2 to judge the right of self-determination of the Serb populations living in the territories of Croatia and Bosnia and Herzegovina, determined that the exercise of such right should have been compatible with the respect of former administrative borders, which had been internationalised as a result of the application of the principle of *uti possidetis*; hence no territorial change could be effected, except by agreement.[39] In its subsequent Opinion No. 3, the Badinter Committee established more in detail the nature and scope of the *uti possidetis* principle and underlined that it is a "general principle [...] which is logically connected with the phenomenon of obtaining independence" and "not a special rule which pertains solely to one specific system of international law".[40] In the same opinion, the Badinter Committee reaffirmed that the alteration of borders through the use of force is contrary to international law.[41] The UN Security Council, in turn, in resolution 787 adopted at the end of 1992 and according to Chapter VII, reaffirmed the territorial integrity of Bosnia and Herzegovina and determined that: "any entities or arrangement in contravention thereof will not be accepted".[42] The Dayton Agreement, which in 1995 put an end to the war in Bosnia, provided for the commitment of the Federal Republic of Yugoslavia, Croatia and Bosnia and Herzegovina to the reciprocal respect of territorial integrity.[43] Annex 4 to the General Framework Agreement established the new constitution of Bosnia and Herzegovina, which was signed by the Republic of Bosnia and Herzegovina, the Federation of Bosnia and Herzegovina and the Republika Srpska, and provided that "[t]he Republic of Bosnia and Herzegovina, the official name of which shall henceforth be "Bosnia and Herzegovina", shall continue its legal existence under international law as a state, with its internal structure modified as provided herein *and with its present internationally rec-*

---

[39] The Badinter Committee "consider[ed] that, whatever the circumstances, the right to self-determination must not involve changes to existing frontiers at the time of independence (*uti possidetis juris*) except where the states concerned agree otherwise" (Badinter Arbitration Committee, Opinion No. 2, ILM, 1992, p. 1488 ff., p. 1497).

[40] "Except where otherwise agreed, the former boundaries become frontiers protected by international law. This conclusion follows from the principle of respect for the territorial status quo and, in particular, from the principle of uti possidetis. Uti possidetis, though initially applied in settling decolonisation issues in America and Africa, is today recognized as a general principle, as stated by the International Court of Justice in its Judgment of 22 December 1986 in the case between Burkina Faso and Mali (Frontier Dispute, (1986) Law Reports 554 at 565). Nevertheless the principle is not a special rule which pertains solely to one specific system of international law. It is a general principle, which is logically connected with the phenomenon of the obtaining of independence, wherever it occurs. Its obvious purpose is to prevent the independence and stability of new states being endangered by fratricidal struggles" (Badinter Arbitration Committee, Opinion No. 3, *ibid.*, p. 1499 ff.).

[41] *Ibid.*

[42] UN Security Council Res. 787 (1992), UN Doc. S/RES/787 (1992), para. 3.

[43] General Framework Agreement for Peace in Bosnia and Herzegovina, 14 December 1995, Arts. I e X (emphasis added).

ognized borders".[44] By adhering to the above agreement, the Republika Srpska renounced to its claim to sovereignty and independence. Finally, in 2008 the Steering Board of the Peace Implementation Council, the group of states and international organiszations supervising the implementation of the Dayton Agreements through the High Representative for Bosnia and Herzegovina "[...] strongly emphasize[d] that under the Dayton Peace Agreement an Entity has no right to secede from Bosnia and Herzegovina".[45] Regardless of any evaluation of the political links between the secessionist republics and the so-called "kin States",[46] the two principles of *uti possidetis* and inadmissibility of acquisition of territory by force not only guided the process of dissolution of the Former Yugoslavia, but also dictated the outcomes of some of the secession processes, by qualifying them in violation of international law.

Another example is that of Abkhazia, which declared independence from Georgia in July 1992.[47] The declaration of independence was followed by a violent conflict with government forces, which lasted until the conclusion of a cease-fire agreement in May 1994, thanks to the mediation of Russia and of the United Nations. The agreement provided for the deployment of a peace-keeping force under the umbrella of the Community of Independent States (CIS), but was mainly comprised of Russian forces. Since 1994 Abkhazia has maintained its claim to sovereignty and it has exercised governmental authority over its territory to the exclusion of the Georgian government (with the exception of the Kodori valley). Notwithstanding the Russian presence and the recurrent diplomatic tensions between Moscow and Tblisi (which resulted in the short-lived military confrontation in August 2008, with Russia intervening in support of Abkhazia and South Ossetia), the political and economic links between Abkhazia and Russia cannot be qualified as being of legally relevant dependence and that is the conclusion also reached by the EU Independent Mission of Enquiry over the Conflict in Georgia.[48] Since the conflict, Abkhazia has been recognised by

---

[44] *Ibid.*, Annex 4, Art. I, para. 1.

[45] Declaration by the Steering Board of the Peace Implementation Council, 27 February 2008, available at: <http://www.ohr.int/pic/default.asp?content_id=41352>.

[46] With regard to the relationship between the Republika Srpska and the Federal Republic of Yugoslavia, according to the ICJ, the latter provided a considerable military and financial support to the political and military apparatus of the Republika Srpska. See *Case Concerning the Application of the Convention on the Prevention and Punishment of the Crime of Genocide (Bosnia and Herzegovina v. Serbia and Montenegro)*, Judgment of 26 February 2007, ICJ Reports, 2007, p. 43 ff., para. 241. However, the Court concluded that the military establishment of the Republika Srpska could not be qualified as *de facto* or *de iure* organ of the FRY, at least in 1995 (*ibid.*, paras. 385-394).

[47] See NUSSBERGER, "Abkhazia", in WOLFRUM (ed.), *Max Planck Encyclopedia of Public International Law*, January 2013, available at: <http://opil.ouplaw.com/view/10.1093/law:epil/9780199231690/law-9780199231690-e2069?rskey=PyCuSn&result=1&prd=EPIL>.

[48] According to the Mission of Enquiry, "[c]ontrary to South Ossetia, the Abkhaz 'government' has expressed its clear will to remain independent from Russia, even if its policies and structures, particularly its security and defence institutions, remain to a large extent under control of Moscow. Abkhazia is more advanced than South Ossetia in the process of state-building and might be seen to have reached the threshold of effectiveness. It may therefore be

Russia, Nicaragua, Venezuela, Nauru, Vanuatu and Tuvalu, the two latter countries subsequently withdrawing recognition. What is important to underline in this case is the repeated and recurrent invocation of the right to territorial integrity by Georgia and by those states intervening in the process (including Russia until 2008); the requests by international organisations addressed to the parties to the conflict to reach a mutually satisfactory solution which should determine the final status of Abkhazia; and yet, at the same time, that such solution shall respect the territorial integrity of Georgia. For instance, in Resolution 1096, the UN Security Council in condemning the elections held in Abkhazia in 1997:

> [r]eaffirm[ed] its commitment to the sovereignty and territorial integrity of Georgia, within its internationally recognized borders, and to the necessity of defining the status of Abkhazia in strict accordance with these principles, and underlines the unacceptability of any action by the Abkhaz leadership in contravention of these principles, in particular the holding on 23 November 1996 and 7 December 1996 of illegitimate and self-styled parliamentary elections in Abkhazia, Georgia.[49]

Thus, also in the case of Abkhazia, we notice the application of the general principle of territorial integrity and that of negotiation in good faith of a mutually satisfactory solution, while safeguarding the territorial integrity of Georgia. The principles of international law have guided and bound the Georgian government, the separatist entity, and the international actors involved in the process. The European Council declaration of September 2008 condemning Russia's recognition of Abkhazia confirms this conclusion.[50]

It is not submitted that the above cases show a regular practice acquiring normativity at the level of general international law, if by that we mean the development of general rules applicable to secession *per se*. It is perfectly possible that international law remains indifferent to a secession process and that states proceed to recognise the seceding entity as a new sovereign state when it displays all the typical features of statehood, namely a population, a territory and an effective and independent government. Per this hypothesis, one can take the example of an autonomous province, with its own, ethnically-distinct population within a federal state, which gradually acquires full autonomy and increasing, effective independence from the central authorities on a constitutional plane, and after having consolidated its prerogatives, unilaterally declares independence. The new entity may also extend its sovereign claim to a tiny portion of territory, outside its regional borders, where the ethnic minority represents a majority and where the regional authorities are already displaying effective control. The

---

qualified as a state-like entity" (Report of the Independent International Fact-Finding Mission on the Conflict in Georgia, September 2009, p. 134, available at: <https://www.echr.coe.int/Documents/HUDOC_38263_08_Annexes_ENG.pdf>).

[49] UN Security Council Res. 1096 (1997), UN Doc. S/RES/1096 (1997), para. 3.

[50] See Conclusions of the Council of the European Union, *cit. supra* note 23.

central government may decide, as a matter of political choice, neither to oppose the state's territorial integrity, nor to oppose the principle of *uti possidetis*, and subsequently to recognise the new independent state. We would be facing a situation in which international law has remained neutral. At the same time, we cannot maintain that this is a general rule in international relations.

A final qualification must be made. What has been argued above relates to unilateral secessions *stricto sensu*. However, we submit that the above conclusions can be extended to processes of dismemberment, a notion which is not always easy to distinguish from secession and is characterised by many similarities. In processes of dismemberment the international community has applied considerations of effectiveness on the ground resulting from the dissolution of federal structures and authority, but also certain requirements of procedural legality such as the prohibition on the use of force between territorial units, respect for the *uti possidetis juris* and respect of popular will on the basis of referenda.[51] On the other hand, these conclusions should not be extended to the numerous cases of agreed devolution with the central government: in this latter scenario, international law does recognise (hence it is not neutral) the sovereign right of a state to dispose of part of its territory, conditioning this right to the procedural principle of respect of popular will.[52]

4. EFFECTIVENESS AND SECESSION BETWEEN LEGAL PRESUMPTIONS AND GAP-FILLING

We must finally identify more precisely the residual role of effectiveness in secession processes. Firstly, we must clarify exactly what we mean by effectiveness. One interpretation of effectiveness, is as a broad notion of political effectiveness, not only characterised by the display of governmental authority over a certain territory and population, but referring also to the power dynamics which influence and determine the process and outcome in instances of secession. When international law is mobilised through a direct involvement of the international community, this interpretation of effectiveness must be considered as one of the important variables, as international law is applied by deduction through general

---

[51] According to Crawford "if it becomes clear that the process of dissolution of the State as a whole is irreversible, the consent of the government of the predecessor State may cease to be required for the separation of its constituent parts. In such a case that government will itself be in the process of dissolution, and may have ceased to represent the former State. But there is strong presumption against dissolution, and the only case of successful separation under these circumstances is that of the constituent republics of the former Yugoslavia" (CRAWFORD, *cit. supra* note 31, p. 418). See also KOHEN, *cit. supra* note 6, pp. 7-8.

[52] For instance, in the cases of Montenegro and in the devolution process in Scotland. See VIDMAR, "Montenegro's Path to Independence: A Study of Self-Determination, Statehood and Recognition", Hanse Law Review, 2007, p. 73 ff.; UK Government, "Scotland analysis: Devolution and the implications of Scottish independence", available at: <https://www.gov.uk/government/publications/scotland-analysis-devolution-and-the-implications-of-scottish-independence>.

principles, which are by nature flexible, but also subject to manipulation by political actors: in this sense, effectiveness is not weakened.

If instead we question the relevance of effectiveness in its traditional sense, namely that of territorial control as a factual precondition for secession to which international law attaches some legal consequences, the conclusion must be that effectiveness has been weakened. That is not tantamount to maintaining that it has no role. In particular, it is submitted that effectiveness continues to be relevant in three respects.

Firstly, while principles of substantive and procedural legality are becoming increasingly important in processes of secession, the factual requirements, often associated with the Montevideo criteria, do continue to play a role, albeit more limited. They reinforce a claim to statehood, in particular when the latter is not strongly contested by the central government; and when the international community does not intervene in the separation. On the other hand, the absence of effectiveness is an *a fortiori* argument to deny recognition as a sovereign state, when statehood is contested due to its violation of the principle of territorial integrity or due to the lack of an adequate degree of support by the population. Effectiveness is not merely the requirement of a rule of general international law; rather the essential component of a legal presumption, which is evaluated and determined on an *ad hoc* basis, and is key to the affirmation of statehood or its denial, especially in the initial phases of independence, in which states and international organisations operate by presumption. The degree and intensity of effectiveness required for the operation of a positive or negative presumption will differ according to the applicability of the principles of general international law, which have been mentioned. Where a "right to secession" arises due to an international agreement or as a consequence of the right of external self-determination arising out of a foreign occupation (an example being the occupation of the Baltic Republics in 1991), the degree of effectiveness required in order to form the legal presumption will be lower, with control over certain parts of the territory, including the capital, and a general support by local population, regardless of the organisation of a referendum.[53] In cases of secession where international law remains neutral,

---

[53] That the degree of effectiveness cannot be merely "nominal", not even in cases in which there is a "right" to create a state, is evident from the events leading to the admission of Palestine as non-member state at the United Nations. The Security Council's Committee on the admission of new member states was divided over the Palestinian request to become a new member of the organisation, as some states opposed the limited authority exercised by the Palestinian Authority, as a result of Israel's occupation of the West Bank and the Hamas authority in Gaza. Even General Assembly Res. 67/19 presents an ambiguous language, where it states "its determination to contribute to the achievement of the inalienable rights of the Palestinian people and the attainment of a peaceful settlement in the Middle East that ends the occupation that began in 1967 and fulfils the vision of two States: an independent, sovereign, democratic, contiguous and viable State of Palestine living side by side in peace and security with Israel on the basis of the pre-1967 borders" (Res. 67/19 (2012), UN Doc. A/RES/67/19, para. 4). Several states, while supporting the resolution, made it clear that Palestine's statehood is a vision and political objective, based on the right of self-determination of the Palestinian people, rather than a reality. According to France "[t]his vision of two States for two peoples must become a reality. The international recognition that the Assembly has today given the proposed Palestinian State

it will be effectiveness in its traditional sense that comes into play, with effective independence over a large part of the territory required and a population which is presumptively or manifestly in favour. Finally, in secession processes where the principle of territorial integrity is violated, it will be only "ultimate success" accompanied by the clear and ascertained will of the population to separate to produce legal consequences.

The second perspective relates to the importance of effectiveness in relation to subsequent recognition in the hypothesis just raised. The more effectiveness corresponds to an irreversible territorial *status quo*, to a definitive separation from the central government and to the effective capacity to maintain international relations *à titre de souverain*, the more the new subject, independently from the original violation of territorial integrity, will be able to receive international recognition from third states, international organisations and, eventually, from the parent state.[54] That is exactly what occurred in Kosovo in the years following the 2008 declaration of independence.[55] One must underline that the norms on territorial integrity and inviolability of international borders, even when framed in terms of *uti possidetis,* are not norms of a peremptory character and no secondary rule of general international law imposes on third states a duty not to recognise the new situation as lawful under international law.[56] The obligation of non-recognition under Article 41 of the ILC Articles on State Responsibility is not generally applicable to cases of secession, unless the violation of territorial integrity is accompanied by a serious violation of a peremptory norm, namely an unlawful use of force in support of secession (as occurred with Crimea's short-lived independence) or a grave form of violation of the right of self-determination of the local population.

Finally, one must mention a third perspective. In a regime, which is informed by legal principles of a general nature, which are variably invoked and applied, effectiveness, precisely because of its flexibility and translation into legal pre-

---

can become fact only through an agreement based on negotiations between the two parties on all final status issues, within the framework of a fair and comprehensive peace settlement that responds to Israel and Palestine's legitimate aspirations" (UN Doc. A/67/PV.44 (2012), para. 14). According to Belgium "[t]oday's vote is a significant step towards the creation of a State of Palestine, which we all look forward to. But Belgium believes that true progress will be made when the Palestinians will be able to benefit on the ground from the existence of a future State that has the necessary institutions, personnel and tools to function properly. Belgium fully shares the goal of resolution 67/19 just adopted – a two-State solution, with Israel living side by side in peace and security with a future State of Palestine that is democratic, viable and sustainable" (*ibid.*, para. 16). See Mancini, "Conseguenze giuridiche dell'attribuzione dello status di stato osservatore presso le Nazioni Unite", RDI, 2013, p. 100 ff.

[54] *Reference re Secession of Quebec, cit. supra* note 18, paras. 143-146.

[55] Milano, *Formazione dello Stato e processi di State-Building nel Diritto Internazionale, Kosovo 1999-2013*, Napoli, 2013, pp. 262-275.

[56] In the ILC project on states' rights and obligations, the obligation of non-recognition was limited to the use of force by states, excluding cases of internal secession: see Yearbook of the International Law Commission, 1949, pp. 112-113. Art. 11 of the draft declaration adopted in 1949 stated: "Every State has the duty to refrain from recognizing any territorial acquisition *by another State* acting in violation of article 9" (emphasis added).

sumptions, tends to fill the gaps left open by the application of the principles of general international law. It does that when those principles are simply not invoked and applied; but it also does that when the application of those principles is particularly contested, for instances in cases of so-called remedial secession; or where in a multinational state, one of the national groups does not support secession; or, finally, where there are doubts on the application of the *uti possidetis* principle. In all these cases, effectiveness fills the gaps left open by international law.

5.   LESSONS FROM CATALONIA AND KURDISTAN

The two recent referenda organised in Catalonia and Kurdish Iraq support the above conclusions. Whereas both cases can be generally considered as cases of attempted separation from the parent state, each of them displays its own features and shows the lack of a general international legal regime concerning secession.

In the case of Catalonia, the process towards independence has remained strictly within the reserved domain of Spain and Spanish law has maintained its exclusive and controlling role over the matter. This is a result of the consistent position of the Spanish central government, which has deployed the means at its disposal under the Spanish legal order in order to suppress the Catalan independence movement, without resorting to international legal arguments or claims; and to the position of the international community, which has consistently stressed the domestic nature of the political conflict.[57] In other words, the lesson that can be drawn from the Catalan experience is that secession attempts, in certain cases, may still be qualified as internal matters, in respect of which international law remains neutral and to a large extent agnostic. This is certainly connected to the subsidiary role played by international law in matters of domestic governance:

---

[57] The Spanish Constitutional Court declared the laws adopted by the Catalonian Parliament "on the self-determination referendum" (Law No. 19/2017 of 6 September 2017), and on the "juridical transition and founding of the Republic" (Law No. 20/2017 of 8 September 2017) as unconstitutional and null. After the declaration of independence of Catalonia, the Spanish Government activated Art. 155 of the Spanish Constitution, which allows the central Government to take "all measures necessary" to compel the self-governing community to meet the obligations imposed to it by the Spanish Constitution, or to protect the general interest of Spain. On the domestic nature of the conflict in Catalonia, see, among others: European Commission, "Statement on the events in Catalonia", available at: <http://europa.eu/rapid/press-release_STATEMENT-17-3626_en.htm>: "this is an internal matter for Spain that has to be dealt with in line with the constitutional order of Spain"; US Department of State, "Press briefing of 26 September 2017", available at <https://www.state.gov/r/pa/prs/dpb/2017/09/274443.htm>: "that is an internal matter for the people of Spain to decide"; Statement of the Chinese Foreign Ministry Spokesperson of 28 September 2017, available at <http://www.fmprc.gov.cn/mfa_eng/xwfw_665399/s2510_665401/t1498012.shtml>: "[t]he issue of Catalonia belongs to the domestic affairs of Spain". For a general comment see LOPEZ-JACOISTE, "Autonomy and self-determination in Spain: Catalonia's claims for independence from the perspective of international law", in HILPOLD (ed.), *Autonomy and Self-Determination: Between Legal Assertions and Utopian Aspirations*, Cheltenham, 2018, p. 283 ff.

where a political process can be channelled and governed through the ordinary and emergency means envisaged by a constitutional legal order, there will be no need to mobilise international legal rules and principles. The most "intrusive" political statement from the international community has been that of the UN High Commissioner for Human Rights and it has not gone further than demanding restraint by the Spanish authorities with regard to pro-independence demonstrators: "I am very disturbed by the violence in Catalonia on Sunday. With hundreds of people reported injured, I urge the Spanish authorities to ensure thorough, independent and impartial investigations into all acts of violence. Police responses must at all times be proportionate and necessary".[58]

On the other hand, in the case of Kurdistan, international law has been mobilised in order to reassert Iraq's sovereignty and territorial integrity. For instance, in a resolution adopted on 14 July 2017, the UN Security Council has "[u]nderscor[ed] the need for all segments of the Iraqi population [...] to develop a just and fair solution for the nation's disputed internal boundaries, and to work to strengthen national unity, including through cooperation between the Government of Iraq and the Kurdistan Regional Government in the spirit of genuine partnership [...]".[59] A few days before the referendum, the President of the Security Council issued a statement in which he stated:

> [t]he members of the Security Council expressed concern over the potentially destabilizing impact of the Kurdistan Regional Government's plans to unilaterally hold a referendum next week. [...] Council members expressed their continuing respect for the sovereignty, territorial integrity, and unity of Iraq and urged all outstanding issues between the federal Government and the Kurdish Regional Government to be resolved, in accordance with the provisions of the Iraqi Constitution, through structured dialogue and compromise supported by the international community.[60]

Apart from being condemned by Iraq's central government, the Kurdish referendum has also been condemned by several other countries, including neighbouring ones, such as Turkey, Iran and Syria. Such practice is indicative of the prevailing attitude of the international community to seek respect for the territorial integrity of states, hence narrowing the scope of application of the right of external self-determination even in cases in which a population has been until recently subjected to discrimination and gross violations of human rights. It is also a result of the fact that the situation in Iraq was already "internationalised": this is because of the cross-border implications of the Kurdish question in the

---

[58] "Comment by the UN High Commissioner for Human Rights Zeid Ra'ad Al Hussein on the situation in Catalonia, Spain", available at: <http://www.ohchr.org/EN/NewsEvents/Pages/DisplayNews.aspx?NewsID=22192&LangID=E>.

[59] UN Security Council Res. 2367 (2017), UN Doc. S/RES/2367 (2017), p. 2.

[60] Security Council Press Statement on Iraq, 21 September 2017, available at: <https://www.un.org/press/en/2017/sc13002.doc.htm>.

Middle East and the fact that the borders of Iraq and Syria have been extremely porous in recent years due to the military conflicts that have engulfed the region; it also has to do with the ambiguous wording of the referendum which referred to "the Kurdistani areas outside the administration of the Region", with the possible implication that the new state could extend to Kurdish areas in neighbouring countries. Certainly, lack of respect for the *uti possidetis* principle may have weakened the chances of the international community turning a blind eye to the independence of Kurdish Iraq.

Another important issue that has been raised by the two cases of Catalonia and Kurdistan is that of territorial referenda, namely whether such referenda are compulsory in case of secession and whether there are any standard under international law they must comply with. While the practice of holding referenda is very widespread, extending from the dissolution of the Soviet Union and the Former Yugoslavia to the more recent cases of Crimea, Catalonia and Kurdistan, it is hard to detect an *opinio juris* pointing to the obligatory nature of this form of ascertainment of popular will. What can be said at best is that when secession is contested and a procedural paradigm is shared and agreed, any presumption or objective determination of popular will suffice. The case of Kosovo is a good case in point: despite the lack of a referendum, the clear will of the people of Kosovo to separate from Serbia was never in doubt.

As for those situations in which a referendum is organised, the Venice Commission of the Council of Europe has established that the minimal international standards for a territorial referendum are the following: a) free and universal suffrage; b) the authorities must provide objective information; c) the public media have to be neutral, in particular in news coverage; d) the authorities must not influence the outcome of the vote by excessive, one-sided campaign; e) the use of public funds for campaigning purposes must be restricted; f) respect for fundamental human rights; g) presence of international observers; and h) availability of an effective appeal system.[61] While those standards are important normative elements concerning the European continent, and they are, at least to some extent, already part of Europe's regional international law, it is doubtful that they would be accepted in the foreseeable future outside Europe; even in Europe, some of the standards are more progressive development than minimum standards with which states comply. In this latter respect, one can point especially to the standard prohibiting excessive, one-sided campaign by the authorities to influence the outcome, which is largely ignored: the case of Catalonia shows that the central government and Catalan's regional government have not spared any means of political campaigning in order to influence the outcome of the referendum (Madrid by demanding people to boycott; Barcelona by inviting people to vote in favour of independence).

---

[61] European Commission for Democracy through Law, Opinion on the Compatibility of the Existing Legislation in Montenegro concerning the Organization of Referendum with Applicable International Standards, 19 December 2005, Opinion No. 343/2005, para. 12.

6. Concluding remarks

Unilateral secession and statehood continue to be contentious issues in international law and international relations. In a legal system dominated by states, it is hardly surprising that the latter are jealously trying to preserve their sovereignty and existing boundaries. And yet states are aware that sovereignty and existing boundaries are not always tenable, when they become themselves a source of instability and conflict. That explains a general "disapproval" of secession and yet the absence of a general prohibition. The ICJ *Kosovo* Advisory Opinion was a lost opportunity to shed light on extremely important international legal issues relating to secession, such as the scope of application of the principle of self-determination of peoples. In truth, it is possible to discern in the parsimonious and narrow scope of the advisory opinion of the Court an extremely prudent attitude, which resulted in part from the contentious narratives presented by states during the proceedings. On the other hand, one must recall that the Court was called upon to pronounce on a specific legal question raised by the General Assembly and could have provided a better answer, without stating any general theory on secession and international law.

The present article has argued that secession remains an enduring, unresolved question in international law. International law still adopts a *sui generis* and casuistic approach to secession, but with the increasing tendency to regulate the process and its outcomes, when contrary to its fundamental principles. The recent cases of Catalonia and Kurdistan confirm that international law does not generally regulate secession as such, but it is put into operation when secession produces regional and international instability and human rights violations.

In the case of Catalonia, the prospects for the foreseeable future are that the separatist movement will remain a Spanish internal matter, also due to the population's lack of clear and overwhelming will in favour of independence. It is unlikely that international law will play any substantive or procedural role. In the case of Kurdistan, the situation is much more volatile and the independence movement in Kurdish Iraq is characterised by a context in which existing states, their governments and their international boundaries have been put under considerable "stress" by internal and external forces; the creation of a *de facto* independent entity in the north of Syria, the so-called Rojava, with no claim to statehood and with a completely different political agenda, is further weakening the cause of Kurdish Iraq. It is to be expected that given the context, the international community will reassert and uphold the territorial integrity of the existing state, in order to avoid a further factor of instability in an area, which has been engulfed in a grave systemic crisis since the overthrow of Saddam Hussein and the Arab Spring a few years later. The Kurdish cause, which goes back in history at least as far as the 1920 Treaty of Sèvres and is rooted in the colonial past of the Middle East, remains unresolved, despite the many fruitful experiments of self-administration both in Iraq and Syria.

THE TREATY ON THE PROHIBITION OF NUCLEAR WEAPONS: A PROMISE, A THREAT OR A FLOP?

MARCO PEDRAZZI[*]

Abstract

On 7 July 2017 a UN Conference, convened in New York by the General Assembly, adopted a Treaty on the Prohibition of Nuclear Weapons, providing for the first total ban on these weapons intended to be global in scale. The Treaty was opened for signature on 20 September 2017. The process and its outcome, were, however, firmly opposed by nuclear-weapon States and by NATO countries, including Italy: they refused to take part in the effort, fearing that it could definitively undermine the stability of the non-proliferation architecture built upon the 1967 Non-Proliferation Treaty. In reality, the Treaty is consistent with the ultimate purpose of the NPT regime, and the obligations assumed by States under the NPT remain untouched. Its main deficiencies relate to its verification apparatus, and it would be advisable to remedy them through future negotiations. Whether this instrument will enter into force is not clear, although it has the potential to acquire, and surpass, the fifty ratifications necessary. However, the absence of support from nuclear-weapon States risks rendering it irrelevant. Nevertheless, it seems plausible that broad support for this new regime, from non-nuclear-weapons States, as well as from civil society, could contribute to exerting pressure towards the adoption of concrete steps in the nuclear disarmament agenda.

Keywords: nuclear weapons; weapons of mass destruction; disarmament; non-proliferation; UN General Assembly; UN Security Council; NATO; law of treaties; international humanitarian law.

1. INTRODUCTION

A UN General Assembly's resolution of 23 December 2016,[1] while recalling that the Treaty on the Non-Proliferation of Nuclear Weapons of 1 July 1968[2] (NPT) "serves as the cornerstone of the nuclear non-proliferation and disarmament regime", acted to convene "a United Nations conference to negotiate a legally binding instrument to prohibit nuclear weapons, leading towards their total elimination". The resolution was adopted with 113 votes in favour, 35 against

---

[*] Professor of International Law, University of Milan.
[1] UN Doc. A/RES/71/258 (2017).
[2] Treaty on the Non-proliferation of Nuclear Weapons, 1 July 1968, entered into force 5 March 1970.

and 13 abstentions.[3] The conference met in New York from 27 to 31 March and from 15 June to 7 July 2017, on which date the Treaty on the Prohibition of Nuclear Weapons (TPNW) was adopted, with 122 votes in favour, one against (the Netherlands) and one abstention (Singapore). None of the nuclear weapons States, or NATO countries (except the Netherlands), or other "nuclear umbrella States", such as Australia, Japan and South Korea, took part in the Conference, however. The Treaty was opened for signature at the UN headquarters on 20 September 2017. It will enter into force after the number of ratifications reaches fifty, according to its Article 15.

The following analysis will briefly trace the origins of the Treaty; it will delineate its structure and main contents, comparing them with other, similar conventional regimes; it will deal with its relationship with the non-proliferation regime, which is the main bone of contention; it will outline the Italian position on this instrument; and it will conclude with a tentative assessment of the prospects for its entry into force and its future universalisation.

2.   THE ORIGINS OF THE TREATY: THE HUMANITARIAN INITIATIVE

The origins of the TPNW can be tracked to the deep dissatisfaction of various non-nuclear-weapon States with what they perceive to be a substantial lack of implementation of Article VI NPT, one of the Treaty's three pillars, which obliges all States Parties to engage in serious disarmament efforts.[4] The International Court of Justice clarified the nature of this obligation in its Advisory Opinion on the *Legality of the Threat or Use of Nuclear Weapons* in the following terms:

> The legal import of that obligation goes beyond that of a mere obligation of conduct; the obligation involved here is an obligation to achieve a precise result – nuclear disarmament in all its aspects – by adopting a particular course of conduct, namely, the pursuit of negotiations on the matter in good faith.[5]

---

[3] However, "[s]ubsequently, the delegations of Albania, Estonia and Italy informed the Secretariat that they had intended to vote against; the delegation of the Comoros had intended to abstain": see UN Doc. A/71/PV.68 (2016), p. 17.

[4] Art. VI NPT reads as follows: "Each of the Parties to the Treaty undertakes to pursue negotiations in good faith on effective measures relating to cessation of the nuclear arms race at an early date and to nuclear disarmament, and on a Treaty on general and complete disarmament under strict and effective international control". See, inter alia, FLECK, International Law Association Committee on Nuclear Weapons, Non-Proliferation and Contemporary International Law, "Second report, Legal Aspects of Nuclear Disarmament", 2014, available at: <http://www.ila-hq.org/index.php/committees>; ROSCINI, "On Certain Legal Issues Arising from Article VI of the Treaty on the Non-Proliferation of Nuclear Weapons", in CARACCIOLO, PEDRAZZI and VASSALLI DI DACHENHAUSEN (eds.), *Nuclear Weapons: Strengthening the International Legal Regime*, The Hague, 2016, p. 15 ff.; MAGI, "L'obbligo di disarmo nucleare quale obbligo a realizzazione progressiva", RDI, 2018, p. 58 ff.

[5] *Legality of the Threat or Use of Nuclear Weapons*, Advisory Opinion of 8 July 1996, ICJ Reports, 1996, p. 226 ff., para. 99.

Undoubtedly, in the close to fifty years since the NPT entered into force in 1970, overall nuclear arsenals have been reduced, in particular on the basis of a series of agreements between the two nuclear superpowers, the US on one side, and the USSR and later Russia on the other side.[6] There has also been progress in relation to nuclear weapon tests, a moratorium on which has been respected by all States for decades notwithstanding the non-entry into force of the Comprehensive Nuclear-Test-Ban Treaty (CTBT),[7] with the notable exception of North Korea. However, while some new *de facto* nuclear-weapon States have proliferated outside the NPT framework, or after having rejected that framework (as in the case of North Korea), other, *de jure* nuclear-weapon States have continued to increase their stockpiles, and several of them are proceeding with the modernization of their arsenals, whose destructive potential has progressively grown over time.[8] Overall, the prospects for nuclear disarmament do not seem much better today than they did in 1968, when the NPT was adopted.

The NPT review conferences did little to improve these prospects, notwithstanding the hopes raised by the Programme of Action agreed to in 1995,[9] the 13-point plan decided in 2000,[10] and, after the 2005 conference's failure, the 64-point Action Plan issued in 2010.[11]

It is also worth recalling that the attempts to obtain authoritative judicial pronouncements "outlawing" nuclear weapons on the basis of their presumed unlawfulness under general international law have failed. The ICJ, in its identical 1974 judgments in the *Nuclear Tests* cases (*Australia v. France* and *New Zealand v. France*) did not pronounce on the merits of the claims (the two countries had asked the Court to declare the illegality of further French nuclear tests in the South Pacific and to order France not to proceed with such tests). Instead, the Court held that France's unilateral declaration announcing the end of its atmospheric tests in the Pacific was a legal undertaking which deprived the parties' claims of their

---

[6] See the data reproduced in CORRALES, "Tratado sobre la prohibición de las armas nucleares: ¿avance hacia el desarme nuclear?", Instituto Español de Estudios Estratégicos, Opinión, available at: <http://www.ieee.es/publicaciones-new/documentos-de-opinion/2017/DIEEEO97-2017.html>, p. 6-9.

[7] Comprehensive Nuclear-Test-Ban Treaty, 10 September 1996, not entered into force, available at: <http://disarmament.un.org/treaties/t/ctbt/text>.

[8] See, *inter alia*, US Department of Defense, "Nuclear Posture Review February 2018", Executive Summary, available at <https://www.defense.gov/News/SpecialReports/2018NuclearPostureReview.aspx>, and Russian president Putin's response in his state of the nation speech of 1 March 2018 (see "Putin's 'Invincible' Missile is Aimed at U.S. Vulnerabilities", The New York Times, available at: <https://www.nytimes.com/2018/03/01/world/europe/russia-putin-speech.html>).

[9] Final Document of the 1995 Review and Extension Conference of the Parties to the Treaty on the Non-Proliferation of Nuclear Weapons, NPT/CONF.1995/32 (Part I), Annex, Decision 2.

[10] Final Document of the 2000 Review Conference of the Parties to the Treaty on the Non-Proliferation of Nuclear Weapons, NPT/CONF.2000/28 (Parts I and II), para. 15.

[11] Final Document of the 2010 Review Conference of the Parties to the Treaty on the Non-Proliferation of Nuclear Weapons, NPT/CONF.2010/50 (Vol. I), p. 19 ff. For a brief survey, see FANIELLE, "Towards Nuclear Disarmament: State of Affairs in the International Legal Framework", Nuclear Law Bulletin, 2016, p. 35 ff, pp. 42-43.

object.[12] In its 1996 Advisory Opinion, the Court, while recognizing that "the threat or use of nuclear weapons would generally be contrary to the rules of international law applicable in armed conflict, and in particular the principles and rules of humanitarian law", left the door open to a possible instance of lawfulness of such threat or use "in an extreme circumstance of self-defence, in which the very survival of a State would be at stake".[13] Finally, in its recent judgments on the claims brought by the Marshall Islands against the UK, India and Pakistan relating to the alleged violation of Article VI NPT, or of the assumed corresponding norm of customary international law, the Court found that it lacked jurisdiction due to the absence of a legal dispute among the parties.[14]

The driving force behind the move towards the Humanitarian Initiative was a clause that was inserted in the Final document of the NPT 2010 Review Conference, which pointed to "the catastrophic humanitarian consequences that would result from the use of nuclear weapons".[15] In addition, in 2011, the Council of Delegates of the International Red Cross and Red Crescent Movement stated in a resolution that it found "difficult to envisage how any use of nuclear weapons could be compatible with the rules of international humanitarian law, in particular the rules of distinction, precaution and proportionality". The resolution also appealed to all States "to pursue in good faith and conclude with urgency and determination negotiations to prohibit the use of and completely eliminate nuclear weapons through a legally binding international agreement".[16] On these bases, a Group of 16 States Parties to the NPT took a firm stand on the "humanitarian dimension of nuclear disarmament", calling for further decisive steps during the 2012 Prep Com for the 2015 Review Conference.[17] Contemporaneously,

---

[12] *Nuclear Tests (Australia v. France)*, Judgment of 20 December 1974, ICJ Reports, 1974, p. 253 ff., paras. 42 ff.; *Nuclear Tests (New Zealand v. France)*, Judgment of 20 December 1974, ICJ Reports, 1974, p. 457 ff., paras. 45 ff.

[13] *Legality of the Threat or Use of Nuclear Weapons*, cit. *supra* note 5, para. 105(E).

[14] *Obligations concerning negotiations relating to cessation of the nuclear arms race and to nuclear disarmament (Marshall Islands v. United Kingdom)*, Preliminary objections, Judgment of 5 October 2016, ICJ Reports, 2016, p. 833 ff., paras. 36 ff.; *Obligations concerning negotiations relating to cessation of the nuclear arms race and to nuclear disarmament (Marshall Islands v. India)*, Preliminary objections, Judgment of 5 October 2016, ICJ Reports, 2016, p. 255 ff, paras. 33 ff.; *Obligations concerning negotiations relating to cessation of the nuclear arms race and to nuclear disarmament (Marshall Islands v. Pakistan)*, Preliminary objections, Judgment of 5 October 2016, ICJ Reports, 2016, p. 552 ff., paras. 33 ff.

[15] 2010 Review Conference, cit. *supra* note 11, para. 80: "The Conference expresses its deep concern at the continued risk for humanity represented by the possibility that these weapons could be used and the catastrophic humanitarian consequences that would result from the use of nuclear weapons".

[16] "Working towards the elimination of nuclear weapons", 26 November 2011, available at: <https://www.icrc.org/eng/resources/documents/resolution/council-delegates-resolution-1-2011.htm>.

[17] See First Session of the Preparatory Committee for the 2015 Review Conference of the Parties to the Treaty on the Non-Proliferation of Nuclear Weapons, Statement of Switzerland on behalf of States parties focusing on The Humanitarian Dimension, 2 May 2012, available at: <https://www.un.org/disarmament/wmd/nuclear/npt2015/prepcom2012-statements/>. The Group included the following States: Austria, Chile, Costa Rica, Denmark, Holy See, Egypt,

Norway, the only NATO member country in the group, called for a conference in spring 2013, "to highlight the humanitarian consequences of nuclear weapons, including the incompatibility of their use under international humanitarian law (IHL)".[18] The Oslo International Conference on the Humanitarian Impact of Nuclear Weapons of 4 and 5 March 2013 was followed by two further conferences in Nayarit, Mexico, on 13 and 14 February 2014, and in Vienna, on 8 and 9 December 2014. They enjoyed broad participation by states, UN bodies, the International Red Cross and Red Crescent Movement and a number of NGOs active in the fight for the elimination of all nuclear arsenals. The process was initially boycotted, however, by the big five: only the UK and the US decided to participate in the final conference in Vienna. The conferences' agenda focused on the dire humanitarian consequences of the use of nuclear weapons on people, the environment and society at large; on the impossibility to provide adequate humanitarian responses to face such consequences; and on the risks that the mere presence of nuclear arsenals entail for the possible accidental outbreak of nuclear war. Their ultimate purpose was clearly to pursue the definitive outlawing of nuclear weapons: the "Austrian pledge", issued at the closure of the Vienna conference, indicated that country's commitment "to cooperate with all relevant stakeholders […] in efforts to stigmatise, prohibit and eliminate nuclear weapons in light of their unacceptable humanitarian consequences and associated risks".[19] After the failure of the 2015 NPT Review Conference, the "humanitarian pledge" was incorporated in a UN General Assembly resolution approved by 139 Member States.[20] This outcome was not acceptable to the nuclear powers and their allies.

Simultaneously, the General Assembly decided to convene an open-ended working group "to substantively address concrete effective legal measures, legal provisions and norms that will need to be concluded to attain and maintain a world without nuclear weapons".[21] In its final report issued in 2016, the open-ended working group recommended "the convening, by the General Assembly, of a conference in 2017, open to all States, with the participation and contribution of international organizations and civil society, to negotiate a legally binding instrument to prohibit nuclear weapons, leading towards their total elimination".[22] This led to the abovementioned General Assembly resolution convening the New York conference for the negotiation of the Treaty.

Indonesia, Ireland, Malaysia, Mexico, New Zealand, Nigeria, Norway, Philippines, South Africa, Switzerland.

[18] See *ibid.*, Statement of Norway, 30 April 2012. See also KMENTT, "The Development of the International Initiative on the Humanitarian Impact of Nuclear Weapons and its Effects on the Nuclear Weapons Debate", IRRC, 2015, p. 681 ff., p. 683.

[19] More information is available at: <https://www.bmeia.gv.at/en/european-foreign-policy/disarmament/weapons-of-mass-destruction/nuclear-weapons-and-nuclear-terrorism/vienna-conference-on-the-humanitarian-impact-of-nuclear-weapons/>.

[20] UN Doc. A/RES/70/48 (2015): the resolution met 29 votes against and 17 abstentions.

[21] UN Doc. A/RES/70/33 (2015), adopted with 138 votes in favour, 12 against and 34 abstentions.

[22] UN Doc. A/71/371 (2016), para. 67.

3. THE NEW YORK CONFERENCE, THE ADOPTION OF THE TREATY, AND ITS
   PURPOSE AND STRUCTURE

The United Nations Conference to Negotiate a Legally Binding Instrument
to Prohibit Nuclear Weapons, Leading Towards their Total Elimination opened
in New York on 27 March 2017. The Conference saw the participation of 125
States, the Agency for the Prohibition of Nuclear Weapons in Latin America and
the Caribbean (OPANAL), the European Union, the International Committee of
the Red Cross (ICRC) and the International Federation of Red Cross and Red
Crescent Societies (IFRC), the Inter-Parliamentary Union and the UN Institute
for Disarmament Research (UNIDIR). NGOs also actively participated in the
conference, producing a relevant number of documents: among these, the proposals produced by the disarmament programme (Reaching Critical Will) of
the Women's International League for Peace and Freedom, a member of the
International Campaign to Abolish Nuclear Weapons (ICAN), are worth mentioning.[23] The crucial role played by NGOs in the whole process, starting with the
Humanitarian Initiative and ending with the TPNW, led ICAN to earn the 2017
Nobel peace prize.[24]

The purpose of the Treaty is clearly enunciated in the second indent of its
Preamble, whereby the drafters, based on their deep concern for "the catastrophic
humanitarian consequences that would result from any use of nuclear weapons",
affirm the "need to completely eliminate such weapons", as "the only way to
guarantee that nuclear weapons are never used again under any circumstances".
In conformity with this stated purpose, the TPNW is both a disarmament and an
international humanitarian law instrument, providing on one side for the total
elimination of nuclear weapons, on the other side for an absolute ban on their
use. The Treaty's nature is therefore comparable to that of such instruments as
the 1993 Chemical Weapons Convention (CWC),[25] the 1997 Anti-Personnel
Mine Ban Convention (APMC)[26] and the 2008 Cluster Munitions Convention
(CMC).[27] At the same time, the TPNW completes the circle of instruments pursuing the total outlawing of all weapons of mass destruction (WMD), adding to

---

[23] See ACHESON, "Banning Nuclear Weapons. Principles and Elements for a Legally
Binding Instrument", March 2017, and ID., "Banning Nuclear Weapons. Prohibitions for a
Nuclear Weapon Ban Treaty", June 2017, both available at: <http://www.reachingcriticalwill.
org/resources/publications-and-research/research-projects/9146-banning-nuclear-weapons>.

[24] ICAN was awarded the prize "for its work to draw attention to the catastrophic humanitarian consequences of any use of nuclear weapons and for its ground-breaking efforts to
achieve a treaty-based prohibition of such weapons". The explanation of the prize is available
at: <https://www.nobelprize.org/nobel_prizes/peace/laureates/2017/ican-facts.html>.

[25] Convention on the Prohibition of the Development, Production, Stockpiling and Use
of Chemical Weapons and on their Destruction, 13 January 1993, entered into force 29 April
1997.

[26] Convention on the Prohibition of the Use, Stockpiling, Production and Transfer of Anti-
Personnel Mines and on their Destruction, 18 September 1997, 3 December 1997, entered into
force 1 March 1999.

[27] Convention on Cluster Munitions, adopted 30 May 2008, 3 December 2008, entered
into force 1 August 2010.

the already mentioned CWC and to the 1972 Biological Weapons Convention (BWC), which, from a formal point of view, is merely a disarmament treaty, as it does not contain an explicit ban on use.[28] From another perspective, we may say that the Treaty aims to universalize the bans already established at the regional level, albeit with different degrees of amplitude and nuances, by the treaties establishing nuclear weapon free zones (NWFZ).[29]

The text of the Treaty contains a long preamble and 20 articles. The core obligations are spelled out in Article 1. The subsequent articles deal with the crucial issue of verification and control, establishing diversified requirements in relation to the different positions of States Parties. Article 5 deals with national implementation and articles 6 and 7 with assistance and remediation. Article 8 inaugurates the procedural part of the Treaty, followed by the final clauses. The TPNW's structure is similar to, although simpler than, that of the CWC, the APMC and the CMC, as the following paragraph will demonstrate.

4. THE CONTENTS OF THE TREATY: THE DISARMAMENT OBLIGATIONS; DURATION AND WITHDRAWAL

As mentioned above, Article 1 is the core of the Treaty, as it traces the fundamental obligations falling on States Parties. The formulations are more detailed than those contained in the CWC, the APMC or the CMC, recalling the provisions of the Pelindaba and Semipalatinsk treaties. In substance, the provisions impose on all States Parties to abstain from any act entailing the opportunity to acquire or receive or develop nuclear weapons or other nuclear explosive devices, to possess or stockpile or test them, to transfer them to any entity, to use or threaten the use of such devices, to assist any entity in one of the abovementioned activities, and to allow them to be stationed at any place under their jurisdiction. The provision is clearly all-encompassing, as no exception is contemplated that would entail the admittance of the prohibited items in any State Party under any form.

---

[28] Convention on the Prohibition of the Development, Production and Stockpiling of Bacteriological (Biological) and Toxin Weapons and on their Destruction, 10 April 1972, entered into force 26 March 1975.

[29] See Treaty for the Prohibition of Nuclear Weapons in Latin America and the Caribbean (so-called Treaty of Tlatelolco), 14 February 1967, entered into force 25 April 1969; South Pacific Nuclear Free Zone Treaty, 6 August 1985, entered into force 11 December 1986; Treaty on the Southeast Asia Nuclear Weapon-Free Zone, 15 December 1995, entered into force 27 March 1997; African Nuclear Weapon Free Zone Treaty (so called Treaty of Pelindaba), 11 April 1996, entered into force on 15 July 2009; Treaty on a Nuclear-Weapon-Free Zone in Central Asia, 8 September 2006, entered into force 21 March 2009. Nuclear weapons are also banned by the Antarctic Treaty, 1 December 1959, entered into force 23 June 1961, and by the Outer Space Treaty, 27 January 1967, entered into force 10 October 1967, from, respectively, Antarctica and outer space (including the Moon and other celestial bodies), and Mongolia, on the basis of a unilateral declaration. For a general analysis, see ROSCINI, *Le zone denuclearizzate*, Torino, 2003.

Some points deserve clarification. A striking difference with respect to most other weapons treaties is the absence of definitions: in particular, "nuclear weapons" and "other nuclear explosive devices" remain devoid of any legal definition. By contrast, not only are other weapons, such as chemical ones, anti-personnel mines and cluster munitions, defined in detail in their respective instruments, but the nuclear weapons themselves are defined in the NWFZ treaties. E.g., under the Semipalatinsk Treaty, "'[n]uclear weapon or other nuclear explosive device' means any weapon or other explosive device capable of releasing nuclear energy, irrespective of the military or civilian purpose for which the weapon or device could be used".[30] At the New York Conference, Sweden proposed the introduction of a definition,[31] but the proposal was not accepted. In fact, the lack of a definition also characterizes the NPT, without prejudicing its interpretation and application: it was evidently felt that a clearly accepted meaning already exists, thanks in part to the supervisory functions performed by the International Atomic Energy Agency (IAEA) under the safeguards agreements.

The all-encompassing Article 1 prohibitions include the ban on allowing the stationing or deployment of any nuclear weapons or nuclear explosive devices on the State Parties' territory. As is well known, no such ban is explicitly spelled out in the NPT's text, giving way to opposing views on the legitimacy of the position of non-nuclear-weapon States, such as Italy, Belgium, Germany, the Netherlands and Turkey, which host on their territory US nuclear weapons, under US control (but subject to local consent in case of use, according to a "double key" system).[32] Now, for the first time, a rule banning nuclear sharing arrangements is being explicitly posed at the universal level.

In line with its purpose, the Treaty "is of unlimited duration" (Article 17(1)). Nonetheless, as with all disarmament treaties, the TPNW contains a withdrawal clause, according to which, as usual, a State party has the right to withdraw "if it decides that extraordinary events related to the subject matter of the Treaty have jeopardized" its "supreme interests." Furthermore, the withdrawal notice "shall include a statement" of such "extraordinary events" (Article 17(2)).[33] The clause is innovative, however, inasmuch as it extends the notice period to up to

---

[30] Art. 1(b). The norm continues specifying: "The term includes such a weapon or device in unassembled or partly assembled forms, but does not include the means of transport or delivery of such a weapon or device if separable from and not an indivisible part of it".

[31] See UN Doc. A/CONF.229/2017/WP.5 (2017). All documents of the New York Conference are available at: <https://www.un.org/disarmament/ptnw/index.html>. The proposal was quite controversial, as it referred to "[weapon] assembly that is *capable of producing* an explosion and *massive damage and destruction* by the sudden release of energy instantaneously released from self-sustaining nuclear fission and/or fusion" (emphasis added). More generally, on the absence of any definition see also the comment of the Netherlands on Art. 1 of the Draft, in Compilation of amendments received from States on the revised draft submitted by the President dated 30 June 2017, UN Doc. A/CONF.229/2017/CRP.1/Rev.1 (2017).

[32] On this point, see ALBERQUE, "The NPT and the Origins of NATO's Nuclear Sharing Arrangements", *Etudes de l'IFRI, Poliferation Papers No. 57*, 2017, available at: <https://www.ifri.org/sites/default/files/atoms/files/alberque_npt_origins_nato_nuclear_2017.pdf>.

[33] See similar formulations, *inter alia*, in Article X NPT; Article XVI CWC; Article IX CTBT. Generally, see, among others, PONTI, "Il recesso dai trattati in materia di disarmo. Il

twelve months and because it provides that if, after the expiration of this period, the State Party is a party to an armed conflict, it "shall continue to be bound by the obligations of the Treaty [...] until it is no longer party to an armed conflict" (Article 17(3)). The restriction in question, whatever its practical effect, is commendable, and providing a possibility of withdrawal was probably unavoidable. All the same, the consistency of such a provision in a treaty bound to totally eliminate a weapon considered radically unlawful (see below) may be called into question. It is further regrettable that the clause does not include a caveat, similar to that enunciated in Article XVI CWC, stating that the withdrawal of a State party "shall not in any way affect the duty of States to continue fulfilling the obligations assumed under any relevant rules of international law".[34]

5. THE BAN ON THE USE OF NUCLEAR WEAPONS AND INTERNATIONAL HUMANITARIAN LAW

As previously mentioned, Article 1 also contains a fundamental international humanitarian law provision, banning any use or threat to use nuclear weapons or other nuclear explosive devices: the ban, qualified by the initial clause "never under any circumstances" obviously applies in any kind of armed conflict (and outside any conflict) and includes a ban on reprisals.[35] These prohibitions are the direct consequence of the statements included in the Preamble, according to which, "any use of nuclear weapons would be contrary to the rules of international law applicable in armed conflict, in particular the principles and rules of international humanitarian law", and "any use of nuclear weapons would also be abhorrent to the principles of humanity and the dictates of public conscience", in total disregard for the Martens' clause precepts.[36] These strong positions represent a step further with respect to the cautious attitude followed by the ICJ in its 1996 Advisory Opinion, pointing to the conviction, shared by many States, in line with ICRC views,[37] that nuclear weapons are already prohibited under international customary law. This is important testimony of *opinio juris* coming from

---

caso della Corea del nord e il futuro del regime di non proliferazione nucleare", in BATSANOV et al., *The Challenges of Disarmament and Non-Proliferation*, Milano, 2007, p. 79 ff.

[34] Indeed, see the proposal of New Zealand to this end, in Compilation of amendments, *cit. supra* note 31.

[35] The text does not contain the prohibition "to engage in any military preparations to use" nuclear weapons, as included in the CWC, Art. I(1)(c), although the insertion of such a rule was proposed: see ICRC comments in UN Doc. A/CONF.229/2017/CRP.2 (2017).

[36] See also the ninth indent of the Preamble, referring to "the principle that the right of parties to an armed conflict to choose methods or means of warfare is not unlimited, the rule of distinction, the prohibition against indiscriminate attacks, the rules on proportionality and precautions in attack, the prohibition on the use of weapons of a nature to cause superfluous injury or unnecessary suffering, and the rules for the protection of the natural environment". For a recent consideration of nuclear disarmament under the lens of humanitarian law and human rights law, see RIETIKER, *Humanization of Arms Control: Paving the Way for a World Free of Nuclear Weapons*, Abingdon, 2017.

[37] See ICRC comments, *cit. supra* note 35.

the majority of the international community, although its relevance is diminished by the fact that it is not supported by the weighty minority of nuclear-weapon States.

6. Verification

With regard to the prohibitions relating to the manufacture, possession and transfer of nuclear weapons and other nuclear explosive devices under Article 1, verification is obviously the core issue. The TPNW's verification system is simpler than that provided by the CWC, but more complex than the ones established by the APMC or the CMC. Its complexities are due to the fact that ratification of the Treaty is open to four different categories of States: 1) States that have never possessed or hosted nuclear weapons; 2) States that have possessed nuclear weapons, and eliminated them before the entry into force of the TPNW for them; 3) States that still possess, own or control nuclear weapons; 4) States hosting in their territory nuclear weapons or other nuclear explosive devices under the control of other States. States Parties are to submit to the UN Secretary General, as soon as they ratify the Treaty, a declaration stating their precise position (Article 2). Two different kinds of verification are therefore necessary, as, according to the situation, controls shall verify either the mere non-diversion from peaceful to military uses of nuclear energy or, in addition, the effective dismantling of existing nuclear arsenals. Differently from the CWC, the TPNW does not create, at least for the moment, any new international organization, but mostly relies on existing mechanisms, i.e. on those belonging to the IAEA.

In fact, as a general rule, States Parties "shall, at a minimum, maintain" their IAEA safeguards obligations in force at the time of entry into force of the TPNW. If they are not yet party to any such agreement, they shall conclude with the IAEA, and bring into force, a comprehensive safeguards agreement (INFCIRC/153 (Corrected)) (Article 3).[38] However, States Parties that have owned, possessed or controlled nuclear weapons or other nuclear explosive devices "after 7 July 2017", i.e. after the date of the adoption of the Treaty, but have eliminated their nuclear-weapon programme before the entry into force of the TPNW for them, and States Parties still owning, possessing or controlling such devices are subject to separate mechanisms and obligations under Article 4. The latter "shall immediately remove" such items "from operational status" and destroy them according to "a legally binding, time-bound plan" (Paragraph 2). The "irreversible elimination of nuclear-weapons programmes" shall be negotiated and verified by a "competent international authority" to be designated by the States Parties (Paragraph 6).[39] The designation of such an authority and, therefore, the defini-

---

[38] For a general survey of the different safeguards agreements see ROCKWOOD, "Legal Framework for IAEA Safeguards", 2013, available at: <https://www.iaea.org/sites/default/files/16/12/legalframeworkforsafeguards.pdf>.

[39] According to JOYNER, "My Impressions on the Second Draft of the NW Ban Treaty", Arms Control Law, 28 June 2017, available at: <https://armscontrollaw.com/2017/06/28/my-

tion of the contours of this second tier of the verification system was evidently postponed, on the basis of an easy prediction that the time for putting it into effect was not imminent. In any case, the same international authority is also to be entrusted with the task of verifying the irreversible elimination of the nuclear-weapon programmes of the former States Parties (Paragraph 1). In addition to that, both categories of States Parties shall conclude with the IAEA a safeguards agreement "sufficient to provide credible assurance of the non-diversion of declared nuclear material from peaceful nuclear activities and of the absence of undeclared nuclear material or activities" in such States "as a whole" (Paragraphs 1 and 3). In this case a clear reference is being made to the Additional Protocols (INFCIRC/540 (Corr.)), the only instruments allowing IAEA to confirm the 'completeness' of States' declarations.[40]

As for States Parties hosting in their territory nuclear weapons owned, possessed or controlled by others, they "shall ensure the prompt removal of such weapons, as soon as possible but not later than a deadline to be determined by the first meeting of States Parties" (Article 4(4)).

7. NATIONAL IMPLEMENTATION, ASSISTANCE AND INTERNATIONAL COOPERATION

All States Parties are also bound to take all legal and administrative measures to implement the Treaty in their national legal order, including the imposition of penal sanctions to prevent and suppress prohibited activities undertaken by persons or on territory under their jurisdiction or control (Article 5). This provision is important, if rather general.

The provisions on victim assistance (Article 6) and on international cooperation and assistance (Article 7) are inspired in particular by the corresponding articles of the CCM (Articles 5 and 6), although they are less developed. Notable aspects of these provisions include the addition to the obligation of the affected State to provide "age and gender-sensitive assistance, without discrimination, including medical care, rehabilitation and psychological support" to victims of use or testing of nuclear weapons, of the duty to take "appropriate measures towards the environmental remediation" of the contaminated areas (Article 6); and the devising of a specific responsibility of the State party that has used or tested such weapons "to provide adequate assistance to affected States Parties", "[w]ithout prejudice to any other duty or obligation that it may have under international law". Since such use or testing would be unlawful under the Treaty, this obliga-

---

impressions-on-the-second-draft-of-the-nw-ban-treaty/>, it is fortunate that IAEA was assigned the role of "administrator of safeguards agreements" and not the very different one of "presumptive verifier of nuclear weapons disarmament".

[40] See, *inter alia*, DUPONT, "Interpretation of Nuclear Safeguards Commitments: The Role of Subsequent Agreements and Practice", in BLACK-BRANCH and FLECK (eds.), *Nuclear Non-Proliferation in International Law, Volume II. Verification and Compliance*, The Hague, 2016, p. 23 ff., p. 24.

tion particularly adds to the content of the international responsibility of the State in question towards the affected States.

8. THE RELATIONSHIP WITH OTHER INTERNATIONAL AGREEMENTS, INCLUDING THE NPT

A core aspect of the TPNW, and one that will be crucial for its future prospects, regards its relationship with other international agreements, in particular with the NPT, with which it has multiple ties. It is, therefore, not astonishing that many of the critiques of the Treaty focus on these relations.[41] The matter is regulated by Article 18 of the Treaty, which reads:

> The implementation of this Treaty shall not prejudice obligations undertaken by States Parties with regard to existing international agreements, to which they are party, where those obligations are consistent with the Treaty.

This is not an uncommon type of conflict clause: it clearly establishes the prevalence of obligations undertaken under the Treaty over those contracted on the basis of any other previous international agreement, among States parties to both instruments, inasmuch as there is incompatibility between the two sets of obligations. Such a provision is, in fact, unnecessary, in light of Article 30(4)(a) of the Vienna Convention on the Law of Treaties, according to which when the parties to a later treaty do not coincide with the parties to an earlier one, relating to the same subject-matter,[42] as between States parties to both "the earlier treaty applies only to the extent that its provisions are compatible with those of the later treaty", in conformity with the *lex posterior* principle. As agreed within the International Law Commission, such a principle would undoubtedly apply when dealing with two treaties belonging to the same legal regime, like the NPT and the TPNW.[43]

---

[41] See the analysis of SOSSAI, "Il rapporto tra il Trattato sul divieto di armi nucleari e gli altri accordi in materia di non proliferazione e disarmo", RDI, 2018, p. 185 ff., p. 192 ff.

[42] On the concept, see KOSKENNIEMI, Report of the Study Group of the International Law Commission on Fragmentation of International Law: Difficulties arising from the diversification and expansion of International Law, UN Doc. A/CN.4/L.682 (2006), paras. 21 ff.

[43] See International Law Commission, Fragmentation of International Law: Difficulties arising from the Diversification and Expansion of International Law, UN Doc. A/61/10, YILC, 2006, Vol. II, Part II, para. 26, where it is stated that "[t]he *lex posterior* principle is at its strongest in regard to conflicting or overlapping provisions that are part of treaties that are institutionally linked or otherwise *intended to advance similar objectives* (i.e. form part of the same regime)" (emphasis added). See, similarly, SOSSAI, *cit. supra* note 41, p. 197. According to MASLEN, "The Relationship of the 2017 Treaty on the Prohibition of Nuclear Weapons with other Agreements: Ambiguity, Complementarity or Conflict?", EJIL: Talk!, 1 August 2017, available at: <https://www.ejiltalk.org/the-relationship-of-the-2017-treaty-on-the-prohibition-of-nuclear-weapons-with-other-agreements-ambiguity-complementarity-or-conflict/>, "[i]n some ways, the provision in Art. 18 is little more than a statement of common sense".

The earlier draft of the Treaty provided a different conflict rule, establishing that it did "not affect the rights and obligations under the Treaty on the Non-Proliferation of Nuclear Weapons".[44] However, as the ICRC pointed out, the proposed norm did not consider the relations with international agreements other than the NPT, and, furthermore, it could "be interpreted as allowing a State Party to the NPT that possesses nuclear weapons to join the convention on the prohibition of nuclear weapons and retain its nuclear weapons, arguing that they have the "right" to do so under the NPT".[45] Therefore, the ICRC suggested a formulation similar to that which was finally adopted, although according to the ICRC proposal the Treaty would have prevailed over "future", as well as over "existing" international agreements.[46] This proposal was, in fact, inserted in the second draft treaty submitted at the end of June,[47] but the term "future" was later deleted.

As for future treaties, the deletion of the mention of "future" agreements in Article 18 does not alter the fact that the conclusion by one or more States Parties to the TPNW of an agreement providing for less extensive disarmament obligations than the TPNW (e.g., the long-planned fissile material cut-off treaty),[48] could never prejudice the stiffer obligations undertaken by States Parties under the TPNW (see also Article 30(5) and Article 41(1)(b) of the Vienna Convention on the Law of Treaties). The prohibition of reservations, under Article 16 TPNW, is another clear sign that the parties are clearly not allowed to restrict, by any means, the assumption of their obligations under the Treaty.[49] Thus, the only possibility for *replacing* the TPNW regime with a more permissive regime would be to form a new agreement involving all the parties to the TPNW.

As the ICRC observed, potential conflicts could also arise in relation to international agreements different from the NPT, specifically with the NWFZ treaties and with the CTBT. In particular, if credit is given to the declaration of Cuba appended to its ratification of the Treaty, according to which the prohibition under Article 1(a), TPNW, "encompasses all forms of testing, including those per-

---

[44] See Draft Convention on the Prohibition of Nuclear Weapons, submitted by the president of the Conference, Art. 19, UN Doc. A/CONF.229/2017/CRP.1 (2017).

[45] On this last point see also JOYNER, "Amicus Memorandum to the Chair of the United Nations Negotiating Conference for a Convention on the Prohibition of Nuclear Weapons", Arms Control Law, 12 June 2017, available at: <https://armscontrollaw.files.wordpress.com/2017/06/amicus-memorandum.pdf>.

[46] See ICRC comments, *cit. supra* note 35. The proposed clause was in fact the same as that contained in the Arms Trade Treaty, 3 June 2013, entered into force 24 December 2014, Art. 26(1).

[47] See Draft Treaty on the Prohibition of Nuclear Weapons, submitted by the president of the Conference, Art. 19, UN Doc. A/CONF.229/2017/CRP.1/Rev.1 (2017). The proposed formulation attracted the criticisms of some delegations. In particular, according to the Dutch delegation, it would have taken away "flexibility to negotiate future arrangements that could take us further on the path towards global zero [...]" (Compilation of amendments, *cit. supra* note 31). On the point see SOSSAI, *cit. supra* note 41, p. 195 ff.

[48] See KIMBALL and REIF, "Fissile Material Cut-off Treaty (FMCT) at a Glance", Arms Control Association, 18 September 2017, available at: <https://www.armscontrol.org/factsheets/fmct>.

[49] See, however, the withdrawal clause, *supra* Section 4.

formed using non-explosive methods such as subcritical testing and computer simulation",[50] the TPNW would establish a broader prohibition on nuclear testing than the CTBT.[51] This interpretation is debatable however, as proposals from Cuba and others to explicitly include "non-explosive methods" of testing in the prohibition were not accepted.[52]

The main issue that has been raised with regard to testing is, however, the danger that States could be induced to ratify the TPNW without ratifying the CTBT, thus further delaying the entry into force of the latter and of its verification mechanism.[53] There may be truth to these concerns, but the risk should not be overemphasized. One should recall that, among the ratifications missing from the CTBT are those of some important nuclear powers, which are not likely to ratify the TPNW in the near future, and probably not the CTBT either. Despite this, the CTBT's verification mechanism is already working, to a certain extent, albeit on a provisional basis.

Undoubtedly, the relationship with the NPT is the major bone of contention. The main accusation coming from nuclear powers and NATO Member States is that the TPNW constitutes a move against the NPT regime, which risks undermining its effectiveness if not prejudicing its very survival.[54] The Preamble to the TPNW reaffirms that "the full and effective implementation of the Treaty on the Non-Proliferation of Nuclear Weapons, which serves as the cornerstone of the nuclear disarmament and non-proliferation regime, has a vital role to play in promoting international peace and security". However,

---

[50] Cuba's declaration is available at: <http://disarmament.un.org/treaties/a/tpnw/cuba/rat/un>.

[51] Under Art. 1 CTBT, all States parties undertake "not to carry out any nuclear weapon test explosion". See, among others, VENTURINI, "Test-Bans and the Comprehensive Test Ban Treaty Organization", in BLACK-BRANCH and FLECK (eds.), *Nuclear Non-Proliferation in International Law, Volume I*, The Hague, 2014, p. 133 ff., p. 144.

[52] See the proposals of Cuba, in Compilation of amendments received from States on the preamble (received as of 29 June), available at: <https://s3.amazonaws.com/unoda-web/wp-content/uploads/2017/06/Preamble-compilation_REV-2.docx>, and of Iran, in Compilation of amendments, *cit. supra* note 31. The current text is at least ambiguous, as the mention of nuclear test "explosions", present in previous drafts, as well as in numerous States' proposals, was deleted, while the CTBT is only referred to in the Preamble, nineteenth indent (see the proposal of the Netherlands, Sweden and Switzerland to include the clause "in accordance with the CTBT" in the test prohibition, *ibid.*).

[53] See the answer of the Italian government (Mr. Giro, Vice Minister for Foreign Affairs) to the Commission on foreign and EU affairs of the Chamber of Deputies (III Commissione (Affari esteri e comunitari)), in Interrogazione a risposta immediata in Commissione 5/11829, 12 July 2017, available at: <http://aic.camera.it/aic/scheda.html?core=aic&numero=5/11829&ramo=CAMERA&leg=17>; see also Permanent Representative of Switzerland to the Conference on Disarmament, "Explanation of vote", 7 July 2012, available at: <https://s3.amazonaws.com/unoda-web/wp-content/uploads/2017/07/Swiss-Explanation-of-Vote2.pdf>.

[54] See, e.g., US Mission to the United Nations, "Joint press statement from the permanent representatives to the United Nations of the United States, United Kingdom, and France following the adoption of a treaty banning nuclear weapons", 7 July 2017, available at: <https://usun.state.gov/remarks/7892>; North Atlantic Council Statement on the Treaty on the Prohibition of Nuclear Weapons, 20 September 2017, available at: < https://www.nato.int/cps/ua/natohq/news_146954.htm>.

it is necessary to examine the realities of the relationship behind this rhetorical statement of principle. On the one hand, the TPNW might be viewed as fulfilling the ultimate purpose of the NPT, as clearly expressed first in its Preamble,[55] and then in binding form in the text of one of its pillars, Article VI. On the other hand, there is no doubt that the aim of the drafters of the TPNW is to completely overcome the NPT regime as it is today, i.e. an international regime codifying a permanent situation of inequality and a deadlock of disarmament prospects, rather than the transitory arrangement suggested by a reading of its text.

From a normative point of view, the TPNW is not incompatible with the NPT, in a strict sense, as it does not prejudice the NPT's States Parties' obligations, but rather complements them by imposing additional, and onerous, obligations, in particular on the nuclear-weapon States Parties to the NPT, and on the non-nuclear-weapon States Parties that host nuclear weapons on their territories, as described above.[56] As mentioned, these provisions prevail, in relation to States Parties to the TPNW, over any right that might be claimed under the NPT, and only with this broader meaning can one speak of an incompatibility.[57] One could question whether the TPNW contradicts Article VII of the NPT, according to which the Treaty does not affect "the right of any group of States to conclude regional treaties in order to assure the total absence of nuclear weapons in their respective territories". Surely, the TPNW is not a "regional treaty", but, on the one hand Article VII is specifically intended to allow for the establishment of nuclear weapon free zones, and does not prohibit agreements with no regional focus; on the other hand, as already mentioned, the TPNW in fact intends to fulfil the NPT's declared final objective, and its negotiations were open to all States, without discrimination.

There are two further, and interconnected objections raised against the TPNW that we must briefly consider. The first relates to the discrimination under the Treaty between the majority of States Parties, which are merely subject to a "lenient" verification system (the comprehensive safeguards agreement), unless they are bound by stricter obligations under the NPT, and a minority (States still

---

[55] See, in particular, the eleventh preambular paragraph: "*Desiring* to further the easing of international tension and the strengthening of trust between States in order to facilitate the cessation of the manufacture of nuclear weapons, the liquidation of all their existing stockpiles, and the elimination from national arsenals of nuclear weapons and the means of their delivery pursuant to a Treaty on general and complete disarmament under strict and effective international control".

[56] See, similarly, DUNWORTH, "The Treaty on the Prohibition of Nuclear Weapons", ASIL Insights, 31 October 2017, available at: <https://www.asil.org/insights/volume/21/issue/12/treaty-prohibition-nuclear-weapons>; MASLEN, *cit. supra* note 43. See also JOYNER, "The Treaty on the Prohibition of Nuclear Weapons", EJIL: *Talk!*, 26 July 2017, available at: <https://www.ejiltalk.org/the-treaty-on-the-prohibition-of-nuclear-weapons/>. An apparently different view is held by TREZZA, "The UN Nuclear Ban Treaty and the NPT: Challenges for Nuclear Disarmament", IAI Commentaries 17, 15 September 2017, available at: <http://www.iai.it/it/pubblicazioni/un-nuclear-ban-treaty-and-npt-challenges-nuclear-disarmament>.

[57] See, among others, on norm conflicts between prohibitive norms, on one side, and permissive norms, on the other, VRANES, "The Definition of 'Norm Conflict' in International Law and Legal Theory", EJIL, 2006, p. 395 ff., especially p. 401 ff.

possessing, or having recently possessed nuclear weapons), which are subject to the much more pregnant Additional Protocol safeguards agreement.[58] Some have raised fears (and this is the second objection) that States Parties to the NPT and subject to an Additional Protocol might be induced to denounce the NPT, while ratifying the TPNW, in order to reduce the scope of their verification obligations. Doing so would result in the collapse of the IAEA verification system, which would in fact mean the collapse of any effective check on respect for non-proliferation obligations.[59]

Maybe the fears of an easy trade between the onerous NPT and the indulgent TPNW are exaggerated, or at least premature.[60] Nonetheless, the lack of agreement on extending to all States Parties the most accurate and all-encompassing verification mechanism is, in fact, unfortunate. Any disarmament agreement, if it aims to be effective, needs to rest on a strong verification system able to guarantee that no dangerous loopholes will open the way to any possible development and spread of prohibited items, and all the more so when the diversion of nuclear energy for military purposes is involved. The TPNW, as it is, is not able to provide such guarantees. All the same, one should take into account the fact that the Treaty does not and could not prejudice the application of the special regimes established by the UN Security Council with regard to specific countries, such as North Korea and Iran, or any additional regimes that the Council might implement in the future. One should also add that it is unfortunate that nuclear powers and their allies have been nearly totally absent from the Treaty negotiation process, as their active role might have generated pressure towards the adoption of, inter alia, a stronger verification apparatus, whatever the results of such a pressure would have been.[61]

---

[58] Various States proposed during the New York Conference an extension of Additional Protocols to all States parties to the TPNW: see, *inter alia*, Need for a verification mechanism at this stage for a treaty prohibiting nuclear weapons – Submitted by Chile, Sweden and Uganda, UN Doc. A/CONF.229/2017/WP.6 (2017); proposals of New Zealand, in Compilation of amendments, *cit. supra* note 52; comments of the Netherlands, in Compilation of amendments, *cit. supra* note 31. See also the criticisms expressed in Sweden, "Explanation of vote", 7 July 2017 available at: <https://s3.amazonaws.com/unoda-web/wp-content/uploads/2017/07/170707-EoV-Sweden.pdf>; and Permanent Representative of Switzerland, *cit. supra* note 52. On the Italian government's criticisms see *infra* Section 9.

[59] See the proposal of Sweden to introduce a second paragraph into the article concerning the relationship with other agreements, stating that the treaty "shall not be cited as grounds for leaving the Treaty of Non-Proliferation", in Compilation of amendments, *cit. supra*, note 52, and the even stronger proposal of the Netherlands, to insert a second paragraph into draft Art. 15 (the current Art. 14, on ratification) providing that "[n]o State may establish its consent to be bound by this treaty unless it has previously established or establishes at the same time its consent to be bound by the NPT", in Compilation of amendments, *cit. supra* note 31. See also US Mission to the United Nations, *cit. supra* note 54.

[60] On this point, see SOSSAI, *cit. supra* note 41, p. 204.

[61] See RONZITTI, "Armi nucleari: ONU discute se abolirle", Affari internazionali, 26 March 2017, available at: <http://www.affarinternazionali.it/2017/03/armi-nucleari-onu-discute-abolirle/>.

9. THE ITALIAN POSITION

As mentioned above, Italy is a non-nuclear-weapon State, which however hosts US nuclear weapons on its territory, as part of a nuclear sharing arrangement. Italy, therefore, unless it decided in the meantime to stop its nuclear sharing, would be directly affected by ratification of the TPNW, as the State would become bound to immediately proceed, under strict international verification, with the removal of the aforementioned weapons and their means of delivery from its territory. Differently from most nuclear powers, Italy participated in the conferences on the Humanitarian Impact of Nuclear Weapons of Oslo, Nayarit and Vienna, while maintaining a low profile. Participation was part of a strategy, consistently pursued by the Italian Government, to keep dialogue open with those civil society initiatives and NGOs engaged in pursuing the goal of complete nuclear disarmament. Italy decided, however, in consonance with all the official and non-official nuclear powers and with almost all the "nuclear umbrella" States (except the Netherlands) not to take part in the UN Conference convened to draft and adopt the TPNW.[62] The Government's position was subjected to debate in Parliament at the time of the adoption of the UN General Assembly resolution convening the abovementioned Conference,[63] at the time of the adoption of the Treaty, and at the time of its opening for signature. In particular, on 19 September 2017, the Chamber of Deputies adopted a majority motion engaging the Government to, first, continue to pursue the objective of a nuclear weapons-free world, through a progressive approach to disarmament, recognizing the centrality of the NPT, and considering the possibility to accede to the TPNW, in conformity with NATO engagements and with the orientation of its allies; and, second, to promote, together with its partners, the universality of the NPT, the entry into force of the CTBT, the conclusion of a Fissile Material Cut-off Treaty (FMCT), the strengthening and extension of NWFZs, especially in the Middle East, and other transparency and confidence-building measures able to lead to a general disarmament.[64] The motion was accepted by the Government.

Although the motion is certainly indicative of the Italian Parliament's sensitivity, shared by other parliaments as well, towards the issue of nuclear disarmament, and even of openness to favourably consider the future universalisation of the TPNW, this should not lead to the conclusion that the Government has modified its position. The motion is formulated in extremely cautious language, and it merely directs the Government to consider future participation in the Treaty,

---

[62] Notwithstanding the invitation of the European Parliament to EU member States "to participate constructively in its proceedings", in Resolution of 27 October 2016 on nuclear security and non-proliferation (2016/2936(RSP)), available at: <http://www.europarl.europa. eu/sides/getDoc.do?pubRef=-//EP//TEXT+TA+P8-TA-2016-0424+0+DOC+XML+V0// EN&language=EN>. On the divided paths followed by EU member States in relation to the New York Conference and Treaty see, among others, RONZITTI, *cit. supra* note 61, and TREZZA, *cit. supra* note 56.

[63] On the Italian vote, see *supra* note 3.

[64] See Italian Chamber of Deputies, Atto Camera – Mozione 1/01699, 19 September 2017, available at: <http://aic.camera.it/aic/query.html>.

"in conformity with the orientation of its allies". By accepting this request the Government is, in reality, confirming its rejection of the Treaty *rebus sic stanti-bus*, i.e. until some fundamental change of circumstances, such as the modification of the position of all NATO countries, and specifically of the nuclear-weapon States among them, could lead it to reopen the issue. The Government's position has always been the same, as expressed various times before Parliament in recent months: Italy pursues a progressive and inclusive path towards nuclear disarmament, through a series of transparent and verifiable steps such as those mentioned in the second part of the motion; it strongly affirms the centrality of the NPT; it adheres to NATO's deterrence doctrine reaffirmed in Warsaw in 2016.[65] Italy has not participated in the UN Conference, considering it to be a divisive move on an issue that would require the full involvement of all military nuclear powers. The Government has also criticized the text of the TPNW, expressing doubts that it could ever lead to an irreversible, transparent and verifiable nuclear disarmament, in particular due to its lack of general acceptance of the highest standards of IAEA verification, and to the lack of verification mechanisms in relation to nuclear tests, which, it claims, threaten to compromise both the NPT and the CTBT regimes. For the above reasons the Italian Government does not intend to sign the TPNW.[66]

Therefore, the Italian position seems consonant with the stance expressed by the North Atlantic Council, including Italy, on 20 September 2017. According to the NATO Council, the TPNW "is at odds with the existing non-proliferation and disarmament architecture", and "risks undermining the NPT [...], and the IAEA Safeguards regime which supports it". The NATO countries, furthermore, assure that there will be no change in their legal obligations "with respect to nuclear weapons", and refuse "any argument that this treaty reflects or in any way contributes to the development of customary international law".[67]

10. Prospects for Entry into Force and Universalisation

By mid-May 2018, nearly eight months after it opened for signature, the TPNW had been signed by 58 States, and ratified by nine: Austria, Cuba, Guyana, Mexico, Palau, Thailand, Venezuela, the Holy See, and the State of Palestine.[68] According to Article 15, the Treaty is to enter into force 90 days after the fiftieth ratification or acceptance: differently from the NPT, which required ratification by the USA, the UK and the USSR, designated as its de-

---

[65] See NATO, Warsaw Summit Communiqué – Issued by the Heads of State and Government participating in the meeting of the North Atlantic Council in Warsaw 8-9 July 2016, 9 July 2016, available at: <https://www.nato.int/cps/en/natohq/official_texts_133169. htm>.

[66] See the answer of the Italian Government, *cit. supra* note 53. According to SOSSAI, *cit. supra* note 41, p. 200, it is surprising that the government does not refer in its statements to the issue of compatibility between its NATO engagements and the TPNW's obligations.

[67] See North Atlantic Council Statement, *cit. supra* note 54.

[68] The status of the Treaty is available at: <http://disarmament.un.org/treaties/t/tpnw>.

positary governments (in this case the depositary is the UN Secretary-General: Article 19), and from the CTBT, which requires ratification from a list of 44 States (which explains why the treaty is not yet in force), the drafters of the TPNW decided to facilitate its entry into force by not requiring acceptance from any particular State. This means that the Treaty may enter into force even without the participation of any nuclear-weapon State. Given that the Treaty, as already recalled, was adopted with positive votes by 122 States, reaching the goal should not be overly difficult, unless other external factors intervene to hinder the process. For the moment, the number of signatures, and even more so of ratifications, is rather low. But it is too early to make any reliable forecasts. One can only note that delays in signing and ratifying multilateral treaties are common, especially in the disarmament and arms control field. Nonetheless, it is notable that a controversial treaty, and one that is still far from being universal, such as the CMC, had been signed by 94 States by the day after its opening for signature, although it required over a year before reaching the thirty ratifications necessary for its entry into force. In the case of the TPNW, the path seems rather slow, for the moment, especially taking into account that the ratification process should not prove any onerous for any of the potential candidates today (presumably all non-nuclear-weapon States already parties to the NPT), as it shall not require the elimination of any arsenals or the subjection to any new verification mechanism. As for the political price to pay, this is obviously a different matter.

Be that as it may, the entry into force of the TPNW, if and whenever it will take place, will not produce any direct consequences for nuclear disarmament, as it is foreseeable that no nuclear-weapon State will accede to the Treaty in the near future. In fact, a multilateral agreement such as the TPNW requires universal participation in order to be effective, even more than the NPT does. The NPT, notwithstanding its flaws and its failures, has produced important results over the years in terms of opposition to the proliferation of nuclear weapons, without having ever reached complete universality. By contrast, a nuclear disarmament agreement will never work unless all nuclear-weapon States, official and non-official, engage in disarmament at the same time; in particular, the big powers are the least likely of all to give up nuclear weapons, unless they can trust that their potential enemies are doing the same. It is, therefore, no wonder that Article 12 explicitly indicates the goal of universality. At the moment, this seems a distant prospect.

Nonetheless, it is foreseeable that the entry into force of the Treaty, and subsequent growth in the number of States Parties, would produce consequences. Even without envisaging that this process might induce a flight from the NPT into the new treaty and thus effect the collapse of the non-proliferation regime, as NATO countries fear, the TPNW would attract more and more attention from international actors, including civil society organizations. Its meetings of States Parties, to be convened every two years, entrusted by Article 8 with the task of making decisions "in respect of any matter with regard to the application or implementation" of the TPNW and "on further measures for nuclear disarmament", and review conferences, to be held five years after entry into force and every six years thereafter,[69] will exercise competences to a large extent overlapping with those of NPT Review Conferences, although real decisions will remain the prerogative of the latter as far as nuclear-weapon States will be concentrated in them. But this process, thanks in part to intense lobbying by representatives of international public opinion, might exert strong pressure on nuclear-weapon States in order to induce them to finally undertake concrete and decisive steps on the way towards nuclear disarmament. They might be induced, *inter alia*, to exercise pressure, in turn, on the States Parties to the TPNW, in order to convince them to adopt amendments to the Treaty to accommodate their own goals, which could ultimately facilitate their acceptance of the Treaty.[70] These are mere speculations that may be belied by reality. The point is that, once a process has started, it is difficult to foresee where it will lead. This will be decided, in the end, not by non-nuclear-weapon States, but rather by the nuclear-weapon ones. It has to be hoped that, even if nuclear-weapon States and their allies will not be motivated by faith in the TPNW, at least their fear, in the face of the potential dismantlement of the non-proliferation architecture, could work, in the long term, as a positive stimulus toward their decisive engagement in disarmament.

---

[69] See Art. 8(4): the conferences shall "review the operation of the Treaty and the progress in achieving the purposes of the Treaty".

[70] Amendments to the TPNW are regulated by Art. 10, which provides for them to be adopted by a meeting of States parties or by a review conference. See the final considerations of JOYNER, *cit. supra* note 56.

THE EU "CONFLICT MINERALS REGULATION": POTENTIALITIES AND LIMITS IN THE LIGHT OF THE INTERNATIONAL STANDARDS ON RESPONSIBLE SOURCING

VALENTINA GRADO[*]

Abstract

Business enterprises involved in the exploitation of mineral resources origi-nating from conflict zones are at risk of financing armed activities and fuelling systematic violations of international law and human rights abuses. This article first analyses the initiatives developed by the UN and OECD aimed at encour-aging companies to respect human rights and avoid contributing to conflict by adopting "supply chain due diligence" practices. Second, it focuses on a recent Regulation adopted by the EU to tackle trade in certain minerals sourced from conflict-affected and high-risk areas in order to highlight its main positive as-pects and challenges and, at the same time, to ascertain whether and to what ex-tent this new legislation is consistent with the UN/OECD international standards on responsible sourcing.

Keywords: conflict minerals; global supply chains; UN Guiding Principles on Business and Human Rights; OECD Due Diligence Guidance; EU Regulation.

1. INTRODUCTION

Natural mineral resources hold great potential for the development of re-source-rich countries but their exploitation can also finance armed activities and fuel human right abuses. A classic example is the role played by diamonds in sustaining conflicts in many African states.

Besides diamonds, tin, tantalum, tungsten and gold (otherwise known as 3TG and labelled "conflict minerals") have also played key roles in fuelling con-flicts and extensive human rights violations, especially since the late 1990s in the Democratic Republic of the Congo (DRC). As is it well documented, the financ-ing of the conflict in DRC through the mining and trading activities of 3TG takes two main forms. First, rebel groups and army units extort cash or minerals from artisanal and small-scale miners who are often children or adults forced to work in the mines. Second, they extort money from traders and intermediaries at all stages of transportation between the mines and the point of export. Subsequently, 3TG are traded – and sometimes partially transformed – in neighbouring coun-tries and then purchased by smelters/refiners mostly located (outside the Great Lakes Region of Africa) in Asia, North America and Europe. Smelters/refiners further process those minerals and others received from different parts of the

---

[*]Associate Professor in International Law at the University of Naples L'Orientale.

world into metals. These metals are then used by component manufacturers before being incorporated into end products such as our electronic devices.

In order to break the link between conflict and the exploitation of these minerals a wide range of international and national initiatives have been taken, including the UN Security Council Resolution 1952 (2010), the UN Guiding Principles on Business and Human Rights, the OECD Due Diligence Guidance for Responsible Supply Chains of Minerals from Conflict-Affected and High-Risk Areas, and Section 1502 of the US Dodd-Frank Wall Street Reform and Consumer Protection Act (known as the "US conflict minerals law"). All these instruments aim to advance "supply chain due diligence" practices when business enterprises source minerals from areas affected by conflict. It is in this context that on 17 May 2017 the European Union (EU) adopted the so-called "Conflict Minerals Regulation".

This article provides an overview of the scope and content of the new EU Regulation, in order to highlight its main potentialities and challenges and, at the same time, to ascertain whether and to what extent this legislation is consistent with the UN/OECD standards on "responsible sourcing". Therefore, the present contribution will, first of all, briefly analyse the concept of "supply chain due diligence", as envisaged in the UN Guiding Principles on Business and Human Rights (Section 2). Second, it will refer to the OECD Due Diligence Guidance for Responsible Supply Chains of Minerals from Conflict-Affected and High-Risk Areas, which – in line with the aforementioned UN Guiding Principles – provides detailed recommendations on due diligence for "responsible sourcing" of minerals from conflict areas (Section 3). Third, it will illustrate the regulatory framework of the EU "Conflict Minerals Regulation" (Section 4), focusing particularly on: i) the material, geographic and personal scope of this new legislation (Section 4.1); ii) the EU importers' obligations under the Regulation (Section 4.2); iii) the member states' obligations under the Regulation (Section 4.3); and iv) the Commission's main commitments under the Regulation (Section 4.4). Lastly, it will conclude by underlining that, even though the new EU Regulation can be considered an important step towards the responsible sourcing of "conflict minerals", its actual contribution to peace and development mostly depends on how many of the Commission's commitments to address its challenges (the latter however not totally consistent with the UN/OECD international standards) will be implemented in the future (Section 5).

2. THE CONCEPT OF "SUPPLY CHAIN DUE DILIGENCE" IN THE UN GUIDING PRINCIPLES ON BUSINESS AND HUMAN RIGHTS

On 16 June 2011 the UN Human Rights Council endorsed the UN Guiding Principles on Business and Human Rights[1] (UNGPs) developed by the Special

---

[1] Human Rights Council, Guiding Principles on Business and Human Rights: Implementing the United Nations "Protect, Respect, Remedy" Framework, UN Doc. A/HRC/17/31 (2011). For a comment see, *ex multis*, MARES (ed.), *The UN Guiding Principles on Business and*

Representative of the Secretary-General on the issue of human rights and transnational corporations and other business enterprises (Professor Ruggie). The UNGPs aim to operationalise the former UN "Protect, Respect and Remedy" Framework developed in 2008.[2] As it is well known, the Framework consists of three pillars: a) the duty of states to "protect" human rights against abuses by third parties, including business enterprises; b) the corporate responsibility to "respect" human rights; and c) access to effective "remedy" for those who are harmed.

As far as the Framework's first pillar is concerned, UNGP 1 reiterates that the state's international human rights obligations require, inter alia, its duty to protect against corporate-related human rights abuses within its territory and/ or jurisdiction by adopting appropriate steps to prevent, investigate, punish and redress such abuses through effective policies, legislation, regulations and adjudication. The UNGPs also recommend that states should, among other things, a) establish a series of regulatory and policy measures to foster business respect for human rights (UNGP 3); b) achieve better alignment among relevant national policy domains and institutions (UNGPs 8-9); and c) promote business respect for human rights through multilateral institutions dealing with business-related issues (UNGP 10). With regard to the scope of the state's duty to protect – an issue relevant to this study as we will see below in Section 5.1 – the first pillar adopts a cautious approach. According to the Commentary to UNGP 2 "states are not generally required under international human rights law to regulate the extra-territorial activities of businesses domiciled in their territory and/or jurisdiction. Nor are they generally prohibited from doing so, provided there is a recognised jurisdictional basis".[3]

With regard to the Framework's second pillar, UNGPs 11-24 set out the responsibility of business enterprises to respect human rights. According to Commentary to UNGP 11, this responsibility to respect human rights is a global standard of expected conduct.[4] It exists independently of states' abilities to meet their own human rights obligations; it extends to all internationally recognised human rights; and it applies to all enterprises, regardless of their size, sector, operational context, ownership and structure (UNGPs 12 and 14). Moreover, the corporate responsibility to respect means that business enterprises "should avoid infringing on the human rights of others and should address adverse human rights

---

Human Rights: Foundations and Implementation, Leiden-Boston, 2012; WETZEL, *Human Rights in Transnational Business: Translating Human Rights Obligations into Compliance Procedures*, Cham, 2016, p. 187 ff.

[2] Human Rights Council, Protect, Respect and Remedy: A Framework for Business and Human Rights, UN Doc. A/HRC/8/5 (2008).

[3] For a critical assessment of such position see, *ex multis*, DE SCHUTTER, "Towards a New Treaty on Business and Human Rights", Business and Human Rights Journal, 2016, p. 41 ff., p. 45 ff.

[4] Professor Ruggie underlines that the UNGPs are not intended to create new obligations under international law (see Human Rights Council, *cit. supra* note 1, p. 6). In order to remark the lack of legal nature of corporate duties, in his Framework states' duties are referred as "obligations" while corporate ones are referred as "responsibilities".

impacts with which they are involved" (UNGP 11). The Interpretative Guide of the corporate responsibility to respect human rights specifies that adverse human rights impacts occur when an action removes or reduces the ability of the individual to enjoy his or her human rights; it refers to both actual impacts (i.e. adverse impacts that have already occurred) and potential ones (i.e. adverse impacts that may occur but has not yet done so, defined as "human rights risks").[5]

The UNGPs identify several ways in which enterprises can be involved in human rights adverse impacts. Indeed, the responsibility to respect requires enterprises to: "avoid causing or contributing to adverse human rights impacts through their own activities, and address such impacts when they occur" (UNGP 13 (a)); and "seek to prevent or mitigate adverse human rights impacts that are directly linked to their operations, products or services by their business relationships, even if they have not contributed to those impacts" (UNGP 13 (b)). Most notably, the Commentary to UNGP 13 stipulates that the term "business relationships" is intended to be understood widely, to include relationships with business partners, "entities" in the value chain, and any other non-state or state entity directly linked to their business operations, products or services.

Under the UNGPs, in order to meet its responsibility to respect, an enterprise should have in place policies and processes, including: a) a human rights "policy commitment"; b) a "human rights due diligence process" to identify, prevent, mitigate and account for how it addresses its human rights impacts; and c) processes to enable the "remediation" of any adverse human rights impacts it has caused or contributed to (UNGP 15).[6] With regard to the "human rights due diligence process", according to UNGPs 17-21 it involves: i) assessing actual and potential human rights impacts; ii) integrating and acting upon the findings; iii) tracking responses; and iv) communicating how impacts are addressed. UNGP 17 defines also the parameters for "human rights due diligence": it should cover both the impacts that the business may cause (or contribute to) through its own activities and those that may be directly linked to an enterprise's operations, products or services through its business relationships. With regard to the nature and extent of the "human rights due diligence", it should be commensurate with the severity (and probability) of the actual and potential adverse impacts;[7] the nature and context of the enterprise's operations; and its size (the first factor being considered by the Interpretative Guide to be the main criterion). Lastly, the timeframe of "human rights due diligence" should be ongoing, because risks may change over time as the enterprise's operations and operating context evolve. In sum, and as already pointed out by scholars, "human rights due diligence" goes beyond business processes to manage enterprise's risks, being primarily aimed

---

[5] Office of the United Nations High Commissioner for Human Rights, The Corporate Responsibility to Respect Human Rights: An Interpretative Guide, UN Doc. HR/PUB/12/02 (2012), pp. 5 and 7.

[6] UNGPs 16-22 elaborate on each element.

[7] The Commentary to UNGP 14 states that severity of impacts will be judged by their scale, scope and irremediable character.

at protecting actual and potential victims of adverse human rights impacts.[8] Such a due diligence underlines the need for preventative identification of risks as a systematic exercise.

In June 2010 Professor Ruggie published a discussion paper which addresses in greater detail the concept of the "corporate responsibility to respect human rights in supply chains".[9] First, he distinguishes two scenarios: whether the enterprise is contributing to the abuse by its own actions and omissions (e.g. where the buyer demands significant last-minute changes in product specifications without adjusting price or delivery dates, thus pushing suppliers to breach international labour standards); or whether the enterprise is implicated in the abuse solely by the link to the goods or services it procures (e.g. without contribution from the enterprise, the product contains components which are manufactured by suppliers using child labour). In the first scenario, the responsibility to respect requires the enterprise to take appropriate steps to address those contributions (such as, inter alia, termination and remediation). In the second scenario, the appropriate action to be undertaken by enterprises – that can be labelled "responsible sourcing" – depends on several factors, including: a) what leverage the enterprise has in changing the behaviour of the entity causing the harm; and b) how crucial the relationship is to the enterprise.[10] The combination of these variables will yield different conclusions as to what action should be taken. Appropriate responses by enterprises may include: mitigating the risk that the adverse impact continues/recurs (when the enterprise possesses the leverage); seeking ways to increase the leverage to enable mitigation (when the enterprise lacks the leverage); and considering ending the relationship either where the enterprise lacks the leverage or where it is unable to increase its leverage or finally because of the severity of the adverse impact.

In addition, the discussion paper underlines that "responsible sourcing" requires the enterprise to carry out due diligence beyond the first tier of business relationships (which are all known to the company). Indeed, with regard to those additional tiers, according to the discussion paper, not knowing about human rights abuses linked to the enterprise's products or services is not a sufficient response by itself if the same enterprise should have reasonably known about them through due diligence. Therefore the company, using due diligence, should first identify general areas of risk of serious human rights abuses in the supply chain (for example, because of the particular region or particular products or materials

---

[8] See, ex multis, MUCHLINKI, "Operationalising the UN Business and Human Rights Framework: The Corporate Responsibility to Respect Human Rights and Due Diligence", in LUNDAN (ed.), Transnational Corporations and Transnational Governance: The Costs of Crossing Borders in the Global Economy, New York, 2015, p. 325 ff.

[9] Special Representative of the Secretary-General on Human Rights and Transnational Corporations and Business Enterprises, "Corporate Responsibility to Respect Human Rights in Supply Chains", discussion paper presented at the 10th OECD Roundtable on Corporate Responsibility, 2010.

[10] The Commentary to UNGP 19 states that appropriate action depends also on the severity of the abuse and whether terminating the relationship with the entity itself would have adverse human rights consequences.

and their known sources) and prioritise these for human rights due diligence.[11] Second, the enterprise should mitigate such risks, by seeking to ensure that intermediary entities in the supply chain are themselves practicing due diligence and following appropriate standards. Finally, the enterprise should identify specific supply chain entities that are abusing human rights and take appropriate efforts to mitigate such abuse (directly or through intermediaries in the relationship chain). If mitigation is impossible, the enterprise should either take steps to end the relationship (whether directly or via intermediaries) or be able to demonstrate efforts made to mitigate the abuse.

In light of the above, the Framework's second pillar seems to provide very useful elements and clarifications in order to qualify and specify the corporate responsibility to respect human rights, a standard that has been endorsed at international and national levels.[12] With regard to the specific issue of "corporate respect in the supply chain", the pillar in question uses two concepts in relation to the attribution of responsibility to the enterprise. The first is "contribution to harm", occurring for example where a decision or action by the enterprise creates strong incentives for a supplier to breach international labour standards. As is self-evident, in this scenario the responsibility to respect is grounded in the enterprise's "own" impacts. The second (but more controversial) concept is the enterprise's responsibility to act in order to seek to mitigate the occurrence of abuses caused by its direct suppliers or sub-tier suppliers, even if it has neither caused not contributed to causing harm. For the purposes of this article, it is enough to underline that the latter responsibility requires corporations to conduct due diligence all along the "global" supply chain, that is, extraterritorially.

3. THE OECD DUE DILIGENCE GUIDANCE FOR RESPONSIBLE MINERAL SOURCING

On 25 May 2011 the OECD Council meeting at the Ministerial level adopted the amendments to the Guidelines for Multinational Enterprises and a new recommendation on Due Diligence Guidance for Responsible Supply Chains of Minerals from Conflict-Affected and High-Risk Areas (OECD Guidance).[13] The latter recommendation, developed through an international multi-stakeholder consultation process, can be regarded as the first example of how the due diligence and supply chain principles contained in the UNGPs (and in the updated

---

[11] UNGP 24 stipulates that where it is necessary to prioritise action to address adverse human rights impacts, the enterprise should first seek to prevent and mitigate those that are most severe.

[12] On this point see, *ex multis*, RUGGIE, "Hierarchy or Ecosystem? Regulating Human Rights Risks of Multinational Enterprises", in RODRÍGUEZ-GARAVITO (ed.), *Business and Human Rights: Beyond the End of the Beginning*, Cambridge, 2017, p. 46 ff., p. 49 ff.

[13] On these two documents see, *ex multis*, LIBERTI, "OECD 50th Anniversary: The Updated OECD Guidelines for Multinational Enterprises and the New OECD Recommendation on Due Diligence Guidance for Conflict-Free Mineral Supply Chains", Business Law International, 2012, p. 35 ff.

OECD Guidelines for Multinational Enterprises) can be translated into operational terms in a specific context (conflict-affected and high-risk areas – CAHR areas) and with regard to risks of adverse impacts associated with a particular sector (the mineral sector). The OECD Guidance has been referred to in other "instruments" aimed at tackling the problem of minerals from conflict zones, such as the "US conflict mineral law",[14] the International Conference on the Great Lakes Region's Certification Mechanism,[15] the Chinese Due Diligence Guidelines for Responsible Mineral Supply Chains[16] and, lastly, the EU "Conflict Minerals Regulation".

Amended twice, the current OECD Guidance consists of: 1) an overarching five-step framework for risk-based due diligence in the mineral supply chain (Annex I); 2) a model supply chain policy for a responsible global supply chain of minerals from CAHR areas (Annex II); 3) principles for risk mitigation (Annex III); and 4) two Supplements on tin-tantalum-tungsten and gold (3TG) containing specific due diligence recommendations tailored to the challenges associated with the structure of the supply chain of those minerals.[17]

Before summarising the detailed requirements set out in the Annexes and Supplements, it is important to highlight the key features of the OECD Guidance. In terms of its "objective", the Guidance provides practical recommendations for companies to ensure they respect human rights and avoid contributing to conflict through their mineral and metal procurement practices ("responsible sourcing"). As far as the "geographic" and "material" scope are concerned, the recommendations apply to all companies that use whatever minerals are sourced from any CAHR area; therefore, the OECD Guidance does not focus either on any particular area, region or country or on 3TG only. The "nature" and "extent" of due diligence it refers to will depend on individual circumstances and will be affected by factors such as the size of the enterprise, the location of the activities, the situation in a particular country and the nature of the products involved. Therefore, the OECD Guidance adopts a flexible approach, allowing for a variety of options, operational schemes and industry collaborative efforts. At the same time, the Guidance points out the "higher risks of significant adverse impacts" which may be associated with the exploitation of minerals from CAHR areas. Consequently, it requires all companies in the mineral supply chain[18] – even those several steps removed from the layer providing the raw material inputs – to take

---

[14] See *infra* note 27.

[15] On this tool see GRADO, *"Conflict minerals e responsabilità sociale d'impresa: le azioni dell'ONU, dell'OCSE e della Conferenza internazionale sulla Regione dei Grandi Laghi"*, Ordine internazionale e diritti umani, 2016, p. 833 ff., p. 856 ff.

[16] On this document see BUHMANN, "Chinese Human Rights Guidance on Minerals Sourcing: Building Soft Power", Journal of Current Chinese Affairs, 2017, p. 135 ff., p. 145 ff.

[17] OECD, *OECD Due Diligence Guidance for Responsible Supply Chains of Minerals from Conflict-Affected and High-Risk Areas*, 3rd ed., Paris, 2016.

[18] It means the process of bringing a raw material to the consumer market. It generally includes the extraction, transport, handling, trading, processing, smelting, refining and alloying, manufacturing and sale of end product.

reasonable steps and make good faith efforts to prevent or mitigate any risks of those adverse impacts. Emphasising progressive improvement over outcomes, the OECD Guidance confirms that "responsible sourcing" requires the adoption of reasonable measures commensurate with the severity of the risks, no matter where these risks may be occurring.[19]

As far as the Annexes and Supplements are concerned, Annex I sets out a five-step framework for risk-based due diligence in the mineral supply chain. According to this framework, all companies in the mineral supply chain that use minerals sourced from CAHR areas should: establish strong company management systems (Step 1); identify and assess risks in the supply chain (Step 2); design and implement a strategy to respond to identified risks (Step 3); carry out independent third-party audit of supply chain due diligence at identified points in the supply chain (Step 4); and publicly report on supply chain due diligence (Step 5).[20] This framework is very similar to the one set up by the UNGPs 15-21, except for the specific expectation concerning auditing.

With regard to Annex II to the OECD Guidance (concerning the model supply chain policy), first it highlights the different risks of "significant adverse impacts" which may be associated with the exploitation of minerals from CAHR areas. These risks are: a) serious abuses of human rights, labour rights and international humanitarian law;[21] b) financing parties to the conflict (direct and indirect support to either non-state armed groups or to public or private security forces); and c) non-conflict specific risks associated with high-risk areas.[22] Second, this Annex provides instructions on how to mitigate the identified risks. It calls on a company to immediately suspend or disengage with suppliers when it identifies a risk that they are sourcing minerals from any party committing serious human rights abuses, or any party providing direct or indirect support to non-state armed groups. It allows instead trade to continue with suppliers where a company identifies a risk that they are sourcing from any party providing direct or indirect support to public or private security forces (not involved in serious human rights abuses), provided that a risk management plan is implemented.

As far as the two Supplements of the OECD Guidance are concerned, they provide specific guidelines on supply chain due diligence for tin-tantalum-tungsten and gold. Both Supplements apply to companies "potentially" using 3TG from CAHR areas. Therefore, companies should preliminarily review their mineral and metal sourcing practices to determine the presence of "red flag indicators" in their supply chain which trigger comprehensive due diligence as envis-

---

[19] Therefore, the OECD Guidance has an extraterritorial reach since due diligence recommendations should be performed by a company throughout its "global" mineral supply chain.

[20] For more details on each step see *infra* Section 4.2.

[21] Serious abuses include: torture, cruel, inhuman and degrading treatment; forced or compulsory labour; the worst forms of child labour; other gross human rights violations such as widespread sexual violence; war crimes, crimes against humanity or genocide.

[22] Significant adverse impacts related to high-risk areas include: corruption; fraudulent misrepresentation of the origin of minerals, money laundering and tax evasion.

aged in the OECD Guidance.[23] Most importantly, if a company in the supply chain is unable to determine whether the minerals in its possession come from "red flag indicators" it should proceed to Step 1 of the Guidance and discontinue due diligence if the subsequent Step 2 can reasonably exclude "red flag indicators" in its supply chain.

Both Supplements distinguish between the due diligence requirements of upstream and downstream companies in the supply chain. "Upstream companies" refers to all companies between the mine and the smelters/refiners (e.g. mining companies, local traders or exporters from the country of mineral origin, international concentrate traders, mineral re-processors and smelters/refiners). "Downstream companies" refers to all companies from smelters/refiners to retailers (e.g. metal traders, component manufacturers, product manufacturers and retailers). In a nutshell, upstream companies should establish a system of control over the minerals in their possession (chain of custody or traceability) and establish on-the-ground assessment teams for generating verifiable, reliable, and up-to-date information on the qualitative circumstances of mineral extraction, trade, handling and export from CAHR areas. They should also provide the results of risk assessment to their downstream purchasers and have the smelters'/refiners' due diligence practices audited by independent third-parties. Downstream companies should establish internal controls over their immediate suppliers and establish a system of transparency that will allow them to identify the smelters/refiners in their supply chains and assess whether they adhere to due diligence measures envisaged in the OECD Guidance. This distinction is based upon the fact that it is at the point of transformation – where minerals are smelted into metals – that the mixing of materials from different regions takes place. The smelters/refiners that handle raw minerals are, often in geographic terms, closer to the original source and they therefore have the primary responsibility to identify, assess, and manage risks that minerals may have financed conflict (or human rights abuses); this is why the Supplements consider them the "choke point" of the 3TG supply chains. By contrast, because after the stage of transformation it is impossible to trace back the origins of minerals, downstream actors' basic role is

---

[23] According to the Supplements, the following checks should raise "red flag locations of 3TG origin and transit": a) the minerals originate from or have been transported via a CAHR area; b) the minerals are claimed to originate from a country that has limited known reserves, likely resources or expected production levels (i.e. the declared volumes of mineral from that country are out of keeping with its known reserves or expected production levels); c) the minerals are claimed to originate from a country in which minerals from CAHR areas are known, or reasonably suspect to transit; and d) only for gold, the mineral is claimed to originate from recyclable/scrap or mixed sources and has been refined in a country where gold from CAHR areas is known or reasonably suspected to transit. The following checks should raise instead "supplier red flags": a) the company's suppliers or other known upstream companies have shareholder or other interests in companies that supply minerals from or operate in one of the above-mentioned red flag locations of mineral origin and transit; and b) the company's suppliers or other known upstream companies are known to have sourced minerals from a red flag location of mineral origin and transit in the last 12 months.

to find out which smelters their metals come from and assess those smelters' due diligence and outcomes based, inter alia, on independent audits.

4. THE REGULATORY FRAMEWORK OF THE EU "CONFLICT MINERALS REGULATION"

On 19 May 2017 the EU published "Regulation (EU) 2017/821 of the European Parliament and of the Council of 17 May 2017 laying down supply chain due diligence obligations for Union importers of tin, tantalum and tungsten, their ores, and gold originating from conflict-affected and high-risk areas"[24] (EU Conflict Minerals Regulation). It establishes a EU system for supply chain due diligence in order to: a) curtail opportunities for armed groups and security forces to trade in the covered minerals; and b) provide transparency and certainty as regards the supply practices of EU importers, and of smelters/refiners sourcing from CAHR areas (Article 1(1)).

Before analysing its main provisions, it is important to highlight that the Regulation is the final result of intense inter-institutional negotiations.[25] On several occasions the European Parliament called for the EU to legislate[26] along the lines of the "US conflict minerals law".[27] On 5 March 2014 the Commission

---

[24] OJ L 130, 2017, p. 1 ff. For a comment see, *ex multis*, VAN DER VELDE, "The End of Conflict Minerals on the EU Market?", ASSER Policy Brief No 3, March 2017; VOLAND and DALY, "The EU Regulation on Conflict Minerals: The Way Out of a Vicious Cycle?", JWT, 2018, p. 37 ff., p. 49 ff.

[25] For more details on these negotiations see, *ex multis*, NOWROT, "Good Raw Materials Governance: Towards a European Approach Contributing to a Constitutionalised International Economic Law", European Yearbook of International Economic Law, 2017, p. 381 ff., p. 392 ff.

[26] See, for example, European Parliament, European Parliament resolution of 5 July 2011 on increasing the impact of EU development policy, available at: <http://www.europarl.europa.eu/sides/getDoc.do?pubRef=-//EP//TEXT+TA+P7-TA-2011-0320+0+DOC+XML+V0//EN>, para. 60.

[27] In 2010 the US Dodd-Frank Wall Street Reform and Consumer Protection Act was adopted (Pub. L. 111-203, 124 Stat. 1376 (2010)). Section 1502 of the Dodd-Frank Act amends Section 13 of the Securities Exchange Act of 1934 and requires the Security and Exchange Commission (SEC) to adopt rules imposing disclosure requirements on SEC reporting companies for which "conflict minerals" are necessary to the functionality or the production of their products. "Conflict minerals" are defined as columbite-tantalite (coltan), cassiterite, gold, wolframite, or their derivatives (3TG), or any other mineral or its derivatives determined by the Secretary of State to be financing conflict in the DRC or an adjoining country (i.e. Angola, Burundi, Central African Republic, Republic of Congo, Rwanda, South Sudan, Tanzania, Uganda, Zambia). The SEC issued the Final Rule in August 2012 (S.E.C., Conflict Minerals: Final Rule, 17 CFR PARTS 240 and 249b). In a nutshell, in-scope companies (approximately 1,200, mostly downstream operators) are required to conduct a reasonable country of origin enquiry design to determine whether any of their minerals originated in the DRC or an adjoining country. If so, they are required to undertake due diligence on the source and chain of custody of the minerals in order to determine whether those minerals directly or indirectly financed or benefitted armed groups in the covered countries. These companies must file a Conflict Minerals Report with the SEC, and make the report publi-

submitted a proposal for a Regulation of the European Parliament and of the Council setting up a EU system on responsible mineral sourcing.[28] This proposal focused on 3TG minerals and metals from CAHR areas; in a nutshell, it envisaged the creation of a "voluntary" self-certification system for importers seeking to import any of the four 3TG raw materials into the EU in a responsible manner. On 20 May 2015 the European Parliament approved amendments reversing the regime proposed by the Commission.[29] Pointing out the need for due diligence along the entire supply chain (from the sourcing site to the final product), the Parliament proposed that both upstream and downstream actors that first place 3TG, including finished products that contain those resources on the EU market, "must" conduct and publicly report on their supply chain due diligence in accordance with the OECD Guidance. Because the Regulation needed to be adopted in co-decision by the European Parliament and the Council, on 20 May 2015 the Parliament decided not to close the first reading position and to enter into informal negotiations with the Council and the Commission (in so-called "trilogue"), to seek agreement on the final version of the Regulation. On November 2016 the EU Council, Commission and Parliament reached an informal final agreement; the latter builds upon the "political agreement" reached in June 2016. The Regulation was formally adopted on 3 April 2017. It entered into force 20 days after its publication and took effect one month after that (9 July 2017); however, its key provisions will apply from 1 January 2021 (Article 20), to allow for sufficient preparation time for, inter alia, member states and economic operators.

---

cally available on their website. The due diligence measures must conform to a nationally or internationally recognised due diligence framework; the Final Rule recognises the OECD Guidance as an international framework for the due diligence standard. For more details of this law, its positive impacts and unintended negative consequences (among the latter, the creation of a market disincentive with regard to sourcing from the Great Lakes Region of Africa and in particular from DRC), see, *ex multis*, SCHWARZ, "The Conflict Minerals Experiment", Harvard Business Law Review, 2016, p. 129 ff.; Progress and Challenges on Conflict Minerals: Facts on Dodd-Frank 1502, Enough Project, June 2017, available at: <https://enoughproject.org/>

[28] European Commission, Proposal for a Regulation of the European Parliament and of the Council setting up a Union system for supply chain due diligence self-certification of responsible importers of tin, tantalum and tungsten, their ores, and gold originating in conflict-affected and high-risk areas, COM(2014) 111 final, 5 March 2014. The Proposal was submitted to those EU institutions because the predominant part covered by the Regulation falls under the common commercial policy of the EU based on Art. 207 TFEU which is subject to the ordinary legislative procedure.

[29] European Parliament, Amendments adopted by the European Parliament on 20 May 2015 on the proposal for a Regulation of the European Parliament and of the Council setting up a Union system for supply chain due diligence self-certification of responsible importers of tin, tantalum and tungsten, their ores, and gold originating in conflict-affected and high-risk areas, P8_TA(2015)0204, May 2015.

4.1. Material, geographic and personal scope of the Regulation

As far as the material scope is concerned, the Regulation applies to tin, tantalum, tungsten and gold (3TG, whether in the form of mineral ores, concentrates or processed metals), as specified in Annex I (Article 1). It does not apply to existing EU stocks created in their current form prior to 1 February 2013, and to recycled metals (with the exception of Article 7(4)).[30] Therefore, this legislation is confined to 3TG; in contrast, the OECD five-step framework for risk-based due diligence covers the responsible management of supply chains of "all" minerals.

With regard to the geographic scope, the Regulation applies to 3TG potentially sourced from CAHR areas worldwide. In alignment with the OECD Guidance, such areas are those "in a state of armed conflict or fragile post-conflict as well as areas witnessing weak or non-existent governance and security, such as failed states, and widespread and systematic violations of international law, including human rights abuses" (Article 2(f)). The Commission is required to prepare non-binding guidelines in the form of a handbook to help economic operators identify CAHR areas, including other supply chain risks triggering "red flag indicators" as defined in the OECD Guidance. It will also provide, with help from external experts, an indicative, non-exhaustive, and regularly updated list of CAHR areas. Nevertheless, EU importers sourcing from areas which are not mentioned on that list will be still responsible for complying with the due diligence obligations under the Regulation (Article 14).

With respect to the personal scope, the Regulation applies to all EU importers of minerals or metals containing or consisting of 3TG into the European market,[31] whose annual import volumes exceed specified thresholds[32] (Article 1). Companies in-scope are: a) upstream operators importing 3TG minerals, including raw material traders and (approximately 20) EU smelters and refiners, as well as b) downstream operators who import 3TG metals processed outside the EU, such as metal traders and component manufacturers. According to the Commission, between 600 and 1,000 EU importers are directly affected by this legislation (out of the 880,000 EU firms that use 3TG in manufacturing consumer products). Downstream users of these commodities operating beyond the metal stage, including EU importers of semi-processed or finished products containing 3TG, do not have compliance obligations under the Regulation. However, EU "big manufacturers" that are subject to the non-financial reporting Directive may need to report on their 3TG due

---

[30] See Art. 2(s) of the Regulation for the definition of recycled metals; Art. 7(4) envisages disclosure requirements. Minerals partially processed, unprocessed or a by-product from another ore are not considered to be recycled metals.

[31] Pursuant to Art. 2(l) Union importer means any natural or legal person declaring minerals or metals for release for free circulation within the meaning of Art. 201 of Regulation (EU) 952/2013, or any natural or legal person on whose behalf such declaration is made.

[32] Annex I to the Regulation contains volume thresholds for some of the listed minerals and metals. For the remaining commodities, the Commission is required to adopt a delegated act, not later than 1 June 2020, in order to establish the required volume thresholds. In any case, the threshold is to cover no less than 95% of the total volumes of each mineral and metal imported into the EU.

diligence.[33] In accordance with the voluntary guidelines on non-financial reporting published by the Commission on 26 June 2017, where relevant and proportionate, companies in-scope are expected to disclose information on due diligence to ensure responsible supply chains for 3TG from CAHR areas.[34]

4.2. EU importers' obligations under the Regulation

The Regulation establishes a complex set of due diligence obligations for EU importers, which – to a large extent – are based on the five-step framework laid out in the OECD Guidance.[35] Specifically, the new legislation imposes on importers: "management system obligations"; "risk management obligations"; "third-party obligations"; and "disclosure obligations". The purpose of the due diligence system is to determine whether 3TG raw materials that are being imported into the EU have been mined and processed responsibly to ensure that they are not funding armed groups and security forces in conflict areas.

With regard to the management system obligations (Article 4), importers are first required to adopt, and clearly communicate to suppliers and the public, up-to-date information on their supply chain policy for 3TG raw materials potentially originating from CAHR areas. Second, they must incorporate in the supply chain policy standards against which supply chain due diligence is to be conducted consistent with the standards set out in the model supply chain policy in Annex II to the OECD Guidance. Third, importers have to structure internal management systems to support supply chain due diligence and maintain records of those systems for a minimum of five years. Fourth, they must strengthen engagement with suppliers by incorporating their supply chain policy into contracts and agreements. Fifth, they must establish a grievance mechanism as an early-warning risk-awareness system. Last but not least, importers have to implement a chain of custody or supply chain traceability system for minerals and metals, supported by documentation, providing information on – among others – the

---

[33] Directive 2014/95/EU of the European Parliament and of the Council of 22 October 2014 amending Directive 2013/34/EU as regards disclosure of non-financial and diversity information by certain large undertakings and groups, OJ L 330, 2014, p. 1 ff. It applies to large public-interest entities with more than 500 employees (approximately 6,000 entities). For more details see, *ex multis*, QUINN and CONNOLLY, "The Non-Financial Information Directive: An Assessment of Its Impact on Corporate Social Responsibility", European Company Law Journal, 2017, p. 15 ff.

[34] See Communication from the Commission, Guidelines on non-financial reporting (methodology for reporting non-financial information), OJ C 215, 2017, p. 1 ff., p. 18. Disclosures should be consistent with the OECD Guidance, including: a) relevant information on the performance of policies, practices and results on conflict minerals due diligence, notably by using performance indicators; and b) the steps taken to implement the OECD Guidance's five-step framework.

[35] For some inconsistencies of the EU Regulation with the OECD Guidance see GRADO, "EU Approaches on 'Conflict Minerals': Are They Consistent with the UN/OECD Supply Chain Due Diligence Standards?", in BONFANTI (ed.), *Business and Human Rights in Europe: International Law Challenges*, New York/London, forthcoming.

supplier and the country of origin (for minerals) or the smelters/refiners (for metals). Additional information is required when 3TG raw materials originate from CAHR areas or where "red flag indicators" listed in the OECD Guidance have been ascertained by the importer.[36]

Using the information retrieved pursuant to Article 4 importers are then required to: i) identify and assess the risks of adverse impacts in their mineral supply chain (Article 5); and ii) implement a strategy to respond to the identified risks, one that prevents or mitigates adverse impacts (Article 5). This strategy involves: a) reporting findings of the supply chain risk assessment to designated senior management; b) adopting risk management measures consistent with the OECD Guidance; c) implementing the risk management plan and tracking its performance; and d) undertaking additional fact and risk assessments for those risks requiring mitigation, or after a change of circumstances. Most notably, risk management measures include consideration of suspension or disengagement with an upstream supplier after failed attempts at risk mitigation.[37]

As to the fourth step of the due diligence system, importers must obtain independent third-party audits pertaining to their supply chain due diligence practices to assess conformity with the Regulation (Article 6(1)[38]). Importantly, importers of metals are exempted from the audit requirements if they make available substantive evidence, including third-party audit reports, demonstrating that all smelters/refiners in their supply chain comply with the Regulation (Article 6 (2)), for example that they source 3TG exclusively from smelters/refiners listed by the Commission as global responsible smelters and refiners (as will be seen below).

With regard to the final step of the due diligence system, importers have specific disclosure obligations to regulators, customers and the public (Article 7). Indeed, they must make available to the relevant member state competent authorities the reports of any third-party audit carried out in accordance with the Regulation (or evidence of conformity with an equivalent scheme). The importers must also make available to their immediate downstream purchasers all information gained pursuant to their supply chain due diligence measures and publicly report these measures as widely as possible, including on the internet, with due regard for business confidentiality.

In light of the above, the Regulation applies directly to all EU importers of 3TG raw materials and indirectly to those involved in the EU supply chain of the import of these materials. Because the EU importers need to make sure that they source responsibly, they are required to influence the conduct of their suppliers in other countries and to impose due diligence requirements upstream in the mineral supply chain.[39] As a result, the Regulation imposes indirect obligations outside

---

[36] See Art. 4(f)(v) and (g)(v) of the Regulation.

[37] See Art. 5(b)(ii) of the Regulation.

[38] The audits should respect the audit principles of independence, competence and accountability set out in the OECD Guidance.

[39] For the potentialities and challenges posed by domestic laws regulating global supply chains with respect to human rights and labour practices, whereby companies are not only regulated entities but also serve as regulators themselves (imposing standards on their sup-

the EU territory on non-EU upstream companies and indirectly forces them to comply with its rules. Therefore, this new piece of legislation increases the number of EU trade rules with extraterritorial reach aimed at pursuing public values (such as the protection of the environment or internationally recognised human rights) outside the EU.

4.3. Member states' obligations under the Regulation

Member states are required to establish competent authorities responsible for the implementation of the Regulation (Article 10). These authorities should: a) carry out *ex-post* checks of importers' compliance, including on-the-spot inspections at the premises of the importer (Article 11[40]); b) keep records of the *ex-post* checks for at least five years (Article 12); and c) exchange information, including with their respective customs authorities, on matters pertaining to supply chain due diligence and *ex-post* checks carried out (Article 13).

Furthermore, member states are required to establish rules applicable to infringements of the Regulation; however, according to Article 16, where infringements are identified, the competent authority must issue a notice of remedial action to be taken by the importer. Finally, member states must report to the Commission on the implementation of the Regulation every year, in particular on notices of remedial action issued and on the third-party audit reports (Article 17).

4.4. Additional Commission's commitments under the Regulation

The EU "Conflict Minerals Regulation" also provides for the adoption of delegated and implementing measures by the Commission aiming, respectively, at supplementing the Regulation's content and ensuring its uniform implementation by member states.

Most significantly, the Commission will adopt delegated acts setting out the methodology and criteria to determine whether supply chain due diligence schemes developed and overseen by governments, industry associations and other organisations (which work mainly with smelters/refiners located outside EU) can be recognised as equivalent to the requirements set out in the Regulation (Article 8[41]). Recital 14 of the Regulation identifies as requisites: a) the presence of overarching due diligence principles; b) the alignment to the specific recommendations of the OECD Guidance; and c) procedural requirements such as stakeholders' engagement, grievance mechanisms and responsiveness.

---

pliers in other countries) see, *ex multis*, SARFATY, "Shining Light on Global Supply Chains", Harvard ILJ, 2015, p. 419 ff., p. 421 ff.

[40] The Commission is required to prepare non-binding guidelines detailing the steps to be followed by competent authorities carrying out the *ex-post* checks.

[41] The Commission is also required to periodically verify the recognised schemes and establish and keep up-to-date a register (publicly available on the internet) of these schemes.

Furthermore, in order to assist companies with their compliance efforts, the Commission is required to establish through an implementing act a list of global responsible smelters and refiners which, at least partially, source minerals from CAHR areas (the so-called "white list") (Article 9). The list will include first of all the EU based smelters/refiners of 3TG covered by the Regulation (if they implement the full range of measures included therein); and second, those smelters/refiners mainly located outside the EU covered by supply chain due diligence industry schemes recognised by the Commission. Articles 8 and 9, dealing mostly with non-EU 3TG smelters/refiners (approximately 480 entities), corroborate the indirect compliance effect of the "Conflict Minerals Regulation". Although not applying directly to 3TG smelters/refiners located outside the EU, the Regulation contributes to the *de facto* extension of the EU regime, given that (as mentioned above) importers of metals which source exclusively from listed responsible smelters/refiners are exempted from the burdensome audit requirements established under Article 6(1). Therefore, the new legislation indirectly promotes the responsible sourcing of smelters/refiners of 3TG based outside EU.

In addition to being empowered to adopt delegated and implementing acts, the Commission is required to review and report to the European Parliament and to the Council on the functioning and effectiveness of the "Conflict Minerals Regulation" by 1 January 2023 and every three years thereafter (Article 17). Notably, reviews are required to include its impact on the ground and on EU economic operators, as well as on the promotion and cost of responsible sourcing of 3TG raw materials from CAHR areas. Reviews must also include an assessment of: a) the proportion of total EU downstream operators with 3TG in their supply chains which have due diligence schemes in place; and b) the adequacy and implementation on these due diligence schemes as well as the need for additional mandatory measures in order to ensure that the EU market has sufficient leverage to influence responsible global supply chains of 3TG.

5. ASSESSMENT OF THE EU "CONFLICT MINERALS REGULATION" AND CONCLUDING REMARKS

Before highlighting the EU Regulation's main positive aspects and some challenges to its effectiveness (Section 5.2), it is important to underline that this piece of legislation, similarly to other EU measures which address social, environmental, and moral concerns regarding production that takes place outside the European market, raises questions of its permissibility under customary international law and GATT obligations (Section 5.1).

5.1. The legal status of the EU Regulation under international law

The EU "Conflict Minerals Regulation", by seeking to ensure that the production and trade of 3TG raw materials do not contribute to the fuelling of armed conflict and human rights abuses, represents a form of "non-product-related process and production methods" (NPR PPMs). As is well known, NPR PPMs mean production requirements for certain products which cannot be traced in the physical characteristics of the product itself, for example, environmental, labour or other social standards for manufacturing processes.[42] Because the new EU Regulation does not impose a trade restriction or a trade embargo on 3TG raw materials originating from CAHR areas, it is not a "country-based measure", that is a measure that seeks to prohibit the import of products because they originated from certain countries. Rather, the EU Regulation belongs to the so-called "producer-based measures"; that is, measures aiming at preventing (foreign) producers that do not comply with certain rules from accessing the market of the importing state.[43] In this respect, it is worth recalling that, under this legislation, EU importers' risk management measures include consideration of suspension or disengagement with an upstream supplier after failed attempts at risk mitigation. This means that under certain circumstances 3TG raw materials from CAHR areas are denied access to the European market if those (foreign) upstream suppliers do not comply with the due diligence obligations laid out in the Regulation.

In light of the above, the EU import regime for 3TG raw materials – like all PPM measures – raises two main questions. First, its legality under customary international law, in particular having regard to, respectively, the rules on sovereignty and international jurisdiction and the principle of non-intervention in internal affairs. Second, its consistency with GATT obligations. These very controversial issues, the subject of intense debate,[44] will be outlined only briefly here because they go beyond the main purpose of this article, that is, the illustration and discussion of the set of rules provided under the EU "Conflict Minerals Regulation".

Starting with the first issue, opponents of PPM measures argue – first of all – that the latter interfere with the exporting country's sovereign right under international law to regulate activities occurring within its jurisdiction and therefore produce extraterritorial effects by prescribing the adoption of a conduct outside the territory of the regulating state.[45] As we have seen, in the case of producer-based measures, producers in an exporting country that do not comply with the production-related requirements established by the importing country cannot ac-

---

[42] For more details on PPMs see, *ex multis*, CONRAD, *Processes and Production Methods (PPMs) in WTO Law: Interfacing Trade and Social Goals*, Cambridge, 2011, p. 20 ff.; COOREMAN, *Global Environmental Protection Through Trade: A Systematic Approach to Extraterritoriality*, Cheltenham, 2017, p. 19 ff.

[43] For the distinction between "country-based measures", "producer-based measures" and "consumer-based measures" see ANKERSMIT, *Green Trade and Fair Trade in and with the EU. Process-based Measures within the EU Legal Order*, Cambridge, 2017, p. 26 ff.

[44] See, *ex multis*, CONRAD, *cit. supra* note 42, p. 147 ff.; ANKERSMIT, *cit. supra* note 43, p. 8 ff.; COOREMAN, *cit. supra* note 42, p. 53 ff.; MAGGIO, *Environmental Policy, Non-Product Related Process and Production Methods and the Law of the Word Trade Organization*, Cham, 2017.

[45] See, *ex multis*, SCHOENBAUM, "International Trade and Protection of the Environment: The Continuing Search for Reconciliation", AJIL, 1997, p. 268 ff., p. 279 ff.; HORN and MAVROIDIS, "The Permissible Reach of National Environmental Policies", JWT, 2008, p. 1107 ff., p. 1125.

cess the latter's market. The second argument asserts that PPM measures have economically coercive effects on developing countries and smaller states heavily dependent on exports for their economy, thus representing a violation of the customary international law principle of non-intervention.[46]

As far as the first argument is concerned, it is important to underline that many domestic regulations may indeed have some effects beyond the territory of the regulating state, but not all of them will be considered as being applied extraterritorially. This is particularly the case of producer-based measures, which prescribe requirements for products to be sold in the territory of the regulating state; they only define the conditions of importation and do not directly regulate activities occurring abroad. Therefore, they are in line with the rules on prescriptive jurisdiction, which include the state's sovereign right to choose its import policies.[47] Moreover, those measures – being enforced either at the border or within the territory of the regulating state – seem also to be consistent with the rules on enforcement jurisdiction.

Turning to the argument that PPM trade measures constitute a violation of the non-intervention norm by inducing changes in the exporting country's internal regulatory regime, it must be underlined that the principle of non-intervention has two elements: an intention to change the policy of the target state and, most importantly, coercion. With regard to the latter, if – on the one hand – it is undisputed that the use of force constitutes a violation of the principle of non-intervention, on the other hand it is unclear if and under which circumstances economic measures amount to coercion.[48] As is well known, in the *Nicaragua* case the ICJ held that the total trade embargo adopted by the United States in order to put pressure on the Sandinista government to achieve political changes in Nicaragua did not constitute a breach of the customary law principle of non-intervention.[49]

---

[46] See GATHII, "Neoliberalism, Colonialism and International Governance: Decentering the International Law of Governmental Legitimacy", Michigan Law Review, 2000, p. 1996 ff., p. 2029 ff.

[47] In the same sense NOLLKAEMPER, "Rethinking States' Rights to Promote Extraterritorial Environmental Values", in WEISS, DENTERS and DE WAART (eds.), *International Economic Law with a Human Face*, The Hague/Dordrecht/London, 1998, p. 175 ff., p. 188 ff.; HOWSE and REGAN, "The Product/Process Distinction – An Illusory Basis for Disciplining 'Unilateralism' in Trade Policy", EJIL, 2000, p. 249 ff., p. 274 ff.; VRANES, *Trade and the Environment: Fundamental Issues in International Law, WTO Law, and Legal Theory*, Oxford, 2009, p. 165 ff. It is worth noting that also Professor Ruggie distinguishes between "domestic measures with extraterritorial implications" and "direct extraterritorial" measures. He points out that the former do not raise the same jurisdictional challenges as the latter, because they rely on territory as the jurisdictional basis; see Human Rights Council, Business and Human Rights: Further Steps Toward the Operationalization of the "Protect, Respect and Remedy" Framework, UN Doc. A/HCR/14/27 (2010), para. 48.

[48] In the same sense see, *ex multis*, CONDON, *Environmental Sovereignty and the WTO: Trade Sanctions and International Law*, Ardsley, 2006, p. 250 ff.; JAMNEYAD and WOOD, "The Principle of Non-Intervention", Leiden JIL, 2009, p. 345 ff., p. 369 ff.

[49] *Military and Paramilitary Activities in and Against Nicaragua (Nicaragua v. United States of America)*, Judgment of 27 June 1986, ICJ Reports, 1986, p. 14 ff., para. 245.

Therefore, it seems highly unlikely that less severe economic actions, like PPM measures, may be qualified as unlawful coercion.

In light of the above brief analysis, it is possible to conclude that the rules on extraterritorial jurisdiction or the principle of non-intervention hardly challenge the permissibility of producer-based measures such as the EU import regime on 3TG raw materials. However, the latter – by addressing situations occurring outside the internal market – can be unlawful on the basis of the EU's treaty commitments. It is thus necessary to examine the "Conflict Minerals" Regulation's consistency with GATT obligations.[50]

Before proceeding with this second issue, it is worth recalling that the new EU Regulation does not prohibit imports of 3TG raw materials sourced from CAHR areas. It imposes on all EU importers of a certain amount of those materials "management system obligations" and "identification and assessment risk obligations". EU importers only have additional obligations where "red flag indicators" are identified in their supply chains, for example because the 3TG raw materials originate from CAHR areas, the most relevant one being the implementation of a strategy to respond to the identified risks which includes consideration of suspension or disengagement with their upstream suppliers abroad. Therefore, certain provisions in the new Regulation bring about different treatment between 3TG raw materials originating from CAHR areas and those sourced from non CAHR-areas. Most notably, this different treatment concerns goods (3TG raw materials originating from CAHR areas and 3TG materials from non-CAHR areas) that seem to be "like" products, according to the main general GATT criteria for likeness.[51]

As is well known, the principle of non-discrimination represents the fundamental pillar in the GATT law. This principle contains two different elements: the most-favoured-nation (MFN) treatment and the national treatment (NT).

The MFN treatment obligation established in Article I:1 GATT essentially requires WTO members not to discriminate between foreign like products on the basis of their origin. Most relevant for our analysis, Article I:1 provides that: "with respect to all rules and formalities in connection with importation and exportation [...] any advantage, favour, privilege or immunity granted by any con-

---

[50] According to the prevailing view NPR PPMs are not covered by the Agreement on Technical Barriers to Trade, which means that they fall within the scope of the GATT. See, *ex multis*, APPLETON, "Private Climate Change Standards and Labelling Schemes under the WTO Agreement on Technical Barriers to Trade", in COTTIER, NARTOVA and BIGDELI (eds.), *International Trade Regulation and the Mitigation of Climate Change: World Trade Forum*, Cambridge, 2009, p. 131 ff., p. 137 ff.

[51] As is well known, the four criteria are: i) the properties, nature and quality of the products; ii) the end-uses of the products; iii) consumers' tastes and habits in respect of the products; and iv) the tariff classification of the products; see e.g. WTO Appellate Body Report, *European Communities – Measures Affecting Asbestos and Asbestos-Containing Products*, 12 March 2001, para. 101. The physical characteristics, end-uses and tariff classification of 3TG raw materials originating from CAHR areas and 3TG materials from non-CAHR areas are essentially the same. For an extensively illustration of these criteria and for further bibliographical references see CHOI, *'Like Products' in International Trade Law: Towards a Consistent GATT/WTO Jurisprudence*, Oxford, 2003, *passim*.

tracting party to any product originating in or destined for any other country shall be accorded immediately and unconditionally to the like product originating in or destined for the territories of all other contracting parties". As already seen, the "Conflict Minerals Regulation" envisages a complex set of obligations for EU importers of 3TG raw materials to ensure they do not contribute – inter alia – to the financing of armed conflict. It establishes rules and formalities in connection to importation; therefore, Article I:1 GATT is applicable. Thus, the next question to be answered is whether this Regulation confers an advantage, that is creates "more favorable import opportunities" for certain products depending on their origin. In the case at hand, 3TG raw materials not sourced from CAHR areas may be marketed in the EU whereas 3TG raw materials sourced from CAHR areas, under certain circumstances, cannot enter the European market in the light of EU importers disengagement obligations. Consequently, the EU import regime on "conflict minerals", by conferring an advantage to certain products, might result in a breach of Article I:1.

Turning to the NT obligation established in Article III:4 GATT, it essentially requires WTO members not to treat foreign products less favourably than like domestic products; it forbids both *de jure* and *de facto* discrimination. Discriminatory treatment is determined through the application of a discriminatory impact test, which compares the treatment of the group of imported products to that of the group of domestic like products. Considering that the EU Regulation excludes from its scope 3TG raw materials sourced within the EU, thereby not posing due diligence obligations for 3TG raw materials of EU origin (for example gold extracted from member states' territories), the group of imported products seems to be more negatively affected than the group of EU products. The EU import regime for 3TG raw materials might therefore be inconsistent also with Article III:4.

In conclusion, the regulatory approach taken by the EU with the "Conflict Minerals Regulation" might raise concerns regarding potential violation of substantive provisions of GATT law; the examination of its possible justifications under Articles XX (general exception) and XXI (security exception) – already conducted by scholars[52] – is therefore particularly relevant.[53]

5.2. The EU Regulation's main positive aspects and challenges

The very relevance of the EU "Conflict Minerals Regulation" as a regulatory instrument emerges, first, from the fact that it establishes due diligence obliga-

---

[52] See PARTITI and VAN DER VELDE, "Curbing Supply-Chain Human Rights Violations Through Trade and Due Diligence. Possible WTO Concerns Raised by the Conflict Minerals Regulation", JWT, 2018, p. 1043 ff., p. 1060 ff.

[53] Pursuant to Art. IX:3 of the WTO Agreement the EU could submit a request for a waiver from Arts. I:1 and III:4 GATT, concerning its import regime on 3TG raw materials. However, in our opinion, such waiver decision has little chance to be granted (for reasons that we cannot explore here due to space limitations).

tions on EU importers of 3TG raw materials (upstream and downstream operators on either side of the "choke point" of the 3TG supply chains), making them
accountable for harm occurring in their supply chains. As we have seen, it attaches legal liability to in-scope companies for failing to comply both with the due
diligence expectations and the reporting requirements.[54] By imposing mandatory
due diligence on those operators, the Regulation extensively relies on business
entities to curb particularly serious crimes and practices occurring in third countries which the EU cannot address directly.

Second, the new Regulation incorporates into law the "risk-based due diligence" international standards envisaged in the UNGPs and the OECD Guidance.
This is very significant at least for two reasons. On the one hand, it "hardens" supply chain due diligence standards, supporting enterprises to meet their commitments to respect human rights also when they are outsourcing their production to
third countries. On the other hand, this piece of legislation makes its requirement
more acceptable for the EU's trading partners, in the light of the OECD Guidance
becoming the leading global due diligence standard for the mineral sector.

Third, the Regulation tries to regulate both the EU's internal market, by ensuring EU imports of 3TG from responsible sources only, and – most notably
– the global market as well, by promoting the responsible sourcing of smelters/
refiners mostly located outside the EU.

Despite the Regulation's positive aspects and opportunities, several provisions therein are problematic in terms of its effectiveness and conformity with
the UN/OECD standards on responsible sourcing. We will confine our remarks
to the most relevant ones.

As mentioned above, according to Article 1, EU companies whose annual
imports of 3TG raw materials fall below established thresholds are not required
to comply with the due diligence system. While the *ratio* here is to avoid the creation of unreasonable administrative burdens for their businesses, this may create
potential loopholes in the system, making it possible for minerals sourced from
CAHR areas to be marketed into the EU through small importers. Considering,
for example, that limited quantities of gold are more likely to be linked to
conflict,[55] this exemption falls short of the international standards on responsible
sourcing. Indeed, the OECD Guidance does not envisage *de minimis* exemptions. Moreover, in the discussion paper mentioned above Professor Ruggie rejects merely numerical or threshold approaches to human rights responsibility

---

[54] On the concept of "supply chain liability", which is broad, varied and, until recently,
merely an academic theory, see, *ex multis*, NOLAN, "Human Rights and Global Corporate
Supply Chains: Is Effective Supply Chain Accountability Possible?", in DEVA and BILCHITZ
(eds.), *Building a Treaty on Business and Human Rights: Context and Contours*, Cambridge,
2017, p. 238 ff.

[55] The threshold for gold imported in mineral or metal form is 100 kg. According to
Amnesty International, approximately 90% of imports of gold into the EU are under this
threshold; see Amnesty International, "Suggested EU Rules on Conflict Minerals Trade Risk
Exclusion of 90% of Importers", available at: <http://www.amnesty.eu/en/news/blog/suggest-
ed-eu-rules-on-conflict-mineral-trade-risk-exclusion-of-90-of-importers00089/>.

and emphasises that the riskiest procurement practices should be subject to basic checks and scrutiny.

In addition, Article 1 only applies to a fraction of the EU 3TG supply chains, excluding downstream companies beyond the metal stage from mandatory due diligence. This is a significant challenge, for several reasons. First of all, in light of the fact that 3TG commodities mostly find their way into the European market through imported semi-processed or end products, the limited personal scope of the Regulation may create further loopholes in the EU system by importing "conflict mineral-derived" products. Second, it severely reduces the impact of the Regulation, by not incentivising EU downstream companies (beyond the metal stage) to create more transparent supply chains and apply joint leverage over upstream suppliers, including those outside of the EU. Third, it does not prevent the aforementioned EU downstream companies from resorting to non-EU smelters/refiners, the majority of which are based in Asian countries that do not have conflict minerals laws in place. Finally, the narrow definition of "importer" is not consistent with the international standards of the OECD Guidance (and of the UNGPs), which point out that "responsible sourcing" of 3TG is the responsibility of the whole supply chain; applying a lower standard could therefore jeopardise a uniform approach towards mineral supply chain due diligence.

The second provision which raises problems is the introduction of a list of CAHR areas (Article 14). Indeed, first, such a list involves the risk of stigmatising certain regions/countries (such as DRC) and thus dissuading companies from sourcing from them. Even if it is only "indicative", the list could create "market distortions" and reverse the (second) aim of the Regulation, which is precisely to encourage responsible sourcing from areas affected by conflict and instability. Second, this list, by including only the region/country of origin of 3TG minerals and leaving out other regions/countries where risk controls should be carried out (e.g. transit regions through which contraband minerals penetrate the international market), may discourage the full implementation by operators of due diligence "throughout their supply chains", as envisaged in the OECD Guidance.

The third provision which may undermine the identification of risks in the importer's supply chain is represented by the so-called "white-list" of responsible smelters/refiners (Article 9), being made up mostly by smelters/refiners located outside the EU that are members of accredited industry schemes. Because the latter do not import minerals into the European market, their due diligence practices will be not subject to *ex-post* checks, in contrast to smelters'/refines' practices located inside the EU. Therefore, infrequent monitoring of industry schemes could allow irresponsible smelters/refiners to operate while being promoted by the Commission as responsible.[56]

The last main problematic aspect of the Regulation is its lack of "teeth". As we have seen, if a member state competent authority finds that an EU importer has not complied with the due diligence expectations and/or the reporting require-

---

[56] Art. 8(4) states that the Commission will "periodically" verify the recognised industry schemes.

ments, it will issue a notice of remedial action to be taken by the company. Thus, the focus is on promoting compliance, rather than punishing non-compliance. Nevertheless, the omission of the standard clause requiring that member states adopt "effective, proportionate and dissuasive penalties" for infringements[57] risks sending the wrong message about the failure to secure traceability and transparency in the 3TG supply chains of EU importers.

In light to the above, it is not surprising that the new EU "Conflict Minerals Regulation" was received with mixed reviews. On the one hand, it was considered a strong demonstration of the EU's commitment to regulate a particularly problematic supply chain where severe human rights abuses are taking place. On the other hand, the importer-focused approach of the Regulation and its further challenges were strongly criticised.[58] With respect to the latter, in our opinion it is important to underline that this legislation envisages many review provisions which could overcome its main shortcomings. As far as its minimum thresholds are concerned, the Commission is empowered to amend the existing thresholds every three years after 1 January 2021 (Article 1(5)) and will, in particular, monitor the gold imports.[59] With regard to its limited personal scope and lack of penalties the Commission will review the Regulation and consider the need to: a) include further mandatory measures for downstream operators with 3TG in their supply chains; and b) give member state authorities the competence to impose penalties on importers that persistently breach their obligations (Article 17). Finally, with respect to its narrow material scope, the review clause opens the door for the inclusion of further minerals. Therefore, it cannot be ruled out that in the future the EU import regime for "conflict minerals" will be more "robust" and in line with the internationally recognised supply chain standards of the UNGPs and the OECD.

---

[57] See, for example, Regulation (EU) 995/2010 of the European Parliament and of the Council of 20 October 2010 laying down the obligations of operators who place timber and timber products on the market, OJ L 295, 2010, p. 13 ff., Art. 19.

[58] See, *ex multis*, EurAc, European Regulation on the Responsible Sourcing of Minerals: The EU Is (Once Again) About to Weaken the Upcoming Regulation, Policy Briefing, 10 November 2016, available at: <http://www.eurac-network.org/sites/default/files/kcfinder/files/Advocacy%20-%20reports%2C%20GTT%20work%20etc/EurAc%20Policy%20Briefing_EU%20Regulation%20on%20Resp%20%20Sourcing_10%20Nov%202016_ENG.pdf>.

[59] Statements by the Council and by the Commission relating to Regulation (EU) 2017/821 of the European Parliament and of the Council of 17 May 2017 laying down supply chain due diligence obligations for Union importers of tin, tantalum and tungsten, their ores, and gold originating from conflict-affected and high-risk areas, OJ C 158, 2017, p. 1.

ITALY'S NEW MIGRATION CONTROL POLICY: STEMMING THE FLOW OF MIGRANTS FROM LIBYA WITHOUT REGARD FOR THEIR HUMAN RIGHTS

Marina Mancini[*]

Abstract

During 2017, the Italian Government adopted a series of controversial measures in order to stem the increasing flow of migrants from Libya, with the full backing of the European Union. The Memorandum of Understanding between Italy and the Libyan Government of National Accord of 2 February 2017 provided the legal basis for most of them. In actual fact, those measures rapidly led to a significant reduction in the number of migrants arriving in Italy, while increasing that of migrants intercepted at sea by the Libyan Coast Guard and transferred to the detention centres managed by the Libyan Department for Combatting Illegal Immigration. As a result, the already inhuman conditions of detention therein further worsened. This article investigates whether and to what extent Italy can be held responsible under international law for human rights violations against migrants on Libyan soil and, at the hands of the Libyan Coast Guard, at sea. It is submitted that, owing to the active support to the Libyan Coast Guard and the adoption of a code of conduct restricting NGOs' search and rescue activities, Italy is complicit in violations of the prohibition of torture and ill-treatment against migrants intercepted at sea and forcibly returned to Libya. It is also stressed that Italy would be responsible for directly violating the prohibition on torture and ill-treatment enshrined in Article 3 of the European Convention on Human Rights, if it were ascertained that Italian military personnel exercise de facto *control over Libyan Coast Guard vessels transporting migrants back to Libyan territory. In the light of this, the author highlights the urgent need for the Italian Government to rethink its migration control policy, amending the said Memorandum of Understanding and modifying the aforementioned measures so as to prioritise the protection of migrants' fundamental human rights.*

Keywords: migrants; refugees; search and rescue at sea; European Convention on Human Rights; State responsibility.

1. INTRODUCTION

Since the beginning of 2017, faced with a dramatic increase in the sea arrivals of migrants from Libya, the Italian Government adopted a series of con-

---

[*] Associate Professor of International Law, Mediterranean University of Reggio Calabria; Adjunct Professor of International Law, LUISS Guido Carli University, Rome. This article was completed before Italy's decision to no longer permit NGO vessels to disembark migrants rescued from the Mediterranean at its ports.

troversial measures aimed at closing off the so-called Central Mediterranean route, with the full backing of the European Union (EU). The Memorandum of Understanding between Italy and the Libyan Government of National Accord on Cooperation in the Field of Development, Fight against Illegal Immigration, Trafficking in Human Beings and Smuggling and on Enhancement of Border Security of 2 February 2017 (MOU) laid down the legal foundations for most of those measures.[1]

Indeed, they had the immediate effect of significantly diminishing the number of irregular migrants arriving in Italy, while boosting that of migrants intercepted at sea by the Libyan Coast Guard and transferred to the detention facilities run by the Department for Combatting Illegal Immigration, a division of the Libyan Ministry of the Interior. As a result, the conditions of detention therein, which were already far short of human rights standards, further worsened.

Against this background, the question arises whether and to what extent Italy can be held responsible under international law for human rights violations against migrants on Libyan soil and, at the hands of the Libyan Coast Guard, at sea. This article tries to answer this question by means of a multilevel analysis. Firstly, the provisions of the MOU are examined thoroughly. Secondly, the EU political and financial support for Italy's new migration control policy is considered. Thirdly, the various measures decided by the Italian Government to curtail the sea crossings are carefully scrutinised.

2.   THE 2017 MEMORANDUM OF UNDERSTANDING BETWEEN ITALY AND LIBYA

The MOU at issue was signed by the Italian Prime Minister, Paolo Gentiloni, and the Prime Minister of the Government of National Accord of Libya, Fayez Mustafa Serraj, in Rome. The Libyan Government of National Accord was formed in January 2016, based on the Libyan Political Agreement that had been concluded in Skhirat (Morocco) on 17 December 2015, thanks to the mediation efforts of the United Nations (UN), in order to overcome the political and institutional chaos of the country.[2] It was recognised as "the sole legitimate government of Libya" by the UN, the African Union, the EU and most of states, including Italy.[3] Despite the international support however, at the time of writing, this Government is far from being in full control of the Libyan territory.

---

[1] The Memorandum of Understanding is available at: <http://itra.esteri.it/vwPdf/wfrm-RenderPdf.aspx?ID=50975>.

[2] The Libyan Political Agreement is available at: <https://unsmil.unmissions.org/sites/default/files/Libyan%20Political%20Agreement%20-%20ENG%20.pdf>.

[3] See the Joint Communiqué adopted at the Ministerial Meeting for Libya, held in Rome, on 13 December 2015, available at: <https://www.diplomatie.gouv.fr/en/country-files/libya/events/2015/article/ministerial-meeting-for-libya-joint-communique-rome-italy-13-12-15>; the Security Council Resolution No. 2259 (2015), UN Doc. S/RES/2259 (2015); the Statement on Libya issued by France, Germany, Italy, the United Kingdom, the United States and the European Union at the Ministerial Meeting held in Paris, on 13 March 2016, available at:

The Gentiloni-Serraj agreement was concluded for a period of three years and entered into force on the date of signature, on 2 February 2017. It will be extended by tacit agreement for a further three-year period, unless it is denounced in writing by one of the parties at least three months before the expiration date (Article 8). It was done in Italian and Arabic, both texts being equally authentic.

The MOU is ideally placed for continuity with the treaties that were concluded between Italy and Gaddafi's Government before the 2011 Libyan revolution. The Preamble stipulates that it aims at implementing the agreements concluded between the parties on the same subject in the past, among which the Treaty on Friendship, Partnership and Cooperation of 30 August 2008 is expressly mentioned.[4]

Nevertheless, on a first reading of the MOU, the broadness and vagueness of the material obligations undertaken by the parties, especially by Italy, appear to be inconsistent with its proclaimed nature as a mere implementing agreement. In particular, the parties commit themselves to launch cooperation initiatives concerning "the support to the security and defense institutions in order to stem the flows of illegal migrants and face the consequences of them", in conformity with the programs of the Libyan Government of National Accord (Article 1(A)).[5] Italy also undertakes "to provide technical and technological support" to the Border Guard and Coast Guard of Libya and the organs of the Libyan Ministry of the Interior in charge of the fight against irregular immigration (Article 1(C)), and to support and finance development programs in the Libyan regions affected by the phenomenon of irregular immigration (Article 1(B)). Moreover, various actions are listed that "the Parties commit themselves to undertake" (Article 2). Actually, however, it is Italy that is primarily burdened with the implementation of such actions. They include: (1) the completion of Libya's southern border control system, as set forth in Article 19 of the 2008 Treaty on Friendship, Partnership and Cooperation; (2) the adaptation and funding of the detention centres run by the Libyan Department for Combatting Illegal Immigration, which are given a respectable veneer with the name "reception centres"; (3) the training of the Libyan staff of those centres; (4) the elaboration of a Euro-African cooperation plan to remove the root causes of irregular immigration, within three months from the signature of the Memorandum; the support to international organisations competent in the field of migration operating in Libya; and (5) the development of

---

<https://www.esteri.it/mae/it/sala_stampa/archivionotizie/comunicati/2016/03/ministerial-meeting-in-paris-france_0.html>.

[4] Treaty between Italy and Libya on Friendship, Partnership and Cooperation, Benghazi, 30 August 2008, available at: <http://itra.esteri.it/vwPdf/wfrmRenderPdf.aspx?ID=49182>. For comment, see RONZITTI, "The Treaty on Friendship, Partnership and Cooperation between Italy and Libya: New Prospects for Cooperation in the Mediterranean?", Bulletin of Italian Politics, 2009, No. 1, p. 125 ff.

[5] The Memorandum repeatedly uses the terms "clandestine migrants", "clandestine immigration", "illegal migrants" and "illegal immigration". These terms, however, are no longer used by international organisations and many states. They have been abandoned in favour of the more neutral terms "irregular migrants" and "irregular immigration". See for example Council of Europe, Parliamentary Assembly, Resolution 1509 (2006), 27 June 2006, para. 7.

initiatives aimed at creating lawful jobs in the Libyan regions where migrant smuggling is an income source for local people (Article 2).

A mixed committee, formed of an equal number of members from Italy and Libya, is established, which is charged with identifying the priorities of action, the sources of funding and the modalities of implementation of the obligations undertaken by the Parties (Article 3).

As for Italy, however, it is specified that the activities provided for in the MOU can be financed with EU funds and cannot entail expenses that are not included in the national budget (Article 4). Since the MOU was concluded in simplified form, this clause aimed at preventing allegations of violation of Article 80 of the Italian Constitution, under which treaties entailing expenses not included in the national budget must be concluded in solemn form: the Head of State may ratify them only after being duly authorised by the Parliament.

Actually, allegations of violation of Article 80 of the Italian Constitution are not completely precluded by the above-mentioned provision. According to that Article, "treaties of political nature" must also be concluded in solemn form: their ratification by the Italian President requires authorisation by the Parliament. As the former Minister of Foreign Affairs Susanna Agnelli made clear in 1995, Article 80 refers to treaties of high political relevance, which involve fundamental foreign policy choices.[6] Given the broadness of the material obligations undertaken by the parties, especially by Italy, the MOU in question certainly falls within this category. Therefore, it should not have been concluded in simplified form. In fact, at the end of February 2018, four members of the Parliament lodged an application with the Italian Constitutional Court, claiming a violation of Article 80. In particular, they complained that, owing to the high political relevance of the MOU, the Government should have submitted a draft law authorising the Head of State to ratify it to the Parliament. The Government omitted to do that and, as a result, it undermined the applicants' prerogatives.[7] At the time of writing, the Constitutional Court has not yet decided on the admissibility of the application.

2.   THE SITUATION IN LIBYA

When reading the Gentiloni-Serraj MOU, one gets the impression that the parties deliberately ignored the complexity of the migration phenomenon affecting Libya and the dire living conditions of irregular migrants in that country. First of all, among the tens of thousands of people who illegally cross Libya's southern border and set off for Italy every year, there are not only so-called economic

---

[6] See Circular of the Minister of Foreign Affairs Susanna Agnelli No. 5 of 19 April 1995.

[7] See Association for Juridical Studies on Immigration, "Technical Note on the Application Relating to the Jurisdictional Dispute between Branches of the State Lodged with the Constitutional Court by the Deputies Brignone, Civati, Maestri and Marcon", 27 February 2018, available at: <https://www.asgi.it/wp-content/uploads/2018/02/2018_2_27_ASGI_Libia_Italia_scheda-tecnica.pdf>.

migrants, but also migrants eligible for international protection, namely refugee status or subsidiary protection as defined by EU rules.[8] The MOU does not envisage any cooperation initiative aimed at identifying the individuals eligible for international protection and establishing an appropriate system of protection for them. Indeed, it does not even mention this category of migrants.

Libya is not a party to either the 1951 Convention relating to the status of refugees or its 1967 Protocol, and it does not recognise the right of asylum. Indeed, it is a party to the 1969 Organization of African Unity Convention Governing the Specific Aspects of Refugee Problems in Africa. This treaty contains the same definition of refugee as the 1951 Convention, as amended by the 1967 Protocol, and it stipulates that the states parties "shall use their best endeavours consistent with their respective legislations to receive refugees and to secure the settlement of those refugees who, for well-founded reasons, are unable or unwilling to return to their country of origin or nationality" (Article 2(1)). Under the 2011 Libyan Constitutional Declaration, "the State shall guarantee the right of asylum by virtue of the law" (Article 10).[9] However, at the time of writing, no law on asylum has been enacted.[10] This fact was totally disregarded by the parties to the MOU.

Moreover, under the Libyan legislation enacted during the Gaddafi regime and still in force, illegal entry or stay in Libya is a criminal offence punishable with imprisonment.[11] Migrants illegally entering Libya are held arbitrarily for indefinite periods in detention centres managed by the Department for Combatting Illegal Immigration or other places of detention run by armed groups, without any possibility to challenge the lawfulness of detention.[12] Migrants rescued or intercepted at sea by the Libyan Coast Guard, too, are routinely transferred to the detention centres run by the Department for Combatting Illegal Immigration.[13]

---

[8] See PALM, "The Italy-Libya Memorandum of Understanding: The Baseline of a Policy Approach Aimed at Closing All Doors to Europe?", EU Immigration and Asylum Law and Policy, 2 October 2017, available at: <http://eumigrationlawblog.eu/the-italy-libya-memorandum-of-understanding-the-baseline-of-a-policy-approach-aimed-at-closing-all-doors-to-europe/>.

[9] Constitutional Declaration, Benghazi, 3 August 2011, available at: <https://www.ndi.org/sites/default/files/Handout%204%20-%20Libya%20Draft%20Interim%20Constitution.pdf>.

[10] See United Nations Support Mission in Libya, Office of the United Nations High Commissioner for Human Rights, "'Detained and Dehumanised': Report on Human Rights Abuses against Migrants in Libya", 13 December 2016, pp. 9 and 12, available at: <https://www.ohchr.org/Documents/Countries/LY/DetainedAndDehumanised_en.pdf>; Report of the Secretary-General pursuant to Security Council Resolution 2312 (2016), UN Doc. S/2017/761, 7 September 2017, para. 45; Amnesty International, "Libya's Dark Web of Collusion. Abuses against Europe-bound Refugees and Migrants", December 2017, available at: <https://www.amnesty.org/en/documents/mde19/7561/2017/en/>, p. 20.

[11] "'Detained and Dehumanised'", *cit. supra* note 10, p. 11; "Libya's Dark Web of Collusion", *cit. supra* note 10, p. 20.

[12] "'Detained and Dehumanised'", *cit. supra* note 10, p. 13; "Libya's Dark Web of Collusion", *cit. supra* note 10, pp. 20 and 24.

[13] "'Detained and Dehumanised'", *cit. supra* note 10, pp. 19-20; Report of the Secretary-General pursuant to Security Council Resolution 2312 (2016), *cit. supra* note 10, para. 40; "Libya's Dark Web of Collusion", *cit. supra* note 10, pp. 28 and 40.

As stated in the 2016 report of the UN Support Mission in Libya and the UN Office of the High Commissioner for Human Rights, conditions of detention in such centres are "generally inhuman, falling far short of international human rights standards".[14] They are characterised by severe overcrowding, little ventilation and poor hygiene. Migrants therein constantly suffer from malnutrition and have limited or no access to medical care. They are generally subjected to torture and other ill-treatment by the guards, mostly in order to extort money from their relatives for their release. Women are often victims of rape or other forms of sexual violence.[15] Similar abuses are committed against migrants held in unofficial detention facilities managed by armed groups.[16]

Migrants rescued or intercepted at sea are usually also victims of abuse by the Libyan Coast Guard members, who do not abstain from using firearms, physical violence and threatening language against them. Their very lives are often endangered by Libyan Coast Guard manoeuvres in flagrant disregard of basic security protocols.[17] This is, *inter alia*, a plain violation of the Protocol against the Smuggling of Migrants by Land, Sea and Air supplementing the 2000 UN Convention against Transnational Organized Crime, to which Libya is a party. Under that Protocol, when taking measures against a vessel suspected of being engaged in the smuggling of migrants by sea, states parties are obliged to "ensure the safety and humane treatment of the persons on board" (Article 9(1)(a)). In addition, as Amnesty International documented in its report of December 2017, some members of the Libyan Coast Guard collude with smugglers, by allowing migrant boats to depart or even escorting them during the initial part of the journey in return for payment.[18]

The parties to the MOU knowingly omitted to take account of the above-described situation. The Gentiloni-Serraj agreement fails to address adequately the problem of the protection of the human rights of migrants in Libya. Under Article 5, Italy and Libya simply commit themselves "to interpret and apply the [...] Memorandum in conformity with the international obligations and the human rights treaties to which they are parties". Only an implicit referral to migrants'

---

[14] "'Detained and Dehumanised'", *cit. supra* note 10, p. 15.

[15] "'Detained and Dehumanised'", *cit. supra* note 10, pp. 15-17; Report of the Secretary-General pursuant to Security Council Resolution 2312 (2016), *cit. supra* note 10, paras. 41-43; "Libya's Dark Web of Collusion", *cit. supra* note 10, pp. 22 and 30-33.

[16] "Libya's Dark Web of Collusion", *cit. supra* note 10, p. 20. In October 2017, the *Corte d'Assise di Milano* ascertained the horrific abuses suffered by hundreds of migrants in an unofficial detention centre in Bani Walid, between the beginning of 2015 and mid-2016. It convicted the former head of the centre, Osman Matammud, of abduction, sexual violence and abetment of illegal immigration, and sentenced him to life imprisonment. See *Corte d'Assise di Milano, Criminal proceedings against Matammud Osman*, Judgment of 10 October 2017, available at: <https://www.penalecontemporaneo.it/upload/1875-sentenza-matammud.pdf>.

[17] See Report of the Secretary-General pursuant to Security Council Resolution 2312 (2016), *cit. supra* note 10, para. 6; "Libya's Dark Web of Collusion", *cit. supra* note 10, pp. 35 and 36.

[18] "Libya's Dark Web of Collusion", *cit. supra* note 10, pp. 37-40. See also "The Kingpin of Libya's Human Trafficking Mafia", TRTWorld, 22 February 2017, available at: <https://www.trtworld.com/magazine/libya-human-trafficking-mafia-in-zawiya-301505>.

right to health is contained in Article 2(2), according to which Italy is bound to contribute medicines and medical equipment, in order to alleviate the conditions of irregular migrants suffering from severe transmissible or chronic diseases in Libya. In the light of the blatant violations of migrants' most fundamental human rights routinely committed in Libya, the aforementioned provisions are thoroughly unsatisfactory.

3. EU SUPPORT FOR ITALY'S MIGRATION CONTROL MEASURES

Despite its flaws, the Gentiloni-Serraj MOU was immediately endorsed by the EU. In the informal summit held the day after its signature, on 3 February 2017, in Malta, the EU Heads of State or Government adopted the so-called Malta Declaration, in which they welcomed the Memorandum, affirmed their readiness to support Italy in its implementation and agreed on a set of measures to stem the flow of irregular migrants from Libya to Italy. Such measures included: (1) training, equipment and support to the Libyan Coast Guard; (2) the implementation of an enhanced operational action against smugglers; (3) support for the development of Libyan local communities, particularly in coastal areas and at land borders on the migratory routes; (4) cooperation with the Government of National Accord and Libya's neighbouring states, in order to reduce migratory pressure on Libyan land borders; (5) assistance in ensuring adequate reception conditions for migrants in Libya; and (6) support to the International Organization for Migration in increasing assisted voluntary return operations.[19]

Following the Malta Declaration, in April 2017, the EU Trust Fund for Africa adopted a 90-million-euro programme to reinforce the protection of migrants in Libya and improve the socio-economic development of Libyan local communities in coastal areas and along migratory routes.[20]

In June 2017, in the light of a substantial increase in the sea arrivals of migrants in Italy from Libya, the European Council decided to step up the implementation of the measures listed in the Malta Declaration.[21] A few days later, the European Commission proposed an action plan to support Italy and accelerate EU efforts aimed at reducing the flow of migrants along the Central Mediterranean route.[22]

---

[19] Malta Declaration by the Members of the European Council on the External Aspects of Migration: Addressing the Central Mediterranean Route, 3 February 2017, available at: <http://www.consilium.europa.eu/en/press/press-releases/2017/02/03/malta-declaration/pdf>.

[20] European Commission, "Press Release: EU Trust Fund for Africa adopts €90 Million Programme on Protection of Migrants and Improved Migration Management in Libya", 12 April 2017, available at: <http://europa.eu/rapid/press-release_IP-17-951_en.pdf>.

[21] European Council Meeting (22 and 23 June 2017) – Conclusions, 23 June 2017, available at: <http://www.consilium.europa.eu/media/23985/22-23-euco-final-conclusions.pdf>.

[22] European Commission, "Action Plan on Measures to Support Italy, Reduce Pressure along the Central Mediterranean Route and Increase Solidarity", 4 July 2017, available at: <https://ec.europa.eu/home-affairs/sites/homeaffairs/files/what-we-do/policies/european-agenda-migration/20170704_action_plan_on_the_central_mediterranean_route_en.pdf>.

On the basis of this action plan, at the end of July 2017, the EU Trust Fund for Africa adopted a 46-million-euro programme to enhance the operational capacities of the Coast Guard and the Border Guard of Libya, which would be co-financed by Italy and implemented by its Ministry of the Interior.[23]

4.   ITALIAN ASSISTANCE TO THE LIBYAN COAST GUARD

Italy's action in support to the Libyan Coast Guard started at the beginning of 2017. On 14 January 2017, Gentiloni's Government decided to establish an assistance mission to the Libyan Coast Guard, on the basis of the Protocol of Cooperation between Italy and Libya and the Additional Technical-Operational Protocol to it, which had been signed in Tripoli at the end of 2007.[24] On 8 March 2017, the Government decision was approved by the Parliament, in accordance with Law No. 145 of 21 July 2016.[25] The assistance mission was entrusted to the Revenue Police (*Guardia di Finanza*) and was to last until 31 December 2017. The Revenue Police were mandated to conduct training cruises and patrolling activities on board ships that had been temporarily ceded by Italy to Libya in 2009 and 2010, and to provide ordinary maintenance of them. In fact, four of those ships, which had been damaged during the 2011 armed conflict, were repaired in Italy and returned to the Serraj Government in April and May 2017.[26] The mandate of the assistance mission was subsequently extended until 31 December 2018.[27]

---

[23] European Commission, "Press Release: EU Trust Fund for Africa Adopts €46 Million Programme to Support Integrated Migration and Border Management in Libya", 28 July 2017, available at: <http://europa.eu/rapid/press-release_IP-17-2187_en.htm>.

[24] Deliberation of the Council of Ministers Relating to the Participation of Italy in International Operations, 14 January 2017, Doc. CCL No. 1, pp. 53 and 54. See Protocol of Cooperation between Italy and Libya, Tripoli, 29 December 2007, available at: <http://briguglio.asgi.it/immigrazione-e-asilo/2009/maggio/prot-italia-libia-2007.pdf>; Additional Technical-Operational Protocol, Tripoli, 29 December 2007, available at: <http://www.asgi.it/wp-content/uploads/public/protocollo.italia.libia.tripoli.dicembre.2007.pdf>.

[25] See Senate, Assembly, Verbatim Record, Meeting No. 780 (Afternoon), 8 March 2017, pp. 23-78; Chamber of Deputies, Verbatim Record, Meeting No. 755, 8 March 2017, pp. 16-41. Law No. 145 of 21 July 2016 (GU No. 178 of 1 August 2016) regulates the deployment of the Italian armed forces abroad. Interestingly, under its Article 1(1), the deployment of Italian forces abroad is allowed, *inter alia*, on condition that their mandate is consistent with international human rights law. On the law at issue, see RONZITTI, "La legge italiana sulle missioni internazionali", RDI, 2017, p. 474 ss.

[26] "Minniti ad Abu Sittah consegna altri due pattugliatori ai libici", Analisi Difesa, 16 May 2017, available at: <http://www.analisidifesa.it/2017/05/minniti-ad-abu-sittah-consegna-altrui-due-pattugliatori-ai-libici/>.

[27] Analytical Report on the Ongoing International Operations and Development Cooperation Actions in Support to Peacebuilding Processes, Approved by the Council of Ministers on 28 December 2017, Doc. CCL-bis No. 1, pp. 173 and 192-193. The Parliament approved the Government's decision to extend the mandate of the assistance mission in January 2018. See Senate, Commissions III (Foreign Affairs, Migration) and IV (Defence), Meeting No. 33, 15

In addition, Italy readily granted the Government of National Accord's request for further support to the Libyan Coast Guard, on the basis of the MOU of 2 February 2017. On 28 July 2017, Gentiloni's Government decided to establish a combined air and naval operation, to be conducted from 1 August to 31 December 2017, with personnel and assets detached from the ongoing operation "Mare Sicuro". The mandate of this new operation included: (1) protecting the Libyan vessels involved in activities against irregular immigration, in the territorial sea and internal waters controlled by the Government of National Accord; (2) providing advice to the Libyan Coast Guard and Navy; (3) supporting the establishment of an operational centre for maritime surveillance and coordination of joint maritime activities in Libya; (4) cooperating in the maintenance and repair of Libyan infrastructures and assets to be used in the fight against irregular immigration.[28] The Parliament rapidly approved the Government decision, in accordance with the above-mentioned Law No. 145 of 2016.[29] Hence, in the first half of August, the patrol boat "Comandante Borsini" and the workshop ship "Tremiti" arrived at the Abu Sittah Naval Base, in Tripoli.[30] A coordination centre was temporarily installed on board the latter. Thanks to the repair work by the Italian personnel, two Libyan patrol boats were made operational again before the end of August.[31] In November, activities aimed at repairing the infrastructures of the Mitiga Airport, in Tripoli, and the C-130H aircraft therein started.[32]

The mandate of the above-described operation was subsequently extended until 30 September 2018.[33] However, the task of cooperating in the maintenance and repair of Libyan infrastructure and assets to be used in the fight against irregular immigration was transferred to another mission in support to the Government of National Accord, which Gentiloni's Government decided to establish at the end of December 2017.[34] This mission was to last until 30 September 2018 and was

---

January 2018, p. 5 ff.; Chamber of Deputies, Verbatim Record, Meeting No. 905, 17 January 2018, p. 2 ff.

[28] Deliberation of the Council of Ministers Relating to the Participation of Italy in the International Operation in Support to the Libyan Coast Guard, 28 July 2017, Doc. CCL No. 2, p. 6.

[29] See Chamber of Deputies, Verbatim Records, Meeting No. 847, 2 August 2017, pp. 1-49; Senate, Assembly, Verbatim Records, Meeting No. 871, 2 August 2017, pp. 41-72.

[30] "Nave Tremiti nel porto libico di Abu Sittah", Analisi Difesa, 10 August 2017, available at: <http://www.analisidifesa.it/2017/08/nave-tremiti-nel-porto-libico-di-abu-sittah/>.

[31] Joint Commissions III and IV of the Senate and III and IV of the Chamber of Deputies, Communication of the Government on the Operation in Support to the Libyan Coast Guard Deliberated by the Council of Ministers on 28 July 2017 (DOC. CCL No. 2), Verbatim Record, Meeting No. 30, 28 September 2017, p. 14.

[32] Analytical Report, cit. supra note 27, p. 101.

[33] Ibid., pp. 173 and 192-193. The Parliament approved the Government's decision to extend the mandate of the assistance mission in January 2018. See Senate, Commissions III (Foreign Affairs, Migration) and IV (Defence), Meeting No. 33, 15 January 2018, p. 5 ff.; Chamber of Deputies, Verbatim Record, Meeting No. 905, 17 January 2018, p. 2 ff.

[34] Deliberation of the Council of Ministers Relating to the Participation of Italy in International Operations to Be Established in 2018, 28 December 2017, Doc. CCL No. 3, p. 4 ff. The Government's decision to establish another mission in support of the Government of National Accord was approved by the Parliament in January 2018. See Senate, Commissions

assigned, *inter alia*, the task of training and providing mentoring to the Libyan security forces in the field of operations against irregular immigration.[35]

In this regard, it is to be stressed that since 2016 Italy has been providing training to the Libyan Coast Guard and Navy also in the framework of the EUNAVFOR MED Operation Sophia, an EU military crisis management operation, whose primary objective is "contributing to the disruption of the business model of human smuggling and trafficking networks in the Southern Central Mediterranean".[36] From September 2016 to October 2017, about one hundred members of the Libyan Coast Guard and Navy attended training courses in Rome, Taranto and on board the Italian ship "San Giorgio".[37]

6. THE ITALIAN CODE OF CONDUCT FOR NGOS INVOLVED IN MIGRANT RESCUE
    AND THE LIBYAN SEARCH AND RESCUE ZONE

As recommended by the European Commission in the above-mentioned action plan, in July 2017, the Italian Ministry of the Interior drafted a code of conduct for NGOs carrying out search and rescue activities in the Mediterranean Sea.[38] Such NGOs were requested to sign the code and comply with it.[39] The signatories commit themselves, *inter alia*, "not to enter Libyan territorial waters, except in situations of grave and imminent danger requiring immediate assistance and not to obstruct search and rescue by the Libyan Coast Guard". In case of non-compliance or failure to subscribe to the code, the Italian authorities may adopt unspecified measures against the relevant vessels "in compliance with applicable domestic and international law and as required in the public interest of saving

---

III (Foreign Affairs, Migration) and IV (Defence), Meeting No. 33, 15 January 2018, p. 5 ff.; Chamber of Deputies, Verbatim Record, Meeting No. 905, 17 January 2018, p. 2 ff.

[35] Deliberation of the Council of Ministers, *cit. supra* note 34, p. 4 ff.

[36] Council Decision (CFSP) 2015/778 of 18 May 2015 (OJ EU L122 of 19 May 2015), Art. 1(1). The mandate of EUNAVFOR MED Operation Sophia was broadened to include the training of the Libyan Coast Guard and Navy, by Council Decision (CFSP) 2016/993 of 20 June 2016 (OJ EU L162 of 21 June 2016). On EUNAVFORMED Operation Sophia see among others: GESTRI, "EUNAVFORMED: Fighting Migrant Smuggling under UN Security Council Resolution 2240 (2015)", IYIL, 2015, p. 21 ff.; D'ARGENT and KURITZKY, "Refoulement by Proxy? The Mediterranean Migrant Crisis and the Training of Libyan Coast Guards by EUNAVFOR MED Operation Sophia", Israel Yearbook on Human Rights, 2017, p. 233 ff.

[37] Analytical Report, *cit. supra* note 27, p. 38.

[38] On the European Commission action plan, see *amplius supra* Section 4.

[39] Code of Conduct for NGOs Involved in Migrant Rescue at Sea, Rome, 7 August 2017, available at: <http://www.interno.gov.it/sites/default/files/codice_condotta_ong.pdf>. For comment, see: PAPANICOLOPULU, "Immigrazione irregolare via mare, tutela della vita umana e organizzazioni non governative", Diritto, Immigrazione e Cittadinanza, 2017, No. 3, p. 1 ff., p. 24 ff.; FERRI, "Il Codice di condotta per le ONG e i diritti dei migranti: fra diritto internazionale e politiche europee", DUDI, 2018, p. 189 ff.; GOMBEER and FINK, "Non-Governmental Organisations and Search and Rescue at Sea", Maritime Safety and Security Law Journal, 2018, No. 4, p. 1 ff., p. 4 ff.; RAMACCIOTTI, "Sulla utilità di un codice di condotta per le organizzazioni non governative impegnate in attività di *search and rescue* (SAR)", RDI, 2018, p. 213 ff.

human lives while guaranteeing shared and sustainable reception of migration flows".[40] Most of the NGOs involved in migrant rescue in the Mediterranean signed the code, including Migrant Offshore Aid Station (MOAS), Proactiva Open Arms, Save the Children and SOS Méditerranée.[41]

Soon afterwards, on 10 August 2017, the Libyan Navy announced the establishment of a Libyan search and rescue region (SAR Region) in accordance with the 1979 International Convention on Maritime Search and Rescue (SAR Convention), to which Libya is a party, and demanded that foreign vessels, in particular NGO ones, should not conduct rescue operations within it, without prior authorisation from the Libyan authorities.[42] In fact, the would-be Libyan SAR Region was notified to the Secretary-General of the International Maritime Organization (IMO) in accordance with the SAR Convention, in July 2017. In December 2017, however, the Libyan communication was withdrawn, as it was inaccurate, and it was replaced with another.[43] The new communication stated that the Libyan SAR Region coincides with the Tripoli Flight Information Region (FIR), already notified to the International Civil Aviation Organization. However, it did not provide any of the information on the national search and rescue service that the SAR Convention requires (Annex, paragraph 2.1.11, as amended).[44]

The adoption of the above-mentioned code of conduct and the Tripoli authorities' insistence that no rescue operation be conducted in the would-be Libyan SAR Region without their prior authorisation severely hampered NGOs search and rescue activities in the Libyan territorial sea and the high seas off the Libyan coast, while simultaneously increasing those of the Libyan Coast Guard, which – as already noted – systematically transfers rescued or intercepted migrants to the detention centres run by the Department for Combatting Illegal Immigration.[45] Apart from any other consideration, such course of conduct by the Libyan Coast Guard, as facilitated by the Italian authorities, amounts to a glaring breach of the SAR Convention, whose Annex, as amended in 1998, defines "rescue" as "an operation to retrieve persons in distress, provide for their initial medical or other needs, and deliver them to a place of safety" (paragraph 1.3.2).[46] According to the Guidelines on the Treatment of Persons Rescued at

---

[40] Code of Conduct for NGOs, cit. supra note 39.

[41] Ministry of the Interior, "Codice di condotta per il salvataggio dei migranti, arriva la firma della Ong Sos Mediterranée", 11 agosto 2017, available at: <http://www.interno.gov.it/it/notizie/codice-condotta-salvataggio-dei-migranti-arriva-firma-ong-sos-mediterranee>.

[42] "Libya Navy Bars Foreign Ships from Migrant 'Search and Rescue' Zone", Daily Mail, 10 August 2017, available at: <http://www.dailymail.co.uk/wires/afp/article-4779316/Libya-navy-bars-foreign-ships-migrant-search-rescue-zone.html>.

[43] Letter of the President of Libyan Ports and Maritime Transport Authority, 14 December 2017.

[44] See also International Maritime Organization, Global Integrated Shipping Information System, available at: <https://gisis.imo.org/Public/Default.aspx>.

[45] See amplius supra Section 3.

[46] Maritime Safety Committee, Resolution MSC.70(69), 18 May 1998, available at: <http://www.imo.org/en/KnowledgeCentre/IndexofIMOResolutions/Maritime-Safety-Committee-(MSC)/Documents/MSC.70(69).pdf>.

Sea, adopted by the IMO Maritime Safety Committee in 2004, "place of safety" means "a place where the survivors' safety of life is no longer threatened and where their basic human needs (such as food, shelter and medical needs) can be met" (paragraph 6.12).[47] In the light of the situation described in the preceding pages, this is certainly not Libya today.[48] As the Office of the UN High Commissioner for Refugees rightly pointed out, this country evidently does not fulfill the criteria for being considered a place of safety for the purpose of disembarkation following rescue at sea.[49]

It is to be noted also that the requirement of prior authorisation from Libyan authorities for NGOs to rescue migrants in the would-be Libyan SAR Region has no legal basis in the SAR Convention. In addition, it is not consistent with the duty to assist persons in distress at sea, which is enshrined in the 1974 International Convention for the Safety of Life at Sea (Chapter V, Regulation 33(1)), the 1982 UN Convention on the Law of the Sea (Article 98(1)) and the 1989 International Convention on Salvage (Article 10(1)) and widely recognised as having customary international law status.[50] The obligation of the shipmaster to render assistance to persons in distress at sea is not geographically limited.[51] In particular, the shipmaster is not released from such obligation in the SAR Region of a coastal State. The SAR Convention stipulates that states parties "shall ensure that assistance be provided to any person in distress at sea" (Annex, paragraph 2.1.10), and only requires them to co-ordinate their search and rescue organisations and, whenever necessary, search and rescue operations with those of neighbouring states (Annex, paragraph 3.1.1, as amended).[52]

---

[47] Maritime Safety Committee, Resolution MSC.167(78), 20 May 2004, available at: <http://www.imo.org/en/OurWork/Facilitation/personsrescued/Documents/MSC.167(78).pdf>.

[48] See *supra* Section 3.

[49] United Nations High Commissioner for Refugees, "UNHCR Position on Returns to Libya, Update I", October 2015, available at: <http://www.refworld.org/docid/561cd8804.html>, para. 33.

[50] See NOYES, "Ships in Distress", Max Planck Encyclopedia of Public International Law, October 2007, available at: <http://opil.ouplaw.com/home/epil>, para. 6; PROELSS, "Rescue at Sea Revisited: What Obligations Exist Towards Refugees?", Scandinavian Institute of Maritime Law Yearbook, 2008, p. 1 ff., p. 9; GALLAGHER and DAVID, *The International Law of Migrant Smuggling*, Cambridge, 2014, p. 446; PAPANICOLOPULU, *International Law and the Protection of People at Sea*, Oxford, 2018, p. 187 ff.

[51] See PROELSS, *cit. supra* note 50, p. 12 ff.; KOMP, "The Duty to Assist Persons in Distress: An Alternative Source of Protection against the Return of Migrants and Asylum Seekers to the High Seas?", in MORENO-LAX and PAPASTAVRIDIS (eds.), *'Boat Refugees' and Migrants at Sea: A Comprehensive Approach*, Leiden/Boston, 2017, p. 222 ff., p. 230; PAPANICOLOPULU, *International Law*, *cit. supra* note 50, p. 187 ff.

[52] See CAMPÀS VELASCO, "The International Convention on Maritime Search and Rescue: Legal Mechanism of Responsibility Sharing and Cooperation in the Context of Sea Migration?", Irish Yearbook of International Law, 2015, p. 57 ff.

7. THE ITALIAN ACTION TO REINFORCE LIBYA'S SOUTHERN BORDER CONTROL
    CAPACITY

Backed by the EU, Gentiloni's Government also took action in order to prevent the illegal entry into Libya of migrants headed to Italy. Every year, tens of
thousands of people illegally enter Libya, through its southern border. Acting
on the basis of the MOU of 2 February 2017, Italy made substantial efforts to
reinforce Libya's capacity to control its southern border, in the belief expressed
by the Minister of the Interior Marco Minniti that "sealing off Libya's southern
border means sealing off Europe's southern border".[53]

Most of the irregular migrants coming from Sub-Saharan Africa enter Libya
through the Fezzan border. Fezzan is a region lying in southwestern Libya, which
is nominally under the authority of the Government of National Accord, but is in
fact controlled by local tribes, often in conflict with each other.[54] Their militias
control the border areas and the smuggling routes. In particular, the Tebu tribe
controls the smuggling routes from Niger up to Sabha, Fezzan's administrative
capital. There migrants are transferred to the Awlad Suleiman tribe.[55]

As a first step, the Italian Government acted as mediator between the Fezzan's
tribes aiming at their reconciliation, with the ultimate purpose of obtaining their
commitment to stop migrant smuggling activities and convert their militiamen
into zealous border guards, in exchange for financial support for the region's
development. A meeting was organised by the Ministry of the Interior in Rome at
the end of March 2017, which was attended by the representatives of about sixty
tribes. During this meeting, representatives of the Tebu and the Awlad Suleiman
signed a peace deal, the text of which however has never been disclosed.[56]

Afterwards, in July and August 2017, Minniti met, respectively, in Tripoli
and Rome with the mayors of the Libyan towns most affected by the phenomenon of irregular immigration, in order to discuss Italy's economic assistance to
Libyan local communities in exchange for their cooperation in the fight against
irregular immigration and migrant smuggling. For such assistance Italy would
use funds made available by the EU Trust Fund for Africa.[57] No details about it
however were revealed.

---

[53] "Libia, le tribù del Sud siglano la pace e si impegnano a bloccare i migranti", La
Stampa, 2 April 2017, available at: <http://www.lastampa.it/2017/04/02/esteri/libia-le-trib-
del-sud-siglano-la-pace-e-si-impegnano-a-bloccare-i-migranti-qzNs23DGe0OSdJi7G285FK/
pagina.html>.

[54] See International Crisis Group, "How Libya's Fezzan Became Europe's New Border",
31 July 2017, available at: <https://d2071andvip0wj.cloudfront.net/179-how-libyas-fezzan-
became-europes-new-border.pdf>.

[55] FRONTEX, "Africa-Frontex Intelligence Community Joint Report 2016", April 2017,
p. 17.

[56] "Libia, le tribù del Sud siglano la pace", cit. supra note 53.

[57] See "Minniti ai sindaci: aiuti in cambio di un'azione di contrasto ai migranti", il
Manifesto, 14 July 2017, available at: <https://ilmanifesto.it/minniti-ai-sindaci-libici-aiuti-in-
cambio-di-unazione-di-contrasto-ai-migranti/>; Ministry of the Interior, "Minniti e i sindaci
delle comunità libiche: i trafficanti sono un nemico comune", 26 August 2017, available at:

Indeed, the Italian Government had no choice but to engage in direct dialogue with the Libyan local communities, since the Government of National Accord has no effective control over its territory. Nevertheless, this very circumstance raises doubts about how it can be ensured that such communities respect their commitments, as they are responsible only to the central Government. Moreover, there is no guarantee that they would make respect for migrants' human rights a priority, when trying to curb irregular immigration and smuggling activities. These concerns are aggravated by the total lack of transparency about the deals that the Italian Government struck with the aforementioned communities.[58]

8. THE ITALIAN ACTION TO REINFORCE CHAD'S AND NIGER'S BORDER CONTROL CAPACITY

In spring 2017, Gentiloni's Government also began cooperation with Chad and Niger, Libya's neighbouring countries through which most of the migrants headed to Italy pass, with the aim of strengthening their border control capacity. On 21 May 2017, in Rome, at the Ministry of the Interior's premises, Minniti met with the Ministers of the Interior of Chad, Libya and Niger. In the joint communiqué issued at the end of the meeting, they stressed the necessity of cooperating in the fight against terrorism and human trafficking, with the objective of ensuring border security, and supporting the training and enhancement of border guards, through regular contact between border control forces. They also announced the decision to create a consultative forum on border security and on the fight against terrorism, human trafficking and irregular immigration.[59]

The involvement of Chad and Niger in the containment of migratory flows was praised by France, Germany, Spain and the EU during the Paris Summit of 28 August 2017. The Heads of State or Government of France, Germany, Italy, Spain, Chad and Niger, the Prime Minister of the Libyan Government of National Accord and the High Representative of the EU for Foreign Affairs and Security Policy attended. In the joint declaration issued after the Summit, France, Germany, Italy, Spain and the EU expressed, *inter alia*, their readiness to further support Chad and Niger in the fight against human trafficking and irregular im-

---

<http://www.interno.gov.it/it/notizie/minniti-e-i-sindaci-comunita-libiche-i-trafficanti-sono-nemico-comune>.

[58] See "Libya's Dark Web of Collusion", *cit. supra* note 10, p. 50.

[59] Joint Communiqué of the Ministers of the Interior of Italy, Chad and Niger, 21 May 2017, available at: <http://www.interno.gov.it/it/sala-stampa/comunicati-stampa/comunicato-congiunto-dei-ministri-dellinterno-italia-ciad-libia-niger>. Subsequently, Mali joined the initiative. In this respect, see Ministry of the Interior, "Incontro al Viminale tra il Ministro Minniti e il Ministro del Mali Coulibaly. Cabina di regia con Italia, Ciad, Libia e Niger", 28 July 2017, available at: <http://www.interno.gov.it/it/sala-stampa/comunicati-stampa/incontro-viminale-ministro-minniti-e-ministro-mali-coulibaly-cabina-regia-italia-ciad-libia-e-niger>; "Immigrazione, seconda riunione della 'Cabina di Regia' dei Ministri dell'interno di Ciad, Italia, Libia, Mali e Niger", 28 August 2017, available at: <http://www.interno.gov.it/it/notizie/immigrazione-riunione-viminale-cabina-regia-ciad-italia-libia-mali-e-niger>.

migration, by strengthening current programmes aimed at improving control of their borders, in particular those with Libya.[60]

Finally, at the end of December 2017, the Italian Government decided to establish a combined air and land operation to support Niger's authorities, at their request, on the basis of the bilateral agreement on security and defence cooperation, which had been signed in September 2017. The Italian forces were tasked with assisting the Nigerien Government in developing national security forces and concurring in territory and border surveillance. The planned duration of the operation was ten months.[61] Despite some opposition, Gentiloni's Government decision received Parliament's approval.[62] At the time of writing, however, the Italian forces have not yet been deployed in Niger.[63] If and when deployment takes place, they will be bound to act in accordance with Italy's human rights obligations. In this respect, participation of Italian military personnel in the surveillance of Nigerien borders might prove problematic, where it implied forcible prevention of migrants' departures from Niger.

9. ITALY'S COMPLICITY IN THE VIOLATIONS OF MIGRANTS' HUMAN RIGHTS IN LIBYA

Italy's new migration control measures, in particular the active support to the Libyan Coast Guard and the adoption of a code of conduct for NGOs involved in migrant rescue, rapidly led to a significant reduction in the number of migrants arriving in Italy (33,288 between July and November 2017, 67% less than in the same period of 2016, according to Amnesty International)[64] and, simultaneously, to a sharp increase in that of migrants intercepted at sea by the Libyan Coast Guard and transferred to the detention centres run by the Department for Combatting Illegal Immigration (19,900 migrants detained at the beginning of November 2017, according to the Department).[65] As a consequence of the growth in the number of migrants held in such centres, the already inhuman conditions of

---

[60] European Commission, "Press Release: Déclaration conjointe 'Relever le défi de la migration et de l'asile'", Paris, 28 August 2017, available at: <http://europa.eu/rapid/press-release_STATEMENT-17-2981_fr.htm>.

[61] Deliberation of the Council of Ministers, *cit. supra* note 34, p. 6.

[62] See Senate, Commissions III (Foreign Affairs, Migration) and IV (Defence), Meeting No. 33, 15 January 2018, p. 5 ff.; Chamber of Deputies, Verbatim Record, Meeting No. 905, 17 January 2018, p. 2 ff.

[63] In March 2017, the Nigerien Minister of the Interior denied that the deployment of Italian troops had been requested by the Nigerien Government. See "Ministro Interni del Niger: nessun accordo con l'Italia per una missione militare", Rainews, 9 March 2018, available at: <http://www.rainews.it/dl/rainews/media/Niger-Ministro-Interni-nessun-accordo-con-Italia-per-missione-militare-b4e83ed6-e3a7-4e87-b59b-0ffd9a410ab3.html>.

[64] "Libya's Dark Web of Collusion", *cit. supra* note 10, p. 43.

[65] Office of the United Nations High Commissioner for Human Rights, "UN Human Rights Chief: Suffering of Migrants in Libya Outrage to Conscience of Humanity", 14 November 2017, available at: <http://www.ohchr.org/EN/NewsEvents/Pages/DisplayNews.aspx?NewsID=22393&LangID=E>.

detention therein further worsened, as denounced by the UN High Commissioner for Human Rights Zeid Ra'ad Al Hussein in November 2017. He affirmed that "the suffering of migrants detained in Libya is an outrage to the conscience of humanity".[66]

Indeed, by providing assistance to the Libyan Coast Guard and restricting NGOs search and rescue activities by means of the said code of conduct, Italy became complicit in the grave violations of human rights against migrants intercepted at sea and transferred to the above-described detention facilities, in particular of the right not to be subjected to torture or ill-treatment.[67]

The prohibition of torture and inhuman or degrading treatment is at the heart of human rights protection. In addition to the Universal Declaration of Human Rights (Article 5), it is enshrined in: the International Covenant on Civil and Political Rights (Article 7), to which both Libya and Italy are parties; the European Convention on Human Rights (ECHR) (Article 3) and the Charter of Fundamental Rights of the European Union (Article 4), by which Italy is bound; and the African Charter on Human and Peoples' Rights (Article 5), to which Libya is a party.[68] It is an absolute prohibition, from which no derogation is allowed even in time of armed conflict or other emergency threatening the life of the nation, including a large and sudden inflow of migrants, according to the International Covenant on Civil and Political Rights (Article 4) and the ECHR (Article 15).[69] The prohibition of torture is a peremptory norm of general international law. Its *jus cogens* status has been asserted by the Human Rights

---

[66] *Ibid.*

[67] On the complicity of Italy and the other EU member states in the violations of migrants' human rights in Libya, see "Libya's Dark Web of Collusion", *cit. supra* note 10, pp. 51 ff., 60.

[68] See also the UN Convention against Torture, to which both Libya and Italy are parties. It requires states parties to prevent in any territory under their jurisdiction acts of torture (Art. 2(1)) and other acts of inhuman or degrading treatment, when committed by or at the instigation of or with the consent or acquiescence of a public official or other person acting in an official capacity (Art. 16(1)). States parties are also obliged to ensure that all acts of torture are criminal offences under domestic law (Art. 4). On the prohibition of torture and inhuman or degrading treatment, see among others: NOWAK, *UN Covenant on Civil and Political Rights. CCPR Commentary*, 2nd revised ed., Kehel, 2005, p. 157 ff.; VAN BOVEN, "The Prohibition of Torture: Norm and Practice", in DUPUY, FASSBENDER, SHAW and SOMMERMANN (eds.), *Common Values in International Law. Essays in Honour of Christian Tomuschat*, Kehel, 2006, p. 91 ff.; VILJOEN and ODINKALU, *The Prohibition of Torture and Ill-treatment in the African Human Rights System*, Geneva, 2006; NOWAK and McARTHUR, *The United Nations Convention against Torture. A Commentary*, Oxford, 2008; KRETZMER, "Torture, Prohibition of", Max Planck Encyclopedia of Public International Law, December 2010, available at: <http://opil.ouplaw.com/home/epil>; DELAPLACE, "Article 7", in DECAUX (ed.), *Le Pact international relatif aux droits civils et politiques. Commentaire article par article*, Paris, 2011, p. 201 ff.; SCHABAS, *The European Convention on Human Rights. A Commentary*, Oxford, 2015, p. 164 ff.; VERMEULEN and BATTJES, "Prohibition of Torture and Other Inhuman or Degrading Treatment or Punishment", in VAN DIJK, VAN HOOF, VAN RIJN and ZWAAK (ed.), *Theory and Practice of the European Convention on Human Rights*, 5th ed., Cambridge-Antwerp-Portland, 2018, p. 381 ff.

[69] See among others: NOWAK, *UN Covenant, cit. supra* note 68, p. 83 ff.; BALGUY-GALLOIS, "Article 4", in DECAUX (ed.), *cit. supra* note 68, p. 147 ff.; SCHABAS, *cit. supra* note

Committee,[70] the International Criminal Tribunal for the former Yugoslavia,[71] the International Law Commission,[72] the Committee against Torture[73] and, more recently, the International Court of Justice in the *Belgium v. Senegal* case.[74] There is some uncertainty only about the peremptory character of the prohibition of inhuman and degrading treatment,[75] which however is without doubt part of customary international law, as was held by the International Court of Justice in the *Diallo* case.[76]

Italy's complicity in violations of the prohibition of torture and ill-treatment against migrants intercepted at sea by the Libyan Coast Guard and transferred to the governmental detention facilities in Libya can be asserted on the basis of the principle laid down in Article 16 of the 2001 International Law Commission's Draft Articles on Responsibility of States for Internationally Wrongful Acts. Under this Article, which the International Court of Justice deemed to reflect a customary rule in the *Genocide* case,[77] "a State which aids or assists another State in the commission of an internationally wrongful act by the latter is internationally responsible for doing so if: (a) that State does so with knowledge of the circumstances of the internationally wrongful act; and (b) the act would be internationally wrongful if committed by that State".[78] In the case at issue, all the aforementioned conditions are fulfilled. Firstly, it is evident that, in order to stem the inflow of irregular migrants from Libya, Italy intended to facilitate their interception by the Libyan Coast Guard and their forcible return to Libyan soil, where they are held in detention centres managed by the Department for Combatting

---

68, p. 587 ff.; SOTTIAUX, "Derogation in Time of Emergency", in VAN DIJK, VAN HOOF, VAN RIJN and ZWAAK (ed.), *cit. supra* note 68, p. 1063 ff.

[70] Human Rights Committee, General Comment No. 24, UN Doc. CCPR/C/21/Rev.1/Add.6, 11 November 1994, para. 10.

[71] Trial Chamber, *Prosecutor v. Anto Furundzija*, Case No. IT-95-17/1-T, Judgment of 10 December 1998, para. 153.

[72] Draft Articles on Responsibility of States for Internationally Wrongful Acts with commentaries, YILC, 2001, Vol. II, Part Two, p. 113, para. 5.

[73] Committee against Torture, General Comment No. 2, UN Doc. CAT/C/GC/2, 24 January 2008, para. 1.

[74] *Questions relating to the Obligation to Prosecute or Extradite (Belgium v. Senegal)*, Judgment of 20 July 2012, ICJ Reports, 2012, p. 422 ff., p. 457, para. 99.

[75] See FOCARELLI, *La persona umana nel diritto internazionale*, Bologna, 2013, p. 13.

[76] *Ahmadou Sadio Diallo (Republic of Guinea v. Democratic Republic of the Congo)*, Judgment of 30 November 2010, ICJ Reports, 2010, p. 639 ff., p. 671, para. 87.

[77] *Application of the Convention on the Prevention and Punishment of the Crime of Genocide (Bosnia and Herzegovina v. Serbia and Montenegro)*, Judgment of 26 February 2007, ICJ Reports, 2007, p. 43 ff., p. 217, para. 420.

[78] Draft Articles on Responsibility of States for Internationally Wrongful Acts with commentaries, *cit. supra* note 72, p. 27. On complicity in an internationally wrongful act, see, among others, DOMINICÉ, "Attribution of Conduct to Multiple States and the Implication of a State in the Act of Another State", in CRAWFORD, PELLET and OLLESON (eds.) *The Law of International Responsibility*, Oxford, 2010, p. 281 ff.; JACKSON, *Complicity in International Law*, Oxford, 2015, p. 135 ss.; LANOVOY, *Complicity and Its Limits in the Law of International Responsibility*, Oxford-Portland, 2016; PUMA, *Complicità di Stati nell'illecito internazionale*, Torino, 2018.

Illegal Immigration. Secondly, there is no doubt that the Italian Government was perfectly aware of the inhuman conditions of detention of irregular migrants in Libya, in the light of the reiterated denunciations by the UN organs,[79] the International Organization for Migration[80] and human rights NGOs.[81] Thirdly, acts of torture and ill-treatment against irregular migrants would constitute internationally wrongful acts even if they were committed directly by Italy.

The state of necessity, to which the Minister of the Interior Minniti implicitly referred in some declarations, could not be invoked as a ground for precluding the wrongfulness of Italy's behaviour. Under Article 26 of the above-mentioned Draft Articles on Responsibility of States for Internationally Wrongful Acts, circumstances precluding wrongfulness cannot justify a breach of a *jus cogens* rule.[82] Therefore, necessity cannot excuse violations of the prohibition of torture.

As to the violations of the obligation not to subject anyone to inhuman or degrading treatment, they could possibly be justified by necessity, if such obligation were deemed not to have attained *jus cogens* status. However, as per Article 26 of the Draft Articles, the state of necessity could be invoked as a ground for precluding the wrongfulness of the aforementioned violations, solely if they were "the only means for the State to safeguard an essential interest against a grave and imminent peril" and did not "seriously impair an essential interest of the State or States towards which the obligation exists, or of the international community as a whole". In the case at issue, what was at stake was Italy's interest in protecting national security, which certainly qualifies as "an essential interest of the State"; however, it is questionable whether, before adopting the aforementioned measures, such interest was threatened by "a grave and imminent peril". Moreover, measures alternative to the transfer of migrants to the Libyan detention centres could be explored, in cooperation with the EU and its member states, in order to ease migratory pressure on Italy, such as the full implementation and the broadening of the relocation scheme for persons in need of international protection, which had been set up by the EU in 2015. As the International Law Commission pointed out in the comment to Article 25, "the plea is excluded if there are other (otherwise lawful) means available, even if they may be more costly or less

---

[79] See in particular "'Detained and Dehumanised'", *cit. supra* note 10, p. 11 ff.; Report of the Secretary-General pursuant to Security Council Resolution 2312 (2016), *cit. supra* note 10, paras. 40-42; "UN Human Rights Chief: Suffering of Migrants", *cit. supra* note 65.

[80] See for example International Organization for Migration, "LIBYA – Migration Crisis Operational Framework 2017-2019", available at: <https://www.iom.int/sites/default/files/our_work/DOE/MCOF/MCOF-Libya-2017-2019.pdf>, p. 25.

[81] See, among others, Human Rights Watch, "Italy: Navy Support for Libya May Endanger Migrants", 2 August 2017, available at: <https://www.hrw.org/news/2017/08/02/italy-navy-support-libya-may-endanger-migrants>; "Libya's Dark Web of Collusion", *cit. supra* note 10, p. 22 ff.

[82] On the state of necessity as a ground for precluding the wrongfulness of an act of a State, see, among others, HEATHCOTE, "Necessity", in CRAWFORD, PELLET and OLLESON (eds.), *cit. supra* note 78, p. 491 ff.; SLOANE, "On the Use and Abuse of Necessity in the Law of State Responsibility", AJIL, 2012, p. 447 ff.; TANZI, "Necessity, State of", Max Planck Encyclopedia of Public International Law, February 2013, available at: <http://opil.ouplaw.com/home/epil>.

convenient"; they include unilateral actions as well as "other forms of conduct available through cooperative action with other States or through international organizations".[83] Finally, the inhuman or degrading treatment of thousands of migrants in the Libyan detention facilities is in stark contrast to the essential interest of the international community as a whole for the protection of human rights of all members of the human family.[84]

10. ITALY'S POSSIBLE INTERNATIONAL RESPONSIBILITY UNDER THE EUROPEAN CONVENTION ON HUMAN RIGHTS

With specific regard to the ECHR, it is worth noting that, in a letter to the Italian Minister of the Interior Minniti of 28 September 2017, the Council of Europe Commissioner for Human Rights Nils Muižnieks stressed that, in facing migration emergencies, "it is imperative that States protect and safeguard the human rights of migrants stemming from, among others, the European Convention on Human Rights".[85] In this respect, he mentioned the 2012 landmark judgment of the European Court of Human Rights in the *Hirsi* case.[86] In that case, the Grand Chamber held that, by returning twenty-four migrants intercepted on the high seas to Libya on board ships of the Italian Revenue Police in 2009, Italy violated, *inter alia*, Article 3 ECHR, which prohibits torture and inhuman or degrading treatment or punishment and, in the Court's interpretation, implies "the obligation not to remove any person who, in the receiving country, would run the real risk of being subjected to such treatment" (obligation of *non-refoulement*).[87] The Grand Chamber found a double violation of Article 3, since the transfer of the said migrants to Libya exposed them to the risk of ill-treatment in Libya, as well as to the risk of arbitrary repatriation to their respective countries of origin

---

[83] Draft Articles on Responsibility of States for Internationally Wrongful Acts with commentaries, *cit. supra* note 72, p. 83, para. 15.

[84] See, for example, New York Declaration for Refugees and Migrants, adopted by the General Assembly on 3 October 2016, UN Doc. A/RES/71/1, paras. 6, 22 and 41; Resolution on Mass Migration, adopted by the Institute of International Law, in the Session of Hyderabad, on 9 September 2017, Art. 13(1).

[85] Letter of the Council of Europe Commissioner for Human Rights, 28 September 2017, available at: <https://rm.coe.int/letter-to-the-minister-of-interior-of-italy-regarding-government-s-res/168075baea>.

[86] European Court of Human Rights, *Hirsi Jamaa and Others v. Italy*, Application No. 27765/09, Grand Chamber, Judgment of 23 February 2012. On the *Hirsi* case, see, among others, GIUFFRÉ, "Watered-Down Rights on the High Seas: *Hirsi Jamaa and Others v Italy* (2012)", ICLQ, 2012, p. 728 ff.; MORENO-LAX, "Hirsi Jamaa and Others v. Italy or the Strasbourg Court versus Extraterritorial Migration Control?", Human Rights Law Review, 2012, p. 574 ff.; PAPASTAVRIDIS, "European Convention on Human Rights and the Law of the Sea: The Strasbourg Court in Unchartered Waters?", in FITZMAURICE and MERKOURIS (eds.), *The Interpretation and Application of the European Convention of Human Rights: Legal and Practical Implications*, Leiden/Boston, 2013, p. 117 ff.

[87] *Hirsi Jamaa and Others v. Italy, cit. supra* note 86, para. 123.

(Eritrea and Somalia), where they could be subjected to the very same treatment.[88]

In his letter, Muižnieks emphasised that "handing over individuals to the Libyan authorities or other groups in Libya would expose them to a real risk of torture or inhuman or degrading treatment or punishment" and warned that "the fact that such actions would be carried out in Libyan territorial waters does not absolve Italy from its obligations under the Convention".[89]

On 11 October 2017, Minniti replied that "neither Italian ships nor ships cooperating with the Italian Coast Guard ever returned rescued migrants to Libya". He also minimised the Italian contribution to the Libyan Coast Guard's operations against irregular immigration, stating that "the Italian authorities' activity aims only at providing training, equipment and logistic support to the Libyan Coast Guard, in close cooperation with the European Union organs".[90]

Indeed, for Italy to be held responsible for violating Article 3 ECHR, at the time of the violation, the victims need to have been within Italy's jurisdiction, that is to say – according to the Court's interpretation of Article 1 ECHR – under the effective control of the Italian authorities, although outside the Italian territory.[91] In the *Hirsi* case, this condition was fulfilled, since the applicants were returned to Libya on board Italian military ships.[92] In contrast, in the instant case, migrants rescued or intercepted at sea are returned to Libya on board Libyan Coast Guard's ships. Minniti's statement on the non-use of Italian ships for returning migrants to Libya aimed precisely at excluding Italian jurisdiction on returned migrants and, consequently, Italy's potential responsibility under the ECHR.

In the framework of the operations supporting the Libyan Coast Guard, Italian military ships are involved in patrolling Libyan territorial waters and the high seas off the Libyan coast. Patrolling, however, does not seem sufficient to trigger Italy's jurisdiction over migrants thereby intercepted, except in the case where they are transferred onto Italian military vessels.[93] This opinion finds support in the 2011 judgment of the European Court of Human Rights in the *Al-Skeini* case. In that judgment, the Grand Chamber stressed that, in the cases where the jurisdiction of a state party to the ECHR was affirmed over individuals outside its territory, by virtue of the conduct of its agents, such state exercised control

---

[88] *Ibid.*

[89] Letter of the Council of Europe Commissioner for Human Rights, *cit. supra* note 85.

[90] Letter of the Italian Minister of the Interior, 11 October 2017, available at: <https://rm.coe.int/reply-of-the-minister-of-interior-to-the-commissioner-s-letter-regardi/168075dd2d>.

[91] On the concept of jurisdiction and the extraterritorial application of the ECHR, see among others: NIGRO, "The Notion of 'Jurisdiction' in Article 1: Future Scenarios for the Extra-territorial Application of the European Convention on Human Rights", IYIL, 2011, p. 11 ff.; BESSON, "The Extraterritoriality of the European Convention on Human Rights: Why Human Rights Depend on Jurisdiction and What Jurisdiction Amounts to", Leiden JIL, 2012, p. 857 ff.; DA COSTA, *The Extraterritorial Application of Selected Human Rights Treaties*, Leiden, 2013, p. 93 ff.; SCHABAS, *cit. supra* note 68, p. 100 ff.

[92] *Hirsi Jamaa and Others v. Italy*, *cit. supra* note 86, paras. 76-82.

[93] On this point, see PAPASTAVRIDIS, "European Convention", *cit. supra* note 86, p. 125; KIM, "Non-Refoulement and Extraterritorial Jurisdiction: State Sovereignty and Migration Controls at Sea in the European Context", Leiden JIL, 2017, p. 49 ff., p. 62 ff.

"over the buildings, aircraft or ship in which the individuals were held", as well as "physical power and control over the person in question".[94]

In this author's opinion, migrants rescued or intercepted at sea and transferred to Libya by the Libyan Coast Guard would fall within Italy's jurisdiction, if Italian military personnel exercised *de facto* control over the Libyan Coast Guard's vessels transporting them back to the Libyan shores. The *Medvedyev* case, decided by the European Court of Human Rights in 2010, is a leading example in this respect.[95] In that case, the Grand Chamber held that France had jurisdiction over the crew members of a Cambodian merchant ship suspected of carrying large quantities of narcotics, which was intercepted by a French frigate off Cape Verde's shores and rerouted to Brest by French military personnel, while the crew were confined to their quarters under French military guard.[96] In the light of the *Medvedyev* case, it is submitted that Italy would certainly have jurisdiction over migrants on board Libyan Coast Guard's vessels, if Italian military personnel boarded such vessels and took control of them, so as to decide their itinerary and their destination.

On the other hand, it is questionable whether Italy's jurisdiction under Article 1 ECHR can be asserted in the absence of physical control over migrants by Italian agents.[97] In particular, it is doubtful whether coordination of search and rescue activities relating to migrant boats in distress on the high seas off the Libyan coast by the Maritime Rescue Coordination Centre Rome (MRCC Rome), under the SAR Convention regime,[98] is sufficient to trigger Italy's jurisdiction over rescued migrants. With regard to such a case, at the beginning of May 2018, seventeen migrants who had been rescued in an operation coordinated by the MRCC Rome filed an application against Italy with the European Court of Human Rights.[99] On 6 November 2017, they were on board a sinking rubber dinghy with dozens of other migrants. Both the NGO vessel "Sea Watch 3" and the Libyan Coast Guard were requested by the MRCC Rome to direct themselves towards the dinghy. According to the applicants, once on the scene, the Libyan Coast Guard ship "Ras Jadir" (one of the four ships provided by Italy to the Serraj Government in spring 2017)[100] obstructed the rescue of migrants by "Sea Watch 3" crew. At least twenty migrants drowned. Forty-seven migrants were taken on board "Ras Jadir"

---

[94] European Court of Human Rights, *Al-Skeini and Others v. the United Kingdom*, Application No. 55721/07, Grand Chamber, Judgment of 7 July 2011, para. 136.

[95] European Court of Human Rights, *Medvedyev and Others v. France*, Application No. 3394/03, Grand Chamber, Judgment of 29 March 2010.

[96] *Ibid.*, paras. 66-67.

[97] See European Court of Human Rights, *Women on Waves and Others v. Portugal*, Application No. 31276/05, Second Section, Judgment of 3 February 2009.

[98] See Maritime Safety Committee, Resolution MSC.167(78), *cit. supra* note 47, Annex, para. 6.7; International Maritime Organization, International Aeronautical and Maritime Search and Rescue Manual, 2013 Edition, Vol. II, paras. 2.25, 3.6.1, 3.6.2 and 3.6.5.

[99] See "Legal Action against Italy over Its Coordination of Libyan Coast Guard Pull-backs Resulting in Migrant Deaths and Abuse", Global Legal Action Network, 8 May 2018, available at: <http://www.glanlaw.org/single-post/2018/05/08/Legal-action-against-Italy-over-its-coordination-of-Libyan-Coast-Guard-pull-backs-resulting-in-migrant-deaths-and-abuse>.

[100] See *amplius supra* Section 5.

and brought back to Libya, where they were detained in inhuman conditions and subjected to serious abuses. The other survivors were transferred to Italy on board "Sea Watch 3".[101] The applicants contend that they were within Italy's jurisdiction under Article 1, at the time of the incident, and allege that they were victims, *inter alia*, of violations of Article 2 and Article 3 ECHR.

11. CONCLUSION

Italy's new migration control policy raises serious human rights concerns. The analysis above shows that the reduction in the number of migrants arriving from Libya has been achieved at the price of their human rights. The 2017 MOU between Italy and the Libyan Government of National Accord, which is the cornerstone of the policy, is based on a deliberately short-sighted vision of the migration phenomenon affecting Libya and the irregular migrants' conditions in that country. In particular, Italy undertakes "to provide technical and technological support" to the Libyan Coast Guard, failing to consider that migrants rescued or intercepted at sea by the latter are routinely transferred to Libyan governmental facilities, where they are arbitrarily detained and subjected to torture and other ill-treatment, and that its members frequently commit abuses against them and collude with migrant smugglers. Indeed, the MOU conspicuously neglects the problem of the protection of migrants' human rights in Libya.

The interception of migrants at sea and their forcible return to Libyan territory by the Libyan Coast Guard constitute typical "pull back" operations carried out by a transit state (Libya) in the interest of a destination state desiring to prevent migrant arrivals without having to engage its own border authorities in unlawful "pushback" operations (Italy).[102] In 2017, such operations intensified significantly, owing to new measures decided by the Italian Government, in particular (1) the active assistance to the Libyan Coast Guard, in terms of supply, maintenance and repair of patrol boats, provision of equipment, training, sea patrolling and sharing of information, and (2) the adoption of a code of conduct restricting NGOs' search and rescue activities in favour of those of the Libyan Coast Guard.

However, as the "pull back" operations at issue usually result in blatant violations of migrants' most fundamental human rights, primarily their right not to be subjected to torture or ill-treatment, these measures actually make Italy complicit in those internationally wrongful acts. As illustrated above, Italy's complicity

---

[101] See a detailed reconstruction of the events in Forensic Oceanography, "Mare Clausum. Italy and the EU's Undeclared Operation to Stem Migration Across the Mediterranean", May 2018, available at: <http://www.forensic-architecture.org/wp-content/uploads/2018/05/2018-05-07-FO-Mare-Clausum-full-EN.pdf>, p. 87 ff.

[102] On the "pull back" operations, see Human Rights Council, Report of the Special Rapporteur on Torture and Other Cruel, Inhuman or Degrading Treatment or Punishment, UN Doc. A/HRC/37/50, 26 February 2018, paras. 56-59. See also General Assembly, Report of the Special Rapporteur of the Human Rights Council on Extrajudicial, Summary or Arbitrary Executions, UN Doc. A/72/335, 15 August 2017, paras. 36-40.

in violations of the prohibition of torture and ill-treatment against migrants intercepted at sea by the Libyan Coast Guard and transferred to the governmental detention centres in Libya can be asserted on the basis of the principle set forth in Article 16 of the 2001 International Law Commission's Draft Articles on State Responsibility.

Interestingly, if it were ascertained that Italian military personnel exercised *de facto* control over Libyan Coast Guard vessels transporting migrants back to the Libyan shores, Italy would be responsible also for directly violating the prohibition of torture and ill-treatment enshrined in Article 3 ECHR. Hence, migrants forcibly returned to Libya on board such vessels might successfully lodge an application with the European Court of Human Rights, claiming to be victims of a violation of Article 3 by Italy.

In addition, Italy's economic assistance to the Libyan local communities, in exchange for their cooperation in the fight against irregular immigration and migrant smuggling, is problematic in the light of the human rights obligations of the former. As noted above, there is no guarantee that those communities make respect for migrants' human rights a priority, when trying to curb irregular immigration and smuggling activities.

Obviously, EU political and financial support for all the aforementioned measures has no influence on the question of the breach of human rights obligations by Italy resulting from them. On the contrary, the European Union action raises doubts as to its consistency with international law.[103]

In conclusion, the investigation above reveals an urgent need for the Italian Government to rethink its migration control policy, prioritizing the protection of migrants' fundamental human rights. The Gentiloni-Serraj MOU should be amended as a matter of urgency: any support offered to the Libyan authorities should be made conditional on the respect for human rights and a monitoring mechanism should be established to this effect, as demanded by the Committee against Torture.[104] Meanwhile, Italy's assistance to the Libyan Coast Guard should be suspended and the code of conduct for NGOs involved in migrant rescue modified; the Italian economic support to the Libyan local communities also should be frozen. Finally, the mandate of Italy's operation in Niger should be carefully tailored, so as to avoid human rights violations by the Italian forces.

---

[103] See "Libya's Dark Web of Collusion", *cit. supra* note 10, p. 60. An investigation on the possible international responsibility of the EU for its support for Italy's new migration control measures is outside the scope of this article.

[104] Committee against Torture, Concluding Observations on the Fifth and Sixth Combined Periodic Reports to Italy, UN Doc. CAT/C/ITA/CO/5-6, 18 December 2017, paras. 22, 23.

PRACTICE OF INTERNATIONAL COURTS AND TRIBUNALS

THE JUDICIAL ACTIVITY OF THE INTERNATIONAL COURT OF JUSTICE IN 2017

SERENA FORLATI[*]

1. INTRODUCTION

The International Court of Justice issued no judgment on the merits of any specific dispute in 2017; differently from past situations, however,[1] this is by no means a sign of a crisis of the principal judicial organ of the United Nations. The Court upheld its jurisdiction in one judgment on preliminary objections and adopted a number of orders, disposing of incidental phases of proceedings in other contentious cases. Moreover, five new contentious cases and one request for advisory opinion have been introduced in the year under review, confirming the high interest of States of different regions of the world in resorting to the ICJ.

As regards the composition of the Court, a significant change occurred in the practice relating to the election of its Members. A new Member, Judge Nawaf Salam from Lebanon, was elected in December 2017 – together with Judges Ronny Abraham (France), Abdulqawi Ahmed Yusuf (Somalia), Antônio Augusto Cançado Trindade (Brazil) and Dalveer Bhandari (India), who stood for re-election.[2] However, for the first time since the Court's establishment, no Member of the Court is of British nationality, as Judge Greenwood withdrew his candidacy after the second round of elections. This shifts away from the tradition that a national of each Permanent Member of the Security Council sits on the Bench while also increasing the number of Judges who are nationals of Asian countries at the expense of the "Western and Others" group.[3]

Under Article 9 of the ICJ Statute, "The General Assembly and the Security Council shall proceed independently of one another to elect the members of the Court". Although Permanent Members of the Security Council hold no right of veto in this kind of deliberation,[4] it is unlikely that the United Kingdom would

---

[*] Associate Professor of International Law, University of Ferrara.

[1] Compare to the pessimistic remarks by VERHOEVEN, "À propos de la fonction de juger en droit international public", in OST and VAN DE KERCHOVE (eds.), *Fonction de juger et pouvoir judiciaire*, Bruxelles, 1983, p. 448 ff., p. 451.

[2] See Security Council, "Press Release: Security Council, General Assembly, Elect Four Judges to International Court of Justice", 9 November 2017, available at: <https://www.un.org/press/en/2017/sc13063.doc.htm>. See the account of AKANDE, "ICJ Elections 2017: UN General Assembly and Security Council Elect Four Judges to the ICJ but Fail to Agree on a Fifth, yet again!", EJIL: Talk!, 11 November 2017, available at: <https://www.ejiltalk.org/icj-elections-2017-un-general-assembly-and-security-council-elect-four-judges-to-the-icj-but-fail-to-agree-on-a-fifth-yet-again-trivia-question/>.

[3] For a discussion of previous practice, see KEITH, "Challenges to the Independence of the International Judiciary: Reflections on the International Court of Justice", Leiden JIL, 2017, p. 137 ff.

[4] See ICJ Statute, Art. 10(2).

have lost support for its candidate within the Security Council for this specific instance. A deadlock between the Council and the General Assembly would have implied the establishment of a Joint Conference of six members with the aim of identifying a single candidate and, as a last resort, the choice would have been entrusted to "those members of the Court who have already been elected".[5] Developments in other fora[6] show the wisdom of this kind of mechanism, which avoids political stalemates on such crucial issue.

2. THE DOCKET

As mentioned above, five new contentious cases were submitted to the Court by unilateral application in 2017, together with one request for an advisory opinion.

2.1. The New Contentious Cases

The first and the last applications submitted to the Court in 2017 are closely connected one with the other; ten years after the judgment in the *Pulau Branca, Middle Rocks and South Ledge* case, Malaysia seeks both the revision[7] and the interpretation[8] of that judgment, in light of the difficulties met by the parties in its implementation.[9] The 2008 Judgment awarded sovereignty over Pedra Branca/Pulau Batu Puteh to Singapore[10] while Malaysia was held to have title over Middle Rocks. However, the status of the waters around the low-tide elevation of South

---

[5] See ICJ Statute, Art. 12.

[6] On the current difficulties concerning the WTO Appellate Body see WTO, "Annual Report 2018", p. 141, available at: <https://www.wto.org/english/res_e/booksp_e/anrep18_e.pdf>.

[7] *Application for revision of the Judgment of 23 May 2008 in the case concerning* Sovereignty over Pedra Branca/Pulau Batu Puteh, Middle Rocks and South Ledge (Malaysia/ Singapore) *(Malaysia v. Singapore)*, filed on 2 February 2017. The case was later removed from the Court's list on 29 May 2018: see "Press Release: Application for Revision of the Judgment of 23 May 2008 in the Case concerning Sovereignty over Pedra Branca/Pulau Batu Puteh, Middle Rocks and South Ledge (Malaysia/Singapore) (Malaysia v. Singapore) Case removed from the Court's List", 1 June 2018. These and the other documents relating to the ICJ's judicial activity in 2017 are available on the Court's website: <www.icj-cij.org>.

[8] *Request for Interpretation of the Judgment of 23 May 2008 in the case concerning* Sovereignty over Pedra Branca/Pulau Batu Puteh, Middle Rocks and South Ledge (Malaysia/ Singapore) *(Malaysia v. Singapore)*, filed on 30 June 2017. Also this case was removed from the Court's list on 29 May 2018: see "Press Release: Request for Interpretation of the Judgment of 23 May 2008 in the case concerning Sovereignty over Pedra Branca/Pulau Batu Puteh, Middle Rocks and South Ledge (Malaysia/Singapore) (Malaysia v. Singapore) Case removed from the Court's List", 1 June 2018.

[9] See the account given *ibid.*, paras. 8-11.

[10] *Sovereignty over Pedra Branca/Pulau Batu Puteh, Middle Rocks and South Ledge (Malaysia v. Singapore)*, Judgment of 23 May 2008, ICJ Reports, 2008, p. 12 ff. See, however, the criticism in the Joint Dissenting Opinion of Jugdes Simma and Abraham, *ibid.*, p. 116 ff., as regards the allocation of sovereignty over Pedra Branca/Pulau Batu Puteh. See also the

Ledge remained partly unclear: as the delimitation of the maritime boundary between the two countries did not fall within the scope of the dispute, the Court held
that sovereignty over South Ledge belongs to the State in whose territorial waters
it lies.[11] Malaysia is now asking for a revision of the finding that sovereignty over
Pedra Branca/Pulau Batu Puteh belongs to Singapore: the judgment's finding in
favour of Singapore was based on a "shared understanding" between the two
countries that this was the situation as from 1953, but according to Malaysia three
new documents, discovered in the United Kingdom National Archives, prove that
in the years immediately after 1953 the Singaporean authorities did not consider
Pedra Branca/Pulau Batu Puteh as belonging to Singapore; this should be considered as a "new fact", or at least as evidence of an "implicit underlying fact"
that could be decisive for the purposes of the decision.[12] Whether the application
meets the stringent admissibility requirements set forth by Article 61 of the ICJ
Statute remains to be seen, especially in light of the rigorous reading of such
requirements in the Court's previous case law on the issue.[13] The same actually
applies to the request for interpretation: according to Malaysia, the Parties are
in disagreement as regards the status of South Ledge and the delimitation of the
maritime boundaries in the area around Pedra Branca/Pulau Batu Puteh, Middle
Rocks and South Ledge, due to their different understanding of the implications
of the Court's 2008 Judgment in this respect.[14] However, the delimitation of the
maritime boundary was deemed to fall outside the scope of the dispute originally
submitted to the ICJ;[15] while according to the Court's case law, the object of applications under Article 60 of the ICJ Statute "must be solely to obtain clarification of the meaning and the scope of what the Court has decided with binding
force, and not to obtain an answer to questions not so decided".[16]

The other three new cases (*Land Boundary in the Northern Part of Isla Portillos
(Costa Rica v. Nicaragua)*, *Application of the International Convention for the
Suppression of the Financing of Terrorism and of the International Convention
on the Elimination of All Forms of Racial Discrimination (Ukraine v. Russia)*, and
the *Jadhav Case (India v. Pakistan)* will be discussed below, as the Court decided
incidental phases of the relevant proceedings in the year under review.

2.2. *The Request of an Advisory Opinion on the Chagos Archipelago*

The Court's advisory function was also revived: on 22 July 2017 the General
Assembly exercised its power under Article 96(1) of the UN Charter to request

---

Separate Opinion of Judge Parra-Aranguren, *ibid.*, p. 107 ff., and the Dissenting Opinion of
Judge *ad hoc* Dugard, *ibid.*, p. 133 ff.

[11] *Malaysia v. Singapore, cit. supra* note 10, p. 102.

[12] *Application for revision, cit. supra* note 7, para. 22.

[13] See KOLB, *The International Court of Justice*, Oxford, 2013, p. 804.

[14] *Ibid.*

[15] *Malaysia v. Singapore, cit. supra* note 10, p. 101.

[16] *Request for Interpretation of the Judgment of 20 November 1950 in the asylum case
(Colombia/Peru)*, Judgment of 27 November 1950, ICJ Reports, 1950, p. 395 ff., p. 402.

an advisory opinion in the *Legal consequences of the separation of the Chagos Archipelago from Mauritius in 1965*. The Court is thus called upon to clarify whether the process of decolonisation of Mauritius was "lawfully completed when Mauritius was granted independence in 1968, following the separation of the Chagos Archipelago from Mauritius and having regard to international law", including obligations reflected in General Assembly resolutions on de-colonization; moreover, a second question is submitted to the Court as to "what are the consequences under international law, including obligations reflected in the above-mentioned resolutions, arising from the continued administration by the United Kingdom of Great Britain and Northern Ireland of the Chagos Archipelago including with respect to the inability of Mauritius to implement a programme for the resettlement on the Chagos Archipelago of its nationals, in particular those of Chagossian origin?" The issue is closely connected to a dispute between Mauritius and the United Kingdom as regards sovereignty over the Chagos Archipelago, which was already at the centre of an inter-State arbitration between Mauritius and the United Kingdom[17] (while the eviction of the Islanders was the object of an unsuccessful application to the European Court of Human Rights[18]). The General Assembly resolution requesting the advisory opinion was met, unsurprisingly, with strong opposition by some States. Specifically the United Kingdom maintained that the request is "a back-door way" to bypass the limitations to the ICJ's contentious competence to decide what is in fact a bilateral dispute, thus undermining the Court's legitimacy;[19] this casts doubts on the propriety of the exercise of the Court's advisory function in these proceedings,[20] within which the United Nations and its Member States,[21] as well as the African Union,[22] have been invited to furnish relevant information.

---

[17] In *Chagos Marine Protected Area Arbitration (Mauritius v. United Kingdom)*, Award of 18 March 2015, the UNCLOS Arbitral Tribunal considered that its jurisdiction did not cover the identification of the coastal State in respect of the Archipelago, while ascertaining that the identification of a maritime protected area by the United Kingdom in the waters surrounding the islands was in breach of its international legal obligations towards Mauritius. See TREVES, "The International Tribunal for the Law of the Sea and other Law of the Sea Jurisdictions (2015)", IYIL, 2015, p. 363 ff.

[18] *Chagos Islanders v. United Kingdom*, Application No. 35622/04, Decision of 11 December 2012, deeming the application inadmissible.

[19] See the declarations of the United Kingdom before and after the vote; the Resolution was adopted by a recorded vote of 94 in favour to 15 against, with 65 abstentions. Other Governments, more or less explicitly, shared the United Kingdom's opinion that the request in fact circumvents the distinction between the ICJ contentious and advisory jurisdiction: see in particular the declarations of the United States of America, Australia, Sweden, Germany, Israel and Canada. Coverage of the debate is available at: <https://www.un.org/press/en/2017/ga11924.doc.htm>.

[20] See *Status of Eastern Carelia*, Advisory Opinion of 23 July 1923, PCIJ Reports, Series B, No. 5, p. 29 ff.

[21] Order of 14 July 2017.

[22] See the Order of 18 January 2018, which followed an express request of the African Union. In line with such request, the deadline for submitting information was postponed by one month.

2.3. Other Relevant Developments

Another noteworthy development relates to the *Gabčíkovo-Nagymaros* case – the oldest on the docket. Slovakia discontinued the procedure it had begun on 3 September 1998 by means of its *Request for an additional judgment* concerning the modalities of implementation of the judgment on the merits.[23] While the Court placed this discontinuance on record on 18 July 2017,[24] the parties reserved the right to submit an analogous request in the future;[25] moreover, the main case is still pending, as negotiations on its implementation and on the issue of reparations have not yet achieved a final settlement.

Last but not least, one should mention an application for revision submitted with regard to the *Genocide (Bosnia v. Serbia)* case, which, eventually, was *not* placed on the docket. A statement by President Abraham of 9 March 2017[26] accounts for the handing in to the Registry of the ICJ of a "document [...] entitled *Application for revision of the Judgment of 26 February 2007 in the case concerning the Application of the Convention on the Prevention and Punishment of the Crime of Genocide (Bosnia and Herzegovina v. Serbia)*", which was signed by the Agent and Co-Agents who had represented the applicant State in the original proceedings, without any new appointment by Bosnia Herzegovina – although the Registrar had previously indicated that such new appointment would be necessary for the purposes of seeking revision of the 2007 judgment.[27] The situation, which is not entirely new for the ICJ,[28] stemmed from an irreconcilable disagreement between the different components of the Presidency of Bosnia and Herzegovina, which could not appoint an Agent in the matter.[29] After seeking information directly from the Bosnian Presidency, the Court considered that

---

[23] *Gabčíkovo-Nagymaros Project (Hungary/Slovakia)*, Judgment of 25 September 1997, ICJ Reports, 1997, p. 7 ff.

[24] See "Press release: The Court places on record the discontinuance by Slovakia of the procedure begun by means of its Request for an additional judgment", 21 July 2017.

[25] This possibility has an express legal basis in Art. 5(3), of the Special Agreement of 7 April 1993 between Hungary and Slovakia.

[26] See "Press Release: Statement by H.E. Judge Ronny Abraham, President of the International Court of Justice", 9 March 2017.

[27] See *ibid.*

[28] See *Certain Questions concerning Diplomatic Relations (Honduras v. Brazil)*, Order of 12 May 2010, ICJ Reports, 2010, p. 303 ff. See for further examples and a thorough discussion HERMET, "Le constat de l'inexistence d'une saisine par la Cour internationale de Justice – À propos d'un communiqué de presse", RGDIP, 2017, p. 393 ss., p. 399.

[29] An account of the situation may be found in the Press Release, *cit. supra* note 26. See MILANOVIC, "The Strangest ICJ Case Got Even Stranger, Or the Revision that Wasn't", EJIL: Talk!, 13 March 2017, available at: <https://www.ejiltalk.org/the-strangest-icj-case-got-even-stranger-or-the-revision-that-wasnt/>; see further AKANDE, "Applications for Revision of the International Court of Justice's Judgments: The Curious 'Case' for Revision of the *Bosnian Genocide* Judgment", *ibid.*, 13 March 2017, available at: <https://www.ejiltalk.org/applications-for-revision-of-the-international-court-of-justice-judgments-the-curious-case-for-revision-of-the-bosnian-genocide-judgment/>.

no decision has been taken by the competent authorities, on behalf of Bosnia and Herzegovina as a State, to request the revision
of the Judgment of 26 February 2007 in the case concerning the
Application of the Convention on the Prevention and Punishment
of the Crime of Genocide (Bosnia and Herzegovina v. Serbia), and
that it is therefore not properly seised of the matter.[30]

This conclusion is in line with the Court's practice, whereby revision proceedings are treated as autonomous cases (therefore requiring a new appointment
of an Agent);[31] moreover, it is not the ICJ's function to find a solution for the
deadlock of the Bosnian constitutional framework. At the same time, the fact that
the Court's decision on this thorny issue was communicated through a statement
of the President, rather than through a formal judicial pronouncement by the
Court as such, is not fully satisfactory from the standpoint of transparency. The
press release indicates that the decision was taken by the Court itself (not by the
President or the Registrar), and clearly implies a legal assessment of the situation
– if only to the effect of ruling out that revision proceedings are simply a phase of
the original case, for which no new appointment of an Agent would be necessary.
The contention that, even under such unusual circumstances, "la décision de ne
pas enregistrer est [...] étrangère au pouvoir de juger"[32] does therefore raise some
doubts: a more formalized procedure of summary dismissal would be more suitable to address this kind of situation.[33]

3. THE JUDGMENT ON PRELIMINARY OBJECTIONS IN THE *SOMALIA V. KENYA*
    CASE

The Judgment of 2 February 2017 concerns the dispute over the establishment of a "single maritime boundary dividing all the maritime areas appertaining
to Somalia and to Kenya in the Indian Ocean, including the continental shelf
beyond 200 M".[34] Somalia sought to found the jurisdiction of the Court on the
unilateral declarations submitted by the two Parties under Article 36 of the ICJ
Statute, and Kenya raised two preliminary objections relating respectively to the
jurisdiction of the Court and to the admissibility of the claim.
We will focus here mainly on the part of the Judgment addressing Kenya's
first objection, which raised the most interesting issues and in respect of which

---

[30] Press Release, *cit. supra* note 26.
[31] See SHAW, *Rosenne's The Law and Practice of the International Court: 1920-2015*, Vol.
3, Leiden, 2016, para. 395.
[32] HERMET, *cit. supra* note 28, p. 406.
[33] For a discussion of this option see SARVARIAN, "Preliminary Report to the ILA
Committee on Rules of Procedure of International Courts and Tribunals", p. 17 ff., available
at: <http://www.ila-hq.org/index.php/committees>.
[34] *Application instituting proceedings*, filed on 28 August 2014, para. 36; Somalia also
requests the Court to determine the "precise geographical co-ordinates of the single maritime
boundary" (*ibid.*, para. 37).

several individual opinions were appended.[35] Kenya relied on a reservation included in its Article 36 declaration, whereby it would not apply to disputes "in regard to which the parties to the dispute have agreed or shall agree to have recourse to some other method or methods of settlement"; the Court was therefore called upon to clarify the impact of such reservation on the relationship between, on the one hand, the competence of the ICJ and, on the other hand, the role of the Commission on the Limits of the Continental Shelf (CLCS) and the dispute settlement procedures established under Part XV of the UNCLOS. Hence, the Court had to determine in the first place whether these procedures amount to "other methods of settlement" that the parties had agreed to.[36]

As regards the first aspect, in 2009 Somalia and Kenya signed a Memorandum of Understanding granting each other "No-Objection" as regards their respective submissions to the Commission, which was duly registered with the UN Secretariat.[37] In 2014, however, Somalia challenged the validity of the Memorandum due to lack of ratification by the Somali Parliament[38] and objected to Kenya's submissions to the CLCS.[39] Shortly before its application to the ICJ, also Somalia presented a submission to the CLCS; both were considered only after the mutual objections were withdrawn.[40] Kenya argued that the Parties had agreed, under paragraph 6 of the MOU, that the delimitation dispute would be settled "by agreement to be concluded by Somalia and Kenya after the CLCS

---

[35] The second preliminary objection, which challenged the admissibility of the claim *inter alia* on the basis of the "clean hands" doctrine (due to the alleged breach by Somalia of the MOU), was rejected unanimously; the Court did not settle the issue of whether, as a matter of principle, the fact that a State comes before the court without "clean hands" could preclude the admissibility of its claims: see *Maritime Delimitation in the Indian Ocean (Somalia v. Kenya)*, Preliminary Objections, Judgment of 2 February 2017, paras. 142-143. See also *Oil Platforms (Islamic Republic of Iran v. United States of America)*, Judgment, ICJ Reports, 2003, p. 161 ff., paras. 30 and 100. See further SCHWEBEL, "Clean Hands, Principle", Max Planck Encyclopedia of Public International Law, March 2013, available at: <http://opil.ouplaw.com/home/EPIL>.

[36] According to BONAFÉ, "Maritime Delimitation in the Indian Ocean (Somalia v. Kenya)", AJIL, 2017 p. 725 ff., p. 728, this reference to "external elements" is at odds with the traditional method of interpretation of optional clauses, that focused "on the declaration itself and on the reservation". However, it would seem that the focus of the Court is precisely on ascertaining whether the intention of Kenya was to exclude the dispute at hand from the scope of its optional clause declaration.

[37] See *Somalia v. Kenya, cit. supra* note 35, paras. 17-18. Rather than being the object of direct negotiations, the MOU was drafted by the Ambassador of Norway, who was assisting Kenya and Somalia in the preparation of their submissions to the CLCS; Vice-President Yusuf's Declaration is critical of the Parties' attitude in this regard, as no Government, and especially those of African States, "can afford today to put its signature to a bilateral legal instrument which it has neither carefully negotiated nor to which it has hardly contributed" (para. 11).

[38] *Somalia v. Kenya, cit. supra* note 35, para. 38.

[39] *Ibid.*, para. 19.

[40] *Ibid.*, paras. 19 ff.

has made its recommendations to them concerning the establishment of the outer limits of the continental shelf beyond 200 nautical miles".[41]

As regards the first aspect, the Court held the MOU to be legally binding in nature, and to be valid even absent ratification by the Parliament of Somalia, as the Minister who had signed it was duly authorised by the Prime Minister who, in turn, was entitled to represent Somalia under international law, on the basis of Article 7 of the Vienna Convention on the Law of Treaties (VCLT).[42] The MOU, moreover, expressly provided it would enter into force upon signature,[43] nor could Article 46 VCLT apply in the instant case. In this specific regard, the Court confirmed its restrictive approach in applying grounds for invalidity of treaties, holding that Kenya could not be bound to seek updated information as to domestic legal requirements for the conclusion of treaties.[44] Furthermore, the Court also posited that the authorities of Somalia had acquiesced to the validity of the MOU under Article 45 of the said Convention.[45]

Discussing the applicability of the Kenyan reservation to the MOU, the Court reiterated that the CLCS's task concerns only the "delineation of the outer limits of the continental shelf, and not delimitation",[46] stressing also that in case of objections States may not even be able to establish the outer limits of their continental shelf through this procedure.[47]

Moreover, after a analysis of the MOU's text in light of the criteria set forth by Articles 31 and 32 VCLT, the Court concluded that paragraph six could apply only to the delimitation of the continental shelf, and that in any case it

> reflected the expectation of the Parties that [...] they would negotiate their maritime boundary in the area of the continental shelf after receipt of the CLCS's recommendations, keeping the two processes of delimitation and delineation distinct. As between States parties to UNCLOS,

---

[41] *Ibid.*, para. 32. Para. 6 of the MOU, which was at stake, reads: "The delimitation of maritime boundaries in the areas under dispute, including the delimitation of the continental shelf beyond 200 nautical miles, shall be agreed between the two coastal States on the basis of international law after the Commission has concluded its examination of the separate submissions made by each of the two coastal States and made its recommendations to two coastal States concerning the establishment of the outer limits of the continental shelf beyond 200 nautical miles".

[42] *Ibid.*, para. 43.

[43] *Ibid.*, paras. 45-47 and 50.

[44] *Ibid.*, para. 49. See already *Land and Maritime Boundary between Cameroon and Nigeria (Cameroon v. Nigeria: Equatorial Guinea intervening),* Judgment of 10 October 2002, ICJ Reports, 2002, p. 303 ff., para. 266.

[45] *Somalia v. Kenya, cit. supra* note 35, para. 49.

[46] *Ibid.*, para. 67 (quoting from *Question of the Delimitation of the Continental Shelf between Nicaragua and Colombia beyond 200 Nautical Miles from the Nicaraguan Coast (Nicaragua v. Colombia),* Preliminary Objections, Judgment of 17 March 2016, ICJ Reports, 2016, p. 100 ff.). A similar conclusion has been reached by the International Tribunal for the Law of the Sea (ITLOS) in the Dispute concerning delimitation of the maritime boundary between Ghana and Côte d'Ivoire in the Atlantic Ocean (Ghana/Côte d'Ivoire), Judgment of 23 September 2017, on which see the comment by TREVES in this Volume, pp. 316-325.

[47] *Somalia v. Kenya, cit. supra* note 35, para. 69.

such negotiations are the first step in undertaking delimitation of the continental shelf. The Court does not, however, consider that the text of the sixth paragraph, viewed in light of the text of the MOU as a whole, the object and purpose of the MOU, and in its context, could have been intended to establish a method of dispute settlement in relation to the delimitation of the maritime boundary between the Parties.[48]

The Dissenting Opinions of Judge Bennouna and Judge *ad hoc* Guillaume were highly critical of this part of the judgment, because of the adopted methodology and the conclusions it reached; Judges Gaja and Crawford, on the other hand, concurred with the Court's findings, arguing however that paragraph 6 was not a *pactum de contrahendo*, and that

> [i]n the context of a declaration concerned with the compulsory jurisdiction of the Court and with alternatives to it, a reservation as to another method of settlement should be construed as referring to a method that will actually settle the dispute when it is resorted to, not to one that is equally consistent with the dispute remaining unsettled in perpetuity.[49]

Moreover, according to Kenya, the reservation included in its unilateral declaration of acceptance would in any case apply with reference to the dispute settlement methods under Part XV of UNCLOS, to which both States are parties – and more specifically Annex VII Arbitration under Article 287(3) UNCLOS, which should apply "as the *lex specialis* and *lex posterior* to the optional clause declarations of the Parties".[50] The Court rejected this contention, holding that "the force of the arguments militating in favour of jurisdiction is preponderant". In its opinion, Article 282 UNCLOS covers also optional clause declarations,[51] and this applies "even when such declarations contain a reservation to the same effect as that of Kenya".[52]

This conclusion was reached on the basis of the argument that, during the negotiation of UNCLOS, "more than half of the [...] optional clause declarations contained a reservation with an effect similar to that of Kenya's reservation" and "there is no indication in the *travaux préparatoires* of an intention to exclude from the scope of Article 282 the majority" of such clauses.[53] Moreover, the Judgment emphasised the need to avoid any "negative conflict of jurisdiction":

---

[48] *Ibid.*, para. 98.

[49] Joint Declaration of Judges Gaja and Crawford, para. 4. The Declaration also expressed the view "that while the Parties, by setting a time-limit in the MOU, had implicitly set a condition for the admissibility of an application to the Court, they set aside that time-limit by agreeing in 2014, without reservation or qualification, to start negotiations in view of seeking an earlier agreement" (para. 12).

[50] *Somalia v. Kenya, cit. supra* note 35, para. 109. According to Kenya, its reservation would prevail over the stipulation of Article 282 UNCLOS (para. 110).

[51] *Ibid.*, paras. 126 ff.

[52] *Ibid.*, para. 130.

[53] *Ibid.*, para. 129.

[a] finding that the Court has jurisdiction gives effect to the intent reflected in Kenya's declaration, by ensuring that this dispute is subject to a method of dispute settlement. By contrast, because an agreed procedure within the scope of Article 282 takes precedence over the procedures set out in Section 2 of Part XV, there is no certainty that this intention would be fulfilled were this Court to decline jurisdiction (see also Article 286 of UNCLOS).[54]

However the risk that, had the Court upheld the preliminary objection, an Annex VII Arbitral Tribunal would also decline jurisdiction seems quite remote; this was stressed by Judge Robinson in his Dissenting Opinion, where he criticised the Court's approach as "untenable"[55] "self-serving"[56] and at risk of defeating "one of the main goals of the UNCLOS States parties in constructing the dispute settlement system in Part XV", since the "States parties did not wish to give any particular prominence to the International Court of Justice in the dispute settlement system".[57]

The Judgment no doubt takes a restrictive approach to the interpretation of Kenya's reservation, with reasons related to the safeguarding of the (Court's) judicial function prevailing over scrupulous respect for States' consent to jurisdiction. As argued by Judge Bennouna, this may in turn give rise to a risk of non-implementation,[58] but the fact that the Court accepts such a risk is in itself an indication of its perceived institutional strength in this phase of its activities.

4.   OTHER JUDICIAL PRONOUNCEMENTS

In the year under review, the International Court of Justice adopted also some pronouncements in incidental proceedings that raise interesting issues of substantive and procedural law. They are discussed here in chronological order.

4.1.   *Joinder of Proceedings: The Maritime Delimitation in the Caribbean Sea and Pacific Ocean and Isla Portillos Cases*

On 16 January 2017, Costa Rica introduced an application against Nicaragua in the *Land Boundary in the Northern Part of Isla Portillos (Costa Rica v. Nicaragua)* case, seeking the precise identification of the land boundary between the two countries in the Los Portillos/Harbor Head Lagoon sandbar and challeng-

---

[54] *Ibid.*, para. 132.
[55] Dissenting Opinion of Judge Robinson, para. 24.
[56] *Ibid.*, para. 36.
[57] *Ibid.*, para. 34.
[58] Dissenting Opinion of Judge Bennouna.

ing the setting up of a Nicaragua military camp on the beach of Isla Portillos[59] (which, Costa Rica contended, was in fact within Costa Rica's territory). Less than 20 days later, on 2 February 2017, the ICJ unanimously adopted an order joining the case to the one relating to the *Maritime Delimitation in the Caribbean Sea and Pacific Ocean* already pending between the same parties.

In the instance under discussion, the ICJ emphasised that Article 47 of the Rules of Court leaves it "a broad margin of discretion"[60] and it decided to join cases on grounds related to the sound administration of justice and judicial economy,[61] without attributing decisive weight to the wishes of the Parties. More specifically, in *Maritime Delimitation/Isla Portillos* the applicant requested the joinder[62] but the respondent considered "that it would not be able to comment on the appropriateness of a joinder [...] until it was in possession of the experts' report and Costa Rica's Memorial".[63] The Court simply took note of this, stressing the discretionary nature of the Court's appraisal and recalling that "any decision to that effect must be taken in light of the specific circumstances of each case".[64] It further considered that

> in view of the claims made by Costa Rica in the case concerning *Isla Portillos* and the close link between those claims and certain aspects of the dispute in the case concerning *Maritime Delimitation*, the proceedings in the two cases should be joined. Such a joinder will allow the Court to address simultaneously the totality of the various interrelated and contested issues raised by the Parties, including any questions of fact or law that are common to the disputes presented.[65]

The Order is consonant with the Court's previous practice as regards joinder of proceedings pending between the same parties[66] as well as with the case law of the Permanent Court of International Justice in cases involving the same parties.[67]

---

[59] See the *Application instituting proceedings*, filed on 16 January 2017, para. 22.

[60] Order of 2 February 2017, para. 16.

[61] *Ibid.* See also *Certain Activities Carried Out by Nicaragua in the Border Area (Costa Rica v. Nicaragua)*, Joinder of Proceedings, Order of 17 April 2013, ICJ Reports, 2013, p. 166 ff., para. 24, and *Construction of a Road in Costa Rica along the San Juan River (Nicaragua v. Costa Rica)*, Joinder of Proceedings, Order of 17 April 2013, para. 18.

[62] Order of 2 February 2017, *cit. supra* note 60, para 13.

[63] *Ibid.*, para. 14. The reference is to the expert opinion arranged for by the Court in *Maritime Delimitation in the Caribbean Sea and the Pacific Ocean (Costa Rica v. Nicaragua)*, Order of 31 May 2016, ICJ Reports, 2016, p. 235 ff.

[64] Order of 2 February 2017, *cit. supra* note 60, para 16.

[65] *Ibid.*, para. 17. See the Orders in *Certain Activities* and *Construction of a Road,*, *cit. supra* note 61, paras. 17 and 23 respectively.

[66] *Ibid.*

[67] Although the agreement of the Parties was recorded in the case of *Certain German Interests in Polish Upper Silesia*, Order of 5 February 1926, PCIJ Reports, Series A, No. 7, Annex I, p. 95 ff., no mention of the issue is made in other cases. See *Legal Status of the South-Eastern Territory of Greenland*, Order of 2 August 1932, PCIJ Reports, Series A/B, No.

On the other hand, it sharply departs from the treatment of joinder in cases involving more than two States.[68]

It is also to be noted that no significant delays were caused by the Court's decision, as in the *Isla Portillos* case proceedings were managed at a particularly rapid pace "taking into account the nature of the case";[69] the judgment on the merits – where the Court identified the land boundary and upheld the contentions of Costa Rica as regards Nicaragua's military camp – was adopted just one year after the Order under discussion.[70]

4.2. *Provisional measures (I): The Order in the case concerning* Application of the International Convention for the Suppression of the Financing of Terrorism and of the International Convention on the Elimination of All Forms of Racial Discrimination (Ukraine v. Russian Federation)

The Order for the indication of provisional measures of 19 April 2017 in the case instituted by Ukraine against the Russian Federation is possibly the most sensitive decision adopted by the ICJ in the year under review. This complaint is one of the several steps taken by Ukraine and Ukrainian nationals – as well as by investors – to submit specific events related to the conflict in Ukraine, including the annexation of Crimea, to international adjudication or arbitration.[71]

The scope of the claims raised by Ukraine before the ICJ is in fact limited to alleged violations of the International Convention for the Suppression of the Financing of Terrorism (ICSFT) and the International Convention on the Elimination of All Forms of Racial Discrimination (CERD),[72] although the Court bears in mind the wider context in which the dispute has arisen: that of the conflict in eastern Ukraine, with "periods of extensive fighting which [...] has claimed a large number of lives", including as a consequence of the destruction

---

48, p. 157 ff.; *Appeals from Certain Judgments of the Hungaro-Czechoslovak Mixed Arbitral Tribunal*, Order of 12 May 1933, PCIJ Reports, Series A/B, No 56, p. 209 ff.

[68] TORRES BERNÁRDEZ, "Bilateral, Plural and Multipartite Elements in International Judicial Settlement" in ANDO, McWHINNEY and WOLFRUM (eds.), *Liber amicorum Judge Shigeru Oda*, The Hague, 2002, p. 995 ff.

[69] See the Order of 2 February 2017, *cit. supra* note 60, para. 15.

[70] See the Judgment of 2 February 2018.

[71] See, as regards cases pending before the ECHR, the Separate Opinion of Judge Cançado Trindade appended to the Order, paras. 60-61. On these and other initiatives see NURIDZHANIAN, "Ukraine vs. Russia in International Courts and Tribunals", EJIL: Talk!, 9 March 2016, available at: <https://www.ejiltalk.org/ukraine-versus-russia-in-international-courts-and-tribunals/>.

[72] See the *Application instituting proceedings*, filed on 16 January 2017, and the *Request for the indication of provisional measures of protection submitted by Ukraine*, submitted on the same day.

of the Malaysia Airlines flight MH17 on 17 July 2014.[73] The Court stressed in this regard that it

> is well aware of the extent of this human tragedy. Nevertheless, the case before the Court is limited in scope. In respect of the events in the eastern part of its territory, Ukraine has brought proceedings only under the ICSFT. With regard to the events in Crimea, Ukraine's claim is based solely upon CERD and the Court is not called upon, as Ukraine expressly recognized, to rule upon any issue other than allegations of racial discrimination.

Ukraine's litigation strategy is functional to establishing an adequate jurisdictional basis in the case: both the Applicant and the Respondent are parties to the Conventions at stake, which include compromissory clauses endowing the ICJ with jurisdiction over disputes relating to their interpretation and application, which could not be settled through negotiations.[74] While jurisdiction *ratione personae* was therefore not controversial, the existence (if only *prima facie*) of jurisdiction *ratione materiae* was disputed by Russia.

As the substantive obligations the two Conventions enshrined do not cover the core of the dispute opposing Ukraine to Russia, it is no surprise that Ukraine has purported a broad reading of the scope of the substantive engagements under those Treaties – arguing, notably, that "the definition of funds contained in the ICSFT is 'extremely broad' and includes in particular such weapons as those which it maintains have been provided by the Russian Federation", and that the obligation of cooperation enshrined in Article 18 "'is a broad one' and includes the obligation to take all practicable measures to prevent individuals from providing or collecting funds for terrorism as well as the State obligation not to finance terrorism directly".[75] Russia, on the other hand, maintained that no actual dispute existed between the parties that would fall under the scope of the two Conventions, since those acts of indiscriminate shelling and other humanitarian law violations could not qualify as "acts of terrorism" under Article 2(1) ICSFT[76] and, furthermore, Russia denied that direct financing of terrorism by States is prohibited under the said Convention.[77] Without taking a stance on either conten-

---

[73] See the Order of 19 April 2017, para. 16. See also the Declaration of Judge Tomka, para. 7, stressing that a prominent aspect of the dispute relates to the issue of sovereignty in Crimea.

[74] See Art. 24(1) ICSFT, and Art. 22 CERD. Both provisions enshrine further limitations to the Court's jurisdiction that are discussed below.

[75] Order of 19 April 2017, *cit. supra* note 73, para. 25.

[76] *Ibid.*, para. 26.

[77] *Ibid.*, para. 27. In the *Bosnian Genocide* case, the ICJ considered that Article I of the UN Convention against Genocide does "prohibit States from themselves committing genocide" although this engagement is not expressly stipulated therein: see *Application of the Convention on the Prevention and Punishment of the Crime of Genocide (Bosnia and Herzegovina v. Serbia and Montenegro)*, Judgment of 26 February 2007, ICJ Reports, 2007, p. 43 ff., para. 166).

tion, the Court considered that a dispute relating to ICSFT existed, at least *prima facie*,[78] and reached the same conclusion as regards the CERD.[79]

As regards the procedural conditions set forth by both the ICSFT and the CERD, Ukraine had made several efforts to negotiate a settlement before seising the Court, also in light of the *Georgia v. Russia* precedent.[80] Russia also relied on the further limitations enshrined in the compromissory clauses: under Article 24 ICSFT arbitration is actually the preferred method of settlement, with the ICJ being endowed with jurisdiction only if arbitral proceedings cannot be organised. Moreover, Article 22 CERD also includes a reference to the "procedures expressly provided for in this Convention"; according to Russia, this implies an obligation to preliminarily begin proceedings prior to the Committee on the Elimination of Racial Discrimination – which Ukraine had not done.[81] Eventually, the Court considered the procedural preconditions to be satisfied, at least *prima facie*[82] (although the issue may be raised again at a later stage of the proceedings).[83]

However, the Court also held that "Ukraine has not put before the Court evidence which affords a sufficient basis to find it plausible"[84] that the elements of intention or knowledge that the "funds" at stake would be used to carry out terrorist acts are present; it therefore rejected the requests for provisional measures under ICSFT.

Judges Owada and Bandhari and Judge *ad hoc* Pocar disagreed on this point, for different reasons. Judge Owada argued that the "plausibility" test applied for the purposes of the adoption of provisional measures should be a low one, distinct from the *prima facie* standard that applies for jurisdiction;[85] he therefore concluded that "the rights asserted by Ukraine concerning the ICSFT should be held to be plausible",[86] as the Court should not have expected Ukraine to show "conclusive evidence that the requirements of intention, knowledge and purposes are satisfied".[87] At the same time, he also considered that there was no risk of irreparable prejudice to the rights asserted by the Applicant, and therefore concurred with the majority in finding that no provisional measures should have been ordered in the light of the ICSFT.

---

[78] Order of 19 April 2017, *cit. supra* note 73, para. 31.

[79] *Ibid.*, para. 38.

[80] *Application of the International Convention on the Elimination of All Forms of Racial Discrimination (Georgia v. Russian Federation)*, Preliminary Objections, Judgment of 1 April 2011, ICJ Reports, 2011, p. 70 ff., para. 184; the ICJ declined to hear the merits of the case as the requirements set forth by Article 22 CERD had not been satisfied. See PALCHETTI, "The Activity of the International Court of Justice in 2011", IYIL, 2011, p. 259 ff., p. 263.

[81] Order of 19 April 2017, *cit. supra* note 73, para. 56.

[82] *Ibid.*, paras. 54 and 60-61.

[83] See LAVAL, "Ordonnance en indication de mesures conservatoirs du 19 avril 2017, *Application de la Convention internationale pour la repression du financement du terrorisme et de la Convention internationale sur l'élimination de toutes formes de discrimination raciale (Ukraine c. Russie)*", RGDIP, 2017, p. 916 ff., p. 918.

[84] Order of 19 April 2017, *cit. supra* note 73, para. 74.

[85] See his Separate Opinion, paras. 15-16.

[86] *Ibid.*, para. 21.

[87] *Ibid.*, para. 24.

Judge Bhandari, on the other hand, considered that provisional measures should have been granted also under ICSFT, as in order to prove plausibility "the applicant State must show that the rights it invokes are not manifestly unfounded, the so-called *fumus non mali iuris*".[88] Moreover, he posited that the relevant part of the order "could have benefited from a closer discussion of the evidence submitted by the parties"[89] (which he does pursue in his long Separate Opinion). In his view, notably, shelling of civilians could be regarded as terrorist acts under the ICSFT, although "they could also be regarded as IHL violations committed by both parties",[90] while "intent or knowledge" by those transferring financial assets through the Russian banking system "could be inferred from a pattern of behaviour relating to the indiscriminate targeting of civilians".[91]

Also Judge *ad hoc* Pocar criticised the Court's "brief reasoning" on the issue of plausibility, as "the frequency of the attacks on civilians and the wide availability of official reports thereon make it at least plausible that the providers of funds were aware that these might likely be used for such attacks";[92] he also took issue with the lack of clarity as to the standard applied for the purposes of the "plausibility" test, leading the parties to "excessively argue the merits" in the provisional measures phase and blur the distinction between these two procedural phases.[93]

As regards the rights invoked under CERD, in the Court's opinion "there is a correlation between respect for individual rights, the obligations of States parties under CERD and the right of States parties to seek compliance therewith";[94] furthermore, "on the basis of the evidence presented before the Court by the Parties, it appears that some of the acts complained of by Ukraine fulfil this condition of plausibility. This is the case with respect to the banning of the *Mejlis* and the alleged restrictions on the educational rights of ethnic Ukrainians".[95]

Also the requirement of a direct link between the measures sought and to the rights at risk of irreparable prejudice was affirmed only for

> the measures aimed at safeguarding the rights of Ukraine under Articles 2 and 5 of CERD with regard to the ability of the Crimean Tatar community to conserve its representative institutions and with regard to the need to ensure the availability of Ukrainian-language education in schools in Crimea.[96]

The Court relied on findings by the OHCHR and OSCE in order to conclude that the abolition of the *Mejlis* and the rapid decline of education in and of the

---

[88] Separate Opinion of Judge Bhandari, para. 16.
[89] *Ibid.*, para. 33.
[90] *Ibid.*, para. 32.
[91] *Ibid.*, para. 34.
[92] Separate Opinion of Judge *ad hoc* Pocar, para. 3.
[93] *Ibid.*, para. 8.
[94] Order of 19 April 2017, *cit. supra* note 73, para. 81.
[95] *Ibid.*, para. 83.
[96] *Ibid.*, para. 86.

Ukrainian language were evidence of an irreparable risk as regards the rights of Crimean Tartars and ethnic Ukrainians in Crimea – who "appear to remain vulnerable".[97] The notion of vulnerability and its importance for the purposes of provisional measures of protection was discussed at length by Judge Cançado Trindade,[98] arguing that "human vulnerability is a test even more compelling than "plausibility" of rights for the indication or ordering of provisional measures of protection".[99]

The Court eventually indicated provisional measures (which "need not be identical to those requested", as stipulated by Article 75, paragraph 2 of the Rules of Court),[100] to the effect that Russia should "[r]efrain from maintaining or imposing limitations on the ability of the Crimean Tatar community to conserve its representative institutions, including the *Mejlis*" and "[e]nsure the availability of education in Ukrainian language". Furthermore, it ordered that both parties "shall refrain from any action which might aggravate or extend the dispute before the Court or make it more difficult to resolve".[101]

Some Judges disagreed with the Court's stance as regards the CERD. Judge *ad hoc* Skotnikov considered that the obligations stemming from this Convention do not cover organisations similar to *Mejlis*, stressing moreover that their dissolution was due "to security grounds and for public order reasons that bore no relation to the ethnicity of the members of the *Mejlis*".[102] Also Judge Tomka, in his Declaration, criticised the "cavalier approach of the Court in requiring the Russian Federation to alter" the decisions of its judicial bodies as regards the suppression of the *Mejlis*,[103] as the Russian Federation is currently exercising sovereignty over Crimea and "must be able to take measures to ensure public order and safety".[104] While agreeing in principle, Judge Crawford argued that measures

> regulating an organization that represents an ethnic group [...] must be carefully justified. In this case, such justification is particularly necessary given the historical persecution of Crimean Tatars and the role of the *Mejlis* in advancing and protecting the rights of

---

[97] *Ibid.*, paras. 96-98.

[98] See his Separate Opinion, paras. 12 ff.

[99] *Ibid.*, para. 44. Judge Cançado Trindade further argued that "amidst generalized violence, the ultimate beneficiaries of obligations under ordered provisional measures of protection are human beings" (para. 68), and reiterated his positions as regards the autonomy of the provisional measures regime under Article 41 ICJ Statute, stressing that any breaches of such measures could be determined by the Court without waiting until the end of proceedings (para. 79) and would directly give rise to international responsibility.

[100] Order of 19 April 2017, *cit. supra* note 73, paras. 100-101.

[101] See *ibid.*, operative part. On the indication by the Court of "general measures" aimed at preventing the aggravation of the dispute see PALCHETTI, "The Power of the International Court of Justice to Indicate Provisional Measures to Prevent the Aggravation of a Dispute", Leiden JIL, 2008, p. 623 ff.; THIRLWAY, *The Law and Procedure of the International Court of Justice: Fifty Years of Jurisprudence*, Oxford, 2013, p. 947 ff.

[102] See his Separate Opinion, para. 2.

[103] Declaration of Judge Tomka, para. 4.

[104] *Ibid.*, para. 7.

the people it represents at a time of disruption and change. In an eventual merits hearing [...] it will be for the Court to assess the evidence provided by the Parties in this regard. At this stage of the proceedings it is sufficient to say that the measure in question, for the reasons given, plausibly affects rights under CERD.[105]

The Court emphasised that it "cannot at this stage make definitive findings of fact. The right of each Party to submit arguments in respect of the merits remains unaffected".[106] Despite this caveat, the rather rigorous approach to provisional measures that is by now typical of the ICJ's case law,[107] and especially the "plausibility" test, imply that the adoption or rejection of specific provisional measures do give important indications as to whether the underlying claims have some chance of being upheld at the merits stage.

The Court also made recommendations to the parties as regards issues that clearly did not fall within the scope of its jurisdiction, namely the conflict in Eastern Ukraine. Besides the expression of concern for the loss of human lives quoted above, it reminded the Parties of the adoption by the Security Council of Resolution 2202 (2015), which endorsed the Package of Measures for the Implementation of the Minsk Agreements, it further stated that it

expects the Parties, through individual and joint efforts, to work for the full implementation of this 'Package of Measures' in order to achieve a peaceful settlement of the conflict in the eastern regions of Ukraine.[108]

These kinds of recommendations or expressions of concern are not infrequent in the recent case law of the ICJ. They can be justified insofar as they are functional to the maintenance of international peace and security and reflect the role of the Court as a principal organ of the United Nations – especially so when they refer to a settlement that was endorsed by the Security Council[109] – although they do raise some difficulties in terms of respect for the principle of consent to international adjudication.[110]

---

[105] Declaration of Judge Crawford, para. 8.

[106] See Order of 19 April 2017, *cit. supra* note 73, para. 90; see also para. 105. A similar caution is called for by Judge *ad hoc* Pocar as regards the applicability of the ICSFT to the shooting down of the MH17 (see his Separate Opinion, paras. 10 ff.).

[107] THIRLWAY, *The Law and Procedure, cit. supra* note 101, p. 394.

[108] Order of 19 April 2017, *cit. supra* note 73, para. 104. See also *Armed Activities in the Territory of the Congo (Democratic Republic of the Congo v. Uganda)*, Judgment of 19 December 2005, ICJ Reports, 2005, p. 168 ff., para. 221.

[109] See OELLERS-FRAHM, "Article 41", in ZIMMERMAN et al. (eds.), *The Statute of the International Court of Justice – A Commentary*, 2nd ed., Oxford, 2012, p. 1026 ff., pp. 1072-1073; COUVREUR, *The International Court of Justice and the Effectiveness of International Law*, Leiden, 2016, p. 119 ss.

[110] See THIRLWAY, "The Recommendations Made by the International Court of Justice: A Skeptical View", ICLQ, 2009, p. 151 ff.

4.3. Provisional Measures (II): The Jadhav Case

The second Order under Article 41 of the ICJ Statute concerns the *Jadhav* case, a relatively less complex dispute – as is shown also by the fact that this Order was adopted unanimously. The proceedings were triggered by an application that India submitted against Pakistan on 8 May 2017, alleging violations of the 1963 Vienna Convention on Consular Relations. The dispute relates the possibility for the State of nationality (India) of a detained individual (Mr. Jadhav) sentenced to the death penalty, to visit him and grant consular assistance under Article 36 of the Vienna Convention; the invoked jurisdictional link is the Optional Protocol to that Convention.[111] The dispute currently pending has many similarities, but also significant differences from the *Breard*, *LaGrand* and *Avena* cases – not only because the respondent State is not the United States of America.[112] On the one hand, the underlying facts are disputed, with India claiming that Mr Jadhav was captured in Iran,[113] while Pakistan argues that he was arrested on Pakistani soil. The case involves also different legal arguments, as according to Pakistan the applicability of the 1963 Convention is precluded, on the one hand, by a Bilateral Agreement on consular access concluded by the Parties in 2008, and, on the other hand, because of the nature of the accusations moved against Mr. Jadhav (espionage).

At least in the provisional measures phase, however, the Court's course of action did not significantly differ from the one it undertook in the three cases against the United States. Although the ICJ did not adopt provisional measures *proprio motu*, as India had asked in line with what happened in the *LaGrand* case, President Abraham addressed a letter dated 9 May 2017 to the Prime Minister of Pakistan, under Article 74(4), of the Rules of Court, calling upon Pakistan "to act in such a way as will enable any order the Court may make on this Request to have its appropriate effects".[114] Furthermore, the Order on provisional measures was adopted, after hearing the parties, on 18 May 2017, only 10 days after the application was submitted – thus confirming the Court's ability to tackle urgent matters swiftly, even if the final settlement of cases may take several years.

With reference to the existence of *prima facie* jurisdiction, the Court deemed it irrelevant to assess whether the dispute would fall under the scope of Pakistan's

---

[111] See the Order on provisional measures of 18 May 2017, par. 3.

[112] On these cases and their impact see, among many other comments, SÉPULVEDA AMOR, "Diplomatic and Consular Protection: the Rights of the State and the Rights of the Individual in the 'LaGrand' and 'Avena' Cases", in *From Bilateralism to Community Interests – Essays in Honour of Judge Bruno Simma*, Oxford, 2011, p. 1097 ff.; HOSS, "*Vienna Convention on Consular Relations* (Paraguay v. United States of America), 1998", in ALMEIDA and SOREL (eds.), *Latin America and the International Court of Justice*, London/New York, 2017, p. 145 ff.

[113] See the *Application instituting proceedings*, filed on 8 May 2017, para. 13, but also the lengthy Declaration appended by Judge Bhandari to the Order on provisional measures, *cit. supra* note 111. No similar issues arose in the cases against the United States.

[114] See the account in the Order on provisional measures, *cit. supra* note 111, para. 8.

and India's respective unilateral declaration of acceptance under Article 36(2) of the ICJ Statute,[115] as India had not relied on that jurisdictional basis.[116] Moreover, the ICJ had little hesitation in assessing that a dispute over the interpretation and application of the Vienna Convention on Consular Relations existed between the Parties when the application was submitted.[117] More specifically, "the alleged failure by Pakistan to provide the requisite consular notifications with regard to the arrest and detention of Mr Jadhav, as well as the alleged failure to allow communication and provide access to him, appear to be capable of falling within the scope of the Vienna Convention *ratione materiae*".[118] The Court also deemed it unnecessary at this stage of the proceedings to determine, on the one side, whether the 1963 Convention applies to persons suspected of espionage or terrorism;[119] nor, on the other side, whether the Bilateral Agreement on consular access, which was registered by Pakistan under Article 102 of the UN Charter only after the beginning of the proceedings, could limit the effects of the said Convention.[120]

The possibility to invoke the 2008 Agreement would seem to be relatively straightforward now that it is registered, but its actual impact on the Vienna Convention regime is in itself open to discussion: under its Article 73(2), the 1963 Convention does not preclude subsequent agreements "confirming or supplementing or extending or amplifying the provisions thereof". Pakistan relies on this clause, and on the stipulation of paragraph (vi) of the 2008 Agreement, which posits that in "case of arrest, detention or sentence made on political or security grounds, each side may examine the case on its own merits", and argues that the Court does not have jurisdiction under Article 36(1) of the 1963 Convention.[121] As was mentioned above, the Court did not address the issue at this stage and concluded "that it has *prima facie* jurisdiction under Article I of the Optional Protocol to entertain the dispute between the Parties".[122] It is in any case difficult to see how the specific interpretation of paragraph (vi) purported by Pakistan could be read as "confirming or supplementing or extending or amplifying" the Convention's

---

[115] The Declaration deposited by Pakistan on 29 March 2017 carves out disputes involving "all matters related to the national security of the Islamic Republic of Pakistan" (letter *e*), whereas India excluded from the scope of its own declaration of 18 September 1974 cases involving two members of the Commonwealth, while including a "multilateral treaty reservation".

[116] See the Order on provisional measures, *cit. supra* note 111, para. 26. India did actually refer to the unilateral declarations at the hearings: see the Verbatim record of the hearing of 15 May 2017, p. 30. However, the Court also observes (para. 26 of the Order on provisional measures) that "any reservations contained in the declarations made by the Parties under Article 36, paragraph 2, of the Statute cannot impede the Court's jurisdiction specially provided for in the Optional Protocol".

[117] *Ibid.*, para. 27.
[118] *Ibid.* para. 30.
[119] *Ibid.*, para. 32.
[120] *Ibid.*, para. 33.
[121] *Ibid*, para. 25.
[122] *Ibid.*, para. 34.

provisions.[123] As regards the plausibility of the rights asserted by India,[124] the Order simply reads:

> It follows from Article 36, paragraph 1, that all States Parties to the Vienna Convention have a right to provide consular assistance to their nationals who are in prison, custody or detention in another State Party. They are also entitled to respect for their nationals' rights contained therein.[125]

This approach confirms that Article 36 of the 1963 Convention confers internationally protected rights both to the States *and* to their nationals.[126] Judge Cançado Trindade dealt extensively with this aspect in his Separate Opinion, stressing that the "right to information on consular assistance is, in the circumstances of the *cas d'espèce*, inextricably linked to the right to life itself, a fundamental and non-derogable one";[127] hence, in this kind of case, any decision on provisional measures "goes well beyond the simple search for a balance of the interests of the contending parties".[128] Albeit without discussing specifically these issues, the Court as such noted that it was not disputed that Pakistan has detained Mr. Jadhav and sentenced him to death without granting him consular access, and thus deemed the plausibility test to be met.[129]

The Court also deemed that a direct link existed between the rights invoked by India and the measures it sought: India seeks to ensure that "the Government of Pakistan will take no action that might prejudice its alleged rights, in particular that it will take all measures necessary to prevent Mr Jadhav from being executed before the Court renders its final decision",[130] with the aim of "preserving the rights of India and of Mr Jadhav under Article 36, paragraph 1, of the Vienna Convention".[131]

Finally, the ICJ had little difficulty in assessing also the condition of urgency, in light of the considerable uncertainties linked to the timing of any decision on Mr. Jadhav's appeal and on the execution date[132] – although it did take care to stress that "the issues brought before it in this case do not concern the question whether a State is entitled to resort to the death penalty".[133]

---

[123] See further, for partially different conclusions, PASCALE, "Sull'obbligo degli Stati di registrare gli accordi internazionali presso il Segretariato generale delle Nazioni Unite: il caso *Jadhav*", RDI, 2017, p. 1175 ff.

[124] See Order on provisional measures, *cit. supra* note 111, para. 43.

[125] *Ibid.*, para. 39.

[126] See *LaGrand (Germany v. United States of America)*, Judgment of 27 June 2001, ICJ Reports, 2001, p. 466 ff., para. 77; *Avena and Other Mexican Nationals (Mexico v. United States of America)*, Judgment of 31 March 2004, ICJ Reports, 2004, p. 12 ff., para. 40.

[127] Separate Opinion of Judge Cançado Trindade, para. 19.

[128] *Ibid.*, para. 23.

[129] See the Order on provisional measures, *cit. supra* note 111, p. 45.

[130] *Ibid.*, para. 47.

[131] *Ibid.* para. 48.

[132] *Ibid.*, paras. 53 ff.

[133] *Ibid.*, para. 56.

After reminding that provisional measures under Article 41 ICJ Statute "create international legal obligations for any party to whom the provisional measures are addressed"[134] the Court thus ordered Pakistan to

> take all measures at its disposal to ensure that Mr. Jadhav is not executed pending the final decision in these proceedings and [...] inform the Court of all the measures taken in implementation of the present Order.

It also decided that, "until the Court has given its final decision, it shall remain seised of the matters which form the subject-matter of this Order".[135]

The content of the Order is similar to the one used in the *Breard, LaGrand* and *Avena* cases: as in those instances, reference is made to an obligation by Pakistan to take "all measures at its disposal" to avoid the execution of Mr Jadhav. This by now familiar language echoes the notion of due diligence – although it would seem more appropriate to frame Pakistan's obligations as obligations of result, rather than of means, as what is to be avoided here is action that would be undertaken by State organs.[136] As regards the indication that the Court will remain "seised of the matter", the exact function of this and similar formulations used in the past is not clear. Arguably "it may indicate that the Court could act *proprio motu* or in coordination with either party if circumstances so require".[137] This may be of some relevance insofar as the power for the ICJ to modify provisional measures *ex officio* is not expressly acknowledged in the ICJ Rules of Court; moreover, Pakistan did not offer assurances that it would not execute Mr. Jadhav during the proceedings, and this is one of the reasons underlying the Court's Order.[138] At the same time, there are no signs that Pakistan will not comply with the Order as such – although it is ultimately difficult to envisage whether the final decision of the case can really lead to a satisfactory outcome for Mr. Jadhav.[139]

4.4   The Order on Counter-Claims in Nicaragua/Colombia

The Order of 15 November 2017 is just one of the several phases of a "judicial saga" relating to the maritime delimitation between Nicaragua and Colombia, which has been under the attention of the Court for about 15 years and led

---

[134] *Ibid.*, para. 59.

[135] Ibid., see the operative part.

[136] India's requests was indeed framed in terms of an obligation of result. See further FORLATI, "Il contenuto degli obblighi imposti dalle misure cautelari indicate nel caso *LaGrand*", RDI, 2001, p. 711 ff., pp. 717-719.

[137] See OELLERS-FRAHM, "Article 41", *cit. supra* note 109, p. 1060.

[138] See *Alleged Violations of Sovereign Rights and Maritime Spaces in the Caribbean Sea (Nicaragua v. Colombia)*, Order of 15 November 2017, para. 54.

[139] See the doubts expressed by BLONDEL, "Cour internationale de justice, Ordonnance en indication de mésures conservatoires du 18 mai 2017, *Affaire Jadhav (Inde c. Pakistan)*", RGDIP, 2017, p. 919 ff., p. 921.

Colombia to denounce the Pact of Bogotá out of dissatisfaction with the merits judgment in the *Territorial and Maritime Dispute (Nicaragua v. Colombia)* case, of 19 November 2012. Nicaragua submitted a further application to the Court on 26 November 2013 (one day before Colombia's denunciation became effective), arguing that Colombia had not implemented the judgment. More specifically, Nicaragua contends that Colombia has infringed

> (a) its obligation not to violate Nicaragua's maritime zones as delimited in paragraph 251 of the Court Judgment of 19 November 2012 as well as Nicaragua's sovereign rights and jurisdiction in these zones; (b) its obligation not to use or threaten to use force under Article 2 (4) of the UN Charter and international customary law; (c) and that, consequently, Colombia has the obligation to wipe out the legal and material consequences of its internationally wrongful acts, and make full reparation for the harm caused by those acts.[140]

Colombia's preliminary objections were rejected by Judgment of 17 March 2016, finding *inter alia* that it had jurisdiction under Article XXXI of the Pact of Bogotá – since its denunciation had not yet come into effect when the application was submitted.[141]

After the 2016 Judgment, however, Colombia included in his counter-memorial a number of counter-claims, seeking an assessment that Nicaragua has infringed "Colombia's sovereign rights and maritime spaces in the Caribbean sea by failing to prevent its flag or licensed vessels from fishing in Colombia's waters" and "from engaging in predatory and unlawful fishing methods in violation of its international obligations"; "by failing to fulfil its international legal obligations with respect to the environment in areas of the Caribbean Sea to which said obligations apply"; "has failed to respect the traditional and historic fishing rights of the inhabitants of the San Andrés Archipelago, including the indigenous Raizal people, in the waters to which they are entitled to said rights"; moreover, in establishing straight baselines Nicaragua allegedly violated "international law and Colombia's maritime rights and spaces".[142]

As the Order under discussion points out, counter-claims are understood by the Court as "autonomous legal acts the object of which is to submit new claims to the Court which are, at the same time, linked to the principal claims, in so far as they are formulated as 'counter' claims that react to those principal claims".[143]

---

[140] These are the submissions as specified in the Memorial, together with the claims as regards reparations: see the Order of 15 November 2017, *cit. supra* note 138, para. 12.

[141] *Alleged Violations of Sovereign Rights and Maritime Spaces in the Caribbean Sea (Nicaragua v. Colombia)*, Judgment of 17 March 2016, ICJ Reports, 2016, p. 3 ff., para. 48.

[142] See the Order of 15 November 2017, *cit. supra* note 138, para. 14. The counter-claims (which were formulated in different ways in different parts of the written defences: see *ibid.*, paras. 26-27) were supplemented by a number of requests in terms of reparations.

[143] See *ibid.*, para 18. As Judge *ad hoc* Caron observed in his Dissenting Opinion, counter-claims are a "construction of the Court rather than a provision of its Statute" (para. 4), since the Statute does not mention them and they are regulated in the Rules of Court.

Under the current text of Article 80(1) of the Rules of Court, "[t]he Court may entertain a counter-claim only if it comes within the jurisdiction of the Court and is directly connected with the subject-matter of the claim of the other party".

The compatibility of Colombia's counter-claims with both these (cumulative) requirements was challenged in the instant case. The Court deemed it appropriate to verify first[144] if a "direct connection" existed between claims and counter-claims, recalling that its previous case law had considered both factual and legal connections to be relevant in this regard: as regards the first aspect, it had notably sought to ascertain "whether the facts relied upon by each party relate to the same factual complex, including the same geographical area or the same time period" and "whether the facts relied upon by each party are of the same nature, in that they allege similar types of conduct",[145] whereas connection in law may be present when there is a connection "in terms of the legal principles or instruments relied upon, as well as whether the applicant and the respondent were considered as pursuing the same legal aim by their respective claims".[146]

In this respect, the counter-claims relating to the behaviour of Nicaraguan fishermen and to the alleged pollution of the Caribbean Sea, the Court opined, did not relate to the same "factual complex" as the claims of Nicaragua (since the alleged violations were of different nature and occurred in different maritime areas),[147] nor was a legal connection present as

> the legal principles relied upon by the Parties are different. In its first two counter-claims, Colombia invokes rules of customary international law and international instruments relating essentially to the preservation and protection of the environment; by contrast, in its principal claims, Nicaragua refers to customary rules of the international law of the sea relating to the sovereign rights, jurisdiction and duties of a coastal State within its maritime areas […]. Secondly, the Parties are not pursuing the same legal aim by their respective claims. While Colombia seeks to establish that Nicaragua has failed to comply with its obligation to protect and preserve the marine environment in the south-western Caribbean Sea, Nicaragua seeks to demonstrate that Colombia has violated Nicaragua's sovereign rights and jurisdiction within its maritime areas.[148]

The Court thus concluded that these counter-claims did not meet the requirement of direct connection and where therefore inadmissible.

On the other hand, the third counter-claim, relating to the traditional fishing rights of the inhabitants of the San Andrés Archipelago, was deemed to be di-

---

[144] *Ibid.*, paras. 22 ff.
[145] *Ibid.*, para. 24.
[146] *Ibid.*, para. 25.
[147] *Ibid.*, para. 37.
[148] *Ibid.*, para. 38.

rectly connected to the principal claims, as the underlying facts relate to the same time-period, the same geographical area and the same kind of behaviours by the naval forces of the two Parties;[149] according to Judge Greenwood and Judge Donoghue, specifically this counter-claim actually falls within the scope of the dispute originally brought before the Court by Nicaragua.[150]

The fourth counter-claim concerns the contention that the adoption of straight baselines through Decree No. 33-2013 violated Colombia's rights, as Nicaragua

> extended its internal waters eastward, thereby 'den[ying] the right of innocent passage and freedom of navigation in vast stretches of sea in which these rights and freedoms should be enjoyed'; secondly, it extended the territorial sea of Nicaragua, having the consequence of unduly restraining Colombia's navigational rights; thirdly, it extended Nicaragua's exclusive economic zone, which 'created an artificial overlap with Colombia's entitlement to its exclusive economic zone and continental shelf'.[151]

The Court held also this counter-claim to meet the "direct connection" test, as it relates to legislative acts adopted in the same time frame as the Colombian legislation on delimitation of maritime areas in dispute and, moreover, both the claims and the counter-claim relate to the "delineation of their respective maritime spaces in the same geographical area".[152]

As regards the third and fourth counter-claims, the Court therefore had to assess whether it had jurisdiction over the counter-claims: in this respect Nicaragua posited that the critical date for determining jurisdiction is the date on which they were submitted – that is, nearly three years after the Pact ceased its effects between the Parties.[153] The Court reached a different conclusion, noting that the counter-claims had been brought under the same head of jurisdiction as the principal claims[154] and that although

> counter-claims are autonomous legal acts the object of which is to submit new claims to the Court, they are, at the same time, linked to the principal claims, and their purpose is to react to them in the same proceedings in respect of which they are incidental. Consequently, the lapse of the jurisdictional title invoked by an applicant in support of its claims subsequent to the filing of the application does not

---

[149] *Ibid.*, paras. 44-46. See also the Declaration of Judge Cançado Trindade, paras. 18 ff.

[150] See the Separate Opinion of Judge Greenwood, para. 12, and the Separate Opinion of Judge Donoghue, para. 2. In their view, the other counter-claims should have been dismissed for lack of jurisdiction, as the Pact of Bogotá was no longer in force between the parties when they were submitted and they did not fall under the scope of the dispute originally introduced by Nicaragua.

[151] Order of 15 November 2017, *cit. supra* note 138, para. 47.

[152] *Ibid.*, paras. 52, 54.

[153] *Ibid.*, para. 59..

[154] *Ibid.*, para. 68.

deprive the Court of its jurisdiction to entertain counter-claims filed on the same jurisdictional basis.[155]

On this basis, the Court went on to assess whether the relevant dispute existed before their submission (and concluded positively on both issues);[156] secondly, it also concluded that the matters raised by the counter-claims "could not 'in the opinion of the Parties [...] be settled by direct negotiations'"[157] as prescribed by Article II of the Pact of Bogotá.[158]

The Court's stance on the issue of jurisdiction met with the joint dissent of Judges Tomka, Gaja, Sebutinde, Gevorgian and Judge *ad hoc* Daudet, who argued that the relevant title of jurisdiction must exist at the time when the counter-claims are submitted – as counter-claims, by their very nature, broaden the scope of the dispute brought before the Court.[159] Moreover, even if an appropriate title of jurisdiction did exist, the Court has "discretion to refuse to deal with a counter-claim".[160] The dissenters further note that

> the Court's decision does not contribute to the good and efficient administration of justice. Filing of counter-claims has already resulted in a one year delay of these proceedings. It is highly likely that this case, brought before the Court in 2013, will be heard and adjudicated only some seven years later.[161]

Indeed, judicial economy is traditionally the main rationale for counter-claims[162] – together with the principle of the "sound administration of justice".[163] The joint Dissenting Opinion rightly points out that the Order under discussion does not fit into this picture, as the autonomy of counter-claims is somehow overshadowed by

---

[155] *Ibid.*, para. 67, where the Court also noted "that the opposite approach would have the disadvantage of allowing the applicant, in some instances, to remove the basis of jurisdiction after an application has been filed and thus insulate itself from any counter-claims submitted in the same proceedings and having a direct connection with the principal claim". This argument was challenged by the Joint Dissenting Opinion, para. 22.

[156] Order of 15 November 2017, *cit. supra* note 138, paras 72-73.

[157] *Ibid.*, para. 74.

[158] *Ibid.*, paras. 75-76. On the obligation of negotiation as a preliminary condition for adjudication see WELLENS, *Negotiations in the Case Law of the International Court of Justice – A Functional Analysis*, Farnham, 2014, p. 99 ff.

[159] Joint Dissenting Opinion, para. 15. See also the stance of Judges Greenwood and Donoghue on this issue, referred to above in the text, adopting a similar approach to the issue of jurisdiction.

[160] *Ibid.*, para. 4.

[161] *Ibid.*, para. 23.

[162] See ANZILOTTI, "La riconvenzione nel processo internazionale", RDI, 1929, p. 307 ff.; *Application of the Convention on the Prevention and Punishment of the Crime of Genocide (Bosnia and Herzegovina v. Yugoslavia), Counter-Claims*, Order of 17 December 1997, ICJ Reports, 1997, p. 243 ff., paras. 27 and 30.

[163] See the Declaration of Judge Cançado Trindade, *cit. supra* note 149, para. 7.

their being accessory to the main claims.[164] This aspect is assessed positively by Vice-President Yusuf,[165] in whose opinion it

> is when the Court is faced with reliance on a different title of juris-
> diction, and in that kind of scenario only, that it will have to address
> the question of jurisdiction over the counter-claims separately from
> the question of jurisdiction over the principal claim. In such a case,
> jurisdiction over the principal claim will not be decisive in terms
> of jurisdiction over a counter-claim based on some other title, and
> the validity of the jurisdictional basis of the counter-claims must
> be assessed at the moment such counter-claims are brought to the
> Court.[166]

At the same time, the broad approach to the issue of jurisdiction may help explaining the rather strict reading of the "direct connection" requirement, which was deemed not to exist as regards the first and second counter-claim. Judge *ad hoc* Caron disagreed with this aspect of the Order, and took issue with the way in which the Court's discretion was exercised on this point. After stressing the importance of articulating the reasons underlying the Court's decisions in this respect,[167] the Judge *ad hoc* argued that specifically the first and second counter-claims should be admitted, as the aim of pursuing the "sound administration of justice" should be read in a broad way, as conducive not only to consistency and procedural economy, but also to a comprehensive settlement of international disputes.[168]

This contention is, as such, convincing; however, precisely the stance on jurisdiction adopted in the Order under discussion would seem to hinder a more flexible approach to the assessment of a "direct connection" – as it would further enhance the advantage for the respondent State which decides to withdraw from the instrument constituting the jurisdictional link for the main claim, while rely-ing on the Court's incidental jurisdiction to raise counterclaims on issues that are only loosely related to the main dispute.

---

[164] See the Joint Dissenting Opinion, *cit. supra* note 159, para. 6.

[165] Declaration of Vice-President Yusuf, paras. 6 and 10.

[166] *Ibid.*, para. 11. The possibility to rely on a jurisdictional basis that is different from the one on which the original claims are based has been called into question in the past: see ANTONOPOULOS, *Counterclaims before the International Court of Justice*, The Hague, 2011; KOLB, *The International Court of Justice*, Oxford, 2013, p. 665.

[167] See his Dissenting Opinion, para. 9.

[168] *Ibid.*, paras. 28 and 30. See also the Declaration of Judge *ad hoc* Guillaume, *Certain Activities Carried Out by Nicaragua in the Border Area (Costa Rica v. Nicaragua)* and *Construction of a Road in Costa Rica along the San Juan River (Nicaragua v. Costa Rica), Counter-Claims*, Order of 18 April 2013, ICJ Reports, 2013, p. 221, para. 17, criticizing the Court for "mov[ing] its case law in a restrictive direction".

5. CONCLUDING REMARKS

The judicial activity of the ICJ in 2017 was mainly focused on issues of jurisdiction, admissibility and on procedural matters – with provisional measures providing, however, important indications as to whether there is any likelihood that specific claims will eventually be upheld. Moreover, the number of cases on the docket and the nature of issues the Court is called upon to address confirm its central role in the realm of international courts and tribunals – a role that the Court is keen to safeguard, as the *Somalia v. Kenya* Judgment clearly shows. In his last address to the General Assembly, President Abraham noted

> the confidence that the international community continues to place in the Court by submitting to it a wide variety of disputes, each raising important legal questions concerning numerous areas of international law. Beyond the clear role the Court has played – and continues to play – in consolidating and developing the law governing issues that could be described as traditional, such as territorial and maritime delimitations, it is increasingly called upon to decide on questions at the heart of the international community's current concerns.[169]

The Court's ability to effectively address such kind of questions remains limited by the principle of consent, as the *Ukraine v. Russia* case shows. At the same time, its docket and the complexity of the disputes it is called upon to address do raise the problem of whether it is possible to further enhance the efficiency – as well as the fairness – of its proceedings. After the Court itself raised the issue in its 2015 "Counsel Survey",[170] reflection continues also in other contexts.[171] The ICJ judicial practice in the year under review confirms, in any case, that the Court can deal swiftly with the issues submitted to it when there are reasons of urgency (such as with the provisional measures adopted in the *Jadhav* case), and that decisions adopted in specific instances (notably as regards joinder in the *Isla Portillos* case) do not necessarily cause undue delay in the hearing of cases on the merits.

---

[169] Speech by H.E. Mr. Ronny Abraham, President of the International Court of Justice, on the Occasion of the Seventy-Second Session of the United Nations General Assembly, 27 October 2017, p. 8.

[170] See CRAWFORD and KEENE, "Editorial", Journal of International Dispute Settlement, 2016, p. 225 ff.

[171] On the work of the ILA Committee on Procedure of International Courts and Tribunals see SARVARIAN, *cit. supra* note 33.

THE INTERNATIONAL TRIBUNAL FOR THE LAW OF THE SEA
AND OTHER LAW OF THE SEA JURISDICTIONS (2017)

TULLIO TREVES[*]

1. 2017 has seen important changes in the composition of the International Tribunal for the Law of the Sea (ITLOS) and developments in dispute-settlement activities under the UN Convention for the Law of the Sea (UNCLOS) in the Tribunal and in another forum.[1]

As regards the composition of the Tribunal, the Parties to UNCLOS in the elections held in 2017 have elected five new Judges, while two Judges have been re-elected. The new Judges are Mr. Oscar Cabello of Paraguay, Ms. Neeru Chadha of India, Mr. Kriangsak Kittchaisaree of Thailand, Mr. Roman Kolodkin of the Russian Federation and Ms. Lisbeth Lijnzaad of the Netherlands. Judges Neeru and Lijzaad had previously represented their countries as agents in cases before the Tribunal. The re-elected Judges are Judges Bouguetaia and Jesus.

In October 2017, the Tribunal elected a new President, Judge Jin-Hyun Paik, a new vice-president, Judge David Attard, and a new President of the Seabed Disputes Chamber, Judge Albert Hoffman. A few weeks after his election the new President delivered an unusually substantive speech to the UN General Assembly, some excerpts of which are reproduced below in paragraph 2.

As regards the Tribunal's judicial activity, the only important development was the handing out, on 23 September 2017, of the Judgment of a Tribunal's

---

[*] Professor Emeritus, University of Milan; former Judge of the International Tribunal for the Law of the Sea (1996-2011). The views expressed are personal.

[1] Previous instalments of the present chronicle are: TREVES, "The International Tribunal for the Law of the Sea (1996-2000)", IYIL, 2000, p. 233 ff.; ID., "The International Tribunal for the Law of the Sea (2001)", IYIL, 2001, p. 165 ff.; ID., "The International Tribunal for the Law of the Sea (2002)", IYIL, 2002, p. 207 ff.; ID., "The International Tribunal for the Law of the Sea (2003)", IYIL, 2003, p. 157 ff.; ID., "The International Tribunal for the Law of the Sea (2004)", IYIL, 2004, p. 289 ff.; ID., "The International Tribunal for the Law of the Sea (2005)", IYIL, 2005, p. 255 ff.; ID., "The International Tribunal for the Law of the Sea and Other Law of the Sea Jurisdictions (2006)", IYIL, 2006, p. 227 ff.; ID., "The International Tribunal for the Law of the Sea and Other Law of the Sea Jurisdictions (2007)", IYIL, 2007, p. 175 ff.; ID., "The International Tribunal for the Law of the Sea and Other Law of the Sea Jurisdictions (2008-2009)", IYIL, 2009, p. 315 ff.; ID., The International Tribunal for the Law of the Sea and Other Law of the Sea Jurisdictions (2010)", IYIL, 2010, p. 315 ff.; ID., "The International Tribunal for the Law of the Sea and Other Law of the Sea Jurisdictions (2011)", IYIL, 2011, p. 275 ff.; ID., "The International Tribunal for the Law of the Sea and Other Law of the Sea Jurisdictions (2012)", IYIL, 2012, p. 245 ff.; ID., "The International Tribunal for the Law of the Sea and Other Law of the Sea Jurisdictions (2013)", IYIL, 2013, p. 354 ff.; ID., "The International Tribunal for the Law of the Sea and Other Law of the Sea Jurisdictions (2014)", IYIL, 2014, p. 341 ff.; ID., "The International Tribunal for the Law of the Sea and Other Law of the Sea Jurisdictions (2015)", IYIL, 2015, p. 354 ff. (TREVES, ITLOS 2015); ID., "The International Tribunal for the Law of the Sea and Other Law of the Sea Jurisdictions (2016)", IYIL, 2016, p. 393 ff.

Special Chamber – chaired by Judge Bouguetaia, and composed by Judges Paik and Wolfrum, and, as *ad hoc* judges, Judges Abraham and Mensah – on the *Dispute concerning delimitation of the maritime boundary between Ghana and Cote d'Ivoire in the Atlantic Ocean*.[2]

Outside the Tribunal, one important development concerning dispute-settlement within the framework of UNCLOS may be signalled and will be examined in the present chronicle. This is the settlement of a dispute between Timor-Leste and Australia, through the work of a Conciliation Commission established under Annex V to the UNCLOS.

Very interesting for the law of the sea is also the Final Award handed out on 29 June 2017 in the *Croatia/Slovenia* case.[3] The jurisdiction of the arbitral tribunal was based on an agreement between the two States signed on 4 November 2009.[4] The Award concerns "the maritime and land boundary" between the two States, "Slovenia's junction to the high seas", and the "regime for the use of the relevant maritime areas".[5] The applicable law was indicated as "the rules and principles of international law" for the maritime and land boundary issues, while it was agreed to be "international law, equity, and the principle of good neighbourly relations in order to achieve a fair and just result by taking into account all relevant circumstances" for the determinations concerning Slovenia's junction to the high seas and the regime of the maritime areas.[6] Notwithstanding the relevance of this case for the law of the sea, as well as for the delimitation of land boundaries, and for its tormented procedural history,[7] we will not examine it in detail because it is not based on the jurisdictional clauses of the UNCLOS and consequently is not encompassed in the scope of the present chronicle.

2. Among the substantive points made by President Paik in his speech to the UN General Assembly,[8] those on delimitation and on subjects which may be submitted to the Tribunal in the future seem particularly interesting.

---

[2] *Dispute concerning delimitation of the maritime boundary between Ghana and Côte d'Ivoire in the Atlantic Ocean*, Judgment of 23 September 2017, unanimously decided by the Special Chamber, with Separate Opinions of Judges Paik and Mensah. On the Order for provisional measures (25 April 2015, ITLOS Reports, 2015, p. 145) see TREVES, ITLOS 2015, *cit. supra* note 1, p. 368.

[3] *In the matter of an Arbitration under the Arbitration Agreement between the Government of the Republic of Croatia and the Government of the Republic of Slovenia, Signed on 4 November 2009*, Final Award of 29 June 2017, PCA Case No. 2012-04.

[4] See Arbitration Agreement between the Government of the Republic of Slovenia and the Government of the Republic of Croatia, 4 November 2009. The text of the Arbitration Agreement is annexed to the Final Award, *cit. supra* note 3.

[5] Arbitration Agreement, Art. 3(1).

[6] *Ibid.*, Art. 4.

[7] See Final Award, *cit. supra* note 3, paras. 145-206 (History of the Proceedings). See also the Partial Award of 30 June 2016.

[8] ITLOS, "Statement by H.E. Judge Jin-Hyun Paik, President of the International Tribunal for the Law of the Sea, on Agenda Item 77(a) 'Oceans and the Law of the Sea' at the Plenary of the Seventy-second Session of the United Nations General Assembly", 5 December 2017,

As regards maritime delimitation, President Paik stated:

> The Tribunal has handled two major cases concerning the delim-
> itation of maritime spaces, the *Bay of Bengal case (Bangladesh/
> Myanmar)* […] and the *Dispute concerning delimitation of the
> maritime boundary in the Atlantic Ocean (Ghana/Côte d'Ivoire)*
> […] Both Judgments demonstrate that the Tribunal sees its role as
> being part of a community of international courts and tribunals and
> takes into account the existing jurisprudence. The Tribunal there-
> fore offers the parties to maritime delimitation cases a fair degree
> of predictability.
> At the same time, the Tribunal and the Special Chamber, in their
> respective Judgments, made important new contributions to the de-
> velopment of international jurisprudence on maritime delimitation.
> This was, for instance, the case when, as I mentioned before, the
> Tribunal in the *Bay of Bengal* case, for the first time in the history of
> international adjudication, proceeded to delimit the continental shelf
> beyond 200 nm. The Special Chamber in the case between Ghana
> and Côte d'Ivoire also provided clarification with regard to legal
> questions that had so far received only limited attention in interna-
> tional jurisprudence, such as the interpretation of article 83, para-
> graph 3, of the Convention. Let me add that the Special Chamber
> also broke new ground in its Order on Provisional Measures in that
> case in which it prescribed, among other measures, that new drill-
> ing activities conducted in the disputed area had to be suspended,
> pending the final judgment.

As regards the "new issues that might be submitted to dispute settlement
before the Tribunal", President Paik stated:

> In this respect, the international community is looking with great
> interest and anticipation at the current negotiations taking place, at
> the initiative of the General Assembly, concerning the development
> of an international legally binding instrument under UNCLOS on
> the conservation and sustainable use of marine biological diversity
> of areas beyond national jurisdiction.
> It is too early to say today what the exact contents of that instru-
> ment will be. It may be anticipated, however, that dispute-settle-
> ment provisions will be an important element of such instrument
> in order to maintain its consistent and efficient interpretation and
> application.

---

available at: <https://www.itlos.org/fileadmin/itlos/documents/statements_of_president/paik/
GA2017_Paik_En.pdf>.

3. The Jurisdiction of the Tribunal's Special chamber in the *Ghana/Côte d'Ivoire* case was based on a Special Agreement concluded by the parties during consultations held with the President of ITLOS following the Notification by Ghana instituting arbitral proceedings under Annex VII of UNCLOS. With the Special Agreement, the parties transferred the arbitral proceeding instituted by Ghana to a Special Chamber of ITLOS.[9] This is the second time that arbitral proceedings instituted under Annex VII were transferred to a Special Chamber of the Tribunal, the first being the *Swordfish* case between Chile and the EU.

The first point dealt with by the Chamber concerns the existence of a tacit agreement for the maritime delimitation whose existence was claimed by Ghana, arguing especially from the practice of oil concessions. The Chamber recalled the statement of the ICJ in *Territorial and Maritime Dispute between Nicaragua and Honduras in the Caribbean Sea (Nicaragua* v. *Honduras)*:[10]

> 'Evidence of a tacit legal agreement must be compelling. The establishment of a permanent maritime boundary is a matter of grave importance and agreement is not easily to be presumed' (Judgment, I.C.J. Reports 2007 (II), p. 659, at p. 735, para. 253).

The Chamber then, in support of its conclusion, set out in para. 228, that there was "no tacit agreement between the Parties to delimit their territorial sea, exclusive economic zone and continental shelf both within and beyond 200 nm" stated, in particular, the following:

> 215. The Special Chamber considers that the oil practice, no matter how consistent it may be, cannot in itself establish the existence of a tacit agreement on a maritime boundary. Mutual, consistent and long-standing oil practice and the adjoining oil concession limits might reflect the existence of a maritime boundary, or might be explained by other reasons. [...]
>
> 225. The Special Chamber observes that States often offer and award oil concessions in an area yet to be delimited. It is not unusual for States to align their concession blocks with those of their neighbouring States so that no areas of overlap arise. They obviously do so for different reasons, but not least out of caution and prudence to avoid any conflict and to maintain friendly relations with their neighbours. To equate oil concession limits with a maritime boundary would be equivalent to penalizing a State for exercising such caution and prudence. It would be contrary to article 74, paragraph 3, and article 83, paragraph 3, of the Convention, which require States, pending agreement on delimitation, in a spirit of understanding and cooperation, not to jeopardize or hamper the reach-

---

[9] Judgment, *cit. supra* note 2, paras. 1-5.

[10] *Ibid.*, para. 212.

ing of the final agreement. It would also entail negative implications for the conduct of States in the area to be delimited elsewhere.

226. The Special Chamber has another reason not to accept Ghana's argument for the existence of a tacit agreement on a maritime boundary. The boundary the Special Chamber has to delimit is a single maritime boundary delimiting the territorial sea, exclusive economic zone and the continental shelf. In the Special Chamber's view, evidence relating solely to the specific purpose of oil activities in the seabed and subsoil is of limited value in proving the existence of an all-purpose boundary which delimits not only the seabed and subsoil but also superjacent water columns. As the ICJ stated in *Maritime Dispute (Peru v. Chile)*, "the all-purpose nature of the maritime boundary [...] means that evidence concerning fisheries activity, in itself, cannot be determinative of the extent of that boundary" (Judgment, I.C.J. Reports 2014, p. 3, at p. 45, para. 111).

The Special Chamber starts its examination of the question of delimitation with the territorial sea. Observing that while one of the parties supported equidistance under Article 15 of UNCLOS, and the other the bisector method, the Judgment states:

257. Both parties, in their final submissions, ask the Special Chamber to draw a single maritime boundary delimiting their territorial seas, exclusive economic zones and continental shelves both within and beyond 200 nm. [...] The Special Chamber notes that the same disagreement over the appropriate delimitation methodology exists between the Parties in respect of the delimitation of the exclusive economic zones and the continental shelves within and beyond 200 nm.

259. The Special Chamber interprets the submissions of both Parties to the effect that it should use the same delimitation methodology for the whole delimitation process, namely the methodology developed for the delimitation of exclusive economic zones and continental shelves.

260. It is for that reason that the Special Chamber will address the question of the appropriate delimitation methodology when it deals with the delimitation of the exclusive economic zones and continental shelves of the Parties.

The Chamber adds, however, two provisos to this statement. The first is in the same paragraph 260:

Nevertheless, the Special Chamber emphasizes that under the Convention different rules apply to the delimitation of territorial seas and the delimitation of exclusive economic zones and continental shelves.

The second proviso is in paragraph 262:

> 262. The Special Chamber considers it important to note that in de-
> limiting the territorial sea it has to be borne in mind that the rights
> of the coastal States concerned are not functional but territorial
> since they entail sovereignty over the seabed, the superjacent wa-
> ters and the air column above. This has been emphasized by the ICJ
> in *Maritime Delimitation and Territorial Questions between Qatar
> and Bahrain (Qatar v. Bahrain)* (Merits, Judgment, I.C.J. Reports
> 2001, p. 40, at p. 93, paras. 173-174). However, neither Ghana nor
> Côte d'Ivoire raised sovereignty-related considerations in respect
> of the delimitation of the territorial sea between them. The Special
> Chamber notes that the Parties, in requesting the Special Chamber
> to delimit a single maritime boundary for their territorial seas, ex-
> clusive economic zones and continental shelves, have implicitly
> agreed that the same delimitation methodology be used for these
> maritime spaces.

Coming to the delimitation of the exclusive economic zone and continental
shelf, the Special Chamber found "no convincing reason to deviate [...] from the
equidistance/relevant circumstances methodology".[11] Côte d'Ivoire had argued
in favour of the application of the "angle bisector methodology".[12] The Special
Chamber noted, however, that the relevant coasts of the Parties are straight and
not unstable, so that, therefore, there was no reason to assume that the identification of base points and the drawing of a provisional equidistance line would
be impossible or inappropriate.[13] After establishing the provisional equidistance
line, the Special Chamber examined "whether relevant circumstances requiring
an adjustment of [...] [that] line [...] exist", and came to the conclusion that no
such circumstance existed.[14] The delimitation line so adopted is an equidistant
line.

In examining the existence of special circumstances which would justify a
deviation from equidistance, the Chamber considered an argument raised by Côte
d'Ivoire based on the location of the oil resources. The Chamber rejected this
argument, as follows:

> 452. According to international jurisprudence, delimitation of mari-
> time areas is to be decided objectively on the basis of the geograph-
> ic configuration of the relevant coasts. Maritime delimitation is not
> a means for distributing justice. In general, the trend – as expressed
> in the *case concerning Continental Shelf (Libyan Arab Jamahiriya/
> Malta)* and reiterated in *Maritime Delimitation in the Area between*

---

[11] *Ibid.*, para. 324.
[12] *Ibid.*, para. 291.
[13] *Ibid.*, paras. 302 and 318.
[14] *Ibid.*, para. 480.

> *Greenland and Jan Mayen (Denmark v. Norway)* (Judgment, I.C.J. Reports 1993, p. 38, at pp. 73-74, paras. 79-80) – was that a maritime delimitation should not be "influenced by the relative economic position of the two States in question, in such a way that the area of continental shelf regarded as appertaining to the less rich of the two States would be somewhat increased in order to compensate for its inferiority in economic resources". [...]
>
> 453. In assessing the international jurisprudence, the Special Chamber wishes to emphasize that such jurisprudence, at least in principle, favours maritime delimitation which is based on geographical considerations. Only in extreme situations – in the words of the Chamber of the ICJ in the *Gulf of Maine* case – if the envisaged delimitation was 'likely to entail catastrophic repercussions for the livelihood and economic well-being of the population of the countries concerned' (see above at para. 452), may considerations other than geographical ones become relevant. In the view of the Special Chamber, Côte d'Ivoire has not advanced any arguments which might lead the Special Chamber to deviate from such jurisprudence.

As regards the delimitation of the continental shelf beyond 200 nautical miles, the Special Chamber is very brief. As far as the "methodology" to be followed is concerned , it

> 526. [...] recalls its position that there is only one single continental shelf. Therefore it is considered inappropriate to make a distinction between the continental shelf within and beyond 200 nm as far as the delimitation methodology is concerned.

From this, as regards the course of the line delimiting the continental shelf beyond 200 nautical miles, according to the Chamber, it follows that:

> 527. [...] the delimitation line for the territorial sea, the exclusive economic zone and the continental shelf within 200 nm as referred to in paragraph 481 continues in the same direction until it reaches the outer limits of the continental shelf.

The Chamber had preliminarily examined whether it had jurisdiction for deciding on delimitation of the continental shelf beyond 200 nautical miles, and whether the submissions concerning it were admissible. As to jurisdiction – although both parties held that jurisdiction existed – the Chamber stated that it had to decide on the subject *proprio motu*.[15] The Judgment recalls its position according to which there is only a single continental shelf. This seems implicitly

---

[15] *Ibid.*, para. 489.

decisive for holding that the Special Chamber had jurisdiction. The Judgment also states:

> 491. The Special Chamber can delimit the continental shelf beyond 200 nm only if such a continental shelf exists. There is no doubt about this in the case before the Special Chamber. Ghana has already completed the procedure before the CLCS. Côte d'Ivoire has made its submission to the CLCS and, although as yet the latter has not issued any recommendation, the Special Chamber has no doubt that a continental shelf beyond 200 nm exists for Côte d'Ivoire since its geological situation is identical to that of Ghana, for which affirmative recommendations of the CLCS exist.

The Judgment also makes interesting remarks about whether a decision of the Chamber on delimitation would interfere with the competence of the Commission for the Limits of the Continental Shelf (CLCS). It states:

> 493. In the view of the Special Chamber, the fact that Côte d'Ivoire has made its submission to the CLCS but that the latter has not yet made its recommendations in respect of Côte d'Ivoire does not call into question the admissibility of the submission on the delimitation of the continental shelf submitted to the Special Chamber by Côte d'Ivoire. It emphasizes that the functions of the CLCS and of the Special Chamber differ and it would like to refer to the Judgment of the Tribunal in *Delimitation of the maritime boundary in the Bay of Bengal (Bangladesh/Myanmar)* [reference to para. 376 of that judgment, whose text is quoted with approval].
> 517. Finally, the Special Chamber reiterates that the functions of the CLCS and those of the Special Chamber differ. Whereas the former deals with the delineation of the continental shelf beyond 200 nm, the latter decides on delimitation with a neighbouring State, that is to say, on the course of the lateral limits. Although those lateral limits have to intersect the outer limit, the Special Chamber would like to point out that its decision is without prejudice to the recommendations of the CLCS and the ensuing legislation as referred to in article 76, paragraph 8, of the Convention.

The last part of the Judgment deals with a claim by Côte d'Ivoire that Ghana had incurred international responsibility. Cote d'Ivoire based its claim on three different grounds:

> 544. […] First, it bases its claim upon an alleged violation of Côte d'Ivoire's sovereign rights by Ghana by conducting or licensing hydrocarbon activities in an area over which Côte d'Ivoire claims

to have sovereign rights; second, it invokes a violation of article 83
of the Convention; and, third, it claims that Ghana acted contrary
to its obligations as set out in the Order of the Special Chamber of
25 April 2015.

The Judgment envisages, preliminarily and *proprio motu*, whether the Special Chamber had jurisdiction to decide on these questions. The Special Chamber underlined "at the outset that jurisdiction to adjudicate over the alleged violation of the provisional measures prescribed by its Order of 25 April 2015 (see final submission no. 3 of Côte d'Ivoire) belongs to the inherent competence of the Tribunal" (paragraph 546).

The Special Chamber then discusses whether it had jurisdiction to decide on the claim of international responsibility. It considered that such a claim was not included in the Special Agreement because the expression "concerning the delimitation" contained therein was not broad enough. In the view of the Special Chamber, "it would stretch the meaning of the words "dispute concerning the delimitation of their maritime boundary" too much to interpret it in such a way that it included a dispute on international responsibility" (paragraph 548). However, in light of the conduct of both parties following the institution of proceedings (paragraphs 551 and 553), and of the jurisprudence on *forum prorogatum* (paragraph 552), the Special Chamber decided that it had jurisdiction on Côte d'Ivoire's claim concerning Ghana's alleged international responsibility (paragraph 554). The Special Chamber made the following remarks of general interest:

> 555. The Special Chamber adds that articles 286 and 288 of the Convention, according to which the jurisdiction of the dispute-settlement bodies under Part XV of the Convention concerns the interpretation and application of the Convention, do not bar it from deciding on international responsibility. Although the Convention does not contain rules concerning international responsibility, article 293, paragraph 1, of the Convention provides for the possibility to have recourse to other rules of international law. Article 293, paragraph 1, of the Convention reads: '[a] court or tribunal having jurisdiction under this section shall apply this Convention and other rules of international law not incompatible with this Convention'.
>
> 556. Following the jurisprudence of the Tribunal (see *M/V 'Virginia G' (Panama/Guinea-Bissau)*, Judgment, ITLOS Reports 2014, p. 4, with reference to earlier jurisprudence of the Tribunal), the Special Chamber will revert to general international law when deciding on issues concerning international responsibility.

As regards the applicable law, the Special Chamber, relying of the remarks of the Seabed Disputes Chamber that several of the International Law Commission's Articles on the Responsibility of States for Internationally

Wrongful Acts are considered to reflect customary international law,[16] stated that it

> 559. [...] will decide on the alleged international responsibility of Ghana on the basis of the relevant customary international law, as reflected in several articles of the ILC Articles on Responsibility of States for Internationally Wrongful Acts.

Coming to the substance of the Côte d'Ivoire claim that certain activities conducted by Ghana in a disputed area which the Judgment declared to belong to Côte d'Ivoire, constituted violations of its sovereign rights on its continental shelf, the Special Chamber stated:

> 590. The Special Chamber agrees with the statements of the two Parties that the sovereign rights which coastal States enjoy in respect of the continental shelves off their coasts are exclusive in nature and that coastal States have an entitlement to the continental shelves concerned without the need to make a relevant declaration. However, the Special Chamber disagrees with both Parties as to the meaning of a judgment on the delimitation of a continental shelf. The Parties both consider such a judgment only to be of a declaratory nature but they disagree as to the consequences to be drawn from such a qualification.
> 591. The Special Chamber emphasizes that in a case of overlap both States concerned have an entitlement to the relevant continental shelf on the basis of their relevant coasts. Only a decision on delimitation establishes which part of the continental shelf under dispute appertains to which of the claiming States. This means that the relevant judgment gives one entitlement priority over the other. Such a decision accordingly has a constitutive nature and cannot be qualified as merely declaratory.
> 592. In the view of the Special Chamber, the consequence of the above is that maritime activities undertaken by a State in an area of the continental shelf which has been attributed to another State by an international judgment cannot be considered to be in violation of the sovereign rights of the latter if those activities were carried out before the judgment was delivered and if the area concerned was the subject of claims made in good faith by both States.

Having so rejected the claim of responsibility for activities in the contested maritime area pending the judgment, the Special Chamber turns to the claim of responsibility under Article 83, paragraph 1, of UNCLOS, for violation of the

---

[16] *Ibid.*, para. 558. *See* ITLOS Seabed Disputes Chamber, *Responsibilities and Obligations of States sponsoring persons and entities with respect to activities in the Area*, Advisory Opinion of 1 February 2011, ITLOS Reports, 2011, p. 10, para. 169.

obligation to negotiate in good faith, and paragraph 3, for violation of the obligation not to jeopardize or hamper the conclusion of an agreement as provided in
that paragraph.

The claim under Article 83, paragraph 1, was rejected for the following reasons:

> 604. The Special Chamber notes that the obligation under article
> 83, paragraph 1, of the Convention to reach an agreement on de-
> limitation necessarily entails negotiations to this effect. The Special
> Chamber emphasizes that the obligation to negotiate in good faith
> occupies a prominent place in the Convention, as well as in general
> international law, and that this obligation is particularly relevant
> where neighbouring States conduct maritime activities in close
> proximity. The Special Chamber notes, however, that the obliga-
> tion to negotiate in good faith is an obligation of conduct and not
> one of result. Therefore, a violation of this obligation cannot be
> based only upon the result expected by one side not being achieved.
> Negotiations took place between Ghana and Côte d'Ivoire over six
> years, with 10 meetings between 2008 and 2014. Those meetings
> all dealt with the issue of maritime delimitation. In the view of the
> Special Chamber, Côte d'Ivoire has not produced any convincing
> arguments that these negotiations were not meaningful. Agreement
> was reached at least on the exact location of the land boundary ter-
> minus (BP 55), for example. The fact that Ghana tried to preserve
> the status quo as it saw it is, in the view of the Special Chamber,
> not a violation of an obligation to negotiate in good faith. Equally,
> the fact that Ghana initially closed off the avenue for a judicial set-
> tlement is not contrary to the obligation to negotiate in good faith,
> as Côte d'Ivoire claims. Article 298 of the Convention explicitly
> permits States Parties to exclude certain disputes from compulsory
> procedures.

As to the claim that Ghana had contravened Article 83, paragraph 3:

> 629. The Special Chamber will now turn to the second obligation
> under article 83, paragraph 3, of the Convention, namely 'during
> this transitional period, not to jeopardize or hamper the reaching of
> the final agreement'. In its view, in interpreting the obligation 'not
> to jeopardize or hamper the reaching of the final agreement', ac-
> count has to be taken of article 83, paragraph 3, of the Convention
> as a whole. This is confirmed by the fact that the first obligation
> (shall make every effort to enter into provisional arrangements of
> a practical nature) and the second (during this transitional period,
> not to jeopardize or hamper the reaching of the final agreement) are
> connected by the word 'and'. This is not without relevance. This
> means, in the view of the Special Chamber, that the two obligations

are connected. The introductory words to the effect that the States concerned have to act in 'a spirit of understanding and cooperation' apply to both. Consequently, the words 'shall make every effort' also apply to the second obligation, qualifying it as an obligation of conduct too.

630. On that basis, the Special Chamber reads the provision of article 83, paragraph 3, of the Convention as follows: the transitional period referred to means the period after the maritime delimitation dispute has been established until a final delimitation by agreement or adjudication has been achieved. Article 83, paragraph 3, covers two situations in this transitional period, namely the situation where a provisional arrangement has been reached which would regulate the conduct of the parties in the disputed area and the situation where no such provisional arrangement has been reached. The obligations States encounter in respect of a disputed maritime area for which no provisional arrangement exists are described by the words 'not to jeopardize or hamper the reaching of the final agreement'. In interpreting these words, account has to be taken of the general obligation under article 83, paragraph 3, of the Convention that in the transitional period States have to act 'in a spirit of understanding and cooperation'.

In any case, according to the Special Chamber, the claim had to be dismissed because the submissions of Côte d'Ivoire under article 83, paragraph 3, concerned activities conducted in Ivorian waters, while all activities conducted by Ghana took place in areas attributed to it by the Judgment (paragraphs 633 and 634).

As regards Côte d'Ivoire's claim that Ghana had contravened the Special Chamber's Provisional Measures Order of 25 April 2015, the Judgment concludes that Ghana was not in contravention. In particular, it did not contravene the prescription not to engage in "new drilling" because the drilling activities that were effected by Ghana were "ongoing activities for which drilling has already been carried out" and were allowed according to paragraphs 99 and 100 of the Provisional Measures Order (paragraphs 650-652).

As an introduction to its consideration of the question of the alleged violation of the Provisional Measures Order, the Special Chamber makes the following statement regarding the effect of Provisional Measures prescribed by ITLOS:

647. As regards the question as to whether Ghana has violated the provisional measures prescribed by the Order of the Special Chamber, the Special Chamber notes that, pursuant to article 290 of the Convention, its Order for the prescription of provisional measures is obligatory in nature, creating legal obligations with which parties have to comply. In this regard, the Special Chamber draws attention to paragraph 6 of article 290, according to which "[t]he parties to the dispute shall comply promptly with any provisional measures prescribed under this article".

4. The years 2016, 2017 and the beginning of 2018 saw the recourse to a dispute-settlement mechanism provided for in UNCLOS but hitherto never applied. This is the so-called compulsory conciliation, whose procedure is set out in Annex V of the Convention and which may be invoked by a party in situations envisaged in Articles 297, paragraphs 2 and 3, and 298, paragraph 1. This procedure is "compulsory" because a party may trigger it unilaterally but it remains a form of conciliation because the final report of the Conciliation Commission is not binding for the parties.[17]

Timor-Leste and Australia were engaged in two different arbitrations,[18] and also in a case, which reached the provisional measures stage but was later withdrawn, before the International Court of Justice.[19] The parties agreed to withdraw both arbitration cases after the beginning of the conciliation procedure.[20]

Timor-Leste initiated the procedure on 11 April 2016 by way of a Notification under section 2 of Annex V of UNCLOS addressed to Australia. The five-member Conciliation Commission was established on 25 June 2016. The Permanent Court of Arbitration acted as Registry. Timor-Leste requested the Commission to act as conciliator for a "dispute concerning the interpretation and application of Articles 74 and 83 of UNCLOS for the delimitation of the exclusive economic zone and the continental shelf between Timor-Leste and Australia including the establishment of the permanent maritime boundaries between the two States". The jurisdictional basis for the request was Article 298(1)(a)(i) of UNCLOS which reads as follows:

> 1. When signing, ratifying or acceding to this Convention or at any time thereafter, a State may, without prejudice to the obligations arising under section 1, declare in writing that it does not accept any one or more of the procedures provided for in section 2 with respect to one or more of the following categories of disputes:
> (a)(i) disputes concerning the interpretation or application of articles 15, 74 and 83 relating to sea boundary delimitations, or those involving historic bays or titles, provided that a State having made such a declaration shall, when such a dispute arises subsequent to the entry into force of this Convention and where no agreement within a reasonable period of time is reached in negotiations between the parties, at the request of any party to the dispute, accept

---

[17] TREVES, "'Compulsory' Conciliation in the U.N. Law of the Sea Convention", in GÖTZ, SELMER and WOLFRUM (eds.), *Liber Amicorum Günther Jaenicke, Zum 85. Geburtstag*, Berlin, 1998, p. 611 ff.; and, in Italian, TREVES, *Le controversie internazionali. Nuove tendenze, nuovi tribunali*, Milan, 1998, pp. 171-193.

[18] *Arbitration under the Timor Sea Treaty (Timor-Leste v. Australia)*, PCA case 2013-16, and *Arbitration under the Timor Sea Treaty (Timor-Leste v. Australia)*, PCA case 2015-42.

[19] *Questions relating to the Seizure and Detention of Certain Documents and Data (Timor-Leste v. Australia)*, Provisional Measures, Order of 3 March 2014, ICJ Reports 2014, p. 147; Discontinuance Order of 11 June 2015, ICJ Reports 2015, p. 572.

[20] Information on the two cases, including the Termination Order of the first one, is available at: <https://pcacases.com/web/view/37> and <https://www.pcacases.com/web/view/141>.

submission of the matter to conciliation under Annex V, section 2; and provided further that any dispute that necessarily involves the concurrent consideration of any unsettled dispute concerning sovereignty or other rights over continental or insular land territory shall be excluded from such submission; [...]

It is noteworthy that Australia, while objecting to the competence of the Commission, declared that:

its objections to competence do not have implications for its participation in any further stage of the proceedings; indeed, Australia has committed that it 'will abide by the Commission's finding as to whether it has jurisdiction to hear matters on maritime boundaries' and that 'if the decision is against us, [Australia] will engage in the conciliation in good faith.'[21]

At the beginning of the conciliation Procedure, the Commission was thus engaged – on the basis of the *Kompetenz-Kompetenz* rule set out in Article 13 of Annex V for Conciliation Commissions engaged in compulsory conciliation – in the determination of its competence in order to deal with an array of jurisdictional objections of Australia. The Commission in this phase of its work functions in a way that is indistinguishable from that followed by an arbitral tribunal, or even ITLOS, in dealing with jurisdictional objections. The Decision on Australia's objections to competence, handed out by the Commission on 19 September 2016, is thus a very interesting contribution to the interpretation of various provisions of Part XV and of Annex V of UNCLOS.

Australia's jurisdictional objection, examined first by the Conciliation Commission, was based on Article 281 of UNCLOS whose paragraph 1 is as follows:

If the States Parties which are parties to a dispute concerning the interpretation or application of this Convention have agreed to seek settlement of the dispute by a peaceful means of their own choice, the procedures provided for in this Part apply only where no settlement has been reached by recourse to such means and the agreement between the parties does not exclude any further procedure.

In Australia's view, Article 281 was applicable on two grounds. First, because an exchange of letters of 2003 between the Prime Ministers of the two countries in which the parties agreed to pursue delimitation by negotiation was an "agreement" for the purposes of Article 281, paragraph (1), even though it was

---

[21], *In the matter of a Conciliation before a Conciliation Commission constituted under Annex V to the United Nations Convention on the Law of the Sea, between the Republic of Timor-Leste and the Commonwealth of Australia,* Decision on Australia's Objections to Competence of 19 September 2016, PCA Case 2016-10, para. 3.

not a binding agreement. Second, because Article 4 of the 2006 Treaty on Certain Maritime Arrangements in the Timor Sea (CMATS) prohibited both parties "to commence or pursue proceedings before any court, tribunal or other dispute settlement mechanism that would raise or result in, either directly or indirectly, issues or findings of relevance to maritime boundaries or delimitation of the Timor Sea". The Commission dismissed the first ground of Australia Objection stating inter alia:

> 56. Although Article 281 does not expressly state that an 'agreement' must be legally binding for the article to apply, the Commission nevertheless considers that Article 281 requires a legally binding agreement. As a matter of the text of the Convention, Article 281 stands adjacent to Article 282, which contemplates formal, binding agreements when it refers to a 'general, regional or bilateral agreement or otherwise, that such dispute shall, at the request of any party to the dispute, be submitted to a procedure that entails a binding decision.' The two provisions use the same terminology of 'have agreed' and 'agreement', and the Commission does not consider that the text of the Convention would support significantly different meanings to the same terms appearing in two parallel articles.
>
> 57. Equally importantly, the Commission does not consider that a reading of Article 281 that would permit a non-binding agreement to preclude the application of the compulsory dispute settlement provisions of Part XV would be consistent with the fact that Part XV of the Convention is itself a binding agreement.
>
> 58. On the basis of the foregoing considerations, the Commission concludes that the 2003 exchange of letters between Prime Ministers Alkatiri and Howard did not constitute an agreement that would have legal effect pursuant to Article 281 of the Convention. Australia does not contend, of course, that the exchange of letters was intended to 'exclude any further procedure.'

The Conciliation Commission rejected also the second ground of Australia's objection based on Article 281. It argued, in particular, that:

> 62. Unlike the exchange of letters, CMATS is a binding treaty between the Parties. Article 4(4) of CMATS also appears to have been intended to exclude recourse to dispute resolution mechanisms, including those of the Convention. In the Commission's view, what CMATS is not – and what Article 281 requires – is an agreement 'to seek settlement of the dispute by a peaceful means of [the Parties'] own choice.' CMATS is an agreement not to seek settlement of the Parties' dispute over maritime boundaries for the duration of the moratorium.
>
> 63. Article 279 of the Convention calls on the Parties to 'seek a solution by the means indicated in Article 33, paragraph 1, of the Charter'

of the United Nations, which include negotiation, enquiry, mediation, conciliation, arbitration, judicial settlement, and resort to regional agencies or arrangements. Article 33 of the Charter and Article 280 of the Convention both make clear that his list is not exhaustive, and that States may settle their disputes through any other 'peaceful means of their own choice.' There is, in short, a great deal of flexibility in the range of approaches to dispute settlement that the Convention will recognize and respect. Nowhere in CMATS, however, is there any procedure intended to provide for the settlement of maritime boundaries. On the contrary, CMATS forecloses all possible avenues for the resolution of disputes relating to maritime boundaries, negating, in Article 4(7), the Parties' 'obligation to negotiate permanent maritime boundaries for the period of this Treaty.' Indeed, even if the Parties had concluded a binding agreement in 2003 to settle their maritime boundary through negotiation, CMATS on its own terms would negate, rather than confirm, such an obligation.
64. Nothing in CMATS constitutes an agreement 'to seek settlement of the dispute by a peaceful means of [the Parties'] own choice.' Nor does the Commission consider that an agreement not to pursue any means of dispute settlement can reasonably be considered a dispute settlement means of the Parties' own choice. Accordingly, the Commission concludes that CMATS is not an agreement pursuant to Article 281 that would preclude recourse to compulsory conciliation pursuant to Article 298 and Annex V.

Other objections to the competence of the Conciliation Commission raised by Australia concern the existence – which Australia denied – of the prerequisites for recourse to the Conciliation Commission set out in Article 298(1)(a)(i). One of these requirements is that the dispute must have arisen "subsequent to the entry into force of the Convention". The question, discussed also in literature, is whether the provision means entry into force of UNCLOS as an international treaty, or as between the parties. The Conciliation Commission accepts the first view and rejects the relevant objection by Australia as follows:

73. In any event, Australia at most invokes only a dispute dating back to Timor-Leste's independence in 2002, prior to the entry into force of the Convention as between the Parties in 2013, but not prior to the entry into force of the Convention in general in 1994. The key question is thus whether the unqualified reference to 'entry into force of this Convention' within the requirement that 'such a dispute arises subsequent to the entry into force of this Convention' refers to the entry into force of the Convention as a whole on 16 November 1994 or to the entry into force of the Convention as between Australia and Timor-Leste on 7 February 2013.
74. For the Commission, the ordinary meaning of the unqualified phrase favours the former interpretation regarding entry into force

of the Convention as a whole, especially when taking into account that the Convention contains various provisions where the phrase 'entry into force' is expressly qualified to indicate that it refers to the entry into force as between the relevant parties. While the Convention is not always consistent in its use of terminology, it does appear to be so in this respect.

The Conciliation Commission further discards Australia's objection alleging that the requirement set out in Article 298(1)(a)(i) of UNCLOS that negotiation be conducted for a reasonable time was not satisfied. The Commission's conclusion is based on the record and an the following argument:

> 78. The requirement under Article 298(1)(a)(i), however, is that 'no agreement within a reasonable period of time is reached in negotiations between the parties.' It does not expressly require that prior negotiations between the parties to the dispute actually take place. Such a requirement would effectively grant a party the right to veto any recourse to compulsory conciliation by refusing to negotiate, contrary to the intention of Article 298. According to the text, the provision merely requires that no agreement be reached within a reasonable period of time in any such negotiations. Furthermore, the 'agreement' envisaged by the provision is an agreement resolving the 'dispute concerning the interpretation or application of articles 15, 74 and 83 relating to sea boundary delimitations' in the sense described above.

Lastly, the Conciliation Commission examined *ex officio* the question from which date would the 12 month maximum duration of conciliation procedures set in Article 7 of Annex V start running. It decided that, in the case before it, it would start running from the day of the Decision on Competence. The following seem particularly relevant reasons:

> 108. On the other hand, the resolution of disagreements over competence can be a central aspect of compulsory conciliation. Indeed, Article 13 is one of only four Articles that make up Section 2 of Annex V, the only portion of the Annex devoted to compulsory conciliation. While the results of such a proceeding are non-binding, it remains the case that an Article 298 procedure is a compulsory process, and one of the parties may be participating against its will. It is neither appropriate that a State be subjected to compulsory conciliation before a commission that lacks competence over the matter, nor is such a conciliation process likely to be effective. As a method for the resolution of disputes, conciliation depends ultimately on the parties' acceptance of the process and willingness to seek agreement and give serious consideration to the recommendations of the commission.

109. Article 13 thus calls for serious attention to any disagreements regarding competence. Article 7 is fixed at the minimum period of time in which a conciliation process could realistically be expected to bear fruit, ensuring that only a productive process will be continued, by agreement, beyond that point. In the Commission's view, the tension between these provisions is resolved by Article 14 of Annex V, which provides that Section 1 of the Annex applies subject to Section 2. The deadline in Article 7 must therefore give way to the time needed to consider and decide objections to competence and is thus properly understood to run only after a Commission has addressed any objections that may be made. Any other approach would run the risk of a commission failing to give proper consideration to a justified objection to competence or, alternatively, of giving such objections appropriate attention only to find that too much time had elapsed for the parties to fairly evaluate whether the conciliation process was likely to prove effective and worthy of extension by agreement.

After the settlement of the issues concerning jurisdiction, the conciliation process proceeded intensively through 2016 and 2017. On 30 August 2017 it reached the conclusion of a "Comprehensive Package Agreement" including the central elements of a treaty on maritime delimitation and other important matters. The text of the delimitation treaty, including the legal status of the controversial Great Sunrise gas field, was finalized on 13 October 2017. A final negotiating session was held from 19 to 23 February 2018. The parties signed the maritime delimitation Treaty in New York at the presence of the UN Secretary General on 6 March 2018.[22] The Conciliation Commission will finalize its report in mid-April 2018.[23]

This first experiment of compulsory conciliation under Annex V of the Convention, on the basis of Article 298(1)(a)(i), has thus been a success. It has eliminated a complex and at times bitter array of disputes between the parties, and shown that there are cases in which, even when parties have excluded delimitation disputes from compulsory settlement utilizing a declaration under Article 298(1), constructive third party involvement is still possible.

---

[22] Julie Bishop, Minister of Foreign Affairs of Australia, Agio Pereira, Minister of the Office of the Prime Minister for Delimitation of Borders and Agent of the Conciliation Process of Timor-Leste, and Kay Rala Xanana Gusmão, Chief Negotiatior for the council for the final delimitation of maritime boundaries of Timor-Leste, "Joint Media Release: Australia and Timor-Leste sign historic Maritime Boundary Treaty", 6 March 2018, available at: <http://timor-leste.gov.tl/?p=19577&lang=en>.

[23] PCA, "Press Release: Conciliation between the Democratic Republic of Timor-Leste and the Commonwealth of Australia", 25 February 2018, available at: <https://pcacases.com/web/sendAttach/2295>.

INTERNATIONAL CRIMINAL JUSTICE (2017)

RAFFAELLA NIGRO[*]

1. INTRODUCTION

The present review provides a summary of the most significant judgments and decisions handed down in 2017 by the international criminal tribunals together with an overview of the main issues relating to their respective activities, in particular: the legacy and impact of the International Criminal Tribunal for the former Yugoslavia (ICTY) (Section 2.2); the decision of the Prosecutor of the International Criminal Court (ICC) to request the authorization to initiate an investigation in Afghanistan (Section 3.2); a meaningful decision of the ICC on the elements of war crimes (Section 3.3); a new decision of the ICC on the immunity of Al-Bashir (Section 3.4); the activation of the crime of aggression by the Assembly of States Parties of the ICC and the introduction of new war crimes in Article 8 of the Rome Statute (Section 3.5); and finally a remarkable notification of the Co-Investigating Judge of the Extraordinary Chambers in the Courts of Cambodia (ECCC) on the interpretation of "civilian population" in the context of crimes against humanity (Section 4.2).

As for the *ad hoc* Tribunals, the ICTY issued two relevant judgments in *Mladić* and in *Prlić et al.* cases before its official closure on 31 December 2017. The Mechanism for International Criminal Tribunals (MICT) continues its judicial work. In addressing the United Nations Security Council, the President of the MICT, Judge Meron, reported a number of rulings issued in the *Stanišić and Simatović* case, the first full trial before the Mechanism, which started on 13 June 2017. The President also reported that the appeal judgment in the *Šešelj* case is expected in the first part of 2018, while the appeal judgment in the *Karadžić* case will be issued by late 2019.[1] With regard to the supervision of sentences imposed by the ICTY, the International Criminal Tribunal for Rwanda (ICTR) and the MICT, President Meron informed that negotiations with several Member States concerning the enforcement of judgments of the remaining prisoners awaiting transfer in Arusha are at an advanced stage.[2] As for the detention by Turkey of Judge Akay of the MICT, after his conviction of terrorism by a criminal court in Ankara on 14 June 2017 and being sentenced to a term of seven years and six months of imprisonment, the Judge was provisionally released pending his appeal. After ascertaining the ability and willingness of the Judge Akay to exercise his judicial function in the *Ngirabatware* case before the MICT, the Appeals

---

[*] Associate Professor of International Law, University *Magna Græcia*, Catanzaro.
[1] UN International Residual Mechanism for Criminal Tribunals, "President Meron Updates UN Security Council on Progress of Work", 6 December 2017, available at: <http://www.un-mict.org/en/news/president-meron-updates-un-security-council-progress-work>.
[2] *Ibid.*

Chamber issued a decision on 19 June 2017 granting a request for review of the judgment in this case.[3]

As for the ICC, on 7 March 2017 the Republic of South Africa notified the Secretary-General of the United Nations in a note verbale as to its decision to revoke the instrument of withdrawal from the Rome Statute.[4] Noteworthy is the request of judicial authorization by the ICC Prosecutor to commence investigation into the situation in Afghanistan for crimes committed by the Taliban and by the United States armed forces in this territory during the conflict in 2003, and also by members of the United States Central Intelligence Agency (CIA) in secret detention facilities outside Afghanistan.[5]

On 27 April 2017 the Extraordinary African Appeals Chamber upheld Hissein Habré's life sentence for crimes against humanity, war crimes and torture, and acquitted him for the charge of direct rape. The Appeals Chamber also confirmed the amounts and types of reparations as decided by the Trial Chamber.[6]

2. THE ICTY AND THE MICT[7]

2.1. Case Law

In 2017, the ICTY handed down two judgments, one of the Appeals Chamber in *Prlić et al.* and one of the Trial Chamber in *Mladić*.

---

[3] *Prosecutor v. Augustin Ngirabatware*, Case No. MICT-19-29-R, Decision on Ngirabatware's motion for review, 19 June 2017. For further details on the detention of Judge Akay, see NIGRO, "International Criminal Justice (2016)", IYIL, 2017, p. 429 ff.

[4] Available at: <https://www.icc-cpi.int/Pages/item.aspx?name=pr1285>.

[5] As for other criminal tribunals, only two decisions were issued in 2017 by the Residual Special Court for Sierra Leone (RSCSL), one on the assignment of a Counsel to Charles Ghankay Taylor (Decision to assign Counsel to Charles Taylor (Case No. RSCSL-04-14-ES-1440, 27 March 2017), and the other on the application for conditional early release of Kondewa (Decision of the President on Application for Conditional Early Release, Case No. RSCSL-04-14-ES-860, 29 May 2017). The Special Tribunal for Lebanon issued a decision on 15 questions of law submitted by the Pre-Trial Judge in order to clarify the crime of criminal association under Article 335 of the Lebanese Criminal Code (Interlocutory Decision on the Applicable Law: Criminal Association and Review of the Indictment, Case No. STL-17-07/I/AC/R176bis, 18 October 2017).

[6] Chambre Africaine Extraordinaire d'Assises d'Appel, *Le Procureur Général c. Hissein Habré*, Judgment of 27 April 2017. For further details on the Chamber's judgment of 30 May 2016, see NIGRO, "International Criminal Justice (2016)", *cit. supra* note 3, p. 445 ff.

[7] Judgments and decisions of the ICTY and MICT are available at: <http://www.icty.org/> and at: <http://www.unmict.org/en> respectively. In the literature, see KING and MEERNIK, *The Witness Experience: Testimony at the ICTY and its Impact*, Cambridge, 2017; JELACIC, "Building a Legacy: The Youth Outreach Program at the ICTY", in RAMIREZ-BARAT and DUTHIE (eds), *Transitional Justice and Education: Learning Peace*, New York, 2017, p. 260 ff.; RADISAVLJEVIĆ and PETROV, "Srebrenica and Genocide Denial in the Former Yugoslavia: What has the ICTY Done to Address it?", in BEHRENS, TERRY and JENSEN (eds), *Holocaust and Genocide Denial: A Contextual Perspective*, Abingdon, 2017, p. 145 ff.; MCDERMOTT, "Fairness Before the Mechanism for the International Criminal Tribunals", QIL, 2017, p. 39 ff.

In its judgment of 29 November 2017, the Appeals Chamber confirmed almost all of the Trial Chamber convictions of Prlić and others serving in the government of a Croatian entity created in Bosnia-Erzegovina in 1993, the "Croats of the Croatian Republic of Herceg-Bosna", in respect to events occurring between 1992 and 1994 in eight municipalities and five detention centres in the territory of Bosnia and Herzegovina.[8] The Appeals Chamber confirmed the accused convictions of crimes against humanity, violation of the law or customs of war and grave breaches of the Geneva Conventions. It also affirmed the conclusion of the Trial Chamber that from mid-January 1993 the accused were participants in a joint criminal enterprise aimed at creating a Croatian entity in Bosnia and Herzegovina with the purpose of facilitating the reunification of the Croatian people, through ethnic cleansing of the Muslim population.

On 22 November 2017, the Trial Chamber I found Ratko Mladić, former Commander of the Bosnian Serbs Army, guilty of genocide, crimes against humanity, and violations of the laws or customs of war committed by Serb forces during the armed conflict in Bosnia Herzegovina from 1992 to 1995.[9] He was in particular convicted of genocide and persecution, extermination, murder, and the inhumane act of forcible transfer in the area of Srebrenica in 1995;[10] of persecution, extermination, deportation, murder and inhumane acts of forcible transfer in municipalities throughout Bosnia and Herzegovina; of murder, terror and unlawful attacks against civilians in Sarajevo; and of hostage-taking of United Nations personnel. The Chamber found that Mladić committed these crimes through his participation in, and contribution to, four joint criminal enterprises, and sentenced him to life imprisonment.

As regard the MICT's case law, on 26 April 2017 the Appeals Chamber issued an interesting decision on a motion to initiate contempt proceedings against the President of Turkey, Recep Tayyip Erdogan, and the Minister of Justice, Bekir Bozdag, for their failure to comply with the Order of 31 January 2017 on the release of Judge Akay of the MICT.[11] The Chamber denied the motion affirming that in matters pertaining to State obligations, it is well-established that State officials are "mere instruments of a State and their official action can only be attributed to the State". Recalling the ICTY's judgment of 1997 in the *Blaškić* case, the Chamber added that State officials cannot be the subject of sanctions

---

[8] *Prosecutor v. Jadrango Prlić, Bruno Stojić, Slobodan Praljak, Milivoj Petković, Valentin Corić, Perislav Pušić* (Case No. IT-04-74-A), Judgment of 29 November 2017.

[9] *Prosecutor v. Ratko Mladić* (Case No. IT-09-92/T), Judgment of 22 November 2017.

[10] As for genocide in Bosnian municipalities other than Srebrenica, the majority of the Chamber (Judge Orie dissenting) found that the physical perpetrators of the killings in the municipalities did have an intention to destroy a part of the Bosnian Muslim group as such (para. 3456 of the Judgment) but it then considered that this intention was not to destroy a substantial part, as required by the jurisprudence of the *ad hoc* Tribunals (para. 3527 ff.). For some critical remarks on this question, see MILANOVIC, "Some Thoughts on the Mladic Judgment", EJIL: Talk!, 27 November 2017, available at: <https://www.ejiltalk.org/some-thoughts-on-the-mladic-judgment/>.

[11] *Prosecutor v. Augustin Ngibaratware* (Case No. MICT-12-29-R), Decision on a motion to initiate contempt proceedings, 26 April 2017.

or penalties for conduct that is not private but undertaken on behalf of the State and cannot suffer the consequences of wrongful acts which are not attributable to them personally but to the State on whose behalf they act. The Appeals Chamber also considered that it is the State which is bound by the obligation to cooperate with the Mechanism under Article 28 of the Statute, and it is the State for which the official or agent fulfils his functions that constitutes the legitimate interlocutor of the Mechanism and shall therefore incur international responsibility for any serious breach of that provision by its officials. Finally, the Chamber explained that, while the Mechanism is endowed with the inherent power to make a judicial finding concerning a State's failure to observe the provision of the Statute, and also has the power to report this finding to the Security Council, it is not vested with any enforcement or sanctionary power *vis-à-vis* States, considering that it is primarily for the Security Council to impose sanctions, if any, against a recalcitrant State.

2.1. *The Legacy and Impact of the ICTY in the Former Yugoslavia*

Following the closure of the ICTY, some authors have discussed its impact in the former Yugoslavia, in terms of its legacy and particularly relating to the public's acceptance of the ICTY findings and reconciliation.[12] According to the public opinion survey conducted in Serbia and published in December 2017, 56% of the respondents find the ICTY to be partial and biased, while only 6% is of the opposite view.[13] Significantly, only 12% believe that what happened in Srebrenica corresponds to what was established by the ICTY in its findings. It has been observed, in this regard, that in amending its Criminal Code, Serbia introduced the criminalization of the public denial of genocide but only when the commission of this crime has been ascertained by Serbian courts or by the ICC.[14] The ethnic bias proved to be the most striking considering that an overwhelming majority of the respondents also believe that non-Serbian war crimes suspects, who were acquitted by the ICTY, are guilty. In this regard, some commentators have stressed that international justice's ability to reach the public in the former Yugoslavia will be tested again after the closure of the ICTY, as the new Special Court for Kosovo will issue its first indictment, in the more general framework of the prosecution of former Kosovo Liberation Army members also for crimes against Serbian victims.[15] Even before the closure of the ICTY, some authors have underlined the ICTY's failure to persuade the relevant target populations that the

---

[12] KOSTIĆ, "Public Opinion Survey in Serbia Sheds Light on ICTY Legacy", EJIL: Talk!, 22 January 2018, available at: <https://www.ejiltalk.org/public-opinion-survey-in-serbia-sheds-light-on-icty-legacy/>.

[13] *Ibid.*

[14] *Ibid.*

[15] "Kosovo war crimes court ready for first indictments: chief judge", Reuters, available at: <https://www.reuters.com/article/us-kosovo-court/kosovo-war-crimes-court-ready-for-first-indictments-chief-judge-idUSKBN1DO199>.

findings in its judgments were true.[16] As for the possible causes of such inability, it has been observed that from its inception, the ICTY was faced with the opposition of those in power in the affected societies for the fear of weakening their influence over their respective communities. In addition, the information about the ICTY would have been processed through a cognitive and emotional filter of prior attitudes and beliefs, and would be skewed to fit those pre-existing beliefs.[17] In this vein, it is a common understanding that the survey of December 2017 does not support the hypothesis that had the ICTY been perceived as impartial it would have persuaded the public in its findings,[18] and that the acceptance of ICTY findings and reconciliation largely depends on how the communities of the former Yugoslavia will decide to use its legacy in the future.[19]

3. THE INTERNATIONAL CRIMINAL COURT (ICC)[20]

3.1. Case Law

While proceedings before the Court and investigations continued in pre-existing situations, on 9 November 2017 the Prosecutor was authorized by the Pre-Trial Chamber to open a *proprio motu* investigation as regard the alleged crimes against humanity committed in Burundi, or by its nationals outside the territory of Burundi from 26 April 2015 to 26 October 2017. The Pre-Trial Chamber found that the Court has jurisdiction over crimes allegedly committed while Burundi was a State party of the ICC Rome Statute until 26 October 2017, when the withdrawal became effective.[21] Furthermore, on 20 November 2017 the Prosecutor requested judicial authorization to commence an investigation into the alleged crimes committed in the territory of Afghanistan since 1 May 2003. As a result

---

[16] MILANOVIC, "Understanding the ICTY's Impact in the Former Yugoslavia", EJIL: Talk!, 11 April 2016, available at: <https://www.ejiltalk.org/understanding-the-ictys-impact-in-the-former-yugoslavia/>; ID., "The Impact of the ICTY on the Former Yugoslavia: An Anticipatory Post-Mortem", AJIL, 2016, p. 233 ff.

[17] MILANOVIC, "Establishing the Facts About Mass Atrocities: Accounting for a Failure of the ICTY to Persuade Targeted Audiences", Georgetown Journal of International Law, 2016, p. 1321 ff.

[18] KOSTIĆ, *cit. supra* note 12.

[19] MILANOVIC, "Understanding", *cit. supra* note 16.

[20] Judgments and decisions of the ICC are available at: <https://www.icc-cpi.int/>. On the ICC, see DE VOS, "The International Criminal Court Between Law and Politics", in KASTNER (ed.), *International Criminal Law in Context*, Abingdon, 2018, p. 240 ff.; LOHNE, "Global Civil Society, the ICC and Legitimacy in International Criminal Justice", in HAYASHI and BAILLIET (eds), *The Legitimacy of International Criminal Tribunals*, Cambridge, 2017, p. 449 ff.; JALLOH and BANTEKAS (eds), *The International Criminal Court and Africa*, Oxford, 2017; RIM, "The Role of the International Criminal Court in Implementing the Responsibility to Protect", Florida Journal of International Law, 2017, p. 69 ff.

[21] Case No. ICC-01/17-X, Public Redacted Version of "Decision Pursuant to Article 15 of the Rome Statute on the Authorization of an Investigation into the Situation in the Republic of Burundi of 25 October 2017" of 9 November 2017. On the withdrawal of Burundi from the ICC, see NIGRO, "International Criminal Justice (2016)", *cit. supra* note 3, p. 435 ff.

of its examination, the Prosecutor has determined that there is a reasonable basis to believe that some categories of crimes within the Court's jurisdiction have occurred, in particular: *a*) crimes against humanity and war crimes by the Taliban and their affiliated Haqqani Network; *b*) war crimes by the Afghan National Security Forces; and *c*) war crimes by the United States armed forces in the territory of Afghanistan and by members of the CIA in secret detention facilities in Afghanistan and on the territory of other States parties to the Rome Statute.[22]

Finally, on 8 February 2018, the Prosecutor announced the opening of preliminary examinations into the situations in the Philippines and in Venezuela. As for the Philippines, the preliminary examination will analyse crimes allegedly committed by this State in the context of the "war on drugs" campaign launched by the government since at least 1 July 2016. The examination of the situation in Venezuela will concern crimes allegedly committed in the context of demonstrations and related political unrest since 1 April 2017.[23]

As for the case law of the ICC, concerning the situation of Côte d'Ivoire, on 19 July 2017 the Appeals Chamber reversed the Trial Chamber decision of 10 March 2017 and requested to carry out a new review as to whether Laurent Gbagbo should continue to be detained or should be released, with or without conditions.[24]

Concerning the situation in Darfur (Sudan), the main question remains the arrest of Al-Bashir and his surrender to the Court. On 26 April 2017, Pre-Trial Chamber II issued a decision inviting the Kingdom of Jordan to provide any further submissions on its failure to arrest and surrender Al-Bashir to the Court.[25] In a note verbale of 28 March 2017 to the Registry of the ICC, the Jordanian authorities stated they had received information that Al-Bashir would have attended the Arab League summit of the 29 March 2017 but to consider that he enjoys sovereign immunity as sitting Head of State under customary international law, and that immunity has not be waived by Sudan nor by the Security Council. Jordan concluded that nothing in Articles 27(2) and 98(1) "mandates the State party to the Rome Statute to waive the immunity of a third State and act inconsistently with its obligations under the rules of general international law on the immunity of a third State".[26] On 11 December 2017, by reasoning that the rights and obligations as provided for in the Statute, including Article 27(2), are applicable to Sudan by imposition of the Security Council, Pre-Trial Chamber II concluded

---

[22] Case No. ICC-02/17, Public Redacted Version of "Request for Authorization of an Investigation Pursuant to Article 15", 20 November 2017. See *infra* Section 3.2.

[23] Available at: <https://www.icc-cpi.int/Pages/item.aspx?name=180208-otp-stat>. For further details on the preliminary examinations before the ICC, see the Report on Preliminary Examinations Activities 2017, 4 December 2017, available at: <https://www.icc-cpi.int/itemsDocuments/2017-PE-rep/2017-otp-rep-PE_ENG.pdf>.

[24] *The Prosecutor v. Laurent Gbagbo and Charles Blé Goudé* (Case No. ICC-02/11-01/15), Judgment of 19 July 2017.

[25] *The Prosecutor v. Omar Hassan Ahmad Al-Bashir* (Case No. ICC-02/05-01/09), Decision inviting the Hashemite Kingdom of Jordan to provide any further submissions on its failure to arrest and surrender Omar Al-Bashir to the Court, 26 April 2017.

[26] *Ibid.*, para. 5.

that the immunities of Al-Bashir as Head of State do not bar States parties to the Rome Statute from executing the Court's request for his arrest and surrender. Having found that the Kingdom of Jordan failed to comply with its obligations under the Statute, the Chamber decided to refer the matter to the Assembly of States parties of the Rome Statute and the Security Council.[27]

On the basis of information received by the Registrar of a possible visit of Al-Bashir to Kazakhstan, Pre-Trial Chamber II issued a decision on 31 August 2017 inviting that State to cooperate with the ICC in the arrest and surrender of Al-Bashir in the event that he would be present on the territory of Kazakhstan.[28] Finally, Pre-Trial Chamber II issued a decision on 13 December 2017 inviting the Republic of Uganda to provide submissions concerning its failure to arrest Al-Bashir and to surrender him to the Court while he was on Ugandan territory on or around 14 November 2017.[29]

On 6 July 2017, Pre-Trial Chamber issued a decision ascertaining the failure of South Africa to comply with its obligations by not arresting and surrendering Al-Bashir to the Court while he was on South African territory between 13 and 15 June 2015. However, the Chamber considered that it is not warranted to refer South Africa's non-compliance to the Assembly of States Parties or the Security Council.[30] First of all, it affirmed that for the purposes of the situation in Darfur, Sudan is in an analogous situation to those of States parties to the Statute as a result of the Security Council resolution adopted under Chapter VII of the UN Charter, triggering the Court's jurisdiction in the situation in Darfur, and imposing on Sudan the obligation to fully cooperate with the Court. In the opinion of the judges, given that Article 27(2) of the Statute is applicable to Sudan, the immunities of Al-Bashir as Head of State under customary international law do not apply *vis-à-vis* States Parties to the Rome Statute for the execution of the Court's request of his arrest and surrender for crimes allegedly committed in Darfur.[31] The Chamber therefore found as a matter of principle that States parties to the Rome Statute are under a duty to execute the warrants of arrest issued by the Court, and to implement the Court's request for the arrest and surrender of Al-Bashir.

---

[27] *The Prosecutor v. Omar Hassan Ahmad Al-Bashir* (Case No. ICC-02/05-01/09), Decision under Article 87(7) of the Rome Statute on the non-compliance by Jordan with the request by the Court for the arrest and surrender of Omar Al-Bashir, 11 December 2017.

[28] *The Prosecutor v. Omar Hassan Ahmad Al-Bashir* (Case No. ICC-02/05-01/09), Request to the Republic of Kazakhstan for cooperation in the arrest and surrender of Omar Hassan Ahmad Al-Bashir, 31 August 2017.

[29] *The Prosecutor v. Omar Hassan Ahmad Al-Bashir* (Case No. ICC-02/05-01/09), Decision inviting the Republic of Uganda to provide submissions concerning its failure to arrest Omar Al-Bashir and surrender him to the Court, 13 December 2017.

[30] *The Prosecutor v. Omar Hassan Ahmad Al-Bashir* (Case No. ICC-02/05-01/09), Decision under Article 87(7) of the Rome Statute on the non-compliance by South Africa with the request by the Court for the arrest and surrender of Omar Al-Bashir, 6 July 2017. For a comment on this specific question see GALAND, "Why the Security Council Should not be Involved Regarding Al-Bashir's Immunity", Opinio Juris, 20 July 2017, available at: <http://opiniojuris.org/2017/07/20/33215/>.

[31] See para. 87 ff. For further comments on this decision, see *infra* Section 3.4.

Despite the absence in the proceedings of submissions regarding the possible effects on the immunity of Al-Bashir arising from the 1948 Genocide Convention, considering that both South Africa and Sudan are States parties to the Convention and that one of the warrants for the arrest of Al-Bashir has been issued for the crime of genocide, the Chamber decided in any case to consider the question. The majority, Judge De Brichambaut dissenting, stressed that, unlike the Statute in Article 27(2), the Genocide Convention does not mention immunities based on official capacity, and in this sense, there was not a convincing basis for an interpretation of the provisions in the Convention such that would give rise to an implicit exclusion of immunities. According to the judges, while Article IV of the Convention speaks of individual criminal responsibility of "persons committing genocide" and can be effective even without reading into it an implicit exclusion of immunities based on official capacity, Article VI of the Convention is concerned with the allocation of competence among the national and international jurisdictions in trying "persons charged with genocide", and, again, does not bear upon immunities. The Chamber therefore concluded that no consequences relevant to the issue of the immunity of Al-Bashir can be derived from the Genocide Convention.[32]

Having said that, the Chamber affirmed that a referral of South Africa's non-compliance to the Assembly of States Parties and/or the Security Council was not warranted. In this regard, it considered of significance that South Africa was the first State Party to seek from the Court a final legal determination on the extent of its obligations to execute a request for arrest and surrender of Al-Bashir. In addition, the Chamber was not convinced that a referral to the Assembly of States Parties and/or the Security Council would be warranted in order to achieve cooperation from South Africa, in the light of the fact that South Africa's domestic courts have already found that State to be in breach of its obligations under its domestic legal framework, and that any remaining issue concerning South Africa's obligations under the Statute was resolved by the Chamber in the decision.[33]

As regards the situation in Central African Republic, on 22 March 2017 Trial Chamber VII delivered its decision on sentencing in the *Bemba et al.* case.[34] Following the judgment of 19 October 2016 in which the accused were found guilty of various offences against the administration of justice,[35] the Trial Chamber delivered its decision on sentencing taking into account the gravity of the offences, the culpable conduct, and the individual circumstances of the convicted person concerned.

Concerning the situation in the Democratic Republic of the Congo, on 24 March 2017 Trial Chamber II issued an order awarding individual and collective reparations to the victims of crimes committed by Germain Katanga in 2003

---

[32] See para. 109 of the decision.

[33] See para. 130 ff. of the decision.

[34] *The Prosecutor v. Jean-Pierre Bemba Gombo, Aimé Kilolo Musamba, Jean-Jacques Mangenda Kabongo, Fidèle Babala Wandu and Narcisse Arido* (Case No. ICC-01/05-01/13), Decision on Sentence pursuant to Article 76 of the Statute, 22 March 2017.

[35] For further details see NIGRO, "International Criminal Justice (2016)", *cit. supra* note 3, p. 433 ff.

during an attack on the village of Bogoro, in the Ituri district of the Democratic Republic of the Congo.[36] The judges awarded 297 victims with a symbolic compensation of USD 250 per victim, and also collective reparations in the form of support for housing, income generating activities, education aid, and psychological support. On 8 March 2018, the Appeals Chamber found that the approach chosen by the Trial Chamber for the reparation proceedings, based on an individual assessment of each application, was not the most appropriate as it has led to unnecessary delays in the award of compensation.[37] However, the Appeals Chamber considered that the Trial Chamber's approach did not amount to an error of law or an abuse of discretion that would justify the reversal of the reparation order.[38] As to the "indirect" victims entitled to reparations, the Appeals Chamber concluded that the Trial Chamber did not err in finding that in the context of Ituri Province, all family members were entitled to reparations for psychological harm from the loss of a family member, presuming psychological harm in respect of all family members of direct victims of the attack of Bogoro.[39] The Appeals Chamber also rejected the grounds of appeal on the alleged error by the Trial Chamber in issuing an order for reparations which was not proportionate to the part the Accused played in the crimes *vis-à-vis* others. According to the Appeals Chamber, when determining liability for reparations, the focus should be on the repair of the harm and not on the mode of liability,[40] nor criteria such as the gravity of the crimes committed or mitigating factors are to be considered relevant to the question at hand.[41] The Appeals Chamber also dismissed the grounds of appeal raised by the Office of Public Counsel for the Victims (OPCV) concerning the alleged procedural error of the Trial Chamber of not appointing a new legal representative for victims immediately after authorising the Former Legal Representative to terminate his mandate in respect of the concerned victims.[42] The Chamber considered in this regard that the period following the withdrawal of the Former Legal Representative was not dedicated to receipt of evidence in relation to specific applications for reparations.[43] Finally, as to the appeal brought by the Legal Representatives of Victims, the Appeals Chamber found that the Trial Chamber erred by failing to properly reason its decision in relation to the causal nexus between the attack on Bogoro and the harm suffered by the Five Applicants.[44]

---

[36] *The Prosecutor v. Germain Katanga* (Case No. ICC-01/04-01/07), Order for Reparations pursuant to Article 75 of the Statute, 24 March 2017.

[37] *The Prosecutor v. Germain Katanga* (Case No. ICC-01/04-01/07), Judgment on the appeals against the Order of the Trial Chamber II of 24 March 2017 entitled "Order for Reparations pursuant to Article 75 of the Statute", 8 March 2018.

[38] *Ibid.*, para. 65.

[39] *Ibid.*, para. 113.

[40] *Ibid.*, para. 182.

[41] *Ibid.*, para. 184.

[42] *Ibid.*, para. 217. On this specific question see YAU, "The Katanga and Al Mahdi Appeals Judgments and the Right of Access to Justice for Victims: Missed Opportunity?", EJIL: Talk!, 9 April 2018, available at: <https://www.ejiltalk.org/the-katanga-and-al-mahdi-appeals-judgments-and-the-right-of-access-to-justice-for-victims-missed-opportunity/>.

[43] Judgment on the appeals, *cit. supra* note 37, para. 219.

[44] *Ibid.*, para. 238.

On 15 December 2017, Trial Chamber II issued a decision setting the amount of Thomas Lubanga Dyilo's liability for collective reparations at USD 10,000,000.[45] The decision completes the order for reparations of 3 March 2015 which awarded collective reparations to the victims of the war crimes committed by Lubanga Dyilo. In view of Lubanga's indigence, the Chamber invited the Board of Directors of the Trust Fund for Victims to examine the possibility of providing an additional amount for the implementation of collective reparations in this case and/or continuing its efforts to raise additional funds. The Chamber also instructed the Trust Fund to make contact with the Government of the Democratic Republic of the Congo to explore a possible contribution to the reparations process by the Government.

As for the situation in Libya, on 15 August 2017, Pre-Trial Chamber I issued a warrant for arrest of Al-Werfalli allegedly responsible under Article 8(2)(c)(i) of the Statute for the war crime of murder in seven incidents against 33 persons which took place in Benghazi in the context of the non-international armed conflict in Libya.[46] On 21 August 2017, the Chamber requested Libya for cooperation in the arrest and surrender of Al-Werfalli to the ICC according to Articles 89(1) and 91 of the Rome Statute.[47] In spite of a statement of the General Command of the National Libyan Army reporting that Al-Werfalli had been arrested and was under investigation by the Libyan military prosecutor, on 13 September 2017 the Prosecutor of the ICC renewed the request for the immediate arrest and surrender of the suspect.[48] In the absence of an admissibility challenge from the competent Libyan authorities and a decision by the ICC judges suspending Libya's obligation to cooperate with the Court, the Prosecutor considered that Libya remains under an obligation to immediately arrest and surrender the suspect to the ICC.

In relation to the situation in Mali, Trial Chamber VIII issued a reparations order concluding that Al Mahdi is liable for 2.7 millions euros in expenses for individual and collective reparations for the community of Timbuktu for intentionally directing attacks against religious and historic buildings in that city.[49] The Chamber ordered reparations in particular for three categories of harm: *i*) damage to the attacked religious and historic buildings; *ii*) consequential economic loss;

---

[45] *Le Procureur c. Thomas Lubanga Dyilo* (Case No. ICC-01/04-01/06), Décision fixant le montant des réparations auxquelles Thomas Dubanga Dyilo est tenu, 15 December 2017. For a comment on this decision see BRODNEY and REGUÉ, "Formal Functional, and Intermediate Approaches to Reparations Liability: Situating the ICC's 15 December 2017 Lubanga Reparations Decision", EJIL: Talk!, 4 January 2018, available at: <https://www.ejiltalk.org/formal-functional-and-intermediate-approaches-to-reparations-liability-situating-the-iccs-15-december-2017-lubanga-reparations-decision/>.

[46] *The Prosecutor v. Mahmoud Mustafa Busayf Al-Werfalli* (Case No. ICC-01/11-01/17), Warrant of Arrest, 15 August 2017.

[47] *The Prosecutor v. Mahmoud Mustafa Busayf Al-Werfalli* (Case No. ICC-01/11-01/17), Request to Libya for cooperation in the arrest and surrender of Mahmoud Mustafa Busayf Al-Werfalli, 21 August 2017.

[48] Available at: <https://www.icc-cpi.int/Pages/item.aspx?name=170913-otp-stat-libya>.

[49] *The Prosecutor v. Ahmad Al Faqi Al Mahdi* (Case No. ICC-01/12-01/15), Reparations order, 17 August 2017. For further details, see NIGRO, "International Criminal Justice (2016)", *cit. supra* note 3, p. 440 ff.

and *iii*) moral harm. According to the judges, reparations are to be collective for rehabilitation of sites and for the community of Timbuktu as a whole to address the financial loss and economic harm as well as the emotional distress suffered as a result of the attack. The Chamber ordered individual reparations for those whose livelihoods exclusively depended upon the attacked buildings and those whose ancestor's burial sites were damaged in the attack. Noting Al Mahdi's indigence, the Chamber encouraged the Trust Funds for Victims to complement the reparations award, directing the Fund to submit a draft implementation plan for 16 February 2018.

Against the Reparation order, the Legal Representative of Victims (LRV) raised two grounds of appeal. First, it was argued that the Trial Chamber erred in limiting individual reparations for economic loss to those whose livelihoods exclusively depended upon the Protected Buildings. Second, the LRV maintained that the Trial Chamber erred in delegating a "power of adjudication" for reparations to the Trust Fund for Victims (TFV), a non-judicial entity. Within the latter, an argument was included challenging the Trial Chamber's findings on the confidentiality of the victims' identifying information.

On 8 March 2018, the Appeals Chamber rendered its decision.[50] It rejected the first grounds of appeal affirming that the LRV had not demonstrated an error in the Trial Chamber's determination of the category of victims entitled to individual reparations for economic loss. In particular, according to the Appeals Chamber, there was no error by the Trial Chamber in considering that the harm caused by the attack on, and destruction of, the Protected Buildings was primarily collective and suffered by the entire community of Timbuktu, and as a consequence that collective reparations were the most appropriate way to address the damage caused in the specific case.[51] On the second grounds of appeal, the Appeals Chamber found that the oversight of the Trial Chamber exercising judicial control over the screening process shall include that it finally endorses the results of the screening, with the possibility of amending the conclusions of the TFV on the eligibility of applicants for individual reparations, upon request of those applicants, or *proprio motu* by the Trial Chamber.[52] The Appeals Chamber was of the view that this will ensure that a contested determination of who should be eligible for individual reparations remains within the scope of judicial control. It also found that the Trial Chamber erred in ordering that access to applicants' identifying information should be granted to Al Mahdi, as a condition for the applicants to have their applications for reparations reviewed by the TFV. This finding was reversed and the Impugned Decision amended to the extent that the TFV is authorised to also consider applications for individual reparations made

---

[50] *The Prosecutor v. Ahmad Al Faqi Al Mahdi* (Case No. ICC-01/12-01/15A), Judgment on the appeal of the victims against the "Reparations order", 8 March 2018. See for a comment YAU, *cit. supra* note 42.

[51] See paras. 33 ff. of the judgment.

[52] *Ibid.*, para. 69.

by applicants who do not wish to have their identifying information disclosed to Al Mahdi.[53]

3.2. The Decision to Request a Judicial Authorization to Commence an Investigation in Afghanistan

The request by the ICC Prosecutor of a judicial authorization to open an investigation into possible international crimes committed in the territory of Afghanistan has raised different legal questions in the literature. While some authors have defined the decision of the Prosecutor as a momentous day for the ICC, considering that the "opening an investigation that could lead to Americans being prosecuted, even if only in theory, is a remarkable act of bravery for a Court that has proven largely impotent with regard to crimes committed by government officials",[54] others asserted that it would be hard to see how the alleged detainee abuses by the United States forces meet the standard of the most egregious and shocking breaches of the law which the ICC was designated to prosecute.[55] In the same vein, also the competence of the ICC according to the complementarity principle under the Rome Statute has been questioned. The United States, as has been reasoned, has one of the most developed and effective military justice systems in the world which also retains the demonstrated ability and willingness to hold its own accountable for violations of the law, including any violations in the context of detention operations.[56] Some have replied, however, that the complementarity analysed by the ICC Prosecutor focuses on the potential cases being considered for investigation by the Office, not on the general availability or effectiveness of the domestic criminal-judicial system of a specific State. Thus the only relevant question would be whether the United States is investigating the same acts as the Prosecutor.[57]

Concerning the Court's jurisdiction, another debated question is whether the Status of Forces Agreement (SOFA) between the United States and Afghanistan precludes the ICC from exercising jurisdiction over American soldiers. Some authors have affirmed that because the SOFA provides the exclusive jurisdiction of the United States on crimes committed by their soldiers, Afghanistan simply

---

[53] *Ibid.*, para. 99.

[54] HELLER, "Initial Thoughts on the ICC's Decision to Investigate Afghanistan", Opinio Juris, 3 November 2017, available at: <http://opiniojuris.org/2017/11/03/otp-decides-to-investigate-the-situation-in-afghanistan/>. See also for some considerations on the meaning of the decision WHITING, "An ICC Investigation of the U.S. in Afghanistan: What Does it Mean", Just Security, 3 November 2017, available at: <https://www.justsecurity.org/46687/icc-investigation-u-s-afghanistan-mean/#more-46687>.

[55] VOGEL, "ICC Prosecutor Advances Examination of U.S. Detention Policies in Afghanistan", Lawfare, 4 December 2014, available at: <https://www.lawfareblog.com/icc-prosecutor-advances-examination-us-detention-policies-afghanistan>.

[56] *Ibid.*

[57] HELLER, "The OTP's Afghanistan Investigation: A Response to Vogel", Opinio Juris, 4 December 2014, available at: <http://opiniojuris.org/2014/12/04/otps-afghanistan-investigation-response-vogel/>.

does not have jurisdiction that it can delegate to the ICC.[58] It has been observed, however, that the Court remains competent to entertain proceedings in such cases, regardless of whether this may cause the State to breach its other treaties.[59] According to some authors, a different situation seems to arise in relation to members of the CIA considering they are not soldiers, and that Lithuania, Poland and Romania, i.e. the States in which secret detention facilities are located and to which the Prosecutor expressly referred, are all parties to the Rome Statute. Moreover, as regards these States, the applicable SOFA NATO provides for a shared rather than an exclusive jurisdiction.[60]

Finally, regarding the prosecution of torture committed by members of the CIA in detention facilities located in Europe, some authors have underlined a possible opportunity for the ICC to weigh in on the debate over the global applicability of international humanitarian law.[61] In order to prosecute such crimes, in fact, the ICC would eventually pronounce itself on the applicability of international humanitarian law beyond the territory where a non-international armed conflict is primarily taking place. While there seems to be no doubt on the existence of a non-international armed conflict in Afghanistan involving the United States at the time when the alleged crimes were committed, it is more difficult to ascertain whether the law of armed conflict also applies in States parties to the Rome Statute which are not directly involved in the same conflict.[62] The current debate seems to support two different approaches, one on the application of international humanitarian law to the national boundaries where the conflict occurs; the other, on the application of international humanitarian law to the conduct of armed conflicts and their effects on individuals, irrespective of their specific geographical location. In this sense, there could be an opportunity for the ICC to pronounce on the approach which allows the application and compliance with international humanitarian law more effectively.

3.3. On the Elements of War Crimes

In a decision issued on 4 January 2017 in relation to the situation in the Democratic Republic of the Congo, Trial Chamber VI found that it has jurisdic-

---

[58] NEWTON, "How the International Criminal Court Threatens Treaty Norms", Vanderbilt Journal of Transnational Law, 2016, p. 371 ff.

[59] O'KEEFE, "Response: 'Quid', Not 'Quantum': A Comment on 'How the International Criminal Court Threatens Treaty Norms'", Vanderbilt Journal of Transnational Law, 2016, p. 433 ff.

[60] HELLER, "Initial Thoughts", cit. supra note 54.

[61] POTHELET, "War Crimes in Afghanistan and Beyond: Will the ICC Weigh in on the 'Global Battlefield' Debate?", EJIL: Talk!, 9 November 2017, available at: <https://www.ejiltalk.org/war-crimes-in-afghanistan-and-beyond-will-the-icc-weigh-in-on-the-global-battlefield-debate/>.

[62] As regards the secret facilities outside Afghanistan, in the 2016 Preliminary Examinations Report, the Prosecutor mentioned in particular those located in the Rome Statute States parties of Poland, Lithuania, and Romania: see para. 199.

tion over the alleged war crimes of rape and sexual slavery that child soldiers were victims of in the *Ntaganda* case.[63] According to the Defence, these crimes do not fall within the jurisdiction of the Court considering that, under Common Article 3 of the Geneva Conventions of 1949, war crimes may not be committed by members of an armed force against fellow members of the same force. In its decision the Chamber asserted at the outset that the Court's statutory framework does not require the victims of the crimes contained in Articles 8(2)(b)(xxii) and 8(2)(e)(vi) to be considered in the limited sense of "protected persons" in terms of Geneva Conventions, or "persons taking no active part in the hostilities" in terms of Common Article 3.[64] Recalling that rape and other forms of sexual violence have long been prohibited by international humanitarian law, the Chamber affirmed that limiting the scope of protection in the manner proposed by the Defence would be contrary to the rationale of international humanitarian law whose purpose is to mitigate the suffering resulting from armed conflict.[65] Interestingly, the Court found that the prohibition of rape and sexual slavery has attained *jus cogens* status under international law with the consequence that such conduct is prohibited at all times, both in times of peace and during armed conflicts, and against all persons, irrespective of any legal status.[66] The Court further concluded that members of the same armed force are not *per se* excluded as potential victims of the war crimes of rape and sexual slavery, whether as a result of the way these crimes have been incorporated in the Rome Statute, or on the basis of the framework of international humanitarian law or international law more generally.[67]

The decision was confirmed in the judgment of 15 June 2017 of the Appeals Chamber which stressed that "if customary or conventional international law stipulates, in respect of a given war crime, an additional element of that crime, the Court cannot be precluded from applying it to ensure consistency of the provision with international humanitarian law, irrespective of whether this requires ascribing to a term in the provision a particular interpretation or reading an additional element into it".[68] The Appeals Chamber clarified that this reasoning does not violate "the principle of legality recognised in Article 22 of the Statute, which protects accused persons against a broad interpretation of the elements of the crimes or their extension by analogy". Having regard to the established framework of international law, the Chamber concluded that members of an armed force or group are not categorically excluded from protection against the war crimes of rape and sexual slavery under Articles 8(2)(b)(xxii) and 8(2)(e)(vi)

---

[63] *The Prosecutor v. Bosco Ntaganda* (Case No. ICC-01/04-02/06), Second Decision on the Defence's challenge to the jurisdiction of the Court in respect of Counts 6 and 9, 4 January 2017.

[64] *Ibid.*, para. 44.

[65] *Ibid.*, para. 48.

[66] *Ibid.*, paras. 51-52.

[67] *Ibid.*, para. 54.

[68] *The Prosecutor v. Bosco Ntaganda* (Case No. ICC-01/04-02/06), Judgment on the Appeal of Mr. Ntaganda against the "Second Decision on the Defence's challenge to the jurisdiction of the Court in respect of Counts 6 and 9", 15 June 2017, para. 1.

of the Rome Statute when committed by members of the same armed force or group. Nevertheless, according to the judges, it must be established that "the conduct in question took place in the context of and was associated with an armed conflict of either international or non-international character" and that "it is this nexus requirement that sufficiently and appropriately delineates war crimes from ordinary crimes".[69]

The reasoning of the Court has been criticized by some authors.[70] Although the judges' legal arguments would seem clearly inspired by the will to guarantee the greatest level of protection to victims of sexual violence in armed conflict regardless of their status, it has been highlighted that such an expansive interpretation of Article 8 of the Rome Statute has not been adequately substantiated by the Court.[71]

3.4. The New Decision of the ICC on the Immunity of Al-Bashir

As mentioned above, in its decision of 6 July 2017 the ICC Pre-Trial Chamber II adopted a new argument on the immunity of Al-Bashir by arguing that the sudanese Head of State does not enjoy immunity because the Security Council's referral of the case to the ICC would place Sudan in a position equivalent to that of a State party to the Rome Statute. In this vein, Al-Bashir would not possess immunity considering that under Article 27(2) of the Statute immunities shall not bar the Court from exercising its jurisdiction. It has been observed by some authors that according to the reasoning of the Chamber, the Council would create obligations for Sudan which are similar to those of a State party under the Statute. It has been underlined, however, that there is no textual argument in the Statute for treating Sudan as a State party, the only effect of the referral being to trigger the Court's jurisdiction.[72] In the same direction is the dissenting opinion of Judge De Brichambaut to the majority of the Chamber.[73] In his view, the referral by the Security Council of the situation in Darfur did not exclusively activate Article 27(2) of the Rome Statute, but preserved the possibility also to apply Article 98(1), which allows a non-State party to invoke the immunities of certain officials *vis-à-vis* the Court. The Judge explained that "in view of the fact

---

[69] *Ibid.*, paras. 2, 63 and 65.

[70] HELLER, "ICC Appeals Chamber Says A War Crime Does Not Have to Violate IHL", Opinio Juris, 15 June 2017, available at: <http://opiniojuris.org/2017/06/15/icc-appeals-chamber-holds-a-war-crime-does-not-have-to-violate-ihl/>.

[71] MCDERMOTT, "ICC Extends War Crimes of Rape and Sexual Slavery to Victims from Same Armed Forces as Perpetrator", Intlawgrrls, 5 January 2017, available at: <https://ilg2.org/2017/01/05/icc-extends-war-crimes-of-rape-and-sexual-slavery-to-victims-from-same-armed-forces-as-perpetrator/>.

[72] KNOTTNERUS, "The Immunity of Al-Bashir: The Latest Turn in the Jurisprudence of the ICC", EJIL: Talk!, 15 November 2017, available at: <https://www.ejiltalk.org/the-immunity-of-al-bashir-the-latest-turn-in-the-jurisprudence-of-the-icc/>.

[73] See Minority Opinion of the Judge Marc Perrin De Brichambaut, available at: <https://www.icc-cpi.int/RelatedRecords/CR2017_04403.PDF>.

that jurisdiction and immunities are distinct concepts, it follows that, once the Court's jurisdiction has been established, it must, subsequently, be established whether any immunities bar the exercise of the Court's jurisdiction". Judge De Brichambaut concluded by affirming: "this means that it need not follow that the mere fact that the Court may exercise jurisdiction on the basis of a referral of the Security Council renders Article 27 of the Statute applicable as if Sudan were analogous to a State Party".[74]

In his opinion, Judge De Brichambaut also disagrees with the majority that the Genocide Convention did not abrogate President Al-Bashir's Head of State immunity. In his view, on the assumption that personal immunities are incompatible with the obligations that the Contracting parties have undertaken under the Genocide Convention, "Sudan must be regarded to have relinquished the immunities of its 'constitutionally responsible rulers' when acceding to the Convention. As Omar Al-Bashir is alleged to have committed the crime of genocide, he no longer enjoys immunity from arrest and surrender". According to the Judge, it then follows that the requirements of Article 98(1) of the Statute have been fulfilled due to the prior accession of Sudan to the Genocide Convention, and that South Africa would not have acted inconsistently with its obligations under international law with respect to the immunity of a person of a third State within the meaning of Article 98(1) of the Statute, had it arrested and surrendered Al-Bashir to the Court.

Following the latest decision on the immunity of Al-Bashir by the Pre-Trial Chamber of the ICC, and taking into account the controversial questions arising from its reasoning, a need for new solutions and clarification has been stressed in the form of an ICC Appeals Chamber decision or through a request for an advisory opinion from the International Court of Justice on the topic.[75]

3.5. The Activation of the Court's Jurisdiction over the Crime of Aggression and the New Amendments to Article 8 of the Rome Statute

On 14 December 2017 the 16th Assembly of States Parties to the Rome Statute decided to activate the Court's jurisdiction over the crime of aggression. The operational paragraph 1 of the resolution adopted by consensus provides the activation as of 17 July 2018.[76] Paragraph 2 confirms that, in accordance with the Rome Statute, the amendments to the Statute regarding the crime of aggression adopted at the Kampala Review Conference shall enter into force for those States parties which have accepted the amendments one year after the deposit of their instruments of ratification or acceptance, and that in the case of a State referral or *proprio motu* investigation the Court shall not exercise its jurisdiction regarding a crime of aggression when committed by a national, or on the territory of a

---

[74] *Ibid.*, para. 56.

[75] KNOTTNERUS, *cit. supra* note 72.

[76] Available at: <https://asp.icc-cpi.int/iccdocs/asp_docs/Resolutions/ASP16/ICC-ASP-16-Res5-ENG.pdf>.

State party that has not ratified or accepted these amendments. As underlined by some commentators, whether or not the Court can exercise its jurisdiction over a crime of aggression committed by a national, or on the territory of a State party to the Rome Statute that has not ratified the crime of aggression amendments, was subject to intense controversy and negotiations before the decision was adopted. It has been suggested that the operative paragraph 2 of the resolution, like paragraph 5 of Article 121 of the Rome Statute on the amendments of the Statute in general, stands in contradiction to paragraph 4 of Article 15 *bis* of the Rome Statute according to which the Court has jurisdiction over a crime "arising from an act of aggression by a State party, unless that State party has previously declared that it does not accept such jurisdiction by lodging a declaration with the Registrar".[77] It would be difficult, in particular, to argue that paragraph 2 of the resolution adopted by the Assembly of the States parties is simply a case of interpreting or clarifying the crime of aggression amendments. If the purpose of paragraph 2 is to amend paragraph 4 of Article 15 *bis*, the problem would be that it was not passed pursuant to the Statute's amendment provisions. The conclusion is that it is now up to the Court to determine the extent of its jurisdiction over acts of aggression by nationals, or on the territory of non-ratifying States parties. And precisely in this direction, the reference to the independence of the judges in operative paragraph 3 of the resolution adopted by the Assembly of States Parties has been considered particularly important. Pending a clear pronouncement by the Court, it has been argued, the only way for any State party to ensure that their nationals will not be prosecuted for the crime of aggression continues to be the procedure provided for in paragraph 4 of Article 15 *bis*.[78]

Another resolution was adopted by the Assembly of States Parties concerning three amendments to Article 8 of the Rome Statute adding new war crimes within the jurisdiction of the Court. The new war crimes relate to the use of prohibited weapons in international and non-international armed conflicts and they concern: 1) employing weapons, which use microbial or other biological agents, or toxins, whatever their origin or method of production (to be inserted as Articles 8(2)(b)(xxvii) and 8(2)(e)(xvi)); 2) employing weapons the primary effect of which is to injure by fragments which in the human body escape detection by X-rays (to be inserted as Articles 8(2)(b)(xxviii) and 8(2)(e)(xvii)); 3) employing laser weapons specifically designed, as their sole combat function or as one of their combat functions, to cause permanent blindness to unenhanced

---

[77] STÜRCHLER, "The Activation of the Crime of Aggression in Perspective", EJIL: Talk!, 26 January 2018, available at: <https://www.ejiltalk.org/the-activation-of-the-crime-of-aggression-in-perspective/>.

[78] See also AKANDE, "The ICC Assembly of States Parties Prepares to Activate the ICC's Jurisdiction over the Crime of Aggression: But Who Will be Covered by that Jurisdiction?", EJIL: Talk!, 26 June 2016, available at: <https://www.ejiltalk.org/the-icc-assembly-of-states-parties-prepares-to-activate-the-iccs-jurisdiction-over-the-crime-of-aggression-but-who-will-be-covered-by-that-jurisdiction/>; BARRIGA, "The Scope of ICC Jurisdiction over the Crime of Aggression: A Different Perspective", EJIL: Talk!, 29 September 2017, available at: <https://www.ejiltalk.org/the-scope-of-icc-jurisdiction-over-the-crime-of-aggression-a-different-perspective/>.

vision, that is to the naked eye or to the eye with corrective eyesight devices (to be inserted as Articles 8(2)(b)(xxix) and 8(2)(e)(xviii)).[79]

Some authors have underscored the controversy in the Assembly of States Parties as to the wisdom and the legality of adding new war crimes in the jurisdiction of the ICC. One of the concerns was that there would be fragmentation of the Rome Statute system with different crimes applicable in differing situations to different individuals. This would be because under the amendment procedure to the Rome Statute these new crimes would not apply to nationals of, or conducted on the territory of, non-ratifying States parties. Another concern was that at least some of the new crimes, in the opinion of a number of States, are not criminalised under customary international law and thus not suitable for inclusion in the ICC Statute.[80] The three amendments are subject to ratification or acceptance and shall enter into force in accordance with Article 121(5) of the Rome Statute.

4. THE EXTRAORDINARY CHAMBERS IN THE COURTS OF CAMBODIA (ECCC)[81]

4.1. Case Law

After a closing order of 22 February 2017 dismissing the case against Im Chaem,[82] on 10 July 2017 the Co-Investigating Judges issued the reasons for the order, clarifying that the accused did not fall into the category of senior leaders of the Democratic Kampuchea nor into the residual category of those who were "most responsible" for the crimes and serious violations of Cambodian penal law, international humanitarian law and custom committed from 1975 to 1979, under Article 1 of the agreement between the United Nations and the government of Cambodia establishing the ECCC.[83]

4.2. On the Interpretation of "Civilian Population" in the Context of Crimes Against Humanity

Following an invitation for submissions from the parties to Cases 003 and 004 and *amici curiae* of 19 April 2016, on 7 February 2017 the Co-Investigating

---

[79] Available at: <https://asp.icc-cpi.int/iccdocs/asp_docs/Resolutions/ASP16/ICC-ASP-16-Res4-ENG.pdf>.

[80] AKANDE, "Customary International Law and the Addition of New War Crimes to the Statute of the ICC", EJIL: Talk!, 2 January 2018, available at: <https://www.ejiltalk.org/customary-international-law-and-the-addition-of-new-war-crimes-to-the-statute-of-the-icc/>.

[81] Judgments and decisions of the ECCC are available at: <https://www.eccc.gov.kh/en>. On the ECCC, see KILLEAN, MOFFETT, "Victims Legal Representation Before the ICC and ECCC", JICJ, 2017, p. 713 ff.

[82] Case No. 004/1/07-09-2009-ECCC-OCIJ, Closing Order (Disposition), 22 February 2017.

[83] Case No. 004/1/07-09-2009-ECCC-OCIJ, Closing Order (Reasons), 10 July 2017.

Judge Bohlander issued a notification on the interpretation of "attack against the civilian population" in the context of crimes against humanity with regard to a State's or regime's own armed forces.[84] The Judge first reviewed evidence of State practice and *opinio juris* pre-1975, in order to determine whether in 1975 "civilian population" included, and could be understood to include, a State or organization's own armed forces.[85] The Judge then analysed the elaboration of the term by the courts who interpreted it, starting from the 1990s.[86] According to the Judge, this review shows that, while nowadays the vast majority of international and hybrid criminal courts define "civilian population" narrowly and based on the meaning of the term from the perspective of international humanitarian law, this jurisprudence originated in the context of cases where crimes against humanity were linked to an ongoing armed conflict. To the contrary, in the opinion of the Judge, the main question to be resolved in the case before the ECCC is whether such an interpretation is appropriate and applicable in times of peace or for crimes against humanity merely committed during an ongoing armed conflict but not contextually connected thereto, and whether it is binding for crimes committed between 1975 and 1979. The Judge also observed that the purpose of the law of crimes against humanity can be characterized as the protection against human rights violations perpetrated on a large scale against individuals including a State's own nationals, who were not otherwise protected by the existing laws and customs of war.[87] On this premise, the Judge considered that, in interpreting the law of crimes against humanity consistently with this objective and purpose, the specific situation criterion, rather than international humanitarian law criterion must be applied, with the consequence of the adoption of a broader definition of the term "civilian population".[88] The Judge concluded that between 1975 and 1979, as a matter of principle, an attack by a State or organization against its own armed forces, when carried out during peacetime, satisfied the *chapeau* requirement of an attack against any civilian population under Article 5 of the ECCC law.[89] He further specified that an attack carried out by a State or regime against its own armed forces during an armed conflict did also, as a matter of principle, satisfy that *chapeau* requirement, unless the attacked armed forces were in fact allied with or otherwise providing military relevant support to an opposing side in the conflict.[90] Finally, the Judge found that his conclusion did comply with the principles of legality,[91] and of *in dubio pro reo*.[92]

---

[84] Case No. 004/07-09-2009-ECCC-OCIJ, Notification on the interpretation of "attack against the civilian population" in the context of crimes against humanity with regard to a state's or regime's own armed forces, 7 February 2017.

[85] *Ibid.*, paras. 29 ff.

[86] *Ibid.*, paras. 29 and 46 ff.

[87] *Ibid.*, paras. 26 and 55.

[88] *Ibid.*, para. 55.

[89] *Ibid.*, para. 56.

[90] *Ibid.*, para. 57.

[91] *Ibid.*, paras. 58 ff.

[92] *Ibid.*, paras. 67 ff.

On 30 June 2017, the Pre-Trial Chamber dismissed the appeal against the Judge's notification.[93] The Co-Lawyers contended in particular that the appeal was admissible as a jurisdictional challenge under internal rule 74(3) since the notification concerned the ECCC's jurisdiction to investigate and prosecute individuals for attacks by a State or regime against its armed forces as a crime against humanity, which if applied would violate the principle of legality.[94] The Pre-Trial Chamber considered that both the title and the form and substance of the impugned notification suggest that it did not amount to a decision "appealable" under internal rule 74(3)(a), but rather to an opinion from which declaratory relief was sought.[95] According to the Pre-Trial Chamber, the Co-Investigating Judge did not explicitly indicate in the notification whether he would apply his conclusion to the case before the ECCC, making "findings as a matter of principle" and calling "for submissions in the abstract as a question of law" with the aim to "benefit international criminal law as a whole".[96] By concluding that the notification cannot be considered as an appealable decision, the Pre-Trial Chamber found no need to examine whether the interpretation of "attack against the civilian population" in the context of crimes against humanity with regard to a State's or regime's own armed forces constitutes a jurisdictional challenge under internal rule 74(3)(a).[97]

As for the Judge's notification, some commentators have confirmed that customary international law applicable from 1975 to 1979 provides a strong case for holding that the purges carried out by the Khmer Rouge against its own armed forces can qualify as an attack against a "civilian population" for the purpose of establishing crimes against humanity. The opportunity of the ECCC to clarify a complex area of law has been underlined, to contribute significantly to the development of the international criminal law, and to counter the regression, in terms of a restrictive interpretation of the "civilian population", that has emerged in the contemporary jurisprudence of other criminal tribunals.[98]

5. CONCLUSION

International criminal tribunals achieved significant results in 2017. Of particular importance is the request of a judicial authorization by the ICC Prosecutor

---

[93] Case No. 004/07-09-2009-ECCC-OCIJ (PTC42), Decision on [...] Appeal against the Notification on the interpretation of "attack against the civilian population" in the context of crimes against humanity with regard to a state's or regime's own armed forces, 30 June 2017.

[94] *Ibid.*, para. 9.

[95] *Ibid.*, para. 12.

[96] *Ibid.*, para. 13.

[97] *Ibid.*, para. 15.

[98] KILLEAN, DOWDS and KRAMER, "Soldiers as Victims at the ECCC: Exploring the Concept of 'Civilian' in the Crimes Against Humanity", Leiden JIL, 2017, p. 685 ff. See also JAMISON, "The Progressive Expansion of Crimes Against Humanity", LOAC Blog, 9 March 2017, available at: <https://loacblog.com/2017/03/10/the-progressive-expansion-of-crimes-against-humanity/>.

to initiate investigations over possible crimes committed in Afghanistan during the armed conflict in 2003. Noteworthy in this regard is the decision to eventually investigate alleged crimes committed by all the actors involved in the conflict, including the United States armed forces and members of the CIA in secret detention facilities even outside the territory of Afghanistan. The decision of the ICC Prosecutor at the beginning of 2018 to initiate investigations in the Philippines and in Venezuela contributes to an extension of the judicial work of the ICC which until last year was almost exclusively focused on the African States. Also relating to the case law, some remarkable decisions and judgments were issued in 2017, such as the sentencing to life imprisonment of Mladić, former Commander of the Bosnian Serbs Army, after being convicted of genocide, war crimes and crimes against humanity by the ICTY, and the ICC decision on its jurisdiction under Article 8 of the Rome Statute over crimes committed by members of an armed force against members of the same group, particularly as for the crimes of rape and sexual slavery. A significant contribution to the interpretation of "civilian population" in the context of crimes against humanity was also provided in the jurisprudence of the ECCC.

THE WTO IN 2017: SYSTEMIC DEVELOPMENTS, DISPUTES AND REVIEW OF THE APPELLATE BODY'S REPORTS

edited by GIORGIO SACERDOTI*

1. THE FUNCTIONING OF THE WTO IN 2017 AND THE CHALLENGES TO THE DISPUTE SETTLEMENT SYSTEM

1.1. The functioning of the WTO in 2017

The most important event in the operation of the WTO was, or rather was supposed to be, the Ministerial Conference in Buenos Aires which took place in the first half of December. The expectations at the opening of the meeting were already low, since a preliminary meeting ("Mini-ministerial") held in Marrakech in October had shown that Members were not engaged in negotiating in such a way as to be able to reach agreements on open issues to be finalized in Buenos Aires. The Ministerial Conference was even more disappointing, to the point of the Members even being unable to issue a final declaration. Procedural agreements were reached just for ongoing negotiations in Geneva on the main open issues where, in theory, an agreement could be reached, notably on regulating (curbing) fishing subsidies. This negative outcome was due not only to the "disengagement" of the United States but also to the unwillingness of most major economies to make efforts to reinforce and expand the multilateral rules.

The WTO system risks to be undermined by the direct challenge to its rules initiated by the Trump administration at the beginning of 2018 with the introduction of substantial anti-dumping duties on washers from Korea and solar panels from India; thereafter with the announcement of safeguards based on the security exception of Article XXI GATT on steel and aluminium imports; and finally with the restrictive measures on a variety of exports from China to the US. Also the attitude of the US towards regional agreements (US withdrawal from the not-yet-in force TPP, the renegotiation of NAFTA accompanied by threats of withdrawing from it, the renegotiation of the FTA with Korea with the aim of rebalancing the trade deficit possibly also through "voluntary" Korean export restraints) shows a "mercantilist" posture which is at odd with the principles underpinning the multilateral trading system.

* Of the Board of Editors. This review was carried out within the framework of the PhD programme in International Law and Economics of the Bocconi PhD School. Professor Giorgio Sacerdoti coordinated the work. The reviews of individual cases were authored by PhD candidates Murielle Bechara, Thi Minh Hoang, Viktoriia Lapa, Andrea Mensi, Victorien Salles, as indicated on the bottom of each review.

1.2.   The Dispute Settlement System in 2017

The WTO dispute settlement system has not remained unaffected by the above trend. While the US is challenging a key element of the system, namely the appointment process for replacing outgoing members of the Appellate Body, the other Members appear uncertain how to respond, inspired by the desire not to frontally antagonise the US, at least not at this stage.

Apparently, the dispute settlement system is functioning well, if one looks at the number of the disputes initiated as an indicator of the existence of trade conflicts and, on the other hand, of the confidence of Members that the system may resolve them satisfactorily. Seventeen new disputes were introduced through requests for consultations in 2017, bringing their total number to 535 from the establishment of the system. The Appellate Body issued five reports. Eleven panel reports were issued in 2017 (two of which in compliance proceedings under Article 21.5 DSU), six of which were not appealed. One arbitration award was issued under Article 21.3(c) DSU for the determination of the "reasonable period of time" to comply.[1] The time frame for panels to complete their work from the moment they are composed to the issuance of the reports of parties and their circulation has somehow shortened, compared to recent years, due to the increase in their staffing undertaken by the Director-General in response to previous complaints by Members. As reported by the Chairman of the DSB at the meeting of 22 November 2017, at that date there were 16 active panels (including four panels under Article 21.5 DSU) that had not yet issued a final report to the parties. Five panel reports had been issued to the parties and were being translated with a view to circulate them. A further four panels were at the composition stage. At the same date, the Appellate Body was dealing with six appeals. Two matters were pending in arbitration under Article 22.6 DSU and one to determine the reasonable period of time under Article 21.3(c) DSU.

1.3.   The paralysis of the Appellate Body's appointment process

The most worrisome feature of the (dys)functioning of the system in 2017, which shows no sign of having been resolved as of April 2018, when this review is being finalized, is the paralysis of the selection process to fill vacancies in the Appellate Body.[2] This unprecedented situation is exclusively due to the US not

---

[1] A review of these non-appealed reports of panels and of the award can be found in the review of the WTO in 2017 edited by the same author, available at: <http://www.ssrn.com>.

[2] On these issues and more generally on proposals for improving the functioning of the system see SACERDOTI, "The Future of the WTO Dispute Settlement System: Confronting Challenges to Consolidate a Success Story", in PRIMO BRAGA and HOEKMAN (eds.), *Future of the Global Trade Order*, 2nd updated ed., Firenze, 2017, p.117 ff.

joining the consensus necessary, in principle, to launch the selection and appointment process because of various grounds of dissatisfaction (however not specified in detail) voiced by the US with the functioning of the Appellate Body. Until these issues are resolved, as the US representatives repeatedly stated at DSB meetings starting in August 2017, the US will continue to block the process.[3] Notwithstanding the isolation of the US in this attitude and the widespread criticism from other members to this linking by the US of what could be proposals for reforming the DSU with the normal functioning of the dispute settlement system, the US has not budged. This has prompted several commentators and the press to speculate that the US – having found a weak point in the rules that is not subject to the reverse consensus principle that in other respects prevents vetoes as to the functioning of the system – is using it to pursue its real aim of undermining the multilateral trading system by blocking and debilitating its dispute settlement mechanism.[4] A desire to go back to the weak power-based system of the GATT, away from the rule-based structure of the WTO, looms in the background.[5]

GIORGIO SACERDOTI[*]

---

[3] The US has referred to various reasons, from the alleged judicial activism of the Appellate Body in "over-reaching", such as improperly filling gaps in its activity and the lack of accountability to the membership, as well as for having the dispute settlement system introduced in its decision obligations upon the US which the US had not agreed to at the negotiating table in the Uruguay Round. This position has apparently not taken into account the fact that in 2017 the US won a series of victories in a row before panels and the Appellate Body in high profile disputes, both as claimant and respondent, notably against China, India, Mexico, Indonesia. Subsequently, for its criticism, the US has relied principally on the fact that the Appellate Body has allowed Mr. Ramirez and Van den Bossche to go on serving in divisions whose work had not been concluded when they had finished their mandate (respectively in June and December 2017). This is however explicitly provided for in Article 15 of the Working Procedure for the Appellate Body. This practice, which has been resorted to in a number of cases in the previous years, has never raised any criticism from WTO Members. See Minutes of the Meeting of the DSB of 22 November 2017, WT/DSB/M/404, p. 18. On the issue see also former Appellate Body member HILLMAN, "Independence at the Top of the Triangle: Best Resolution of the Judicial Trilemma", AJIL Unbound, 2017, p. 364 ff.

[4] At the end of 2017, the Appellate Body was operating with four of seven members, due to the non-replacement of Ricardo Ramirez, Peter Van den Bossche and Hyun Chon Kim. The latter, who had replaced Seung Wha Chang (also of Korea) when the US had blocked his reappointment for a second term in 2016, resigned abruptly, effective 31 July 2017, having been appointed foreign trade minister of Korea. Currently the work of the Appellate Body is obviously slowed down, but it could cease to be operational altogether in 2019, when only two members would remain in office, should the paralysis go on until then.

[5] See for instance "America holds the WTO hostage. The rule-based system of trade faces threat beyond Trump's tariffs", The Economist, 23 September 2017.

[*] Of the Board of Editors.

2. APPELLATE BODY REPORT, *RUSSIAN FEDERATION – MEASURES ON THE IMPORTATION OF LIVE PIGS, PORK AND OTHER PIG PRODUCTS FROM THE EUROPEAN UNION* (DS475)[6]

2.1. Introduction and Main Facts of the Dispute

The present case concerns the "the EU-wide ban" imposed by Russia on the importation of live pigs, pork and certain pig products from the entire EU as well as the country-specific importation ban on the products at issue from Estonia, Latvia, Lithuania and Poland, following outbreaks of African swine fever (ASF) in certain regions of the European Union. One condition that has to be met in veterinary certificates for live pigs and pig products to be imported into Russian territory is that the entire EU, except the island of Sardinia, must have been free of the ASF for the previous 3 years. The EU claimed that the measures at issue were contrary to the SPS Agreement. In particular, the EU argued that Russia, by imposing the EU-wide ban, had failed to take into account that there were areas within the EU which are free from the ASF. The EU asked for consultations with Russia on 8 April 2014. At its meeting on 22 July 2014, the DSB established the Panel, which issued its report on 19 August 2016. Russia and the European Union appealed the Panel Report on 23 and 28 September 2016 respectively. The Appellate Body circulated its report on 23 February 2017. Pursuant to Article 21.3(b) of the DSU, the Russian Federation and the European Union agreed on the reasonable period of time to implement the DSB's recommendations and rulings in this dispute that expired on 6 December 2017.

The dispute was, however, not thereby resolved. Russia informed that it fully implemented the DSB's rulings and recommendations in this dispute on 13 December 2017. On 19 December 2017 the European Union had recourse to Article 22.2 of the DSU and requested authorization from the Dispute Settlement Body to suspend concessions with regard to the Russian Federation, submitting that the latter had failed to comply with the Appellate Body Report. On its part, Russia on 3 January 2018 disagreed with the allegations of the European Union as to non-compliance and objected to the European Union's level of suspension. Moreover, on 30 January 2018 Russia requested consultations pursuant to Article 21.5 of the DSU.

2.2. The Panel Report

The European Union claimed that the Russian ban on pigs and pig products from the EU is not consistent with its SPS obligations. In line with this, the EU maintained that Russia breached its commitment to ensure that its SPS measures

---

[6] Appellate Body Report, *Russian Federation – Measures on the Importation of Live Pigs, Pork and Other Pig Products from the European Union*, adopted on 23 February 2017, WT/DS/475/AB/R.

protecting animal life and health are (1) based on scientific principles and on sufficient scientific evidence, and are (2) neither discriminative, (3) nor more trade restrictive than necessary. Against these allegations, Russia argued that the measure could not be attributed to it since Russia was merely following what was agreed in the requirements of the bilateral veterinary certificates and the terms of its Accession Protocol. In this regard, the Panel ruled that the EU-wide ban was a measure susceptible to challenge under the WTO dispute settlement mechanism. The main complaints of the EU, though, were related to Articles 2, 3 and 6 of the SPS Agreement.

2.2.1. Articles 6.1, 6.2 and 6.3 of the SPS Agreement

The core of the case concerned the regionalization requirement under Article 6 of the SPS Agreement. In particular, Article 6.1 of the SPS Agreement requires that the WTO Members shall ensure that their SPS measures are "adapted" to the SPS characteristics of the area, whether all of a country, part of a country, or all or parts of several countries from which the product originated and to which it is destined. Article 6.2. goes further by stating that "Members shall, in particular, recognize the concepts of pest- or disease-free areas or areas of low pest or disease prevalence". Article 6.3 states that "exporting Members claiming that areas within their territories are pest- or disease-free areas or areas of low pest or disease prevalence shall provide the necessary evidence thereof in order to objectively demonstrate to the importing Member that such areas are, and are likely to remain, pest- or disease-free areas or areas of low pest or disease prevalence, respectively".

First, the EU, as the exporting Member, had the obligation of providing the necessary evidence to objectively demonstrate that there are areas within the EU, outside Estonia, Latvia, Lithuania, and Poland that are free of ASF and are likely to remain so within the meaning of Article 6.3. The Panel concluded that the EU, indeed, had objectively demonstrated to Russia that there are areas within the EU outside Estonia, Lithuania and Poland that are free of ASF and are likely to remain so. However, the EU failed to demonstrate that the ASF-free areas within Latvia were likely to remain so. It should be mentioned that this was the first time a Panel interpreted the term to "objectively demonstrate". The Panel explained that to "objectively demonstrate" means to "prove something in an impartial manner".

As to Article 6.2. of the SPS Agreement, the Panel found that Russia's legislative framework recognized the concepts of pest- or disease-free areas and areas of low pest or disease prevalence in respect of ASF. Therefore, the EU-wide ban was not inconsistent with Article 6.2.

Taking into account the above-mentioned conclusion under Article 6.3 of the SPS Agreement, the Panel concluded that Russia had not adapted its measure to the sanitary and phytosanitary characteristics of the European Union territory outside Estonia, Lithuania, Latvia and Poland, contrary to Article 6.1. of the SPS Agreement.

2.2.2. "Arbitrary or Unjustifiable Discrimination" against Imported Products

SPS Article 2.3 provides that Members must ensure that their SPS measures do not "arbitrarily or unjustifiably discriminate between Members where identical or similar conditions prevail, including between their own territory and that of other Members" and cannot be "applied in a manner which would constitute a disguised restriction on international trade".

The EU argued that Russia breached Article 2.3 of the SPS Agreement as "Russia bans imports of the products at issue from the entire territory of the European Union, while it allows for trade in the products at issue from non-affected areas within Russia." The Panel considered that there was "a clear distinction in the treatment of the products under the same conditions, i.e. imports of products from areas not affected by ASF". It noted that it was an "undisputed fact" that ASF has been present in Russia since 2007. It observed that the "imported products coming from non-ASF affected areas within the European Union are not allowed to enter into Russia's market, while intra-Russian trade is possible for those products coming from non-ASF affected areas".[7] The Panel concluded that "the EU-wide ban discriminates against products originating in the non-ASF affected areas of the European Union and domestic trade of the products at issue from non ASF-affected areas within Russia",[8] in breach of Article 2.3.

2.2.3. Articles 3.1 and 3.2 and 5.1 and 5.7 of the SPS Agreement

Article 3.1 of the SPS Agreement provides in part that Members shall base their SPS measures on "international standards, guidelines or recommendations, where they exist". The Panel noted that the World Organization for Animal Health (OIE) Terrestrial Animal Health Code "sets out standards for the improvement of terrestrial animal health and welfare and veterinary public health worldwide, including through standards for safe international trade in terrestrial animals".[9] The Panel found that the Russian ban breached Russia's obligations under Article 3.1 since it was not based on the relevant international standard.

Moreover, Article 5.1 of the SPS Agreement provides that Members shall ensure that their SPS measures are based on a risk assessment. Further, Article 5.7 of the SPS Agreement allows the Members to provisionally adopt SPS measure on the basis of "available pertinent information". Russia acknowledged that it had not conducted any risk assessment, but justified its measure by reference to Article 5.7 of the SPS Agreement by claiming that it had adopted the measure as a precautionary one. According to the Appellate Body case law, Article 5.7 of the SPS Agreement sets out four cumulative requirements to justify a precautionary measure. In particular, the Appellate Body checks whether (i) it is imposed in respect of a situation where relevant scientific evidence is insufficient; (ii) it

---

[7] Panel Report, circulated on 19 August 2016, WT/DS/475/R, para. 7.1339.
[8] *Ibid.*, para. 7.1344.
[9] WT/DS/475/R, para. 7.284.

is provisionally adopted on the basis of available pertinent information; (iii) the Member maintaining the measure seeks to obtain the additional information necessary for a more objective assessment of risk; and (iv) the Member reviews the measure within a reasonable period of time. The Panel underlined the Appellate Body's finding that the four requirements are "cumulative in nature" and that "whenever one of these four requirements is not met, the measure at issue is inconsistent with Article 5.7". After reviewing the evidence, the Panel concluded that Russia did not satisfy any of the four requirements and therefore the measure was not justified under Article 5.7 of the SPS Agreement.

2.2.4. Standard of Review under the SPS Agreement

When reviewing Russia's compliance with Article 6.1 of the SPS Agreement, the Panel first dealt with the relevant procedural matter – the standard of review. In essence, under Article 11 of the DSU, the standard of review implies that the Panel has to "make an objective assessment of the matter before it, including an objective assessment of the facts of the case and the applicability of and conformity with the relevant covered agreements". Russia claimed that the Panel must determine whether the totality of the circumstances and evidence (or lack thereof) was sufficient to support the objectivity of Russia's decision in light of the relevant provisions of the Terrestrial Code and SPS Agreement Article 6 criteria and the available information. The Panel referred to the Panel report in *US – Animals* to shed some light on the standard of review under Article 6.1. The Panel needs to examine the evidentiary record and carry out an objective assessment, pursuant to its obligation under Article 11 of the DSU, of whether the challenged measure is adapted to the relevant ASF characteristics of the area where the products at issue originate and of the area to which they are destined. Such an objective assessment is framed in the broader context of panels' standard of review, which has been described by the Appellate Body in respect of fact-finding, "as neither de novo review as such, nor 'total deference', but rather the 'objective assessment of facts'".[10] In the end, the WTO-consistency of an SPS-measure will depend on whether it has a valid scientific basis. In the present case, both the Panel and the Appellate Body concluded that the Russian Federation's ban fell short of this standard.

2.3. The Appellate Body Report

2.3.1. Articles 6.1, 6.2 and 6.3 of the SPS Agreement

Russia appealed the Panel's finding on Article 6.3 of the SPS Agreement by claiming that the Panel failed to take into account (1) the evidence, relied on by

---

[10] Appellate Body Report, *European Communities – Measures Concerning Meat and Meat Products (Hormones)*, adopted on 16 January 1998, WT/DS26/AB/R, para. 117.

the importing Member and (2) the fact that Article 6.3 of the SPS Agreement provides for a certain period of time for the importing Member to assess the evidence provided by the exporting Member and to adapt its measure. The Appellate Body disagreed with Russia and stated that Article 6.3 focuses on the obligations of the exporting Member. Moreover, the Appellate Body rejected Russia's argument as to the certain period of time for the importing Member stating that it is not mentioned in Article 6.3.

Russia also appealed the Panel's finding under Article 6.1 of the SPS Agreement. Russia disagreed with conclusion as to the adaptation of its measure to the imports coming from Latvia. Taking into account the fact that the European Union did not demonstrate that the ASF-free areas within Latvia are likely to remain so, Russia was not able to adapt its measure in this respect. On this point the Appellate Body sided with Russia. In essence, the Appellate Body concluded that an obligation to adapt the SPS measure is on the exporting Member (in the present case, the European Union), but the compliance with this obligation is dependent on the importing Member, i.e. Russia. In other words, Russia could not be expected to adapt its measure to products coming from Latvia, since the EU did not demonstrate that the ASF-free areas within Latvia are likely to remain so. Therefore, the Appellate Body stated that the Panel erred by not taking into account its own conclusion with regard to Latvia.

The European Union appealed the Panel's interpretation of the concept "to recognize" under Article 6.2. The Panel had stated that Article 6.2 imposes the obligation to acknowledge the concept as an abstract idea. However, the Appellate Body considered that this obligation is not an abstract one and corresponds to "render operational" the concepts of pest- or disease-free areas and areas of low pest or disease prevalence. The Appellate Body reversed the Panel's finding that the Russian measures were consistent with Article 6.2., but it did not complete the legal analysis.

2.3.2. Other Provisions

A number of rulings of the Panel were neither appealed by Russia nor by the EU. These included the Panel's finding that the EU-wide ban was inconsistent with Russia's obligation to base its SPS measures on international standards pursuant to Article 3.1; and that Russia did not base the EU-wide ban on a risk assessment, in breach of SPS Articles 5.1, 5.2 and 2.2.

2.4. Concluding Remarks

In order to fully understand this case, one should grasp the broader context. The Russian ban was imposed in 2014 at the same time of the sanctions imposed by the European Union on Russia in relation to the Ukrainian conflict. It might thus seem plausible that Russia responded to EU sanctions by imposing a ban on the imports of pig products from the EU. And the Russian authorities, to be sure, called out the decision of the Panel as politically motivated.[11] However, after the Appellate Body Report confirmed most of the findings of the Panel, it is hard to say that the Panel Report is based on political considerations since it follows established case law on these matters. It seems that high politics did not contaminate the Panel discussion in this case. The political context, though, might have implications in the compliance stage. Indeed, as for now, the parties to the dispute have not found an agreement as to the compliance.

Furthermore, an important consideration that can be drawn from the case concerns the relevance of the regionalization requirement for SPS measures under Article 6 of the SPS Agreement. By interpreting this provision, the Panel and the Appellate Body once again demonstrated its importance for large and diverse WTO Members like the EU where a pest might be present in some parts and absent in others.

Finally, the Appellate Body's approach to the standard of review under the SPS agreement deserves attention. As already noted by Ming Du in relation to the Appellate Body Report in *EC – Hormones II*, the Appellate Body follows a less intrusive standard of review for SPS cases, which offers more policy space to WTO Members in SPS related issues.[12] It appears that the Appellate Body's conclusions in *Russia – Pigs (EU)* on the standard of review under Article 6.3 of the SPS Agreement followed that previous case law by adopting a special standard of review which offers Members more deference.[13]

VIKTORIIA LAPA[*]

3. APPELLATE BODY REPORT, *UNITED STATES – CERTAIN METHODOLOGIES AND THEIR APPLICATION TO ANTI-DUMPING PROCEEDINGS INVOLVING CHINA* (DS471)[14]

3.1. Introduction and Main Facts of the Dispute

The dispute revolved around several methodologies used by the United States Department of Commerce (USDOC) in anti-dumping investigations involving Chinese imports. More specifically, the USDOC's three challenged methodologies are: (1) its use of the weighted average-to-transaction (W-T) methodology, (2) its treatment of multiple exporters from a non-market economy (NME) as a single NME-wide entity (the Single Rate Presumption) and (3) its use of facts

---

[11] Rosselkhoznadzor says that the WTO's decision on pigs is politically motivated in "Россельхознадзор назвал политическим решение ВТО по свиньям", Lenta, 18 August 2016, available at: <https://lenta.ru/news/2016/08/19/pigpolicy/> (in Russian).

[12] DU, "Standard of Review under the SPS Agreement after EC-Hormones II", ICLQ, 2010, p. 458 ff.

[13] FURCULIȚĂ, "Regionalization Within the SPS Agreement After Russia – Pigs (EU)", Legal Issues of Economic Integration, 2018, p. 101 ff.

[*] Ph.D. Candidate in International Law and Economics, Bocconi University, Milan.

[14] Appellate Body Report, *United States — Certain Methodologies And Their Application To Anti-Dumping Proceedings Involving China,* adopted on 22 May 2017, WT/DS471/AB/R.

available in determining anti-dumping duty rates for NME-wide entities (called the "Adverse Facts Available Norm" or the AFA Norm) and the level of such duty rates. On 26 March 2014, the Panel was established; its Report was circulated on 19 October 2016 and thereafter appealed by China. The Appellate Body Report was circulated and then adopted on 11 May 2017 and on 22 May 2017 respectively.

3.2. The Panel Report

China held the view that the measures at issue were inconsistent with Articles 2.4.2, 6.1, 6.8, 6.10, 9.2, 9.3 and 9.4 of the Anti-Dumping Agreement (ADA) and Annex II thereto and Article VI:2 of the GATT 1994.

First, regarding the USDOC's use of the W-T methodology, on the one hand, the Panel found it inconsistent with Article 2.4.2 of the ADA due to various reasons, including the fourth quantitative flaw with the Nails test[15] leading to the omission of non-target prices below the "alleged target prices" under the price gap test, the first programming error in price gap test application, its use of W-T methodology with zeroing, its exclusion of the transaction-to-transaction (T-T) methodology from cases with significant gaps in relevant export prices and application of the W-T methodology to all export transactions. The Panel, on the other hand, rejected the other challenges brought by China, holding that China had not demonstrated the breaches of Article 2.4.2 it alleged the United States had committed in the investigations at issue.

Secondly, the Panel ruled that the USDOC use of zeroing in the W-T methodology infringed on Article 9.3 of ADA and Article VI:2 of the GATT 1994. Additionally, in footnote 385 of its Report, the Panel suggested that the W-T methodology applied to "pattern transactions" might be combined with the W-W or the T-T methodology applied to "non-pattern transactions" to determine dumping margins.[16]

Thirdly, as a measure of general and prospective application, the Single Rate Presumption "as such" and "as applied", both constituted a breach of Article 6.10 and 9.2 of the ADA. The Panel did not rule on the claim on Article 9.4 of the ADA for judicial economy.

Fourthly, the Panel judged that, as the AFA Norm was not evidenced by China as a norm of general and prospective application, it was not "as such" at odds with Article 6.8 of the ADA and paragraph 7 of Annex II thereto. Neither was it "as applied" due to the judicial economy.

---

[15] The Nails test – using the USDOC terminology – was used by the USDOC to find a pattern of export prices which differed significantly among different purchasers or across different time periods.

[16] Panel Report, *United States – Certain Methodologies And Their Application To Anti-Dumping Proceedings Involving China,* adopted on 19 October 2016, WT/DS471/R, fn. 385 to para. 7.220.

In sum, at the Panel procedure, China won partially on its claim against the Nails test and the use of W-T methodology, succeeded completely in its Single Rate Presumption arguments and lost completely on its last point on the AFA Norm.

3.3. The Appellate Body Report

Having won on just a part of its claim at the Panel procedure, China appealed on the other points it lost. More specifically, challenges by China were grouped into two clusters in relation to Articles 2.4.2 and 17.6(i) of the ADA and Article 6.8 and paragraph 7 of Annex II thereto.

In the first cluster, China objected to the Panel's findings under Article 2.4.2 of the ADA pertaining to the USDOC application of the Nails test and its use of the W-T methodology in the three challenged investigations. In particular, China claimed that the Panel erred in its findings regarding (1) the first[17] and third[18] qualitative flaws with the Nails test, (2) omission of certain qualitative factors when establishing the "significance" feature of pricing differences and (3) the use of averages to determine a "pattern". Additionally, China pointed out the wrongfulness of the Panel's suggestion to combine methodologies of comparison to measure dumping margins in footnote 385 of the Panel Report.

In its Report, the Appellate Body rejected first of all the allegations by China on the first and third alleged quantitative flaw with the Nails test, considering that the Panel was correct in its interpretation and application of the second sentence of Article 2.4.2 of the ADA.[19] More specifically, the first alleged quantitative flaw did not prevent an anti-dumping "investigating authority from finding that the export prices to the 'target' differ significantly from the other export prices and form a pattern".[20] Moreover, the Appellate Body upheld the Panel's finding that China had failed to prove that the assumption on which the third alleged quantitative flaw was based was "factually correct insofar as the three challenged investigations are concerned".[21]

Secondly, as far as qualitative factors in determining the "significance" of price differences under the second sentence of Article 2.4.2 of the ADA were concerned, the Appellate Body rejected China's claim in that the relevant pro-vision of the ADA "neither requires that an investigating authority ascertain the cause of (or objective reasons for) the price differences, nor does it require that an authority ascertain the motivation for (or intent behind) the difference

---

[17] The first quantitative flaw related to the Nails test's "assumption that the examined export price data were, in terms of statistics, normally distributed, or at least single-peaked and symmetric around the mean". See WT/DS471/R, para. 7.56.

[18] The third quantitative flaw "related to the manner in which the USDOC calculated the weighted-average non-target price gap and the alleged target price gap and then compared them". See WT/DS471/R, para. 7.75.

[19] WT/DS471/AB/R, paras. 5.31 and 5.45.

[20] *Ibid.*, paras. 5.31.

[21] *Ibid.*, para. 5.45 and WT/DS471/R, para. 7.82.

in prices".[22] In other words, the Appellate Body supported the exclusion of the so-called "objective reasons" – to use China's terminology – for pricing differences, from the scope of the notion "objective market factors".[23] The Appellate Body, by echoing the previous Appellate Body ruling in *US – Washing Machines*, confirmed that the inclusion in or exclusion from the notion of "objective market factors" depended on the relevance of a certain factor in assisting an investigating authority in examining the significance of pricing differences.[24] The Appellate Body rejected factors that explained reasons for differences in prices and the (dis-)connection with "target dumping" as being relevant to determining price difference significance.[25] As to seasonality and market-driven fluctuations – the two concrete instances of "objective reasons" cited by China – the Appellate Body, while turning down the latter altogether, considered the former as relevant insofar as it was useful in assessing "the significance, or lack thereof, of such price differences".[26]

Thirdly, in terms of the use of weighted-average export prices in determining the existence of a pattern or "targeted dumping"[27] within the meaning of the second sentence of Article 2.4.2 of the ADA, the Appellate Body disfavoured China's arguments. The Appellate Body referred to its decision in *US – Washing Machines* and upheld the Panel's findings by interpreting the second sentence of Article 2.4.2 as giving investigating authorities discretion to determine a pattern on a basis of individual export prices or average prices.[28] In the view of the Appellate Body, "the pattern clause focuses on the price differences among different purchasers, regions or time periods, not the differences within the prices for the 'targeted' purchaser, region, or time period".[29] Added to that, a pattern, determined on the basis of average prices, itself includes individual export prices. The Appellate Body rejected the argument that the parallelism between the two parts of the provision limited the discretion of the investigating authority to individual export prices in determining a pattern and confirmed that, notwithstanding the use of individual or average prices, a pattern would consist of all export prices for the "targeted" purchaser, region or time period.[30] The Appellate Body turned down China's claim under Article 17.6(i) of the ADA as China neither pointed out any specific instance of the Panel's assessment of the facts nor put

---

[22] WT/DS471/AB/R, para. 5.61.

[23] *Ibid.*, para. 5.66.

[24] *Ibid.*, para. 5.67.

[25] *Ibid.*

[26] *Ibid.*, para. 5.68.

[27] The Appellate Body in *US – Washing Machines* interpreted the second sentence of Article 2.4.2 as being purported to identify and address "targeted dumping". See Appellate Body Report, *United States – Washing Machines*, adopted on 26 September 2016, WT/DS464/AB/R, paras. 5.17 and 5.28.

[28] WT/DS471/AB/R, para. 5.83.

[29] *Ibid.*, para. 5.82.

[30] *Ibid.*, para. 5.90 refers to WT/DS464/AB/R, para. 5.36.

forth separate or different reasoning, but just echoed its own arguments under Article 2.4.2.[31]

Fourthly, China's claim against the Panel's suggestion to combine comparison methodologies to measure dumping margins was the least problematic issues in the appeal procedure, as even the United States did not oppose China's challenge. Accordingly, the Appellate Body declared moot the Panel's suggestion and re-affirmed the prohibition of comparison methodology combination under Article 2.4.2 of the ADA.[32]

In the second cluster of claims regarding the AFA Norm, China requested the Appellate Body to reverse the Panel's finding that China had failed to establish the essence of general and prospective application of the Norm. Furthermore, China requested the Appellate Body to complete the analysis by ruling that the Norm, with its general and prospective application, could be subject to "as such" claims in WTO dispute settlement and was inconsistent "as such" with Article 6.8 and paragraph 7 of Annex II to the ADA.

Firstly, the Appellate Body reversed the Panel's ruling and found that the Norm was of general and prospective application based on the interpretation of the relevant terms. "General application" is read as affecting "an unidentified number of economic operators"[33] while "a rule or norm has 'prospective application' to the extent that it applies in the future".[34] The requirement to show with "certainty" that a given measure would apply in future situations was dismissed.[35] The pure potential for a rule or norm to be altered or withdrawn did not deprive the measure of its prospective application.[36] A variety of factors could contribute to the nature of prospective application of a norm, including its underlying policy, its systematic application, its design, architecture and structure, its provision of administrative guidance for future conduct and the expectation it created among economic operators about its future application.[37] The Appellate Body further clarified that the determination of general and prospective application of a norm is to be made on a case-by-case basis and might take into account other additional relevant factors depending upon the concrete facts and situation of the case at issue.[38]

Secondly, the Appellate Body recognized the general and prospective application of the Norm as requested by China. The general application of the Norm was less disputed thanks to the findings in the Panel Report and undisputed facts about the Norm, including its unappealed precise content without any explicit limitation on scope of application in terms of subjects, its wide and diverse coverage of 73 anti-dumping determinations put forth by China and the support-

---

[31] *Ibid.*, para. 5.99.
[32] *Ibid.*, para. 5.108.
[33] *Ibid.*, para. 5.130.
[34] *Ibid.*, para. 5.131.
[35] *Ibid.*, para. 5.132.
[36] *Ibid.*
[37] *Ibid.*
[38] *Ibid.*, para. 5.133.

ive effect of the Panel's finding on the general application of the Single Rate Presumption.[39] Although being more contentious, the prospective application of the Norm was recognized by virtue of its underlying policy, its 12-odd-year consistent application, its provision of administrative guidance for future actions and the formation of expectations among economic operators about its future application which were proven beforehand by the Panel's certain findings and statements.[40] Consequently, the Appellate Body, in sharp contrast to the Panel, recognized the possibility of the AFA Norms to be challenged "as such" in WTO dispute settlement.[41]

Lastly, the Appellate Body nevertheless dismissed China's request to complete the analysis regarding the inconsistency with Article 6.8 and paragraph 7 of Annex II to the ADA of the AFA Norm due to "the absence of Panel findings and sufficient undisputed facts on the Panel record, as well as the arguments made by the participants on appeal",[42] which in turn precluded the Appellate Body from reaching accurate determination.

3.4. Concluding Remarks

In the end, basically, China lost most of its appeal claim. Except for the point on combination of comparison methodology, China lost on remaining points including the first and third qualitative flaws with the Nails test, consideration of some qualitative factors when establishing the "significance" feature of pricing differences and the use of averages to determine a "pattern". Regarding the AFA Norm, China just achieved a partial win as the Appellate Body recognized the general and prospective application of the Norm and its susceptibility to "as such" claims in WTO dispute settlement but declined to complete the analysis to declare the noncompliance "as such" of the Norm with Article 6.8 and paragraph 7 of Annex II of the ADA.

The resolution on this dispute plays a significant role as it deals with methodologies systematically used by the USDOC within the ambit of certain ADA provisions. The methodology to identify a pattern or "targeted dumping" under the second sentence of Article 2.4.2 of the ADA prescribed by the Appellate Body in *US – Washing Machines* was consistently advocated by the Appellate Body in this case. However, this methodology is aggressively contested by the United States as being unused by any WTO Member States to date. The reading of the second sentence of Article 2.4.2 of the ADA clarifies that the W-T methodology is applicable conditionally to exceptional cases where "export transactions to the targeted purchaser or in the targeted time period form the relevant pattern of export prices which differed significantly among different purchasers or different

---

[39] *Ibid.*, paras. 5.152-5.155.
[40] *Ibid.*, paras. 5.159-5.162.
[41] *Ibid.*, para. 5.164.
[42] *Ibid.*, paras. 5.178 and 5.184.

time periods".[43] This articulation thereby restricts the discretion of an anti-dumping investigative authority in resorting to the methodology. Furthermore, since the Single Rate Presumption used by the USDOC to treat multiple exporters from NME as a single NME-wide entity was found ADA-inconsistent, exporters from a non-market economy are, from now on, subject to individual investigation. This ruling will further burden the workload of domestic anti-dumping investigators in Member States when the case involves a large quantity of exporters from NMEs. The declaration of the AFA Norm as having general and prospective application makes it subject to "as such" challenges, whose scope can be broad but the final outcome is undetermined due to the incompleteness of the analysis by the Appellate Body.

HANG THI MINH HOANG[*]

4. APPELLATE BODY REPORT, *UNITED STATES – CONDITIONAL TAX INCENTIVES FOR LARGE CIVIL AIRCRAFT* (DS487)[44]

4.1. Introduction and Main Facts of the Dispute

This case was between the United States and the European Union on the very complex and expensive subject of subsidies in the Large Civil Aircraft (LCA) Industry. In particular, it involved tax incentives offered by the US State of Washington to commercial airplane manufacturers that were allegedly conditioned on local content requirements, which are prohibited by the WTO Agreement on Subsidies and Countervailing Measures (the SCM Agreement). Thus, on 19 December 2014, the European Union filed a dispute against the United States, and on 23 February 2015, the Dispute Settlement Body (DSB) established a panel to examine the European Union complaint with respect to these tax incentive measures.[45]

On 28 November 2016, the WTO issued the Panel Report. The Panel found that all the aerospace tax measures at issue constituted a subsidy within the meaning of Article 1 of the SCM Agreement. It also found that the European Union had failed to demonstrate that any of the aerospace tax measures were *de jure* contingent upon the use of domestic over imported goods with respect to two provisions of the Washington Engrossed Substitute Senate Bill 5952 (ESSB 5952).[46] However, the Panel found that one of the measures providing a reduction in the business and occupation tax rate for the manufacturing or sale of commercial

---

[43] WT/DS471/R, para. 8.1.a.iii.

[*] Ph.D. Candidate in International Law and Economics, Bocconi University, Milan.

[44] Appellate Body Report, *United States – Conditional Tax Incentives for Large Civil Aircraft*, adopted on 4 September 2017, WT/DS487/AB/R.

[45] Request for the Establishment of a Panel by the European Union of 12 February 2015, WT/DS487/2.

[46] Engrossed Substitute Senate Bill 5952, Chapter 2, Laws of 2013 3rd Special Session, 2014 Wash. Sess. Laws. 2, codified in the Revised Code of Washington (Panel Exhibit EU-3).

airplanes (the "B&O aerospace tax rate") under Boeing's 777X aircraft program is a subsidy *de facto* contingent upon the use of domestic over imported goods within the meaning of Article 3.1(b) of the SCM Agreement.

On 16 December 2016, the United States filed a notice of appeal[47] against the Panel ruling and, on 17 January 2017, the European Union also notified the DSB of its intention to appeal certain issues of law and legal interpretations developed by the Panel.[48]

Finally, on 4 September 2017, the Appellate Body issued its report and upheld the United States' appeal while rejecting a cross-appeal by the European Union,[49] as shown hereafter.

4.2. The Panel Report

Before the Panel, the European Union challenged certain tax measures provided by the State of Washington in ESSB 5952. They include the B&O aerospace tax rate and a set of other tax credits or exemptions relating to product development activities, property and leasehold taxes, and sales and use taxes (collectively, the "aerospace tax measures"). According to the European Union, these tax incentives are governed by two siting provisions set out in ESSB 5952. One of them was made available upon the siting of a significant commercial airplane manufacturing program in Washington State (the "First Siting Provision"), that uses goods (i.e. fuselages and wings) produced in the United States in the subsidized aircraft. The second set of tax incentives provided that the reduced B&O aerospace tax rate will apply as long as there is no determination by the Washington Department of Revenue "that any final assembly or wing assembly of any version or variant of a commercial airplane that is the basis of a siting of a significant commercial manufacturing program" under the First Siting Provision has been sited outside of Washington (the "Second Siting Provision"; collectively with the First Siting Provision, the "Siting Provisions").

The European Union argued that these Siting Provisions were prohibited under Article 3.1(b) of the SCM Agreement which defines the prohibited import substitution subsidies as subsidies contingent whether solely or as one of several other conditions, upon the use of domestic over imported goods. Specifically, the European Union advanced both a claim of *de jure* and *de facto* contingency by discussing first the legal standard set out in Article 3.1(b), followed by a discussion on the application of that legal standard to the facts of the case. Thus, to establish a *prima facie* case in respect of *de jure* contingency, the European Union based its analyses on the wording of the provisions of ESSB 5952: under the First Siting Provision, "the tax incentives would not have been extended in duration through 2040 if Boeing had decided to 'use' imported wings and fuselages in the assembly of the 777X, nor would the scope of the sales and use tax exemption

---

[47] Notice of Appeal, WT/DS487/6.
[48] Notice of Appeal, WT/DS487/7.
[49] WT/DS487/AB/R, para. 6.

for construction services and materials have been expanded to cover Boeing's work on the 777X manufacturing facilities in 2015 and 2016".[50] Similarly, it argued that under the Second Siting Provision, "Boeing benefits from the reduced B&O tax rate for the 777X so long as it *uses* wings assembled exclusively in Washington State for the 777X".[51] To support its arguments, the European Union took the example of wings produced in Japan for the manufacture and sale of the 777X, and argued that if Boeing were to use any wings made in Japan, as it does for the 787, it would lose its entitlement to the preferential B&O tax rate.

In response to the European Union's arguments, the United States submitted that the European Union's claims were based on an incorrect interpretation of Article 3.1(b) of the SCM Agreement: the United States asserted that wings and fuselages are not "goods" and are not "used" in the production of the 777X, contrary to the arguments of the European Union. The United States considered that the European Union failed to establish each element of its claims and therefore to make a prima facie case. As a result, it requested the Panel to reject the European Union's claim and find that the litigious measures are not within the realm of Article 3.1(b) of the SCM Agreement.[52]

4.3. Analysis and Findings of the Panel

In light of each party's arguments, the Panel concluded that the European Union failed to demonstrate that the aerospace tax measures were *de jure* contingent upon the use of domestic over imported goods with respect to the First Siting Provision, on the grounds that

> nowhere in the words used in the First Siting Provision does the Panel find a requirement that makes the entry into force of the challenged measures contingent upon a determination that domestic goods will be used instead of imported products. Nor do the terms of the First Siting Provision impose any such requirement in respect of the 'significant commercial airplane manufacturing program' that would be the basis for the Department of Revenue's determination.[53]

Indeed, the First Siting Provision does not mention the use of imported or domestic goods and "does not make the receipt of subsidies dependent on refraining from using imported goods".[54] Similarly, the Panel also did not find that the B&O aerospace tax rate was *de jure* contingent upon the use of domestic over

---

[50] Panel Report, adopted on 28 November 2016, WT/DS487/R, para. 37.

[51] *Ibid.* para. 38.

[52] First Integrated Executive Summary of the arguments of the United States, WT/DS487/R/Add.1, para.38.

[53] WT/DS487/R, paras. 7.290 and 7.291.

[54] *Ibid.*, para. 7.291.

imported goods with respect to the Second Siting Provision. It considered that contrary to the European Union's assertion, the Second Siting Provision "does not indicate on its face that the B&O aerospace tax rate would cease to apply if the aircraft manufacturer in question "uses" imported products instead of domestic products. Moreover, it does not inevitably result from the terms of the Second Siting Provision that the importation of wings would amount to the "siting" of production activities outside the state of Washington, even if such an outcome is not excluded by the text of the Second Siting Provision".[55]

However, after examining in detail the potential existence of factual evidence suggesting any requirement to use domestic goods with regards to the First Siting Provision, and after analysing the manner in which the Second Siting Provision operates in practice, the Panel found that the B&O aerospace tax rate was a subsidy *de facto* contingent upon the use of domestic over imported goods within the meaning of Article 3.1(b) of the SCM Agreement[56] and as a result recommended the withdrawal of the prohibited B&O aerospace tax without delay.[57]

4.4. The Appellate Body Report

4.4.1. Arguments of the Parties

On 16 December 2016, the United States filed a Notice of Appeal to the Appellate Body in respect of the Panel findings that the Washington State B&O aerospace tax rate is inconsistent with Articles 3.1(b) and 3.2 of the SCM Agreement because it is *de facto* contingent on the use of domestic over imported goods.

The United States argued that the Panel erred in interpreting and applying Article 3.1(b) of the SCM Agreement in considering that it prohibited subsidies conditional on the domestic siting of production activities. Second, it estimated that the Panel erroneously considered that the B&O aerospace tax rate for Boeing's 777X aircraft program is contingent upon the "use" of wings because "in Boeing's production of the 777X, the wing is [...] the output of Boeing's production process, and not an input or instrumentality"[58] as suggested by the ordinary meaning of "use". Moreover, the United States claimed that by not establishing whether or not the 777X wing was a "domestic good", the Panel failed to correctly apply the legal standard set out in Article 3.1(b) to the facts of the case and lacked evidentiary support to reach its finding when it comes to analyzing whether the Second Siting Provision was *de facto* contingent on the use of domestic over imported goods, which was dependent on the meaning of the terms

---

[55] *Ibid.*, para. 7.310.
[56] *Ibid.*, para. 8.5.
[57] *Ibid.*, para. 8.6.
[58] Executive summary of the United States' appellant's submission, WT/DS487/AB/R/Add.1, para. 4.

"domestic" and "imported", and simultaneously failed to "make an objective assessment of the matter under Article 11 of the DSU".[59]

On 17 January 2017, the European Union also filed a Notice of Other Appeal with respect to the Panel's finding that the European Union failed to demonstrate that the First Siting Provision makes the subsidies either *de jure* or *de facto* contingent on the use of domestic over imported goods.

First, the European Union claimed that the Panel erred on its interpretation of Article 3.1(b) in the sense that the object and purpose of the provision would be defeated following the interpretation of the Panel which considers that as long as the subsidy recipient may use some imported goods in addition to domestic goods, the subsidy is not contingent on the use of domestic over imported goods. Secondly, it also claimed that the Panel erred in finding that the Second Siting Provision does not make the B&O tax rate reduction *de jure* contingent on the use of domestic over imported goods, on the basis (i) of the same interpretative error that it claims for the First Siting Provision and (ii) the United States' admission before the Panel that "the Second Siting Provision, properly interpreted, would deprive Boeing of the B&O tax rate reduction if the wings for the 777X were imported".[60]

4.4.2. Findings of the Appellate Body

The Appellate Body started by developing its own interpretation of Article 3.1(b) of the SCM Agreement. By using the ordinary meaning of "contingent", it considered that "a subsidy would be 'contingent' upon the use of domestic over imported goods if the use of those goods were a condition, in the sense of a requirement, for receiving the subsidy".[61] It also added, through reference of two precedents, namely *Canada – Aircraft*[62] and *Canada – Autos*,[63] that the legal standard of the term "contingency" should be the same for *de jure* and *de facto* contingency. As a result, in order to reach a conclusion as to whether a subsidy is contingent upon the use of domestic over imported goods, there must be an assessment of the words used in the relevant legislation, regulation or other legal instrument constituting the measure.

In light of its interpretation of Article 3.1(b), the Appellate Body addressed the issue raised by the European Union. According to the European Union, the Panel confined the applicability of Article 3.1(b) "to those situations where the subsidy recipient is required under the terms of the subsidy measure, for a given

---

[59] *Ibid.*, para. 16.

[60] Executive summary of the European Union's other appellant's submission, WT/DS487/AB/R/Add.1, para. 21.

[61] WT/DS487/AB/R, para. 5.7.

[62] Appellate Body Report, *Canada – Measures Affecting the Export of Civilian Aircraft*, adopted on 20 August 1999, WT/DS70/AB/R, p. 1377.

[63] Appellate Body Report, *Canada – Certain Measures Affecting the Automotive Industry*, adopted on 19 June 2000, WT/DS139/AB/R and WT/DS142/AB/R, p. 2985.

good, to use domestic goods to the complete exclusion of imported goods"[64] and articulated a legal standard requiring the use of domestic goods to the complete exclusion of imported goods in its *de jure* and *de facto* contingency analyses of the Siting Provisions. The Appellate Body recognized that if read out of context, the statements with which the European Union takes issue, could be interpreted as a legal standard "under 3.1(b) that requires the use of domestic goods to the complete exclusion of imported goods".[65] However, the Appellate Body concluded that when these words are examined in the context of the Panel's analysis, no said legal standard was in fact asserted by the Panel.

The Appellate Body addressed thereafter the second issue raised by the European Union, namely that the Panel erred in its application of Article 3.1(b) of the SCM Agreement in finding that the First Siting Provision did not make the aerospace tax measures *de jure* contingent upon the use of domestic over imported goods. The Appellate Body considered that even though the requirement to produce wings and fuselages in Washington under the First Siting Provision would have resulted in the use of domestically produced wings and fuselages in the assembly of the 777X, this is not in itself "sufficient to establish the existence of a condition, reflected in the measure's terms or arising by necessary implication therefrom, requiring the use of domestic over imported goods".[66]

Thirdly, concerning the claim of the European Union that the Panel erred in its application of Article 3.1(b) of the SCM Agreement in finding that the Second Siting Provision did not make the aerospace tax measures *de jure* contingent, the Appellate Body rejected the European Union's claim because it did not consider that the scope of application of said provision was limited to the relocation of specific assembly operations that had been previously sited in Washington.[67] The Appellate Body also found they "do not consider that the Panel erred in its application of Article 3.1(b) by not examining the United States' responses to its questions in the context of its de jure contingency analysis of the Second Siting Provision".[68]

Fourthly, the Appellate Body upheld the US claim with regards to the *de facto* contingency issue. Indeed, the Appellate Body considered that "it is the location of production, not the imported or domestic origin of the resulting product, that would trigger the loss of the B&O aerospace tax rate", and emphasized that "although conditions for eligibility and access to a subsidy may entail certain consequences for a domestic producer's sourcing decisions between domestic and imported goods, this alone does not equate to a condition requiring the use of domestic over imported goods".[69]

The Appellate Body thus found that the challenged Washington State tax measures were consistent with the provisions of the SCM Agreement.

---

[64] European Union's other appellant's submission, para. 40.
[65] WT/DS487/AB/R, para. 5.26.
[66] *Ibid.*, para. 5.40.
[67] *Ibid.*, para. 5.55.
[68] *Ibid.*, para. 5.57.
[69] *Ibid.*, para. 5.75.

4.5. Concluding Remarks

For more than a decade, the disputes between the US and the EU over subsidies in the LCA industry have become notorious for being the most complex and expensive disputes brought before the WTO. Both the United States and the European Union took turns to bring new arguments either about the subsidies provided by the EU and member state governments to Airbus companies or the incentives brought by US federal and state governments to Boeing and its related companies, thus violating Article 3.1 of the SCM Agreement.

These disputes have been brought in the context of the withdrawal of the United States from a 1992 bilateral agreement concluded with the European Communities,[70] which provided progressive limitations on government support for large civil aircraft programs. Following its withdrawal, the United States decided to file a complaint with the WTO and claimed that Airbus had received several billions of dollars in illegal subsidies whose economic benefit were estimated at more than $200 billion. These subsidies included the Launch Aid, which funded the development of new products through very favourable loans, contributing to the faster introduction into the market of new products, all of which posed a significant risk to the competitiveness of the United States within the LCA industry. In June 2010,[71] the Appellate Body ruled in favour of the United States, acknowledging that Airbus had received $18 billion of illegal subsidies. However, the European Union did not meet the compliance deadline to remedy the harmful effects of these illegal subsidies, as concluded by the compliance panel on 22 September 2016.[72] On 13 October 2016 and 21 December 2016, the European Union and the United States respectively appealed and cross-appealed certain issues of law and legal interpretations developed by the compliance panel. Due to the complexity of these compliance proceedings, the Appellate Body has yet to provide the circulation date of its report.

Similarly, on 27 June 2005, the European Union launched its own WTO case against subsidies given to Boeing, as a response to the WTO dispute initiated by the United States.[73] According to the European Union, these federal, local subsidy programs totalled between $5-6 billion and gave Boeing a competitive advantage, causing Airbus to lose market shares and adversely impacting its sales. In its report, the Appellate Body found that these tax breaks were actionable subsidies and should be removed.[74] In June 2017, a compliance panel found that 28 out of the 29 subsidy programs challenged by the European Union had been put in compliance with the WTO rules, except the B&O aerospace tax rate. The

---

[70] EU-US Bilateral Agreement on Trade in Large Civil Aircraft, 17 July 1992.

[71] Appellate Body Report, *European Communities – Measures Affecting Trade in Large Civil Aircraft*, adopted on 18 May 2011, WT/DS316/R.

[72] Report of the Panel, *European Communities and Certain Member States – Measures Affecting Trade in Large Civil Aircraft – Recourse to article 21.5 of the DSU by the United States*, WT/DS316/RW, para. 7.1.

[73] Appellate Body Report, *United States – Measures Affecting Trade in Large Civil Aircraft*, WT/DS353/AB/R, adopted 12 March 2012.

[74] *Ibid.*, para. 1350.

European Union and the United States notified the DSB respectively on 29 June 2017 and on 10 August 2017 of their decisions to appeal the findings of the compliance panel. This case is pending.

Thus, all these legal disputes are correlated and nourished by the fact that both companies have invested multiple billions of dollars for the development of new aircrafts. Within the LCA industry, Airbus is the largest exporting manufacturer in Europe and similarly for Boeing in the United States. Any slight competitive advantage could lead one of the parties to reap significant economic benefits and, as a result, neither is disposed to give up any benefit.

Although this present decision is the latest on this topic, it is highly probable that for all the reasons listed above, and until concrete and successful bilateral agreements are negotiated between the United States and the European Union, additional disputes will arise in the foreseeable future, making any prospective final and general settlement less and less likely to be reached.

MURIELLE BECHARA*

5. APPELLATE BODY REPORT, *EUROPEAN UNION – ANTI-DUMPING MEASURES ON IMPORTS OF CERTAIN FATTY ALCOHOLS FROM INDONESIA* (DS442)[75]

5.1. Introduction and Main Facts of the Dispute

On 13 August 2010, the European Union Commission started an anti-dumping investigation concerning imports of certain fatty alcohols from Indonesia, India and Malaysia.[76] In its Preliminary Determination, the EU Commission imposed a provisional anti-dumping duty of 6.3% on imports of products from the Indonesian exporter PT Musim Mas (PT Musim) in accordance with Article 2(20) of the EU Basic Anti-Dumping Regulation.[77] The mark-up paid by PT Musim to Inter-Continental Oils & Fats Pte Lte (ICOF-S), a related trading company based in Singapore, has been qualified by the EU Commission as a commission paid in respect of export sales to the EU internal market. Consequently, the mark-up has been treated as a difference affecting price comparability for which a downward adjustment to the export price was warranted. Therefore, the EU Commission rejected the argument submitted by PT Musim that no adjustments should have

---

* Ph.D. Candidate in International Law and Economics, Bocconi University, Milan.

[75] Appellate Body Report, *European Union – Anti-Dumping Measures on Imports of Certain Fatty Alcohols from Indonesia,* adopted on 5 September 2017, WT/DS442/AB/R. Short title: *EU – Fatty Alcohols (Indonesia).*

[76] European Commission, Notice of initiation of an anti-dumping proceeding concerning import of certain fatty alcohols and their blends originating in India, Indonesia and Malaysia, Official Journal of the European Union, C Series, No. 219, 13 August 2010, pp. 12-16. Fatty Alcohols are products obtained by natural fats, oils, coal and natural gas and are mainly used to produce household, personal care and detergents products.

[77] Article 2(20)(i) of the Council Regulation (EC) No. 1225/2009 of 30 November 2009 on protection against dumped imports from countries not members of the European Community, Official Journal of the European Community, L Series, No. 343, 22 December 2009, p. 51.

been made and applied a definitive 4.2% anti-dumping duty rate on their products.[78]

5.2. The Panel Report

On 13 July 2015, a Panel was established to examine the complaints brought by Indonesia against the anti-dumping measures imposed by the EU Commission. Before the Panel, Indonesia submitted that the EU would have acted inconsistently with Articles 2.3, 2.4, 3.1, 3.5 and 6.7 of the Anti-Dumping Agreement (ADA).[79]

5.2.1. Articles 2.3 and 2.4 of the ADA

Pursuant to Indonesia, the EU Commission acted inconsistently with Articles 2.3 and 2.4 of the ADA by making an improper deduction for a factor that did not affect price comparability.[80] Indonesia claimed that the EU Commission's explanation in the investigation on anti-dumping measures was not adequate because PT Musim and ICOF-S formed a "single economic entity" that precluded the EU Commission from making allowance for the mark-up. The Panel found that Indonesia failed to prove that the EU acted inconsistently with Article 2.4 and consequently, with Article 2.3.[81]

5.2.2. Articles 3.1 and 3.5 of the ADA

In addition, Indonesia challenged the downward adjustments made to the export price of fatty alcohols sold in the EU arguing that EU Commission violated Article 3.5 of the ADA because they did not conduct a proper non-attribution analysis with respect to two "known factors": the "economic crisis" and the EU

---

[78] The EU Commission imposed a definitive 7.3% anti-dumping duty also on the other Indonesian exporter PT Ecogreen Oleochemicals (Ecogreen). In their revised Determination, following the judgment of the European Court of Justice in the *Interpipe* case, the EU Commission found that the dumping margin established for Ecogreen was *de minimis*. Therefore, the anti-dumping duty imposed to Ecogreen was eliminated but the one applicable to PT Musim was confirmed.

[79] The EU requested that the Panel reject Indonesia's claims in their entirely. Moreover, on 8 January 2015, the EU demanded to issue a preliminary ruling that its authority had lapsed pursuant to Article 12.12 of the DSU, following an alleged suspension of the Panel proceedings for more than 12 months. The Panel found that the EU had not demonstrated that the correspondence sent by the Permanent Mission of Indonesia to the WTO Secretariat on 11 July 2013 constituted a request to suspend the work.

[80] Appellate Body Report, *United States – Zeroing (European Communities)*, adopted on 18 April 2006, WT/DS294/AB/R, para. 157.

[81] Panel Report, *EU – Fatty Alcohols (Indonesia)*, adopted on 16 December 2017, WT/DS442/R, paras. 7.160 and 7.161.

domestic industry's "access to raw materials".[82] Consequently, Indonesia asserted that the EU Commission acted inconsistently with Article 3.1 by failing to conduct an "objective examination" on the basis of a "positive evidence". The Panel concluded that Indonesia did not prove that the EU Commission acted inconsistently with the ADA provisions in their analysis of the factors in object.[83]

5.2.3. Article 6.7 of the ADA

Finally, Indonesia claimed that the EU Commission violated Article 6.7 of the ADA as they did not disclose the results of inspections to the companies under investigation. Indonesia submitted that no separate report had been made available to the producers following the on-the-spot visits and that the communications contained only general statements that did not properly disclose the results of such verifications. The Panel accepted Indonesia's claim and found that the EU Commission failed to disclose the results of their investigations according to Article 6.7, concluding that the documents issued by the EU Commission as part of the investigations did not satisfy the EU's obligation under Article 6.7.[84] Indeed, the documents did not clarify what information the EU Commission had sought to verify during the visits and whether the EU was able to confirm the accuracy of the information provided by PT Musim. Therefore, the Panel recommended that the EU bring its measures into conformity with its obligations under the ADA.[85]

5.3. The Appellate Body Report

On 28 February 2017, the EU and Indonesia each filed an appellant's submission concerning certain issues of law and legal interpretations developed in the Panel Report.

5.3.1. Article 2.4 of the ADA

(i) Interpretation of Article 2.4

According to Indonesia the Appellate Body's finding in *US – Hot Rolled Steel* supported the assertion that a price charged by one company within a "sin-

---

[82] Panel Report, *China – X-Ray Equipment*, adopted on 26 February 2013, WT/DS425/R, para. 7.267.

[83] WT/DS442/R, paras. 7.189 and 7.205.

[84] Panel Report, *United States – Anti-Dumping Duty on Dynamic Random Access Memory Semiconductors of One Megabit or Above from Korea*, adopted on 29 January 1999, WT/DS99/R, para 6.78 and Panel Report, *Argentina – Ceramic Tiles*, adopted on 28 September 2001, WT/DS189/R, para. 6.57.

[85] WT/DS442/R, paras. 7.236 and 8.3.

gle economic entity" to another within the same entity might not reflect commercial considerations.[86] The Appellate Body underlined that Article 2.4 does not make explicit reference to the words "single economic entity" and that the provision prescribes to the investigating authorities to ensure the fairness of the comparison between the normal value and the export price.[87] In order to be fair a comparison should be "unbiased, objective and even-handed" in light of the specific circumstances of each case.[88] The Appellate Body then stated that *US – Hot Rolled Steel* did not provide a general legal concept under the ADA in respect of which certain consequences would automatically follow if a single economic enterprise existed. Therefore, the existence of a close relationship between transacting companies would be pertinent to the extent that the relationship affects the relevant transactions in such a way as to condition the comparability of the export price and the normal value. Thus, the Panel did not err in rejecting Indonesia's argument that the existence of what Indonesia denoted as a "single economic entity" was dispositive of whether a given mark-up qualifies as a difference which affects price comparability under Article 2.4.[89] The Appellate Body found that the Panel was correct in its interpretation of Article 2.4 of the ADA. Accordingly, Indonesia argued that the Panel erred as it articulated a legal standard that contained no reference to whether the existence of a single economic entity could determine whether a factor affected price comparability.

(ii)   Application of Article 2.4

Secondly, Indonesia challenged the Panel's review on whether the EU Commission provided sufficient evidentiary basis to prove that the mark-up paid by PT Musim to ICOF-S was a difference affecting price comparability.[90] The Appellate Body found that Indonesia had not demonstrated that the Panel erred in its application of Article 2.4 of the ADA. Indeed, the Appellate Body underlined that the Panel critically examined the findings by the EU Commission. The Panel had properly found that the EU Commission relied on evidentiary basis in their conclusion that ICOF-S had functions similar to an agent working on a commis-

---

[86] Appellate Body Report, *United States – Anti-Dumping Measures on Certain Hot-Rolled Steel Products from Japan*, adopted on 24 July 2001, WT/DS184/AB/R, para. 177.

[87] Panel Report, *Egypt – Steel Rebar*, adopted on 8 August 2008, WT/DS211/R, para. 7.333.

[88] Appellate Body Report, *United States – Softwood Lumber V (Canada)*, adopted on 15 August 2006, WT/DS264/AB/RW, para. 138.

[89] WT/DS442/AB/R, para. 5.44.

[90] According to Indonesia: (i) the EU Commission failed to prove a sufficient evidentiary basis for treating the mark-up paid by PT Musim to ICOF-S as a difference affecting price comparability; (ii) the existence of a single economic entity precluded the EU Commission from making an allowance for the mark-up; (iii) the allowance resulted in an asymmetrical comparison with the normal value. Indonesia challenged also the Panel's rejection that: "the existence of a single economic entity precluded the EU Commission from making an allowance for the mark-up and that the allowance resulted in an asymmetrical comparison with the normal value".

sion basis and that the mark-up constituted a difference affecting price comparability.[91] Indonesia also asserted that the Panel was mistaken in its analysis of whether the allowance for the mark-up resulted in an asymmetrical comparison with the normal value. For the Appellate Body, the Panel's finding that ICOF-S general and administrative costs and profit represented a reasonable basis for the EU Commission to calculate the value of the mark-up was correct. Therefore, the Appellate Body rejected Indonesia's claim that the Panel erred in reviewing the EU Commission's evaluation, including the evidence that they identified as the basis for their findings.[92]

(iii)   Articles 17.6 (i) of the ADA and 11 of the DSU

Pursuant to Indonesia, the Panel acted inconsistently with Articles 17.6 (i) of the ADA and 11 of the DSU in its analysis of Indonesia's claim under Article 2.4. First, Indonesia alleged that the Panel made intermediate findings in contrast with its duties on due process and on the allocation of the burden of proof. The Appellate Body underlined that panels enjoy discretion in determining the structure of their decisions and that intermediate findings are not a final conclusion.[93] Therefore, the Appellate Body found that the Panel did not act inconsistently with Article 11.[94] Secondly, Indonesia asserted that the Panel conducted a *de novo* analysis at different times as if it were the investigating authority. The Appellate Body underlined that no provisions of the DSU and the ADA prevented the Panel from examining evidence that was on the investigation record but not expressly reflected in the investigation authorities' determination. Therefore, the Appellate Body found that the Panel did not conduct a *de novo* review of the record evidence and did not substitute the EU Commission's judgement with its own.[95] Finally, Indonesia argued that the Panel dismissed or ignored fundamental arguments and evidence related to the Sale and Purchase Agreement between PT Musim and ICOF-S. The Appellate Body rejected Indonesia's claim and found that the Panel had evaluated the relevant evidence in an objective and unbiased manner.[96]

5.3.2. Article 6.7 of the ADA

The EU claimed that the Panel erred in interpreting Article 6.7 of the ADA as it imposed an obligation to provide a document setting out a complete description

---

[91] WT/DS442/AB/R, para. 5.59.

[92] *Ibid.*, para. 5.68.

[93] Particularly, Indonesia underlined that the Panel used the words "we conclude" in its intermediate findings.

[94] WT/DS442/AB/R, para. 5.82.

[95] *Ibid.*, para. 5.100.

[96] *Ibid.*, para. 5.107.

of the on-the-spot investigations. Pursuant to the EU, the term "results" in Article 6.7 refers to the information related to "essential facts" within the meaning of Article 6.9. Therefore, the "results" to be disclosed would only be those that may have a bearing on the authorities' decision whether or not to impose anti-dumping measures.[97] Moreover, the EU asserted that the interaction between the EU Commission and PT Musim would have shown that PT Musim understood which parts of the questionnaire response had been verified. First, the Appellate Body found that Articles 6.7 and 6.9 contain different obligations and that the information to be disclosed according to Article 6.7 are not limited to the "essentials" but vary from case to case. Accordingly, investigated firms must be informed of the results in sufficient detail and in a timely manner.[98] Secondly, the Panel found that the disclosure of the results of the investigations did not allow PT Musim to understand whether the EU Commission had been able to confirm the accuracy of the information. Therefore, the Appellate Body concluded that Panel was correct in its interpretation and application of Article 6.7.[99]

5.3.3. Article 3 of the DSU

The EU asserted that Indonesia acted inconsistently with Article 3 of the DSU. According to the EU, the appeal submitted by Indonesia was inappropriate and inconsistent because the measure at issue had been withdrawn in the course of the Panel's proceedings.[100] Pursuant to the EU, the withdrawal of the measure determined the achievement of a positive solution to the dispute, making the appeal pointless rather than "fruitful" as required by Article 3.7. The EU also appealed on the principle of good faith in the effort to resolve the disputes required by Article 3.10. In response, the Appellate Body underlined that the fact that a measure has expired is not dispositive in determining whether a panel can address claims in respect of it.[101] Moreover, the Appellate Body specified that a Panel has discretion in deciding how to take into account expired measures, also considering the possibility that they could easily be re-imposed.[102] Therefore, the Appellate Body found that Indonesia did not act inconsistently with Article 3 and rejected the EU's claim.

---

[97] Pursuant to Indonesia, the EU Commission conflates the different requirements of Article 6.7 on the disclosure of the investigation results, with those of Article 6.9 regarding the disclosure of essential facts.

[98] WT/DS442/AB/R, para. 5.140.

[99] *Ibid.*, paras. 5.164-5.165.

[100] On 16 November 2016, the EU sent an e-mail to the Panel to communicate that the measures expired on 12 November 2016.

[101] WT/DS442/AB/R, para. 5.179, citing Appellate Body Report, *European Communities – Bananas III*, adopted on 9 September 1997, WT/DS27/AB/R, paras. 135 and 270.

[102] WT/DS442/AB/R, para. 5.180, citing Panel Report, *India – Additional Import Duties*, adopted on 9 June 2008, WT/DS360/R, paras. 7.69 and 7.70.

5.3.4. Article 19.1 of the DSU

Pursuant to the EU, the Panel acted inconsistently with Articles 11 and 19.1 of the DSU, in making a recommendation to the EU with respect to an expired measure. Indonesia requested the Panel to reject the EU's claim because the EU notified the expiry of the measure more than three months after the interim report had been issued to the parties.[103] The Appellate Body highlighted that the EU sent its communication to the Panel on 16 November 2016 informing it that the measure at issue had expired on 12 November 2016, while the Panel has issued its final report to the parties to the dispute on 23 September 2016. Moreover, the information regarding the expiry of the measure at issue was submitted after the time prescribed by paragraph 7 of the Panel's Working Procedures and the EU did not provide any explanation for the late submission.[104] To conclude, the Appellate Body rejected the EU's claim, finding that it was within the Panel's discretion to decide how to take into account subsequent modifications to the measure at issue.[105]

5.3.4. Articles 11 and 12.12 of the DSU

The EU requested the Appellate Body to reverse three findings: (i) that the EU failed to demonstrate that the correspondence sent by the Indonesia's permanent mission to the WTO Secretariat in July 2013 constituted a request to suspend the work of the Panel according to Article 12.12 of the DSU; (ii) that the work of the Panel was not suspended; (iii) that the authority of the establishment of the Panel had not lapsed.[106] According to Indonesia the email was not a request to suspend the work of the Panel under Article 12.12 but a response to the WTO Secretariat to attend the meeting regarding the Panel composition.[107] The Appellate Body found that Article 12.12 reveals that the possibility that a panel "may suspend its works" involves a decision of a panel that has already been composed.[108] Therefore, the WTO Secretariat's response to Indonesia was not a decision by the Panel that was still not constituted. Therefore, the Appellate

---

[103] Indonesia cited Panel Report *China – Goes (United States)*, adopted on 15 June 2012, WT/DS414/R, and Panel Report *European Communities – Bananas (United States)*, adopted on 19 May 2009, WT/DS27/RW/USA.

[104] According to the Panel's Working Procedures, exceptions could be granted in case of a good cause.

[105] WT/DS442/AB/R, para. 5.208.

[106] On 11 July, Indonesia sent an email in which it affirmed that it would like "to suspend the meeting [regarding the Panel composition] while waiting for developments from Brussels".

[107] WT/DS442/R, para. 7.15. Indonesia declared that its position was based on the possibility to delay the Panel composition in order to reach an amicable solution.

[108] WT/DS442/AB/R, para. 5.227. The EU claimed that the reference to suspension of work "at any time" in Article 12.12 suggested that a panel's work could be suspended before its formal composition.

Body declared moot and of no legal effect the first Panel's finding and upheld the second and third findings.

5.4. Concluding Remarks

The OECD's most recent data show an increase in the number of anti-dumping investigations initiated by G-20 members.[109] Within the EU, anti-dumping measures are the most frequently used trade defence instruments. In December 2017, the EU adopted the new Regulation (EU) 2017/2321 which contains new methodologies to calculate dumping margins for imports. According to the EU Commission, the new rules represent a balanced outcome that will take into account the interests of EU producers, users and importers. In *EU – Fatty Alcohols (Indonesia)*, the aim of balancing conflicting interests seems to be at the base of many findings on anti-dumping investigation procedures.[110] As stated by Article 6.7, investigating authorities may conduct on-the-spot inspections to ensure the accuracy of information provided by interested parties. In this context, the interpretation of Article 6.7 of the ADA provided by the Appellate Body is relevant. Indeed, the Appellate Body underlined that the rules governing on-the-spot investigations are part of the broader set of provisions of Article 6 regulating the process of identifying evidence in anti-dumping cases. Previously, in *China – HP-SSST (EU)* it was noted that Article 6 refers to the due process rights enjoyed by the parties during the inspections.[111] In *EU – Fatty Alcohols (Indonesia)*, the Appellate Body found that the due process is based on the possibility for investigated firms to defend their own interests throughout the duration of investigations.[112] Therefore, the disclosure of results of the on-the-spot investigations has a fundamental importance in making the evidence available to investigated firms. On this point, the Appellate Body stated that the results disclosed must be "sufficiently specific for the interested parties to understand at a minimum those parts of the questionnaire response or other information supplied for which supporting evidence was requested".[113] Overall, the Appellate Body's conclusion on this point could have important consequences on practical implementation. Indeed, these findings seem to create a new minimum standard of treatment not strictly limited to on-the-spot investigations but able to become a new legal basis for an increasing protection of investigated firms' interests. As shown by the Appellate

---

[109] OECD's Reports on G20 Trade and investment measures, 30 June 2017, available at: <http://www.oecd.org/daf/inv/investment-policy/g20.htm>. The period covering July-December 2016 shows an 11% increase in the number of AD investigations initiated by G-20 members compared to the previous six-month period (January-June).

[110] EU Commission Press release, "Commission welcomes landmark deal modernising the EU's trade defence", 5 December 2017.

[111] Appellate Body Report, *China – Measures Imposing Anti-Dumping Duties on High-Performance Stainless Steel Seamless Tubes from the European Union*, adopted on 28 October 2015, WT/DS460/AB/R, para. 5.73.

[112] WT/DS442/AB/R, para. 5.139.

[113] WT/DS442/R, para. 228.

Body's findings, transparency and predictability are two factors that trade defence instruments will need to take into account of in the near future.

ANDREA MENSI*

6. APPELLATE BODY REPORT, *INDONESIA – IMPORTATION OF HORTICULTURAL PRODUCTS, ANIMALS AND ANIMAL PRODUCTS* (DS477/DS478)[114]

6.1. Introduction and Main Facts of the Dispute

The present case, involving Indonesia against New Zealand and the United States, pertains to eighteen measures imposed by Indonesia on the importation of horticultural products, animals and animal products.

More precisely, Indonesia, by the enactment of several regulations and legislative amendments, implemented different measures which constituted, for most of them, discrete elements of Indonesia's import-licensing regime for horticultural products (Measures 1 through 8) and for animals and animal products (Measures 10 through 16). In addition, two others measures – measure 9 for horticultural products and measure 17 for animals and animal products – concerned the import-licensing regime *as a whole*. Finally, measure 18 conditioned the importation of the above-mentioned products on Indonesia's determination of the sufficiency of domestic supply to satisfy domestic demand.

Hence, on 8 May 2014, New Zealand[115] and the United States[116] requested consultations on the inconsistency of these measures with Indonesia's WTO obligations. However, as a consequence of the unsuccessfulness of the consultations, the co-complainants requested, on 18 March 2015, the establishment of a Panel.[117] According to them, measures implemented by Indonesia were contrary to Article XI:1 of the GATT 1994 and Article 4.2 of the Agreement on Agriculture. Following these requests, the Dispute Settlement Body (DSB) established, on 20 May 2015, a single Panel, which issued its report on 22 December 2016.[118] Indonesia, which raised several disagreements pertaining to the legal interpretation by the Panel of the GATT 1994 and Agreement on Agriculture provisions, appealed the Panel Report on 17 February 2017.[119] The Appellate Body report, adopted on 12 October 2017, confirmed the findings of the Panel. Finally, on 15 December 2017, Indonesia requested a reasonable period of time (RPT) from the

---

* Ph.D. Candidate in International Law and Economics, Bocconi University, Milan.

[114] Appellate Body Report, *Indonesia – Importation Of Horticultural Products, Animals And Animal Products*, adopted on 12 October 2017, WT/DS477/AB/R and WT/DS478/AB/R.

[115] Request for Consultations by New Zealand, WT/DS477/1.

[116] Request for Consultations by the United States, WT/DS478/1.

[117] Request for the Establishment of a Panel by New Zealand, WT/DS477/9 and Request for the Establishment of a Panel by the United States, WT/DS478/9.

[118] Panel Report, adopted on 22 December 2016, WT/DS477/R and WT/DS478/R.

[119] Notification of an Appeal by Indonesia, WT/DS477/11 and WT/DS478/11.

co-complainants in order to comply with the recommendations and rulings of the DSB.[120]

6.2.   The Panel Report

6.2.1.   Arguments of the Parties

The co-complainants claimed the inconsistency of the measures with Article XI:1 of the GATT 1994 and Article 4.2 of the Agreement on Agriculture. In particular, New Zealand argued that, owing to their design, architecture and structure, the measures at issue constituted quantitative restrictions contrary to the WTO obligations of Indonesia and were not justified under Article XX and XI:2(c)(ii) of the GATT 1994. Furthermore, New Zealand considered the limited application windows (Measure 1) and validity periods (Measure 11) as "administrative measures", and claimed the inconsistency of these measures with Articles 3.2, or 2.2(a)ii of the Import Licensing Agreement. Finally, New Zealand argued that Measures 6, 14, and 15 were inconsistent with Article III:4 of the GATT 1994.[121] Similarly to New Zealand, the United States claimed the inconsistency of Indonesia's import regimes with Article XI:1 of the GATT 1994 and with Article 4.2 of the Agreement on Agriculture. Therefore, the Parties requested the Panel to find the measures at issue inconsistent with WTO obligations of Indonesia.

In response to the co-complainants' claims, Indonesia asserted that the regulations and legislative amendments supporting the implementation of the eighteen measures were consistent with its WTO obligations. It further claimed that the measures aimed to facilitate importers' administrative requirements[122] as well as to ensure food safety and security.[123] Therefore, Indonesia requested the Panel to begin the legal analysis with Article 4.2 of the Agreement on Agriculture and not with Article XI:1 of the GATT 1994,[124] and argued that the measures fell outside the scope of both Article 4.2 of the Agreement on Agriculture and of Article XI:1 of the GATT 1994 inasmuch as they constituted an automatic import licensing regime.[125] In the alternative, Indonesia claimed that the measures at issue fell within the exceptions provided in the subparagraphs (a), (b) and (d) of Article XX of the GATT 1994. In addition, Indonesia claimed that the non-trade restrictive design of the measures prevented them from being inconsistent with Article 3.2 of the Import Licensing Agreement and are thus "expressly permitted" by Article

---

[120] Communication from Indonesia concerning Article 21.3(b) of the DSU, WT/DS477/16 and WT/DS478/16.

[121] Second part of the executive summary of the arguments of New Zealand, WT/DS477/R/Add.1 and WT/DS478/R/Add.1, paras. 83-89.

[122] First part of the executive summary of the arguments of Indonesia, para. 4, WT/DS477/R/Add.1 and WT/DS478/R/Add.1.

[123] *Ibid.*, para. 7.

[124] *Ibid.*, para. 9.

[125] *Ibid.*, para. 22.

2.2 of the same Agreement.[126] Finally, Indonesia claimed the consistency of the Measures 6, 14 and 15 with Article III:4 of the GATT 1994 as they fell within the exceptions of Article XX(a) and (b) of the GATT 1994. Hence, Indonesia requested the Panel to reject all co-complainants' claims.

6.2.2. Analyses and Findings of the Panel

Within the framework of the analysis of the claims, the Panel first addressed the delicate issue of the order of the analysis. On the one hand, the co-complainants requested the Panel to commence the claims' analysis with Article XI:1 of the GATT 1994, as they considered it more specific than Article 4.2 of the Agreement on Agriculture as regards quantitative restrictions. On the other hand, Indonesia requested, for efficiency and judicial economy considerations, to commence with Article 4.2. Thus, after recalling that panels have discretion with regard to the order of the analysis of the parties' claims, as highlighted in *Canada – Wheat Exports and Grain Imports*,[127] the Panel concurred with *India – Autos*[128] by considering whether the order "is compelled by principles of valid interpretative methodology, which, if not followed, might constitute an error of law".[129] On this basis, the Panel, considering the scope of Article XI:1 of the GATT 1994 narrower than that of Article 4.2 of the Agreement on Agriculture, decided to begin the analysis of the claims of the Parties with Article XI:1 of the GATT 1994.[130] Furthermore, the Panel justified this approach by considering that if the measures were to be inconsistent with Article XI:1 of the GATT 1994, the analysis under Article 4.2 of the Agreement on Agriculture would be unnecessary as the Panel would have to examine Indonesia' defence under Article XX of the GATT 1994.[131]

Hence, after assessing, through a two-step analysis, the compatibility of the measures with Article XI:1 of the GATT 1994,[132] as well as rejecting Indonesia' contention that Article XI:2(c)(ii) of the GATT 1994 excluded Measures 4, 7 and 16 from the scope of Article XI:1, the Panel made the following findings.

First, with regard to the alleged inconsistency of the measures with Article XI:1 of the GATT 1994, the Panel found Measures 1 through 7, 9, and 11 through 17 inconsistent because, "by virtue of their design, architecture, and revealing structure they constitute[d] a restriction having a limiting effect on importation".[133] Similarly, the Panel found Measures 8 and 10 inconsistent, since they constituted

---

[126] *Ibid.*, paras. 30 and 31.
[127] Appellate Body Report, *Canada – Wheat Exports and Grain Imports*, adopted on 27 September 2004, WT/DS276/R, para. 126.
[128] Panel Report, *India – Autos*, adopted on 21 December 2001, WT/DS146/R and WT/DS175/R, para. 7.154.
[129] WT/DS477/R and WT/DS478/R, paras. 7.28 and 7.31.
[130] *Ibid.*, para. 7.32.
[131] *Ibid.*, para. 7.33.
[132] *Ibid.*, paras. 7.40-7.50.
[133] *Ibid.*, para. 8.1.

a prohibition on importation. Finally, and for the same reasons, Measure 18 was considered inconsistent *as such* with Article XI:1 as it constituted a restriction having a limiting effect on importation. Secondly, with regard to Indonesia's defence under Article XX of the GATT 1994, the Panel found that Indonesia failed to demonstrate that Measures 1 to 18 were justified under subparagraphs (a), (b) or (d) of this article. Finally, the Panel declined to rule on the co-complainants' claims under Article III:4 of the GATT 1994 and under Article 3.2 of the Import Licensing Agreement.

6.3.   The Appellate Body Report

6.3.1.   Arguments of the Parties

The Appellant, Indonesia, argued that the Panel, by considering Article XI:1 of the GATT 1994 to be more specific with quantitative restrictions than Article 4.2 of the Agreement on Agriculture, erred in law and thus failed to apply the principle of *lex specialis derogat lege generali* "as reflected in Article 21.1 of the Agreement on Agriculture".[134] Secondly, Indonesia raised that "a complainant must demonstrate both elements set out in footnote 1 to Article 4.2 of the Agreement on Agriculture", and hence, that the Panel erred in law by allocating to it the burden of proof of the second part of footnote 1 to Article 4.2.[135] Thirdly, Indonesia claimed that the Panel failed to make an objective assessment, under Article 11 of the Dispute Settlement Understanding (DSU), both of the applicability of Article 4.2 of the Agreement on Agriculture and of the allocation of the burden of proof under the second element of the footnote 1 of the same provision.[136] Fourthly, Indonesia claimed that, in the alternative where the Panel was correct as regards the applicability of Article XI:1 of the GATT 1994, the Panel erred in law with regard to its conclusion under Article X1:2(c) of the GATT 1994.[137] Finally, Indonesia claimed that, by assessing Measures 9 through 17 only with respect to the requirements under the *chapeau* of Article XX of the GATT 1994, and not the defences of Indonesia under the subparagraphs of the same article, the Panel erred in law in finding the measures not to be justified under the subparagraphs (a), (b) or (d) of Article XX of the GATT 1994.[138] Hence, Indonesia requested the Appellate Body to reverse the conclusions of the Panel related to its appeal claims.

In response, New Zealand argued that the Panel had not erred by beginning its analysis with Article XI:1 of the GATT 1994, rather than with Article 4.2 of the Agreement on Agriculture, since, first, panels have a "margin of discretion"

---

[134] Indonesia's Notice of Appeal, WT/DS477/AB/R/Add.1 and WT/DS478/AB/R/Add.1, Section I.
[135] *Ibid.*, Section II.
[136] *Ibid.*, Section III.
[137] *Ibid.*, Section IV.
[138] *Ibid.*, Section V.

in structuring their analyses and, second, the obligations of these provisions are cumulative and apply concurrently.[139] Furthermore, with regard to the allocation of the burden of proof under the second part of footnote 1 to Article 4.2 of the Agreement on Agriculture, New Zealand recalled that Article XX of the GATT 1994 constitutes an affirmative defence and thus the Panel did not err in law in its conclusion.[140] Moreover, New Zealand considered that since Indonesia had failed to distinguish its claim under Article 11 of the DSU from the two previous one, the claim should fail.[141] Finally, New Zealand estimated that since the sequence of the analysis conducted by the Panel with regards to Measures 9 through 17 had "no repercussions for the substance", the Panel did not err by assessing these measures only with respect to the requirements of the chapeau of Article XX of the GATT 1994.[142] Similarly to New Zealand, the United States markedly disagreed with all issues raised by Indonesia, in particular as regards the order of the analysis.[143] Therefore, the Appellees requested the Appellate Body to reject all of Indonesia's claims on appeal.

6.3.2. *Analysis and Findings of the Appellate Body*

The Appellate Body commenced its analyses with the claims under Article XI:1 of the GATT 1994. Precisely, after recalling the abundant WTO jurisprudence dealing with the relationship between the provisions of the GATT 1994 and those of the Agreement on Agriculture,[144] the Appellate Body considered that, due to the "same substantive obligations in relation to these claims",[145] Article XI:1 of the GATT 1994 and Article 4.2 of the Agreement on Agriculture apply cumulatively in the dispute at issue. Further in the analysis, the Appellate Body, after referring to the *Canada – Wheat Exports and Grain Imports* and *Canada – Renewable Energy/Canada – Feed-in Tariff Program* decisions, estimated that there is no mandatory sequence of analysis between the above-mentioned provisions.[146] Therefore, the Appellate Body found that Article 4.2 of the Agreement on Agriculture does not apply to the exclusion of Article XI:1 of the GATT 1994 with respect to the measures at issue and that Indonesia failed to substantiate its claims under Article 11 of the DSU.[147] Hence, it decided to uphold the Panel findings.[148]

---

[139] Executive summary of New Zealand's Appellee's submission, WT/DS477/AB/R/Add.1 / WT/DS478/AB/R/Add.1, Section II.

[140] *Ibid.*, Section III.

[141] *Ibid.*, Section IV.

[142] *Ibid.*, Section V.

[143] Executive summary of the United States' Appellee's submission, WT/DS477/AB/R/Add.1/ WT/DS478/AB/R/Add.1, Section II.

[144] WT/DS477/AB/R and WT/DS478/AB/R, paras. 5.8-5.11.

[145] *Ibid.*, para. 5.18.

[146] *Ibid.*, paras. 5.23-5.25.

[147] *Ibid.*, paras. 5.28-5.30.

[148] *Ibid.*, para. 5.32.

With respect to the second issue raised by Indonesia, namely the allocation of the burden of proof under the second part of footnote 1 to Article 4.2
of the Agreement on Agriculture, the Appellate Body rejected Indonesia's request to reverse the finding of the Panel.[149] Accordingly, the incorporation of
Article XX of the GATT 1994, recognized as an *affirmative defence* by the WTO
jurisprudence,[150] by reference to Article 4.2 of the Agreement on Agriculture implies allocating the burden of proof to the respondent.[151] Finally, the Appellate
Body found that Indonesia failed to substantiate its claims under Article 11 of
the DSU.[152]

Next, the Appellate Body considered Indonesia's alternative claim, raised
in the event that the Panel did not err in addressing the claim under Article XI:I
of the GATT 1994. According to this claim, the Panel erroneously found that
Article XI:2(c) of the GATT 1994 has been rendered inoperative by Article 4.2
of the Agreement on Agriculture. Hence, the Appellate Body, after recalling that
Article XI of the GATT 1994 and Article 4.2 of the Agreement on Agriculture
contain the same prohibitions of quantitative restriction "as far as the importation
of agricultural products is concerned",[153] estimated that the prohibition of specific
measures under Article 4.2 of the Agreement on Agriculture cannot benefit from
the derogations laid down in Article XI:2(c) of the GATT 1994.[154] Furthermore,
as Article 21.1 of the Agreement on Agriculture established the prevalence of
the Agreement on Agriculture in the event of a conflict with the provisions of
the GATT 1994, the Appellate Body estimated that Indonesia could not rely on
Article XI:2(c) of the GATT 1994 in order to justify the measures prohibited under Article 4.2 of the Agreement on Agriculture.[155] Therefore, the Appellate Body
upheld the Panel's finding.[156]

With respect to the last issue raised by Indonesia, namely the order of the
analysis of the claim under Article XX of the GATT 1994, the Appellate Body
declined to rule and declared the Panel's finding, in paragraph 7.830 of the
Panel Report, moot and of no legal effect.[157] Interestingly, after recalling the
normal sequence of analysis of Article XX of the GATT 1994 in light of the
WTO jurisprudence,[158] the Appellate Body estimated that, depending on the circumstances of the dispute, a deviation by the Panel from the normal sequence
of analysis is not automatically synonymous with a reversible legal error.[159]
However, as a consequence of Indonesia's contention that it would not be possible for the Appellate Body to complete the legal analysis on the consistency of

---

[149] *Ibid.*, paras. 5.56-5.57.
[150] *Ibid.*, para. 5.42.
[151] *Ibid.*, para. 5.46.
[152] *Ibid.*, para. 5.55.
[153] *Ibid.*, para. 5.74.
[154] *Ibid.*, para. 5.79.
[155] *Ibid.*, paras. 5.80-5.83.
[156] *Ibid.*, para. 5.85.
[157] *Ibid.*, para. 5.103.
[158] *Ibid.*, paras. 5.97-5.99.
[159] *Ibid.*, para. 5.100.

the Measures 9 through 17 with the subparagraphs (a), (b) or (d) of the GATT 1994, the Appellate Body declined to rule. Therefore, the Appellate Body, at the exception of the last issue apropos the sequence of order of analysis where it declined to rule, upheld the Panel's findings.

6.4. Concluding Remarks

The significance of the *Indonesia – Import Licensing Regimes* case relates to the fact that for the first time it addresses some important procedural issues. Indeed, while the Appellate Body approach and conclusion, a propos the first four legal issues, were consistent with previous WTO jurisprudence, a significant jurisprudential departure on the sequence of order of analysis of Article XX of GATT 1994 may be observed.

The "normal" sequence of analysis of Article XX under GATT 1994 was first addressed in the *US – Gasoline* case where the Appellate Body specified that a measure, to be justified under Article XX of GATT 1994, must fall within the exception of its subparagraphs (a) to (j) and must "also satisfy the requirements imposed by the opening clauses of Article XX".[160] This two-tiered analysis, always confirmed since, evolved through the guidance of the Appellate Body on the interpretation of the *chapeau* of Article XX of GATT 1994 in the *Brazil – Tyres* case.[161] Notwithstanding this normal sequence of analysis, the Appellate Body in *Indonesia – Import Licensing Regimes* proposes, at paragraph 5.100 of the report, a novel interpretation of the sequence of order of analysis of Article XX of GATT 1994. More precisely, the Appellate Body estimated that deviating from the normal sequence of analysis, in analysing the claims only under the *chapeau* and not under the relevant subparagraphs of Article XX, does not automatically constitute a reversible legal error if the panel "has made findings on those elements under the applicable paragraphs that are relevant for its analysis of the requirements of the chapeau".[162] As a consequence, this interesting legal novelty, also emphasised by legal practitioners,[163] would provide, if confirmed in future reports, two possible sequences of analysis of order of Article XX of GATT 1994, respectively a "normal sequence of analysis" and a "derogatory" one depending on the circumstances of the case. Hence, these two sequences of analysis could potentially lead futures panels to balance, in light of the requirement of the *chapeau* but with less degree of accuracy than under the subparagraphs of Article XX of GATT 1994, the pro and cons of the measure at issue. The consequences of this potential "derogatory sequence of analysis of order of Article XX of GATT

---

[160] Appellate Body Report, *United States – Gasoline*, adopted on 20 May 1996, WT/DS2/AB/R, p. 22.

[161] Appellate Body Report, *Brazil – Measures Affecting Imports of Retreaded Tyres*, adopted on 17 December 2007, WT/DS332/AB/R.

[162] *Ibid.*, paras. 5.99 and 5.100.

[163] McGIVERN, "Indonesia – Import Licensing Regimes", White & Case Publications, 16 November 2017.

1994" are, nevertheless, relativized at paragraph 5.100 of the report where the Appellate Body considered the difficulties of assessing the measure at issue under the *chapeau*. Undoubtedly innovative, the sequence of analysis of order of Article XX of GATT 1994, as raised in the *Indonesia – Import Licensing Regimes* case, would need to be reaffirmed in future reports to be considered as a lasting WTO jurisprudential departure.

VICTORIEN SALLES*

* Ph.D. Candidate in International Law and Economics, Bocconi University, Milan.

INVESTMENT ARBITRATION IN 2017: TOWARDS ADULTHOOD?

GIOVANNI ZARRA[*]

1. INTRODUCTION

2017 was a very rich year for investment arbitration. The International Centre for the Settlement of Investment Disputes (ICSID) registered 49 new cases, administered 258 disputes and concluded 44 arbitrations.[1] In addition, several investment disputes have been brought before the Arbitration Institute of the Stockholm Chamber of Commerce (SCC), the Permanent Court of Arbitration (PCA), and *ad hoc* arbitration panels (usually regulated by the UNCITRAL Rules).

While the debate on the need to reform the system of investor-State dispute settlement (ISDS) continues incessantly,[2] numerous investors still start arbitration proceedings aimed at settling disputes regarding their foreign business. This is a confirmation of the fact that, still, investment arbitration is perceived as the most neutral and efficient form for the resolution of this kind of dispute, not-

---

[*] Adjunct Professor of Private International Law and International Litigation, University of Naples Federico II. The Author would like to point out that, with respect to previous editions of the present review, not only we analysed ICSID case law but the entirety of publicly available investment decisions. This choice is due to the fact that, first of all, there is an enormous amount of cross-referencing among decisions rendered by different institutions. Secondly, and most importantly, considering that usually all investment tribunals apply the same substantive law (i.e. international law), it is possible to affirm that all forms of investment arbitration equally contribute to the development of international investment law. In addition to the above, this paper will exceptionally take into account one decision issued on 27 December 2016 (*Blusun v. Italy*) but which has only recently become public, in light of the fact that it has been the first ICSID case in which Italy acted as a Respondent and, therefore, it is of particular importance for the IYIL mission.

[1] See ICSID 2017 Annual Report, available at: <https://www.openknowledge.worldbank. org/handle/10986/28558>. In comparison with last year, ICSID registered four more cases and concluded 7 less cases. See ZARRA, "The Relevance of State Interests in Recent ICSID Practice", IYIL, 2016, p. 487 ff.

[2] See, *inter alia*, DI BENEDETTO, *La proposta europea di una corte multilaterale sugli investimenti: tra critiche all'attuale sistema di ISDS e rischi di future inefficienze*, federalismi.it, 2017, p. 1 ff., available at: <www.federalismi.it>; FONTANELLI, AMELI, BANTEKAS, CIURTIN, LAVRANOS, RUBINO-SAMMARTANO and SPITERI-GONZI, "Lights and Shadows of the WTO-Inspired International Court System", European Investment Law and Arbitration Review, 2016, p. 189 ff.; BERNARDINI, "Reforming Investor-State Dispute Settlement: The Need to Balance Both Parties' Interests", ICSID Review – Foreign Investment Law Journal, 2017, p. 38 ff.; ID., "The European Union's Investment Court System – A Crytical Analysis", ASA Bulletin, 2017, p. 812 ff.; VAN DEN BROEK and MORRIS, "The EU's Proposed Investment Court and WTO Dispute Settlement: A Comparison and Lesson Learned", European Investment Law and Arbitration Review, 2017, p. 35 ff.; ZARRA, "The New Investor-State Dispute Settlement Mechanisms Proposed by the EU and the Geneva Centre for International Dispute Settlement. A Step Forward or a Hasty Reform?", Studi sull'integrazione europea, 2018, p. 389 ff.

withstanding the fact that awards upheld claims (in part or in full) in only 48% of cases.[3]

The reading of awards issued in 2017, in addition, is interesting from the perspective of the development of the subject of international investment law as a whole. Indeed, while in the past it often happened that tribunals were in strong disagreement among themselves with regard to the regulation of similar (if not identical) matters, the analysis of the most recent investment case law shows that such disharmony is substantially decreasing. This circumstance has two important consequences: firstly, it increases the perception that – as stated by various authors some time ago[4] – arbitral tribunals dealing with investment disputes behave as if they *were* a single system of dispute resolution; secondly it ensures the predictability of arbitral decisions and, therefore, reinforces the perception of legal certainty in relation to the settlement of investment disputes.

In this regard, it is interesting to put this perceived development of the investment system in relation to a somehow prophetic paper written by Anthea Roberts for the American Journal of International Law in 2013.[5] In this article, she wrote that investment arbitration had passed its infancy, in which it was largely inspired by the paradigm of international *commercial* arbitration, where each tribunal decided the dispute brought before it without consideration of the systemic implications of its decision. Investment arbitration was facing its adolescence with investment arbitrators becoming more aware of the public nature of investment disputes (which is now an undisputed assumption)[6] and largely applied mechanisms of decision-making that, first, widely consider the work of previous tribunals (as is typical of any real system of adjudication), and, second, take into account the wider implications of the decisions which are going to be assumed (both for future tribunals and for the public interests at stake). Investment awards issued in 2017 show that the ISDS mechanism is probably in its late-adolescence phase and is currently approaching its adulthood. Indeed, many issues which have been considered unsettled for a long time and generated inconsistent decisions are now being treated as less problematic subjects, due to the consolidation of the case law regarding them. This is not surprising: international investment law is a relatively new area of the law, largely unexplored by scholarship until the second half of the 1990s, and therefore necessitating some time to refine the appropriate mechanisms of "checks and balances" among the various forces which compose it.

---

[3] See The ICSID Caseload – Statistics, Issue 1, 2018, p. 15, available at: <https://icsid.worldbank.org/en/Documents/resources/ICSID%20Web%20Stats%202018-1(English).pdf>.

[4] See, *inter alia*, PALOMBINO, *Il trattamento giusto ed equo degli investimenti stranieri*, Bologna, 2012, p. 195 (the book has been now re-edited in English under the name *Fair and Equitable Treatment and the Fabric of General Principles*, Heidelberg, 2018); SAVARESE, *La nozione di giurisdizione nel sistema ICSID*, Naples, 2012, pp. 26 and 233.

[5] ROBERTS, "Clash of Paradigms: Actors and Analogies Shaping the Investment Treaty System", AJIL, 2013, p. 45 ff., p. 75.

[6] See, *inter alia*, DE BRABANDERE, *Investment Arbitration as Public International Law*, Cambridge, 2014.

The present paper will be divided into three sections, which will respectively analyse the improvements of the system in approaching jurisdictional, procedural and substantive issues. Each of these sections will be divided into subsections devoted to more specific subjects pertaining to the macro-area of analysis.

2. JURISDICTION

Jurisdiction is the first essential step of all arbitrations: prior to analysing the merits of disputes, all arbitral tribunals have to ascertain that they have been empowered by the parties to do so. In the context of investment arbitration, it is required (i) that the parties have expressed their consent to such a form of dispute resolution, as well as that they meet the (ii) *ratione materiae* and (iii) *ratione personae* requisites set forth in any applicable bilateral investment treaty (BIT), regional agreements (e.g. NAFTA, ECT) and in the ICSID Convention (if applicable). The above requirements are cumulative. Usually, respondents try to challenge tribunals' jurisdiction with the aim of avoiding the discussion on the merits or – in any case – of postponing it as much as possible, arguing that one of the above elements is lacking in the case at hand. In the present section we will analyse, first of all, the recent developments concerning the requirement of consent (as expressed either in an investment contract or in a BIT), and then move on to analyze cases regarding *ratione materiae* and *ratione personae* jurisdiction.

2.1. Consent

Consent is the cornerstone of arbitration. National laws and judicial authorities accept that jurisdiction of domestic courts may be waived only in cases where there is a *clear* manifestation of such a waiver.[7] Problems may therefore arise when consent is allegedly expressed through a mechanism of incorporation by reference, typical of commercial schemes in which the parties refer to standard contracts, or when the validity of consent expressed by a State in a BIT[8] is put into question due to the entry into force of another treaty (not containing an arbitration clause) with supposedly the same object and purpose. This latter circumstance allegedly takes place in the case of intra-EU BITs signed by new EU members prior to their accession to the Union: in this regard it has to be as-

---

[7] LEW, MISTELIS and KRÖLL, *Comparative International Commercial Arbitration*, The Hague, 2003, p. 129 ff.; PUNZI, *Disegno sistematico dell'arbitrato*, Padova, 2012, p. 319 ff.; DIMUNDO, "Il mandato ad arbitrare", in ALPA and VIGORITI (eds.), *Arbitrato. Profili di diritto sostanziale e di diritto processuale*, Turin, 2013, p. 460 ff.; RUBINO-SAMMARTANO, *Il diritto dell'arbitrato*, Padova, 2010, p. 419 ff.

[8] In this regard it is worth recalling that consent in investment treaty arbitration is regulated by the so-called doctrine of arbitration without privity: by signing bilateral investment treaties States make general offers to all investors of the other contracting party of the BIT, who match that offer when they start arbitration proceedings, thus perfecting bilateral consent to arbitration.

certained whether the fact that both parties to the previous BIT also became parties of the Treaty of Lisbon (establishing the EU competence in matters relating to foreign investments) has determined that the consent prior expressed through the BIT is now invalid or ineffective. These two scenarios will be the subject of analysis of the present section.

2.1.1. *Consent Expressed Through Incorporation by Reference*

Consent to investment arbitration has rarely been asserted by a claimant on the basis of a reference, in a contract, to another legal instrument that provides for such a form of dispute resolution. In *CSOB v. Slovakia*,[9] one of the earliest ICSID cases, the Tribunal, also by analysing the negotiating history of the relevant contract, found that the referral therein to the Czech-Slovak BIT as applicable law was sufficient grounds for establishing consent to the Centre's jurisdiction.

The abstract possibility of expressing consent through incorporation by reference has been recently reaffirmed in *Lighthouse v. Timor-Leste*,[10] notwithstanding the fact that – *in concreto* – the actual existence of consent was denied by the Tribunal considering that there was no evidence that the Respondent actually agreed (even implicitly) to ICSID arbitration. In this case, a dispute arising from a supply agreement, Claimants tried to affirm the Tribunal's jurisdiction[11] on the basis of either (i) the reference to certain standard terms (providing for ICSID arbitration) contained in an unsigned ancillary document that regarded some technical specification of a diesel generator; or (ii) the reference, in an *addendum* to the main supply agreement, to a document containing the Lighthouses' general terms and conditions, which, however, were amended *after* the signing of the *addendum*. In this regard, the Respondent respectively argued[12] that (i) the reference to certain standard terms, of which Timor-Leste was allegedly unaware, in an unsigned ancillary document may not be considered as an expression of consent to arbitration; and (ii) the general terms and conditions to which the Claimants referred did not exist at the time of the signing of the *addendum*.

The Tribunal, insofar as relevant to this paper's purpose, recognized that it is possible – in investment arbitration – to establish consent on the basis of incorporation by reference.[13] In this regard, it stated that

> incorporation by reference of an arbitration clause into a contract is indeed one of the methods by which contracting parties can express

---

[9] *Ceskoslovenska Obchodni Banka SA v. Slovak Republic*, ICSID Case No. ARB/97/4, Decision on Objections to Jurisdiction of 24 May 1999, para. 53 ff.

[10] *Lighthouse Corporation Pty Ltd and Lighthouse Corporation Ltd, IBC v. Democratic Republic of Timor-Leste*, ICSID Case No. ARB/15/2, Award of 22 December 2017. The Tribunal was composed of Gabrielle Kaufmann-Kohler (President), Stephen Jagusch and Campbell McLachlan.

[11] *Ibid.*, para. 196 ff.

[12] *Ibid.*, para. 155 ff.

[13] *Ibid.*, para. 142 ff.

their agreement to arbitrate future disputes; in other words, it is a method of expressing consent.[14]

In addition, arbitrators referred to the provision of Article 7(6) of the UNCITRAL Model Law on International Commercial Arbitration (as amended in 2006) where it is said that "[t]he reference in a contract to any document containing an arbitration clause constitutes an arbitration agreement in writing, provided that the reference is such as to make that clause part of the contract" in order to acknowledge that there is "*a transnational consensus allowing for the conclusion of arbitration agreements by way of incorporation*".[15] While this conclusion might appear foreseeable for practitioners involved in international commercial arbitration, it is nevertheless worth highlighting the results of this award in light of the fact that, while in commercial arbitration the validity of an incorporation by reference is to be ascertained through the application of a system of domestic law,[16] in investment arbitration "[t]he determination of whether this condition has been met is governed by international law":[17] this means that, according to what is affirmed in the *Lighthouses* award (and the previous *CSOB* decision), there seems to be agreement on the possibility of establishing consent in ICSID arbitration (i.e. according to international law) by explicitly referring to a legal instrument which provides for such a form of dispute resolution.

2.1.2. Consent Revoked Through Subsequent Treaties? The Case of Intra-EU BITs

As is well-known, in the vast majority of cases, investment arbitration proceedings are started by investors, who never had a legal relationship with the host State, on the basis of the general "offers to arbitrate" contained in BITs. This is the so-called mechanism of "arbitration without privity".[18] It may happen, however, that a subsequent treaty, whose content totally or partially overlaps with the one of the BIT, allegedly sets forth a different mechanism for the resolution of investor-State disputes, thus putting into question the validity and/or effectiveness of the offer to arbitrate contained in the BIT. The matter is regulated, in the cases of total overlap, by Article 59(1)(b) of the 1969 Vienna Convention on the Law of Treaties (VCLT) which provides that a treaty shall be considered as terminated (and therefore invalid) if the provisions of the later treaty are so far incompatible with those of the earlier one that the two treaties are not capable of being applied synchronously. Contrariwise, if there is only a partial incompat-

---

[14] *Ibid.*, para. 144.

[15] *Ibid.*, para. 147 (emphasis added).

[16] VAN HOUTTE, "Consent to Arbitration Through Agreement to Printed Contracts: The Continental Experience", Arbitration International, 2000, p. 2 ff.

[17] *Lighthouse* Corporation, *cit. supra* note 10, para. 142.

[18] PAULSSON, "Arbitration Without Privity", ICSID Review – Foreign Investment Law Journal, 1995, p. 232 ff.; SAVARESE, *cit. supra* note 4, p. 101 ff.

ibility between clauses of the first and the second treaties, Article 30(3) VCLT applies, with the consequence that "when all the parties to the earlier treaty are parties also to the later treaty but the earlier treaty is not terminated or suspended in operation under article 59, the earlier treaty applies only to the extent that its provisions are compatible with those of the later treaty".

This issue emerged in the context of disputes arising from intra-EU BITs, i.e. investment treaties concluded by EU States (such as Slovakia and Czech Republic) prior to their accession to the Union with other States that were already Members of the EU, as well as in disputes based on the arbitration clause contained in the Energy Charter Treaty (which also involves, on the one hand, a number of States which have been parties to the EU since long time, and, on the other hand, several States which at the time of signing the treaty were not members of the EU and then became parties of it).[19] When intra-EU investment disputes have been started before arbitral tribunals, both respondent States and the EU Commission (acting as *amicus curiae*) objected the jurisdiction of arbitral tribunals by saying that the above mentioned provisions of the VCLT rendered arbitration clauses contained in BITs invalid or ineffective. This in light of the facts that (i) the protection of intra-EU investments is now subject to the regulation of the Treaty on the Functioning of the European Union (TFEU), (ii) the only judicial organ deputed to have the final say on the provisions of EU treaties is the Court of Justice of the European Union, and (iii) the principle of mutual trust, which governs relationship among EU Member States, requires that intra-EU disputes are subject to the jurisdiction of Member States. In addition, they averred that, should intra-EU disputes be arbitrated, this would constitute a violation of Article 344 TFEU, setting forth the monopoly of the CJEU for the interpretation of EU Treaties, to be exercised through the mechanism of preliminary rulings (set forth by Article 267 TFEU). Finally, the EU Commission also stated in several proceedings that the payment by Respondent States of obligations arising from intra-EU arbitral awards would constitute an unlawful State aid.[20]

In 2017, seven publicly available awards – rendered by very authoritative Tribunals – have analysed the issue of intra-EU BITs.[21] All of them, also by re-

---

[19] For some recent papers concerning the issue see, *inter alia*, BINDER, "A Treaty Law Perspective on Intra-EU BITs", Journal of World Investment & Trade, 2016, p. 964 ff.; CILIBERTO, "Intra-EU BIT's Arbitration Clause and EU Law: the Countdown for the CJEU's Final Say", DCI, 2018, p. 217 ff.

[20] High Court of Justice, Queen's Bench Division, Commercial Court, *Viorel Micula et al. v. Romania (and European Commission as Intervener)*, Decision of 20 January 2017, [2017] EWHC 31 (Comm), para. 7; United States Court of Appeal for the Second Circuit, *Ioan Micula et al. v. Republic of Romania*, Brief of *Amicus Curiae* the Commission of the European Union in Support of the Defendant Appellant of 4 February 2016, available at: <https://www.italaw.com/sites/default/files/case-documents/italaw9198.pdf>.

[21] *PL Holdings S.à.r.l. v. Republic of Poland*, SCC Arbitration No. V 2014/163, Partial Award of 28 June 2017, para. 306 ff. (Tribunal composed of G. Bermann as President, Julian Lew and Michael Schneider); *WNC Factoring LTD (United Kingdom) v. The Czech Republic*, PCA Case No. 2014-34, Award of 22 February 2017, para. 294 ff. (Tribunal composed of Gavan Griffith as President, Robert Volterra and James Crawford); *Jurgen Wirtgen, Stefan Wirtgen, Gisela Wirtgen, JSW Solar (zwei) GmbH & Co. KG v. The Czech Republic*, PCA Case

ferring to previous arbitral decisions concerning the matter, reached *exactly* the same results, namely that intra-EU BITs (and *mutatis mutandis* the ECT) remain in force and applicable with the effect that investment arbitral tribunals retain jurisdiction.[22] In particular all tribunals stated that:

1. Article 59 VCLT requires that the two allegedly incompatible treaties relate to the same subject matter. This is not the case for BITs (aimed at protecting foreign investments after their establishment) and the TFEU (regarding, at most, the initial phase of investments). Moreover, Article 59 requires, for the effectiveness of the treaty termination, that a formal denunciation process is started in accordance with the procedure set forth in Article 65 VCLT and in none of these cases did this happen.

2. Article 30(3) VCLT does not have the effect that arbitration clauses in BITs are ineffective, considering that Article 344 – i.e. the treaty clause allegedly superseding consent to arbitration – affirms that "*Member States* undertake not to submit a dispute concerning the interpretation or application of the Treaties to any method of settlement other than those provided for therein" and, therefore, does not overlap with a mechanism of dispute resolution involving States, on the one side, and individual investors, on the other.

3. As said above, Article 344 TFEU refers only to disputes among Member States and, in any case, "no other jurisdiction in the world has asserted a monopoly – much less succeeded in asserting a monopoly – over the interpretation of its law, even though it may of course claim to have 'the last word' on the meaning of the law".[23]

No. 2014-03, Final Award of 11 October 2017, para. 241 ff. (Tribunal composed of Gabrielle Kaufmann-Kohler as President, Gary Born and Peter Tomka); *Eiser Infrastructure Limited y Energia Solar Luxembourg S.à.r.I. v. Reino de Espana*, ICSID Case No. ARB/13/36, Award of 4 May 2017, para. 160 ff. (Tribunal composed of John Crook as President, Stanimir Alexandrov and Campbell McLachlan); *Anglia Auto Accessories Limited v. The Czech Republic*, SCC Arbitration No. V 2014/181, Final Award of 10 March 2017, para. 98 ff. (Tribunal composed of Yas Banifatemi as President, August Reinisch and Philippe Sands); *I.P. Busta & J.P. Busta v. The Czech Republic*, SCC Arbitration No. V 2015/014, Final award of 10 March 2017, para 95 ff. (Tribunal composed of Yas Banifatemi as President, August Reinisch and Philippe Sands). In addition, it is worth here mentioning the only recently available decision *Blusun S.A., Jean-Pierre Lecorcier and Michael Stein v. Italian Republic*, ICSID Case No. ARB/14/3, Award of 27 December 2016, para. 277 ff. (Tribunal composed of James Crawford as President, Stanimir Alexandrov and Pierre-Marie Dupuy).

[22] See, *inter alia, Eureko B.V. v. The Slovak Republic*, PCA Case No. 2008-13, Award on Jurisdiction, Arbitrability and Suspension of 26 October 2010, para. 65 ff.; *Eastern Sugar B.V. (Netherlands) v. The Czech Republic*, SCC Arbitration No. 2004/088, Partial Award of 27 March 2017, para. 168 ff.

[23] *PL Holdings, cit. supra* note 21, para. 315.

Notably, the above conclusions have been also shared by the EU Advocate General Melchior Wathelet in his opinion delivered in the case *Slowakische Republik v. Achmea BV*,[24] in which the CJEU has been called upon to rule on the compatibility of intra-EU BITs and EU law. Surprisingly enough, however, the CJEU has recently boldly declared that intra-EU BITs are incompatible with EU law.[25] Indeed, according to the Court, the EU is an autonomous legal order based on the principle of primacy on Member States' law[26] and such a feature may only be granted by ensuring the monopoly of the CJEU, which – in the opinion of the Judges – would be prejudiced by a system of arbitration which derogates from the general jurisdiction of Member States.

In addition to the strong criticisms which may be moved against this decision, *inter alia*, as it completely ignores the treaty law perspective outlined above, for its disregard of the fact that (at least in non-ICSID cases) the national court of the seat of arbitration may have a say in investment disputes, as well as for its unmotivated departure from its case law[27] which admitted the compatibility of commercial arbitration with EU law,[28] it is likely that this decision will not be the final episode of the intra-EU BITs saga. Indeed, in two arbitral decisions issued in 2017, tribunals – acknowledging the pendency of the *Achmea* case before the CJEU – expressly stated that their jurisdiction is based on the consent (still validly) expressed in relevant BITs and therefore they would disregard the possible prevalence of a different view expressed by the CJEU.[29]

2.2. *Jurisdiction* Ratione Materiae

As is well-known, jurisdiction *ratione materiae* of investment treaty tribunals is grounded on the existence of an investment. While *all* arbitrators will have

---

[24] Case C-284/16, Opinion of the AG of 19 September 2017, para. 138 ff. The AG's opinion has been welcome with enthusiasm by scholarship, at least for the results it reached. See, in this regard, the comment by CILIBERTO, *cit. supra* note 19.

[25] Case C-284/16, *Slowakische Republik v. Achmea BV*, Judgment of 6 March 2018, para. 33 ff.

[26] On the principle of primacy see ARENA, "Sul carattere 'assoluto' del primato del diritto dell'Unione europea", Studi sull'integrazione europea, 2018, p. 317 ff.

[27] Case C-126/97, *Eco Swiss China Time Ltd v. Benetton International NV*, Judgment of 6 March 1999, ECR, 1999, I-03055, paras. 35-36 and 40.

[28] In this regard, the clarification contained at para. 55 of the judgment (saying that "[h]owever, arbitration proceedings such as those referred to in Article 8 of the BIT are different from commercial arbitration proceedings. While the latter originate in the freely expressed wishes of the parties, the former derive from a treaty by which Member States agree to remove from the jurisdiction of their own courts, and hence from the system of judicial remedies which the second subparagraph of Article 19(1) TEU requires them to establish in the fields covered by EU law, disputes which may concern the application or interpretation of EU law") appears hardly understandable.

[29] See *WNC*, *cit. supra* note 21, para. 311; *PL Holdings*, *cit. supra* note 21, para. 316. For a completely contrary opinion see MUNARI and CELLERINO, "EU Law Is Alive and Healthy: The *Achmea* Case and a Happy Good-Bye to Intra-EU Bilateral Investment Treaties", 2018, available at: <http://www.sidiblog.org/2018/04/17/eu-law-is-alive-and-healthy-the-achmea-case-and-a-happy-good-bye-to-intra-eu-bilateral-investment-treaties/>.

to look at the definition of investment contained in the relevant BIT, ICSID tribunals shall, additionally, take into account ICSID case-law which has gradually shaped a so-called "objective" definition of investment referring to Article 25 of the ICSID Convention.[30]

2017's practice has significantly contributed to the definition of protected investments (pointing towards the system's maturity) in three ways: first of all by precisely explaining in which circumstances a trademark can be qualified as an investment; secondly, by reinforcing the (somehow questioned) idea that commercial arbitral awards may qualify as investments; and, third, by offering a meaningful analysis of the so-called "legality requirement", according to which, in order to be protected under a BIT, an investment shall be established in accordance with the law of the host State.

2.2.1. In What Circumstances Does a Trademark Qualify as an Investment?

BITs' wording usually includes, among the examples of protected investments, "intellectual property rights". Some arbitral cases already confirmed such a qualification.[31] It has never happened, however, that a tribunal was called upon to shape the circumstances in which a trademark could be considered an investment. This has been the task of the arbitrators in the *Bridgestone v. Panama* case,[32] who had to decide whether the Bridgestone and Firestone trademarks (related to the commerce of tires) registered in Panama may be qualified as investments for the purpose of the United States-Panama Trade Promotion Agreement signed on 28 June 2007 and in force on 31 October 2012 (TPA). The TPA contains, at Article 10.29, a definition of investment referring to "every *asset* that an investor owns or controls [including] […] (f) intellectual property rights; (g) licenses, authorizations, permits, and similar rights conferred pursuant to domestic law" (emphasis added). According to Panama, the fact that the Claimants merely had a license conferring revenue sharing and intellectual property rights is insufficient to identify an investment, considering that this license cannot be considered as an "asset" as required by the *chapeau* of the TPA's provision.

---

[30] SAVARESE, *cit. supra* note 4, p. 56 ff.

[31] See *Mr. Frank Charles Arif v. Republic of Moldova*, ICSID Case No. ARB/11/23, Award of 8 April 2013, para. 326 ff.; *Philip Morris Brand Sàrl et al. v. Oriental Republic of Uruguay*, ICSID Case No. ARB/10/7, Decision on Jurisdiction of 2 July 2013, para. 24. On this topic see VADI, "Trade Mark Protection, Public Health and International Investment Law: Strains and Paradoxes", EJIL, 2009, p. 773 ff.; LIBERTI, "Intellectual Property Rights in International Investment Agreements: An Overview", OECD Working Papers on International Investment, 2010, available at: <https://www.oecd.org/daf/inv/investment-policy/WP-2010_1.pdf>.

[32] *Bridgestone Licensing Services, Inc. and Bridgestone America, Inc. v. Republic of Panama*, ICSID Case No. ARB/16/34, Decision on Expedited Objections of 13 December 2017, para. 163 ff. At para. 222, the Tribunal expressly stated that "[s]o far as the Tribunal is aware, this is the first case in which it has been necessary to analyse the different types of investments that can arise in relation to trademarks".

The Tribunal started its analysis[33] by recalling the requirements for ascertaining the existence of an international investment, including the commitment of capital or other resources, the expectation of gain or profit, the assumption of risk, the reasonable duration of the investment, and the contribution to the host State's development.[34] It further pointed out that "[t]he Tribunal is of the view, in agreement with most previous decisions, that there is no inflexible requirement for the presence of *all* those characteristics, but that an investment will normally evidence most of them". Arbitrators then passed to analysing which one of these requirements are present with regard to trademarks. They stated that

> [a] trademark identifies the features that a consumer will expect to find in a product that bears the mark. Where consumers consider those features to be desirable, the trademark enables the seller to profit from the goodwill that attaches to products that bear the trademark. That goodwill can be generated in two ways. The first is by designing, manufacturing and selling products that contain the desirable features. [...] The other way of generating goodwill is by promoting the brand by advertising and other means so that the purchaser is led to anticipate that an article bearing the trademark will contain those desirable features. Whichever way the trademark is promoted, the promotion involves the commitment of resources over a significant period, the expectation of profit and the assumption of the risk that the particular features of the product may not prove sufficiently attractive to enable it to win or maintain market share in the face of competition.[35]

On the basis of the above, the Tribunal arrived at the conclusion that the mere registration of a trademark in a country *manifestly* does not amount to, or have the characteristics of, an investment. This is because the registration has only a "negative" effect consisting in preventing competitors from using that trademark and does not generate any expectation of profits. The situation is, however, different where the trademark is exploited through the manufacture, promotion and sale of goods that bear the mark. Such activity is the core of exploited trademarks and involves devotion of resources, benefices for the development of the host State and an assumption of risk. An exploited trademark is, therefore, an investment.[36] In the present case, considering that both Bridgestone and Firestone trademarks were exploited in Panama, the Respondent's objection to jurisdiction has been dismissed.

---

[33] *Ibid.*, paras. 164-165.

[34] The Tribunal recalled, in this regard, the well-known decision *Salini Costruttori S.p.A. and Italstrade S.p.A. v. Kingdom of Morocco*, ICSID Case No. ARB/00/4, Decision on Jurisdiction of 23 July 2001.

[35] *Bridgestone Licensing Services*, *cit.* supra note 32, paras. 167-169.

[36] *Ibid.*, paras. 171-172.

2.2.2. Awards as investments

The possibility that the non-enforcement (or the annulment) of a commercial arbitral award by a domestic court is seen as a violation of rights conferred to investors by BITs (and in particular either as a measure tantamount to expropriation or as a denial of justice involving a violation of the fair and equitable treatment standard) is a subject which has been debated in scholarship[37] and brought arbitral tribunals to reach very different conclusions. In three cases,[38] Tribunals recognized that the entirety of economic operations which lead to the non-enforced (or annulled) awards may be considered as investments; therefore, while avoiding pronouncing that commercial awards may be classified as investments, they functionally applied international investment law in order to take jurisdiction on the dispute.[39] Another decision, contrariwise, refused to assert jurisdiction on a similar case. According to the Tribunal

> the fact that the Award rules upon rights and obligations arising out of an investment does not equate the Award with the investment itself. In the Tribunal's view, the two remain analytically distinct, and the Award itself involves no contribution to, or relevant economic activity within, Ukraine such as to fall – itself – within the scope of Article 1(1) of the BIT or (if needed) Article 25 of the ICSID Convention.[40]

The issue has been recently analysed in the *Anglia Auto v. Czech Republic* Final Award,[41] where the Tribunal made a further step towards the recognition of arbitral awards as investment protected under a BIT. In this instance, the Claimant's case concerned its efforts to enforce an arbitral award that it obtained in December 1997 against its business partner in the Czech Republic, a company named VDI Kyjovan. Although the Claimant was granted several of the enforcement orders it sought, it argued that Czech courts unduly delayed in issuing such orders and that – during this time – Kyjovan became bankrupt. Accordingly, the

---

[37] See MISTELIS, "Award as an Investment: The Value of an Arbitral Award or the Cost of Non-Enforcement", ICSID Review – Foreign Investment Law Journal, 2013, p. 1 ff., p. 10 ff.

[38] *Saipem S.p.A. v. People's Republic of Bangladesh*, ICSID Case No. ARB/05/7, Decision on Jurisdiction and Recommendation on Provisional Measures of 21 March 2007, para. 110 ff.; *ATA Construction, Industrial and Trading Company v. Hashemite Kingdom of Jordan*, ICSID Case No. ARB/08/2, Award of 18 May 2010, para. 113 ff.; *White Industries Australia Limited v. The Republic of India*, UNCITRAL, Award of 30 November 2011, para. 7.6.10.

[39] It is worth here quoting para. 167 of the *Saipem* Award, *cit. supra* note 38, where it was said that "the rights embodied in the ICC Award were not created by the Award, but arose out of the Contract. The ICC Award crystallized the parties' rights and obligations under the original contract. It can thus be left open whether the Award itself qualifies as an investment, since the contract rights which are crystallized by the Award constitute an investment within Article 1(1)(c) of the BIT".

[40] *GEA Group Aktiengesellschaft v. Ukraine*, ICSID Case No. ARB/08/16, Award of 31 March 2011, para. 162.

[41] *Anglia Auto*, *cit. supra* note 21, paras. 149-154.

Claimant argued that it had been deprived of the value of the arbitral award by the Courts. The Tribunal had therefore to understand whether an investment actually existed, by interpreting the definition of investment contained at Article 1(a) of the BIT between the United Kingdom and the Czekoslovakia of 10 July 1990, which provides, as many other BITs do, that investment is "every kind of asset belonging to an investor of one Contracting Party in the territory of the other Contracting Party" including "claims to money or to any performance under contract having a financial value". By applying the criteria of interpretation set forth at Articles 31 and following of the VCLT, the Tribunal found that the words "claim to money" encompass a party's right under an award to be paid a sum of money, a right which can be claimed in enforcement proceedings. It follows that the Claimant had a claim to money to be enforced before Czech Courts. The Tribunal, therefore, assumed jurisdiction over the claim (even if, however, the Respondent prevailed at the merit stage considering that the Claimant failed to establish that the behaviour of Czech Courts can be considered tantamount to expropriation).

2.2.3. The Legality Requirement

Many BITs contain provisions setting forth that only investments made in compliance with the host State's law may be considered as "investments" for the purpose of the BIT. It sometimes happened, therefore, that arbitral tribunals dismissed jurisdiction due to the illegality of the investment (at the time it was established) from the perspective of the law of the host State.[42]

The issue recently emerged in *Vladislav Kim et al. v. Uzbekistan*,[43] a case arisen under the BIT between Kazakhstan and Uzbekistan of 8 September 1997. Article 12 of the treaty, entitled "Application of the Agreement", stated that it applied only to foreign investment made in one of the Contracting Parties "in compliance with its legislation". The Respondent argued that, for various reasons, the Claimants' investment was not established in compliance with Uzbek law.[44]

Faced with this issue, the Tribunal took note of the fact that previous case-law usually analysed the matter of legality *in abstracto*, i.e. by saying that the substantive scope of the legality requirement is limited to fundamental laws of the host State, and there is a variety of predetermined scenarios whereby the first proposition may be applied.[45] Arbitrators then expressly stated that, while it is obvious that minor or trivial acts of non-compliance do not involve a violation of

---

[42] See the debate and the cases reported in MOLOO and KHACHATURIAN, "The Compliance with the Law Requirement in International Investment Law", Fordham International Law Journal, 2011, p. 1473 ff.

[43] ICSID Case No. ARB/13/6, Decision on Jurisdiction of 8 March 2017, para. 384 ff. (Tribunal composed of David Caron as President, Yves Fortier and Toby Landau).

[44] See *ibid.* para. 171.

[45] *Ibid.*, para. 384 ff.

the legality requirement,[46] they are not satisfied by this approach for it being often too far from the particularities of the case at hand.[47] For this reason, the Tribunal affirmed that the best way to approach the legality requirement is to apply the principle of proportionality. As a consequence

> [t]he Tribunal must balance the object of promoting economic rela-
> tions by providing a stable investment framework with the harsh
> consequence of denying the application of the BIT in total when
> the investment is not made in compliance with legislation. The
> denial of the protection of the BIT is a harsh consequence that is
> a proportional response only when its application is triggered by
> *noncompliance with a law that results in a compromise of a cor-
> respondingly significant interest of the host State.*[48]

Such a test based on proportionality allows arbitrators to decide on the legality requirement on a case-by-case basis and to evaluate its violations taking into
account the overall outcome of the investor's behaviour. The concrete analysis
proposed by the Tribunal would be based on three steps:[49] (i) the Tribunal must
assess the significance of the obligation with which the investor is alleged to not
comply; (ii) the Tribunal must assess the seriousness of the investor's conduct;
and (iii) the Tribunal must evaluate whether the combination of the investor's
conduct and the law involved results in the prejudice of a significant interest of
the host State to such an extent that the harshness of the sanction of placing the
investment outside of the protections of the BIT is a proportionate consequence
for the violation examined. On the basis of the above balancing, the majority of
the Tribunal concluded that, in view of the facts of the case (the investors had
been accused of violating, in the acquisition of their investment, Uzbek securities law and the antifraud provisions of the Uzbek legal system: see paras 419
ff. of the Decision) the claim was admissible because the "Respondent either has
failed to establish that Claimants acted in noncompliance with various laws or
that such acts of noncompliance do not result in a compromise of an interest that
justifies, as a proportionate response, the harshness of denying application of the
BIT" (para. 541).

This approach is to be generally welcomed, considering that it is arguable
that the consequences of *all* violations of the law should be evaluated in light of
their concrete effects and not on the basis of the abstract importance of the violated provision;[50] hence, the sacrifice imposed to an investor who is deprived of

---

[46] *Ibid.*, para. 390.

[47] *Ibid.*, para. 396 ff.

[48] *Ibid.*, para. 396 (emphasis in original). The Tribunal also referred, at para. 397, to *Metalpar S.A. and Buen Aire S.A. v. Argentine Republic*, ICSID Case No. ARB/03/5 Decision on Jurisdiction of 27 April 2006, paras. 83-84, which somehow applied a similar approach.

[49] *Vladislav Kim, cit. supra* note 43, para. 405 ff.

[50] The necessity to base the solution of *all* legal cases on the balance of the various inter-
ests at stake is proposed as a generally applicable method of decision making by PERLINGIERI, *Profili applicativi della ragionevolezza nel diritto civile*, Naples, 2015, p. 17 ff.

BITs' protection should be considered in light of the importance of the interests of the host State which are at stake and of the concrete prejudice that the investor's conduct has generated to such interests.

2.3. *Jurisdiction* Ratione Personae

Jurisdiction *ratione personae* is based, in investment arbitration, on the circumstance that the investor is a national of the other Contracting Party *or*, as stated in Article 25(2)(b) of ICSID Convention, is a juridical person which had the nationality of the Contracting State party to the dispute who, because of foreign control, the parties have agreed should be treated as a national of another Contracting State. It is not easy, however, to understand – for the purpose of jurisdiction of arbitral tribunals – which is the nationality of juridical persons who have their *siège statutaire* in a certain country but are actually managed (*siège réel*) in another country. This matter, on which there is no unanimous consensus among arbitral tribunals, was widely debated in 2017 and deserves some analysis in the present section. In addition, we will also briefly introduce a recent decision which shed light on the possibility to consider a trustee as a foreign investor for the purpose of the ICSID Convention.

2.3.1. *Siège Statutaire v. Siège Réel: is national or international law applicable?*

Three awards issued in 2017 had to consider whether, for the purpose of the relevant BIT, the concept of statutory seat shall be interpreted as a reference to the *siège statutaire* or to the *siège réel*.[51] This issue is more complicated than it appears at first glance, because – in order to understand the concept to which BITs make reference – it is necessary to understand which law shall be applied to this test: do we have to refer to an autonomous standard enshrined in international law or shall we refer to the national law of the place of incorporation of the claimant?

Tribunals did not reach the same conclusion on this matter. In a very well-motivated decision, Arbitrators in *Orascom v. Algeria* had to apply Article 2 of the BIT between Algeria and the Belgium-Luxembourg Economic Union (BLEU) of 24 April 1991, which stated that

---

[51] The reference applies to *Capital Financial Holdings Luxembourg SA v. Republique du Cameroun*, ICSID Case No. ARB/15/18, Award of 22 June 2017, para. 197 ff. (Tribunal composed of Pierre Tercier as President, Alexis Mourre and Alain Pellet); *Orascom TMT Investment S.à.r.l. v. People's Democratic Republic of Algeria*, ICSID Case No. ARB/12/35, Award of 31 May 2017 (Tribunal composed of Gabrielle Kaufmann-Kohler as President, Albert Jan van den Berg and Brigitte Stern); *Eskosol S.p.A. in liquidazione v. Italian Republic*, ICSID Case No. ARB/15/50, Decision on Respondent's Application Under Rule 41(5) of 20 March 2017 (Tribunal composed of Jean Kalicki as President, Fuido Santiago Tawil and Brigitte Stern).

> [l]e domicile de toute société commerciale est situé au siège de
> l'administration centrale de la société. L'administration centrale
> d'une société est présumé, jusqu'a preuve du contraire, coïncider
> avec le lieu du siège statutaire de la société.

Having to understand whether the company Orascom, actually managed
from Egypt but with its statutory seat in Luxembourg, was to be considered an
entity entitled to get protection from the BIT, the Tribunal refused to consider
that the Treaty drafters intended to refer to the definition of *siège social* under
Luxembourg law.[52] According to the arbitrators

> the grammatical and syntactic structure of the provision and the
> context in which the term *siège social* is employed make it clear
> that for corporations the BIT provides its autonomous or treaty-
> specific requirement *ratione personae*. [...] Had the Contracting
> Parties wished to refer to the domestic nationality criteria, they
> would have linked the BIT requirements ratione personae to their
> domestic law.

The Tribunal further noted that there is nothing unusual in creating autonomous notions in international law,[53] detached from any domestic legal system:
this is the approach very often employed in private international law matters by
the CJEU, which generally prefers to give an autonomous EU interpretation to
words used in EU regulations instead of referring to the contradictory meanings
derived from different national law conceptions.

Having established this, the Tribunal tried to understand whether the BIT
refers to the concept of *siège statutaire* or *siège réel*. After having analysed several dictionaries (in French, Dutch and Arabic, i.e. the three official languages in
which the treaty was drafted), all pointing towards the interpretation favouring
the concept of *siège statutaire*, arbitrators devoted significant space to the ICJ's
Barcelona Traction decision[54] and to the International Law Commission (ILC)
Draft Articles on Diplomatic Protection, both confirming the conclusion which
the Tribunal had already reached on the issue. Indeed, the *Barcelona Traction* decision, supported by the ILC Draft Articles, sustains the idea that the "traditional
approach" in international law is to give weight – for the purpose of the exercise
of diplomatic protection – to the place of incorporation or the registered office of
a company. According to the Tribunal, this interpretation is also compliant with
the principle of *effet utile*[55] because it represents the actual willingness of the
Contracting Parties, as confirmed also by a reading of the *traveaux preparatoires*

---

[52] *Orascom, cit. supra* note 51, para. 278 ff.

[53] *Ibid.*, para. 280.

[54] *Barcelona Traction, Light and Power Company, Limited (Belgium v. Spain)*, Judgment
of 5 February 1970, ICJ Reports, 1970, p. 3 ff.

[55] *Orascom, cit. supra* note 51, paras. 287-289.

of the BIT, where Belgium insisted on the application of the *Barcelona Traction* ruling to the concept of *siège social* contained in the BIT.[56]

A similar approach has also been applied in *Eskosol*, where the Tribunal – having to determine whether a company was submitted to foreign control for the purpose of the application of Article 25(2)(b) of the ICSID Convention – expressly stated that foreign control is an issue to be determined in accordance with international law and not domestic law.[57]

Contrariwise, in *Capital Financial Holdings*, the Tribunal had to apply Article 1(2) of the BIT between the Belgium-Luxembourg Economic Union (BLEU) and Cameroon of 1 November 1981, stating that *sociétés* are to be considered,

> [e]n ce qui concerne l'Union Economique Belgo-Luxembourgeoise, toute personne morale constituée conformément à la législation de Belgique ou du Luxembourg et ayant son siège social sur le territoire de Belgique ou du Luxembourg.

According to the Arbitrators,[58] the ambiguous formulation in the BIT refers to Luxembourg's definition of *siège social* instead of to an autonomous international law standard. The Tribunal found support for this opinion in several arbitral precedents[59] and in the Treaty wording (saying that the companies shall be *constituée conformément*), which seems to somehow refer to domestic law. Adjudicators then applied the test already carried out in *Tenaris and Talta* and reached the conclusion that Luxembourg law is based on the concept of *siège réel*. For this reason, due to the fact that the claimant was only a shell company with its seat in Luxembourg but was effectively managed from Cameroon, the Tribunal declined its jurisdiction.

Both the above approaches present advantages and criticalities. While, as a matter of principle, the *Orascom* approach seems more suitable for an international law framework because it allows one to avoid the subjectivities of domestic law systems, it is not satisfactory for the results that the Tribunal reached. Indeed, the application of the *Barcelona Traction* principle is probably outdated in international investment law, as confirmed by the several decisions and scholarly works where it is perfectly explained that the "piercing of the corporate veil" is a test which may find a place for the purpose of establishing jurisdiction in international investment law.[60] Moreover, the approach endorsed in *Orascom* continues

---

[56] *Ibid.*, para. 299 ff.

[57] *Eskosol*, *cit. supra* note 51, para. 106.

[58] *Capital Financial Holdings*, *cit. supra* note 51, para. 203 ff.

[59] The Tribunal notably referred to *Tenaris S.A. and Talta-Trading E Marketing Sociedade Unipessoal LDA v. Venezuela*, ICSID Case No. ARB/11/26, Award of 29 January 2016, para. 169; *Abaclat et al. v. Argentina*, ICSID Case No. ARB/07/5, Award on Jurisdiction and Admissibility of 4 August 2011, para. 257; *Gaëta v. Republique de Guinee*, ICSID Case No. ARB/12/36, Award of 21 December 2015, para. 135.

[60] See the debate reported in VALASEK and DUMBERRY, "Developments in the Legal Standing of Shareholders and Holding Corporations in Investor-State Dispute", ICSID Review – Foreign Investment Law Journal, 2011, p. 34 ff.

to lay the ISDS system open to abuses of foreign investors who may improperly gain the BITs' advantages simply by establishing a shell company where the BIT with the host State is favourable. Contrariwise, the *Capital Financial Holdings* approach seems misplaced in its reliance on domestic law concepts but reaches, from the substantive point of view, a more satisfactory conclusion, considering that the concept of *siège réel* is more apt to avoid abuses of investment arbitration.

In conclusion, this seems to be a matter on which arbitrators still have to reach agreement and – in this regard – the ISDS system is far from maturity.

2.3.2. *Trustees as investors?*

In *Blue Bank v. Venezuela*,[61] the Tribunal had to face a case in which the Claimant brought the action as trustee for the Qatar Trust. It did not invoke an investment made on its own account or on its own behalf, the alleged investment being the acquisition of two companies on behalf of the settlor. For this reason, the Respondent asked the Tribunal to reject its jurisdiction on the basis of the lack of an investor for the purpose of the BIT between Barbados and Venezuela of 15 July 1994. In order to understand whether Blue Bank could be understood as an investor, the Tribunal applied a test based on the evaluation of whether a business carried out by a trustee can be considered as an investment. It therefore somehow mixed the *ratione personae* and *ratione materiae* jurisdictional requirements. According to the Tribunal, as a trustee, the Claimant did not own the assets but simply administered them for the specific purpose of the benefit of the beneficiary. It follows that Blue Bank cannot be considered as having committed any assets in its own rights, having incurred any risk or been due to share the loss or profits resulting from the investment. Article 8 of the BIT allows the filing of ICSID arbitration proceedings to investors who made an investment in accordance with the definition contained at Article 1 of the BIT, which requires the investment of an asset in the host State. In the present case, Blue Bank's business in Venezuela lacked all the characteristics of an investment; in addition, the trust lacks legal personality and is not a company.[62] For this reason, the Tribunal rejected its jurisdiction on the claim.

3. PROCEDURE

Recent investment practice has shown significant improvements from the point of view of the management of arbitral procedure. Indeed, the case law shows that tribunals are uniformly applying certain essential procedural rules

---

[61] *Blue Bank International & Trust (Barbados) Ltd. v. Bolivarian Republic of Venezuela*, ICSID Case No. ARB/12/20, para. 134 ff. (Tribunal composed of Christer Söderlund as President, George Bermann and Loretta Malintoppi).

[62] *Ibid.*, para. 165.

whose role and applicability in the previous jurisprudence was not clearly established. The reference mainly applies to the principle of judicial economy and the management of parallel proceedings (both between arbitral proceedings and between arbitrations and domestic trials).[63]

3.1. Judicial Economy

The principle of judicial economy, which in international adjudication "requires the judge to obtain the best result in the management of a controversy with the most rational and efficient use possible of his or her powers",[64] has rarely received *explicit* attention in international arbitration practice. On the one hand, this is surprising, considering that efficiency is a core issue in the management of all arbitration proceedings; on the other hand, however, time and costs often drive the choices made by international arbitrators in dealing with matters of procedure.[65] In this regard, it is worth mentioning Article 17 of the UNCITRAL Arbitration Rules, which requires that

> The arbitral tribunal, in exercising its discretion [in the management of procedure], shall *conduct the proceedings so as to avoid unnecessary delay and expense and to provide a fair and efficient process for resolving the parties' dispute* (emphasis added).

Recent arbitral practice, however, has overcome this problem and, indeed, very often the Tribunal expressly mentioned the principle of judicial economy.

The reference applies, first of all, to the *Eli Lilly v. Canada* Award,[66] where the Tribunal had to rule on the Respondent's objection that States' liability may arise from the conduct of the judiciary *only* in cases of denial of justice. In this regard, the Tribunal acknowledged that the parties made very lengthy submissions on this matter but – finding the answer to the issue quite straightforward (in the sense that behaviours of the judiciary may give rise also to other forms of State responsibility) – it refused to do so in light of the principle of judicial economy. Indeed, the analysis of the entire parties' submission would have involved a sub-

---

[63] Developments have occurred also with regard to the interference of arbitral provisional measures and domestic criminal proceedings; however, due to the complexity of the topic, for reasons of space it is not possible to analyse this practice in the present paper. The relevant cases, however, are *Nova Group Investments, B.V. v. Romania*, ICSID Case No. ARB/16/19, Procedural Order No. 7 of 29 March 2017; *Sergei Viktorovich Pugachev v. The Russian Federation, Ad Hoc* Arbitration under UNCITRAL Rules, Interim Award of 7 July 2017.

[64] See PALOMBINO, "Judicial Economy and Limitation of the Scope of the Decision in International Adjudication", Leiden JIL, 2010, p. 909 ff., p. 909.

[65] See in this regard ZARRA, *Parallel Proceedings in Investment Arbitration*, Turin-The Hague, 2017, p. 42 ff.

[66] *Eli Lilly and Company v. Government of Canada*, ICSID Case No. UNCT/14/2, Final Award of 16 March 2017, para. 220 ff. (Tribunal composed of Albert Jan van den Berg as President, Daniel Bethlehem and Gary Born).

stantial expense (both in matters of time and costs) which the Tribunal did not consider necessary to incur.

In *Eiser v. Spain*,[67] the Claimant submitted to the Tribunal various possible violations of the Energy Charter Treaty all arising from the same facts. The Tribunal, instead of addressing such facts in light of *all* the various standards recalled by Eiser stated that the fair and equitable treatment

> [p]roporciona el contexto jurídico más adecuado para evaluar la compleja situación de hecho que se presenta en este caso.

For this reason, considerations of judicial economy may dictate that a Tribunal departs from the Claimant's request and addresses only the issues which are essential for its decision.[68]

A similar approach was also endorsed in *Ampal v. Egypt*,[69] where, having found that a Respondent's behaviour fell into the scope of application of the full protection and security standard, the Tribunal – expressly mentioning the canon of procedural economy – avoided addressing whether the same behaviour could also constitute a FET violation.

Finally, in *Burlington v. Ecuador*, the Tribunal had to consider whether it was worth reopening a matter already decided in an interim award.[70] While analysing its inherent power of reconsideration,[71] the Tribunal based its decision on the opportunity of reopening a decided matter on the canon of procedural efficiency: while in certain cases efficiency dictates that an already decided matter is not reopened, in other cases it is the same principle which requires that there is an exception to the binding force of interim awards. In this regard, arbitrators noted that – in presence of exceptional circumstances of fact, such as new essential evidence – it is better to avoid that the Tribunal's decision is called into question in subsequent proceedings (e.g. annulment) when it is simply possible to reopen an already closed issue.

---

[67] *Eiser, cit. supra* note 21, paras. 353-354.

[68] In this regard the Tribunal also referred to *SGS Société Générale de Surveillance S.A. v. Paraguay*, ICSID Case No. ARB/07/29, Award of 19 February 2012, para. 161; *Ioan Micula et al. v. Romania*, ICSID Case No. ArB/05/20, Award of 11 December 2013, para. 874.

[69] *Ampal-American Israel Corp., EGI-FUN (08-10) Investors LLC, EGI-Series Investments LLC, and BSS-EMG Investors LLC v. Arab Republic of Egypt*, ICSID Case No. ARB/12/11, Decision on Liability and Head of Loss of 21 February 2017, para. 291 (Tribunal composed of Yves Fortier as President, Campbell McLachlan and Francisco Orrego Vicuna).

[70] *Burlington Resources Inc v. Republic of Ecuador*, ICSID Case No. ARB/08/5, Decision on Reconsideration and Award of 7 February 2017, para. 91 ff. (Tribunal composed of Gabrielle Kaufmann-Kohler as President, Brigitte Stern and Stephen Drymer).

[71] The Tribunal recognized that, as stated by previous decisions, it had such power in exceptional circumstances: indeed, while it is not possible to say that interim awards have *res judicata* effects, the Tribunal stated that they shall be anyway considered as binding for the parties and generally not open for a second discussion. See, on this matter, CANTELMO, "The Inherent Power of Reconsideration in Recent ICSID Case Law", Journal of World Investment & Trade, 2017, p. 232 ff.

All the above decisions show that the canon of judicial economy is starting to find a place as a general principle of procedure of international arbitration law, or, as Fulvio Palombino puts it, as one of the "general canons of adjudication – that is, those canons which are inherent in the judicial function and that the judge takes into account in the exercise of his duties, regardless of what the written procedural law establishes".[72] The wide application of this principle in investment arbitration, however, might also be considered from the wider perspective of public international law: the fact that the canon of judicial economy is being applied constantly also in this area of international adjudication might be seen as an *indicium* towards the affirmation of a general principle of procedure before international courts and tribunals.[73]

3.2. Parallel Proceedings

Parallel proceedings are one of the major issues concerning international arbitration. They can be defined as proceedings pending before two (or more) arbitral tribunals, in which the parties, the legal basis and one (or more) of the issues are the same or substantially the same.[74] The problem, however, may also regard concurrent proceedings between international arbitrators and domestic courts, in which there is also the necessity of coordinating proceedings arisen in different legal orders. The risk of conflicting results (as well as the great rise of costs) deriving from this phenomenon is one of the main reasons why the legitimacy of international investment arbitration has been put into question.[75] It is not by chance that parallel proceedings are one of the subjects of analysis of UNCITRAL for possible reforms to the ISDS mechanism[76] and it is also not fortuitous that arbitral tribunal which recently dealt with this issue conveniently devoted particular attention and careful analysis to this issue, trying to find an appropriate solution for it. Such a case law, therefore, requires a detailed study, which – anyway – imposes a differentiation between parallel arbitration proceedings and parallel domestic and arbitration proceedings.

---

[72] PALOMBINO, *cit. supra* note 64, p. 910.

[73] See, in general terms on the effects of international investment law on general international law SCHREUER, "The Development of International Law by ICSID Tribunals", ICSID Review – Foreign Investment Law Journal, 2016, p. 728 ff.

[74] In investment arbitration, this phenomenon has arisen in three different scenarios: (i) the same party starts, in parallel, a contract and a treaty claim against the host State; (ii) various shareholders of the same company operating a foreign investment start several parallel claims against the host State; (iii) different companies of the same group (composing a chain terminating with the corporation which actually owns the investment) start parallel claims against the host State. See, in this regard, ZARRA, *cit. supra* note 65, p. 3 ff.

[75] See, *inter alia*, CARVER, "How to Avoid Conflicting Awards: The Lauder and CME Cases", Journal of World Investment & Trade, 2004, p. 23 ff.

[76] See United Nations Commission for International Trade Law, Possible future work in the field of dispute settlement: Concurrent proceedings in international arbitration, UN Doc. A/CN.9/915 (2017).

3.2.1. Parallel Arbitration Proceedings

While it does not seem possible to find a solution to the problem of parallel proceedings at the jurisdictional stage of arbitrations, possible responses to this issue may be found at the admissibility phase.[77] In this regard, the mechanisms of abuse of process, *res judicata* and collateral estoppel, together with a less strict application of the traditional triple identity test (requiring, for the application of such doctrines, the identity of parties, *petitum* and *causa petendi*), have been sometimes proposed as valuable tools for the avoidance of duplicative proceedings and awards. Satisfactorily enough, various decisions in 2017 have applied (or at least taken into consideration) this proposed approach in order to solve the problem of parallel proceedings.

The first notable decision in this regard is, again, *Orascom v. Algeria*.[78] In this case, brought under the BLEU-Algeria BIT, the Respondent contended that the claims were inadmissible, the Claimant having lost its standing to bring arbitration proceedings (*intérêt pour agir*) against the Respondent, because Mr. Sawiris (i.e. the final owner of the Claimant company) had already started two other sets of proceedings against Algeria for the same facts through other companies of the group (OTH and Weather Investments), respectively on the basis of the Egypt-Algeria BIT and the Italy-Algeria BIT. In the Respondent's opinion, such a conduct constituted an abuse of process. The Tribunal started its analysis by noting that the three companies complained of the same measures taken by Algeria and, in the Tribunal's view, while the parties to the dispute and the legal bases for the claims (the BITs) were different, the dispute in the three arbitrations was effectively one and the same.[79] In light of this circumstance, the Tribunal pointed out that

> the existence of several legal foundations for arbitration does not necessarily mean that the various entities in the shareholder chain could make use of the existing arbitration clauses to assail the same measures and to recover the same economic loss under any circumstances. Indeed, the purpose of investment treaty arbitration is to grant full reparation for injuries that a qualifying investor may have suffered as a result of a host state's wrongful measures. If the harm incurred by one entity is fully repaired in one arbitration, the claims brought by other members of the vertical chain in other arbitral proceedings may become inadmissible depending on the circumstances.[80]

---

[77] ZARRA, *cit. supra* note 65, p. 58 ff. and p. 103 ff. See, on this matter, also GAILLARD, "Abuse of Process in International Arbitration", ICSID Review – Foreign Investment Law Journal, 2017, p. 32 ff. On the distinction between jurisdiction and admissibility, see, *inter alia*, PAUKER, "Admissibility of Claims in Investment Treaty Arbitration", Arbitration International, 2018, p. 1 ff.; FONTANELLI, *Jurisdiction and Admissibility in Investment Arbitration: The Practice and the Theory*, The Hague, 2018, p. 2 ff.

[78] *Orascom*, *cit. supra* note 51, para. 411 ff., and para. 488 ff.

[79] *Ibid.*, para. 488.

[80] *Ibid.*, para. 495.

On the basis of the above, the Tribunal noted that Mr. Sawiris' attempt to multiply the claim's chances of success in the dispute against Algeria was an abuse of process and therefore declared Orascom's claim inadmissible.

Moving to the principle of *res judicata*, it has found application in the *Ampal* case.[81] In this dispute, also characterized by the concurrency of several proceedings based on arbitration clauses contained both on BITs and investment contracts, an International Chamber of Commerce (ICC) Tribunal (ICC Case 18215/GZ/MHM) already issued an Award on 4 December 2015 at the end of a contractual dispute involving one of the companies of Ampal's group (as Claimant) and three Egyptian State companies (as Respondents). Faced with the question of the appropriateness of duly taking into account such a decision, the Tribunal showed its concern for overlaps and inconsistent findings[82] and therefore determined that

> [w]here the parties have chosen the forum to decide their contractual dispute, the findings of that court or tribunal will be entitled to *res judicata* effect within the legal order in which they were rendered. Accordingly, where a contractual claim between an investor and the host State has been the subject of an authoritative determination by an arbitral tribunal appointed under the contract, 'the authority as *res judicata* of a decision given by another competent jurisdiction between the same parties, concerning the same claims and based on the same factual and legal bases, prohibits a party from reintroducing a new action that is similar on all points'.[83]

As a consequence, for all matters related to the application of the contract, the investment Tribunal declared itself to be bound to respect the previous findings of the ICC tribunal. Such a conclusion is not limited by the fact that the parties in the two proceedings are formally different: recalling the common law doctrine of "privity of interests" and the *RSM v. Grenada*[84] and *Apotex v. USA*[85] decisions, the Tribunal found that when parties representing the same substantial interests start two subsequent arbitration proceedings, the finding of the first tribunal shall be binding on the second. This is because

> since, in the context of investment arbitration, a shareholder is entitled to pursue a claim for investments that are indirectly held through a corporation, it must also be subject to defences that

---

[81] *Ampal, cit. supra* note 69, para. 248 ff.

[82] *Ibid.*, para. 252.

[83] *Ibid.*, para. 258, quoting also *Malicorp Limited v. Arab Republic of Egypt*, ICSID Case No. ARB/08/18, Award of 7 February 2011, para. 103(b).

[84] *RSM Production and Others v. Grenada*, ICSID Case No. ARB/10/6, Award of 10 December 2010, para. 7.1.5. ff.

[85] *Apotex Holdings Inc. v. United States of America*, ICSID Case No. ARB(AF)/12/1, Award of 25 August 2014, para. 7.40 ff.

would be available against the corporation, including the defences of estoppel based on a prior judgment.[86]

For this reason, the ICSID Tribunal expressly quoted, in its Decision, all the parts of the ICC Award which it found relevant for the present dispute and did not reopen all the matters discussed by the ICC Tribunal.[87]

Finally, as to the applicability of collateral estoppel in investment arbitration, it has been discussed in two awards (in which, however, Tribunals found that the evidence presented by the parties did not support the applicability of the doctrine). In *Caratube v. Kazakhstan (II)*,[88] the Tribunal started its analysis by saying that it did not feel comfortable in affirming that such a doctrine is "a general principle of law applicable in investment arbitration proceedings".[89] However, on the basis of the findings of the abovementioned *Apotex* decision – where it was said that "international tribunals regularly look to the prior tribunal's reasons and indeed also to the parties arguments, in order to determine the scope of what was finally decided in that earlier proceeding" – and of the ILA Final Report on *res judicata* and arbitration[90] – where a "more extensive" notion of *res judicata* was endorsed and it was said that arbitral awards have conclusive and preclusive effects in further proceedings as to issues of fact or law which have actually been determined and arbitrated by it – the Tribunal declared that it was ready to accept the applicability of collateral estoppel in investment arbitration.[91] The same conclusion was reached in *Eskosol v. Italy*,[92] where the Tribunal did not deny that – in the case where a real privity of interest exists – the effects of a prior finding should be bound on subsequent Tribunals.

3.2.2. *Parallel domestic and arbitration proceedings*

It is often said that investment arbitration and domestic proceedings do not operate in the same legal order. As a consequence, first of all, the findings of each of them may have the force of *res judicata* with regard to the system in which it operates:[93] investment tribunals are bound by the determination

---

[86] *Ampal, cit. supra* note 69, para. 266.

[87] A similar issue arose in *Lao Holdings B.V. v. The Government of the Lao People's Democratic Republic*, ICSID Case No. ARB(AF)/12/6, Decision on the Merits of the Claimants' second material breach application of 15 December 2017, para. 105 ff. (Tribunal composed of Ian Binnie as President, Bernard Hanotiau and Brigitte Stern). In this case the Tribunal did not reach the same conclusion of the *Ampal* Tribunal, but in any case stated (para. 113) that it would have not second guessed the conclusions reached by the previous Stockholm Chamber of Commerce Award in the matters pertaining to its competence.

[88] *Caratube International Oil Company LLP and Mr Devincci Salah Hourani v. Republic of Kazakhstan*, ICSID Case No. ARB/13/13, Award of 27 September 2017, para. 458 ff.

[89] See, for a similar conclusion, ZARRA, *cit. supra* note 65, p. 162 ff.

[90] Reported in Arbitration International, 2014, p. 67 ff., Recommendation No. 4.

[91] Caratube, *cit. supra* note 88, para. 464.

[92] *Eskosol, cit. supra* note 51, para. 168 ff.

[93] *Helnan v. Egypt*, ICSID Case No. ARB/05/19, Award of 3 July 2008, para. 121 ff.

reached by domestic courts with regard to matters of national law, and domestic courts are bound by investment tribunals' conclusion on matters of international law. [94] Secondly, exactly in virtue of the different legal order in which they operate, arbitral tribunals have usually refused to consider that domestic and international disputes may actually overlap and, therefore, be considered as identical for the purpose of the application of mechanisms of prevention of parallel proceedings.

Such a conclusion, which has been quite unanimously applied in investment arbitration,[95] seems to have been put into question in the *Supervision y Control S.A. v. The Republic of Costa Rica* Award,[96] a contractual case where – in presence of a fork-in-the-road clause – an ICSID Tribunal declared (by majority) inadmissible a claim on the basis of the fact that the Claimant required the same damages that it had already asked (without success) before Costa Rican administrative courts. After having found that the actions brought before domestic courts and the arbitral tribunal pursued ultimately the same purposes[97] and were essentially the same[98] the Tribunal stated that this conclusion is not put into question by the fact that domestic proceedings were brought by the majority shareholder of the company who acted as Claimant in the arbitration. According to the Tribunal, there is a general presumption that a majority shareholder controls the company[99] (they are, therefore, in privity of interests) and – in order to (i) prevent a situation in which such a majority shareholder starts more than one claim in relation to the same facts and (ii) interpret fork-in-the-road clauses in a way which helps in rendering them effective – a less strict application of the triple identity test is required. The claim was, therefore, declared inadmissible.

As for the case law regarding parallel arbitration proceedings, this decision, which let the substantial identity of the two sets of proceedings prevail over their formal diversity, is to be welcome as a praiseworthy attempt aimed at avoiding the abusive practice of investors who start multiple claims in relation to the same dispute.

---

[94] As a consequence, an investment Tribunal cannot second-guess State acts validated in domestic proceedings, unless such acts and their validation constitute a violation of international law. See *Fouad Alghanim et al. v. Hashemite Kingdom of Jordan*, ICSID Case No. ARB/13/38, Award of 14 December 2017, para. 318 (Tribunal composed of Cambpbell McLachlan as President, Yves Fortier and Marcelo Cohen).

[95] For a confirmation see also *UAB E Energija (Lithuania) v. Republic of Latvia*, ICSID Case No. ARB/12/33, Award of 22 December 2017, paras. 563-572 (Tribunal composed of Paolo Michele Patocchi as President, August Reinisch and Samuel Wordsworth). A partial critic to this approach may be found in Zarra, *cit. supra* note 65, p. 154 ff.

[96] ICSID Case No. ARB/12/4, Award of 18 January 2017, para. 308 ff. (Tribunal composed of Claus von Wobeser as President, Joseph Klock and Eduardo Silva Romero).

[97] *Ibid.*, para. 315.

[98] *Ibid.*, para. 317.

[99] *Ibid.*, para. 328.

4. SUBSTANCE

Important clarifications have occurred also with regard to substantive matters concerning investment arbitration proceedings. They regarded, mainly, the arbitrators' approach to issues of applicable law and, partially, also the contours of standards of treatment enshrined in BITs (on which the debate was already at a quite advanced stage). We will analyse them in the following subsections.

4.1. Applicable Law

Developments concerning how arbitral tribunals deal with issues of applicable law have regarded the applicability of the principle *iura novit curia* in international arbitration, the interplay between domestic and international law, and the role of precedent in investment arbitration. All these developments show that these issues, which once upon a time were subject to huge discussions, may now be considered as settled.

4.1.1. Iura Novit Curia

The applicability in international arbitration of the principle *iura novit curia*, according to which adjudicators are not bound by the issues of law as presented by the parties and may independently investigate the legal framework surrounding the dispute before them, has been largely discussed in scholarship.[100] The problem mainly arose in international commercial arbitration due to the fact that – as is well known – there is no uniformity among civil law and common law systems concerning the status of foreign law: while the former apply it as a law, and therefore consider that judges have a duty to investigate on its content, the latter apply it as a fact, and hence base their determination on the evidence presented by the parties. The place of the seat and the background of arbitrators might be therefore crucial in the determination of the applicability of the *iura novit curia* maxim in commercial arbitration.

The solution to this problem seems to be more straightforward in investment arbitration (and, in particular, in ICSID cases, which are fully grounded in international law) where the question seems to be answered in the affirmative; 2017 cases strongly contribute to this solution. Indeed, in several cases (all of which

---

[100] GIOVANNINI, "International Arbitration and Jura Novit Curia – Towards Harmonization", Transnational Dispute Management, 2012, p. 1 ff.; KURKELA, "'Jura Novit Curia' and the Burden of Education in International Arbitration – A Nordic Perspective", ASA Bulletin, 2003, p. 486 ff.; KAUFMANN-KOHLER, "The Arbitrator and the Law: Does He/She Know It? Apply It? How? And a Few More Questions", Arbitration International, 2005, p. 631 ff.; CARLEVARIS, "L'accertamento del diritto nell'arbitrato internazionale tra principio *jura novit curia* e onere della prova", Rivista dell'arbitrato, 2007, p. 505 ff.

are characterised by the Presidency of Gabrielle Kaufmann-Kohler), it is possible to find disclaimers with the following content:

> *Iura Novit Curia*: When applying the governing law, the Tribunal is not bound by the arguments or sources invoked by the Parties. Under the maxim *iura novit curia* – or, better, *iura novit arbiter* – the Tribunal is required to apply the law of its own motion, provided always that it gives the Parties an opportunity to comment if it intends to base its decision on a legal theory that was not addressed and that the Parties could not reasonably anticipate.[101]

In other cases, Tribunals have, without so much detail, simply declared that they considered the principle as applicable and that it allowed them to refer either to previous decisions not addressed by the parties[102] or to general principles of international law.[103] As previously stated with regard to the principle of judicial economy, these precedents (should they find confirmation in the future) seem to constitute good *indicia* pointing towards the recognition of *iura novit curia* as a general principle of international arbitration law. This would be an important development for ensuring the effective management of arbitral proceedings and the correct resolution of disputes.

4.1.2. Interplay of National and International Law

The applicability of international law in investment treaty arbitration is today a settled issue, which does not require further discussion.[104] More problematic remained only the question of the possible applicability of public international law in presence of an express choice of law operated in a contract. Prof. Schreuer, in this regard, pointed out that international law should be applicable in any case, because otherwise one would have to uphold discriminatory and arbitrary action by the host State amounting to breaches of public international law standards of protection of foreign investments. Hence, according to Schreuer, the obligatory nature of these standards is not open to the disposition of the parties.[105]

---

[101] *Lighthouses, cit. supra* note 10, para. 109. An identical statement may be found in *Wirtgen, cit. supra* note 21, para. 179; *Burlington, cit. supra* note 70, paras. 45 and 115.

[102] *Capital Financial Holdings, cit. supra* note 51, para. 135.

[103] *Ampal, cit. supra* note 69, para. 262.

[104] GAILLARD and BANIFATEMI, "The Meaning of 'and' in Article 42(1), Second Sentence, of the Washington Convention: The Role of International Law in the ICSID Choice of Law Process", ICSID Review – Foreign Investment Law Journal, 2003, p. 375 ff.; PAUCIULO, "Il diritto applicabile dai tribunali arbitrali ICSID nella soluzione delle controversie tra Stato e investitore privato", in DEL VECCHIO and SEVERINO (eds.), *Tutela degli investimenti tra integrazione dei mercati e concorrenza di ordinamenti*, Bari, 2017, p. 71 ff.

[105] SCHREUER, *The ICSID Convention: A Commentary*, Oxford, 2009, p. 585 ff.

The issue arose in *Caratube v. Kazakhstan*,[106] where the Tribunal had to consider the applicability of customary international law in a contractual dispute in which the parties expressly provided for the applicability of Kazak law. The Tribunal, while noting that in presence of a choice of law made by the parties Article 42 seems to exclude the applicability of customary international law, nevertheless expressly quoted Schreuer's opinion and stated that it would be improper to disregard public international law, which has been duly taken into account in its decision.[107]

This *obiter dictum* is, therefore, an important clarification concerning the role of public international law in all ICSID disputes.

4.1.3. The "Taking into Account" Approach

Another matter on which investment practice seems to have reached its full maturity concerns the role of precedents. Among the opinions which recognized a quasi-binding force to previous awards[108] and those who denied any importance to them,[109] the approach which prevailed is the one which recognizes the necessity for arbitrators to take previous awards into consideration with the possibility to depart from them (duly motivating such a choice) if compelling reasons require to do so.[110] This is largely confirmed by 2017 practice.

Among the various decisions which addressed the issue, it is worth mentioning the *Spence International Investments LLC, Berkowitz et al. v. the Republic of Costa Rica* Award.[111] The dispute concerned an alleged expropriation due to environmental reasons of certain villas in the western coast of Costa Rica. The Tribunal noted that a very similar issue was already debated in a previous case[112] and therefore stated:

> [w]hile not in any way controlling of liability issues in these proceedings, having regard to the bearing that the *Unglaube* case narrative has on the present proceedings, the Tribunal has had regard to the discussion in the *Unglaube* award of issues that overlap with the present case.

---

[106] *Caratube, cit. supra* note 88, paras. 288-290.

[107] *Ibid.*, para. 290.

[108] KAUFMANN-KOHLER, "Arbitral Precedent: Dream, Necessity or Excuse?", Arbitration International, 2007, p. 357 ff., p. 373 ff.

[109] TEN CATE, "The Costs of Consistency: Precedent in Investment Treaty Arbitration", Columbia Journal of Transnational Law, 2013, p. 418 ff., p. 425.

[110] PALOMBINO, *Fair and Equitable Treatment, cit. supra* note 4, p. 151 ff.

[111] ICSID Case No. UNCT/13/2, Interim Award of 30 May 2017, para. 30 ff. (Tribunal composed of Daniel Bethlehem as President, Mark Kantor and Raul Vinuesa).

[112] *Marion Unglaube and Reinhard Unglaube v. the Republic of Costa Rica*, ICSID Consolidated Cases No. ARB/08/1 and ARB/09/20, Award of 16 May 2012.

This is an emblematic example of how arbitral tribunals should conciliate their role of *ad hoc* adjudicators with the expectations of the parties arising from previous decisions and the systemic implications of their awards.

Significantly, Awards in which Prof. Kaufmann-Kohler acted as President often contain statements saying that

> The Tribunal considers that it is not bound by previous decisions. At the same time, it is of the opinion that it should pay due consideration to earlier decisions of international tribunals. It believes that, subject to compelling contrary grounds, it should be respectful of the reasoning and solutions established in a series of consistent cases. It also believes that, subject to the circumstances of an actual case, it has a duty to seek to contribute to the harmonious development of investment law and thereby to meet the legitimate expectations of the community of States and investors towards certainty of the rule of law.[113]

The confirmation of the applicability of the taking into account approach in investment arbitration shall be warmly welcomed: through this mechanism, arbitral awards show the arbitrators' consideration of the more general consequences of their decisions in the development of international investment law and ensure the coherent development of this subject.

4.2. Standards of Treatment (in brief)

With regard to standards of treatment, there have been numerous awards discussing the scope of application of the legitimate expectations arising from the fair and equitable treatment, as well as the level of deference that tribunals shall pay to States' sovereignty. These discussions, however, just contributed in reinforcing already consolidated approaches to the matters and therefore do not deserve a detailed analysis. Indeed, as to legitimate expectations deriving from normative acts, 2017 practice confirms that investors may never take the stability of the legal framework of the host State as guaranteed (indeed, legal changes are part of the business risk assumed by them): expectations are legitimate only when – through *specific* statements – the host State *induced* the investor to make a certain choice ensuring him that the legal framework will not change (legitimate expectations by induction).[114] With regard to expropriation, the recent case

---

[113] *Lighthouses*, *cit. supra* note 10, p. 111. Similarly see *Burlington*, *cit. supra* note 70, p. 111. This well-known quote comes from the authoritative and often reported precedent *Saipem v. Bangladesh*, ICSID Case No. ARB/05/07, Decision on Jurisdiction and Recommendation on Provisional Measure of 21 March 2007, para 67 (the President of the Tribunal was, also in that case, Prof. Gabrielle Kaufmann-Kohler).

[114] See *Teinver S.A. et al. v. The Argentine Republic*, ICSID Case No. ARB/09/1, Award of 21 July 2017, para. 667 (Tribunal composed of Thomas Buergenthal as President, Henri

law confirms that tribunals are currently more willing than before to pay due deference towards the legitimate policy objectives of Respondent States and to balance the importance of such policies with the interests of the investors.[115]

Having said the above, the most significant developments concerning standards of treatment have regarded the recognition of a higher role for the principle of proportionality in international investment law, both in cases of alleged FET violations and in cases of alleged expropriations. Indeed, while the structure of the principle of proportionality – based on the tripartite test composed of suitability, necessity and proportionality *stricto sensu* – is a settled issue in international investment law,[116] the case law applying this test in cases of alleged FET violations is quite poor; moreover, some authors even doubted of the applicability of the principle of proportionality in cases of alleged expropriations.[117]

As to the relationship between proportionality and FET, it is worth mentioning the *PL Holdings* Award,[118] where the Tribunal examined whether certain measures assumed by the *Komiska Nadzoru Finanswego* (KNF – i.e. the Polish regulatory authority) towards the Claimant (consisting in (i) an order prohibiting its exercise of voting rights in connection with its shareholding in the Polish bank FM Bank PBP and (ii) an order to PL Holdings compelling it to sell its shares in this Bank) were to be considered as a violation of the FET. Considering that the Respondent argued that KNF's measures were adopted in response to certain misconduct by the Claimant which led the FM Bank to face grave financial problems, the Tribunal conducted its evaluation in light of the principle of proportionality: was the KNF's reaction proportional to PL Holdings misconduct? According to the Tribunal, in light of the factual background surrounding the case, the Claimant suffered a damage which was not proportional to (i.e. bigger than) its previous conduct. Indeed, PL Holdings was already carrying out measures aimed at resolving FM Bank's crisis when the regulatory authority took the disputed actions. For this reason, the Tribunal considered that – at the time they were adopted – KNF's measures were not suitable to achieve their purpose, could have been substituted by less intrusive measures (they were, therefore, not necessary) and were – *in concreto* – not proportional *stricto sensu* as they caused grievous damage to the Claimant. To this author's knowledge, this is the first

---

C. Alvarez and Kamal Hossain); *UAB, cit. supra* note 95, para. 835 ff.; *Blusun, cit. supra* note 21, para. 365 ff.; *Wirtgen, cit. supra* note 21, para. 407 ff. In scholarship see, *inter alia*, PALOMBINO, *Fair and Equitable Treatment, cit. supra* note 4, p. 113 ff.

[115] In *Koch Minerals Sàrl and Koch Nitrogen International Sàrl v. The Bolivarian Republic of Venezuela*, ICSID Case No. ARB/11/19, Award of 30 October 2017, para. 7.22 (Tribunal composed of V.V. Veeder as President, Marc Lalonde and Zachary Douglas) the Tribunal even recognized the existence of a "*jurisprudence constante* on deference".

[116] PALOMBINO, *Fair and Equitable Treatment, cit. supra* note 4, p. 127 ff.

[117] TITI, "Refining the Expropriation Clause: What Role for Proportionality?", 2017, p. 1 ff., available at <https://papers.ssrn.com/sol3/papers.cfm?abstract_id=2978530>. *Contra* see ZARRA, "Right to Regulate, Margin of Appreciation and Proportionality: Current Status in Investment Arbitration in Light of *Philip Morris v. Uruguay*", Brazilian Journal of International Law, 2017, p. 95 ff.

[118] *PL Holdings, cit. supra* note 21, para. 354 ff.

investment award in which a so detailed analysis of the proportionality principle for the purpose of assessing a FET violation has been carried out, as well as one of the first investment disputes to be decided on the basis of such a principle.[119]

With regard to the role of proportionality in expropriation cases, the *Blusun v. Italy* Award[120] deserves some analysis. In this case, the Tribunal had to evaluate whether certain reduction of the feed-in tariffs and limitations of the use of agricultural lands related to the production of renewable energy were to be considered as expropriatory measures, in particular in light of the previous Italian regulation which strongly incentivized foreign investments in this area of the market. In order to assume its decision, the Tribunal considered the legitimate public purposes behind Italy's choices, i.e. the necessity to face a problematical economic situation (the Tribunal talked about "a genuine fiscal need") and the willingness to address valid rural planning concerns and compared such purposes to the sacrifices imposed on the investor, taking in due account the alleged promises that Italy made at the time the investment was started. According to the Tribunal, investors did not suffer a damage which was disproportionate to the Italian public needs, considering that the reduction in incentives was less than the reduction of the costs of photovoltaic technology of which Blusun benefited, Italy maintained a 20 year period of incentives for the Claimant's activity (as undertook when the investment was made) and Italian reduction of subsidies was comparably less than it has been in other European countries. As a consequence, the Tribunal said that no expropriation had taken place.

The above Awards are noteworthy because they show that Tribunals are starting to give due weight to the principle of proportionality, which, as it has been demonstrated in scholarship,[121] is potentially a very valuable tool in order to pay due deference to States' sovereignty and helps in addressing the concrete reasonableness of measures affecting foreign investors.

5. CONCLUSIONS

As the present paper has attempted to demonstrate, 2017 has been a year rich in debate concerning investment arbitration law. Arbitral practice has not only

---

[119] One of the few significant precedents is *Continental Casualty Company v. Argentina*, ICSID Case No. Case No. ARB/03/9, Award of 5 September 2008, para. 227, which applied the proportionality test in relation to the model of exception enshrined in art. XX GATT; see also *Glamis Gold Ltd v. United States*, UNCITRAL, Award of 8 June 2009, para. 803 ff.; *Azurix v. Argentina*, ICSID Case No. ARB/01/12, Award of 14 July 2006, para. 311 ff.; *Occidental Petroleum Corp., Occidental Exploration and Production Company v. Ecuador*, ICSID Case No. ARB/06/11, Award of 5 October 2012, para. 404 ff.

[120] *Blusun, cit. supra* note 21, paras. 342-343. A notable precedent in this regard is *Técnicas Medioambiente Tecmed S.A. v. Mexico*, ICSID Case No. ARB (AF)/00/2, Award of 29 May 2003, para. 122.

[121] See, *inter alia*, STONE SWEET and DELLA CANANEA, "Proportionality, General Principles of Law, and Investor-State Arbitration: A Response to Jose Alvarez", NYU Journal of International Law and Politics, 2014, p. 911 ff.

developed new approaches to issues faced by arbitral tribunals but has mainly demonstrated that many of the questions that were subject to huge debate in the past may now be considered settled.

This seems to be the natural evolution of a system which saw its infancy in the sixties, actually started developing – and facing its adolescence – only during the late 1990s (when the ICSID started to register a higher number of arbitrations) and obviously needed some time in order to get settled and improve mechanisms of checks and balances aimed at pondering all the various interests at stake. The sensibility shown by arbitrators for the systemic implications of arbitral awards, as well as the development of more precise principles and rules aimed at regulating the various issues arisen during arbitral proceedings, shows that the system is significantly improving, reacting to the strong criticisms that it faces and, probably, approaching its adulthood. This is, finally, a clear signal of the fact that, probably, a drastic reform of the entire ISDS system is not the only way to be pursued in order to address the criticisms that it is facing: any system of adjudication needs time in order to find its proper way of functioning. Hence, before totally subverting and/or replacing the existing system, it would probably be worth waiting for its full maturation to then evaluate its validity and efficiency in light of its defined features.

ITALIAN PRACTICE
RELATING TO INTERNATIONAL LAW

Classification Scheme

I. INTERNATIONAL LAW IN GENERAL

II. INTERNATIONAL CUSTOM, LAW OF TREATIES AND OTHER SOURCES OF INTERNATIONAL LAW

III. STATES AND OTHER INTERNATIONAL ENTITIES

IV. DIPLOMATIC AND CONSULAR RELATIONS

V. IMMUNITIES

VI. TERRITORY

VII. LAW OF THE SEA

VIII. ENVIRONMENT

IX. CULTURAL HERITAGE

X. AIR AND SPACE LAW

XI. TREATMENT OF ALIENS AND NATIONALITY

XII. HUMAN RIGHTS

XIII. INTERNATIONAL CRIMINAL LAW

XIV. CO-OPERATION IN JUDICIAL, LEGAL, SECURITY, AND SOCIO-ECONOMIC MATTERS

XV. INTERNATIONAL ECONOMIC LAW

XVI. INTERNATIONAL ORGANIZATIONS

XVII. RELATIONSHIP BETWEEN MUNICIPAL AND INTERNATIONAL LAW

XVIII. USE OF FORCE AND PEACE-KEEPING

XIX. ARMED CONFLICT, NEUTRALITY, AND DISARMAMENT

XX. INTERNATIONAL RESPONSIBILITY

XXI. INTERNATIONAL DISPUTE SETTLEMENT

JUDICIAL DECISIONS

(edited by *Daniele Amoroso* and *Andrea Caligiuri*)

II. INTERNATIONAL CUSTOM, LAW OF TREATIES AND OTHER SOURCES OF INTERNATIONAL LAW

1. SUCCESSION TO BILATERAL TREATIES: THE CONSENT OF THE "NEW" STATE IS A NECESSARY BUT NOT SUFFICIENT CONDITION

Succession of States in respect of treaties – Unilateral declarations of succession – Bilateral Treaties – Extradition – Reciprocity – Articles 9 and 24 of the 1978 Vienna Convention on Succession of States in Respect of Treaties

Corte di Cassazione (Sez. VI Penale), 3 February 2017, No. 14237
Republic of Mauritius v. Soornack Nandanee

With the Judgment under comment, the *Corte di Cassazione* dismissed the appeal lodged by the Republic of Mauritius against the decision of the Court of Appeals of Bologna which had rejected, in turn, an extradition request made by the appellant State.

On 22 May 2015, the Republic of Mauritius submitted to Italy an extradition request against Ms. Soornack Nandanee, who was charged with criminal conspiracy and money laundering. The request was based on the Bilateral Agreement between Italy and the United Kingdom for the Mutual Extradition of the Offenders, 5 February 1873, applicable, under Article 18, to foreign possessions and colonies of both parties. According to the Court of Appeals, the Bilateral Agreement was not applicable to the case, since Italy was not bound by the unilateral declaration of 1968, by which the Republic of Mauritius stated that it succeeded to all treaties to which its predecessor State, the United Kingdom, was a party. In the opinion of the Court, Italy had never shown a will to accept such a declaration and, consequently, no succession to the Bilateral Treaty had occurred. The Court of Appeals considered nonetheless admissible the participation of the Republic of Mauritius in the proceedings, since it met the conditions set forth in Article 702 of the Italian Code of Criminal Procedure. Under this provision, "[t]he requesting State shall be entitled to participate to the proceedings before the Court of Appeal and the Court of Cassation, represented by a lawyer entitled to plead before the Italian judicial authority, *provided that there is reciprocity*" (translation by GIALUZ, LUPARÌA and SCARPA (eds.), *The Italian Code of Criminal Procedure. Critical Essays and English Translation*, Padova, 2014, p. 473, emphasis added). The Court of Appeals deemed the diplomatic note sent by the Mauritius High Commission of Pretoria on 8 August 2016 to fulfil the condition of reciprocity laid down by Article 702 of the Code of Criminal Procedure. This note stated that in case Italy submitted an extradition request to the Republic of Mauritius and extradition proceedings were initiated, the former State could apply before Mauritian courts to formally take part in the proceedings as a third party.

In the appeal lodged with the *Corte di Cassazione*, the Republic of Mauritius reiterated its status as a successor State to the abovementioned Bilateral Agreement on Extradition, by reason of the unilateral declaration issued in 1968. Before the *Corte di Cassazione*, moreover, Ms. Soornack Nandanee challenged the participation of the appellant State in the extradition proceeding, claiming that the condition of reciprocity laid down in Article 702 of the Code of Criminal Procedure was not satisfied at all.

The *Corte di Cassazione*, on the one hand, declared the appeal inadmissible (*In Law,* para. 1), considering that the Court of Appeals correctly excluded that the Bilateral Agreement of 1873 was in force between Italy and the Republic of Mauritius; on the other hand, it stated that the condition of reciprocity was not fulfilled. The latter conclusion is based on a *substantive*, rather than formal, approach: the Court assessed that the Mauritian legal system would not have granted Italy with procedural guarantees that were *substantially* comparable to those enshrined in Art 702 of the Code of Criminal Procedure (see PORRO, ILDC 2818 (IT 2017), A7).

The first – and most notable, in terms of international law – set of arguments regards the question of whether the Republic of Mauritius could be considered as the successor State of Great Britain in relation to the Bilateral Treaty of 1873. According to the Court, this question should be answered in the negative. Under Articles 9 and 24 of the 1978 Vienna Convention on Succession of States in Respect of Treaties, the maintaining in force of a treaty to which the predecessor State was a Party depends entirely on the mutual consent of both the successor State and the other State party to that treaty (*In Law*, para. 2.2). For the Court, this is the approach persistently held by Italian courts (*In Law*, para. 2.3), first in *Bottali* (*Corte d'appello di Roma*, Judgment of 17 October 1980, in RDI, 1981, p. 882 ff.), where the 1873 Bilateral Treaty between Italy and Great Britain was deemed to be inapplicable to the relations between India and Italy. The Court relied also on two of its previous judgments: in *Jadranko* (*Corte di Cassazione, Sez. VI Penale*, Judgment No. 2828, 17 July 1995), the *Corte di Cassazione* held that the Bilateral Agreement between Italy and the Kingdom of Serbs, Croats and Slovenes, concluded on 6 April 1922 was applicable to the relations between Italy and the "new" Republic of Croatia as concerns extradition. But, according to the Court, this case is different from that concerning the relations with the Republic of Mauritius: the Republic of Croatia, in fact, had issued a unilateral declaration in relation to the treaties of the former Socialist Federal Republic of Yugoslavia, and Italy *had accepted* such declaration by concluding facts, by publishing it in its official journal (*Gazzetta Ufficiale della Repubblica Italiana*). Furthermore, the *Corte di Cassazione* reminded its decision in the *Glicic* case (*Corte di Cassazione*, No. 4353, 19 December 1995, in *Cassazione Penale*, 1996, p. 2629 ff.), where an extradition request submitted by the Federal Republic of Yugoslavia had been rejected by the Court, by reason of the non-applicability of the Bilateral Agreement between the Kingdom of Italy and the Kingdom of Serbs, Croats and Slovenes.

The Court of Cassation emphasized that the Federal Republic of Yugoslavia had not yet issued any declaration of will to be a successor State to the treaties of the former Socialist Federal Republic of Yugoslavia. It is therefore clear that for the *Corte di Cassazione* a succession in a bilateral treaty is admissible only where the requirement of "double consent" of both the successor State and the original Parties is met. According to the Court, "[t]he diplomatic procedures concerning, in particular, the international succession in bilateral treaties require, therefore, the convergence of two acts of will: that of the successor State and that of the State with which the predecessor State had originally concluded the treaty subject to succession" (*In Law*, para. 2.2).

The arguments set forth by the Court may be scrutinized on several grounds. First of all, the *Corte di Cassazione* rightly observed that this is a case of succession regarding a Newly Independent State – since the Republic of Mauritius is a former Colony of Great Britain – which falls, in principle, under Part III of the Vienna Convention on Succession of States of 1978. In this regard, it is worth noting that Italy is not a Party to this Convention. Furthermore, the treaty applies only to hypotheses of succession occurring after its entry into force (6 November 1996), so that the situation under consideration would, in any case, have been outside its scope of application *ratione temporis*. It must be emphasized, however, that many of the rules set forth in that Convention, mentioned by the *Corte di Cassazione*, reflect customary international law. Article 16 of the Convention establishes that "[a] newly independent State is not bound to maintain in force, or to become a party to, any treaty by reason only of the fact that at the date of the succession of States the treaty was in force in respect of the territory to which the succession of States relates". This article codifies the so-called *clean slate* principle (on the customary *status* of which see HENRY, "Article 16", in DISTEFANO, GAGGIOLI and HÊCHE (eds.), *La Convention de Vienne de 1978 sur la succession d'États en matière de traités. Commentaire article par article et études thématiques*, Bruxelles, 2016, vol. I, p. 561 ff., pp. 575-586) which is deemed, by the Court and by some authors, to be applicable to *all* situations of succession, even to those occurring outside the decolonization process (see, among others, CONFORTI (ed. by IOVANE), *Diritto internazionale*, 11th ed., Napoli, 2018, p. 127). As correctly assessed by the Court, the succession to bilateral treaties, such as the Agreement under consideration, is regulated by Articles 9 and 24 of the Convention. Under Article 24, a bilateral treaty "is considered as being in force between a newly independent State and the other State party when: (a) they expressly so agree; or (b) by reason of their conduct they are to be considered as having so agreed". The consent of *both* States involved – the new State and the original State party – is an essential condition for the maintenance in force of a bilateral treaty (International Law Commission, Draft articles on Succession of States in respect of Treaties with commentaries, YILC, 1974, Vol. II, Part. 1, p. 174 ff., p. 238). This requirement is particularly strict in bilateral agreements due to the fact that, in such treaties, the succession determines a significant change in the identity of the parties. As persuasively argued, a bilateral treaty is characterized by a sort of "personal equation" in which reciprocity plays a decisive role: the object of most bilateral treaties is to regulate the mutual rights and obligations of the parties by reference principally to their own particular relations and interests (DI STEFANO, "Article 24", in DISTEFANO, GAGGIOLI and HÊCHE (eds.), *cit. supra*, p. 833 ff., pp. 847-848 and p. 852; see also the ILC Draft articles on Succession of States, *cit.*, p. 237) .

As regards the consent of the successor State, the *Corte di Cassazione* rightly found it in the unilateral declaration issued by the Republic of Mauritius in 1968. This kind of declaration – very common during the 1960s in the practice of newly independent States – looks similar to a "corollary" of the *clean slate* principle, giving rise to a "voluntary" succession of the new State. The declarations at issue did not fall into any established form or procedure, but rather pursued the aim to declare the intention of a new State to succeed in treaty obligations of the predecessor State. These acts were formally addressed to the UN Secretariat "as the *convenient diplomatic channel* for circulating to all States Members [...] notifications of such acts" (WALDOCK, Second Report on Succession in Respect of Treaties, UN Doc. A/CN.4/214 and Add.1 & 2, YILC, 1969, Vol. II, p. 45 ff., p. 66, para. 5, emphasis added). Article 9 of the 1978 Convention, on the one hand, reflects this practice, taking into account unilateral declarations as a valid tool to assess the *intention* of a new State in respect of treaties concluded by its predecessor. On the other hand, however, it clearly establishes that such a declaration is not sufficient for the continuance in force of a given treaty, since the consent of the other State party is indispensable (on the effect of unilateral declarations see KALLIOPOULOS, "Article 9", in DISTEFANO, GAGGIOLI, HÊCHE (eds.), *cit. supra*, p. 295 ff., p. 329 ff).

What is missing for the Court is the other side of the coin, that is to say Italy's consent to be bound by the 1873 Extradition Treaty. Article 24 of the 1978 Convention provides that the consent of the other Party may take both an *express* and a *tacit* form. As for the express form, exchange of diplomatic notes or joint declarations may be mentioned. It is clear, as correctly stressed by the Court (*In Law*, para. 2.4), that Italy had never expressed its consent to be bound by the 1873 Treaty with the Republic of Mauritius. In this perspective, the Court underlined the difference between this case and other instances where succession in bilateral treaties actually occurred, such as the exchange of diplomatic notes with Kenya (22 September and 8 December 1967), by which the parties agreed to keep in force, in their mutual relations, the 1873 Extradition Treaty under consideration.

Tacit consent under Article 24 of the 1978 Vienna Convention may consist of an *active* conduct – such as the publication of the treaty into the official report of treaties in force, the conclusion of a subsequent agreement which refers to the bilateral treaty – or a *passive* behaviour, giving rise, for example, to acquiescence (DI STEFANO, *cit. supra*, p. 870 ff.). There is no evidence of a tacit consent, by which Italy could have agreed to keep in force the Extradition Treaty under its scrutiny. Correctly, therefore, – and coherently with its previous case law – the Court concluded that such a consent could not be presumed and, accordingly, that the Extradition treaty was not in force between Italy and the Republic of Mauritius (*In Law*, para. 2.5). Nonetheless, some of the arguments employed by the Court raise at least two observations. On the one hand, the *Glicic* case, recalled by the Court, does not seem to be relevant for the case under consideration, since it concerned a case of succession occurring *outside* the decolonization process. Furthermore, in that case the Italian Government claimed that no succession had occurred for the lack of a unilateral declaration by the new Republic of Yugoslavia. In other words, the *Glicic* case was based more on the consent of the new State, rather than on that of the other party to the bilateral treaty, namely Italy. On the other hand, it is interesting to notice that the Court confirmed the narrow reading of succession rules adopted in 1980 in the *Bottali* case, where the Court of Appeals of Rome stated that the 1873 Treaty was not in force between India and Italy, despite the opposite opinion expressed by the Italian Ministry of Justice (see the opinion of 7 June 1980, quoted in the judgment of the Court of Appeals of Rome, *cit.*, p. 883: "between Italy and India is still applicable the Bilateral Agreement between Italy and the United Kingdom for the Mutual Extradition of the Offenders, signed in Rome on 5 February 1873, given that India has not so far denounced it") (The Italian text of the judgment is published in *Cassazione Penale*, 2017, p. 3128 ff.; English excerpts are available at: <http://opil.ouplaw.com/page/ILDC/oxford-reports-on-international-law-in-domestic-courts>).

GIUSEPPE PUMA

V. IMMUNITIES

1. CONFLICTING APPROACHES OF THE COURT OF CASSATION TO STATE IMMUNITY IN EMPLOYMENT DISPUTES

Immunity of foreign States from jurisdiction – Employment disputes – Restrictive immunity – Article 11 of the UN Convention on Jurisdictional Immunities of States and Their Property of 2 December 2004 (UNCSI) – Customary international law – Article 10 of the Italian Constitution

Corte di Cassazione (Sezioni Unite Civili), 27 February 2017, No. 4882
Embassy of Qatar v. Mohamed Hasan Mohamed Awad

Corte di Cassazione (Sezioni Unite Civili), 6 June 2017, No. 13980
Cleopatra Mutinta Chibomba v. Embassy of the Republic of Zambia to the Italian Republic

In two decisions rendered in the course of 2017, the *Corte di Cassazione* adopted contrasting approaches to the immunity of foreign States in employment disputes. In Order No. 4882 of 27 February, the court seemed to implicitly depart from its precedents where, from 2014 onwards, it had applied the provisions of the UN Convention on Jurisdictional Immunities of States and Their Property (UNCSI) regarding contracts of employment (i.e. Article 11) *qua* codification of customary international law, incorporated in the Italian legal system pursuant to Art. 10 of the Constitution. Instead of the UNCSI, the *Cassazione* applied the precepts of its pre-2014 jurisprudence in the field of employment disputes. In Judgment No. 13980 of 6 June, however, the court ignored Order No. 4882 and went back to applying Article 11 UNCSI. As will be seen, on top of the bewilderment caused by the apparent jurisprudential inconsistency, both rulings also stand out for the court's reliance on a congeries of weak or incorrect legal arguments.

The facts of Order No. 4882 played out as follows. The claim had been brought by Mohamed Hasan Mohamed Awad, who had been in charge of the public relations of the Embassy of Qatar in Italy from 1994 to 2015. After the termination of his employment relationship, he sued the Embassy before the *Tribunale di Roma* alleging that he was entitled to various pecuniary benefits by reason of the duties he had performed and seeking monetary compensation. He did not challenge the lawfulness of his termination of employment. At the request of the Embassy, which contended that the Italian courts lacked jurisdiction over the claims brought by the plaintiff, the *Corte di Cassazione* was asked to deliver a preliminary ruling on jurisdiction.

The Cassation affirmed the jurisdiction of the Italian courts and returned the case to the *Tribunale* for a decision on the merits. It motivated this conclusion by referring to a long-standing line of its own case law where it had adapted the distinction between *acta jure imperii* and *acta jure gestionis* to the context of labour claims. Pursuant to this case law, the immunity of the State employer should be excluded in two distinct cases: when the employment relationship concerns "activities merely auxiliary to the institutional functions of the defendant bodies", or when the subject-matter of the claim involves "purely pecuniary aspects" and is incapable of affecting or interfering with the State's sovereign functions (see *Corte di Cassazione (Sezioni Unite Civili), Federative Republic of Brazil v. De Vianna Dos Campos Riscado*, 13 February 2012, No. 1981; *Corte di Cassazione (Sezioni Unite Civili), Embassy of the Republic of Korea v. B.S.*, 17 January 2007, No. 880; *Corte di Cassazione (Sezione Unite Civili), Consulate of the Republic of Tunisia v. A.M.*, 10 July 2006, No. 15628). Noting that the claim brought by Mr Awad only concerned economic treatment, the Cassazione concluded that this claim fell outside the realm of *acta jure imperii* because the organisation of the Embassy "could not be affected by an order to pay compensation, because the employment relationship has already ceased, so that the asserted relevance and confidentiality of the functions once performed by the employee are irrelevant" (pp. 2-4).

As noted above, the approach adopted by the *Cassazione* seems to depart from a more recent line of precedents in which the court applied Article 11 UNCSI *qua* codification of customary international law, despite the fact that the UNCSI has not yet entered into force (see *Corte di Cassazione (Sezioni Unite Civili), Embassy of Spain to the Holy See v. De la Grana Gonzales*, 18 April 2014, No. 9034; *Corte di Cassazione (Sezioni Unite Civili), Académie de France à Rome v. Galamini di Recanati*, 18 September 2014, No. 19674 ("*Galamini*"); *Corte di Cassazione (Sezioni Unite Civili), Lasaracina v. Embassy of the United Arab Emirates*, 27 October 2014, No. 22744, IYIL, 2014, p. 468 ff., with a comment by ROSSI; *Corte di Cassazione (Sezioni Unite Civili), Ranasinghe Arachchige*

Neil Rohitha v. Embassy of the Republic of Korea to the Holy See, 9 June 2016, No. 11848, IYIL, 2016, p. 529 ff., with a comment by ROSSI). But such a change might be more apparent than real. The *Cassazione* did not clarify why it chose not to conform to its recent case law concerning the application of Article 11 UNCSI. The failure to adequately explain this choice may be a sign that the court was simply unaware of the differences between its pre-2014 jurisprudence and the UNCSI, so that the departure from the post-2014 precedents was in fact purely unintentional.

This may find confirmation in a second perplexing feature of this judgment, i.e. the fact that the Court did refer to Article 11 in passing when it stated that, in the present case, the subject matter of the claim did not interfere with the "security interests of the state". Pursuant to Article 11(2)(d) UNCSI, if "the subject-matter of the proceeding is the dismissal or termination of employment of an individual", the forum State's jurisdiction should be denied only if the employer State notifies the Court that such a proceeding would interfere with its security interests. By referring to this provision, the *Cassazione* seemed to imply that the jurisdiction of the Italian courts should have been ruled out if the Qatari authorities had made such a notification to the court.

Such a reference to Article 11(2)(d) UNCSI is faulty on several counts. Firstly, the Cassation did not clarify the legal basis for invoking the UNCSI and only referred to it *en passant*. Secondly, Article 11(2)(d) was manifestly inapplicable to the case, because the subject-matter of the proceedings was not "the dismissal or termination of employment of an individual". Indeed, the plaintiff did not complain about the legitimacy of the termination of his employment relationship, but merely asked for pecuniary benefits accrued as a result of his work for the Embassy. Thirdly, the effects of the inappropriate reference to Article 11(2)(d) are alarming, in that this provision leaves the choice to invoke an interference with "security interests" entirely at the foreign State's discretion (FOAKES and O'KEEFE, "Article 11", in O'KEEFE and TAMS (eds.), *The United Nations Convention on Jurisdictional Immunities of States and Their Property: A Commentary*, Oxford, 2013, p. 183 ff., pp. 204-205). In future cases, the application of this provision could become a dangerous weapon in the hands of employer States willing to evade proceedings.

Were it not for these inconsistencies, the discontinuation of the previous precedents concerning Article 11 UNCSI could be regarded as a largely positive development in itself, and this for mainly two reasons. Firstly, such precedents rested on weak legal grounds, in that the court never put forward any persuasive argument to demonstrate the correspondence between Article 11 and customary international law. Instead, it merely relied on some decisions in which the European Court of Human Rights (ECtHR) held that Article 11 UNCSI corresponds to customary international law in its entirety (see e.g. *Cudak v. Lithuania*, Application No. 15869/02, Judgment of 23 March 2010; *Guadagnino v. Italy and France*, Application No. 2555/03, Judgment of 18 January 2011; and *Sabeh El Leil v. France*, Application No. 34869/05, Judgment of 29 June 2011. The ECtHR more recently confirmed this view in *Naku v. Lithuania and Sweden*, Application No. 26126/07, Judgment of 8 November 2016). In their turn, the

ECtHR's findings on Article 11 have been criticized as being largely inaccurate (PAVONI, "The Myth of the Customary Nature of the United Nations Convention on State Immunity: Does the End Justify the Means?", in VAN AAKEN and MOTOC (eds.), *European Convention on Human Rights and General International Law*, Oxford, 2018, forthcoming; BEDERMAN, "Sabeh El Leil v. France", AJIL, 2012, p. 125 ff., pp. 129-130).

Secondly, the regime set forth by the pre-2014 jurisprudence of the *Cassazione* is for the most part more progressive and more favourable to the rights of employees than Article 11 UNCSI (with a notable exception in the area of compensation for unfair dismissal, where the jurisdiction of the Italian courts, which was routinely denied before 2014, has recently been affirmed pursuant to the relevant provisions of the UNCSI. A more detailed analysis of this point is developed below, with regard to Judgment No. 13980). Suffice it to point to the following difference between the two regimes. On the one hand, the order under scrutiny applied the maxim whereby States do not enjoy immunity in disputes regarding only pecuniary compensation, regardless of whether the plaintiff's duties involve the performance of acts *jure imperii* (see *Corte di Cassazione (Sezioni Unite Civili)*, *Vespignani v. Bianchi*, 22 July 2004, No. 13711, IYIL, Vol. XV, 2005, p. 317 ff., with a comment by PALOMBINO; FOCARELLI, ILDC 556 (IT 2004)). On the other hand, Article 11(2)(a) UNCSI excludes the jurisdiction of the forum State whenever "the employee has been recruited to perform particular functions in the exercise of governmental authority". The application of Article 11(2)(a) UNCSI to the case at hand might have resulted in the Cassation ruling in favour of immunity, had the court found that the duties performed by Mr. Awad fell into the realm of *acta jure imperii*. In this regard, it should also be noted that the problem of establishing whether an employee's duties require the performance of governmental authority is left completely unresolved by Article 11.

If Order No. 4882 gave the impression that the *Corte di Cassazione* did not really intend to depart from its precedents concerning Article 11 UNCSI once and for all, any doubt was dispelled by Judgment No. 13980. On that occasion, barely three months after delivering Order No. 4882, the Cassation handled the UNCSI in a completely different fashion and returned to applying Article 11 as the sole rule of decision.

Turning briefly to the facts of the case, Cleopatra Mutinta Chibomba was an Italian national working at the Embassy of the Republic of Zambia in Rome, where she performed administrative functions. Having been fired by the Embassy shortly after giving birth, she initiated proceedings before the *Tribunale di Roma* seeking to be reinstated in her job and to obtain pecuniary compensation for discriminatory dismissal. The Tribunal upheld Ms. Chibomba's claims because it found her dismissal to be in violation of the norms prohibiting dismissal during maternity leave and on return to work. It therefore held in favour of her reinstatement to her employment and of the payment of compensation. The Embassy appealed the first instance judgment before the *Corte d'appello di Roma*, alleging that the Italian courts lacked jurisdiction. The Court of Appeals held that any decisions concerning the termination of employment entailed an exercise of the foreign State's sovereign powers, hence it reversed the first instance judgment and upheld the immunity of the Embassy. Ms. Chibomba filed an appeal with the *Corte di Cassazione*.

The *Cassazione* developed a long and convoluted legal reasoning, starting with a truly baffling incipit. It began by recalling the principle of customary international law *par in parem non habet jurisdictionem* and by citing the judgment of the International Court of Justice in the case *Jurisdictional Immunities of the State, Germany v. Italy (Greece Intervening)*, ICJ Reports, 2012, p. 99 (*Germany v. Italy*), as the main authority in support of the existence of this norm. It then qualified the acts ascribable to the Embassy as a violation of the Convention on the Elimination of All Forms of Discrimination Against Women (CEDAW). Immediately afterwards, it stated, without further clarification, that the aforementioned principle of State immunity could not have any derogation even in the case of violations of CEDAW.

It is hard to understand what the court really meant to say. It could be conjectured that it was implicitly referring to its precedents in which it held that State immunity for *acta jure imperii* did not extend to claims of compensation brought by victims of grave breaches of fundamental human rights (most notably, *Corte di Cassazione (Sezioni Unite Civili), Ferrini v. Repubblica Federale di Germania*, 11 March 2004, No. 5044, on which see IOVANE, "The Ferrini Judgment of the Italian Supreme Court: Opening Up Domestic Courts to Claims of Reparation for Victims of Serious Violations of Fundamental Human Rights", IYIL, 2004, p. 165 ff.). If this interpretation is correct, the *Cassazione* likely meant to argue that violations of CEDAW could not be invoked to limit State immunity, because the ICJ judgment in *Germany v. Italy* held that such an exception was not admissible under customary international law. This argument, however, is perplexing on at least two grounds: firstly, both *Ferrini* and *Germany v. Italy* did not deal with State immunity in employment disputes and only concerned immunity for acts undisputedly to be qualified as *iure imperii*; and secondly, the Cassation made no mention of the landmark judgment in which the Italian Constitutional Court declared the *Germany v. Italy* judgment unconstitutional and barred its implementation by the Italian judges (*Corte Costituzionale, Simoncioni, Alessi and Bergamini v. Federal Republic of Germany and Presidency of the Council of Ministers*, 22 October 2014, No. 238, IYIL, 2014, p. 1 ff., with comments by FRANCIONI, PISILLO, BOTHE, CATALDI, and PALCHETTI; PAVONI, "Simoncioni v. Germany", AJIL, 2015, p. 400 ff.).

Be that as it may, the puzzling arguments put forward in the initial part of the decision did not appear to have any influence on the final outcome of the case. Indeed, shortly afterwards, and rather inconsistently, the *Corte di Cassazione* affirmed that its long-established case law favoured the application of the principle of restrictive immunity, which the court went on to apply. In particular, the *Cassazione* affirmed its intention to apply the principle of restrictive immunity as enshrined in Article 11 UNCSI. The court motivated this intention in the following terms:

> [Article 11 UNCSI] entered into force thirty days after the date of deposit of the thirtieth instrument of ratification, acceptance, ap-

proval or accession to the Secretary-General of the United Nations (Article 30 of the Convention). On the other hand, Article 4 of the Convention provides for its non-retroactivity, prescribing that it does not apply to any claim of immunity of States and their property raised in proceedings instituted against a State before a court of another State before the entry into force of the Convention. Nevertheless, this Court (Case No. 9034 of 18 April 2014), recalling the case law of the ECtHR, has held that Article 11 of the Convention reflects the evolution of customary law in the field under consideration and serves as a parameter of the compatibility of the judicial immunity of the defendant State with the guarantees of due process (pp. 10-11).

The logic of this passage is bizarre. To start with, the statement according to which the UNCSI would be already in force is plainly wrong: indeed, at the time of writing, the UNCSI has been ratified by only twenty-one States, compared to the thirty ratifications required by Article 30 for its entry into force. Moreover, the court errantly hinted at the impossibility of applying the Convention to the present case not to incur a violation of the principle of non-retroactivity set forth by Article 4, thus informing the reader that the fabled entry into force of the UNCSI would have occurred after the case at hand was brought to court. But overcoming Article 4 was a cakewalk for a particularly imaginative *Cassazione*: the relevant provisions of the UNCSI could nonetheless be applied thanks to their full correspondence to customary international law. In sum, such a labyrinthine reasoning led the court to nothing other than restating the arguments put forward in its aforementioned precedents where it held that Article 11 UNCSI should be applied as codification of customary international law.

Ultimately, the court found that, because Ms. Chibomba was an employee performing administrative functions, her tasks were not connected to the sovereign functions of the Embassy and, therefore, Article 11(2)(a) UNCSI (pursuant to which the State is immune from claims brought by employees "recruited to perform particular functions in the exercise of governmental authority") did not bar her claims. The Italian courts, however, retained jurisdiction only over the pecuniary claims related to the allegedly wrongful dismissal, while they lacked jurisdiction over the claim for reinstatement in employment, a conclusion which is once again fully in line with the *Cassazione*'s recent jurisprudence (see *Galamini, cit.*). The court reached this outcome by applying the combined provisions of Article 11(2)(c) UNCSI (barring the jurisdiction of the forum State over claims relating to the recruitment, renewal of employment, or reinstatement of an individual) and Article 11(2)(d) UNCSI (pursuant to which, if "the subject-matter of the proceeding is the dismissal or termination of employment of an individual", the forum State's jurisdiction is denied only if the employer State notifies the court that such a proceeding interferes with its security interests), even though – for some reason – it did not expressly refer to Article 11(2)(c) UNCSI and only mentioned Article 11(2)(d) UNCSI.

The usual caveat applies to the Cassation's reliance on the UNCSI to rule over this case, i.e. that this provision's purported correspondence to customary international law is to a large degree inaccurate. However, as briefly noted above, it should also be acknowledged that the UNCSI's provisions governing claims of compensation for wrongful dismissal are more favourable to the rights of the employees than the pre-2014 jurisprudence of the *Corte di Cassazione*. Before starting to apply the UNCSI in the context of employment disputes, the Cassation had constantly held that any inquiry into the reasons for dismissal would amount to unlawful interference with the sovereign authority of a foreign State and that, for this reason, the Italian courts lacked jurisdiction with regard to claims for compensation for wrongful dismissal (see, e.g., *Corte di Cassazione (Sezioni Unite Civili), Embassy of the Republic of Korea v. B.S.*, 17 January 2007, No. 880; *Corte di Cassazione (Sezione Unite Civili), Consulate of the Republic of Tunisia v. A.M.*, 10 July 2006, No. 15628; *Corte di Cassazione (Sezioni Unite Civili), Canadian State v. Cargnello*, 20 April 1998, No. 4017, IYIL, 1999, p. 152 ff., with a comment by IOVANE). The denial of jurisdiction over such claims was a rather self-contradictory feature of the court's pre-2014 take on this matter, as it ran counter to the principle whereby the pecuniary nature of the claim constituted the decisive criterion for assessing the jurisdiction of the Italian courts (for a criticism of this approach, see PAVONI, "La jurisprudence italienne sur l'immunité des États dans les différends en matière de travail: tendances récentes à la lumière de la Convention des Nations Unies", AFDI, 2007, p. 211 ff., pp. 217-219). This position on damages for wrongful dismissal was finally overturned in *Galamini*, the second case where the Cassazione applied the UNCSI *qua* customary international law.

However, the wording of Article 11 may cause the actual impact of this breakthrough to wear off. Firstly, as recalled above, Article 11(2)(d) entitles the employer State to designate a claim for wrongful dismissal damages as one that would interfere with its security interests, thus barring the jurisdiction of the courts of the territorial State. Secondly, the jurisdiction should be declined in all compensation claims submitted by unlawfully dismissed employees whom the court deems to fall under Article 11(2)(a), i.e. whose duties require the performance of acts qualified as *jure imperii*.

To conclude, the foregoing shows that Order No. 4882 comes across as destined to remain an isolated precedent and that the *Corte di Cassazione* will probably continue applying Article 11 UNCSI *qua* customary international law along the lines of Judgment No. 13980. But looking at this seeming jurisprudential inconsistency as no more than an involuntary bump in the road does not dispel all misgivings – and not just for the court's recurrent reliance on obscure or unsound legal arguments. In fact, two irreconcilable legal regimes currently coexist and overlap in the jurisprudence of the *Cassazione* and, what is worse, the court does not even seem to be aware of this (the Italian texts of the decisions are available at: <http://www.italgiure.giustizia.it>).

PIERFRANCESCO ROSSI

XII.   HUMAN RIGHTS

1. THE CARRYING OF A *KIRPAN* BETWEEN FREEDOM OF RELIGION, PUBLIC SAFETY AND THE (ALLEGED) DUTY OF MIGRANTS TO CONFORM TO THE VALUES OF THE "WESTERN WORLD"

Religious symbols – Article 9 of the European Convention on Human Rights (ECHR) – Public order – Values of the Western world

Corte di Cassazione (Sez. I Penale), 15 May 2017, No. 24084
Criminal proceedings against Singh Jatinder

In this judgment, the *Corte di Cassazione* ruled that carrying a *kirpan* – a curved knife considered a religious symbol – in public places is contrary to public safety and peaceful co-existence, as part of the notion of public order. Although the result reached by the *Cassazione* can in principle be shared, the underpinning legal reasons are rather questionable due to the inaccurate reference to the case-law of the European Court of Human Rights (ECtHR) concerning Article 9(2) the European Convention of Human Rights (ECHR). This shortcoming is also related to the affirmation whereby migrants would have a duty to conform their own values to those of the "Western world".

Prior to examining these critical aspects, it is worth summarising the factual and procedural background of the judgment under scrutiny. In 2013 the Italian police found that S.J., an adherent of Sikhism, was carrying a *kirpan* in public places. In 2015, the *Tribunale di Modena* sentenced S.J. to pay 2,000 euros as a fine for the crime provided by Article 4(2) of Law No. 110 of 18 April 1975. This provision prohibits carrying dangerous instruments in public places if such instruments, although not expressly qualified as weapons, can be used to wound people (so-called *"arma impropria"*). The only exonerating circumstance of the unlawfulness is the presence of a justified reason for carrying these tools. According to the *Tribunale*, the *kirpan* carried by S.J. was an instrument suitable to hurt people and the manifestation of the right of freedom of religion under Article 19 of the Italian Constitution did not constitute a justified reason to exempt the conviction. The *Tribunale di Modena* based its decision on the qualification of wearing religious symbols simply as a custom that, as such, cannot derogate from a criminal provision whose aim is protecting public security.

J.S. lodged an appeal before the *Corte di Cassazione* asking for the annulment of the first instance judgment on the grounds that carrying the *kirpan* is justified under his right of freedom of religion, whose manifestation is protected under Article 19 of the Italian Constitution. Furthermore, S.J. underlined that the *kirpan* is a religious symbol that orthodox Sikhs are obliged to wear as a mandatory religious requirement. The *Cassazione* upheld the first instance decision by stating that the symbolism related to wearing the knife does not constitute a justified reason under Article 4(2) of Law No. 110/1975, since no religious belief can be deemed as a legitimate ground to carry harmful instruments in public places. This conclusion was reached on the basis of the (alleged) duty of migrants to conform their own values to those of the "Western world", on the concept of public order, deemed as including the notion of public safety and peaceful co-existence, and on the case-law of the ECtHR concerning the restriction of the manifestation of the right of freedom of religion and belief under Article 9(2) ECHR.

As mentioned above, although the outcome can in principle be shared, the legal bases underlying the judgment are characterized by the inaccurate reference to the jurisprudence of the ECtHR on Article 9(2) ECHR. The *Corte di Cassazione* recalled that

> [t]he jurisprudence of the European Court of Human Rights concerning the Islamic veil in *Leyla Şahin Turkey*, Application No. 44774/98, Judgment of 10 November 2005, para. 111; *Refah Partisi (the Welfare Party) and Others v. Turkey*, Applications Nos. 41340/98, 41342/98, 41343/98 and 41344/98, Judgment of 13 February 2003, para. 93, acknowledges that a State can limit the manifestation of the right of freedom of religion if the exercise of that right hinders the aim of protecting the rights and freedom of others, public order and public safety. In the case of *Eweida and Others v. the United Kingdom*, Applications Nos. 48420/10, 59842/10, 51671/10 and 36516/10, Judgment of 15 January 2013, the Court deemed the restriction on the wearing of visible necklaces with Christian crosses at work as legitimate. The Court supported this outcome by recalling that, in the same work environment, employees adherent to Sikhism had complied with the request not to wear turbans or *kirpan* (a circumstance that demonstrates that the mandatory religious commandment of wearing the *kirpan* is not absolute and can be subjected to legitimate limitations (para. 2.6).

It is worth underlining that, while referring to a number of ECtHR judgments, the *Cassazione* omitted to mention either the factual backgrounds or the argumentative path underlying them, which are manifestly dissimilar to each other and to those of the case at hand. Indeed, the *Leyla Şahin* case concerned the prohibition for a student to wear the Islamic headscarf at university. The grounds for the compliance of the ban with Article 9 ECHR rely on the purpose of avoiding proselytism and the rise of fundamentalist religious movements, as well as of preserving the principle of secularism (*Leyla Şahin, cit. supra* para. 116). The *Refah Partisi* case concerned the Turkish Constitutional Court's decision to dissolve a political party whose members' actions and speeches were aimed at setting up a regime based on *sharia* law and which did not exclude the use of force in order to gain and retain political power. It is worth highlighting that the ECtHR declared that the judicial decision complied with Article 11 ECHR (freedom of association) and, at the same time, deemed the separate examination of the complaints under – *inter alia* – Articles 9 ECHR as unnecessary. The

Court's reasoning in these cases relies on the principles of democracy, among which the principle of secularism (*Refah Partisi, cit.*, paras. 120-123), and on the "pressing social need" underpinning the judicial decision (*Refah Partisi, cit.*, para. 133). Lastly, the *Eweida* case concerned the manifestation of freedom of religion at work. With reference to the second applicant's claim, a geriatric nurse whose employer requested to remove her necklace with the Christian cross, the ECtHR asserted the compliance of the request of the hospital manager with Article 9 ECHR since it pursued the legitimate aim of protecting health and safety (*Eweida, cit.*, paras. 99-100).

This brief overview outlines the controversial reference by the *Corte di Cassazione* to the ECtHR's case law. Taking into account the different circumstances and lines of reasoning featuring in each of the aforementioned ECtHR cases and in the case at hand, the *Corte* might have recalled other ECtHR judgments whose factual background or reasoning were closer to the ones of the case at hand. The reference is to *S.A.S. v. France* (Application No. 43835/11, Judgment of 26 June 2014), a case concerning the full-face veil ban in which the ECtHR restated its well-established case-law on the connection between religious expression and pluralism, according to which, as general principles, pluralism is one of the hallmarks of democratic societies, and democracy "does not simply mean that the views of a majority must always prevail". Against this background, the role of national authorities is "to ensure that the competing groups tolerate each other" (*S.A.S., cit.*, paras. 124-128). Moreover, in *S.A.S.* the ECtHR held that there had been no violation of Article 9 ECHR since, under certain conditions, the respect of "living together" may constitute the legitimate aim of the "protection of the rights and freedoms of others" under Article 9(2) ECHR (*S.A.S., cit.*, para. 121; for a different outcome, see the recent *Hamidović v. Bosnia and Herzegovina*, Application No. 57792/15, 5 December 2017, paras. 41-43).

Perhaps, quoting the *S.A.S.* case could have avoided the improper value-centred analysis outlined by the *Cassazione* in the judgment under scrutiny. Indeed, according to the *Corte*, the pluralism characterizing a multi-ethnic society, as protected under Article 2 of the Italian Constitution, is limited by the need to guarantee that the hosting society's legal culture is respected. Against this background, migrants are under the duty to conform their own values to those of the Western World and to respect the values of the hosting society (para. 2.3).

This statement raises several criticisms. Aside from the shift from the legal-based assessment to the ethical one and from the uncertainty surrounding the countries belonging to the "Western World" (see also e.g. NICO, "Ordine pubblico e libertà di religione in una società multiculturale", Osservatorio Costituzionale, 2017, available at: <https://www.olir.it/areetematiche/73/documents/kirpan.pdf>), the main shortcoming bears upon the challenging identification of a list of core values common to the states included in this notion (see e.g. CAVAGGION, "Diritto alla libertà religiosa, pubblica sicurezza e 'valori occidentali'. Le implicazioni della sentenza della Cassazione nel 'caso *kirpan*' per il modello di integrazione italiano", federalismi.it, 2017, available at: <http://www.federalismi.

it/>). This last critical aspect splits into two. The first is the general remark that the right to "keep and bear arms" is protected under the Second Amendment of the US Constitution. The second is specifically referred to the carrying of the *kirpan* as a religious symbol, that both European and other countries belonging to the "Western World" consider as legitimate (see e.g. Belgium, Court of appeal of Antwerp, 2009-01-14, No. 1204 P 2007 and No. 1205 P 2007; England, Wales and Northern Ireland, Criminal Justice Act 1988, Article 139(5); Scotland, Criminal Law (Consolidation) Act 1995, Article 49(5); Australia, Controls of Weapons Act 1990, section 8(B); United States, *New York v. Partap Singh*, 516 N.Y.S.2d 412 (1987); Canada, *Multani v Commission scolaire Marguerite-Bourgeoys*, (2006) 1 S.C.R. 256, 2006 SCC 6).

The *Cassazione*'s value-centred analysis and the following reference to the alleged duty to conform to the values of the "Western World" highlights a restrictive approach to the right enshrined in Article 9 ECHR, which is contrary to the ECtHR's case-law according to which "the reference to a tradition cannot relieve a Contracting State of its obligation to respect the rights and freedoms enshrined in the Convention and its Protocols" (see e.g. *Lautsi and Others v. Italy*, Application No. 30814/06, Judgment of 18 March 2011, para. 68). Furthermore, it is worth noting that this position differs from the line of reasoning of the previous case-law of the *Corte di Cassazione*, which in two earlier judgments reached the same outcome as the one under scrutiny by simply balancing the right to freedom of religion guaranteed by the Italian Constitution with that of public safety (*Corte di Cassazione (Sezione I penale)*, 24 February 2016, No. 25163; *Corte di Cassazione (Sezione I penale)*, 1 March 2016, No. 24739). Hence, even if the determination of the Court can in principle be shared, the reasoning behind it is rather controversial.

The last consideration bears upon the different outcome that the *Corte di Cassazione* could have reached by referring to *Ahmet Arslan and Others v. Turkey* (Application No 41135/98, Judgment of 23 February 2010) and *Hamidović v. Bosnia and Herzegovina* (Application No. 57792/15, Judgment of 5 December 2017) before the ECtHR. In the first judgment, the applicants complained about their conviction for wearing religious symbols in a public place. The Court found a violation of Article 9 ECHR due to the absence of a threat to public order, although among the religious symbols worn there was also a baton. In the second judgment, the applicant was convicted of contempt of court and fined for refusing to remove his skullcap. The Court upheld the applicant's position and found a violation of Article 9 ECHR, since the measure was not "necessary in a democratic society". Had the *Corte di Cassazione* followed this case-law, it would have either overruled its previous case-law or, at least, ascertained the disproportion of the fine imposed on the defendant. (The Italian text of the judgment is available at: <http://www.italgiure.giustizia.it/sncass/>).

GIULIA CILIBERTO

2. THE "INTERNATIONALISATION" OF THE PUBLIC POLICY CLAUSE IN THE
    RECENT DEVELOPMENTS OF THE ITALIAN CASE LAW: A BRIEF OVERVIEW

*Public policy – Internationalization – Punitive damages – Surrogate mother-
hood procedure – IVF program – Status filiationis – Best interest of the child*

Corte di Cassazione (Sezioni Unite Civili), 5 July 2017, No. 16601
Axo Sport Soc. v. Nosa Inc.

Corte di Cassazione (Sez. I Civile), 15 June 2017, No. 14878
S.F v. Procuratore Generale presso la Corte di Cassazione et al.
Corte Costituzionale, 22 November 2017, No. 272
A.L.C. v. curatore speciale di L.F.Z.

Whenever values which are totally alien to a legal tradition are to be taken
into account or foreign judgments have to be recognised, the public policy exception responds to the need to protect the coherence and to safeguard the fundamental principles of the relevant domestic legal system in a specific historical
moment (indeed, public policy is an ever-changing concept).

In modern times, due to the fact that each domestic legal system has increasingly opened to the other national legal systems but also to the international
legal order (conventions and general international law), these values go beyond
the mere principles recognised by national constitutions, since, over the years,
the domestic systems have been enriched by other fundamental principles deriving from European and international legal sources. In this respect, the critical
point is to understand to what extent the public policy clause, traditionally strictly
connected with domestic sovereignty, may be affected and broadened reflecting
these international values. In other words, it is interesting to question if these
international values may completely replace the domestic ones and lead to the
extreme consequence of creating a common notion of public policy which, due
to this process of "internationalisation", would be endorsed by a majority of the
legal systems (see CONTALDI, "Ordine Pubblico", in BARATTA (ed.) *Dizionario
di diritto internazionale privato*, Milano, 2010, p. 273 ff.; and FERACI, *L'ordine
pubblico nel diritto dell'Unione europea,* Milano, 2012, p. 19 ff.).

It is worth noting that in this particular historical moment the Italian legal
system is going through a highly challenging period. In fact, from the one side
it faces other European legal systems having introduced innovative solutions in
terms of same-sex marriages, surrogate motherhood or *in vitro* fertilization (IVF)
programs. From the other side, it has to deal also with legal instruments peculiar
to third countries, such as the US punitive damages or Islamic legal traditions
and related discrimination issues (see CONTALDI and GRIECO, "Art. 35 – Public
Policy", in CALVO CARAVACA, DAVÌ and MANSEL (eds.), *The EU Succession
Regulation. A Commentary*, Cambridge, 2016, p. 512 ff.).

Based on the above assumption, it is particularly interesting to understand
how the Italian courts are dealing with these increasingly frequent issues and how
they apply the "international" public policy clause to different sorts of cases.

The following comments regard three judgments, respectively on punitive damages, on the recognition of *status filiationis* acquired through an IVF program and on the deletion of a *status filiationis* recognised abroad on the basis of a surrogate motherhood procedure.

At long last, following other countries such as Spain, France, Slovenia, with the first judgment under consideration (No. 16601 of 5 July 2017), the *Corte di Cassazione* has shown openness to recognizing a judgment awarding punitive damages in the Italian legal system.

The Court examined the case of a US company (*Nosa Inc.*) which applied to the *Corte d'Appello di Venezia* to obtain enforcement of three different judgments delivered in the United States, having acquired the authority of final decisions. With these judgments US Courts accepted the request, promoted by *Nosa Inc.,* to approve a settlement agreement amounting to one million dollars, without specification of the different components of the damages awarded, concluded to the advantage of a motorcyclist, who was severely injured during a motocross competition due to an alleged flaw of the helmet produced by *Axo Sport*, an Italian firm, distributed by *Helmet House* and sold by *Nosa*. The American courts considered that *Nosa Inc.* was supposed to be guaranteed by *Axo Sport*. In this respect, *Nosa Inc.* obtained the recognition of the American judgments from the Court of Appeal of Venice. Nevertheless, *Axo Sport* promoted a further appeal in front of the *Corte di Cassazione*. According to the applicant's perspective, the *Corte d'Appello di Venezia* erred in the application of the potential liability test and neglected to consider the validity of the claim for guarantee. Moreover, the applicant alleged that the recognition of that sort of judgment was incompatible with public policy, pursuant to Article 64(g) of the Italian Statute on Private International Law (Law No. 218 of 31 May 1995).

In the case at hand, the Court recalled that the notion of public policy as concerns the recognition and enforcement of foreign judgments shall be intended as referred solely to the inviolable principles safeguarding the right to access to justice and the right of defence, but not also to the way in which these individual rights are protected in a specific legal system. The Italian court recalled the interpretation adopted by the ECJ as concerns the corresponding EU rules, even if these are not relevant to the present case being the judgment issued in a third country. According to those rules, up to a certain extent even the right of defence may be subjected to restrictions and/or conditions (see in this respect Case C-394/07, *Gambazzi v. Daimler Chrysler Canada Inc. and CIBC Mellon Trust Company*, ECR, 2009, I-2563). Furthermore, according to the previous case law of the Italian Court concerning *exequatur*, a violation of the right of defence may not be alleged in respect of each single infringement of foreign procedural rules, but solely for those which, considering their relevance, have caused a manifest violation of the right of defence affecting the entire trial (Judgment of 3 September 2015, No. 17519).

The applicant also claimed that the US judgments, considering the high amount of money recognised by way of compensation to the injured party, was a conviction for punitive damages, which should be considered as not allowed under the Italian legal system (see SARAVALLE, "I *punitive damages* nelle sentenze delle corti europee e dei tribunal arbitrali", RDIPP, 1997, p. 867 ff.).

Firstly, the Court recalled that it is not possible for the Italian court to proceed with a new reassessment of the damage since this aspect falls under the competence of the US Supreme Court. Secondly, the Italian court acknowledged that even in the absence of a clear specification of the different components of the damages awarded in the relevant judgment, it is not possible to presume a punitive aim in the conviction.

In this respect, it is possible to underline a *revirement* by the Italian *Corte di Cassazione*. In fact, in 2007 (Judgment of 19 January 2007, No. 1183) and in 2012 (Judgment of 8 February 2012, No. 1781), the Court refused to recognise a judgment concerning the same matter. Namely, in taking those decisions, the Court underlined that the role of civil liability within the Italian legal system was to restore the patrimonial situation of the damaged party by excluding any punitive purpose.

On the contrary, in this case, the Court has underlined that this approach shall be considered obsolete and no longer appropriate for this specific matter (the ever-changing nature of the public policy clause is particularly noticeable in this statement). Taking into consideration the legal development of modern society, civil liability has nowadays a new multi-purpose role, equally deterrent and reparatory. In this respect, the Court recalled that even within the Italian legal system there are several legislative examples in which civil liability goes beyond an aim of mere restoration (see e.g. Article 187-*undecies*(2), Legislative Decree No. 58 of 24 February 1998, concerning financial intermediation rules).

Formerly, the Italian Constitutional Court underlined, regarding Article 96 of the Italian Code of Civil Procedure, the deterrent rather than restorative aim of this specific rule (Judgment of 23 June, No. 152). Furthermore, the *Corte di Cassazione* itself recognised "punitive damages" as an instrument to prevent the violation of European Union law (Judgment of 15 March, No. 5072).

In conclusion, the *Corte di Cassazione* finally clarified this long-standing issue as follows:

> Given that civil liability has not just a restoration aim but also a deterrent and reparatory function, the US instrument of punitive damages may not be considered, *per se*, contrary to the Italian legal system. In this respect, in order to recognise a foreign judgment which includes a conviction for punitive damage, it is necessary to ensure that such a judgment has been delivered in the legal system of origin on a clearly determined legal basis and in compliance with a foreign procedural system which guarantees clear and foreseeable legislative rules and certain quantitative limitations to the conviction (para. 8).

On a completely different issue, with the second judgment under consideration (No. 14878 of 15 June 2017), the *Corte di Cassazione* addressed the case of

S.F. and *M.R.*, a married same-sex couple of Italian citizens habitually resident abroad, who applied to the Italian competent authority, pursuant to Articles 95 ff. of D.P.R. No. 396 of 3 November 2000, for the amendment of the birth certificate of the child *S.E.* Particularly, according to the birth certificate delivered by the competent UK authority, initially *S.E.* was registered as the biological son of *S.F.* following an IVF program. Later, the UK authorities clarified that the registration was incomplete. Given this, the child should have been registered as the son of both *S.F.* and *M.R.,* even if the latter had no biological connection with the child but just an "affective" one.

The registry officer (*Ufficiale di stato civile*) refused the amendment and, subsequently, the *Tribunale di Venezia* rejected the application for an order providing for the amendment because this would have been in contrast with the Italian public policy. The same stance has been taken on appeal by the *Corte d'Appello di Venezia*, which clarified that the measure requested was not a mere amendment but implied the evaluation of the validity of the same-sex marriage within the Italian legal system. Particularly, in order to support its decision the Court recalled a consolidated Italian case law, which considers the different sex of the spouses a basic precondition for the validity of the marriage (*Corte Costituzionale*, Judgment of 14 April 2010, No. 138, and *Corte di Cassazione*, Judgment of 15 March 2012, No. 4184).

It appears appropriate to underline that at the time that the Court of Appeal of Venice delivered its decision, the law on same-sex registered partnerships (*unioni civili*; Law No. 76 of 20 May 2016, so-called *Legge Cirinnà*) had not been adopted yet in Italy, and allegedly this circumstance affected the Court's perspective. In the same terms, the *Corte di Cassazione* underlined that the amendment of the birth certificate of the child in question necessarily required an examination of the validity, or, rather, of the effectiveness of a same-sex marriage within the Italian legal system, even if the applicants did not require the registration of the marriage itself. But, differently from the *Corte d'Appello di Venezia*, the Court underlined that a same-sex marriage within the Italian legal system shall not be considered invalid but merely ineffective.

This decision is a coherent and mindful development of a previous judgment whereby the Court adopted the same restrictive approach to the public policy clause in order to recognize a foreign judgment (see in this respect *Corte di Cassazione (Sez. I.), Procuratore Generale della Repubblica presso la Corte di Appello di Torino v. B.L.I.M. and R.V.M.,* 30 September 2016, No. 19599, IYIL, 2016, p. 542 ff., with a comment by Tonolo).

In the judgment under consideration, differently from the one examined above on punitive damages, the Court expressly recalled the traditional distinction between domestic and international public policy clauses, which it qualified as follows: there are two different concepts of public policy, a domestic one which operates as a limit to party autonomy, to be intended as subject to the national mandatory rules, and an international one which operates as a limit to the application of foreign law or to the recognition of a foreign judgment. Referring to the latter, the Court argued that reference shall be made to the "international" notion of public policy in the sense explained above, which requires an in-depth evaluation of the Italian constitutional principles but also of the relevant international legal sources.

> In order for an Italian court to deem a judgment as contrary to public policy, it must refer to our constitutional principles, but also, among others, to the UN Declaration on Human Rights, the European Convention on Human Rights, the European Treaties and the European Charter on Fundamental Rights and, as particularly concerns children and their interests, to the UN Declaration on the Rights of the Child, the UN Convention on the Rights of the Child and the procedural guarantees provided for by the European Convention on Human Rights (p. 15).

The Court recalled the European Convention on Human Rights (ECHR), particularly Articles 12, 8 and 14, referring respectively to the right to marry and found a family, to the right to respect for private and family life and to the prohibition of discrimination. Besides, the Court referred also to Articles 2, 3, 6 and 7 of the Convention on the Rights of the Child. According to the latter, the best interest of the child has to be a primary consideration. In this respect, the Court recalled also EC Regulation No. 2201/2003 and the Hague Convention of 29 May 1993 on Protection of Children and Co-operation in Respect of Intercountry Adoption, both of which provide that the evaluation of compatibility with public policy has to be made taking into consideration the best interest of the child. Moreover, the Court referred also to the Italian national system, reminding that the recent legislative reform has led to a single *status filitiationis* in order to avoid any sort of discrimination among children.

With respect to the recognition of same-sex marriages, the Court recalled the position adopted by the ECtHR, which on several occasions (e.g. *Schalk and Kopf v. Austria*, Application No. 30141/04, Judgment of 24 June 2010) underlined that the right to have a family shall not be limited to heterosexual couples. However, it should also be borne in mind that the ECtHR finds that Article 12 of the Convention does not impose an obligation on governments to grant same-sex couple marriage, since marriage has deep-rooted social and cultural connotations which may differ largely from one society to another (Legislative Decree No. 154 of 28 December 2013, No. 154).

Referring particularly to the public policy clause, the ECtHR clarified that its application must be evaluated taking into account the *best interest of the child* and the parental relationship (*Mennesson v. France* and *Labassée v. France*, Application No. 65941/11 and Application No. 65942/11, Judgments of 26 June 2014; and also, for a recent application of the same principle, *Paradiso and Campanelli v. Italy*, Grand Chamber, Application No. 25358/12, Judgment of 27 January 2015).

Given the above, the *Corte di Cassazione* underlined that, even if the Italian Law No. 40 of 19 February 2004 governing IVF program requires the diversity of sex within the couple,

[i]n this case, since the program was completed abroad, and the results have been already certificated by the competent authorities of a foreign country, the amendment of the birth certificate shall not be considered in contrast with the international public policy clause (p. 23).

This decision is noteworthy. The Italian Court in this case applied a truly international concept of public policy by recalling almost solely international legal sources instead of domestic ones. Moreover, the Court has strengthened the role of same-sex partnerships in the Italian legal system by emphasizing the similarities with the traditional marriage reserved to heterosexual couples, based on Article 1, para. 20, Law No. 76 of 20 May 2016, which, even if with some exceptions, extends the rights and duties of spouses to same-sex couples. This question is distinct from the *status filitiationis* issue, since the latter, from the perspective of the Italian legislator, is completely apart from the relationship between the parents. On the contrary, the decision does not properly address the profile of "social parenting" or "affective parenting", which nowadays, given the various concepts of families relied upon as part of the domestic legal systems, is a crucial aspect.

In the latter respect, this decision represents a missed opportunity for the Italian *Corte di Cassazione*, even in consideration of the position adopted by the ECtHR on this specific issue.

By means of the third and last judgment under consideration (No. 272 of 22 November 2017), the Italian *Corte Costituzionale* addressed an issue concerning the possibility to delete from the Italian civil status records the registration of a birth certificate (made abroad) regarding a child who was born following a surrogate motherhood program but who was registered in Italy as the biological son of both parents (while just the father had a biological connection). Nowadays, surrogacy is a widespread practice for childless parents and surrogacy laws vary widely from State to State (see TONOLO, "Identità personale, maternità surrogata e superiore interesse del minore nella più recente giurisprudenza della Corte europea dei diritti dell'uomo", DUDI, 2015, p. 208 ff.).

The detection of this circumstance led the *Tribunale di Milano* to declare that the surrogate motherhood program was based on an agreement contrary to Italian public policy. For this reason, the registration of the birth certificate should have been deleted from the relevant records. The *Corte d'Appello di Milano*, having doubts concerning the legitimacy of such a measure, referred the issue to the *Corte Costituzionale*. The Court of Appeal underlined that it was not about questioning the possibility to register a birth certificate made abroad in a country where surrogate motherhood is allowed, but about the possibility to withdraw a *status* already recognized since it was discovered as certainly untrue.

According to the *Corte Costituzionale*, it is imperative to guarantee an appropriate balance between the interest of the legal system to seek the truth and the best interest of the child. However, Article 263 of the Italian Civil Code, which provides for the right to appeal against the recognition of a biological child when the declared circumstances turn out to be untrue, is not in contrast with the Italian Constitution for the sole reason that it does not subject that right to appeal to the condition of meeting the best interest of the child. For the Italian Constitutional Court, in fact, the national and the international legal frameworks do not require, in every legal action concerning the removal of a *status filiationis,* the absolute and indiscriminate priority of this assessment. In this respect, the Court argued that where there is a divergence between biological identity and legal identity it is necessary to proceed with an appropriate balancing among the different needs at stake (see MARONGIU BUONAIUTI, "Il riconoscimento delle adozioni da parte di coppie di persone dello stesso sesso al vaglio della Corte costituzionale", Ordine internazionale e diritti umani, 2014, p. 1135 ff.).

It is worth noting that the Court referred to a changed legal framework by recalling the relevant international legal sources (the above mentioned conventions plus the Recommendation adopted by the Committee of Ministers of the Council of Europe, on 17 November 2010, for a child-friendly Justice, available at: <https://rm.coe.int/16804b2cf3>). The Court also expressly underlined that the *best interest of the child* is a recognised principle thanks to the consolidated case law of the ECtHR (*Mennesson v. France* and *Labassée v. France, cit.*). At present, given the relevant international legal framework, the *best interest of the child* must be held as a recognized principle in the Italian legal system as well, and it must be taken into consideration in all legal actions aimed to withdraw a *status filiationis*, even if this has been recognised abroad.

Nevertheless, in the Court's view, this means that the best interest of the child might also be identified in the right for the child to become aware of his or her true personal biological story. In addition, the Court argued that in the development of a modern concept of family, the genetic bond is not a necessary requirement for the existence of a family. However, it cannot be underestimated that in some cases the interest of the legal system for the truth conveys a public value, especially when reference is made to some specific cases, such as surrogate motherhood which is expressly forbidden under the Italian legal system (according to Article 12, para. 6, Law No. 40/2004) since, in the Court's view, it intolerably violates women's dignity and jeopardizes human relationships.

The *Corte Costituzionale*, in rejecting the issue of constitutionality concerning Article 263 of the Italian Civil Code, concludes by underlining that sometimes the balancing among different values shall be done directly by the legislator, but in other cases, such as that under consideration, a specific comparative evaluation shall be made by the judge on a case-by-case approach, by taking into account on the one side the best interest of the child and on the other side the general interest in legal certainty. Aprioristically, none of these demands shall take precedence over the other. The Italian texts of the decisions of the Court of Cassation are available at: <http://www.italgiure.giustizia.it/sncass/>; the judgment of the Constitutional Court is available at: <www.corte-costituzionale.it>).

CRISTINA GRIECO

XIII. INTERNATIONAL CRIMINAL LAW

1. Germany Held Responsible for the Nazi Massacre of Pietransieri

Immunity of foreign States from jurisdiction – Judgment No. 238/2014 of the Italian Constitutional Court – International crimes – Admission of responsibility

Tribunale di Sulmona, 2 November 2017, No. 20
Comune di Roccaraso and others v. Germany and Ministry of Foreign Affairs of Italy

By Order delivered on 2 November 2017, the Italian *Tribunale di Sulmona* ordered Germany to pay about 7 million euros as compensation to the town of Roccaraso and to the heirs of more than 100 civilian victims of the massacre known as *"Eccidio dei Limmari"*, carried out in the village of Pietransieri, municipality of Roccaraso, between 16 and 21 November 1943, by the Nazis' armed forces.

The *Tribunale di Sulmona* reaffirmed the approach followed by the Italian *Corte Costituzionale* by means of the Judgment No. 238/2014, and then abided by the Italian courts in several disputes on cases related to serious crimes committed in Italy by Nazis' armed forces during World War II (a number of cases are reported and commented in Pavoni, "How Broad is the Principle Upheld by the Italian Constitutional Court in Judgment No. 238?", JICJ, 2016, p. 573 ff.; and Forlati, IYIL, 2015, p. 497 ff.).

As is well known, after the 2012 ICJ Judgment (ICJ, *Jurisdictional Immunities of the State (Germany v. Italy: Greece intervening)*, Judgment, 3 February 2012, ICJ Reports, 2012, p. 99 ff.), the *Corte Costituzionale*, by its Judgment No. 238/2014, found that Italian courts have jurisdiction on claims for compensation filed against foreign States, related to the commission of an international crime by State agents *(jure imperii)*. The *Corte Costituzionale* ruled that in such cases, relying upon the "counter-limits doctrine", the principle of jurisdictional immunity of the States should not be applied (on these topics see the wide discussion in IYIL, 2014, with contributions by Francioni, Pisillo Mazzeschi, Bothe, Cataldi, and Palchetti. See also Pavoni, "Simoncioni v. Germany. Judgment No. 238/2014", AJIL, 2015, p. 400 ff.).

These are the facts around which the dispute took place: the town of Roccaraso (along with the village of Pietransieri) is located near the Gustav Defence Line that ran across Italy and in the Abruzzo region coincided with the mouth of the Sangro river. The Gustav Line was built by the Nazis in the Autumn of 1943 to halt or hinder the advance of the Allied forces from the South to Northern Italy. At that time, the Nazis' 3rd Battalion belonging to the 1st Regiment of the 1st paratroopers Division, under the command of the Field Marshal Kesselring, was stationed there. With the purpose of ensuring a "security zone" near the Gustav Line, on 3 October 1943 Kesselring ordered the town of Roccaraso, including the village of Pietransieri, to be evacuated by the following day, and, as reported by the *Tribunale di Sulmona*, he also warned that "after the aforementioned date and time, all those who will still be in the village or in the surrounding mountains will be considered rebels and they shall be subjected to the laws of war established by the German army" (Order No. 20/2017, para. IV-8). For 15 days the Nazis tolerated disobedience to the evacuation order, without forcibly evicting the civilian population remained in their homes, but from 16 November onwards they began to capture and kill many inhabitants. On 20 November, along the Sangro river, clashes between Nazis and the Allied forces began. At that point, the Nazis, no longer intending to postpone the liberation of the security zone, in the morning of 21 November carried out the killing of over one hundred inhabitants who had taken refuge in some farmhouses located outside the village, in the area known as "*Limmari*". It is estimated that between 16 and 21 November 1943, 128 members of the population of Pietransieri, mostly elderly, women and children, were exterminated.

The massacre was neither a reprisal to the killing of German soldiers (not even recorded in the war diaries of Nazi paratroopers), nor a reaction to the assistance provided by civilians to partisan Resistance groups (they never claimed any activity in the area), nor a way to punish disobedience with respect to the evacuation order (even by applying the German legislation in force at that time, there was no legal basis for the killing of civilians, nor a court martial had been previously convened). Instead, according to the *Tribunale di Sulmona*, this massacre was the instrument through which the Nazis, frightened by the advance of the Allied forces, arbitrarily solved the problem of the persistent presence of civilians in the security zone closest to the Gustav Line (Order No. 20/2017, *cit. supra*, para. IV-13). The *Tribunale* held that the extermination of Pietransieri's civilians amounted to a war crime and a crime against humanity, and, at the same time, as a crime under the Italian Criminal Code and Military Criminal Code applicable in time of war, both of them in force at the time of those events.

Germany, as successor of the Third Reich, was found responsible for the crimes committed in Pietransieri. Therefore, the heirs of the victims and the municipality of Roccaraso, were awarded compensation, quantified at about 7 million euros, for the harm caused by the Nazis' acts, plus 150,000 euros for litigation costs.

The Order No. 20/2017 deals with some elements of interest and originality that are worth dwelling on. In the first place, it should be noted that the *Tribunale*, while reaffirming the principle stated in the Judgment No. 238/2014, curiously goes so far as to question the current persistence of the customary norm on the jurisdictional immunity of the States as construed by the ICJ. The *Tribunale* justifies this finding by referring to the time now elapsed since the ICJ 2012 Judgment, and to the case law of the Italian courts that have largely adhered to the principle affirmed by the *Corte Costituzionale*'s 2014 Judgment. It would seem appropriate to point out that the *Corte Costituzionale*, in trusting that the principle at stake could have contributed to the development of the international law on immunity (Judgment No. 238/2014, *In Law*, para. 3.3), seemed not to have relied only on its endorsement within national borders. On the contrary, the *Corte Costituzionale* was likely to expect such a development of the international law only if the principle at hand was also backed within other States.

To date it seems that the principle at stake, as literally affirmed in the Judgment No. 238/2014, did not go beyond national borders, but was only endorsed in Italian domestic case law. However, it should be recalled that there are cases outside Italy in which, although in different contexts, exceptions to the law on jurisdictional immunity have been allowed, as it happens in the US and Canada, under the practice of the "terrorism exception" to State immunity (ESPOSITO, "Jus Cogens and Jurisdictional Immunities of States at the International Court of Justice: 'A Conflict Does Exist'", IYIL, 2011, p. 161 ff.). Nevertheless, such exceptions to State immunity, developed within the Italian and North American context, do not seem yet suitable to lead to the conclusion that the international law on jurisdictional immunity has somehow evolved. However, a kind of "persistent dynamism" of the law on immunity might be inferred from this practice (PAVONI, "After *Sentenza 238*: A Plea for Legal Peace", in VOLPE, PETERS, and BATTINI (eds.), "Remedies against Immunity? Reconciling international and domestic law after the Italian Constitutional Court's *Sentenza 238/2014*", 2018, forthcoming).

The second question to be highlighted concerns the impact within the lawsuit at hand of a sort of admission of responsibility entered by Germany in a previous proceeding stemmed from the slaughter of Pietransieri, as well, and concerning the same facts, subsequently discontinued after the ICJ 2012 Judgment (*Tribunale di Sulmona, Comune di Roccaraso and others v. Germany, Presidency of the Council of Ministers of Italy, Ministry of Finance of Italy and Ministry of Foreign Affairs of Italy*, Case No. 83/2012, cancelled).

Appearing in this civil lawsuit, Germany filed a statement of defence dated 26 November 2012 in which it declared that "the terrible crimes perpetrated against the unarmed civilian population, constitute an incontrovertible reality, the moral weight of which falls on the German people and for whose responsibility Germany also here asks for the forgiveness of the victims, their relatives and all the Italian people" (Order No. 20/2017, para. IV-2). Such an argument, as Germany maintained in the same statement, could not be questioned by its defence strategy that was based on the international law on State immunity, and aimed at denying the Italian courts' jurisdiction.

On the contrary, throughout the proceeding here debated, that resulted in the 2017 Order, as well as the others that arose all over Italy after Judgment No. 238/2014, Germany failed to attend or take action, so the lawsuit continued *in absentia*. Germany merely transmitted an act (*Nota verbale*, 17 July 2015, No. 2/15, sent by post to the *Tribunale di Sulmona* and to the Italian Ministry of Foreign Affairs) unsuitable to be qualified as an act of proceeding, and unfit to be used therein, through which it announced that it would not have filed further documents during the proceeding, as it did not recognize the Italian jurisdiction in that lawsuit, according to the ICJ 2012 Judgment. Instead, the Italian Ministry of Foreign Affairs intervened, appearing in the *Tribunale*, and filed a third party statement, in which it maintained to be interested in the rejection of the plaintiffs' claim. The latter, according to the Ministry's view, was filed in breach of the immunity to which foreign States are entitled under international customary law. The Ministry also stressed the risk that Italy would have been held responsible for an internationally wrongful act if Germany had been ordered to compensate the plaintiffs. Despite Germany's default, the *Tribunale di Sulmona* acquired Germany's statement of defence submitted in the previous lawsuit No. 83/2012. While not qualifying it as a sort of admission of responsibility, as it was signed only by Germany's counsel, the *Tribunale* considered it as a clue, to be taken into account along with the evidence adduced by the plaintiffs, anyhow useful for the decision (the Italian text of the decision is available at: <http://www.europeanrights.eu/public/sentenze/ITA-Tribunale_di_Sulmona_strage_di_pietransieri_Sulmona.pdf>).

FERDINANDO FRANCESCHELLI

XVII. RELATIONSHIP BETWEEN MUNICIPAL AND INTERNATIONAL LAW

1. TO LUXEMBOURG AND BACK: HOW JUDICIAL DIALOGUE AVOIDED A NORMATIVE CLASH BETWEEN THE EU AND ITALIAN LEGAL ORDERS

"Taricco" judgment – Article 325 of the Treaty on the Functioning of the European Union – Financial interests of the European Union – Limitation periods – Primacy of EU law – Preliminary reference – Counter-limits doctrine – Supreme constitutional principles – Principle of legality in criminal matters – Article 25(2) of the Italian Constitution – Article 7 of the European Convention on Human Rights – Article 49 of the Charter of Fundamental Rights of the European Union – Article 4(2) of the Treaty on European Union – "National identity" clause

Corte Costituzionale, 26 January 2017, No. 24
Criminal proceedings against Mauro Bertoni and others
Criminal proceedings against D.B.C. and others

It is an established practice of the Italian Yearbook of International Law not to review Italian judicial decisions dealing with issues of pure EU law. Still, the *Taricco* saga – of which the Order under comment represents one the latest developments – certainly deserves to be an exception, since it raises a number of unprecedented and fundamental problems concerning the relationship between domestic and EU legal orders, with particular regard to the so-called "counter-limits doctrine". The counter-limits doctrine, as it is known, is designed to shield national fundamental values from external interferences, by requiring domestic judges to refrain from applying international and supranational norms (even through a declaration of unconstitutionality if required) which do not conform with the national Constitution, or at least with its core principles.

The beginning of the second decade of the 2000s witnessed an unusual recurrence, in Italian case law, of requiem for this doctrine. This trend was ushered in by the *Corte di Cassazione*, which noted how, in the light of the enhanced role of the Court of Justice of the EU (CJEU) in the protection of human rights and the transformation of the EU Charter of Fundamental Rights into binding primary law, the "theory of counter-limits [...] seems now in open contradiction with the very notion of integration [...], to the point that a conflict between EU and domestic law does not appear to be conceivable in a truly integrated European legal space" (*Corte di Cassazione (Sez. Tributaria)*, 19 November 2010, No. 23418, para. 8.3; see also, in the very same terms, *Corte di Cassazione (Sez. Tributaria)*, *Formazione Innovazione Lavoro s.p.a. v. Agenzia delle Entrate*, 16 May 2012, No. 7659, para. 9). This view was reaffirmed, about a year later, by the *Consiglio di Stato*, which in 2011 stressed its "decline", mainly due to the fact that the notion of counter-limit "implies a pre-established hierarchy of the sources relating to the protection of fundamental rights", while sources of law should be seen "in virtuous competition with each other" in order to ensure the fullest enjoyment of these rights (*Consiglio di Stato (Sez. VI)*, *Di Lenardo Adriano Srl and Dilexport Srl v. Ministero dello sviluppo economico*, 9 August 2011, No. 4723, para. 7.3., IYIL, 2011, p. 382 ff., with a comment by AMOROSO; CHECHI, ILDC 1957 (IT 2011)). In a similar vein, the First President of the *Corte di Cassazione*, in his Report on the Administration of Justice in 2012, branded this doctrine as "outdated", to the extent that it is based on concerns that no longer reflect the current status of the relationships among legal orders (LUPO, *Relazione sull'amministrazione della giustizia nell'anno 2012*, Roma, 2013, p. 17).

In fact, the death bell of the counter-limits doctrine was rung too early. Aside from the fact that the above remarks overlook that the doctrine is applicable – *and has been renownedly applied* – also to general international law (*Corte Costituzionale, Simoncioni, Alessi and Bergamini v. Federal Republic of Germany and Presidency of the Council of Ministers*, 22 October 2014, No. 238, IYIL, 2014, p. 1 ff., with comments by FRANCIONI, PISILLO, BOTHE, CATALDI, and PALCHETTI; CHECHI, ILDC 2237 (IT 2014)) and treaty law (*Corte Costituzionale, Ministro degli Interni v. Lorenzon Guido Luciano*, 28 November 2012, No. 264, IYIL, 2011, p. 454 ff., with a comment by PALOMBINO; NESSI, ILDC 2062 (IT 2012)), there was no reason to consider it obsolete with regard to EU law. As it was aptly noted, its *raison d'être* will cease only when the EU integration process is finalised with "the dissolution of the integrated legal orders into the integrating one" – a "federalist" outcome that is far from being realised in the EU (MODUGNO, "Ancora sui «controlimiti» alla c.d. primarietà o primazia (preminenza) del diritto comunitario", in BARGIACCHI et al. (eds.), *Studi in onore di Augusto Sinagra*, Roma, 2013, p. 11 ff., p. 26).

And indeed, as the Order under comment highlights, the counter-limits doctrine is still alive and well, although it should be acknowledged that the *Corte Costituzionale* is clearly reluctant to activate it in relation to EU law.

The legal and factual background of the *Taricco* saga is widely known and, at the same time, slightly intricate. Only a brief outline will be here provided (for a fuller account see BERNARDI, "I controlimiti al diritto dell'Unione europea e il loro discusso ruolo in ambito penale", in BERNARDI (ed.), *I controlimiti. Primato delle norme europee e difesa dei principi costituzionali*, Napoli, 2017, p. VII ff., pp. XCIII-CXXVII). In 2014 the *Tribunale di Cuneo* submitted to the CJEU a request for a preliminary ruling concerning the compatibility with EU law of the Italian regime on limitation periods for criminal offences, set out by Articles 160(3) and 161(2) of the Criminal Code, insofar as it granted impunity to the perpetrators of tax fraud aimed at evading VAT. On the premise that the collection of VAT revenue represents a EU budgetary resources, the CJEU found that the aforementioned provisions of the Italian Criminal Code give rise to serious issues of compatibility with the obligation of Member States to "counter fraud and any other illegal activities affecting the financial interests of the Union" under Article 325(1) and (2) of the Treaty on the Functioning of the European Union (TFEU). In particular, the CJEU held that the Italian regime on limitation period for criminal offences:

> […] is liable to have an adverse effect on fulfilment of the Member States' obligations under Article 325(1) and (2) TFEU if that national rule prevents the imposition of effective and dissuasive penalties in a significant number of cases of serious fraud affecting the financial interests of the European Union, or provides for longer limitation periods in respect of cases of fraud affecting the financial interests of the Member State concerned than in respect of those affecting the financial interests of the European Union, which it is for the national court to verify (Case C-105/14, *Criminal proceedings against Ivo Taricco and others*, 5 September 2015, para. 58).

Accordingly, it instructed Italian courts to disapply Articles 160(3) and 161(2) of the Criminal Code whenever their application would prevent the fulfillment of the obligations arising under Article 325(1) and (2) TFEU. In the aftermath of this ruling, some Italian courts adhered – more or less faithfully – to the CJEU's *dictum* (see the judgments analysed by RUOPPO, "I giudici di legittimità tra 'primato' del diritto dell'Unione Europea e principio di legalità in materia penale", Giur. It., 2017, p. 193 ff.). Yet, the *Corte di appello di Milano*, and at a later time the Third Criminal Section of the *Corte di Cassazione*, questioned the compatibility of the rule asserted in *Taricco* with the Italian Constitution. Therefore, they referred to the *Corte Costituzionale* a question of constitutionality with respect to Article 2 of the law implementing the Lisbon Treaty (Law No. 130 of 2 August 2008), to the extent that it gave legal effect to Article 325 TFEU as interpreted by the CJEU. To put it bluntly, they asked the *Corte* to trigger the counter-limits doctrine.

The doubts of constitutionality raised by the referring courts revolved around the principle of legality under Article 25(2) of the Italian Constitution, having regard to the principles – deriving therefrom – of precision of criminal law (*principio di determinatezza*) and non-retroactivity *in mala partem*. On the one hand, indeed, they complained that the CJEU left too much discretion to national criminal judges, as it did not clarify under what conditions a fraud qualifies as "serious" or the application of the Italian regime on limitation periods grants impunity to wrongdoers "in a significant number of cases". On the other hand, they underscored that the CJEU ordered national judges to apply a stricter regime on limitation periods to offences committed before the *Taricco* judgment was handed down.

While sharing the concerns voiced by the *Corte di appello* and the *Corte di Cassazione*, the *Corte Costituzionale* declined the invitation to resort to the counter-limits doctrine, by preferring to seek – with the Order under analysis – another preliminary ruling from the CJEU. The reasoning followed by the *Corte Costituzionale* to support this (further) request is condensed in few, but substantial, pages and may be summarised as follows.

At the outset the *Corte* recalled that, in the Italian legal order, the regime on limitation period for criminal offences is conceptualised in substantive terms, and thus it is subject to the principle of legality under Article 25(2) of the Constitution. That such an approach is at variance with the one taken by other EU Member States, the CJEU and European Court of Human Rights (for which limitation periods are a procedural matter, unrestrained by the principle of legality) is, in the opinion of the *Corte*, ultimately immaterial. Since "there is no requirement whatsoever for uniformity across European legal systems regarding this aspect", the *Corte* argued, "[e]ach Member State is therefore free to conceptualise the limitation of criminal offences in either substantive or procedural terms, in accordance with its own constitutional tradition" (para. 4). The *Corte* also noted that this point was not addressed in *Taricco*, where the issue was analysed only from the angle of Article 49 of the Charter of Fundamental Rights of the European Union (CFREU) and Article 7 of the European Convention on Human Rights.

The *Corte* then proceeded to assess whether the directions given by the CJEU to Italian courts in *Taricco* were compatible with the principle of legality. In this respect, it should be noted that the *Corte* dwelled mostly (if not exclusively) on the principle of precision of criminal law, somehow leaving the principle of non-retroactivity in *malam partem* in the background. This could be explained with the fact – underlined by the same *Corte* (paras. 7 and 9) – that the CJEU ruled out the incompatibility between the rule asserted in *Taricco* and the principle of legality solely with regard to the prohibition of retroactivity, and not with the principle of precision.

The *Corte Costituzionale* examined this aspect in two steps. In the first one, it gauged the foreseeability of the interpretation of Article 325(1) and (2) TFEU set forth in *Taricco*, having particular regard to its repercussions on the Italian regime of limitation periods. After underlining that this was in no way aimed at questioning the authoritative interpretation of EU law provided by the CJEU, the *Corte* reached the conclusion that

> an individual could not have reasonably considered, prior to the judgment given in the Taricco case, that Article 325 TFEU required the courts to disregard Articles 160, last paragraph, and 161(2) of the Criminal Code in situations in which this would have resulted in an exemption from punishment in a considerable number of cases involving serious fraud affecting the financial interests of the Union, specifically in breach of the principle of assimilation (para. 5).

In the second step, the *Corte Costituzionale* tested the rule asserted in *Taricco* against the principle of the rule of law in criminal matters (*riserva di legge in materia penale*). In this regard, it upheld the doubts raised by the referring judges and observed that the requirement set out by the CJEU as a condition to disapply the Italian regime on limitation period (i.e. that it granted impunity in "a significant number of cases of serious fraud") was too vague and ends up endowing criminal judges with a veritable legislative competence, in blatant disregard of the principle of separation of powers. In the *Corte*'s words,

> it is not possible for EU law to set an objective as to the result for the criminal courts and for the courts to be required to fulfil it using any means available within the legal order, without any legislation laying down detailed definitions of factual circumstances and prerequisites (para. 5).

Having ascertained that the *Taricco* judgment actually posed a problem of compatibility with the Italian Constitution, the *Corte* addressed the gist of its request in a preliminary ruling. Notably, it wondered whether the CJEU intended to direct Italian judges to abide by its interpretation of Article 325 TFEU even when it conflicted with a core constitutional principle, such as that of legality. Significantly enough, the discussion of this point was opened by a remark which appears to be halfway between a diplomatic plea and a threat: "This Court thinks that [the CJEU] did not [intend to do so], but considers that it is in any case appropriate to bring the doubt to [its] attention" (para. 6). To justify this conclusion, the *Corte* referred to the EU's motto "United in diversity", as well as to a number of foundational principles enshrined in the Lisbon Treaty, namely the principles of pluralism (Article 2 of the Treaty on European Union, TEU), of sincere cooperation (Article 4(3) TEU), of respect for national identities (Article 4(2) TEU). Relying on these principles, in particular, the *Corte* made the case for a substantive (rather than merely formal) conception of the primacy of EU law in a passage that deserves to be quoted in full:

> The primacy of EU law does not express a mere technical configuration of the system of national and supranational sources of law. It rather reflects the conviction that the objective of unity, within the context of a legal order that ensures peace and justice between nations, justifies the renunciation of areas of sovereignty, even if defined through constitutional law. At the same time, the legitimation for (Article 11 of the Italian Constitution) and the very force of unity within a legal order characterised by pluralism (Article 2 TEU) result from its capacity to embrace the minimum level of diversity that is necessary in order to preserve the national identity inherent within the fundamental structure of the Member State (Article 4(2) TEU) (para. 6).

The primacy of EU law, in other words, could not be construed so as to compel a Member State to renounce its fundamental principles. But what court should be competent to establish whether EU law conflicts with a domestic fundamental principle? According to the *Corte Costituzionale*, this assessment should be entrusted to national courts (in Italy the *Corte Costituzionale* itself), without prejudice to the competence of the CJEU to ensure the uniform interpretation of EU law and to define its scope of application (para. 6). Should the CJEU confirm this understanding of the relationship between EU law and domestic fundamental principles, the *Corte* concludes, "no grounds for contrast would remain" and there would be no reason to invoke the counter-limits doctrine (para. 7).

At this juncture, the *Corte* made a further, two-pronged argumentative effort. On the one hand, it suggested that its view was somehow implied in the same *Taricco* judgment (para. 7), insofar as the CJEU stated that "if the national court decides to disapply the national provisions [on limitation periods], it must also ensure that the fundamental rights of the persons concerned are respected" (*Taricco, cit.*, para. 53) and that the disapplication of national norms on limitation periods is "subject to verification by the national court" (*ibid.*, para. 55).

On the other hand, it bothered to distinguish the present case from *Melloni* (Case C-399/11, *Stefano Melloni v. Ministerio Fiscal*, 26 February 2013), where it was ruled out that the provisions of a national constitution could integrate the regime of the European arrest warrant by imposing requirements for its enforcement other than those provided by Framework Decision 2009/299/JHA of 26 February 2009. Indeed, the *Corte* pointed out that, unlike in *Melloni*, the legal issue at stake (i.e. whether the regime on limitation periods belongs to substantive criminal law and it is thus subject to the principle of legality) was "extraneous to EU law", viz. it was not harmonised by it (para. 8). As a consequence, the primacy of EU law was not challenged in the case at hand; to be under discussion, rather, was "the existence of a constitutional bar" on the direct application of Article 325 TFEU by Italian courts (*ibidem*). Furthermore, none of this was meant to downsize the responsibility of the Italian State for failing to provide an effective remedy against serious tax fraud affecting EU financial interests (para. 7).

In the light of the foregoing, the *Corte Costituzionale* requested the CJEU to clarify whether Article 325 TFEU had to "be interpreted as requiring the criminal courts to disregard national legislation concerning limitation periods" even when "there is not a sufficiently precise legal basis for setting aside such legislation"; or "limitation is part of the substantive criminal law in the Member State's legal system and is subject to the principle of legality". Also, it sought a preliminary ruling on whether the *Taricco* judgment had to "be interpreted as requiring the criminal courts to disregard national legislation concerning limitation periods" even when "the setting aside of such legislation would contrast with the supreme principles of the constitutional order of the Member State or with the inalienable human rights recognised under the Constitution of the Member State".

Much has been written about Order No. 24/2017 (see, in addition to the works referred to in this note, the valuable contributions collected in Bernardi and Cupelli (eds.), *Il caso* Taricco *e il dialogo tra le corti. L'ordinanza 24/2017 della Corte Costituzionale*, Napoli, 2017). And rightly so, since it represents an unprecedented attempt to engage the CJEU in a critical discussion over one of its most successful (and most stoutly defended) creatures: the primacy of EU law. Of course, it will not be possible to give here a full account of this debate, nor to analyse in depth the various issues raised by the Order under comment. We will hence limit ourselves to making some remarks on the merits of the dialogical strategy adopted by the *Corte Costituzionale*, also in the light of the ensuing preliminary ruling issued by the CJEU (Case C-42/17, *Criminal proceedings against M.A.S. and M.B.*, 5 December 2017, on which see LAZZERINI, "Il rapporto tra primato del diritto dell'Unione europea e tutela costituzionale dei diritti fondamentali nella sentenza *Taricco-bis*: buona la seconda?, RDI, 2018, p. 234 ff.).

In this respect, it should be first stressed that the very decision to foster a dialogue with the CJEU, through a second request for a preliminary ruling, was anything but foregone. As some Italian constitutional lawyers pointed out (see, in particularly neat terms, LUCIANI, "Il brusco risveglio. I controlimiti e la fine mancata della storia costituzionale", Rivista dell'Associazione Italiana dei Costituzionalisti, No. 2/2016), the considerations made by the *Corte Costituzionale* in paragraphs 4 and 5 of the Order unambiguously supported the conclusions that the rule asserted in *Taricco* was contrary to the principle of legality as understood in the Italian legal order.

Also, in promoting this dialogue, the *Corte* generally took a non-confrontational posture, which is revealed from a number of argumentative choices. First, it expressed more than once an open deference with regard to the CJEU's interpretation of EU law (*in casu* Article 325 TFEU, see paras. 5 and 8). Second, it strove to play down the elements of disagreement with the CJEU by lingering on an aspect of the principle of legality – that of precision of criminal law – which had not been addressed in *Taricco*. Third, and relatedly, it leveraged on the margin of uncertainty left by some passages of the *Taricco* judgment in order to suggest that the solution proposed in Order No. 24/2017 had been already envisaged – at least in an embryonic form – by the same CJEU. Fourth, it bothered to demonstrate the consistency of its approach with the case law of the CJEU, in particular by distinguishing the legal issue at stake from the one dealt with in *Melloni*. Fifth, and remarkably enough, the *Corte* carefully avoided to use the (taboo) word "counter-limits" (RUGGE, "The Italian Constitutional Court on Taricco: Unleashing the normative potential of 'national identity'"?, QIL, Zoom-in 37, 2017, p. 21 ff., p. 22; CUPELLI, "*Ecce Taricco II*. Fra dialogo e diplomazia, l'attesa sentenza della Corte di Giustizia", Diritto penale contemporaneo, 2017, p. 177 ff., p. 182), but substantiated its insistence on the need to safeguard fundamental domestic legal values by making reference to EU law, and notably to some basic provisions of the Lisbon Treaty (PARIS, "Carrot and Stick. The Italian Constitutional Court's Preliminary Reference in the Case Taricco", QIL, Zoom-in 37, 2017, p. 5 ff., p. 15).

As aptly noted by many commentators (see e.g. PARIS, *cit. supra*, pp. 16-17), all of this was instrumental to provide the CJEU with a comfortable argumentative path to disavow *Taricco* without "losing face". In the same perspective, one should read the emphasis placed by the *Corte* on the fact that the *real* responsibility for the potential damages to EU financial interests, as well as for the intricate legal problems raised by the *Taricco* judgment, lies with the Italian legislator (one author saw therein a sort of pledge for an inter-judicial alliance, PARIS, *cit. supra*, p. 17).

This strategy proved successful. Instead of focusing on the weaknesses of some interpretations of EU law put forth by the *Corte Costituzionale* (see e.g. BERNARDI, "Note critiche sull'ordinanza *Taricco* della Corte Costituzionale", in BERNARDI and CUPELLI (eds.), *cit. supra*, p. 17 ff., pp. 22-34), the CJEU disregarded the contrary advice provided by Advocate General Yves Bot (Opinion of 18 July 2017) and took a likewise dialogical attitude, by rendering a judgment that seeks to fine-tune the rule asserted in *Taricco* with the concerns voiced by Italian courts. Indeed, while reiterating *verbatim* the duty of disapplication affirmed in *Taricco*, it added a crucial saving clause relieving national courts from such a duty whenever it "entails a breach of the principle that offences and penalties must be defined by law because of the lack of precision of the applicable law or because of the retroactive application of legislation imposing conditions of criminal liability stricter than those in force at the time the infringement was committed".

It is noteworthy that, in reaching this conclusion, the CJEU took advantage of some of the "escape lines" (PARIS, *cit. supra*, p. 16) drawn by the *Corte Costituzionale*. In the first place, the CJEU conceded to the *Corte Costituzionale* that, at the time the *Taricco* judgment was issued, "the limitation rules applicable to criminal proceedings relating to VAT had not been harmonised by the EU legislature" (*M.A.S. and M.B.*, para. 44), with the consequence that Italy was "free to provide that in its legal system those rules [...] form part of substantive criminal law, and are thereby [...] subject to the principle that offences and penalties must be defined by law" (*ibid.*, para. 45; at para. 44, however, the CJEU specified that this situation has partially changed after the enactment of Directive (EU) 2017/1371). Furthermore, the CJEU – as suggested by the *Corte Costituzionale* – relied on para. 53 of the *Taricco* judgment to (re-)affirm that national courts are endowed with the task of verifying that the disapplication of domestic rules on limitation periods does not entail a breach of the fundamental rights of the accused. In this way, the conclusion reached by the CJEU did not come across as a spectacular (and somewhat dishonorable) *revirement*, but rather as a mere clarification of the principles already stated in 2015.

Yet, the CJEU preferred not to go down the whole path traced by the *Corte Costituzionale*. The Luxembourg Court, indeed, did not even mention the latter's attempt to "Europeanise" the counter-limits doctrine in the light of the national identity clause under Article 4(2) TEU. On balance, this appears to have been a wise choice, if we consider the potentially disrupting effects of a too broad interpretation of this clause on the unity of the EU legal order (MARTINICO, "Il potenziale sovversivo dell'identità nazionale alla luce dell'ordinanza 24/2017 della Corte Costituzionale", in BERNARDI and CUPELLI (eds.), *cit. supra*, p. 241 ff.).

Can we say that the crisis has thus been averted? For the time being yes, but the issue seems far from being definitively settled. Less than ten days after the *M.A.S.* judgment was handed down, the *Corte Costituzionale* came back to the relationship between the Italian Constitution and EU law in a controversial *obiter dictum*, where it arguably advocated a "prioritisation" of the "*erga omnes*" constitutional review of legislation over that of conformity to the CFREU, also hinting at the opportunity to interpret the rights guaranteed by the Charter "in a way consistent with constitutional traditions" (*Corte Costituzionale*, Joined cases *Ceramica Sant'Agostino Spa v. Autorità garante della concorrenza e del mercato* and *Bertazzoni spa v. Autorità garante della concorrenza e del mercato*, 14 December 2017, No. 269, para. 5.2). The CJEU almost immediately retorted by reiterating, a few days later, the duty of national courts of final instance "to refer a question for a preliminary ruling concerning the interpretation of EU law even if, in the course of the same national proceedings, the constitutional court of the Member State concerned has assessed the constitutionality of national rules in the light of regulatory parameters with content similar to rules under EU law" (Case C-322/16, *Global Starnet Ltd v. Ministero dell'Economia e delle Finanze and Amministrazione Autonoma Monopoli di Stato*, 20 December 2017, para. 26; on this point see LAZZERINI, *cit. supra*, p. 242). That seems to suggest that another confrontation, perhaps in less diplomatic tones, is looming large in the "complicated relationship" between the *Corte Costituzionale* and the CJEU (an English translation of the Order is available at: <https://www.cortecostituzionale. it/documenti/download/doc/recent_judgments/O_24_2017.pdf>).

DANIELE AMOROSO

2. THE FORESEEABILITY OF PREVENTIVE MEASURES UNDER ITALIAN CRIMINAL LAW IN THE LIGHT OF THE EUROPEAN PRINCIPLE OF LEGALITY

Principle of legality – Foreseeability of criminal law – Consistent interpretation – Preventive measures – Special police supervision – Obligations to live honestly and within the law – Article 2 of Protocol No. 4 to the European Convention on Human Rights

Corte di Cassazione (Sezioni Unite Penali), 27 April 2017, No. 40076
Criminal proceedings against Andrea Paternò

In the judgment under scrutiny, the *Corte di Cassazione* assessed the compatibility of Article 75(2) of Legislative Decree No. 159 of 6 September 2011 with the principle of legality as construed by the European Court of Human Rights (ECtHR). Under Article 75(2), in particular, the breach of obligations and provisions related to the preventive measure of special police supervision (*sorveglianza speciale di pubblica sicurezza*) with mandatory residence or a prohibition of residence is punished with one to five years' detention. In the case at hand, the *Corte di Cassazione* was asked to determine whether the obligations to "live honestly" and to "respect the law" (*"vivere onestamente"* and *"rispettare le leggi"*) imposed with any judicially-established measure of prevention pursuant Article 8(4) of Legislative Decree No. 159/2011 were also included within the scope of application of Article 75(2). Until then, such an inclusion had been supported by Italian jurisprudence.

The factual background of the case concerned the conviction of Mr. Paternò for the aggravated crime of causing bodily harm (*lesioni personali aggravate*) while he was under special police supervision, on the grounds of Articles 582 and 585 of the Italian Criminal Code and of Article 75 of Legislative Decree No. 159/2011, taken alone and in accumulation. From the outset, the *Corte di Cassazione* observed that Legislative Decree No. 159/2011 is the result of several reforms. Most notably, Law No. 155 of 31 July 2005 modified Law No. 1423 of 27 December 1956 (which was subsequently replaced by Legislative Decree No. 159/2011) in the sense of converting all breaches of obligations related to special police surveillance from misdemeanours to criminal offences. The *Corte Costituzionale* had upheld this stricter approach towards individuals considered to be particularly dangerous as compatible with the Constitution, deeming it as a reasonable exercise of the legislator's discretional power (*Corte Costituzionale*, Judgment of 18 May 2009, No. 161). The obligations related to special police surveillance referred to by Article 75(2) of Legislative Decree No. 159/2011 are specified by its Article 8. Among such obligations, it is possible to find both specific provisions (such as mandatory residence, the prohibition to bear arms, and so forth) and the generic obligations of living honestly and respecting the law. The *Corte Costituzionale* (*G.D. v. Presidenza del Consiglio dei Ministri*, 7 July 2010, No. 282) had ruled that the obligations to live honestly and within the law do not breach the principle whereby the law must exhaustively define the situations to which it is applicable (the so-called *principio di tassatività e determinatezza*). Indeed, an interpretation of such a norm in the light of the context provided by Law No. 1423/1956 (applicable at the time) allowed to specify their content, consisting respectively in the duty to comply with all the obligations established in the context of the measure of special police supervision pursuant Article 5 of the Law (now Article 8 of Legislative Decree No. 159/2011) and to respect all laws whose breach further denotes that the individual is a danger to society. This interpretation had also been repeatedly upheld by the *Corte di Cassazione* itself (see for instance *Sezione I Penale, Criminal proceedings against Lungari*, 6 November 2008, No. 47766; *Sezione I Penale, Criminal proceedings against Iuosio*, 27 January 2009, No. 8412; *Sezione VII Penale, Criminal proceedings against Rosario Polimeni*, 29 January 2014, No. 11217).

Against the background of this consistent Italian jurisprudence, the *Corte di Cassazione* in the *Sinigaglia* case (*Sezioni Unite Penali, Criminal proceedings against Giulio Sinigaglia*, 29 Aprile 2014, No. 32923) had carried out a divergent interpretation. In particular, it had held that the criminal offence of violating the obligations related to special police supervision must be understood as referring only to those breaches that show a willingness to evade this preventive measure, substantially undermining it. This conclusion, in the Court's view, was also supported by the principle of proportionality as interpreted by ECtHR in *Labita v. Italy* (Application No. 26772/95, Grand Chamber, Judgment of 6 April 2000). On that occasion, the ECtHR had examined the restrictions on freedom of movement implied by the preventive measure of special police supervision (as regulated by the then in force Art. 3 of Law No. 1423/1956) from the point of view, among other provisions, of the right to freedom of movement recognised by Article 2 of Protocol No. 4 to the ECHR. In particular, it had established that the adoption of this measure against a person after his acquittal from the charge of being a member of a mafia-type organisation could be considered as necessary in a democratic society only in presence of evidences substantiating the reasonable fear that further criminal offences would be committed.

In the judgment under review, the *Corte di Cassazione* observed that the principles established in the *Sinigaglia* judgment support a restriction of the scope of application of Article 75(2) of Legislative Decree No. 159/2011, so as to include only those conducts that constitute criminal offences or serious administrative offences. In the Court's view, however, these criteria may be appropriate for specific obligations but not for generic ones, because they would leave an excessive discretionary power to criminal courts in the enforcement of this norm. Most importantly, they do not solve the main issue of Article 75, namely, the generic character of the obligations of living honestly and within the law.

In this respect, the *Corte di Cassazione* extensively recalled the ECtHR judgment of *De Tommaso v. Italy* (Application No. 43395/09, Grand Chamber, Judgment of 23 February 2017). In this judgment, the ECtHR had reproached the lack of foreseeability of the obligations to live honestly and within the law, enshrined in Article 9 of Law 1423/1956 (now Article 75(2) of Legislative Decree No. 159/2011). On these grounds, the ECtHR had recognised a breach of Article 2 of Protocol No. 4 to the ECHR, whose paragraph 3 requires all restrictions to freedom of movement to be "in accordance with the law", because the restrictions to freedom of movement related to the preventive measure of special police surveillance were not clear enough to qualify as law for this purpose. In the judgment under review, the *Corte di Cassazione* observed that:

> the ECtHR has specifically insisted on the concept of European legality, upholding its own jurisprudence whereby the requirement of being in accordance with the law should not be understood as referring exclusively to the legal foundation of a provision, but rather to the quality of the law, which must be accessible to persons who have an interest in it and predictable as to its effects (para. 8)

The *Corte di Cassazione* shared the ECtHR's view that the obligations to live honestly and within the law had not been sufficiently clarified neither by Italian law nor by its constitutional jurisprudence. The Court, then, recalled that its duty of consistent interpretation of Italian law in the light of the European Convention on Human Rights (ECHR) provided that such an interpretation is in compliance with the Constitution (*Corte Costituzionale, R.A. v. Comune di Torre Annunziata; Comune di Montello v. A.C.; M.T.G. v. Comune di Ceprano*, 24 October 2007, No. 348; *Corte Costituzionale, E.P et al. v. Comune di Avellino et al.; A. G. et al. v. Comune di Leonforte et al.*, 24 October 2007, No. 349, IYIL, 2007, p. 292 ff. with a comment by CATALDI). In the Court's view, this duty requires a definition of the boundaries and characteristics of the conducts punished by Article 75(2) of Legislative Decree No. 159/2011. In this light, it concluded that the generic character of this norms' reference to the obligations related to special police supervision (pursuant Article 8 of the same Legislative Decree) made it impossible to anticipate the consequences of one's actions and granted an excessively wide discretionary power to criminal courts as to the determination of which offences must be included within its scope of application. The Court noted that neither the obligation to live honestly nor that to respect the law, in particular, required any specific behaviour, and thus they could be considered as having a moral value but not as criminal law provisions. Therefore, the *Corte di Cassazione* concluded that Article 75(2) of Legislative Decree No. 159/2011 should not be understood as referring also to the generic obligations to live honestly and within the law, because only those obligations envisaged by Article 8 that have a clear prescriptive content can be included within the scope of application of Article 75(2). Breaches of the obligations to live honestly and within the law, on the other hand, could be taken into consideration by criminal courts in the assessment of the dangerousness of involved individuals, serving as possible grounds to establish stricter measures of special surveillance.

In the case under review, the *Corte di Cassazione* extensively relied on the ECtHR judgment of *De Tommaso v. Italy* to fulfil its duty of consistent interpretation of Italian criminal law with Italy's obligations under Article 2 of Protocol No. 4 to the ECHR. The judgment by the *Corte di Cassazione* resonates with the broader scholarly debates concerning the progressive affirmation of a "concept of European legality" – as defined by the Court itself – over the principle of legality as understood in civil law traditions. The consolidated jurisprudence by the ECtHR as well as by the European Court of Justice has indeed interpreted this principle as requiring not only the formal legal recognition of a certain measure, but also the respect of qualitative standards in their content, which must make its provisions accessible and foreseeable (SANZ-CABALLERO, "The Principle of *Nulla Poena Sine Lege* Revisited: The Retrospective Application of Criminal Law in the Eyes of the European Court of Human Rights", EJIL, 2017, p. 787 ff.). According to this construction, law is not simply made up of legal provisions but also of domestic judgments that interpret them. With specific reference to criminal law, it has been rightly observed that the European understanding of the principle of legality is not necessarily incompatible with the formal concept of law that grounds this principle as affirmed by Article 25 of the Italian Constitution. Rather, this principle can be considered as a further source of guarantees for individuals, requiring not only the existence of legislation that criminalise certain conducts and establish related punishments but also that the content of such legislation is clear enough to make it accessible and foreseeable. Following this interpretation, the principle of European legality construed by the ECtHR and the Court of Justice of the European Union does not give rise to issues of compatibility with constitutional principles that would prevent its application in the Italian order (FLICK, "The Principle of Legality: Reflections on the Dialogue between the Court of Justice, the European Court of Human Rights and the Italian Constitutional Court", New Journal of European Criminal Law, 2015, p. 553 ff.).

The judgment under review appears to constitute a further step towards the recognition of a substantive notion of legality by Italian higher courts (some previous examples have been discussed by LUPO and PICCIRILLI, "The Relocation of the Legality Principle by the European Courts' Case Law", European Constitutional Law Review, 2015, p. 55 ff.). Here, the Court was not satisfied with assessing the existence of legislation criminalising the breach of obligations related to the preventive measure of special police surveillance. Instead, it went on to examine the content of said legislation in the light of the standards of accessibility and foreseeability established by the ECtHR in the *De Tommaso* judgment. In such an assessment, it correctly considered the interpretation carried out by the *Corte Costituzionale* in judgment No. 282/2010 as insufficiently clear to comply with these standards. While not questioning the European understanding of the principle of legality in itself, indeed, the latter had offered a rather tautological and generic definition of the obligations of living honestly and within the law. Therefore, the conclusion of the *Corte di Cassazione* that such obligations are too vague to be included within the scope of the criminal offence of breaching the duties related to special police surveillance appears overall correct.

An important point, however, concerns the objectionable character of the *obiter dictum* whereby the violation of the obligations to live honestly and within the law could be taken into consideration by criminal courts as possible grounds to adopt stricter measures in connection to special police supervision. The review of this preventive measure, for instance with the aim to add compulsory residence or a prohibition of residence, is allowed by Article 11(2) of Legislative Decree No. 159/2011 (among other things) precisely in case of repeated breaches of the obligations related to this measure. According to the *Corte di Cassazione*, then, the indeterminate character of the duties to live honestly and within the law prevents their framing as a criminal offence under Article 75(2) of Legislative Decree No. 159/2011, but not their inclusion among the obligations envisaged by its Article 11 whose breach may give rise to further restrictions of the liberty of movement of an individual under police supervision. This conclusion appears to rest on the questionable assumption that the principle of legality as construed by European jurisprudence exclusively applies in relation to provisions on criminal offences rather than to criminal law in its entirety. The *Corte Costituzionale*, instead, has consistently applied the principle of legality in relation to preventive measures, examining their clarity and specificity in the light of Articles 13 and 25(3) of the Constitution (*Corte Costituzionale, Gaetano Raddato, Carmela Sciancalepore and Pietro Comizzoli v. Presidenza del Consiglio dei Ministri*, 4 March 1964, No. 23; *Corte Costituzionale, Vincenzo Miliucci v. Presidenza del Consiglio dei Ministri*, 16 December 1980, No. 177). Therefore, a more coherent solution in relation to norms considered to be unforeseeable would have been to simply state their character of moral exhortations (as the *Corte di Cassazione* did when it analysed Article 8 of Legislative Decree No. 159/2011) without allowing them to constitute grounds for the adoption of stricter obligations towards individuals already under police supervision, *de facto* reviving them in a different normative context (the Italian text of the judgment is available at: <http://www.italgiure.giustizia.it/sncass/>).

FULVIA STAIANO

DIPLOMATIC AND PARLIAMENTARY PRACTICE

(edited by *Pietro Gargiulo*, *Marco Pertile* and *Paolo Turrini*)

III. STATES AND OTHER INTERNATIONAL ENTITIES

1. THE REFERENDUM ON THE SELF-DETERMINATION OF CATALONIA

In September 2017 the Parliament of Catalonia, a region enjoying autonomous status within Spain,[1] passed legislation to enable the holding of a binding referendum on self-determination.[2]

Claiming a breach of the indissoluble unity of the Spanish Nation,[3] the Spanish Government brought the law before the Spanish Constitutional Court and threatened to suspend the regional autonomy of Catalonia should the referendum be held.[4] The Court pre-emptively suspended the law,[5] and later declared it unconstitutional and void due to both the lack of competence of the Government of Catalonia in calling a referendum on a matter of Spanish sovereign authority and the fact that its approval by the Parliament of Catalonia did not comply with voting procedures.[6]

In the weeks preceding the referendum, Spanish law enforcement authorities started to seize ballot boxes and occupy Catalan ministries to search for evidence of the breach of Spanish law. Some of the key figures of the Catalan pro-independence movement were arrested and accused of sedition. Tension between the parties rose, and people started to take to the streets both in Madrid and Barcelona.

On 29 September 2017, during an urgent question time taking place at the *Camera dei Deputati* (Chamber of Deputies, 861st Meeting, XVII Legislature),

---

[1] The Statute of Autonomy of Catalonia (2006) gives the *Generalitat de Catalunya* (composed of the Parliament, the President and the Government) self-government powers in accordance with the Spanish Constitution of 1978. The competences of the autonomous community are partly exclusive, partly concurrent and partly shared with the central government in Madrid. The Statute of Autonomy is available at: <https://web.gencat.cat/en/generalitat/estatut/estatut2006/>.

[2] The Law on the Referendum on Self-determination of Catalonia is available at: <http://exteriors.gencat.cat/web/.content/00_ACTUALITAT/notes_context/Llei-del-Referendum_ENGLISH.pdf>.

[3] Guaranteed by Art. 2 of the Spanish Constitution.

[4] Art. 155 of the Spanish Constitution provides that if a self-governing community does not fulfil the obligations imposed upon it by the Constitution or other laws, or acts in a way that is seriously prejudicial to the general interest of Spain, the Government may take all measures necessary to compel the Community to meet said obligations, or to protect the above-mentioned general interest, including issuing instructions to all the authorities of the self-governing community.

[5] The provisional decision is available at: <https://www.tribunalconstitucional.es/NotasDePrensaDocumentos/NP_2017_062/NOTA INFORMATIVA N° 62-2017.pdf>.

[6] The final decision can is available at: <https://www.tribunalconstitucional.es/NotasDePrensaDocumentos/NP_2017_074/2017-4334STC.pdf>.

the *Sottosegretario di Stato per gli Affari esteri e la Cooperazione internazionale* (Undersecretary of State for Foreign Affairs and International Cooperation), Mr. Vincenzo Amendola, was asked about the Italian Government's position on the promotion of the referendum on self-determination by the Catalan authorities. More specifically, he was asked whether the Government planned to undertake any politico-diplomatic initiative aimed at stopping the spiral of actions and re-actions characterizing the situation; whether the Government deemed useful to raise at the European level the possibility of adopting sanctions against Spain in light of what looked like criminal repression of the legitimate Catalan authori-ties' right to self-determination; whether the Government was considering the option of recalling the Italian Ambassador to Spain; and whether and how the Government intended to support internal dialogue in Spain, with the aim of guar-anteeing that Catalans could legitimately decide their own future.

First of all, it is worth highlighting that, in his reply, Mr. Amendola framed the issue as one of autonomy as opposed to one of self-determination – as per the question he was asked – or independence – as per the Catalan claim.[7] The Undersecretary's response was generally quite evasive. He called for dialogue among the parties but at the same time made it clear that any breach of the Spanish Constitution would be seen as illegitimate and that the unity of the Spanish state could not be put into question. In particular, Mr. Amendola stated the following:

> In executing the judicial decisions that declared autonomy illegiti-mate, the action of Rajoy's Government is in full coherence with the political thesis laying in the background – that is, the constitu-tional incompatibility of any kind of autonomy.

Having stressed that the status of Catalonia could only be discussed in the framework of a concerted political dialogue, Mr. Amendola praised the way the situation had been managed by adding:

> To be honest, up to now we have witnessed balance and measure on the side of the law enforcement authorities within the complex sys-tem of local governmental forces and their respective competences – that are local as regards law enforcement but central as regards the execution of judicial decisions.

On 1 October 2017, the day of the referendum, voters occupied polling sta-tions in order to keep them open notwithstanding police attempts to suppress the voting. Images of police repression and violence circulated all over the world. According to the Catalan Government, out of a turnout of 42.3% of voters, 90% voted for independence. The President of Catalonia, Mr. Carles Puidgemont, sub-

---

[7] The autonomous status of Catalonia was however not in question. While the Spanish Constitution rules out the possibility of an autonomous region of Spain becoming an indepen-dent state, it expressly provides for regional autonomy by recognizing and guaranteeing in Art. 2 the right to self-government of the nationalities and regions composing the Spanish Nation.

sequently declared that Catalonia had conquered its right to be an independent state in the form of a republic. His declarations were opposed by the central government in Madrid. Over the following days, the European Commission expressed the position that the referendum was illegal and that the situation had to be dealt with by Spain as an internal matter, calling both parties to resume dialogue.[8] At the same time, the King of Spain Felipe VI strongly condemned the Catalan government and its attempt to threaten Spain's stability, urging the state to defend the constitutional order.

On 4 October 2017, during a question time taking place at the Chamber of Deputies (864th Meeting, XVII Legislature), Mr. Angelino Alfano, *Ministro degli Affari esteri e della Cooperazione internazionale* (Minister of Foreign Affairs and International Cooperation), was asked about any political and diplomatic activity that the Government intended to adopt in order to guarantee the right to peaceful and democratic self-determination of the Catalan people. Mr. Alfano's statement largely reflected what the Under-Secretary had said some days before, but rightly brought back to the fore the question of independence as opposed to autonomy. Although not expressly taking sides, the Minister clearly framed the matter as one of management and containment of autonomist claims rather than one of unilateral self-determination.

In particular, he stated the following:

> The Italian Government does not want to discuss the merits of what is an internal Spanish question. However, I cannot but share the words of the President of the Italian Republic who said that, these days, Europe has once more experienced that, when clash prevails and positions are exacerbated, it is more difficult to find any positive solution. The same concepts were repeated by the Prime Minister, in the context of the forum for dialogue between Italy and Spain held in Rome last Monday 2 October. The Italian Government, as the European Union, therefore strongly wishes for dialogue between the parties in order to prevent the further deterioration of a situation that is already serious. In our view, it is possible to see the initiative of President Rajoy, who called the parties to inclusive political dialogue, against the background of such aim. We are indeed convinced that the choice of the method used to manage Catalan autonomist claims is the key element in order to keep centrifugal forces within Spain – a country whose unity is guaranteed by the king – under control.

In the same context, Mr. Alfano was later asked about the Italian Government's position and intended course of action vis-à-vis the violent repression of the referendum held in Catalonia. Without making reference to the violence, the Minister

---

[8] The statement is available at: <http://europa.eu/rapid/press-release_STATEMENT-17-3626_en.htm>.

reiterated that the situation was to be considered an internal constitutional matter within Spain. He carefully framed the question as a political one, to be resolved through dialogue between the parties rather than through unilateral decisions. In particular, he stated the following:

> The situation in Spain, and in particular the referendum in Catalonia, are of the outmost importance for the Italian Government. I wish to stress again that, although the Government considers the matter as one of internal politics, we are fully aware of the importance of political dialogue between the parties. [...]
> President Gentiloni himself expressed the wish that dialogue could bring politics back to the fore, in the search of a solution that needs to be in total compliance with the laws, the rule of law and the unitary Constitution of Spain.[9] The same position was expressed by the European Union which, without interfering with the Catalan question, declared to believe that such a situation calls for unity and stability rather than division and fragmentation. As already mentioned, we find ourselves in line with this European position.

As emerges from the statements issued by the Ministry of Foreign Affairs and International Cooperation in dealing with the question of the referendum, the Italian Government decided to use the lexicon of constitutional law and internal politics rather than the one of international law and self-determination. Without mentioning the right of the Catalan people to determine their own future, the Government automatically removed unilateral action from the range of admissible options. Rather, it seemed to imply that room for discussion over Catalan independence would only lie in the context of a constitutional dialogue involving both parties. In this sense, the Italian Government's position on the Catalan referendum was overall very much in line with the one expressed by the European Union. This is easily understandable in light of the autonomist and secessionist claims currently spreading across European societies.

BIANCA MAGANZA

VI. TERRITORY

1. THE STATUS OF JERUSALEM

On 6 December 2017, the United States (US) President, Mr. Donald Trump, put into effect his presidential campaign promise to effectively recognize Jerusalem as the capital of Israel, thereby indicating a future move there for

---

[9] The Prime Minister expressed his position in the framework of the Italo-Spanish forum held in Rome in October 2017. The statement is available at: <http://www.ansa.it/english/news/politics/2017/10/02/mattarella-on-catalonia-4_81d82a38-41b1-4abb-8595-38a91a5b6b71.html>.

the US embassy from Tel Aviv. Such a decision has been interpreted by many as marking a turning point in the US approach towards the Israeli-Palestinian issue. Indeed, even though the 1995 Jerusalem Embassy Act adopted by the US Senate and House of Representatives committed the Federal Government to moving the US Embassy to Jerusalem, since its enactment every US President has regularly availed himself of the possibility to invoke a six-month waiver of the application of the law. President Trump himself signed such a waiver twice, before (June 2017) as well as after (December 2017) his own declaration. Nonetheless, his announcement sparked controversy and many countries voiced their dissent. Italy is among those States and its stance will be discussed below. However, in order better to understand the dissent it expressed along with a number of other countries, it is useful to provide a factual and legal context, starting with Mr. Trump's actual words.

In his speech, Mr. Trump motivated his decision as follows:

> Israel is a sovereign nation with the right, like every other sovereign nation, to determine its own capital. [...] But today we finally acknowledge the obvious. That Jerusalem is Israel's capital. This is nothing more or less than a recognition of reality. It is also the right thing to do. It's something that has to be done.

However, he also added:

> We are not taking a position of any final status issues including the specific boundaries of the Israeli sovereignty in Jerusalem or the resolution of contested borders. Those questions are up to the parties involved.

This specification seems to downplay the bearing of Mr. Trump's declaration and to move it closer to the position of other States as well as of previous US administrations. Indeed, it must be recalled that, until the early Eighties, the US abstained on some resolutions in which the United Nations (UN) Security Council condemned the Israeli presence in the Palestinian territory.[10] Although the threat of veto made it impossible for the Security Council to approve similarly phrased resolutions for about 35 years,[11] in December 2016, one year before Mr. Trump's

---

[10] For example, Security Council Resolution 478 of 20 August 1980, paras. 1 and 2, "[c] ensure[d] in the strongest terms the enactment by Israel of the 'basic law' on Jerusalem", which it deemed to constitute "a violation of international law" (the so-called Jerusalem Law was passed by the Knesset on 30 July 1980 and established Jerusalem as the capital of Israel). The same document, at para. 2, referred to "the Palestinian and other Arab territories occupied since June 1967, including Jerusalem": an expression that can be found in other resolutions of the same period that determined "that all measures taken by Israel to change the [...] status of the Palestinian and other Arab territories occupied since June 1967, including Jerusalem, or any part thereof have no legal validity".

[11] But see, e.g., Security Council Resolution 1073 of 28 September 1996, "[r]ecalling [the] resolutions on Jerusalem and other relevant Security Council resolutions" (third recital of

declaration, his predecessor at the White House, Mr. Barak Obama, opted for his country to abstain on a resolution condemning the policy of Israel towards the occupied territories. By means of Resolution 2334 (2016),[12] the Security Council:

> 1. Reaffirm[ed] that the establishment by Israel of settlements in the Palestinian territory occupied since 1967, including East Jerusalem, has no legal validity and constitutes a flagrant violation under international law [... and]
> 3. Underline[d] that it will not recognize any changes to the 4 June 1967 lines, including with regard to Jerusalem, other than those agreed by the parties through negotiation.

Despite the recent recognition of Jerusalem as the capital of Israel, a certain degree of continuity can be discerned in the US position on this issue. Apparently, part of the international community, including the US until the end of 2016, considers the 1967 lines – which divided Jerusalem between a Western part under the authority of Israel and an Eastern part annexed by Jordan – as the starting point for the determination of the borders of a Palestinian State. By refusing to address the question of contested borders and leaving it to the disputants, Mr. Trump's declaration seems to take a similar approach. Indeed, if it is true that the declaration did not specifically mention the 1967-lines benchmark, it should also be noted that such lines are sometimes considered as susceptible of being modified by agreement of the parties (though the criteria against which the modifications are to be assessed are not always spelled out).[13]

For instance, on 6 April 2017 the Russian Federation issued an official *communiqué* specifically making reference to "West Jerusalem" as the capital of Israel, with no prejudice, however, to a negotiated solution of the territorial con-

---

the preamble), and Security Council Resolution 1322 of 7 October 2000, expressly recalling Resolution 478 (1980) (first recital of the preamble). The United States abstained on both.

[12] Security Council Resolution 2334 of 23 December 2016.

[13] A criterion (that of "equivalent land swaps") can be found in the joint declaration of 8 December 2017 whose text is below. Sometimes, the very possibility of changing the lines is not explicitly stated, though indirect support might perhaps be inferred from reference to Security Council resolutions or other international documents. For instance, the Members States of the Organization of the Islamic Cooperation issued on 13 December 2017 a statement by which they said to "[c]onsider that th[e] dangerous [Trump] declaration, which aims to change the legal status of the City of Al-Quds Al-Sharif, is null and void and lacks any legitimacy, as being a serious violation of the international law, and the Fourth Geneva Convention in particular, and all relevant resolutions of international legitimacy, particularly the UN Security Council resolutions No. 478 (1980) and 2334 (2016)" (para. 5). The statement also backed up the establishment of an "independent and sovereign Palestinian State on the borders of 4 June 1967, with Al-Quds Al-Sharif as its capital" (para. 2). *Rectius*: its Eastern part, as the Members of the Organization also "[r]eaffirm[ed] [their] attachment to the just and comprehensive peace based on the two-state solution with east Jerusalem as the capital of the State of Palestine" (para. 3) and "[d]eclare[d] East Jerusalem as the capital of the State of Palestine" (para. 8). The full text of the statement is available at: <https://www.oic-oci.org/docdown/?docID=1699&refID=1073>.

troversy.[14] The European Union (EU) stance, too, to which Italy strictly adheres, stresses the need for the issue of borders to be settled through direct negotiations between Israel and Palestine, starting from the 1967 ceasefire lines. However, both the EU and Italy refrain from recognizing Israel's sovereignty over Jerusalem. It is worth quoting in full the Italian reaction to the Trump declaration, as expressed on three occasions. On 7 December 2017, the *Ministro degli Affari esteri e della Cooperazione internazionale* (Minister of Foreign Affairs and International Cooperation), Mr. Angelino Alfano, issued the following statement:[15]

> Italy's position on Jerusalem remains anchored to that of Europe and to the international consensus gathered within the UN.
> A solution for Jerusalem as the future capital of two States is to be sought in negotiations between Israelis and Palestinians within the peace process based on the two-State solution, taking into account the legitimate expectations of both sides.
> Until this occurs, Italy will continue to abide by the relevant UN resolutions and maintain its Embassy to the State of Israel in Tel Aviv.
> We are concerned about the repercussions that the announcement of the United States' new approach can have on the ground. We call on the sense of responsibility of all the players in Palestine and in the region to avoid accidents and acts of violence that would benefit no one.
> Italy, together with its EU partners – and in contact with regional and international actors – will assess the situation and reflect on possible European initiatives aiming at contributing to a substantial resumption of the peace process in the prospect of a two-State solution, which must be upheld as it is the only one realistically viable.

The following day, 8 December 2017, the Italian Permanent Representative to the UN Security Council, Ambassador Sebastiano Cardi, together with his French, German, Swedish and British colleagues, adopted the following joint statement,[16] which was said to represent the position of the whole EU:

> We disagree with the US decision to recognize Jerusalem as the capital of Israel, and to begin preparation to move the American embassy from Tel Aviv to Jerusalem. It is not in line with Security Council resolutions and is unhelpful in terms of prospects for peace in the region.

---

[14] The full text of the statement is available at: <http://www.mid.ru/en/foreign_policy/news/-/asset_publisher/cKNonkJE02Bw/content/id/2717182>.

[15] The statement is available at: <https://www.esteri.it/mae/en/sala_stampa/archivionotizie/comunicati/2017/12/dichiarazione-del-ministro-alfano_0.html>.

[16] The statement is available at <https://consgerusalemme.esteri.it/consolato_gerusalemme/it/consolato/news/dal_consolato/8-december-2017-un-security-council.html>.

The status of Jerusalem must be determined through negotiations between Israelis and Palestinians leading to a final status agreement. It is a constant position of EU Members that, within this framework, Jerusalem should ultimately be the capital of both Israeli and Palestinian states. Until then, we recognize no sovereignty over Jerusalem.

In line with international law and relevant Security Council Resolutions, notably resolutions 476, 478 and 2334, we consider East Jerusalem as part of the Occupied Palestinian Territories. An agreement on the borders of the two states should be based on the 4 June 1967 lines with equivalent land swaps as may be agreed between the parties. The EU will not recognize any changes to the pre-1967 borders, including with regard to Jerusalem, other than those agreed by the parties.

Given the volatile situation on the ground, we call on all parties and all regional stake holders to work together to maintain calm.

We all share a willingness to put an end to the conflict. We note the commitment made by President Trump to support a two-state solution if agreed to by both sides and his clear acknowledgement that the specific boundaries of the Israeli sovereignty in Jerusalem must be subject to negotiations between the Israelis and the Palestinians. We stand ready to contribute to all credible efforts to restart the peace process, on the basis of internationally agreed parameters, leading to a two-State solution. We encourage the US Administration to now bring forward detailed proposals for an Israel-Palestinian settlement.

Ten days later, on 18 December 2017, Mr. Cardi reiterated this position by indicating Italy's support for a draft resolution, tabled by Egypt, that would have called upon all States to refrain from establishing diplomatic missions in Jerusalem (the resolution, however, was unsurprisingly vetoed by the US).[17]

This is a stance that Italy has consistently taken with regards to the Israeli-Palestinian question, both at the domestic and international levels, before as well as after the Trump declaration. In 2017, for instance, Italy intervened several times before the UN Security Council on this issue. On the occasion of the Security Council Open Debate on the Middle East, including the Palestinian question, of 25 July 2017, the Italian Deputy Permanent Representative to the United Nations Security Council, Ambassador Inigo Lambertini expressed

full adherence to Italy's long established position on the Middle East peace process, including with regard to the 1967 lines and to

---

[17] The full text of the statement is available at: <https://consgerusalemme.esteri.it/consolato_gerusalemme/it/consolato/news/dal_consolato/18-december-2017-un-security-council.html>.

East Jerusalem as set out in the relevant conclusions of the Council of the European Union.[18]

Almost the same words were pronounced by Mr. Lambertini during the Security Council Open Debate on the Middle East, including the Palestinian question, of 18 October 2017.[19] Interestingly, on two other occasions, in April and June 2017, reference was made by Mr. Cardi not to the 1967 borders but, rather, to the Oslo accords:

> Any new approach that leads to a just and lasting peace will be welcome and Italy will contribute to it, as long as it remains within the Oslo framework and it pursues the two-State solution.[20]

Indeed,

> we are open to considering new diplomatic schemes aimed at achieving a negotiated solution, provided that they remain within the boundaries of the Oslo framework.[21]

It is worth recalling that, according to the 1995 Israeli-Palestinian Interim Agreement on the West Bank and the Gaza Strip (also known as Oslo II Accord), "[n]othing in th[e] Agreement shall prejudice or preempt the outcome of the negotiations on the permanent status [of the West Bank and the Gaza Strip]. Neither Party shall be deemed, by virtue of having entered into this Agreement, to have renounced or waived any of its existing rights, claims or positions". Such negotiations should have covered, *inter alia*, the issues of Jerusalem and the borders between Israel and Palestine (Article XXXI, paras. 5 and 6). Therefore, even though the Accord provisionally put a large share of the West Bank under Israeli control, it can be said that Italy's stance is not contradictory.

The same position was put forth at the domestic level. On 13 December 2017, before the *Camera dei Deputati* (Chamber of Deputies, 900th Meeting, XVII Legislature), Minister Alfano reiterated Italy's adherence to the EU and the UN consensus, as well as the idea of Jerusalem as the capital of both the Israeli and

---

[18] The full text of the statement is available at: <https://italyun.esteri.it/rappresentanza_onu/it/comunicazione/archivio-news/2017/07/consiglio-di-sicurezza-open-debate.html> (the Council of the European Union routinely issues conclusions on foreign affairs). In his speech, Mr. Lambertini also said that "Italy supports President Abbas as the legitimate representative of the Palestinian leadership, and we uphold the goal of increased pressure by the Palestinian authority on Hamas in order to retake control over the Gaza Strip and restore the whole Palestine under a single, democratic and legitimate authority".

[19] The full text of the statement is available at: <https://italyun.esteri.it/rappresentanza_onu/it/comunicazione/archivio-news/2017/10/consiglio-di-sicurezza-medio-oriente.html>.

[20] The full text of the statement is available at: <https://italyun.esteri.it/rappresentanza_onu/it/comunicazione/archivio-news/2017/06/consiglio-di-sicurezza-briefing_26.html>.

[21] The full text of the statement is available at: <https://italyun.esteri.it/rappresentanza_onu/it/comunicazione/archivio-news/2017/04/consiglio-di-sicurezza-dibattito_10.html>.

Palestinian States, in the framework of a mutually agreed-upon solution. He also defined this stance as consistent with the two parliamentary motions (Motions nos. 1-00745 and 1-00746) passed by Chamber of Deputies on 27 February 2015,[22] whereby the Parliament committed the Italian Government "to promote the recognition of Palestine as a democratic and sovereign State within the 1967 borders and with Jerusalem as a shared capital", "including possible territorial exchanges between the parties", but only under certain (vaguely posited) circumstances. On 15 March 2017, before the Chamber of Deputies (760th Meeting, XVII Legislature), the *Ministra per i Rapporti con il Parlamento* (Minister for the Relations with Parliament), Ms. Anna Finocchiaro, confirmed the intention of the Government to comply with the directives set out by the motions. In particular, she said:

> This is a commitment that the Government made in Parliament, by which it is willing to abide under the conditions set out in the motion of February 2017 itself […], that is, 'at the right time and in the appropriate conditions'. All European governments stuck to this rule, that is, to save the card of formal recognition so as to be able to play it when it will be most useful and essential to give a real boost to the peace process, rather than merely making a token gesture.

Here, too, it clearly emerges that the position of Italy is overtly anchored to that of the EU. All its salient features (the 1967 lines as the starting point to solve the dispute on borders, Jerusalem as the capital shared by both Israel and Palestine, the need for a negotiated solution and the abstention from recognition of the claims of both parties until such solution is in sight) are common to most EU Member States, though not all of them.[23] This willingness to adhere to a shared European position, as well as a politically- rather than legally-motivated approach to recognition (i.e., qualification of facts), have been demonstrated by Italy in other circumstances.[24] Interestingly, such an intention to conform to a common EU stance had already become, in late October 2016, the object of a direct accusation by the then *Presidente del Consiglio dei Ministri* (President of the Council of Ministers) Matteo Renzi. On 13 October 2016, Italy abstained on a UNESCO resolution on the "Temple Mount" question.[25] A week later –

---

[22] The English translation of the full text of both motions can be found in IYIL, XXV (2015), pp. 546–550.

[23] For instance, in October 2014 Sweden recognized the State of Palestine. Moreover, the positions of the EU countries on recognition is possibly less homogeneous than Italy claims it to be (Ms. Finocchiaro's words are identical to those uttered by the then Minister of Foreign affairs, Mr. Paolo Gentiloni, in October 2016: see IYIL, XXVI (2016), pp. 596–599).

[24] For example, on 8 March 2017, before the Chamber of Deputies (755th Meeting, XVII Legislature), speaking of the massacre of the Yazidis beginning in 2014, Minister Alfano said: "We are paying close attention to what our partners are meant to do, and how, about the recognition of those facts as a genocide, also with a view to ensuring coherence to actions on the international plane".

[25] See IYIL, XXVI (2016), pp. 596–599.

as newspapers reported – Mr. Renzi defined this episode "unreal", scolding the Italian diplomacy, and indirectly the then Minister of Foreign Affairs, Mr. Paolo Gentiloni, for driving on "autopilot". In Mr. Renzi's view, this term also covered the European guidance, and he called for discontinuity: "I expressly asked to stop taking such positions. We cannot continue to support such motions that are aimed at attacking Israel. If, on this issue, we must break the European unity, then we will break it". On 17 January 2017, before the *Commissioni riunite – Affari esteri e comunitari (III) della Camera dei Deputati; Affari esteri, Emigrazione (3a) del Senato della Repubblica* (Joint Commissions – Foreign and European Affairs (III) of the Chamber of Deputies; Foreign Affairs, Emigration (3rd) of the Senate of the Republic), the Minister of Foreign Affairs, Mr. Alfano,[26] rejected this criticism. More specifically, he stressed that Italy had manifested its reservations about the way the UNESCO resolution had been originally drafted, and clarified that "being in an open field" – that is, having no prejudiced position – requires that forces be joined with all like-minded countries.

Finally, it must be noted that, on 12 December 2017, the *Senato della Repubblica* (Senate of the Republic, 915th Meeting, XVII Legislature) passed a motion (Motion No. 6-00269, first signatories Zanda, Bianconi, Zeller, Barani), also approved by the *Sottosegretario di Stato per gli Affari esteri e la Cooperazione internazionale* (Undersecretary of State for Foreign Affairs and International Cooperation), Mr. Benedetto della Vedova, on behalf of the Government, which, recalling a 2014 resolution of the European Parliament,[27] committed the Italian Government to

> promote at the EU level all actions aimed at resuming a credible negotiating process between Israelis and Palestinians and prevent new hostilities between them.

A few days later, on 20 December 2017, at the 919th Meeting of the Senate of the Republic, Ms. Laura Puppato posed an interpellation (No. 2-00493) whereby the Government was asked

> which diplomatic measures it intends to take to ensure compliance with international law, especially with respect to the status of Jerusalem as a shared capital, and to sustain the efforts of the international community for a peaceful resolution of the Israeli-Palestinian conflict, with a view to recognizing the State of Palestine.

On 28 December 2017 the *Presidente della Repubblica* (President of the Republic), Mr. Sergio Mattarella, dissolved the Parliament, before the interpellation could be answered.

PAOLO TURRINI

---

[26] In December 2016 a new Government took office.
[27] European Parliament resolution on recognition of Palestine statehood, 2014/2964(RSP), approved on 17 December 2014.

XI. TREATMENT OF ALIENS AND NATIONALITY

1. THE VENEZUELAN CRISIS

Popular protests have been taking place in Venezuela at least since 2014: their targets are the Government's crackdown on civil and political liberties and the grave economic crisis afflicting the country, which has *inter alia* resulted in skyrocketing inflation and a persistent lack of essential goods.

In December 2015, parliamentary elections were held and won by the Democratic Unity Roundtable (MUD), a coalition of parties opposing President Nicolás Maduro and his United Socialist Party (PSUV). In the following months, President Maduro declared a state of emergency and assumed more powers, while the MUD started to collect signatures for a referendum to remove him from office before the natural end of his term. In October 2016, however, the National Electoral Council suspended the referendum process; new demonstrations against this decision took place.

After a year-long tug-of-war between the National Assembly (the Venezuelan Parliament) and the Supreme Court (controlled by President Maduro), on 29 March 2017, the Court stripped the Assembly of its legislative powers and assumed them. The decision was reversed shortly afterwards, but popular discontent did not diminish. Shortly before, fourteen members of the Organization of American States had urged the Venezuelan Government to release all political prisoners, recognize the legitimacy of the National Assembly and hold the local elections originally scheduled for December 2016 and postponed by the Government.[28] The statement followed a critical report by the Secretary of the Organization, Luis Almagro.[29] A mediation attempt led by the Vatican had already failed in January 2017.

On 1 May 2017, President Maduro announced his intention to establish a Constituent Assembly with the mandate to draft a new Constitution. The MUD organized an informal referendum against the proposed Constituent Assembly in July 2017, but elections for the new Assembly were held nonetheless at the end of the same month. Notwithstanding the boycott of the opposition and the controversy surrounding turnout figures, the Constituent Assembly officially took office on 4 August 2017. Over the following days, it revoked the legislative powers of the National Assembly and voted to proceed against the opposition leaders for high treason.

In Italy, these developments have been followed closely. Concern was expressed for the limitations imposed on democracy, the separation of powers, the rule of law, and individual freedoms, as well as for the grave economic crisis plaguing the country. As emphasized by both the Government and the Parliament, Italy's interest in the situation in Venezuela is reinforced by the considerable

---

[28] The joint statement, issued on 23 March 2017, is available at the website of the US Department of State: <https://www.state.gov/p/wha/rls/prsrl/2017/269071.htm>.

[29] The report, dated 14 March 2017, is available at: <http://www.oas.org/documents/eng/press/Informe-VZ-II-English-Final-Signed.pdf>.

number of Italian citizens and descendants living in the country, as well as Italian companies operating there: initiatives were thus taken to ensure their security and well-being. More generally, the Italian authorities expressed their hope for a political solution to the crisis and their willingness to participate in the mediation efforts of the international community, while recognizing the principle of non-interference with the internal affairs of Venezuela.

As to the role of the international community, and of Italy in particular, on 24 January 2017, the *Ministro degli Affari esteri e della Cooperazione internazionale* (Minister of Foreign Affairs and International Cooperation), Mr. Angelino Alfano, briefly illustrated before the *Senato della Repubblica* (Senate of the Republic, 746th Meeting, XVII Legislature) the Italian position:

> The question arises of what role the international community can play. The Italian Government believes that the international community must in the first place strongly support a dialogue between the [Venezuelan] Government and the opposition and contribute to overcome the economic and social crisis which is a cause for great concern for the entire South American region.

He further discussed the issue before the *Camera dei Deputati* (Chamber of Deputies). On 18 July 2017 (836th Meeting, XVII Legislature), Mr. Alfano took the floor to report on the latest developments in Venezuela, starting from the raid on 5 July of the Venezuelan National Assembly by supporters of President Maduro, which resulted in the wounding of various members of the Assembly:

> When a parliament, the place for democratic choices, is breached by violence, I believe we cannot remain indifferent, and that is why I wanted to publicly and strongly condemn this incident. [...] We cannot stand idle in the face of the violations of the Venezuelan people's right to live in peace and security and to freely choose its representatives.

Mr. Alfano then outlined two ways forward for the mediation efforts: one involving Latin American States only; the other also supported by countries outside of the region, including Italy:

> We must seek as much as possible to involve regional organizations and, even more, the United Nations, by offering our readiness to participate in possible mediation initiatives for which we have the necessary professional competences and experience.

He concluded:

> One thing is certain: should violence persist, we will not look away nor remain silent, and I am happy to say it in front of a Parliament that I feel as being ideally very close to the one in Caracas.

The *Ministro*, however, also clarified the limits of the Italian Government's action, in compliance with the principle of non-interference with (or non-intervention in)[30] the domestic affairs of other States. In his January speech before the Senate of the Republic, he stressed that:

> It is not however our intention to interfere with the internal affairs of a government, since history will judge the merits of President Chavez and of his successor, as it is for any other government experience. Italy has always respected the sovereign choice of the Venezuelan people for their representatives and cooperated constructively with any legitimate government without entering into a political and ideological debate. I think no one can deny that the Italian Government has always maintained relationships with both the Venezuelan authorities and the opposition parties.

The principle of non-interference is considered a fundamental norm of customary international law, but its content remains controversial in light of the vague language of the relevant declarations and the uncertain practice of States. While it is generally recognized that the principle of non-interference is not limited to the prohibition of the use of force, there is no agreement on what political, economic and other measures might breach the principle.[31] It has been argued that an element of coercion is required for a violation of the principle to take place,[32] but the existence of such element is not always easy to assess in practice and depends at any rate on the concrete circumstances of each case. Measures to promote a political regime change or a State's compliance with its human rights obligations can be particularly sensitive, and there is a fine line between lawful and unlawful interference. Despite the Minister's reassurances, doubts can be raised about whether the Italian stance finds itself within or beyond that line.

First of all, Italy seemed to set out the requirements to be met for any mediation between the parties to take place. Recalling the efforts of the Holy See, which managed to arrange the first meeting between the Government and the opposition on 30 October 2016, in the above-mentioned speech before the Senate of the Republic, the *Ministro* endorsed the conditions laid down by the Vatican:

> Let me remind that, for the mediation to be fruitful, the Secretary of State, Monsignor Parolin, asked by means of a letter addressed

---

[30] The two terms are commonly used as synonyms: at times, "intervention" still refers chiefly to military action, while "interference" is considered as having a broader meaning.

[31] For a thorough analysis of the content and ambiguities of the principle of non-interference, see JAMNEJAD and WOOD, "The Principle of Non-intervention", Leiden JIL, 2009, p. 345 ff. See also, for a useful summary: KUNIG, "Intervention, Prohibition of", Max Planck Encyclopedia of Public International Law, April 2008, available at: <http://opil.ouplaw.com/home/EPIL>.

[32] *Military and Paramilitary Activities in and Against Nicaragua (Nicaragua v. United States of America)*, Judgment of 27 June 1986, ICJ Reports, 1986, p. 14 ff., para. 205.

to President Maduro that four crucial points be complied with: respect for the institutions (and for the Parliament's autonomy in particular), the release of all political prisoners, the admission of humanitarian aid for the Venezuelan population, and the adoption of a definite electoral calendar.

On subsequent occasions, Mr. Alfano reiterated Italy's support for those four conditions. Moreover, in his July statement before the Chamber of Deputies, he asserted that "the Government must take into account the will of the people, as expressed on Sunday,[33] to find a political solution to the crisis", and criticized the envisaged Constituent Assembly. He stated that

> One additional condition must be added to [the other four], namely the interruption of the constituent process. At the same time, both parties must act urgently to stop any violent action in the country. It is at any rate clear that in Venezuela too, as in every sovereign State, the greatest responsibility for the maintenance of peace and security lies with the Government.

Indeed, the *Ministro* clarified:

> While we respect the principles of sovereignty and self-determination, we must express our concern for the electoral system established for the Constituent Assembly: it does not appear to comply with the principles of universal suffrage and free and equal participation in the expression of individual choices, which are essential in the context of the rule of law.

With regard to the constituent process, Minister Alfano also mentioned the open letter signed by the Italian President of the Council of Ministers, Mr. Paolo Gentiloni, and his Spanish counterpart, Mr. Mariano Rajoy, and published in the Italian newspaper *Corriere della Sera* on 18 June 2017.[34] In the letter, it is stated *inter alia* that

> Italy and Spain strongly ask the Venezuelan Government to reconsider its decision to establish a Constituent Assembly. The 1999 Constitution, which must be respected in its letter and spirit by all parties – already provides for mechanisms to find a political solution for the diverse interests, in compliance with the institutions, the laws, and popular sovereignty. The decision to convene – at such

---

[33] Reference is here made to the informal referendum organized by the opposition on 16 July 2017, where 98% of the voters rejected the creation of the Constituent Assembly.

[34] The text of the letter is available at: <http://www.corriere.it/esteri/17_giugno_18/maduro-ripensaci-lettera-gentiloni-rajoy-f173b00c-5392-11e7-8a99-4abe2a560c36.shtml>.

> a critical juncture – the Constituent Assembly divides the country instead of uniting it.

As is apparent, the Italian Government put great emphasis on democratic procedures and the respect for the will of the people stemming therefrom. On 17 May 2017 (Senate of the Republic, 825th Meeting, XVII Legislature), Mr. Alfano noted, again with reference to the Constituent Assembly, that

> there is the well-founded concern that this initiative is aimed at depriving the legislative power of its prerogatives and postponing new elections indefinitely.

On that occasion, he reasserted the Italian Government's compliance with the principle of non-interference: "in accordance with the prerogatives of a sovereign State, it is not for me to assess the constitutional legitimacy of such a decision". Nonetheless, he gave account of his actions to tackle this issue:

> I called on the Venezuelan Government to listen to the demands of the population and of its elected representatives. To use the words of the President of the Italian Republic, Mr. Sergio Mattarella: 'we see the need, which cannot be disregarded, for respect for the popular will, respect for the separation of powers, respect for genuine democracy, all things that are seriously put into question'. Finally, I invited the Venezuelan Government not to fuel internal contrasts, which could result in further violence, and to ensure that the people are called to a universal, free, direct, and secret vote. Unfortunately, this plea of mine, which is in line with the position of the international community, has been rejected by the Venezuelan authorities, who defined my statement as 'pernicious and inspired by interventionist goals'. The [Venezuelan] Government reiterated the concept by means of a public communication regarding my statements, including those that I gave before this House.

Criticism was also levelled at the modalities of the regional elections held in October and won by President Maduro's party (17 governorships out of 23) in contrast with consistent poll results. On 5 December 2017 (Chamber of Deputies, 897th Meeting, XVII Legislature), the *Sottosegretario di Stato per gli Affari esteri e la Cooperazione internazionale* (Undersecretary of State for Foreign Affairs and International Cooperation), Mr. Benedetto Della Vedova, spoke of "the deplorable conditions under which the regional elections of 15 October [2017] took place, which testify to the democratic regression under way".

Therefore, on the one hand, the Italian Government has exerted pressure on President Maduro to restore full democracy in Venezuela and resume the mediation with the opposition. On the other hand, the Government has focused on the safety of the Italian community living in the country as well as on the protection of its interests. This two-pronged approach is reflected, in an exemplary manner, in a parliamentary motion (Motion No. 709, first signatory Casini[35]), which Minister Alfano endorsed on behalf of the Government in January. The motion reads as follows:

> [...] Notwithstanding an increasingly serious humanitarian crisis, resulting in the lack of food, medicines and medical devices, the [Venezuelan] Government hinders the entry of humanitarian aid in the country and various international initiatives, including non-governmental ones, supporting the population;
> Concern for the Venezuelan situation is shared by the international community, including the European Union, the United Nations, the Organization of American States and the G7;
> The declaration of the 'state of exception and economic emergency' confers on the Government extraordinarily extensive powers in all fields, thereby unacceptably limiting constitutional guarantees and civil and political rights;
> The separation of powers, which is essential to the rule of law, is severely limited, in light of the strong control exercised by the Government over the judiciary, the National Electoral Council and the Supreme Tribunal especially;
> The constitutional prerogatives of the National Assembly, where the democratic opposition holds the majority, are systematically infringed upon by decisions from both the Government and the Supreme Tribunal that prevent the exercise of the Assembly's legislative and monitoring functions and have laid the basis for the adoption by the Assembly of measures that further exacerbate the current institutional fracture. [...]
> [The Senate] commits the Government:
> 1) to urgently adopt any useful initiative, also at the European Union level and in collaboration with international organizations, to obtain the cooperation of the Venezuelan Government to overcome the country's critical situation; to commit the Venezuelan Government to restore the separation of powers and protect the attributions of the various constitutional bodies; to promote an effective and close dialogue between the different governmental levels, the democratic opposition and civil society; to obtain the release of all political prisoners;
> 2) to urgently adopt any useful initiative, also at the European Union level and in collaboration with international organizations, to alleviate the grave humanitarian crisis in the country, particularly in support of the most vulnerable members of society;

---

[35] The motion was passed with 184 votes in favour, 41 against and 10 abstentions.

3) to prepare an extraordinary plan to assist our fellow citizens residing in Venezuela, including by strengthening our diplomatic and consular offices;

4) to continue to support the legitimate interests of the Italian companies that operate in the country and have claims against the Government.

As put by Minister Alfano on the same occasion:

We must, as a country, take on the responsibility not to abandon [the 160.000 Italian citizens living in Venezuela]. These are Italians who are appealing to their country of origin and we have a duty to help them, while respecting the principles of sovereignty and non-interference.

In a context of heated protests and violent repression, the security of Italian citizens and descendants residing in the country was a primary concern for the Italian Government. During his January speech before the Senate of the Republic, Mr. Alfano welcomed a parliamentary initiative for the recruitment of additional personnel in Venezuela and the reinforcement of the diplomatic offices' security. The *Ministro* also made reference to the unresolved death of an Italian consular official in Caracas, Mr. Mauro Monciatti, and stated the strong commitment of the Italian Government to clarify the circumstances of the incident. In December, before the Chamber of Deputies, Mr. Della Vedova detailed further security measures adopted by the Italian Government, including the upgrade of emergency satellite communication systems and the increase in the number of *Carabinieri* deployed at the Italian Embassy and Consulate General. As clarified by the *Sottosegretario*, funds earmarked for international peacekeeping missions were used to implement these measures.

The Italian Government also strived to provide the Italian community with essential medicines. As reported by Mr. Alfano in January:

We have been asking [local authorities] for over a year to allow us to provide for the medical needs of the Italian community by lifting the ban on the import of medicines, but our request was rejected.

Minister Delcy Rodriguez made a personal commitment to my predecessor to addressing the needs of the [Italian] community and a list of essential and urgent medicines was delivered to her, but these have never been distributed. Nor was our readiness to alleviate – through the United Nations – the lack of essential goods in the country more successful.

The repeated attempts of the Italian Government in this respect met with the persistent refusal of Venezuelan authorities to acknowledge the existence of a health emergency in the country, as admitted by Mr. Della Vedova in December. Nonetheless, the *Sottosegretario* restated the willingness of the Government to exert pressure on its Venezuelan counterpart in order for such aid to be allowed into the country. Conversely, the Italian Government's interventions in the area of social and economic assistance yielded more substantial results: in January, Mr. Alfano referred in particular to the supplement to those pensions that had been most affected by the rising inflation.

Finally, the protection of the interests and claims of Italian companies operating in Venezuela is a common thread of all Government statements before the Parliament. In January, in his speech before the Senate of the Republic, Mr. Alfano stated:

> We pointed out on multiple occasions to the Venezuelan Government that the claims of almost all of our companies are growing untenably. We are well aware of the financial situation of Venezuela, but we keep asking at least for a sign of goodwill to reassure those Italian companies that believed in Venezuela and its development. Meanwhile, I asked for an assessment of the outstanding claims of our companies and citizens in Venezuela in order to identify possible means for redress among the tools provided for by the law.

The Italian Government seemed thus to exercise its diplomatic protection prerogatives, even though recourse to this traditional instrument was not mentioned explicitly. It remains that the two bilateral investment treaties signed between Italy and Venezuela, in 1990 and 2001 respectively, have never entered into force, while the European Union-Mercosur Cooperation Agreement entrusts the promotion and protection of investment to bilateral agreements between the parties. Nonetheless, the *Ministro* reiterated on multiple occasions the commitment of the Italian Government to raise the issue of Italian companies' claims with the Venezuelan authorities "at the highest level" and to explore possible means of redress "with due regard to budget constraints".

The direct interest of Italy in the solution of the political and economic crisis in Venezuela, due to the large Italian community residing there, appears further to justify the adoption of bilateral restrictive measures by the Italian Government – i.e. limitations on the export of defense equipment to Venezuela. As highlighted by Mr. Della Vedova in December, these measures were followed by the sanctions decided by the European Union Foreign Affairs Council on 13 November 2017. Council Regulation (EU) 2017/2063 and Council Decision (CFSP) 2017/2074 include an embargo on arms and related material and a legal framework for individual travel bans and assets freezes. With regard to the latter, it was only in January 2018 that seven Venezuelan officials were put on the sanctions list, as persons responsible for serious human rights violations and the repression of the opposition.[36]

CHIARA TEA ANTONIAZZI

---

[36] The list is included in Council Implementing Regulation (EU) 2018/88 and Council Decision (CFSP) 2018/90, both adopted on 22 January 2018.

XII. HUMAN RIGHTS

1. THE RIGHT OF DEFENSE BEFORE THE ROMAN ROTA

On 10 March 2017, during a meeting of the *Camera dei Deputati* (Chamber of Deputies, 757th Meeting, XVII Legislature), Mr. Renato Brunetta, a member of the Italian Parliament, posed an interpellation to the *Sottosegretario di Stato per la Giustizia* (Undersecretary of State for Justice), Mr. Gennaro Migliore, regarding the right of defense before the Roman Rota[37] in trials aimed at obtaining a declaration of nullity of marriage. In particular, Mr. Brunetta drew the Government's attention to the fact that the *Decano del Tribunale della Rota Romana* (Dean of the Ecclesiastical Court), through a decree issued in December 2015, was preventing the parties to such trials from appointing their own defenders by claiming that prerogative for himself. The right of defense is enshrined in Article 6 of the European Convention for the Protection of Human Rights and Fundamental Freedoms (ECHR), to which the Holy See is not a party. The ECHR, however, is binding upon Italy, for which the same right is also a fundamental principle at the constitutional level.[38] Therefore, according to Mr. Brunetta, a problem emerges for Italy, as once a declaration of matrimonial nullity is pronounced by the Roman Rota, the decision is considered a judgment of a foreign court by the Italian legal order and may be recognized therein. This is done through a special procedure laid down in Article 8 of the *Accordo di Villa Madama* (Villa Madama Agreement) signed by Italy and the Holy See in 1984.[39] Such procedure differs from the automatic recognition of foreign judgments provided for by Articles 64 and 65 of *Legge 31 maggio 1990, n. 218* (Law No. 218 of 31 Maj 1990) on private international law. According to the Villa Madama Agreement, judgments declaring matrimonial nullity are recognized through the *exequatur* of the Italian *Corti d'Appello* (Courts of Appeal), under Articles 796 and 797 of the Italian Civil Procedure Code, and produce civil effects in the Italian legal order. Mr. Brunetta therefore asked what measures the Italian Government was planning to take to ensure compliance with the right of defense, as protected by both the Italian Constitution and the ECHR.

---

[37] As defined by Can. 1443 of the Code of Canon Law, the Roman Rota (*Tribunal Apostolicum Rotae Romanae*) "is the ordinary tribunal established by the Roman Pontiff to receive appeals". A claim may be addressed to the Pope – "the supreme Judge for the entire Catholic world" – who can handle the case personally or through ordinary tribunals like the Roman Rota (Can. 1442). The Rota was established in the 13th century and it is called like this (Rota is Latin for "wheel") because the judges originally met in a round room to hear cases.

[38] As affirmed by the Italian Constitutional Court: see Judgment of 22 January 1982, No. 18 and, more recently, Judgment of 16 January 2003, No. 29.

[39] *Accordo tra la Santa Sede e la Repubblica italiana che apporta modificazioni al Concordato Lateranense*. The Agreement was signed by Cardinal Agostino Casaroli and Prime Minister Bettino Craxi in Rome on 18 February 1984 in order to revise the previous Concordat (see next footnote).

In answering the question, Mr. Migliore began by saying that, since the Lateran Pacts of 1929,[40] the Italian State has considered the Catholic Church as an independent and sovereign entity. Such stance did not change with the signing of the Villa Madama Agreement. Moreover, the sovereignty of the Holy See over the State of Vatican City is recognized by Article 7 of the Italian Constitution. Having stressed this, the Undersecretary added:

> Within such legislative framework, the separation between the legal orders of the Republic and the Holy See does not allow the Government to interfere in issues pertaining to the independence and sovereignty of the Holy See, also with regards to jurisdictional powers. Thus, the Government may directly inspect neither the initiative of the Roman Rota's Dean as to the appointment of the defender in trials for the declaration of matrimonial nullity held before Ecclesiastical Tribunals, nor the compliance of the Ecclesiastical proceedings with the principles expressed in the European Convention on Human Rights. The issue of the restriction of the right of defense, stemming from the Dean's decree, may, instead, have relevance with regard to the *exequatur* of the Ecclesiastical judgments by the Italian judges and this is a general principle, which applies to all cases of reciprocity between two sovereign States' jurisdictional systems. [...] In order for the judgment to be recognized, the Italian judge shall assess, specifically, whether during the proceedings in front of Ecclesiastical Tribunals the right of action as well as defense of the parties was respected, in a manner not dissimilar to what is prescribed by the fundamental principles of the Italian order [...] and, therefore, whether, despite the restriction to the right to appoint a private defense lawyer introduced by the Ecclesiastical jurisdiction, the proceedings were fully respectful of the right of defense.

In conclusion, Italy's compliance with the right of defense stemming from both the ECHR and its constitutional law principles is to be ensured through the *exequatur* of the Italian judges. More specifically, the Courts of Appeal, which are in charge of *exequatur* proceedings, will determine whether and to what extent each declaration of nullity of marriage complies with international and domestic principles concerning the right of defense. In this regard, it is worth noting that the *Corte di Cassazione* (Court of Cassation) has already identified cases where

---

[40] The Lateran Pacts were signed by the Prime Minister Benito Mussolini and Cardinal Pietro Gasparri in the Lateran Palace on 11 February 1929. They contained three different documents: the Treaty; the Concordat and the Financial Convention. Art. 34 of the Concordat laid down the rules on Catholic matrimony and the declaration of its nullity.

granting the *exequatur* of Ecclesiastical judgments would have been contrary to the Italian public order for breaching supreme principles of constitutional law.[41]

FEDERICO DI DARIO and LUIGI D'ETTORRE

XIV. CO-OPERATION IN JUDICIAL, LEGAL, SECURITY, AND SOCIO-ECONOMIC MATTERS

1. ITALY'S INVOLVEMENT IN POST-CONFLICT LIBYA. THE LIBYAN COAST GUARD TRAINING MISSION

Post-conflict Libya has been riven by internal conflict, institutional, political and social instability as well as a grave humanitarian crisis. The achievement of stability in Libya has been of concern to the international community, in particular in light of the serious consequences of internal conflict and fragmentation on, *inter alia*, the fight against terrorism and the Islamic State, as well as against human trafficking and migrant smuggling across the Mediterranean Sea.[42]

Historically a prominent international actor in the country, Italy has strongly supported the Government of National Accord, formed under the terms of the Libyan Political Agreement signed in Skhirat, Morocco, on 17 December 2015,[43] and endorsed by the United Nations (UN) Security Council as the sole legitimate executive authority in Libya.[44] On 8 May 2017, during a briefing at the UN Security Council on the situation in Libya (7934th Meeting),[45] the Permanent Representative of Italy to the United Nations, Ambassador Sebastiano Cardi, declared:

> There is a need for a sustainable political solution to the crisis in Libya, one based on the Libyan Political Agreement. That is the sole framework in which solutions to the most pressing issues can be found, and the Presidency Council and the Government of National Accord, headed by Prime Minister Serraj, are the sole legitimate executive authorities of Libya, in line with resolution 2259 (2015).

In particular with regard to the fight against human trafficking and migrant smuggling, Italy took initiative both at the European Union level and bilaterally

---

[41] See, for example, *Corte di Cassazione (Sezioni Unite Civili)*, 17 July 2014, Nos. 16379 and 16380.

[42] For a recent description of the situation in Libya, see for instance the Report of the Secretary-General on the United Nations Support Mission in Libya, UN Doc. S/2017/726 (2017).

[43] An unsigned version of the Libyan Political Agreement is available at the website of the United Nations Support Mission in Libya (UNSMIL): <https://unsmil.unmissions.org/sites/default/files/Libyan%20Political%20Agreement%20%20ENG%20.pdf>.

[44] UN Security Council Resolution 2259 (2015) of 23 December 2015, para. 3.

[45] UN Doc. S/PV.7934 (2017).

with Libya. At the European level, Italy supported, *inter alia*, the strengthening of the EUNAVFOR MED operation Sophia.[46] On 8 March 2017, in answering a parliamentary question at the *Camera dei Deputati* (Chamber of Deputies, 755th Meeting, XVII Legislature), the *Ministro degli Affari esteri e della Cooperazione internazionale* (Minister of Foreign Affairs and International Cooperation), Mr. Angelino Alfano, explained:

> Italy has promoted and continues to work for the transition to phase three of the EUNAVFOR MED operation Sophia, which, as is well known, provides for the entry of the vessels of the Operation into Libyan territorial waters in order to stop smugglers and their boats straight off the Libyan coast. So, this is our position. It also serves to dismantle more efficiently the business model of human trafficking networks. These tasks would be in addition to what Sophia has already been doing, namely the prevention of arms trafficking and the crucial task of training the Libyan Coast Guard so that it can itself operate within its own territorial waters as soon as possible.

Mr. Alfano stressed the importance of certain legal requirements for the development of the operation advocated by Italy:

> It does not depend only on us; that is to say, we need the consent of the Libyan institutions and we need, this is essential, a vote by the United Nations Security Council.

At the bilateral level with Libya, a memorandum of understanding (MoU) was signed on 2 February 2017 between the *Presidente del Consiglio dei Ministri* (President of the Council of Ministers), Mr. Paolo Gentiloni and the Libyan Prime Minister Fayez al-Sarraj.[47] As explained by the *Ministro dell'Interno* (Minister of Internal Affairs), Mr. Marco Minniti, on 5 July 2017 before the *Senato della*

---

[46] The EUNAVFOR MED operation was first established by Council Decision (CFSP) 2015/778 of 18 May 2015 on a European Union military operation in the Southern Central Mediterranean (EUNAVFOR MED), lastly amended by Council Decision (CFSP) 2017/1385 of 25 July 2017. Its mission, as laid down in Article 1 of Decision 2015/778, is to "contribut[e] to the disruption of the business model of human smuggling and trafficking networks in the Southern Central Mediterranean [...], achieved by undertaking systematic efforts to identify, capture and dispose of vessels and assets used or suspected of being used by smugglers and traffickers, in accordance with applicable international law, including UNCLOS and any UN Security Council Resolution".

[47] The full title of the MoU is *Memorandum d'intesa sulla cooperazione nel campo dello sviluppo, del contrasto all'immigrazione illegale, al traffico di esseri umani, al contrabbando e sul rafforzamento della sicurezza delle frontiere tra lo Stato della Libia e la Repubblica Italiana* (Memorandum of Understanding on cooperation in the field of development, in the fight against illegal immigration, human trafficking, smuggling, and on the strengthening of the security of the borders between the State of Libya and the Italian Republic). The text of the MoU is available (in Italian) at the website of the Italian Government: <http://www.governo.it/sites/governoNEW.it/files/Libia.pdf>. On this issue see the comment by MANCINI in this Volume, pp. 259 ff.

Repubblica (Senate of the Republic, 852th Meeting, XVII Legislature), the MoU was based on three cornerstones:

> Its first cornerstone, the control of Libyan territorial waters, is dependent upon the strengthening, the training and the enhanced capacity for action of the [Libyan] Coast Guard.

The Minister then outlined the second key element of the MoU:

> Since the goal is to have the Coast Guard control the [migratory] flows leaving from the northern coast of Libya and return them back to Libya, it is paramount not to open new reception centers, since there are so many in Libya, but to guarantee the respect of human rights.

Finally, Mr. Minniti laid out the third element, the control of the southern border of Libya:

> The Sub-Saharan border is a fundamental element for the control of human trafficking as well as for anti-terrorism activities. [...] In the past weeks, the main tribes, the so-called guardians of the desert – the Tebus, the Tuaregs, the Suleimans – who were at war against each other, came to Rome and signed a peace agreement before the Italian Government. [...] Those tribes may constitute, in the future, the backbone of a modern Libyan border guard protecting the southern borders of Libya, together with two key countries with which we have concluded a cooperation agreement, i.e. Niger and Chad.

On 23 July 2017, the Libyan Prime Minister Al-Sarraj sent a letter to Italy requesting technical assistance for the Libyan Coast Guard in the Libyan territorial waters, within the framework of the MoU. The details of the request were reported on 1 August 2017 before the *Commissioni Riunite – Affari esteri e comunitari (III) e Difesa (IV) della Camera dei Deputati; Affari esteri, Emigrazione (3a) e Difesa (4a) del Senato della Repubblica* (Joint Commissions – Foreign and European Affairs (III) and Defense (IV) of the Chamber of Deputies; Foreign Affairs, Emigration (3rd) and Defense (4th) of the Senate of the Republic, 28th Meeting, XVII Legislature) by Mr. Alfano as well as the *Ministro della Difesa* (Minister of Defense), Ms. Roberta Pinotti. Mr. Alfano explained:

> The Libyan President has called on the Italian Government to send naval support that is technically suited to provide all the necessary assistance in fighting human traffickers and illegal immigration, thus providing the necessary assistance to the Libyan vessels that are operating in these very areas. The assistance we are asked to provide, therefore, concerns the activities of the Libyan Coast Guard.

He continued:

> I would like to reiterate and underline that this is the first time that
> we have received such a request and that an action such as the one
> that is envisaged would have been impossible without a specific
> request from the Libyan side, and indeed has never been carried
> out in the past.

This request for assistance sparked controversy in Libya. In particular,
General Khalifa Haftar, arguably the most powerful opponent of al-Sarraj's leadership in Libya, spoke of interference in Libya's sovereignty and hinted at the
fact that Italy might be using the pretext of combatting illegal immigration to
intervene and change the balance of power in the country.[48] Ms. Pinotti, without
referring directly to such controversies, addressed the issue of potential interference with state sovereignty:

> In order to carry out this activity, the Libyan authorities asked us
> to operate in their territorial waters and ports as well. This will en-
> tail the deployment of our vessels to carry out the abovementioned
> support functions, in particular in the port of Tripoli and in the area
> east and west of Tripoli. All activities will be carried out on the ba-
> sis of the needs expressed by the Libyan authorities, and therefore
> in close coordination with them. There is no issue of interference
> with, or prejudice to, the Libyan sovereignty, not least because our
> objective is, if anything, to strengthen that sovereignty by provid-
> ing support for all the activities that are typical of fully sovereign
> States.

Ms. Pinotti added with regard to the rules of engagement applicable to the
mission:

> International law explicitly allows for extended self-defense, which
> requires in any event at all times a graduated, limited and propor-
> tionate use of force. Also in this regard, the details will need to
> be discussed with the Libyans, in the sense that just like in *Mare
> Sicuro*,[49] if it were to happen that smugglers would shoot at one of
> our vessels, we could take action on the basis of this rule of interna-
> tional law. The same must apply if Libyan vessels are put at risk.

---

[48] The declarations of General Haftar, and the subsequent reaction of the Libyan Presidential
Council, were mentioned and discussed during the above-mentioned debate before the Joint
Commissions.

[49] *Mare Sicuro* (Safe Seas) is an operation launched by the Italian Navy on 12 March 2015
with the task of carrying out, pursuant to national legislation and international agreements in
force, maritime surveillance and safety-related activities in the central Mediterranean Sea.

Ms. Pinotti denied that the mission could have a "Search and Rescue" objective:

> It is not our task or the task of the mission. Our task is to help the Libyans, both with regard to the rescue and with regard to the fight against smugglers as [we/they][50] are attacked.

Again on the issue of consent and state sovereignty, Mr. Alfano also intervened and concluded:

> We are managing this whole matter consensually with the legitimate Libyan authorities. That is the essential point. Any action involving armaments and naval units or aircrafts, without consent, as Minister Pinotti said, would assume a different profile under international law.

On 2 August 2017, the Chamber of the Deputies and the Senate of the Republic gave their authorization to the mission, in line with *Legge 21 luglio 2016, n. 145* (Law No. 145 of 2016).

ALESSIO GRACIS

XV. INTERNATIONAL ECONOMIC LAW

1. CHINA'S MARKET ECONOMY STATUS

China joined the World Trade Organization (WTO) in 2001. As an economy undergoing transformation, special trade rules were negotiated and agreed with China to safeguard the interests of the existing WTO membership. Article 15 of China's WTO Accession Protocol sets out that modified rules for imposing anti-dumping tariffs (less favorable to China) will apply for a period of fifteen years from the accession date. This period expired on 11 December 2016 and since then the interpretation of the provisions in Article 15 of the Accession Protocol has become a bone of contention. The dispute over granting China market economy status (MES), which is associated with the expiry of the special conditions in Article 15 of the Accession Protocol, affects directly the legal basis of EU's trade (defense) policy towards China.

On 1 February 2017, shortly after the fifteenth anniversary of China's WTO membership, during a meeting of the *Camera dei Deputati* (Chamber of Deputies, 734th Meeting, XVII Legislature), Mr. Raffaello Vignali, a member of the Italian Parliament, posed an interpellation to the *Ministro dello Sviluppo economico* (Minister of Economic Development), Mr. Carlo Calenda, regarding the issue of

---

[50] The Italian version reads "in quanto attaccati" and does not specify the subject of the verb. There are two possibilities: "attacked" can refer either to the Libyans or the Italians.

granting China MES – which would potentially weaken the competitiveness of Italian companies – and the initiatives undertaken at the European Union (EU) level to achieve a balanced solution.

The legal context for such interpellation and the Government's response thereto needs to be clarified in more detail. Under standard WTO rules (Article VI of the General Agreement on Tariffs and Trade (GATT) and the related Anti-Dumping Agreement (ADA)), where products of one country are introduced into the market of another country at less than their "normal value" (i.e. dumping), and this threatens or causes injury to an industry in the importing country, the latter is authorized to levy duties to offset or prevent such practice. Anti-dumping duties should not be higher than the margin of dumping in respect of the product at issue and, as a general principle, duties at a level lower than the margin of dumping are desirable – but not mandatory – if this level is adequate to remove injury (lesser duty rule, Article 9 ADA). The so-called normal price sets the basis for calculating the scale of dumping.

The relevant WTO provisions indicate different ways to determine the normal price of a product, first, as the "domestic price" of the product in the exporting country (Article VI(1)(a) of the GATT) and second, in the absence of a domestic price, as either the "highest comparable price for a like product for export", or the cost of production in the country of origin plus a reasonable addition for selling cost and profit (Article VI(1)(b) of the GATT). The Interpretative Note *Ad* Article VI, however, also recognizes that, where imports originate from "a country which has a complete or substantially complete monopoly of its trade and where all domestic prices are fixed by the State" a strict comparison with domestic prices may not be appropriate, and a comparison with prices in a third country can be used to determine the "normal value". In all these cases, the country imposing the anti-dumping duty bears the burden of proof that dumping which caused material injury to a domestic industry has taken place.

Article 15 of the WTO Accession Protocol acknowledges State control of the prices of land, capital and energy in China and sets out different rules for establishing the normal value of products: first, by introducing a legal presumption that China is not a market economy and, second, by shifting the burden of proof on Chinese firms or the government. Article 15 of the Accession Protocol establishes that if the producers under investigation can clearly show that market economy conditions prevail in the relevant industry, the importing WTO Member must use Chinese domestic prices as a basis for anti-dumping duties (Article 15(a)(i)). The comparison criterion is the same as under general WTO rules (i.e. domestic price) but a different standard of proof applies. Where Chinese producers cannot offer such evidence, the importing WTO country can apply a standard other than domestic prices or costs in China, for instance, third-country price comparison (Article 15(a)(ii)). Anti-dumping duties determined this way are notably higher than those that would apply under standard WTO rules and this makes Chinese products less competitive. This latter provision was set to expire fifteen years after China's date of accession to the WTO (Article 15(d)).

The ambiguity regarding the interpretation of the Accession Protocol arises from the fact that the provision in Article 15(d) contains two limbs, one on granting MES to China once it has fulfilled the conditions set out in the domestic legislation of the importing WTO Member, and the other on the elimination of the legal basis for applying third-country price comparison methodology under Article 15(a)(ii), starting from 11 December 2016. The relationship between the two provisions remains unclear, i.e. whether the expiry of Article 15(a)(ii) amounts to an automatic fulfillment of MES conditions. If this interpretation is valid, Article 15(a) will cease to apply in its entirety, the special treatment of China will terminate vis-à-vis the importing State, and China's position in this respect will become equal to that of most other WTO members. Significantly, on 12 December 2016 China notified the WTO Secretariat of a request for consultations with the United States and the EU regarding special calculation methodologies used by the United States and the EU in anti-dumping proceedings.

The position of the Italian government on this issue was made clear by Mr. Calenda before the *Commissione X – Attività produttive* (Commission X – Economic Activities) of the Chamber of Deputies, on 31 January 2017:

> Given that the text of Article 15 is actually drawn up in an unclear way, in our interpretation, the deadline of 12 December 2016 does not imply the obligation to use the Chinese prices and costs for the calculation of the normal value in investigations using standard methodology, which would be equivalent to a 'recognition of the status of a market economy'.

Some countries (notably Australia) have granted recognition of MES to China, mainly granting the status as a condition for negotiating free trade agreements (FTA) with China. The EU (similarly to the United States) has established domestic criteria for granting MES and has been in dialogue with China regarding their fulfillment.[51] At the same time, however, to avoid open conflict, most recently, the EU has modernized its instruments on the methodology for determining cost and price distortions related to dumping.

In this regard, at the above-mentioned meeting of the Chamber of Deputies (734th Meeting, XVII Legislature), Mr. Calenda reported that:

> Italy, in fact, has blocked an attempt by the European Commission, which dates back to the middle of last year, to recognize, in practice, market economy status to China, through a mechanism that, while recognizing it as a market economy, would have included

---

[51] Council Regulation (EC) No 905/98 of 27 April 1998 amending Regulation (EC) No 384/96 on protection against dumped imports from countries not members of the European Community. See in particular the revised Art. 2.7(c). The regulation has not been in force since 10 January 2010 but the same conditions were replicated in subsequent regulations. Recently, Regulation (EU) 2017/2321 of the European Parliament and of the Council of 12 December 2017 introduced a new methodology and removed all references to market economy conditions in Regulation (EU) 2016/1036 on protection against dumped imports from countries not members of the EU (see *infra*).

so-called mitigation clauses, i.e. safeguarding the anti-dumping duties imposed. We have considered this case as potentially disastrous for the Italian and European industry. The Italian government was the first and for a long time the only one to talk openly about it, to mobilize the press and to take concrete steps, which ultimately achieved a result, because the Commission stopped and proposed today a Regulation, that will need to be approved by the European Parliament, which is totally different and somewhat similar to that of the United States, and uses an analysis of average prices compared to the country's prices, in the calculation of dumping mechanisms. However, we are not comfortable with how this Regulation is developing, because we still think that it is too weak. In particular, we believe that the regulatory text must maintain a clear anchoring to the five criteria on the basis of which a market economy is evaluated.[52] We must strongly limit the discretion of the Commission, in the sense that, when there is dumping, dumping must be sanctioned; in this sense we are concerned about the idea of a macroeconomic study to be produced by the Commission before being able to operate with a non-market economy methodology.[53]

The Minister added that:

In our opinion, the new situation of international trade policy urges a strengthening of all instruments of commercial defense, also because the United States goes towards this path […]. On this, the Italian government has the strongest position in Europe and continues to support it with the hope of achieving what we have experienced in the last year, namely that slowly other countries start to follow and agree on strengthening these instruments.

Among such trade defense instruments, the Italian Government had proposed to limit the use of the lesser duty rule in anti-dumping cases where there are structural raw material distortions. The rule is not mandatory under WTO law as such, but is a criterion included in EU trade defense regulations, praised by the EU as a positive instrument that reduces trade distortions. At the above-mentioned meeting of the Commission X – Economic Activities, Mr. Calenda summarized the Italian position on this issue:

Unfortunately, this attempt got stuck as a result of the ideological and preconceived opposition of some Member States, who simply rejected the idea of partially reducing the application of the so-called 'lesser duty rule' […].

---

[52] Such criteria are listed in Art. 2.7(c) of Regulation (EC) No 384/96 as amended by Council Regulation (EC) No 905/98.

[53] The new mechanism is explained below.

Unfortunately, despite the political pressure and the economic interests at stake, which also involve the employment of many European
citizens, the position of some Member States has remained ideo-
logically anchored to the principle of not changing the provisions
relating to the lesser duty rule. However, this rule cannot be considered an intangible principle, because it is a WTO-plus guarantee,
therefore not mandatory, that numerous and important international
partners, starting from the United States, do not apply.

It should be recalled that the EU speaks with one voice at the WTO level and
the solution eventually pursued by the EU institutions is partially different from
what Italy had foreseen, even though it is equally aimed at maintaining protection standards against Chinese products similar to the ones previously in force.
On the one hand, the EU has substantially revised its anti-dumping legislation by
removing all references to MES, and on the other, it has incorporated in a current
draft legislation the Italian proposal to derogate from the lesser duty principle,
where there are raw material distortions in the exporting country, and where this
(the non-application of the lesser duty rule) is in the EU's interest.[54]

To continue defending the interests of EU firms in compliance with WTO
obligations, a new regulation (EU Regulation 2017/2321) was adopted on 12
December 2017, amending the methodology that the European Commission uses
to calculate price distortions for all WTO countries alike. The previous Anti-
Dumping Regulation applied, for all countries qualified by the EU as "Non-Market
Economy", the "analogue country" methodology to calculate normal prices or
costs. The new legislation removes the source of the conflict with China, namely
all reference to MES (a distinction repeatedly labeled as discriminatory by China)
and introduces a "neutral" mechanism that will purportedly apply equally to all
WTO Members. A standard methodology based on domestic market prices for
dumping calculation purposes will apply to all WTO Members, with a non-stan-
dard methodology being used where "significant distortions" caused by government intervention are established. Where the Commission has "well founded indications of the possible existence of significant distortions", it shall make public
and regularly update a report describing the distorted market circumstances and
use as a basis for anti-dumping duties certain international benchmarks, including costs/prices in an appropriate third country with a similar level of economic
development. On 20 December 2017 the Commission published its first report,
concerning China, and announced the preparation of the next one, on Russia.

Despite these efforts, which are intended to solve some of the issues covered
by China's legal action before the WTO, the real matter at the core of the dispute,

---

[54] See the Provisional agreement resulting from inter-institutional negotiations: Proposal
for a regulation of the European Parliament and of the Council amending Council Regulation
(EC) No 1225/2009 on protection against dumped imports from countries not members of the
European Community and Council Regulation (EC) No 597/2009 on protection against sub-
sidised imports from countries not members of the European Community (COM(2013)0192
– 2013/0103(COD)), AG\1142795EN.docx, 10 January 2018.

i.e. the level of duties to be imposed on Chinese products in the future, remains open. The EU solution is as close as it gets to the third-country price comparison standard in Interpretative Note *Ad* Article VI, but the Non-Market Economy definition therein contained sets a higher threshold than the requirement of "significant distortions" caused by government intervention in Regulation No. 2017/2321. The EU's approach, which has been – only partly – successfully contested by Italy throughout the negotiations of the new legislative framework,[55] was finally hailed by Mr. Calenda as "the best possible result considering the various interests involved". He also added that "the level of alert must remain high and the task of the Government and the other actors is now to ensure that the new legislation is rigorously applied".[56]

JULINDA BEQIRAJ

XVII. RELATIONSHIP BETWEEN MUNICIPAL AND INTERNATIONAL LAW

1. PRESIDENT MATTARELLA'S REFUSAL TO PROMULGATE A LAW ON THE FINANCING OF THE ARMS INDUSTRY

On 27 October 2017, the *Presidente della Repubblica Italiana* (President of the Italian Republic, hereinafter President), Mr. Sergio Mattarella, refused to promulgate the law[57] drafted and approved by the Parliament titled "*Misure per contrastare il finanziamento delle imprese produttrici di mine antipersona, di munizioni e submunizioni a grappolo*" (Measures to combat the financing of firms manufacturing antipersonnel landmines, cluster munitions and submunitions, hereinafter Law No. 57).[58] In the Italian constitutional system, in order for

---

[55] In mid-September 2017, Mr. Calenda was still hoping for a "significant improvement of the text". See the Press release available at: <http://www.sviluppoeconomico.gov.it/index.php/it/194-comunicati-stampa/2037067-mes-cina-calenda-bene-proposta-commissione-su-investimenti-analoga-fermezza-su-commercio>.

[56] See the texts of the declarations available at: <https://it.finance.yahoo.com/notizie/ue-calenda-ora-applicazione-rigorosa-su-metodologia-antidumping-173116786.html> and <https://finanza.repubblica.it/News/2017/10/03/anti_dumping_calenda_raggiunto_miglior_compromesso_possibile-263/>.

[57] The word "law" is used to refer to a bill passed by the Parliament even though not yet signed and, therefore, promulgated by the President, whereas the term "bill" refers to a legislative proposal that has not been passed by both Houses of the Parliament yet. This terminology is in accordance with the English translation of the Italian Constitution provided for by the International Affairs Service of the Senate of the Republic: Servizio Affari internazionali, Senato della Repubblica, *Constitution of the Italian Republic. Costituzione Italiana Edizione in Lingua Inglese*, available at <http://www.senato.it/application/xmanager/projects/leg18/file/repository/relazioni/libreria/novita/XVII/COST_INGLESE.pdf>. This translation is used throughout the whole text to render the Italian legal vocabulary.

[58] This is the name given to the bill during the preparatory works. For more details, see Parlamento Italiano, "Disegno di Legge S. 57 – 17a Legislatura", available at <http://www.senato.it/leg/17/BGT/Schede/Ddliter/39361.htm>.

a law to enter into force the President has to promulgate it, according to Article 73 of the Constitution. To this end, Article 74 confers the President the power to require that the law undergoes a new debate in the two Houses of the Parliament, expressing the reasons for such a request. As explained in the opinion sent to the *Senato della Repubblica* (Senate of the Republic) and the *Camera dei Deputati* (Chamber of Deputies), the President identified two problematic features of the law, which are here illustrated.

In the first place, there was a lack of coherence between the main purpose of the law and some measures adopted to pursue that purpose. Secondly, a specific provision of Law No. 57, i.e. Article 6(2), appeared to clash with two norms of the Constitution: Article 117(1), regarding the status of Italy's international obligations vis-à-vis domestic legislation, and Article 3, establishing the principle of equality of all citizens before the law.

The President opened his opinion describing the relevant provisions:

> The law (composed of seven articles) was approved on 6 October 2016 by the *6ªCommissione permanente* [6th Permanent Committee] of the Senate through the deliberative process,[59] and definitively on 3 October 2017 by the Chamber of Deputies. By means of Article 1 of this law, a comprehensive prohibition is introduced for authorized intermediaries[60] [...] on financing those firms that, in Italy or abroad, directly or through (other) controlled or associated firms, perform activities that are in any way connected to the production or distribution or commercialization of antipersonnel landmines, cluster munitions and submunitions.

President Mattarella appreciated this innovation and affirmed:

> The law contains innovative aspects, which undoubtedly appear positive as they strengthen the measures to combat the manufacturing of these dangerous and insidious warfare devices, providing for, among other things, administrative liability for legal persons.

However, a few lines below, the President introduced his first ground of concern:

---

[59] In the original version of the opinion, the expression "*sede deliberante*" is used. Such an expression refers to the procedure in which a bill is voted and approved within the competent committee of a House of the Parliament in a legislative capacity, without passing through the plenary assembly of the House itself. Such a possibility is admitted by Art. 72 of the Italian Constitution.

[60] Article 2 of the law defines the expression "*intermediari abilitati*" (authorized intermediaries). The provision lists different kinds of companies, banks, financial intermediaries, bank foundations, pension funds and other entities that are involved with the investment of money.

> At the same time, the presence, within the law, of a provision that appears to clash with the declared aims of this legislative intervention and seems to be characterized by significant critical aspects should be noticed.
> I am speaking of Article 6, titled "*Sanzioni*" [Sanctions], which, at paragraph 2, decriminalizes those operations of financing firms that produce antipersonnel landmines and cluster bombs, whenever those operations are carried out by subjects at the head of authorized intermediary bodies.

The President continued describing the content of the provision taken into consideration:

> In that paragraph, an administrative monetary sanction between € 50,000 and € 250,000 is provided for physical persons who have managerial or directorial roles of authorized intermediary bodies or who, on behalf of them, perform control functions, in the case the prohibition on financing firms that operate in the field of antipersonnel landmines and cluster munitions is violated.

In this respect, as noted above, the President took the view that the administrative sanctions provided for the conduct covered by the law were inconsistent with its purpose, spelt out by Article 1 quoted above.

President Mattarella also manifested a second ground of concern, by highlighting the incompatibility of Article 6(2) with two articles of the Italian Constitution. As far as Article 117(1) is concerned, it must be noted that Article 6(2) of Law No. 57 was at odds with some laws enacted by the Parliament in order to incorporate into the Italian legal system some international obligations regarding anti-personnel landmines and cluster munitions. The President explained this point as follows:

> The issue at the center of the provision cited earlier is already generally regulated by the criminal provisions contained in Law No. 374 of 1997 and Law No. 95 of 2011. This latter provides for the ban of cluster munitions, as well as ratifies and implements the Oslo Convention (made in Dublin on 30 May 2008), criminalizing, at Article 7, the financial assistance in favor of whoever employs, develops, produces, acquires in any way, stockpiles, stores or transfers, directly or indirectly, cluster munitions or parts of them, and punishing such conducts with the imprisonment between three and twelve years and a fine from € 258,228 to € 516,456. Therefore, the conduct of 'financial assistance' (included among those that are prohibited by the Oslo Convention) fully corresponds to the one prohibited by Article 1 of the law under review, for which only an administrative sanction is provided by Article 6, paragraph 2, if committed by those authorized subjects indicated above.

In this passage, President Mattarella referred to the law of the Parliament that incorporated the 2008 Convention on Cluster Munitions (Oslo Convention),[61] whose Article 9 requires States to adopt "all appropriate legal, administrative and other measures to implement th[e] Convention, including the imposition of penal sanctions to prevent and suppress any activity prohibited to a State Party" under its provisions. By means of the law cited by the President – *Legge 15 giugno, n. 95* (Law No. 95 of 15 June 2011)[62] – Italy implements this obligation, establishing a criminal liability regime for the financing of behaviors that are proscribed by the Oslo Convention. In light of this, Article 6(2) of Law No. 57 appeared to be incompatible with the obligations arising out of the domestic implementation of the convention, as it regulated a specific conduct already criminalized by Law No. 95/2011, downgrading the related sanction from a penal to an administrative one.

A similar problem arose also with regard to the regulation of the conduct involving anti-personnel landmines. In 1997, with regard to these items, Italy enacted *Legge 29 ottobre 1997, n. 374* (Law No. 374 of 29 October 1997),[63] and subsequently ratified and implemented the Ottawa Convention on Landmines[64] by means of *Legge 26 marzo, n. 106* (Law No. 106 of 26 March 1999).[65] President Mattarella explained the incompatibility in the following passage of his message:

> For what regards antipersonnel landmines, Article 7 of Law No. 374 of 1997 criminalizes, with similar penalties, whoever uses, sells, gives at any title, exports, imports, and possesses antipersonnel landmines or parts of them, or uses or gives away, directly or indirectly, patent rights or manufacturing technologies, in Italy or abroad. Such a regulation is confirmed by Article 9 of Law No. 106 of 1999 that ratified and implemented the Convention regarding the

---

[61] Convention on Cluster Munitions, 30 May 2008, entered into force 1 August 2010 (Cluster Munitions Convention or Oslo Convention).

[62] Law No. 95 of 2011, titled "*Ratifica ed esecuzione della Convenzione di Oslo sulla messa al bando delle munizioni a grappolo, fatta a Dublino il 30 maggio 2008, nonché norme di adeguamento dell'ordinamento interno*" (Ratification and implementation of the Oslo Convention on the ban on cluster munitions, done in Dublin on 30 May 2008, and norms for bringing the domestic order in compliance).

[63] Law No. 374 of 1997, titled "*Norme per la messa al bando delle mine antipersona*" (Norms for the ban on antipersonnel landmines).

[64] Convention on the Prohibition of the Use, Stockpiling, Production and Transfer of Anti-Personnel Mines and on their Destruction, 18 September 1997, entered into force 1 March 1999 (Ottawa Convention).

[65] Law No. 106 of 1999, titled "*Ratifica ed esecuzione della Convenzione sul divieto d'impiego, di stoccaggio, di produzione e di trasferimento delle mine antipersona e sulla loro distruzione, firmata ad Ottawa il 3 dicembre 1997. Modifiche alla legge 29 ottobre 1997, n. 374, riguardante la disciplina della messa al bando delle mine antipersona*" (Ratification and implementation of the Convention on the Prohibition of the Use, Stockpiling, Production and Transfer of Anti-Personnel Mines and on their Destruction, signed in Ottawa on 3 December 1997. Amendments to Law No. 374 of 1997, concerning the regulation of the ban on anti-personnel mines).

prohibition of using, stockpiling, producing and transferring anti-personnel landmines and their destruction, signed in Ottawa on 3 December 1997. Financing the conducts prohibited by Article 7 is considered among the behaviors listed by Article 1, paragraph 1, of the Ottawa Convention, which explicitly obligates the States to forbid, among other things, to 'assist, encourage or induce, in any way, anyone to engage' in the activities prohibited by the Convention itself.[66]

According to Article 117(1) of the Constitution, the legislation enacted by the Parliament must comply with Italy's international obligations.[67] Such a provision grants a special status to international treaties ratified and implemented by Italy. Domestic laws that clash with these international norms can be struck down as unconstitutional, in that they are deemed to be conflicting with Article 117(1) itself. President Mattarella referred to this issue in his message:

The two incriminating provisions[68] are the outcome of the implementation of international obligations contained within the two conventions, ratified by Italy, which explicitly require, both at Article 9, the imposition of penal sanctions in order to prevent and suppress the activities they prohibit.[69]
Therefore, the normative core of the provisions cannot be modified without directly harming the principle defended by Article 117 of the Constitution, which provides for the obligation to exercise the legislative power 'in compliance with the constraints deriving from EU legislation and international obligations'.[70]

The President also highlighted that this principle is strengthened by two judgments of the Italian Constitutional Court of 2007:[71]

Since the Judgments Nos. 348 and 349 of 2007, the Constitutional Court has clarified that Article 117 of the Constitution is capable

---

[66] The President's words recall those of Article 1(c) of the Ottawa Convention.

[67] Article 117(1) states: "Legislative powers shall be vested in the State and the Regions in compliance with the Constitution and the constraints deriving from EU legislation and international obligations". See Servizio Affari internazionali, Senato della Repubblica, *cit. supra* note 57.

[68] That is, Art. 7 of Law No. 374/1997 and Art. 7 of Law No. 95/2011, already mentioned by the President earlier in his message.

[69] Both the 1997 Ottawa Convention and the 2008 Cluster Munitions Convention contain a similar Art. 9, titled "National implementation measures", whose content is described above.

[70] This sentence of Art. 117(1) reads in full: "Legislative powers shall be vested in the State and the Regions in compliance with the Constitution and the constraints deriving from EU legislation and international obligations". See Servizio Affari internazionali, Senato della Repubblica, *cit. supra* note 57.

[71] On these two judgments see IYIL, XVII (2007), p. 292 ff., with a comment by CATALDI.

of granting international norms a particular position in the system of the sources, as interposed norms in a possible judgment of constitutionality, so that the acts that clash with international treaties that have been executed in the domestic legal system are unconstitutional.

Applying this principle to the international as well as national norms on anti-personnel landmines and cluster munitions, President Mattarella explained that Article 6(2) of Law No. 57 may not exclude the criminal relevance of the conduct it regulates. Indeed, such criminal relevance is provided by domestic laws implementing international obligations and thus, as explained above, is required and protected by Article 117(1) of the Constitution. Furthermore, the President stressed that the particular status of those laws does not permit the removal of criminal liability, which is an effective tool to combat financial assistance to conduct related to the use and circulation of anti-personnel landmines and cluster munitions.

As President Mattarella explained, within the Italian legal system, the adoption of administrative sanctions for a certain conduct, without considering the simultaneous applicability of relevant criminal provisions, leads to excluding criminal liability altogether. With regard to the norms of interest here, the President clarified this issue as follows:

> The norm contained in Article 6, paragraph 2, of the law under review, which does not provide for a 'safeguard clause in criminal matters'[72] (unless the fact constitutes a criminal offence), exerts its effect in the described normative framework. Because of the principle of specialty of the administrative wrongdoing dictated by Article 9 of Law No. 689 of 1981, this would have the effect of depriving the intentional conducts of financing, brought about by authorized subjects, of their criminal relevance, as they would be sanctioned only by administrative means, in contrast with international obligations. This would concern not only the future conducts that violate the prohibition of financing, but also those carried on before the entry into force of the present law, with respect to which, lacking a transitory regulation, not even the administrative offence regime would be applicable (*Corte di Cassazione, Sezioni Unite Penali*, Judgment No. 25457 of 2012).

---

[72] The expression "safeguard clause in criminal matters" translates the Italian "*clausola di salvaguardia penale*". As the President explained, there would have been no issue if Art. 6(2) of Law No. 57 had included a provision, called "safeguard clause in criminal matters", keeping the previous relevant criminal liability regime in force. On the contrary, the absence of any mentions to earlier criminal provisions in the law under review is problematic. Indeed, such law would abrogate earlier criminal provisions and substitute them with administrative sanctions.

As anticipated above, a conflict of Article 6(2) of Law No. 57 with Article 117(1) of the Constitution is not the only ground of incompatibility with the fundamental text. Indeed, the President explained to the Houses that the promulgation of Law No. 57 would unjustifiably create two different legal regimes for the same conduct, whose application would depend on the role played by the subject involved. Such a situation would not be in line with Article 3 of the Constitution, which sanctions the principle of equality of every citizen before the law:

> With regard to a different, but connected, aspect, I must again highlight that the creation for the same financing-related conduct of two different sanctioning systems – one criminal and the other administrative – only depending on the different role played by the subject acting within the scope of an authorized intermediary or on the status of the user (a firm and not an individual entrepreneur), raises doubts about its compatibility with Article 3 of the Constitution. Indeed, the physical persons exercising managerial and directorial functions of authorized intermediaries or undertaking control functions on their behalf would benefit, by effect of the regulation contained in Article 6, paragraph 2, from a solely administrative sanctioning regime. Vice versa, all other subjects who provide financial assistance outside the circuit of authorized intermediaries (that is, because of the absence of an authorizing administrative act) would remain subjected to the abovementioned criminal sanctions.

In light of the above, the President exercised his power under Article 74 of the Constitution and requested a new deliberation by the Houses.

All in all, President Mattarella's intervention appeared to be a balancing exercise between the safeguard of constitutional norms and respect of the legislative initiative. Indeed, the President explained his choice according to constitutional principles but, at the same time, he hinted at how the problems he identified could be avoided. Speaking about the "safeguard clause in criminal matters",[73] he seemed to suggest that the Parliament should have coordinated Law No. 57 with the earlier laws implementing the Oslo Convention and the Ottawa Convention. It is noteworthy that the choice not to promulgate such law possibly prevented a subsequent ruling of the Constitutional Court. Indeed, the Court would have likely considered the law as unconstitutional because of its clashing with Article 117(1) of the Constitution on identical or similar grounds as those spelt out by President Mattarella.

RICCARDO LABIANCO

---

[73] See previous footnote.

XVIII. USE OF FORCE AND PEACE-KEEPING

1. THE USE OF CHEMICAL WEAPONS AT KHAN SHAYKHUN AND THE US ATTACK ON A SYRIAN AIRFIELD

On 4 April 2017, it was reported that the Syrian town of Khan Shaykhun – controlled at the time by the Tahrir Al-Sham Alliance – had been the object of an airstrike by the air force of the Government of President Bashar Al Assad.[74] As a result of the airstrike, chemical agents poisoned large numbers of civilians.

In a report released on 30 June 2017, the Fact-Finding Mission of the Organization for the Prohibition of Chemical Weapons (OPCW) estimated the number of deaths "as approximately 100 people" and determined that "Sarin or a Sarin-like substance" had been used as a weapon in Khan Shaykhun.[75] It took until 27 October 2017 for the OPCW-United Nations Joint Investigative Mechanism to take position on the responsibility for the attack and affirm that the Leading Panel of the mechanism itself was "confident that the Syrian Arab Republic is responsible for the release of Sarin at Khan Shaykhun on 4 April 2017".[76]

In the aftermath of the attack, however, several countries condemned the action and the United States (US), the United Kingdom and France openly called into question the responsibility of the Syrian Government.[77] The US President, Mr. Donald Trump, condemned the attack as "intolerable" and openly blamed the inaction of his predecessor Barack Obama, who, after establishing "a 'red line' against the use of chemical weapons did nothing".[78] On its part, the Syrian government denied any involvement in the use of chemical weapons.[79] The Government of the Russian Federation offered alternative explanations of the events, mentioning the fact that the Syrian Air Force could have "bombed an underground factory producing chemical warfare agents" or alluding to a pos-

---

[74] "Death toll rises in Syria 'gas attack'", Deutsche Welle, 4 April 2017, available at: <http://www.dw.com/en/death-toll-rises-in-syria-gas-attack/a-38282661>.

[75] Report of the OPCW Fact-Finding Mission in Syria regarding an alleged incident in Khan Shaykun, Syrian Arab Republic, April 2017, Annex to Letter dated 30 June 2017 from the Secretary-General addressed to the President of the Security Council, UN Doc. S/2017/567, paras. 1.7 and 5.80.

[76] Seventh report of the Organisation for the Prohibition of Chemical Weapons–United Nations Joint Investigative Mechanism, Annex to Letter dated 26 October 2017 from the Leadership Panel of the Organisation for the Prohibition of Chemical Weapons–United Nations Joint Investigative Mechanism addressed to the Secretary-General, UN Doc. S/2017/904, para. 46.

[77] "Attaque au gaz toxique en Syrie: la communauté internationale met en cause Assad et ses soutiens", Le Monde, available at: <http://www.lemonde.fr/syrie/article/2017/04/04/attaque-au-gaz-toxique-en-syrie-la-communaute-internationale-met-en-cause-assad-et-ses-soutiens_5105868_1618247.html>.

[78] "Statement from President Donald J. Trump", 4 April 2017, available at: <www.white-house.gov/briefings-statements/statement-president-donald-j-trump-3>.

[79] "Observatory says 58 killed in suspected chemical attack in Syria, military source denies", Reuters, 4 April 2017, available at: <https://af.reuters.com/article/worldNews/idAFKB-N1760V4>.

sible "provocation by the terrorists".[80] Within the United Nations (UN) Security Council, a draft resolution condemning the attack – tabled by France, the United Kingdom and the US – was vetoed by the Russian Federation, with the abstention of China, Ethiopia and Kazakhstan.[81]

Two days after the event, the US launched a Tomahawk missile attack from two destroyers in the Mediterranean Sea. 59 Tomahawk missiles targeted the Shayriat Syrian Air Force airfield. The strike was described by the US Department of Defense as "a proportional response to Assad's heinous act".[82] It was also added that the Airfield "was used to store chemical weapons and Syrian air forces" and that "[t]he U.S. intelligence community assesses that aircraft from Shayrat conducted the chemical weapons attack on April 4".[83] Finally, according to the same statement, "[t]he strike was intended to deter the regime from using chemical weapons again".[84]

The US President's decision to attack was neither authorized by the UN Security Council nor did it have Congressional backing in the US. That notwithstanding, it was met favorably by a large number of States, with statements ranging from open support for the attack to statements qualifying the US reaction as "understandable".[85] However, legal scholars expressed severe doubts as to the legality of the action.[86]

On 7 April, a press release by the *Ministro degli Affari Esteri e della Cooperazione Internazionale* (Minister for Foreign Affairs and International

---

[80] "Remarks by Russia's Permanent Representative at the OPCW, Ambassador Alexander Shulgin, at the 54th Meeting of the OPCW Executive Council", 13 April 2017, available at: <http://www.dw.com/en/death-toll-rises-in-syria-gas-attack/a-38282661>. This Russian narrative was however quickly dismissed when it was shown that there was no evidence of any buildings being hit in the area. See "'The dead were wherever you looked': inside Syrian town after gas attack", The Guardian, 6 April 2017, available at: <https://www.theguardian.com/world/2017/apr/06/the-dead-were-wherever-you-looked-inside-syrian-town-after-chemical-attack>.

[81] "Security Council Fails to Adopt Resolution Condemning Chemical Weapons Use in Syria, Following Veto by Russian Federation", Press release of 12 April 2017, SC/12791.

[82] US Department of Defense, "Statement from Pentagon Spokesman Capt. Jeff Davis on U.S. strike in Syria", available at: <https://www.defense.gov/News/News-Releases/News-Release-View/Article/1144598/statement-from-pentagon-spokesman-capt-jeff-davis-on-us-strike-in-syria>.

[83] *Ibid.*

[84] *Ibid.*

[85] For example, the statement issued on 7 April 2017 by the German Minister for Foreign Affairs, Sigmar Gabriel: "It is understandable that the United States has now responded with an attack on the military structures of the Assad regime which were the source of this horrific war crime", available at: <https://www.auswaertiges-amt.de/en/Newsroom/170407-bm-luftschlaege-syr/289136>. For an overview of the position of States on the attack, see: "Which Countries Support and Which Oppose the U.S. Missile Strikes in Syria", The New York Times, 9 April 2017, available at: <https://www.nytimes.com/interactive/2017/04/07/world/middleeast/world-reactions-syria-strike.html>.

[86] KU, "Trump's Syria strike clearly broke international law – and no one seems to care", Vox, 19 April 2017, available at: <https://www.vox.com/the-big-idea/2017/4/19/15345686/syria-un-strike-illegal-un-humanitarian-law>.

Cooperation), Mr. Angelino Alfano, clarified the Italian position on the matter. The relevant part of the press release reads:

> Italy understands the reasons of a US military action, proportion-ate in time and manner, in response to an unacceptable sense of impunity and as a sign of deterrence against the risk of a further use of chemical weapons by Assad, in addition to the cases already ascertained by the United Nations. The air raids conducted on Khan Sheikhoun on 4 April were ruthless and cruel for the high death toll they caused, including many children. They are vile actions that Italy and the European Union have firmly condemned and that add on to Assad's reiterated violations of the ceasefire and the atro-cious violence repeatedly perpetrated by his Armed Forces on ci-vilians. Our Government is closely following the events unfolding in the Mediterranean, in consideration of its many and direct inter-ests in the security and stability of the region. It is now necessary and urgent to reactivate the UN Security Council and make it fully functional in reaching a consensual resolution in order to identify the parties responsible and avert future atrocities. As a member of the Security Council, Italy will continue to work towards this end. Moreover, Italy strongly wishes for the international community to resume its commitment – on the basis of a renewed USA–Russia dialogue – to achieve a UN-led political transition in Syria in com-pliance with Resolution 2254 of the UN Security Council and the 2012 Geneva Communiqué.[87]

Subsequently, on 10-11 April, Italy hosted the G7 Ministerial Meeting on Foreign Affairs. Understandably, the attention of the Ministers focused *inter alia* on the situation in Syria and their "Statement on Non-Proliferation and Disarmament" made direct reference to the facts of Khan Shaykhun. In their joint statement, the Ministers affirmed:

> We are shocked and horrified by the reports of use of chemical weapons in an airstrike in the Khan Shaykhun area of southern Idlib on 4 April. Syria's possession of chemical weapons and their means of delivery are illegal under UN Security Council Resolution 2118 and the Chemical Weapons Convention. The subsequent US mili-tary action against Shayrat Airfield was a carefully calibrated, lim-ited in scope response to this war crime and was directed against Syrian military targets directly connected to the 4th April chemical

---

[87] The statement is available at: <https://www.esteri.it/mae/en/sala_stampa/archiviono-tizie/comunicati/2017/04/siria_0.html>. On 12 April 2017, the Minister expressed the same concepts in Parliament, during a communication before the *Senato della Repubblica* (Senate of the Republic, 807th Meeting, XVII Legislature).

weapons attack in order to prevent and deter the proliferation and use of deadly chemical weapons in Syria.[88]

Somewhat paradoxically, after having endorsed the US military action, the G7 statement also expressed full support for the OPCW Fact Finding Mission which should have identified the perpetrators and called upon "the Syrian Arab Republic and all parties in Syria to cooperate fully with the OPCW to allow a prompt conclusion of its investigation on this heinous incident".[89]

MARCO PERTILE

XIX. ARMED CONFLICT, NEUTRALITY, AND DISARMAMENT

1. THE LEGALITY OF ITALY'S EXPORT OF ARMS

On 17 July 2017, during a Parliamentary debate on the ongoing war in Yemen, the *Sottosegretario di Stato per gli Affari esteri e la Cooperazione internazionale* (Undersecretary of State for Foreign Affairs and International Cooperation), Mr. Vincenzo Amendola, presented the stance of the Italian Government vis-à-vis the conflict between the Houthi rebels and the government of President Abdrabbuh Mansur Hadi. The request for military support from President Hadi's government, which enjoys wide international recognition, has been accepted by a coalition of States, led by Saudi Arabia. Before the *Camera dei Deputati* (Chamber of Deputies, 835th Meeting, XVII Legislature) Mr. Amendola qualified the government as the legitimate authority in Yemen. He described the situation as follows:

> In 2014, there was a true subversion of the institutional order from the Houthis, carried out by paramilitary militias. The coup interrupted the process of transition that was in place and resulted in the destitution of President Hadi and the fall of the Yemeni Parliament. Given the situation and the worsening of the terrorist threat brought about by Al Qaeda in great part of the Yemeni territory, which took advantage of the power vacuum in the country, a military intervention upon request and sustained by the legitimate government was launched by a coalition of States formed by Saudi Arabia, United Arab Emirates, Bahrain, Qatar, Kuwait, Sudan, Egypt and Morocco.

Allegations of a violation of international humanitarian law as a result of the bombings carried out by Saudi Arabia led to questioning the export of arms

---

[88] G7 Statement on Non-Proliferation and Disarmament, Lucca, 11 April 2017, available at: <http://www.g7italy.it/sites/default/files/documents/NPDG_Statement_Final.pdf>.

[89] *Ibid.*

to Riyadh. On this issue, too, the Undersecretary explained the Italian position. The obligations applicable to Italy as to the export of arms derive from domestic, European and international legal instruments. However, Mr. Amendola only mentioned the domestic framework and reminded that:

> The exports of arms are governed by Law No. 185 of 1990 and its subsequent amendments, and the authorizations for licenses involve different Ministries and authorities, as to the analysis of the content of the single operation as well as in terms of opinions for the export to non-EU/NATO countries.

He also highlighted the fact that Italy coordinates its arms export policies with other countries:

> In the matter of arms policies, Italy operates in strict connection with the partners of the European Union, with whom there are periodical coordination meetings in Brussels, and we operate also in strict coordination with our main allies.

Indeed, the role played by Italy's European and extra-European partners is explicitly recognized in *Legge 9 luglio 1990, n. 185* (Law No. 185 of 1990).[90] Pursuant to Article 1(6)(c) of that law, embargos imposed by the United Nations, the European Union (EU) or the Organization for Security and Cooperation in Europe are to be taken into account when assessing the legality of arms exports: if such embargos are in place, any exports are prohibited. The importance of such an evaluation was made clear by the Undersecretary, with reference to the Yemeni case:

> I want to remind that there are no embargos or other sanctions adopted on an international and European level towards single members of the coalition [that operates in Yemen]. In the case of specific members of the coalition, which, in addition, are also part of the coalition against Daesh, the requests of Italian companies for obtaining the license for arms export are evaluated in a very rigorous and articulated way, case by case, on the basis of the Italian, European and international rules [...]. Obviously, should potential violations be detected in the context of the United Nations or the European Union, Italy would immediately abide by the prescriptions or bans adopted.

---

[90] Law No. 185 of 1990, as amended by, in chronological order: Law No. 222 of 27 February 1992, Presidential Decree No. 373 of 20 April 1994, Law No. 148 of 17 June 2003, Legislative Decree No. 66 of 15 March 2010, Legislative Decree No. 105 of 22 June 2012, Law Decree No. 114 of 10 October 2013.

The same prohibition is binding upon Italy due to some of the international commitments to which Mr. Amendola referred. Article 2(1)(a) of EU Council Common Position 944/2008 of 8 December 2008 (compliance with which is also demanded by Article 1(11-bis) of Law No. 185 of 1990), as well as Article 6 of the Arms Trade Treaty[91] also ban arms exports when the above-mentioned international organizations set up an embargo. Although Mr. Amendola's reasoning seemed to rely largely on the absence of any embargo towards Yemen, the "Italian, European and international rules" he hinted at provide for other standards against which the legality of arms exports is to be judged. For example, Article 1(6) of Law No. 185 of 1990 requires the competent national organs to also address other considerations in their assessments. More specifically,

> The export, the transit, the transfer within the European Union and the brokering of armament materials[92] are also prohibited:
> a) towards countries involved in an armed conflict, in contrast with the principles enshrined in Article 51 of the United Nations Charter, without prejudice to compliance with Italy's international commitments and to the divergent deliberations of the Council of Ministers to be adopted following the opinion of the Chambers [the Chamber of Deputies and the Senate]. [...]
> d) towards countries whose governments are responsible of grave violations of international conventions in the matter of human rights, as established by the competent organs of the United Nations, of the European Union or of the Council of Europe [...].

Further prohibitions are listed under Article 1(5), whereby the export and transit of armament materials are

> prohibited when they contrast with the Constitution, with Italy's international commitments, with agreements on non-proliferation, with its fundamental interests in the matter of national security, with the fight against terrorism and with the maintenance of good relationship with other nations, as well as when proper guarantees about the final destination of such materials are lacking.

In turn, according to Article 2(a)(c) of EU Council Common Position 944/2008, Member States shall

---

[91] Ratified by Italy by means of Law No. 118 of 2013; ratification deposited on 2 April 2014.

[92] Armament materials are defined by Art. 2(1) of Law No. 185 of 1990 as follows: "For the purposes of the present law, armament materials are those materials that, for their technical-manufacturing or design requirements or features, are considered to be built for mainly military or police usage". Art. 2(2) further specifies the categories under which the armament materials are classified. Such classification is wider than the one provided by the Arms Trade Treaty and encompasses also items, such as electronic, electro-optical and photographic systems, that could be classified as non-lethal.

deny an export license if there is a clear risk that the military technology or equipment to be exported might be used in the commission of serious violations of international humanitarian law.

The same risk-based approach is also adopted by Article 7 of the Arms Trade Treaty, which requires the exporting State to assess whether the arms it is planning to sell could be used to commit or facilitate serious violations of humanitarian law and human rights law or to undermine peace and security. If an overriding risk that this will occur exists, the State must refrain from any arms export. The same is required if, under Article 6 of the treaty, the State has knowledge that the arms would be used to commit an international crime.

Thus, the legality of arms transfer has to be assessed against a number of parameters that encompass, but are not limited to, arms embargos. The criterion related to grave breaches of international humanitarian law was indeed mentioned in a motion of the Chambers of Deputies (Motion No. 1-01695, first signatories Quartapelle Procopio, Alli, Marazziti, Locatelli) endorsed by the Italian Government (853th Meeting, XVII Legislature) on 19 September 2017, where it was recalled:

> the Resolution of the European Parliament of 25 February 2016 on the humanitarian situation in Yemen (2016/2515(RSP)) calls on the Vice President/High Representative to launch an initiative aimed at imposing an EU arms embargo against Saudi Arabia, given the serious allegations of breaches of international humanitarian law by Saudi Arabia in Yemen and the fact that the continued licensing of weapons sales to Saudi Arabia would therefore be in breach of Council Common Position 2008/944/CFSP of 8 December 2008.

The motion also warned that

> In December 2016 the US Administration decided to temporarily suspend the provision of some precision ammunitions to Saudi Arabia, specifically the sale by Raytheon of 16,000 kits of guided ammunitions for the value of 350 million dollars, having assessed that the Saudi aviation appears not to have been able to correctly locate its objectives.

Therefore, the motion committed the Government to

> foster, in the context of the regular consultations promoted by the EU in Brussels, a shared line of action on the matter of arms export, by giving concrete support to international initiatives for the cessation of the hostilities and complying promptly with the prescriptions or bans that were to be adopted in the context of the United Nations or of the European Union.

A confirmation that the assessment carried out by the Italian authorities as to the legality of arms export does not need to be based solely on the existence of an embargo comes from Italy's position with regards to the situation in Venezuela. Restrictive measures were adopted at the EU level by means of Council Regulation No. 2017/2063 of 13 November 2017; however, the Undersecretary of State for Foreign Affairs and International Cooperation, Mr. Benedetto Della Vedova, explained in front of the Chamber of Deputies on 5 December 2017 (897th Meeting, XVII Legislature) that the measures taken by Italy preceded those adopted by the EU:

> In November, at the last Council of Foreign Affairs, a system of individual sanctions was approved that could be applied to those who bear the largest share of responsibility for the current situation, together with a ban on the export of arms and other instruments for the repression of dissent. From the Italian side, however, bilateral restrictive measures for the export of materials for defense had already been adopted in the previous weeks.

In conclusion, the Yemeni case confirms that the existence of a UNSC embargo or other restrictive measure plays a fundamental role in the legality assessment of arms export carried out by Italy. The other criteria put forth by the applicable rules are not explicitly recalled in the statements.

However, the Venezuelan case suggests that even in the absence of international restrictive measures, the Italian Government may still be prepared to adopt unilateral sanctions. In this case, political considerations linked to the presence of a large Italian community in Venezuela may have prompted the adoption of measures before concerted action could take place in Brussels. Whether the driving force of this decision is political interest rather than compliance with the other legal obligations applicable to arms exports is unclear.

IOTAM ANDREA LERER

TREATY PRACTICE

(edited by *Marina Mancini*)

XII. HUMAN RIGHTS

MEMORANDUM OF UNDERSTANDING BETWEEN ITALY AND THE LIBYAN GOVERNMENT OF NATIONAL ACCORD ON COOPERATION IN THE FIELD OF DEVELOPMENT, FIGHT AGAINST ILLEGAL IMMIGRATION, TRAFFICKING IN HUMAN BEINGS AND SMUGGLING AND ON ENHANCEMENT OF BORDER SECURITY OF 2 FEBRUARY 2017

(Cf. *supra* in this volume MANCINI "Italy's New Migration Control Policy: Stemming the Flow of Migrants from Libya Without Regard for Their Human Rights")

LEGISLATION

(edited by *Pia Acconci*)

XI. TREATMENT OF ALIENS AND NATIONALITY

Law No. 47 of 7 April 2017
New Protective Measures for Unaccompanied Foreign Minors

With Law No. 47 of 7 April 2017 (hereinafter, Law No. 47/2017),[1] the Italian government addressed the issue of protection and assistance of the increasing number of foreign minors who enter Italy unaccompanied by an adult entitled to custody.[2] These minors are in a state of particular vulnerability,[3] due to their age, the distance from home, the terrible migration route they have often undertaken and their uncertain future. Because of this peculiar vulnerability, the Law grants them the same rights to protection as Italian and European minors.

The new Law reforms the Italian legal asylum system through the amendment and integration of the law in force as well as through the adoption of new procedural provisions.

Unaccompanied foreign minors are defined by the Law as minors who are not Italian or European citizens and who for whatever reason are in the Italian territory or subjected to Italian jurisdiction without the assistance or representation of parents or other adults responsible for them according to Italian legislation.[4] This definition complies with the European notion of unaccompanied minor, enshrined in the EU Qualification Directive[5] and in the Reception Conditions

---

[1] Law No. 47/2017 (G.U. no. 93 of 21 April 2017), also called "Zampa Act", was proposed by Save the Children in July and submitted at the Chamber of Deputies on 4 October 2013. The proposal was approved by the Senate with amendments on 1 March 2017 and by the Chamber of Deputies on 29 March 2017. The Law passed almost unanimously with 375 votes in favour and 13 against. It entered into force on 6 April 2017.

[2] According to the Italian National Authority for the Protection of Childhood and Adolescence, 26,000 unaccompanied foreign minors entered Italy in 2016 (available at: <https://www.west-info.eu/files/Autorità-Garante-per-l'Infanzia-e-l'Adolescenza-Relazione-al-Parlamento-2016.pdf>).

[3] The status of "extreme vulnerability" of unaccompanied minors has been repeatedly recognised by the European Court of Human Rights, *Mubilanzila Mayeka and Kaniki Mitunga v. Belgium*, Application No. 13178/03, Judgment of 12 October 2006, para. 55; *Popov v. France*, Applications No. 39472/07 and 39474/07, Judgment of 19 January 2012, para. 91; see also European Court of Justice, Case C-648/11, *M.A., B.T. and D.A. v. Secretary of State of the Home Department*, 6 June 2013, para. 55.

[4] Art. 2 of Law No. 47/2017.

[5] Art. 2(1)(l) of the EU Directive of the European Parliament and of the Council of 13 December 2011 on standards for the qualification of third-country nationals or stateless persons as beneficiaries of international protection, for a uniform status for refugees or for persons eligible for subsidiary protection, and for the content of the protection granted (2011/95/EU) qualifies as an unaccompanied minor: "[a] minor who arrives on the territory of the Member

Directive[6] as well as with international law.[7] All of these definitions place importance on the lack of any adults responsible for minors in the territory of the State
and include both minors who arrived alone in the territory of the State and minors
left alone after their arrival.

One of the most relevant novelties provided for by Law No. 47/2017 concerns
the "absolute prohibition of refoulement".[8] This prohibition modifies Article 19
of Law Decree No. 286/1998 and strengthens the protection of the child, without
exceptions, not even for public security reasons. The favourable attitude of the
Law for minors dispels all doubts about the predominance of children's interests
over national security safeguards.[9]

Furthermore, the Law, although maintaining the State's right to expulsion for public order or national security reasons,[10] limits the circumstances
in which an unaccompanied minor can be expelled and introduces procedural
safeguards: the expulsion can be issued by a juvenile court, within thirty days
from the expulsion decision, only if the decision will not entail risk of serious

---

States unaccompanied by an adult responsible for him or her whether by law or by the practice
of the Member State concerned, and for as long as he or she is not effectively taken into the
care of such a person; it includes a minor who is left unaccompanied after he or she has entered
the territory of the Member States".

[6] Art. 2(1)(e) of the EU Directive of the European Parliament and of the Council of 26
June 2013 laying down standards for the reception of application for international protection
(2013/33/EU) states that: "'unaccompanied minor' means a minor who arrives on the territory
of the Member States unaccompanied by an adult responsible for him or her whether by law or
by the practice of the Member State concerned, and for as long as he or she is not effectively
taken into the care of such a person; it includes a minor who is left unaccompanied after he or
she has entered the territory of the Member States". The same definition was adopted by Art.
1 of EU Council Resolution of 26 June 1997 on unaccompanied minors who are nationals of
third countries states (97/C 221/03).

[7] The UN Committee on the Right of the Child in the General Comment No. 6 of 2005,
paras. 7-8, identifies the unaccompanied minors as children "who have been separated from
both parents and other relatives and are not being cared for by an adult who, by law or
custom, is responsible for doing so". The Committee distinguished also "unaccompanied
minors" from "separated children", who, instead, are not necessarily separated from their
relatives.

[8] This prohibition is enshrined in Art. 33 of the 1951 United Nations Convention Relating
to the Status of Refugees, 28 July 1951, entered into force 22 April 1954; Art. 3 of the United
Nations Convention against Torture and Other Cruel, Inhuman or Degrading Treatment or
Punishment, 10 December 1984, entered into force 26 June 1987; Art. 19 of the Charter of
Fundamental Rights of the European Union, OJ 2000/C 364/01, 7 December 2000. On the
cogens nature of the principle of *non-refoulement* see GIANELLI, "Il carattere assoluto dell'obbligo di non refoulement: la sentenza Saadi della Corte europea dei diritti dell'uomo", RDI,
2008, p. 449 ff.

[9] SENIGALLIA, "Considerazioni critico-ricostruttive su alcune implicazioni civilistiche
della disciplina sulla protezione dei minori stranieri non accompagnati", Jus Civile, p. 712 ff.;
CASCONE, "Brevi riflessioni in merito alla legge n. 47/17 (disposizioni in materia di protezione
dei minori stranieri non accompagnati): luci e ombre", Diritto, immigrazione e cittadinanza,
2017, available at: <https://www.dirittoimmigrazionecittadinanza.it/>, p. 8.

[10] Art. 13, Law Decree No. 286/1998.

damages for the minor.[11] Moreover, return can be ordered only when family reunification in the country of origin or in a third country suits the best interests of the child. In case of prohibition of refoulement or expulsion of the minor, the minor is entitled to obtain a residence permit.

Specific procedures are set for the identification[12] and age assessment[13] of unaccompanied minors in cases of serious doubts about the declared age. Following the guarantee of immediate humanitarian assistance, the Law provides for the inference of the minor's age through a three step procedure. The procedure starts with a preliminary interview conducted by qualified personnel of the first reception centre and is aimed to let all the elements of his personal and family story, useful to his protection, come out.[14] To better enable the minor to express themselves, the involvement of a cultural mediator shall be guaranteed during this interview.

At the end of the procedure, the interviewers draft a "Social Folder", a new tool introduced by the Law, which highlights all the elements necessary to identify the best long-term solution in the best interest of the child.

Following the interview, the confirmation of the declared age depends on the age record and, also, on the assistance of diplomatic authorities.[15] Thereafter, if serious doubts endure,[16] the Public Prosecutor's Office of the juvenile Court can order social-medical examinations aimed at establishing the age of the child. The

---

[11] Art. 3(3)(b) of Law No. 47/2017. For the purpose of this law, as highlighted by CORDIANO, "Prime riflessioni sulle nuove disposizioni in materia di misure di protezione dei minori stranieri non accompagnati", La nuova giurisprudenza civile commentata, 2017, p. 1304 ff., there is a difference between return and expulsion. This different lies in the moment of the decision issuance, in fact the return is strictly related to the moment of crossing the border or immediately after.

[12] The identification is established through the involvement of public security authorities, a cultural mediator and the guardian or temporary guardian (if already appointed) after the adequate assistance of the minor (Art. 5(3) of Law No. 47/2017).

[13] Age assessment aims at determining the immigration procedures and rules to be followed. The European Court of Human Rights in the case *Mahamad Jama v. Malta*, Application No. 10290/13, Judgment of 26 November 2015, para. 150, stated that the age assessment is a preliminary step "given that a number of procedural safeguards are attached to asylum claims lodged by minors".

[14] Where possible, the personnel of the first reception centre are assisted also by organizations, authorities or associations with demonstrated and specific experience in the protection of minors (Art. 5(1) of Law No. 47/2017).

[15] This assistance must be exceptionally avoided in some circumstances: if the minor expressed his will to apply for international protection, if a possibility of international protection emerged from the interview or if risks of persecutions may arise from this cooperation. In the end the assistance of diplomatic authorities must be avoided if the minor declares his refusal to take advantage of diplomatic authority (Art. 5(3) of Law No. 47/2017).

[16] Law No. 47/2017 uses the term "serious doubts" instead of the expression "reasonable doubt" of the Decree of the President of the Council of Ministers no. 234/2016. DI NAPOLI, "Riflessioni a margine della «nuova» procedura di accertamento dell'età del minore straniero non accompagnato ai sensi dell'art. 5 della legge 47/2017", Diritto, immigrazione e cittadinanza, 2017, available at: <https://www.dirittoimmigrazionecittadinanza.it>, p. 16, expresses her concerns about the elements which integrate the "serious doubts" and the lack of the duty to justify these doubts.

final report shall indicate the margin of error and the procedure has to be completed with the adoption of a decision,[17] which determines the age of the child. If it cannot be ascertained, the reasons for this impossibility shall be expressed. Among the guarantees recognised to the minors during this stage is the right to appeal this decision.

If doubts persist about the applicant's age, a minor age shall be assumed.[18] The presumption of minor age is particularly relevant in the pursuit of the principle of the best interest of the child. This principle, regulated in Italy by Article 28(3) of the Law Decree No. 286/1998, represents a milestone in the international protection of children's rights since the entry into force of the United Nations Convention on the Rights of the Child. It is a well-established principle of international[19] and EU[20] law and its primacy has been frequently stated by the

---

[17] According to a recent interpretation of Art. 19 by an Italian court (Trieste Juvenile Court, Decree of 12 July 2017), the decision should be issued by a Juvenile court at the end of the age examination supervised by the Prosecutor's Office of the Juvenile court.

[18] The Italian law complies with the position expressed by the UN Committee on the Rights of the Child about the initial age assessment of the unaccompanied minors: see United Nations Convention on the Right of the Child, General Comment No. 6, para. 31(a). The UN expressed the same position in the Guidelines on International Protection No. 8, para. 75: "The margin of appreciation inherent to all age-assessment methods needs to be applied in such a manner that, in case of uncertainty, the individual will be considered a child". Also European Union law (Art. 5(5) of the Directive 2013/32/EU of the European Parliament and of the Council of 26 June 2013 on common procedures for granting and withdrawing international protection) provides that if, after all the investigations, member States are still in doubt on the age of the child, he must be assumed minor.

[19] Art. 3(1) United Nations Convention on the Rights of the Child, 20 November 1989, entered into force 2 September 1990, states that "In all actions concerning children, whether undertaken by public or private social welfare institutions, courts of law, administrative authorities or legislative bodies, the best interests of the child shall be a primary consideration", it also details the way to implement this interest "taking into account the rights and duties of his or her parents, legal guardians, or other individuals legally responsible for him or her, and, to this end, shall take all appropriate legislative and administrative measures". It finally provides the obligation of contracting State to "ensure that the institutions, services and facilities responsible for the care or protection of children shall conform with the standards established by competent authorities, particularly in the areas of safety, health, in the number and suitability of their staff, as well as competent supervision". The UN Committee on the Rights of the Children in the General Comment No. 14 (2013) on the right of the child to have his or her best interests taken as a primary consideration (Art. 3(1)), also declared that the child should have his or her best interests taken as a primary consideration.

[20] Art. 3(3) of the Treaty on European Union; Art. 24 of the Charter of Fundamental Rights of the European Union: "In all actions relating to children, whether taken by public authorities or private institutions, the child's best interests must be a primary consideration". Art. 31 EU Directive 2011/95/UE, *cit. supra* note 5; Art. 6 EU Regulation No. 604/2013 of the European Parliament and of the Council of 26 June 2013 establishing the criteria and mechanisms for determining the Member State responsible for examining an application for international protection lodged in one of the Member States by a third-country national or a stateless person, which listed also factors that States have to take into consideration in assessing the best interest of the child: family reunification possibilities, the minor's well-being and social development, safety and security considerations, in particular where there is a risk of the minor being a victim of human trafficking, the views of the minor, in accordance with his or her age and maturity. Art. 25(5) and (6) of the EU Directive 2013/32/UE, *cit. supra* note 18, states that: "If, thereafter,

European Court of Human Rights jurisprudence; the Court has recently affirmed in *Rahimi v. Greece*: "dans toutes les décisions concernant des enfants, leur intérêt supérieur doit primer".[21]

Having acknowledged the lack of a specific definition of the content of the child's interest, the Court has clarified the importance of a case by case approach:

> The child's best interests, from a personal development perspective, will depend on a variety of individual circumstances, in particular his age and level of maturity, the presence or absence of his parents and his environment and experiences [...] For that reason, those best interests must be assessed in each individual case.[22]

If, as it has been correctly maintained,[23] the principle of best interest constitutes a criterion for assessing the laws of the States for all measures related to the child, the positive assessment of Italian legislation is undoubtedly linked to the role ascribed to this principle at a crucial stage for the determination of future solutions for the minor, that of age assessment.

The regulation of this stage adopted by Law No. 47/2017 borrowed the holistic method of the so-called *Protocollo Ascone*, an Italian agreement among different Ministries, which promoted a multidisciplinary approach to the assessment of unaccompanied minors' age.

Compared to the *Protocollo Ascone* and to the Decree of the President of the Council of Ministers No. 234/2016, concerning "Rules on determining the age of unaccompanied children victims of trafficking", Law No. 47/2017 aims to overcome the fragmentation of age assessment regulation, linked to the different statuses of minors (victims of trafficking, sexual abuse, etc.) and to establish a homogeneous legal framework.[24] However, there are still unfilled gaps, notably in the definitions of competencies of the different authorities involved in the procedure (juvenile court, tutelary court, prosecutor's office and administrative officials).

Scepticism on the regulation of the age assessment has also been expressed by some scholars,[25] who have emphasized how some steps of the procedure (the

---

Member States are still in doubt concerning the applicant's age, they shall assume that the applicant is a minor" and that "The best interests of the child shall be a primary consideration for Member States when implementing this Directive".

[21] *Rahimi v. Greece*, Application No. 8687/08, Judgment of 5 April 2011, para. 108.

[22] *Neulinger and Shuruk v. Switzerland*, Application No. 41615/07, Judgment of 6 July 2010, para. 138. On the content of the child's best interest see also *Gnahoré v. France*, Application No. 40031/98, Judgment of 19 September 2000, para. 59; *Maumousseau and Washington v. France*, Application No. 39388/05, Judgment of 6 December 2007, para. 74.

[23] SCIACOVELLI, "Minori stranieri non accompagnati: criticità e nuovi sviluppi giurisprudenziali", Studi sull'integrazione europea, 2018, p. 502.

[24] DI NAPOLI, *cit. supra* note 16, p. 9.

[25] SENIGALLIA, *cit. supra* note 9, p. 733.

identification, for instance), due to their complexity, negatively interfere in its celerity and therefore in the prompt protection of the primary interest of the child.

During the identification and age assessment procedure, in order to ensure rescue and immediate protection, unaccompanied minors are welcomed in a first reception centre. In compliance with Article 37 of the United Nations Convention on the Rights of the Child, the Law provides for the establishment of appropriate host communities for unaccompanied minors, where they are separated from adults. This provision shows the effort to correct the gaps of the former regulation already stressed by the European Court of Human Rights. In the recent case *Darboe and Camara v. Italy*,[26] two minors residing in a reception centre for adults in Cona complained about the conditions of the reception facilities in the host community; in response to their request, the Court applied an interim measure and ordered the transfer of the minors to a reception centre adequate for children.[27]

The choice of the adequate centre, according to the Law, shall take into consideration the facilities offered by the reception structure and be tailored to the needs and characteristics of the child, as revealed in the interview.

According to the Law, the allocation in the reception centre should be avoided if relatives of the unaccompanied minors are identified. In fact, the law promotes family foster care more than that of host communities and, where possible, care by relatives more than allocation in reception centres.

A pivotal role in the Italian system of protection of unaccompanied minors is played by volunteer guardians, persons introduced by Article 11 of the Law, who provide their availability to protect unaccompanied minors. These volunteers are in charge of legal representation of minors and their task is to promote the recognition of minors' rights, the guarantee of their psycho-physical well-being, the surveillance of their education, integration, reception and safety conditions. According to the Law, every Juvenile Court should have a list of volunteer guardians – private citizens, selected and appropriately trained by regional authorities.

Also the European Commission stressed the importance of the guardian as one of the key points of the proposed revision of the European asylum system.[28] Although the Zampa Act grants, in many ways, more guarantees than the system

---

[26] *Darboe and Camara v. Italy*, Application No. 5796/2017, Communication of 14 February 2017. Relying on Art. 3 of the European Convention on Human Rights, the applicants complained about the conditions of accommodation, referring in particular to the overpopulation of the centre, the lack of heating, the poor hygiene conditions, the conditions of promiscuity and violence, which would expose them to inhuman and degrading treatment. A similar complaint was submitted to the European Court of Human Rights against Italy on 5 July 2017: see *Trawalli and Others v. Italy*, Application No. 47287/17.

[27] Criticism of the European Court of Human Rights' decision was expressed by D'ALCONZO, INVERNO, "Le nuove norme sulla protezione dei minori stranieri non accompagnati: contenuto e riflessioni sull'attuazione", Minorigiustizia, 2017, p. 65 ff., p. 74.

[28] European Commission, Communication from the Commission to the European Parliament and the Council, The protection of Children in Migration, 14 April 2017, COM(2017) 211.

envisaged by the Commission,[29] it still lacks a mechanism of monitoring and control of the guardian activity.

In sum, this Law enforces the minimum core rights guaranteed during the period of time necessitated for the identification of appropriate durable solutions: access to legal assistance (through the legal aid benefit),[30] to education (educational institutions should activate all the necessary measures for the fulfilment of the educational duty of the minor) and access to health. To implement the latter, the director of the first reception centre, or the person in charge of minor care, can request the registration of minors to the National Healthcare Service. This right is recognised to every unaccompanied minor and not only to minors with permission of residence, as provided for by the Law Decree No. 286/1998.

Special protection is granted to unaccompanied minors who are victims of human trafficking: in this case a particular assistance plan must assure adequate conditions of reception and psychosocial, legal and health assistance.

Law No. 47/2017 has been welcomed by different organisations for minority rights protection,[31] as well as by scholars,[32] as the first legal general intervention in Europe in the field of protection of unaccompanied minors. In effect, this Law safeguards the obligation of non refoulement and the centrality of the best interest and it implements in the Italian legal system fundamental principles of international law and of the European common system of asylum, moving forward in the direction recently suggested by the European Commission.[33]

In 2014, the United Nations High Commissioner for Refugees, while noting the conformity of the Italian legal system to international and European law,[34]

---

[29] SCIACOVELLI, *cit. supra* note 23, p. 514.

[30] In conformity with the position expressed by the UN Committee on the Rights of the Child, General Comment No. 12 (2009): The right of the child to be heard, 20 July 2009, unaccompanied minors have the right to participate, through a legal representative, to all the jurisdictional and administrative procedures concerning their persons and to be listened. In order to assure this right, a cultural mediator should also be involved (Art. 15 of Law No. 47/2017).

[31] The United Nation Children's Emergency Fund (UNICEF) considered the Law not only a "historic law to boost support and protection for the record number of foreign unaccompanied and separated children who arrived in Italy" but also as "a model for how other European countries could put in place a legislative framework that supports protection" (available at: <https://www.unicef.org/media/media_95485.html>); Save the Children noted that this new Law "encompasses all the basic elements for a good integration" (available at: <http://legale. savethechildren.it/enUS/News/Details/3ad3b3bb82184a27a6f6a6f5b827f666?container=g enerica-news>). The Italian association for immigration studies hailed the new Italian age assessment procedure as a model for Europe (although under the condition of its practical implementation): see ROSSI, "The new Italian law on unaccompanied minors: a model for the EU?", Eumigrationlawblog.eu, 13 November 2017, available at: <http://eumigrationlawblog. eu>. For a comparative approach to the regulation of unaccompanied minor status in other States see ROSSKOPF (ed.), *Unaccompanied Minors in International, European and National Law*, Berlin, 2016.

[32] DI NAPOLI, *cit. supra* note 16, p. 4.

[33] European Commission, *cit. supra* note 28.

[34] See United Nations High Commissioner for Refugees, "L'accertamento dell'età dei minori stranieri non accompagnati e separati in Italia", March 2014, available at: <https://www. unhcr.it/wp-content/uploads/2016/01/accertamento.pdf>.

made some remarks concerning the lack of procedural guarantees during the age assessment stage[35] and the fragmentation of the regulatory framework of the protection of minors. Although the new Law introduces additional procedural safeguards for minors, some concerns nevertheless remain with reference to the implementation of these guarantees without the allocation of additional costs for public finances. Indeed, there is the risk that the assistance recognised to unaccompanied minors in theory, could lack a real possibility of practical implementation.

As to the fragmentation of the Italian regulatory framework, the capacity of this Law to fill the gap of the Italian legal system and harmonise the various applicable rules of the matter is highly questionable and the distribution of competences between judicial authorities involved in the protection of unaccompanied minors is one of the least clear points.[36]

In conclusion, progress has been achieved by this new Law for protection and identification of unaccompanied minor arriving in Italy, but there is still a long way to go.

CHIARA CIPOLLETTI

XII. HUMAN RIGHTS

Law No. 110 of 14 July 2017
Introduction of the Crime of Torture into the Italian Legal Order

Law No. 110 of 14 July 2017, passed with 198 votes in favour, 35 against and 104 abstentions, introduces the crime of torture into the Italian legal order,[37] thus implementing the provision enshrined in Article 4(1) of the Convention against Torture and Other Cruel, Inhuman or Degrading Treatment or Punishment (CAT), adopted in 1984 under the aegis of the United Nations, according to which "each State Party shall ensure that all acts of torture are offences under its criminal law".[38]

---

[35] For instance, to carry out the age assessment procedure only as *extrema ratio*, if after listening to the minor and examining his or her documents, there is still a serious doubt about his or her age or the need to guarantee humanitarian assistance before the age assessment or the adequate information of the minor on his rights.

[36] The involvement of two different jurisdictional authorities (Juvenile Court, Tutelary Court) can determine the practical overlapping of judicial processes with all the consequences related to communications, listening and notices. In light of this problem, CASCONE, *cit. supra* note 9, considered this Law as a missed opportunity to harmonise the regulation in this field. *Contra* see BONIFAZI and DEMURTAS, "I minori stranieri non accompagnati: dimensioni e caratteristiche nello scenario europeo e italiano", Minorigiustizia, 2017, p. 33 ff.

[37] On the laboured parliamentary procedure, see the reconstruction by GONNELLA, "Storia, natura e contraddizioni del dibattito istituzionale che ha condotto all'approvazione della legge che criminalizza la tortura", Politica del diritto, 2017, p. 415 ff.

[38] See MARCHESI, "Implementing the UN Convention Definition of Torture in National Criminal Law (with Reference to the Special Case of Italy)", JICJ, 2008, p. 195 ff.

The punishment is increased – from 5 to 12 years imprisonment – if the acts "are committed by a public official or a person acting in an official capacity abusing of his or her powers, or acting in violation of the duties connected with the function or office". On the contrary, "Suffering resulting solely from the execution of lawful measures in deprivation or limitation of rights" is exempted from punishment.

Article 613-*bis* of the Italian Criminal Code (hereinafter cited as Article 613-*bis*) calls for 4 to 10 years imprisonment of whomever "through serious threats or acts of violence, or acting with cruelty, provokes acute physical suffering or a verifiable psychic trauma in anybody deprived of personal liberty or entrusted to his or her custody, authority, vigilance, control, care or assistance, or who in conditions of permanent or temporary disability, […] if the act is committed by means of several conducts, or if it produces an inhuman and degrading treatment for the dignity of the person".[39]

Further aggravating factors are provided for some special consequences arise, notably: a) a bodily injury: increase in sentence up to one third; b) a grievous bodily injury: increase of one third; c) a very grievous bodily injury: increase of a half; d) death as an unintended consequence: 30 years imprisonment; e) death as an intentional consequence: life imprisonment.

Article 613-*ter* of the Italian Criminal Code is also introduced, establishing that imprisonment from 6 months to 3 years is handed to any public official or person acting in an official capacity "who, in the exercise of his or her function or office, in a practically suitable way, instigates another public official or other person acting in an official capacity, to commit the crime of torture, if the instigation is not accepted or, if the instigation is accepted but the crime is not committed".

Moreover, Law No. 110 modifies Article 191 of the Italian Code of Criminal Procedure in matters relating to illegally obtained evidence: the latest paragraph 2-*bis* sets forth the non-usability of the declarations or any information obtained by means of torture, except as against the persons accused of that crime and for the sole purpose of proving their criminal responsibility.

In addition, Law No. 110 envisages two further provisions. In the first place, a second paragraph is added to Article 19 of the Consolidated Law on the regulations on immigration and rules on the condition of the foreigner (Legislative Decree No. 286 of 25 July 1998). This provision establishes the prohibition of *refoulement*, expulsion or extradition of a person towards a State in case there are "justified reasons to believe that he or she is likely to be subjected to torture"; to that end, the existence in that State of systematic and serious violations of human rights shall be considered.[40] In the second place, the acknowledgment of any form of diplomatic immunity is excluded for foreigners subjected to criminal procedure or sentenced for torture in another State or by an international tribunal; in such cases the foreigner is extradited to the requiring State in which the

---

[39] Among the first commentaries see MARCHI, "Il delitto di tortura: prime riflessioni a margine del nuovo art. 613-bis c.p.", Diritto penale contemporaneo, 7-8 2017, p. 155 ff.

[40] On these specific issues see ZAGATO and DE VIDO (eds.), *Il divieto di tortura e altri comportamenti inumani o degradanti nelle migrazioni*, Padova, 2012.

criminal procedure is pending or the sentence for torture has been pronounced or, in cases of a procedure before an international tribunal, to the tribunal itself, or to the State identified according to the Statute of the same tribunal.

The final text approved by the Chamber of the Deputies had been under discussion since July 2013 as it arrived at the Commission for Justice of the Senate. It took four years for it to be approved, and the final result is quite different from the proposal presented through parliamentary initiative.[41] The debate on torture was sped up in April 2015, as the European Court on Human Rights condemned Italy because of police conduct during the raid on the Diaz School during the "G8" Summit in Genoa in 2001, where, according to the Strasbourg judges, police actions had "punitive purposes [...] geared to causing humiliation and physical and mental suffering on the part of the victims".[42] The Court spoke therefore of "torture" and invited Italy "to introduce into the Italian legal system legal mechanisms capable of imposing appropriate penalties on those responsible for acts of torture and other types of ill-treatment under Article 3 and of preventing the latter from benefiting from measures incompatible with the case-law of the Court".[43]

Still with regard to the violent break-in by the police into the Diaz School, approving the request presented by 42 persons who were inside the said school on the night between 20 and 21 July 2001, on 22 June 2017 the Strasbourg Court, defining Italian laws as "inadequate" to punish and prevent the acts of torture committed by police forces, ordered Italy once again to compensate 35 victims with a total of two million euros.[44]

---

[41] Such amendments are certainly what induced the Senator of the Partito Democratico Luigi Manconi, first signer of the original bill, to abstain from voting on the amended text: the grounds of such disapproval are explained in depth by the Senator in his article "Nella vostra legge 'tutto il male del mondo'" ["Inside your law 'all the evil of the world'"], Il Manifesto, 18 May 2017, available at: <https://ilmanifesto.it/nella-vostra-legge-tutto-il-male-del-mondo/>. After the difficult step at the Senate, the Chamber of the Deputies preferred not to modify the text anyway, ignoring the serious concerns set out by the Commissioner for Human Rights of the Council of Europe, Nils Muižnieks, whose letter, addressed to the Presidents of the two Chambers of the Italian Parliament, is available at: <https://rm.coe.int/letter-from-nils-muiznieks-council-of-europe-commissioner-for-human-ri/1680727baf>.

[42] Cestaro v. Italy, Application No. 6884/11, Judgment of 7 July 2015, para. 177. On this case, see CAROLEI, "Cestaro v. Italy: The European Court of Human Rights on the Duty to Criminalise Torture and Italy's Structural Problem", International Criminal Law Review, 2017, p. 567 ff.

[43] Cestaro v. Italy, cit. supra note 42, para. 246.

[44] Bartesaghi Gallo and Others v. Italy, Application No. 12131/13 and 43390/13, Judgment of 22 June 2017. Recently, on 26 October 2017, the First Section of the European Court of Human Rights rendered three judgments with which it unanimously condemned Italy for the violation – both under the procedural and the substantive point of view – of the prohibition of torture as set forth in Article 3 of the European Convention on Human Rights: see Azzolina and Others v. Italy, Applications Nos. 28923/09 and 67599/10; Blair and Others v. Italy, Application No. 1442/14, both concerning the abuses that occurred at the Bolzaneto barracks during the "G8" Summit in Genoa in 2001, as well as the case Cirino and Renne v. Italy, Applications Nos. 2539/13 and 4705/13, relating to the ill-treatment inflicted on two prison detainees in Asti in 2004. The three judgments have in common some remarks which the Strasbourg judges addressed to Italy. From the substantive point of view, the acts of torture impugned were put in practice by police forces in a systematic and organized manner towards

Actually, already at the end of 1988, Italy ratified the Convention against Torture (CAT),[45] whose Article 1(1) envisages that "the term 'torture' means any act by which severe pain or suffering, whether physical or mental, is intentionally inflicted on a person for such purposes as obtaining from him or a third person information or a confession, punishing him for an act he or a third person has committed or is suspected of having committed, or intimidating or coercing him or a third person, or for any reason based on discrimination of any kind, when such pain or suffering is inflicted by or at the instigation of or with the consent or acquiescence of a public official or other person acting in an official capacity. It does not include pain or suffering arising only from, inherent in or incidental to lawful sanctions".[46]

In fact, by confronting the offence of torture as delineated by the CAT and the elements of the offense introduced in the Italian legal order, several incongruities emerge. Recently, some of these have even been accurately stressed by the UN Committee against Torture in its "Concluding observations on the fifth and sixth combined periodic reports of Italy".[47]

In the first place, within the Italian legal order, torture cannot be considered as a proper offense (*reato proprio*), i.e. ascribable exclusively to an official or to a person exercising public functions, abusing his or her powers towards a person in a condition of deprivation of liberty: in Article 613-*bis* the offense is rather

---

individuals deprived of their personal liberty. Under the procedural point of view, the Court has found that, despite the effort made by Italian jurisdictional authorities to ascertain the facts and identify the persons responsible, on the one hand, the response by the criminal legal order has been inadequate because of the lack, at the time of the events, of the provision on torture (obviously not amended, nor amendable through the subsequent introduction of Article 613-*bis*). On the other hand, even the disciplinary judgments charged to the persons responsible have revealed to be ineffective: either for no disciplinary measure being in fact adopted; or for the proceedings having had no suspensory effect upon the office of the person responsible. It shall be also observed that Article 613-*bis* is completely silent upon the suspension as well as the removal of public officials sentenced for torture or inhuman and degrading treatment.

[45] Authorization to ratification and writ of execution carried out in Italy with Law No. 489 of 3 November 1988 (GU No. 271 SO of 18 November 1988). Among many authors, see ZAGATO and PINTON (eds.), *La tortura nel nuovo millennio. La reazione del diritto*, Padova, 2010.

[46] The first attempt to implement the CAT within the Italian legal order was in 1989. Since then, according to the databank of the Senate, available at: <https://www.senato.it>, 88 bills have been presented on this subject. However, the offence of torture should have already been introduced as a fulfilment and specification of Article 13(4), of the Italian Constitution, according to which every form of physical as well as moral violence on persons under restrictions of liberty shall be punished. On Italy'slate fulfilment of the prescriptions provided for by the CAT, see PUGIOTTO, "Repressione penale della tortura e Costituzione: anatomia di un reato che non c'è", Diritto penale contemporaneo, 2/2014, p. 129 ff.; COLELLA, "La repressione penale della tortura: riflessioni *de iure condendo*", Diritto penale contemporaneo, 2014, available at: <https://www.penalecontemporaneo.it/upload/1406048334COLELLA_2014a.pdf>; TRONCONE, "Notazioni sulla mancata previsione del reato di tortura: un vuoto nella tutela dei diritti fondamentali della persona", federalismi.it, 2014, available at: <http://www.federalismi.it>.

[47] Committee against Torture, Concluding observations on the fifth and sixth combined periodic reports of Italy, adopted by the Committee at its sixty-second session (6 November – 6 December 2017).

a common one (*reato comune*), i.e. it can be committed by anyone exercising a sort of "surveillance, control, care or assistance". As a corollary, contrary to the CAT provisions, this formulation is completely silent on the purpose of the act in question, i.e. the aims pursued and the grounds motivating the resorting to torture in the definition of the elements of crime required by the international instruments which stigmatise it: I refer here to the four – alternative – purposes of 1) obtaining a confession or information, 2) punishing; 3) intimidating or coercing; 4) discriminating.[48] Actually, Article 613-*bis* provides for harsher sentences if the acts are committed by a public official or by a person acting in an official capacity, but it does not seem sufficient to cover the provisions of the CAT. This conclusion can be drawn in the light of two considerations. Under a first point of view, the disvalue of the conduct is sensibly increased when the perpetrators of the offence are members of police forces, or, better said, those who actually have the task to protect the psycho-physical integrity of individuals making up a given community. On the other hand, qualifying torture as a common offense marginalizes, if not even wipes out, the specificity of its disvalue, for in this way no adequate prominence is given to the fact that the torture carried out by *State agents* violates – *inter alia* – legally protected rights transcending the individual sphere (first of all, the legitimacy of the action carried out by public powers and the very trust of citizens in State authorities and in the rule of law). In other words, torture, correctly intended as an act of physical or psychological violence arising from an abuse of power, committed by a person who has the legal authority to deprive a person of his/her personal liberty – therefore from an asymmetry in the positions of power between the author of the offense and the victim – hurts the collective sensibility and represents an injury to society. Instead, characterising it as a common offense, every person acting with special cruelty can be sentenced for torture although, for this kind of offence, he or she could be prosecuted through the rules which already sanction threat, grievous or very grievous injuries or attempted murder.

Under a second point of view, if members of a police force have committed acts of torture, the legal framework of Article 613-*bis* not only implies the possibility of being subjected to the balance evaluation and the applicability of extenuating circumstances,[49] but is even mitigated if compared with the regulations

---

[48] Such discrepancy was well known to the Studies Service of the Chamber of Deputies, which, in the report adopted in support and explication of the text passed by the Senate, stresses that the bill transmitted from the Senate to the Chamber of Deputies, "from a systematic point of view, connotes the offence in a manner not exactly coinciding with that provided by the UN Convention and seems to extend the elements of crime, given that the torture could be committed by anyone and irrespective of the possible purpose pursued by the individual through his or her conduct": see the report "Introduzione del delitto di tortura nell'ordinamento italiano", 23 June 2017, available at: <http://documenti.camera.it/leg17/dossier/pdf/GI0210C. pdf>, especially p. 2.

[49] In fact, neither the balance of evaluation nor the applicability of the extenuating circumstances have been expressly excluded in the wording of Article 613-*bis*, with a concrete possibility of very mild sanctions.

provided for in other countries in Europe.[50] Suffice it to remind that in the United Kingdom, according to Article 134 of the Criminal Justice Act of 1988, "a public official or person acting in an official capacity […], who commits the offence of torture shall be liable on conviction on indictment to imprisonment for life";[51] or that in France, where the offence of torture or barbaric acts, as set forth in Article 222 of the *Code pénal*, is sanctioned by a "minimum" punishment of 15 years detention without the possibility to benefit from suspension of the sentence nor its service in instalments,[52] and the punishment can be extended to 20 years if the offence was committed by a public authority or a public official or on a minor or a physically or mentally disabled person (up to 30 years if the offense is committed by a parent, or in a habitual manner towards a person vulnerable because of his or her age, illness or infirmity)[53], while life imprisonment is provided also if the unintentional death of the victim occurs.[54]

Therefore, conveniently the UN Committee against Torture affirms that "the definition set forth in new article 613-*bis* of the [Italian] Criminal Code is incomplete inasmuch as it fails to mention the purpose of the act in question, contrary to what is prescribed in the Convention. Moreover, the basic offence does not include specifications relating to the perpetrator, namely, reference to the act being committed by, at the instigation of, or with the consent or acquiescence of a public official or other person acting in an official capacity. […] [T]he Committee considers that this definition is significantly narrower than the one contained in the Convention, establishing a higher threshold for the crime of torture by adding elements beyond those mentioned in its article 1".[55] The Committee against Torture stresses, thence, that Italy "should bring the content of article 613-*bis* of the Criminal Code in line with article 1 of the Convention by eliminating all superfluous elements and identifying the perpetrator and the motivating factors or reasons for the use of torture […]" and calls for attention to the previous "general comment No. 2, in which it states that serious discrepancies between the Convention's definition and that incorporated into domestic law create actual or potential loopholes for impunity".[56]

A second critical point of the formulation of Article 613-*bis* relates to the qualifications of the consequences of torture upon the victim, for a causal nexus is

---

[50] For a critical review of the legislation on torture set forth in other European countries see: SERGES, "L'introduzione dei reati di tortura in Italia ed in Europa quale corollario della tutela «fisica e morale» della persona umana «sottoposta a restrizioni di libertà»", Costituzionalismo. it, 2/2015, available at: <http://www.costituzionalismo.it/articoli/522/>.

[51] Available at: <https://www.legislation.gov.uk/ukpga/1988/33/section/134>.

[52] French Criminal Code, Article 222(1)

[53] *Ibid.*, Article 222(3).

[54] *Ibid.*, Article 222(6).

[55] Committee against Torture, *cit. supra* note 47, para. 10.

[56] *Ibid.*, para. 11. Among the scholars see PINESCHI, "Tortura e trattamenti o punizioni crudeli, disumani e degradanti: il Commento generale n. 2 del Comitato contro la tortura", in VENTURINI and BARIATTI (eds.), *Diritti individuali e giustizia internazionale – Individual Rights and International Justice – Droits individuels et justice internationale, Liber Fausto Pocar*, Vol. I, Milano, 2009, p. 695 ff.

necessary between the action carried out by the agent and both the acute physical suffering or the verifiable psychological trauma. On the one hand, it is required that the inflicted suffering is "acute" (rather than "severe", as set forth in the CAT), unduly raising, in this way, the "lowest threshold of gravity" and without putting in evidence its protraction in time; on the other hand, as regards mental suffering, for the offense to occur, it must have produced a "verifiable psychological trauma", the evidence of which is burdened upon the victim. Such a formulation is too restricted if compared with psychological torture in such a way that makes the norm almost inapplicable: either because the effects of a psychological trauma may vanish after some time, or emerge several years later; or in the light of the time gap between the procedures and the facts that gave rise to them, which makes it almost impossible to verify and ascertain traumas that occurred a long time before.

Furthermore, it shall be stressed that the violence and threats inflicted on the victim must be carried out "with cruelty", a difficult circumstance to prove for public prosecutors, and are punishable "if committed by means of several conducts". Such a vague formulation, however, makes it even more difficult to ascertain whether an action that falls under the offense of torture has effectively been carried out. What is more, the necessity of a plurality of conducts, in order to make the application of the rule on torture possible, departs from the CAT according to which "any act", if sufficiently serious on the basis of international standards, constitutes torture. It is true that the previous draft required that the serious threats and the violence were "repeated", but the formulation of the present text seems not to give relevance to the single act of brutal violence, as for instance, a sole slap,[57] or even the mere threat to put electrodes on genitals, followed by immediate confession (what renders further threats, and *a fortiori*, the shift to action, useless),[58] leaving it thence unpunished, or at least not capable to be subsumed under the elements of "torture". In fact, such an action could be sanctioned as an "inhuman and degrading treatment for the dignity of the person", in accordance with the last words of the first paragraph of Article 613-*bis*. Concerning this last issue, however, it is necessary to point out the substitution of the disjunctive conjunction ("or") between the two elements of crime – as according to CAT – through a correlative one ("and"), which transforms them into a restraint of the hypothesis under which the crime can occur. Moreover, the interpretation of Article 1 of the CAT unanimously intends the definition of torture within this norm as comprehensive of suffering caused by omissions (as for instance deprivation of food and water): but such an orientation could not be confirmed with regard to Article 613-*bis*, short of violating the principle of strict construction of criminal statutes, given that the current provision contains no explicit reference to omission in conduct, excepted a link with Article 40 of

---

[57] See *Bouyid v. Belgium*, Application No. 23380/09, Judgment of 28 September 2015.

[58] However, on the impossibility to use evidence extorted by torture, see, for instance, among the cases brought before the European Court for Human Rights, *Othman (Abu Qatada) v. The United Kingdom*, Application No. 8139/09, Judgement of 17 January 2012.

the Italian Criminal Code regarding the causal nexus – but the application of this reference is made difficult by the necessity to identify a plurality of conducts.[59]

Lastly, the Parliament has rejected the proposal to redouble the deadline of the statutory limitation for the offense of torture, notwithstanding the necessity to guarantee that the persons guilty of such a serious crime do not escape justice. So, an ordinary limitation of time is established for torture, although in a country like Italy, which is infamous for exorbitantly long proceedings, such a provision produces the concrete risk that some cases of torture remain unpunished and that justice and compensation are denied to the victims.[60] This concern is quite clear to the UN Committee against Torture, which has recommended Italy to "ensure that the offence of torture is not subject to any statute of limitations in order to preclude any risk of impunity in relation to the investigation of acts of torture and the prosecution and punishment of perpetrators".[61]

Among the recommendations expressed by the Committee against Torture, a further two deserve to be stressed: the call for ensuring that the complaints for torture, ill-treatments and an excessive use of violence are examined in an impartial way;[62] and the recommendation to guarantee that all victims of torture and ill-treatment obtain reparation.[63] Special attention is then paid to Article 41-*bis* of the Italian Prison Order[64] and to the necessity to modify the imprisonment regime in emergency situations (so called "hard prison") in order to adequate it to the minimum standard on human rights;[65] also, both the treatment reserved to migrants in reception structures[66] and the *Memorandum* between Italy and Libya (which does not seem to guarantee adequate protection to migrants) are considered.[67]

In conclusion, the new domestic criminal provision on torture on the basis of Article 613-*bis* seems neither to identify with the necessary precision the elements constituting the crime, nor to fulfil the obligation set forth in Article 1(2) of the CAT, according to which "each State Party shall take effective legislative, administrative, judicial or other measures to prevent acts of torture in any territory under its jurisdiction".[68] With the awareness that possible gaps in

---

[59] Article 40 of the Italian Criminal Code states: «No one can be punished for an act envisaged as an offence by the law, if the harmful or dangerous event is not a consequence of his or her action or omission. Not preventing an event, which one has the legal obligation to prevent, is equivalent to causing it».

[60] On this aspect it shall be reminded that, according to Article 29 of the Statute of the International Criminal Court, the crime of torture is exempt from any statute of limitation.

[61] Committee against Torture, *cit. supra* note 47, para. 13.

[62] *Ibid.*, paras. 39 and 41.

[63] *Ibid.*, paras. 43 and 45, with special regard to the cases of gender violence, reference to which is moreover completely lacking in Article 613-*bis*. On this question, see PINTON, "La riparazione dovuta alle vittime di tortura", in PINTON and ZAGATO (eds.), *La tortura nel nuovo millennio, cit. supra* note 45, p. 95 ff.

[64] Committee against Torture, *cit. supra* note 47, para. 35.

[65] *Ibid.*, para. 33.

[66] *Ibid.*, paras. 25, 27 and 29.

[67] *Ibid.*, para. 23. On this point, see the comment by MANCINI in this Volume, p. 259 ff.

[68] See LOBBA, "Punire la tortura in Italia. Spunti ricostruttivi a cavallo tra diritti umani e diritto penale internazionale", Diritto penale contemporaneo, 10/2017, p. 181 ff., whose analy-

the range of protection will not be filled through the application of analogy, some commentators have nevertheless welcomed the introduction of the offense of torture into the Italian legal order, for it represents, despite of its – so to say – weakened form, a step forward which avoids it being put off for the nth time;[69] while another part of civil society holds it as a false and self-defeating step.[70]

AGOSTINA LATINO

Law No. 167 of 20 November 2017, n. 167
New Legislative Measures against Holocaust Denial-Negationism

In the Legislation's Review of last year (see IYIL, 2016, pp. 633-634) we reported that by Law No. 115 of 16 June 2016 Italy had at last enacted as law the crime of Holocaust denial, or "negationism", as well as the denial of the crime of genocide, crimes against humanity and war crimes as defined in the Statute of

---

sis reveals how the innovations created through Law No. 110 of 14 July 2017 produce paradoxical effects because, on the one hand, despite the declared legislative intentions, it leaves room for an excessive criminalisation of operations by police forces; on the other hand, it does not extinguish glimmers of impunity with respect to conducts clearly qualified and persecuted as torture at the international level.

[69] On 29 June 2017, Professor Antonio Marchesi, President of Amnesty International Italia, affirmed: "we do not like this law [...]. We believe that, however, it represents a little step forward. Amnesty is a pragmatic organization, it gives itself practical goals [...]. Between nothing and this rubbish, Amnesty chooses to have something": see the text of the interview available at: <http://www.radioradicale.it/scheda/513420/lo-stato-del-dirit-to-trasmissione-curata-e-condotta-da-irene-testa>. The same opinion, at least in part, is shared by Patrizio Gonnella, President of the NGO Associazione Antigone, who declared on 6 July 2017: "now it is up to [...] the judges to demonstrate that, through interpretation, a very, very fearful legislation can be brought a step forward": see the text available at: <http://it.radiovaticana.va/news/2017/07/06/tortura,_amnesty_e_antigone_meglio_questa_legge_che_nulla/1323564>. For Cittadinanzattiva as well, although Article 613-*bis* is the fruit of a "law full of limits, [...] it shall be recognized that today an *ad hoc* provision against torture exists also in the Italian legal order, even if it is a blunt tool": the interview is available at: <http://www.cittadinanzattiva.it/comunicati/giustizia/10414-cittadinanzat-tiva-su-legge-tortura-piena-di-limiti-uno-strumento-spuntato-ora-occorre-farla-applicare.html>.

[70] Article 613-*bis* is considered the outcome of a "swindle-law". Among others, Enrico Zucca, Substitute General Attorney in Genoa, former prosecuting attorney for the "Diaz" proceeding, shares the opinion according to which Article 613-*bis* is a "rule which seems to have been written specifically not to be applied". A similar position is expressed by Roberto Settembre, former judge at the appeal proceedings for the affair in Bolzaneto; Lorenzo Guadagnucci, member of the Committee "Verità e giustizia per Genova"; Tomaso Montanari, President of "Libertà e Giustizia": see <https://altreconomia.it/no-legge-tortu-ra/>. Ilaria Cucchi, President of the Association "Stefano Cucchi Onlus" has written: "better nothing than a useless law", considering Article 613-*bis* as "an insult" in itself: see the text available at: <http://www.lapresse.it/tortura-ilaria-cucchi-questa-legge-e-un-offesa.html>.

the International Criminal Court in compliance with the above EU Framework Decision.

Implementation was however not fully compliant because, due to some opposition in Parliament, the criminal law provision which was adopted was limited to "denial" proper and to acts of "propaganda, instigation and incitement". The "European Law" of 2017, Law No. 167, which provides for the implementation by a single statute of a number of provisions of various directives and similar EU acts, as is now the practice in Italy every year, covers also the loophole left by Law No. 115 of 2016. Article 5 of Law 167 makes an addition to the implementing provision of the Framework Decision adopted in 2016 by Law No. 115, which in turn modified Law No. 654 of 1975 adding to Article 3 a new Article 3-*bis*. This law, which had been originally enacted in order to enforce in Italy the UN Convention of 1966 on the Elimination of All Forms of Racial Discrimination, had been considerably reinforced already by Law No. 295 of 1993 (*Legge Mancino*). The new addition consists in punishing also whomever publicly condones *(apologia)* or grossly trivializes (*minimizzazione in modo grave*) the above mentioned international crimes. Finally, the new provisions extend the coverage of the regulation concerning the liability for certain crimes by legal entities, including companies (Legislative Decree No. 231 of 2001), also to the crimes listed in Article 3-*bis* of Law No. 654, as modified.

GIORGIO SACERDOTI

BIBLIOGRAPHIES

ITALIAN BIBLIOGRAPHICAL INDEX
OF INTERNATIONAL LAW 2017

(edited by *Giulio Bartolini* and *Alessandro Chechi*)

This bibliography includes books and articles published during the year 2017, with some exceptions going back to 2016.

Items are listed only once, under their most appropriate heading. Headings correspond to the Classification Scheme adopted for the Italian practice relating to international law.

Unless otherwise specified, texts are in the same language as corresponding entries in the bibliography. When available, translations of titles have been reproduced from the original source.

The bibliography includes only works on public international law. Works considered as belonging to European Union law and to private international law are generally omitted.

Any indication of items inadvertently omitted will be appreciated with a view to publication in the next volume of the *Yearbook*.

I. INTERNATIONAL LAW IN GENERAL

CASSESE A. (FRULLI M. ed.), *Diritto internazionale* (International Law), 3rd ed., Bologna, 2017, pp. 464.

CREMA L., *La prassi successiva e l'interpretazione del diritto internazionale scritto* (The Subsequent Practice and the Interpretation of Written International Law), Milano, 2017, pp. 364.

FOCARELLI C., "*Jus gentium* in Alberico Gentili: A Call for Prudence and the Common Sense of Humanity", RDI, 2017, p. 329 ff.

FOCARELLI C., *Diritto internazionale* (International Law), 4th ed., Padova, 2017, pp. 710.

FOCARELLI C., *Giurisdizioni internazionali* (International Juridictions), Padova, 2017, pp. 398.

FRANCIONI F., "Ricordo di Benedetto Conforti", in PINESCHI L. (ed.), *La tutela della salute nel diritto internazionale ed europeo tra interessi globali e interessi particolari*, Napoli, 2017, p. 31 ff.

MARCHISIO S., *Corso di diritto internazionale* (Course of International Law), 2nd ed., Torino, 2017, pp. 434.

MURA E., *All'ombra di Mancini. La disciplina internazionalistica in Italia ai suoi albori* (On Mancini's Shadow. At the Dawn of International Law Studies in Italy), Pisa, 2017, pp. 401.

PANEBIANCO M., "Il diritto internazionale codificato del 1900 nel 'codice' Kandler" (The International Codified Law of 1900 in the Kandler 'Code'), RCGI, 2017, p. 9 ff.

PANEBIANCO M., "Una rilettura del diritto internazionale codificato fra codicismo ed anticodicismo (secoli XIX-XX)" (A New Reading of International Codified Law between 'Codicism' and 'Anti-Codicism' (XIX-XX Centuries)), Studi sull'integrazione europea, 2017, p. 455 ff.

SACERDOTI G., "Ricordo di Luigi Ferrari Bravo", in PINESCHI L. (ed.), *La tutela della salute nel diritto internazionale ed europeo tra interessi globali e interessi particolari*, Napoli, 2017, p. 35 ff.

SALERNO F., *Diritto internazionale. Principi e norme* (International Law. Principles and Norms), 4th ed., Padova, 2017, pp. 670.

SALVATI P., "The 2016 US Presidential Election and Russia's (Alleged) Interference through Cyber Intelligence Collection: A Perspective of International Law", CI, 2017, p. 17 ff.

TANZI A., *International Law. A Concise Introduction*, Bologna, 2017, pp. 203.

TRIGGIANI E. et al. (eds.), *Dialoghi con Ugo Villani* (Dialogues with Ugo Villani), Bari, 2017, pp. 1244.

VADI V., "'Grotius' Book Chest, International Law and Material Culture", Northern Ireland Legal Quarterly, 2017, p. 317 ff.

VADI V., "International Law and Its Histories: Methodological Risks and Opportunities", Harvard International Law Journal, 2017, p. 301 ff.

II. INTERNATIONAL CUSTOM, LAW OF TREATIES AND OTHER SOURCES OF INTERNATIONAL LAW

BORLINI L., "Soft law, soft organizations e regolamentazione 'tecnica' di problemi di sicurezza pubblica e integrità finanziaria" (Soft Law, Soft Organizations and "Technical" Rules on Issues of Public Security and Financial Integrity), RDI, 2017, p. 356 ff.

PANTALEO L., "The Provisional Application of CETA: Selected Issues", QIL, Zoom-out 41, 2017, p. 59 ff.

PASCALE G., "Sull'obbligo degli Stati di registrare gli accordi internazionali presso il Segretariato generale delle Nazioni Unite: il caso *Jadhav*" (On the Obligation for States to Record International Treaties at the UN General-Secretariat: The *Jadhav* Case), RDI, 2017, p. 1175 ff.

SCALESE G., "La problematica dei c.d. 'accordi non vincolanti' nel diritto internazionale: un potenziale paradosso" (The Problem of So-Called "Non-Binding Treaties" in International Law: A Potential Paradox", RCGI, 2017, p. 9 ff.

VIOLI F., "Formal and Informal Modification of Treaties before Their Entry Into Force: What Scope for Amending CETA?", QIL, Zoom-out 41, 2017, p. 5 ff.

III. STATES AND OTHER INTERNATIONAL ENTITIES

ALÌ A., "Lo Stato, il territorio, l'accesso e la localizzazione dei dati ai tempi del cloud computing" (The State, the Territory, Data Access and Localization at the time of Cloud Computing), *Gnosis*, 2, 2017, p. 143 ff.

AMOROSO D., "Muddying the 'Bright Lines': The Crimean Claim to Self-Determination in a Policy-Oriented Perspective", in CZAPLINSKI W. et al. (eds.), *The Case of Crimea's Annexation Under International Law*, Warsaw, 2017, p. 105 ff.

CARBONE S.M., "I diritti degli individui e delle imprese nell'evoluzione del diritto internazionale dell'economia: alcuni cenni" (Rights of Individuals and Corporations in the Evolution of International Law: Some Remarks), Rivista del commercio internazionale, 2017, p. 3 ff.

MILANO E., "Unfreezing and Settling the Conflict over Kosovo", GYIL, 2016, p. 163 ff.

PASCALE G., "Su alcune recenti vicende riguardanti i rapporti dell'Ordine di Malta con l'Italia e con la Santa Sede" (Some Recent Events Concerning the Relationship of the Order of Malta with Italy and the Holy See), CI, 2017, p. 191 ff.

VALENTI M., *La questione del Sahara occidentale alla luce del principio di autodeterminazione dei popoli* (The Question of Western Sahara in the Light of the Self-Determination Principle), Torino, 2017, pp. 194.

VIGNI P. and FRANCIONI F., "Territorial Claims and Coastal States", in DOODS K. et al. (eds.), *Handbook on the Politics of Antarctica*, Cheltenham, 2017, p. 241 ff.

ZECCA M.V., "Il ruolo delle organizzazioni non governative nella riforma del processo di Kimberley" (The Role of Non-Governmental Organisations in the Reform of the Kimberley Process), CI, 2017, p. 343 ff.

IV. DIPLOMATIC AND CONSULAR RELATIONS

NESI G. and BALDI S. (eds.), *Diplomatici in azione. Aspetti giuridici e politici della prassi diplomatica nel mondo contemporaneo* (Diplomats in Action. Legal and Political Aspects of Contemporary Diplomatic Practice), Vol. III, Napoli, 2017.

PANEBIANCO M., *Codici diplomatici internazionali e diritto europeo* (International Diplomatic Codes and European Law), Napoli, 2017, pp. 176.

V. IMMUNITIES

CATALDI G., "Immunités juridictionnelles des Etats étrangers et droit de l'homme: quel équilibre entre les valeurs fondamentales de l'ordre national et le droit international coutumier?", in CRAWFORD J. et al. (eds.), *The International Legal Order: Current Needs and Possible Responses, Essays in Honour of Djamchid Momtaz*, Leiden/Boston, 2017, p. 571 ff.

DE SENA P., "The Judgment of the Italian Constitutional Court on State Immunity in Cases of Serious Violations of Human Rights or Humanitarian Law: A Tentative Analysis under International Law", in ACCONCI P. et al. (eds.), *International Law and the Protection of Humanity: Essays in Honour of Flavia Lattanzi*, Leiden, 2017, p. 61 ff.

PAVONI R., "Immunità e responsabilità dell'ONU per l'introduzione del colera ad Haiti: la sentenza d'appello nel caso *Georges*, il 'rapporto Alston' e le 'scuse' del Segretario generale" (Immunity and Responsibility of the United Nations for the Spread of Cholera in Haiti: The Judgment of the Court of Appeals in *Georges*, the "Alston Report" and the Secretary-General's "Apologies"), RDI, 2017, p. 133 ff.

PISILLO MAZZESCHI R., "The Functional Immunity of State Officials from Foreign Jurisdiction: A Critique of the Traditional Theories", in ACCONCI P. et al. (eds.), *International Law and the Protection of Humanity: Essays in Honour of Flavia Lattanzi*, Leiden, 2017, p. 507 ff.

SCARPA S., "Immunità dello Stato straniero, licenziamento e discriminazione della lavoratrice" (Immunity of the Foreign State, Dismissal and discrimination of Female Workers), Giur. it., 2017, Issue No. 12, pp. 2707 ff.

VII. LAW OF THE SEA

CALIGIURI A., "La Charte de Lomé comme instrument pour une nouvelle gouvernance maritime en Afrique", PSEI - Paix et Sécurité Européenne et Internationale, No. 6, 2017.

CATALDI G., "Il contributo di Benedetto Conforti al diritto internazionale del mare" (Benedetto Conforti's Contribution to the International Law of the Sea), RDI, 2017, p. 98 ff.

LANDO M., "The Croatia/Slovenia Arbitral Award of 29 June 2017: Is there a Common Method for Delimiting All Maritime Zones under International Law?", RDI, 2017, p. 1184 ff.

LEANZA U., "Il confine marittimo tra Italia e Francia: il negoziato dell'Accordo di Caen" (The Maritime Borders between Italy and France: The Caen Agreement Negotiations), CI, 2017, p. 5 ff.

MANEGGIA A., "Il controllo 'preventivo' nella zona contigua" ("Preventive" Control in the Contiguous Zone), RDI, 2017, p. 23 ff.

MAROTTI L., "Esaurimento dei ricorsi interni e controversie in materia di interpretazione e applicazione della Convenzione sul diritto del mare: riflessioni a margine del caso M/V '*Norstar*'" (Exhaustion of Local Remedies and Disputes Relating to the Interpretation and Application of the Convention on the Law of the Sea: Reflections on the Norstar Case), RDI, p. 141 ff.

SONDRA F., "The South China Sea Arbitration Award of July 12, 2016: The Unbearable Lightness of Being a Rock", CI, 2017, p. 623 ff.

VIII. ENVIRONMENT

ALLENA M., "Le droit à un environnement salubre: quels nouveaux enjeux Nord-Nord et Nord-Sud?", in MANDERIEUX L. and VELLANO M. (eds.), *Étique globale, bonne gouvernance et droit international économique*, Torino, 2017, p. 107 ff.

ARCURI A., "Is CETA Keeping Up with the Promise? Interpreting certain Provisions Relating to Biotechnology", QIL, Zoom-out 41, 2017, p. 35 ff.

BOCCHI M., "La dimensione internazionale del principio di precauzione e la sua applicazione nel diritto europeo e statunitense alla prova del negoziato sul TTIP" (The International Dimension of the Precautionary Principle and Its Application in EU Law and in US Law in Light of the TTIP Negotiations), CI, 2017, p. 255 ff.

CORDINI G., FOIS P. and MARCHISIO S., *Diritto ambientale. Profili internazionali, europei e comparati* (Environmental Law. International, European and Comparative Perspectives), 3rd ed., Torino, 2017, pp. 172.

FASOLI E., "Review and Adjustment Procedures under the Climate Change Treaty Regimes", Carbon and Climate Law Review, 2017, p. 261 ff.

FASOLI E., "Review and Adjustment under the UN-ECE Transboundary Air Pollution Treaty Regimes and the Implementing EU Legislation", European Environmental Law Review, 2017, p. 130 ff.

FASOLI E., "The Possibilities for Nongovernmental Organizations Promoting Environmental Protection to Claim Damages in Relation to the Environment in France, Italy, the Netherlands and Portugal", RECIEL, 2017, p. 30 ff.

FASOLI E., "The UNECE Convention on Access to Information, Public Participation in Decision- Making and Access to Justice in Environmental Matters", in FITZMAURICE M., TANZI A. and PAPANTONIOU A. (eds.), *Multilateral Environmental Treaties*, Cheltenham, 2017, p. 422 ff.

FRANCIONI F., "Da Rio a Parigi: cosa resta della Dichiarazione del 1992 su ambiente e sviluppo?" (From Rio to Paris: What Is Left of the 1992 Declaration on Environment and Development?), in TRIGGIANI E. et al. (eds.), *Dialoghi con Ugo Villani*, Bari, 2017, p. 779 ff.

GIUFFRIDA R., "Il dovere di prevenzione del danno da inquinamento per la tutela dell'ambiente nel diritto internazionale generale ed europeo" (The Obligation to Prevent Damage Deriving from Pollution for the Protection of the Environment in General International Law and European Law), in TRIGGIANI E. et al. (eds.), *Dialoghi con Ugo Villani*, Bari, 2017, p. 789 ff.

LEANZA U., "Le tre generazioni dei diritti umani e la genesi del diritto all'ambiente*" (The Three Generations of Human Rights and the Genesis of Environmental Law), in TRIGGIANI E. et al. (eds.), *Dialoghi con Ugo Villani*, Bari, 2017, p. 799 ff.

MARRANI D. (ed.), *Il contributo del diritto internazionale e del diritto europeo all'affermazione di una sensibilità ambientale* (The Contribution of International and European Law to the Development of Environmental Understanding), Napoli, 2017, pp. 168.

MONTINI M., "Riflessioni critiche sull'Accordo di Parigi sui cambiamenti climatici" (Some Critical Reflections on the Paris Agreement on Climatic Changes), RDI, 2017, p. 719 ff.

MONTINI M., "The Double Failure of Environmental Regulation and Deregulation and the Need for Ecological Law", IYIL, 2016, p. 265 ff.

ODONI M., "The Protection of the Environment against Harmful Effects of Peacetime Military Training Activities: The Role of International Law", in ACCONCI P. et al. (eds.), *International Law and the Protection of Humanity: Essays in Honour of Flavia Lattanzi*, Leiden, 2017, p. 262 ff.

TANZI A., *The Consolidation of International Water Law. A Comparative Analysis of the UN and UNECE Water Conventions*, Napoli, 2017, pp. 266.

TURRINI P., "Virtual Water: A Global Economic Solution to a Local Environmental and Political Problem?", in CHAISSE J. (ed.), *Charting the Water Regulatory Future: Issues, Challenges and Directions*, Cheltenham/Northampton, 2017, p. 55 ff.

IX. CULTURAL HERITAGE

CARACCIOLO I., "Il caso *Al Mahdi*: responsabilità penale internazionale per crimini di guerra e distruzione intenzionale del patrimonio culturale" (The *Al Mahdi* Case: International Criminal Responsibility for War Crimes and Intentional Destruction of Cultural Heritage), in TRIGGIANI E. et al. (eds.), *Dialoghi con Ugo Villani*, Bari, 2017, p. 101 ff.

CHECHI A. and RENOLD M.-A. (eds.), *Cultural Heritage Law and Ethics: Mapping Recent Developments*, Zurich, 2017, pp. 244.

CONFORTI R., "Il contrasto del traffico di beni culturali durante i conflitti armati" (The Fight against the Trafficking in Cultural Objects in Times of Armed Conflict), in CARACCIOLO I. and MONTUORO U. (eds.), *L'evoluzione del peacekeeping. Il ruolo dell'Italia*, Torino, 2017, p. 155 ff.

FIORENTINI F. and JAKUBOWSKI A., "Istria's Artistic and Spiritual Heritage in Abeyance: International Cooperation and Cultural Community Rights", IYIL, 2016, p. 211 ff.

FRANCIONI F., "Cultural Property in International Law", in GRAZIADEI M. and SMITH L. (eds.), *Comparative Property Law. Global Perspectives*, Cheltenham, 2017, p. 374 ff.

FRANCIONI F. and LIXINSKI L., "Opening the Toolbox of International Human Rights Law in the Safeguarding of Cultural Heritage", in DURBACH A. And LIXINSKI L. (eds,), *Heritage, Culture and Rights*, Oxford, 2017, p. 11 ff.

GAGLIANI G., "*Pro bono pacis*? Le interazioni tra diritto internazionale degli investimenti e patrimonio culturale" (*Pro bono pacis*? Interactions between International Investment Law and Cultural Heritage), RDI, 2017, p. 756 ff.

LEANZA U., "La proposta italiana per i Caschi blu della cultura" (The Italian Proposal for the Blue Helmets for Culture), in CARACCIOLO I. and MONTUORO U. (eds.), *L'evoluzione del peacekeeping. Il ruolo dell'Italia*, Torino, 2017, p. 139 ff.

LENZERINI F., "Distruzione intenzionale del patrimonio culturale: crimine contro i popoli e contro l'umanità complessivamente intesa" (Intentional Destruction of Cultural Heritage: Crime against Peoples and against Humanity as a Whole), in BARSOTTI V. (ed.), *Arte e Diritto. Quaderni del dottorato fiorentino in Scienze Giuridiche. Seminario conclusivo del Dottorato in Scienze*

Giuridiche, Firenze, 27 maggio 2016, Santarcangelo di Romagna, 2017, p. 27 ff.

LENZERINI F., "Intentional Destruction of Cultural Heritage, Crimes against Humanity and Genocide: Towards an Evolutionary Interpretation of International Criminal Law", Europa Ethnica, 2017, n. 3/4, p. 66 ff.

LENZERINI F., "Reparations for Wrongs against Indigenous Peoples Cultural Heritage", in XANTHAKI A. et al. (eds.), *Indigenous Peoples' Cultural Heritage. Rights, Debates, Challenges*, Leiden/Boston, 2017, p. 327 ff.

MANCINI M., "Corte Penale Internazionale" (International Criminal Court), in *Libro dell'anno del Diritto 2017, Supplemento di Enciclopedia Giuridica*, Rome, 2017, p. 785 ff.

MANCINI M., "The Memorandum of Understanding between Italy and UNESCO on the Italian 'Unite4Heritage' Task Force", IYIL, 2016, p. 624 ff.

MONTUORO U., "Ulteriori ipotesi applicative e di 'completamento' in merito all'impiego dei Caschi blu della cultura" (Further Thoughts on the Deployment of the Blue Helmets for Culture), in CARACCIOLO I. and MONTUORO U. (eds.), *L'evoluzione del peacekeeping. Il ruolo dell'Italia*, Torino, 2017, p. 167 ff.

MUCCI F., "La reazione della Comunità internazionale alle distruzioni massicce intenzionali del patrimonio culturale" (The Reaction of the International Community to the Intentional Massive Destruction of Cultural Heritage), in CARACCIOLO I. and MONTUORO U. (eds.), *L'evoluzione del peacekeeping. Il ruolo dell'Italia*, Torino, 2017, p. 173 ff.

RONZITTI N., "Sunken Warships and Cultural Heritage", in CRAWFORD J. et al. (eds.), *The International Legal Order: Current Needs and Possible Responses. Essays in Honour of Djamchid Momtaz*, Leiden/Boston, 2017, p. 476 ff.

SCOVAZZI T., "Il traffico illecito di beni culturali: non soltanto una minaccia alla pace e alla sicurezza internazionali" (The Illicit Trafficking in Cultural Objects: Not Just a Threat to International Peace and Security), in TRIGGIANI E. et al. (eds.), *Dialoghi con Ugo Villani*, Bari, 2017, p. 197 ff.

SCOVAZZI T., "The Relationship between Two Conventions Applicable to Underwater Cultural Heritage", in CRAWFORD J. et al. (eds.), *The International Legal Order: Current Needs and Possible Responses. Essays in Honour of Djamchid Momtaz*, Leiden/Boston, 2017, p. 504 ff.

SILVI M., "La proposta italiana dei Caschi blu della cultura presso l'UNESCO" (The Italian Proposal for the Blue Helmets for Culture at the UNESCO), in CARACCIOLO I. and MONTUORO U. (eds.), *L'evoluzione del peacekeeping. Il ruolo dell'Italia*, Torino, 2017, p. 145 ff.

XI. TREATMENT OF ALIENS AND NATIONALITY

ALÌ A., "Divieto di ingresso ed espulsione dello straniero dal territorio dello Stato per motivi di terrorismo: la sicurezza nazionale nella recente giurisprudenza della Corte di giustizia dell'Unione europea" (Prohibition of Entry and Expulsion of Foreigners from the Territory of the State on Grounds of Terrorism: National Security in the Recent Case Law of the Court of Justice of the European Union), in CORTESE F. and PELACANI G. (eds.), *Il diritto in migrazione. Studi sull'integrazione giuridica degli stranieri, Quaderni della Facoltà di Giurisprudenza di Trento*, Vol. 30, 2017, p. 519 ff.

CARACCIOLO I., "Migration and the Law of the Sea: Solutions and Limitations of a Fragmentary Regime", in CRAWFORD J. et al. (eds.), *The International Legal Order: Current Needs and Possible Responses. Essays in Honour of Djamchid Momtaz*, Leiden/Boston, 2017, p. 274 ff.

CATALDI G., "Migrations in the Mediterranean between Protection of Human Rights and Border Control. An Italian Perspective", in HILPOLD P. (ed.), *Europa im Umbruch*, 2017, p. 119 ff.

CATALDI G., LIGUORI A. and PACE M., *Migration in the Mediterranean Sea and the Challenges for "Hosting" European Society*, Napoli, 2017, pp. 228.

CELLAMARE G., "Sul rilascio di visti di breve durata (VTL) per ragioni umanitarie" (Observations on the Issuance of Short Stay Visas (LTV) on Humanitarian Grounds), Studi sull'integrazione europea, 2017, p. 527 ff.

FAVILLI C., "Visti umanitari e protezione internazionale: così vicini così lontani" (Humanitarian Visa and International Protection: So Close, So Far), DUDI, 2017, p. 553 ff.

GORNATI B., "'Paesi terzi sicuri', respingimenti a catena e detenzione arbitraria: il caso *Ilias e Ahmed*" ('Safe Third Countries', Chain-Refoulement and Arbitrary Detention: The Ilias and Ahmed Case), DUDI, 2017, p. 543 ff.

MARCHEGIANI M. (ed.), *Antico mare e identità migranti: un itinerario interdisciplinare* (Ancient Sea and Migrants Identity: A Interdisciplinary Journey), Torino, 2017, pp. 228.

MARCHESI A., "Close and Enduring Connections: Expulsion Procedures and the Ties between Non Citizens and Host States in the Practice of the Human Rights Committee", in ACCONCI P. et al. (eds.), *International Law and the Protection of Humanity: Essays in Honour of Flavia Lattanzi*, Leiden, 2017, p. 152 ff.

MASELLIS F., "L'illegittimità della 'tassa' italiana sui permessi di soggiorno" (The Unlawfulness of the Italian 'Tax' on Residence Permits), DUDI, 2017, p. 562 ff.

MAURO M.R., "A Step Back in the Safeguard of Migrants' Rights: The Grand Chamber's Judgment in *Khlaifia v. Italy*", IYIL, 2016, p. 289 ff.

NIGRO R., "La sentenza della Corte di giustizia dell'Unione europea nel caso *Lounani* e le controverse motivazioni giuridiche al fine di escludere lo status di rifugiato per presunti terroristi (The Judgment of the EU Court of Justice in the *Lounani* Case and the Controversial Legal Reasons in Order to Exclude Suspected Terrorists from Refugee Status), RDI, 2017, p. 565 ff.

PISTOIA E., "Procedural Rights of Illegal Migrants Facing Expulsion in Contemporary Times: Exploring Synergies between the ILC Draft Articles and the EU Returns Directive", in ACCONCI P. et al. (eds.), *International Law and the Protection of Humanity: Essays in Honour of Flavia Lattanzi*, Leiden, 2017, p. 182 ff.

RUOZZI E., "La Dichiarazione di New York sui rifugiati e sui migranti: verso un modello condiviso di gestione del fenomeno migratorio?" (The New

York Declaration on Refugees and Migrants: Toward a Shared Model for the Management of Migrant Flows?), OIDU, 2017, p. 24 ff.

SCOVAZZI T., "Some Cases in the Italian Practice Relating to Illegal Migration at Sea", in ACCONCI P. et al. (eds.), *International Law and the Protection of Humanity: Essays in Honour of Flavia Lattanzi*, Leiden, 2017, p. 196 ff.

XII. HUMAN RIGHTS

ACCONCI P. et al. (eds.), *International Law and the Protection of Humanity: Essays in Honour of Flavia Lattanzi*, Leiden, 2017, pp. 564.

ACCONCI P., "The Safeguard of Social Rights within the Activity of the Security Council", in ACCONCI P. et al. (eds.), *International Law and the Protection of Humanity: Essays in Honour of Flavia Lattanzi*, Leiden, 2017, p. 1 ff.

ALÌ A., "Commento all'art. 22" (Comment to Article 22), in MASTROIANNI R. et al. (eds.), *Carta dei diritti fondamentali dell'Unione europea*, Milano, 2017, p. 436 ff.

ARCARI M., "UN Security Council Resolutions before the European Court of Human Rights: Exploring Alternative Approaches for the Solution of Normative Conflicts", in ACCONCI P. et al. (eds.), *International Law and the Protection of Humanity: Essays in Honour of Flavia Lattanzi*, Leiden, 2017, p. 24 ff.

BALBONI M. (ed.), *The European Convention on Human Rights and the Principle of Non-Discrimination*, Napoli, 2017, pp. 328.

BASSAN F., "Legal Options and Models in the Design of a Sovereign Wealth Fund, and Their Implications for Human Rights Protection", in ACCONCI P. et al. (eds.), *International Law and the Protection of Humanity: Essays in Honour of Flavia Lattanzi*, Leiden, 2017, p. 38 ff.

BEVILACQUA G., "Partecipazione ai processi decisionali e accesso alla giustizia delle associazioni ambientali a tutela degli habitat naturali di importanza europea" (Participation to Decisional Procedures and Access to Justice of Environmental Organizations for the Protection of Natural Habitats of European Interest), DUDI, 2017, p. 497 ff.

BONFANTI A., "Intercettazione di comunicazioni telematiche e acquisizione di dati: sullo studio dell'Unione europea su *Legal Frameworks for Hacking by Law Enforcement*" (Hacking by Law Enforcement Agencies: Remarks about the European Union Study on Legal Frameworks for Hacking by Law Enforcement), DUDI, 2017, p. 506 ff.

BOSCHIERO N., "Intellectual Property Rights and Public Health: An Impediment to Access to Medicines and Health Technology Innovation?", in PINESCHI L. (ed.), *La tutela della salute nel diritto internazionale ed europeo tra interessi globali e interessi particolari*, Napoli, 2017, p. 259 ff.

BURCI G.L., "Tutela della salute ed evoluzione della sicurezza collettiva" (Protection of Health and the Evolution of Collective Security), in PINESCHI L. (ed.), *La tutela della salute nel diritto internazionale ed europeo tra interessi globali e interessi particolari*, Napoli, 2017, p. 67 ff.

BUSACCA A., "'Diritto di accesso' alla rete internet" (Right to Access to the Internet), OIDU, 2017, p. 345 ff.

BUTTARELLI G., "Diritto alla salute e tutela dei dati personali" (The Right to Health and the Protection of Personal Data), in PINESCHI L. (ed.), *La tutela della salute nel diritto internazionale ed europeo tra interessi globali e interessi particolari*, Napoli, 2017, p. 205 ff.

CAGGIANO G., "L'applicazione della Convenzione europea dei diritti umani ai Rom tra principio di non-discriminazione e azioni positive a favore dei gruppi vulnerabili" (The Application of the European Convention on Human Rights to Roma: The Principle of Non-discrimination and Positive Actions in Favor of Disadvantaged Minority Groups), Studi sull'integrazione europea, 2017, p. 33 ff.

CANNONE A., "La sentenza della Grande camera della Corte europea dei diritti dell'uomo del 3 luglio 2014, *Georgia c. Russia* (I) (merito): brevi osservazioni" (The Judgment of the Grand Chamber of the European Court of Human Rights of 3 July 2014, *Georgia v. Russia* (I) (merits)), in TRIGGIANI E. et al. (eds.), *Dialoghi con Ugo Villani*, Bari, 2017, p. 243 ff.

CAPONE F., "From the Justice and Peace Law to the Revised Peace Agreement between the Colombian Government and the FARC: Will Victims' Rights Be Satisfied at Last?", ZAÖRV, 2017, p. 125 ff.

CATALDI G., "Immunités juridictionnelles des États étrangers et droit de l'homme: quel équilibre entre les valeurs fondamentales de l'ordre national et le droit international coutumier?", in CRAWFORD J. et al. (eds.), *The International Legal Order: Current Needs and Possible Responses. Essays in Honour of Djamchid Momtaz*, Leiden/Boston, 2017, p. 571 ff.

CATALDI G., "La deroga francese alla Convenzione europea dei diritti dell'uomo. Un precedente da non seguire" (The French Derogation From the European Convention on Human Rights. A Precedent Not To Be Followed), in TRIGGIANI E. et al. (eds.), *Dialoghi con Ugo Villani*, Bari, 2017, p. 271 ff.

CATALDI G., "La giurisprudenza della Corte europea dei diritti dell'uomo in materia di diagnosi genetica preimpianto" (The Case Law of the European Court of Human Rights in matters of Pre-Implantation Genetic Diagnosis), in FATTIBENE R. (ed.), *La diagnosi genetica preimpianto tra normativa e giurisprudenza*, Napoli, 2017, p. 183 ff.

CORCIONE E., "Nuove forme di schiavitù al vaglio della Corte europea dei diritti umani: lo sfruttamento dei braccianti nel caso *Chowdury*" (Modern Slavery Before the European Court of Human Rights: The Exploitation of Agricultural Workers in the Chowdury Case), DUDI, 2017, p. 516 ff.

D'ONGHIA M. and ZANIBONI E. (eds.), *Tutela dei soggetti deboli e trasformazioni del lavoro tra diritti e libertà. Prospettive nazionali e internazionali* (Protection of Vulnerable Subjects and Transformations of Labour between Rights and Freedom. National and International Perspectives), Napoli, 2017, pp. 218.

DANISI C., "Contextualising Non-Discrimination: Towards A New Approach for Sexual Minorities under the ECHR?", in BALBONI M. (ed.), *The European*

Convention on Human Rights and the Principle of Non-Discrimination, Napoli, 2017, p. 192 ff.

DE FAZIO R.S., "La tutela e la memoria delle vittime del terrorismo internazionale" (The Protection of Victims of Intenational Terrorism and of Their Memory), OIDU, 2017, p. 42 ff.

DELLA FINA V., CERA R. and PALMISANO G. (eds.), *The United Nations Convention on the Rights of Persons with Disabilities. A Commentary*, 2017, pp. 769.

DI LIETO A., "L'arcipelago Chagos: vecchio e nuovo colonialismo" (Chagos Archipelago: Old and New Colonialism), in TRIGGIANI E. et al. (eds.), *Dialoghi con Ugo Villani*, Bari, 2017, p. 299 ff.

DI MATTEO F., "La raccolta indiscriminata e generalizzata di dati personali: un vizio congenito nella direttiva PNR?" (The Massive and Indiscriminate Collection of Passengers' Data: A Congenital Defect Within the EU PNR Directive?"), DUDI, 2017, p. 213 ff.

DI PAOLO C., "I diritti delle donne in materia di interruzione volontaria di gravidanza: la situazione in Italia nella prospettiva della Carta sociale europea" (Women's Rights within the Italian Legal Order in Matters of Voluntary Termination of Pregnancy), Studi sull'integrazione europea, 2017, p. 97 ff.

DI TURI C., "Ancora sul caso *Chowdury*: quale tutela per i diritti dei lavoratori migranti irregolari vittime di sfruttamento? L'art. 4 CEDU e le forme contemporanee di schiavitù" (On the Chowdury Case Once Again: What Legal Protection for the Rights of Irregular Migrant Workers? Article 4 of the European Convention on Human Rights and Contemporary Forms of Slavery), CI, 2017, p. 565 ff.

FABBRICOTTI A. (ed.), *Il diritto al cognome materno. Profili di diritto civile italiano, di diritto internazionale, dell'Unione europea, comparato ed internazionale privato* (The Right to the Maternal Surname. Remarks on Italian Civil Law, International Law, European Union Law, Comparative Law and International Private Law), Napoli, 2017, pp. 224.

FABBRICOTTI A., "The Transmission of the Mother's Surname Under the CEDAW", DUDI, 2017, p. 465 ff.

FASCIGLIONE M., "Il Piano d'azione nazionale italiano su impresa e diritti umani e l'attuazione dei Principi guida ONU del 2011" (The Italian National Action Plan on Business and Human Rights and the Domestic Implementation of the 2011 UN Guiding Principles), DUDI, 2017, p. 277 ff.

FRANCHI M. and VIARENGO I., *Tutela internazionale dei diritti umani: casi e materiali* (The International Protection of Human Rights: Cases and Materials), Torino, 2016, pp. 338.

GERACI A., "Il minore straniero non accompagnato nel diritto internazionale, dell'Unione Europea e italiano: criticità attuali e prospettive future" (Unaccompanied Minors in International, European and Italian Law: Current Weaknesses and Future Prospects), CI, 2017, p. 585 ff.

GIUFFRÉ M., "Deportation with Assurances and Human Rights: The Case of Persons Suspected or Convicted of Serious Crimes", JICJ, 2017, 75 ff.

GIUFFRIDA R., "La tutela delle minoranze e il principio di non discriminazione nel diritto internazionale" (The Protection of Minorities and the Principle of Non Discrimination in International Law), in MARCHEGIANI M. (ed.), *Antico mare e identità migranti: un itinerario interdisciplinare*, Torino, 2017, p. 74 ff.

GIUFFRIDA R., "Subsidiary Protection in International and European Law", in ACCONCI P. et al. (eds.), *International Law and the Protection of Humanity: Essays in Honour of Flavia Lattanzi*, Leiden, 2017, p. 105 ff.

GRAZIANI F., "L'introduzione del reato di tortura nel codice penale italiano, ovvero del funambolismo e altri equilibrismi" (On the Inclusion of the Crime of Torture in the Italian Penal Code, or rather on Practising Funambulism and Juggling), CI, 2017, p. 421 ff.

GRECO R., "The Silala Dispute: Between International Water Law and the Human Right to Water", QIL, Zoom-in 30, 2017, p. 23 ff.

GRIECO C. AND MUSSO F., "An International and European Perspective on the Right to Food and to Adequate Food for Elderly People and Its Justiciability. Food Common Policy and Strategies", OIDU, 2017, p. 373 ff.

GUSMAI G., "Acqua e cibo: alcune irragionevoli 'divergenze' di tutela nella prospettiva giuridica interna e sovranazionale" (Water and Food: Some Unreasonable "Differences" of Safeguard in the National and Supranational Legal Perspective), Studi sull'integrazione europea, 2017, p. 193 ff.

IANNUZZI L., "Alcune considerazioni sul meccanismo di revisione periodica universale nell'ambito delle Nazioni Unite" (Some Remarks on the Universal Periodic Review Mechanism within the United Nations), in TRIGGIANI E. et al. (eds.), *Dialoghi con Ugo Villani*, Bari, 2017, p. 307 ff.

IOVANE M., "L'affaire de l'immunité juridictionnelle de l'Allemagne devant les tribunaux italiens: une tentative extrême d'assurer le respect du droit international des droits de l'homme ou un exemple de protection diplomatique par les juges?", in TRIGGIANI E. et al. (eds.), *Dialoghi con Ugo Villani*, Bari, 2017, p. 313 ff.

IPPOLITO F., "Mainstreaming Human Rights in EuroMed Bilateral Relations: The Road to Hell Is Paved with Good Intentions", The Global Community, 2016, p. 83 ff.

LA ROSA E., "È giunto finalmente il momento di introduzione del reato di tortura?" (Is It Time for the Crime of Torture?), OIDU, 2017, p. 360 ff.

LATINO A., "The Principle of Non-Refoulement between International Law and European Union Law", in ACCONCI P. et al. (eds.), *International Law and the Protection of Humanity: Essays in Honour of Flavia Lattanzi*, Leiden, 2017, p. 131 ff.

LEANDRO A., "Arbitration, Multi-Tier Waiver of the Access to Courts and the European Convention on Human Rights: Some Remarks on the Tabbane Decision", in TRIGGIANI E. et al. (eds.), *Dialoghi con Ugo Villani*, Bari, 2017, p. 321 ff.

LENZERINI F., "The Land Rights of Indigenous Peoples under International Law", in GRAZIADEI M. and SMITH L. (eds.), *Comparative Property Law. Global Perspectives*, Cheltenham, 2017, p. 393 ff.

LIGUORI A., "Il Muslim Ban di Trump alla luce del diritto internazionale" (Trump "Muslim Ban" and International Law), DUDI, 2017, p. 173 ff.

LIZZI L., "The (Mal)Functioning of the Russian Justice System in Cases Involving Political Opponents and the European Court of Human Rights", CI, 2017, p. 59 ff.

LUGATO M., "Diritto alla salute, scelte etiche e margine di apprezzamento dello Stato" (Right to Health, Ethical Choices and the State's Margin of Appreciation), in PINESCHI L. (ed.), *La tutela della salute nel diritto internazionale ed europeo tra interessi globali e interessi particolari*, Napoli, 2017, p. 161 ff.

MARCHEGIANI M., "Tendenze evolutive nel ricorso al principio della protezione equivalente da parte della Corte europea dei diritti dell'uomo" (Evolutive Trends in References to the Principle of Equivalent Protection Made by the European Court of Human Rights), RDI, 2017, p. 447 ff.

MARINAI S., *Perdita della cittadinanza e diritti fondamentali: profili internazionalistici ed europei* (Loss of Citizenship and Fundamental Rights: International and European Perspectives), Milano, 2017, pp. 310.

MARRELLA F., "Protection internationale des droits de l'homme et activités des sociétés transnationales", RCADI, Vol. 385, 2016, p. 33 ff.

MATONTI A.I., "Garanzie procedurali derivanti dall'art. 4 del Protocollo n. 4 CEDU: il caso *Khlaifia*" (Procedural Guarantees Stemming from Article 4 of Protocol No. 4 to the ECHR: The Khlaifia Case), DUDI, 2017, p. 523 ff.

PADELLETTI M.L., "Significant Disadvantage and Admissibility of Applications to the European Court of Human Rights: Effects on Domestic Legal Orders", in ACCONCI P. et al. (eds.), *International Law and the Protection of Humanity: Essays in Honour of Flavia Lattanzi*, Leiden, 2017, p. 75 ff.

PALMISANO G., "L'obbligo dello Stato di tutelare il diritto alla salute ai sensi della Carta sociale europea" (The Obligation of the State to Protect the Right to Health according to the European Social Charter), in PINESCHI L. (ed.), *La tutela della salute nel diritto internazionale ed europeo tra interessi globali e interessi particolari*, Napoli, 2017, p. 189 ff.

PALMISANO G., "La protezione dei diritti dei Rom nella prassi applicativa della carta sociale europea" (The Protection of Roma Rights within the Implementation Framework of the European Social Charter), Studi sull'integrazione europea, 2017, p. 47 ff.

PALMISANO G., "Protecting the Rights of Persons with Autism: The Role of the European Committee of Social Rights", in ACCONCI P. et al. (eds.), *International Law and the Protection of Humanity: Essays in Honour of Flavia Lattanzi*, Leiden, 2017, p. 90 ff.

PALOMBINO F.M., "Il diritto umano all'acqua nella prospettiva della Corte europea dei diritti dell'uomo: in margine al caso *Otgon*" (Human Right to Water Under the Perspective of the European Court of Human Rights: About the *Orgon* Case), RDI, 2017, p. 149 ff.

PANEBIANCO M., "Soft Law and Hard dei diritti umani: l'età della crisi" (Soft Law and Hard Law in Human Rights Law: The Crisis Era), RCGI, 2017, p. 22 ff.

PANNARALE L., "La sfida dei diritti umani" (The Human Rights Challenge), in TRIGGIANI E. et al. (eds.), *Dialoghi con Ugo Villani*, Bari, 2017, p. 345 ff.

PASCALE G., *La tutela internazionale dei diritti dell'uomo nel continente africano* (The International Protection of Human Rights in the African Continent), Napoli, 2017, pp. 438.

PINESCHI L. (ed.), *La tutela della salute nel diritto internazionale ed europeo tra interessi globali e interessi particolari*, Napoli, 2017, pp. 496.

PISILLO MAZZESCHI R., "Sicurezza umana e diritto internazionale" (Human Security and International Law), in TRIGGIANI E. et al. (eds.), *Dialoghi con Ugo Villani*, Bari, 2017, p. 353 ff.

POGGI F., "Violenza di genere e Convenzione di Istanbul: un'analisi concettuale" (Gender Violence and Istanbul Convention: A Conceptual Analysis), DUDI, 2017, p. 51 ff.

RUSSO D., "Lo sfruttamento del lavoro negli Stati membri del Consiglio d'Europa: una riflessione a margine del caso *Chowdury*" (Work Exploitation in the Member States of the Council of Europe: Reflections on the *Chowdury* Case), RDI, 2017, p. 835 ff.

SACCUCCI A., "The European Court's Afterthoughts on the Khlaifia Case: The Prohibition of Degrading and Inhuman Treatment and of Collective Expulsions in the Context of the Migration Emergency", RDI, 2017, p. 552 ff.

SAVARESE E., "Questioni sul fine vita a vent'anni dalla Convenzione di Oviedo: consolidati principi e permanenti incertezze" (Questions on End-of-life Situations Twenty Years after the Oviedo Convention: Stated Principles and Permanent Uncertainties), DUDI, 2017, p. 321 ff.

SCALI L., "The Impact of Conditionality on Economic, Social and Cultural Rights in the Latest Reports of the UN Independent Expert on Foreign Debt and Human Rights", DUDI, 2017, p. 532 ff.

SCOVAZZI T., "Il diritto umano all'acqua e all'igiene personale" (The Human Right to Water and Personal Hygene), in PINESCHI L. (ed.), *La tutela della salute nel diritto internazionale ed europeo tra interessi globali e interessi particolari*, Napoli, 2017, p. 231 ff.

SINAGRA A., "Il Consiglio dei diritti umani e il *diritto alla pace*" (The Human Rights Council and the *Right to Peace*), in TRIGGIANI E. et al. (eds.), *Dialoghi con Ugo Villani*, Bari, 2017, p. 381 ff.

SPAGNOLO A., "Human Rights Implications of Autonomous Weapon Systems in Domestic Law Enforcement: Sci-Fi Reflections on a Lo-Fi Reality", QIL, Zoom-in 43, 2017, p. 33 ff.

TINO E., "Il diniego di accesso alla giustizia per i soggetti privati nella SADC: alcune considerazioni sul nuovo Protocollo sul Tribunale" (The Denial of Access to Justice for Individuals Within the SADC: Some Considerations on the New Protocol on the Tribunal), DUDI, 2017, p. 477 ff.

VANNUCCINI S., "Roma-Strasburgo-Roma. Il viaggio del 'figlio di ignoti' alla scoperta della verità sulla propria ascendenza" (Rome-Strasbourg-Rome. The Journey of the "Child of Unknown Parents" to the Discovery of Truth about His/Her Genealogy), CI, 2017, p. 369 ff.

VERDASCHI A. and FABBRINI F., "Secrecy and Accountability for Extraordinary Renditions to Torture: Italy, the European Court of Human Rights and the Abu Omar Case", European Journal of Human Rights, 2017, p. 3 ff.

VERDASCHI A. and MARINO NOBERASCO G., "From DRD to PNR: Looking for a New Balance Between Privacy and Security", in COLE D., FABBRINI F. and SCHULHOFER S. (eds.), *Surveillance, Privacy and Trans-Atlantic Relations*, Oxford, 2017, p. 67 ff.

VERDASCHI A., "Cronaca di una condanna annunciata: Abu Omar a Strasburgo, l'ultimo atto" (Account of an Announced Ruling: Abu Omar in Strasbourg, Last Stand), DPCE online, 2016, No. 1, p. 265 ff.

VERDASCHI A., "State Secret Privilege versus Human Rights: Lessons from the European Court of Human Rights Ruling on the Abu Omar Case", European Constitutional Law Review, 2017, p. 166 ff.

ZICCARDI CAPALDO G., "Giudice interno, reato di tortura e maltrattamenti: un nuovo approccio allo *jus cogens human rights* per contrastare l'impunità" (Domestic Judge, Crime of Torture and Mistreatments: A New Approach to *Jus Cogens Human Right* in order to Fight Impunity), in TRIGGIANI E. et al. (eds.), *Dialoghi con Ugo Villani*, Bari, 2017, p. 399 ff.

ZICCARDI CAPALDO G., "Novelty in ECtHR Case Law on Torture, But It Is Not Enough - Reopening Domestic Proceedings to End Impunity", The Global Community, 2016, p. 3 ff.

XIII. INTERNATIONAL CRIMINAL LAW

AZAROVA V. and MARINIELLO T., "Why the ICC Needs a 'Palestine Situation' (More than Palestine Needs the ICC): On the Court's Potential Role(s) in the Israeli-Palestinian Context", DUDI, 2017, p. 115 ff.

BARTOLINI G., "'Il mancato processo al Kaiser' nella prassi e nella dottrina italiana" ("The Failed Trial to the Kaiser" in the Italian Pratice and Academic Writings), in TRIGGIANI E. et al. (eds.), *Dialoghi con Ugo Villani*, Bari, 2017, p. 81 ff.

BONAFÉ B.I., "Sentencing Practice and the Contribution of International Criminal Tribunals to the Maintenance of Peace", DUDI, 2017, p. 101 ff.

CAPONE F., "La qualificazione del delitto di strage come crimine contro l'umanità" (The Qualification of the Crime of Massacre as a Crime against Humanity), Giurisprudenza italiana, 2016, Issue No. 11, pp. 2498 ff.

CARCANO A., "Of Efficiency and Fairness in the Administration of International Justice: Can the Residual Mechanism Provide Adequately Reasoned Judgments?", QIL, Zoom-in 40, 2017, p. 40 ff.

CIMIOTTA E., "Giustizia penale internazionale e mantenimento della pace: qualche riflessione conclusiva" (International Criminal Justice and the Maintenance of Peace: Some Concluding Thoughts), DUDI, 2017, p. 447 ff.

CUSATO E.T., "Beyond Symbolism: Problems and Prospects with Prosecuting Environmental Destruction before the ICC", JICJ, 2017, p. 491 ff.

DELLA MORTE G., "La preuve à l'épreuve: trois cas-limites pour le juge international (pénal)", in ACCONCI P. et al. (eds.), *International Law and the*

Protection of Humanity: Essays in Honour of Flavia Lattanzi, Leiden, 2017, p. 339 ff.

DONAT CATTIN D., "Intervention of Humanity or the Use of Force to Halt Mass-Atrocity Crimes, the Peremptory Prohibition of Aggression and the Interplay between Jus ad Bellum, Jus in Bello and Individual Criminal Responsibility on the Crime of Aggression", in ACCONCI P. et al. (eds.), *International Law and the Protection of Humanity: Essays in Honour of Flavia Lattanzi*, Leiden, 2017, p. 353 ff.

FASOLI E. and MITSILEGAS V., "Historical Pollution in the UK (England and Wales): The Residual Role Played by Criminal Law", in CENTONZE F. and MANACORDA S. (eds.), *Historical Pollution. Comparative Legal Responses to Environmental Crimes*, Zurich, 2017, p. 227 ff.

FASOLI E., "Environmental Criminal Law in the United Kindgdom", in FARMER A., FAURE M. and VAGLIASINDI G.M. (eds.), *Environmental Crime in Europe*, Oxford, 2017, p. 243 ff.

GIANELLI A., "The Place of Rehabilitation of the Offender among the Purposes of Penalties according to International Law", in ACCONCI P. et al. (eds.), *International Law and the Protection of Humanity: Essays in Honour of Flavia Lattanzi*, Leiden, 2017, p. 397 ff.

NESI G., "Introduzione" (Introduction), in WENIN R. and FORNASARI G. (eds.), *Diritto penale e modernità. Le nuove sfide fra terrorismo, sviluppo tecnologico e garanzie fondamentali. Atti del convegno, Trento, 2 e 3 ottobre 2015*, Napoli, 2017, p. 1 ff.

NESI G., "La repressione dei crimini di sfruttamento e abusi sessuali da parte dei *peacekeepers*. Recenti sviluppi e prospettive future" (The Repression of the Crimes of Sexual Exploitation and Sexual Abuse Committed by Peacekeepers. Recent Developments and Future Prospects), in TRIGGIANI E. et al. (eds.), *Dialoghi con Ugo Villani*, Bari, 2017, p. 173 ff.

NESI G., "The Repression of the Crimes of Sexual Exploitation and Abuse Committed by Peacekeepers: Recent Developments", CI, 2017, p. 327 ff.

PAPA M.I., "L'iniziativa dell'Assemblea generale dell'ONU di istituire un 'Meccanismo' di sostegno nelle indagini sui crimini internazionali commessi in Siria a partire da marzo 2011" (The Institution by the General Assembly of the United Nations of a "Mechanism" to Support Enquiries into International Crimes Committed in Syria after March 2011), RDI, 2017, p. 827 ff.

POCAR F., "Reflections on International Criminal Justice Twenty Years Later", in ACCONCI P. et al. (eds.), *International Law and the Protection of Humanity: Essays in Honour of Flavia Lattanzi*, Leiden, 2017, p. 488 ff.

PROSPERI L. and TERROSI J., "Embracing the 'Human Factor': Is There New Impetus at the ICC for Conceiving and Prioritizing International Environmental Harms as Crimes against Humanity?", JICJ, 2017, p. 509 ff.

RASI A., "Principio di complementarietà e interpretazione dello Statuto di Roma" (The Principle of Complementarity and Interpretation of the Rome Statute), DUDI, 2017, p. 5 ff.

RICCARDI A., "Sull'esistenza di un obbligo generale di prevenire e reprimere il fenomeno dei *foreign fighters* alla luce della vicenda della guerra civile spagnola" (Some Remarks on the Existence of a General Duty to Prevent the Phenomenon of Foreign Fighters in Light of the Spanish Civil War), CI, 2017, p. 213 ff.

ROSSI P., "The Al Mahdi Trial Before the International Criminal Court: Attacks on Cultural Heritage Between War Crimes and Crimes Against Humanity", DUDI, 2017, p. 87 ff.

SCOVAZZI T., "The First Judgment of the International Criminal Court on the Destruction of Cultural Property", DUDI, 2017, p. 77 ff.

SPAGNOLO A., "La criminalizzazione degli attacchi ai peacekeepers nella prospettiva della funzione della giustizia penale internazionale al fine del mantenimento della pace" (The Criminalization of Attacks Against Peacekeepers in the Light of the Function of International Criminal Justice to Maintain Peace), DUDI, 2017, p. 151 ff.

SULLO P., "The ICC as a Transitional Justice Actor: New Space for Victims?", DUDI, 2017, p. 239 ff.

VERDASCHI A., "Da al-Qaida all'IS: il terrorismo internazionale si è fatto Stato?" (From al-Qaida to IS: Has International Terrorism Acquired Statehood?), Rivista trimestrale di diritto pubblico, 2016, No. 1, p. 41 ff.

VERDASCHI A., "Dalla global war al global law" (From Global War to Global Law), Quaderni costituzionali, 2017, No. 2, p. 424 ff.

VERDASCHI A., "Osama Bin Laden: l'ultimo targeted killing. Gli Stati Uniti hanno dunque la licenza di uccidere?" (Osama Bin Laden: The Last Targeted Killing. Do the United States Have the Authorization to Kill?), in BAGNI S., FIGUEROA MEJÍA G. and PAVANI G. (eds.), *La ciencia del derecho constitucional comparado. Estudios en Homenaje a Lucio Pegoraro*, Tomo III, Ciudad de México, 2017, p. 1479 ff.

VERDASCHI A., "The Dark Side of Counter-Terrorism: The Argument for a More Enlightened Approach Based on a Constitutional Law Paradigm", in SHETREET S. and MCCORMACK W. (eds.), *The Culture of Judicial Independence in a Globalised World*, Leiden-Boston, 2016, p. 94 ff.

ZAMUNER E., "L'applicazione nel tempo della Convenzione sul genocidio: una retrospettiva sulla giurisprudenza della Corte internazionale di giustizia" (The Temporal Scope of Application of the Genocide Convention: A Retrospective Assessment of the ICJ Case Law), DUDI, 2017, p. 361 ff.

XIV. CO-OPERATION IN JUDICIAL, LEGAL, SECURITY, AND SOCIO-ECONOMIC MATTERS

BARTOLINI G., "Il progetto di articoli della Commissione del diritto internazionale sulla 'Protection of Persons in the Event of Disasters'" (The ILC Draft Articles on the Protection of Persons in the Event of Disasters), RDI, 2017, p. 677 ff.

MASTRACCI M., "L'Accordo quadro tra USA e UE sul trasferimento dei dati personali per il contrasto della Criminalità" (The US-EU Umbrella Agreement on Data Protection Rights in Law Enforcement Cooperation), CI, 2017, p. 37 ff.

ODDENINO A., "Reflections on Big Data and International Law", DCI, 2017, p. 777 ff.

XV.   INTERNATIONAL ECONOMIC LAW

ARRIGO G. and CASALE G., *International Labour Law Handbook*, Torino, 2017, pp. 328.
ACCONCI P., "La tutela della salute nel diritto internazionale e dell'Unione europea in materia di investimenti" (The Protection of Health in International and European Law concerning Investments), in PINESCHI L. (ed.), *La tutela della salute nel diritto internazionale ed europeo tra interessi globali e interessi particolari*, Napoli, 2017, p. 295 ff.
BARONCINI E., "The Relation between the Marrakesh System and Regional Trade Agreement in the WTO Case-Law", in TRIGGIANI E. et al. (eds.), *Dialoghi con Ugo Villani*, Bari, 2017, p. 835 ff.
BERNARDINI E., "Da una sentenza di arbitrato commerciale internazionale: riflessioni sul funzionamento delle norme limite internazionali al potere sovrano degli stati in materia di investimenti stranieri" (From a Judgment dealing with International Commercial Arbitration: Reflections on the Functioning of International Rules Limitign State Soveregnity concerning Foreign Investments), RCGI, 2017, p. 15 ff.
BORLINI L. and DORDI C., "Deepening International Systems of Subsidy Control in EU PTAs: A Comparative Analysis. Normative Rationales and Legal Implications", Columbia Journal of European Law, 2016/2017, p. 551 ff.
BORLINI L. and MONTANARO F., "Climate Change and Trade: Challenges and Lingering Questions on the Relationship between Renewable Energy Subsidies and WTO Disciplines", China EU-Journal, 2017, p. 1 ff.
BORLINI L. and MONTANARO F., "The Evolution of the EU Law against Criminal Finance: The 'Hardening' of FATF Standards within the EU", Georgetown Journal of International Law, 2017, p. 1009 ff.
BORLINI L., "La disciplina delle State-Owned Enterprises nel diritto del commercio internazionale tra stallo degli accordi commerciali multilaterali e accordi preferenziali di nuova generazione" (The Regulation of State-Owned Enterprises in International Trade Law between Stalled Multilateral Trade Agreements and New Generation Preferential Agreements), DCI, 2017, p. 967 ff.
BORLINI L., "Regulating Criminal Finance in the EU in the Light of the International Instruments", YEL, 2017, p. 553 ff.
BORLINI L., "State Aid Control and Subsidies Regulation in EU Agreements: Substance, Procedure and Policy Space in the 'New Generation' EU FTAs", The Global Community 2016, p. 145 ff.
BORLINI L., "Tutela della privacy e protezione dei dati personali a fronte della sicurezza pubblica e dell'integrità del sistema finanziario europeo" (Rights to Privacy and Data Protection v. Public Security and the Integrity of the European Financial System), DUDI, 2017, p. 23 ff.

BUONOMENNA F., "Limiti della governance economica nel regime internazionale ed europeo The Limits of the Economic Governance in the International and European System", Studi sull'integrazione europea, 2017, p. 605 ff.

CARBONE S.M., "I diritti degli individui e delle imprese nell'evoluzione del diritto internazionale dell'economia: alcuni cenni" (The Rights of Individuals and Corporations in the Evolution of International Economic Law: Some Remarks), in TRIGGIANI E. et al. (eds.), Dialoghi con Ugo Villani, Bari, 2017, p. 251 ff.

CARREA S., Coordinamento e integrazione fra ordinamenti: il caso del GECT (Coordination and Integration of Legal Orders: The European Grouping for Territorial Cooperation), Torino, 2017, pp. 318.

DE STEFANO C., "Reforming the Governance of International Financial Law in the Era of Post-Globalization", JIEL, 2017, p. 509 ff.

DI BENEDETTO F., "Reciprocity in International Trade and Investment Law and the Establishment of a European Committee on Foreign Investment", DCI, 2017, p. 573 ff.

DORDI C., "Le droit international et la corruption: perspectives historiques et considérations actuelles", in MANDERIEUX L. and VELLANO M. (eds.), Étique globale, bonne gouvernance et droit international économique, Torino, 2017, p. 85 ff.

GAGLIANI G., "Regards croisés sur les conventions UNESCO et le droit international de l'économie: entre interactions pratiques et gouvernance mondiale", in MANDERIEUX L. and VELLANO M. (eds.), Étique globale, bonne gouvernance et droit international économique, Torino, 2017, p. 57 ff.

MALAGUTI M.C., "'Sviluppo' e diritto internazionale dell'economia" ("Development" and International Economic Law), in TRIGGIANI E. et al. (eds.), Dialoghi con Ugo Villani, Bari, 2017, p. 873 ff

MANDERIEUX L. and VELLANO M. (eds.), Étique globale, bonne gouvernance et droit international économique, Torino, 2017, pp. 192.

MARCHISIO S., "Lo sfruttamento delle risorse minerarie dei corpi celesti nel diritto internazionale" (The Exploitation of the Mineral Resources of Celestial Bodies in International Law), in TRIGGIANI E. et al. (eds.), Dialoghi con Ugo Villani, Bari, 2017, p. 881 ff.

MARRELLA F., Manuale di diritto del commercio internazionale (International Trade Law Handbook), Padova, 2017, pp. 800.

MARRELLA F. and VETTOREL A., "Banca mondiale e diritti umani: il ruolo dell'Inspection Panel" (The World Bank and Human Rights: The Role of the Inspection Panel), in MANDERIEUX L. and VELLANO M. (eds.), Étique globale, bonne gouvernance et droit international économique, Torino, 2017, p. 39 ff.

PALMISANO G., "Reflections on the Implementation Procedures of the OECD Guidelines for Multinational Enterprises", in TRIGGIANI E. et al. (eds.), Dialoghi con Ugo Villani, Bari, 2017, p. 909 ff.

SACERDOTI G., "Has China Become 'Legally' a Market-Economy Country on 11 December 2016 under the WTO Antidumping Agreement? Analyzing an Open Question", Yearbook on International Investment Law and Policy, 2015-2016, p. 356 ff.

SACERDOTI G., "The Future of the WTO Dispute Settlement System: Confronting Challenges to Consolidate a Success Story", in BRAGA C. and HOEKMAN B. (eds.), *Future of the Global Trade Order*, San Domenico di Fiesole, 2017 p. 117 ff.

SACERDOTI G., "The WTO Dispute Settlement System: Consolidating Success and Confronting New Challenges", in ELSIG M. et al., *Assessing the World Trade Organization: Fit for Purposes?*, Cambridge, 2017, p. 147 ff.

SACERDOTI G., "The Prospects: The UK Trade Regime with the EU and the World. Options and Constraints Post-Brexit", in FABBRINI F. (ed.), *The Law and Politics of Brexit*, Oxford, 2017, p. 72 ff.

SCISO E., *Appunti di diritto internazionale dell'economia* (Notes of International Economic Law), 3rd ed., Torino, 2017, pp. 348.

SCISO E. (ed.), *Accountability, Transparency and Democracy in the Functioning of the Bretton Woods Institutions*, Torino, 2017, pp. 268.

VADI V., "Culture", in NADAKAVUKAREN SCHEFER K. and COTTIER T. (eds.), *Encyclopaedia of International Economic Law*, Cheltenham, 2017, p. 246 ff.

VADI V., "Local Communities, Cultural Heritage and International Economic Law", in BIUKOVIC L. and POTTER P. (eds.), *Local Engagement with International Economic Law and Human Rights*, Cheltenham, 2017, p. 150 ff.

VELLANO M., "Alla ricerca di un'etica globale nel diritto internazionale dell'economia" (Seeking a Global Ethic in International Economic Law), in TRIGGIANI E. et al. (eds.), *Dialoghi con Ugo Villani*, Bari, 2017, p. 929 ff.

VELLANO M., "Religione, etica e sovranità economica e finanziaria nel mondo Contemporaneo" (Religion, Ethics and Economic and Financial Sovereignty in Contemporary World), in MANDERIEUX L. and VELLANO M. (eds.), *Étique globale, bonne gouvernance et droit international économique*, Torino, 2017, p. 13 ff.

ZAMUNER E., "Gli effetti della denuncia della convenzione ICSID sul consenso all'arbitrato in materia di investimenti" (The Effects of the Denunciation of the ICSID Convention on the Consent to Arbitration in Investments), DCI, 2017, p. 181 ff.

XVI. INTERNATIONAL ORGANIZATIONS

BORLINI L., "The North Korea's Gauntlet, International Law and the New Sanctions Imposed by the Security Council", IYIL, 2016, p. 319 ff.

CONFORTI B. and FOCARELLI C., *Nazioni Unite* (United Nations), 11th ed., Padova, 2017, pp. 550.

INGRAVALLO I., "UNIDROIT at Ninety: An International Institutional Law Perspective", Uniform Law Review, 2017, p. 158 ff.

SEATZU F., "On the Unbeareable Lightness of the Effects of Public International Law within the Andean Legal System", IYIL, 2016, p. 191 ff.

SPAGNOLO A., "The Loan of Organs between the European Union and Other International Organizations as a Bridge: Some Remarks on Recent Developments", IYIL, 2016, p. 171 ff.

XVII. RELATIONSHIP BETWEEN MUNICIPAL AND INTERNATIONAL LAW

CALVANO R., "Una questione pregiudiziale al quadrato… o forse al cubo: sull'ordinanza n. 24/2017 della Corte costituzionale" (Question for a Preliminary Ruling (Squared or Even Cubed): The Order No. 24/2017 of the Italian Constitutional Court), DUDI, 2017, p. 301 ff.

CATALDI G., "La mise en oeuvre des décisions tribunaux internationaux dans l'ordre interne", RCADI, Vol. 386, 2017, p. 267 ff.

DEL VECCHIO A., "Recenti sviluppi della giurisprudenza costituzionale in materia di applicazione della CEDU nell'ordinamento italiano" (Recent Developments in the Case Law of the Constitutional Court relating to the Application of the ECHR in the Italian Legal System), in TRIGGIANI E. et al. (eds.), *Dialoghi con Ugo Villani*, Bari, 2017, p. 965 ff.

DI STASI A., "L'art. 6 della CEDU come 'cerniera' normativa tra ordinamento nazionale, sistema CEDU e ordinamento giuridico dell'Unione europea: brevi considerazioni in tema di mancata motivazione del rifiuto di rinvio pregiudiziale" (Article 6 ECHR as Legal "Connector" between the National Legal System, the ECHR System and the Legal System of the European Union: Brief Considerations on the Lack of Motivation of the Refusal to Refer for a Preliminary Ruling), in TRIGGIANI E. et al. (eds.), *Dialoghi con Ugo Villani*, Bari, 2017, p. 973 ff.

GALLO D., "Controlimiti, identità nazionale e i rapporti di forza tra primato ed effetto diretto nella saga *Taricco*" (Counter-limits, national identity and the tense relationship between primacy and direct effect in the Taricco saga), Il Diritto dell'Unione europea, 2017, p. 249 ff.

GUIDI M., "L'interpretazione 'costituzionalmente orientata' quale chiave di lettura obbligatoria delle sentenze della Corte europea di Strasburgo nell'ordinamento italiano" (The "Constitutionally Oriented" Interpretation of the Judgments of the European Court of Strasbourg in the Italian Legal System), in TRIGGIANI E. et al. (eds.), *Dialoghi con Ugo Villani*, Bari, 2017, p. 991 ff.

MORI P., "La Corte costituzionale chiede alla Corte di giustizia di rivedere la sentenza *Taricco*: difesa dei controlimiti o rifiuto delle limitazioni di sovranità in materia penale?" (The Constitutional Court Requests the Court of Justice to Review the Taricco Judgment: Defending Restrictions to Supremacy Rooted in Municipal Law or Refusing to Accept Limitations to Sovereignty with regard to Criminal Matters?), RDI, 2017, p. 409 ff.

PAPPONE M., "Il recepimento della CEDU nell'ordinamento interno: un'analisi di diritto comparato" (The Reception of the ECHR in the Italian Legal System: A Comparative Law Analysis), OIDU, 2017, p. 90 ff.

PARIS D., "Carrot and Stick. The Italian Constitutional Court's Preliminary Reference in the Case Taricco", QIL, Zoom-in 37, 2017, p. 5 ff.

RUGGE G., "The Italian Constitutional Court on Taricco: Unleashing the Normative Potential of 'National Identity'?", QIL, Zoom-in , 2017, p. 21 ff.

SINAGRA A. and VALVO A.L., "Internal Law and International Law: From Common Law to Civil Law", RCGI, 2017, p. 107 ff.

TERRASI A., "Note a margine dell'ordinanza della Corte costituzionale sul caso Taricco: l'effetto delle norme dei trattati istitutivi dell'UE sulla legge penale sostanziale italiana" (Brief Observations on Italian Constitutional Court Preliminary Ruling in *Taricco* Case: The Effect of EU Primary Law on Domestic Substantive Criminal Law), DUDI, 2017, p. 308 ff.

TIZZANO A., "Diritti fondamentali e corti supreme europee. Qualche considerazione dal versante lussemburghese" (Fundamental Rights and European Supreme Courts. Some Remarks from the Luxembourg Side), in TRIGGIANI E. et al. (eds.), *Dialoghi con Ugo Villani*, Bari, 2017, p. 1037 ff.

VILLANI U., "Limitazioni di sovranità, 'controlimiti' e diritti fondamentali nella Costituzione italiana" (Limitations to Sovereignty, 'Counter-limits' and Fundamental Rights in the Italian Constitution), Studi sull'integrazione europea, 2017, p. 489 ff.

ZANGHÌ C., "La progressiva frenata della giurisprudenza costituzionale introdotta dalle sentenze gemelle del 2007" (The Progressive Slowing Down of the Constitutional Jurisprudence Introduced by the Twin Decision of 2007), in TRIGGIANI E. et al. (eds.), *Dialoghi con Ugo Villani*, Bari, 2017, p. 1063 ff.

ZARRA G., "ICSID Provisional Measures and Interference with National Criminal Proceedings", IYIL, 2016, p. 83 ff.

XVIII. USE OF FORCE AND PEACE-KEEPING

ARCARI M., "La risposta statunitense all'uso di armi chimiche in Siria e la (con)fusione delle categorie dello *ius ad bellum*" (The United States Reaction to the Use of Chemical Weapons in Syria and the (Con)Fusion in the Legal Categories of *Ius ad bellum*), DUDI, 2017, p. 375 ff.

AVENIA C., "L'intervento francese in Mali alla luce del principio di autodeterminazione dei popoli", RCGI, 2017, p. 121 ff.

BRANCA E., "Recenti sviluppi in materia di repressione degli abusi sessuali commessi dai caschi blu nel corso delle missioni di pace delle Nazioni Unite" (Recent Developments Concerning the Repression of Sexual Abuses Committed by Blue Helmets during United Nations Peacekeeping Missions), RDI, 2017, p. 68 ff.

BUONOMO V., "Un *Accordo* per contribuire alla pace, secondo il diritto internazionale" (An *Agreement* to Contribute to Peace, according to International Law), in TRIGGIANI E. et al. (eds.), *Dialoghi con Ugo Villani*, Bari, 2017, p. 91 ff.

CARACCIOLO I. and MONTUORO U. (eds.), *L'evoluzione del peacekeeping. Il ruolo dell'Italia* (The Evolution of Peacekeeping. The Role of Italy), Torino, 2017, pp. 424.

CIMIOTTA E., "Alcune novità nei rapporti tra Nazioni Unite, organizzazioni regionali e sub-regionali per il mantenimento della pace in Africa" (Some Innovations in the Relations between the United Nations, Regional and Sub-

Regional Organizations for Peacekeeping in Africa), in TRIGGIANI E. et al. (eds.), *Dialoghi con Ugo Villani*, Bari, 2017, p. 111 ff.

DI STASI A., "L'operato dei peacekeeper nella giurisprudenza della Corte europea dei diritti dell'uomo" (The Work of Peacekeepers in the Jurisprudence of the European Court of Human Rights), in CARACCIOLO I. and MONTUORO U. (eds.), *L'evoluzione del peacekeeping. Il ruolo dell'Italia*, Torino, 2017, p. 273 ff.

FORNARI M., "Conflitto in Ucraina, orsi fantasiosi e programmi malevoli" (The Conflict in Ukraine, Fantasious Bears and Malwares), RDI, 2017, p. 1156 ff.

GARGIULO P., "Il mantenimento della pace nei rapporti tra l'ONU e le organiz-zazioni regionali" (Maintaining Peace in the Relations between the UN and Regional Organizations), in TRIGGIANI E. et al. (eds.), *Dialoghi con Ugo Villani*, Bari, 2017, p. 135 ff.

GREPPI E., "International Humanitarian Law and Criminal Justice: International, Domestic and Comparative Law at a Crossroads", in TRIGGIANI E. et al. (eds.), *Dialoghi con Ugo Villani*, Bari, 2017, p. 155 ff.

GREPPI E., "*Peacekeeping* e violazione dei diritti umani" (Peacekeeping and Violations of Human Rights), in CARACCIOLO I. and MONTUORO U. (eds.), *L'evoluzione del peacekeeping. Il ruolo dell'Italia*, Torino, 2017, p. 195 ff.

MARCHISIO S., "Le Nazioni Unite e il mantenimento della pace e della sicurezza internazionale tra luci e ombre" (The United Nations and the Maintenance of Peace and International Security: Bright and Dark Sides), in CARACCIOLO I. and MONTUORO U. (eds.), *L'evoluzione del peacekeeping. Il ruolo dell'Ita-lia*, Torino, 2017, p. 35 ff.

NALIN E., "L'intervento militare della coalizione anglo-americana in Iraq del 2003 alla luce del rapporto Chilcot e degli sviluppi della prassi in tema di le-gittima difesa preventiva" (The Military Intervention of the Anglo-American Coalition in Iraq in 2003 in the light of the Chilcot Report and of the Developments in matters of Preventive Legitimate Defense), in TRIGGIANI E. et al. (eds.), *Dialoghi con Ugo Villani*, Bari, 2017, p. 163 ff.

NESI G., "The Repression of the Crimes of Sexual Exploitation and Abuse Committed by Peacekeepers. Recent Developments", CI, 2017, p. 327 ff.

NOVI C., "Brevi considerazioni sulle missioni militari dell'Unione euro-pea volte a supportare operazioni multifunzionali delle Nazioni Unite" (Brief Considerations on the European Union's Military Missions Aimed at Supporting the Multi-Functional Operations of the United Nations), in TRIGGIANI E. et al. (eds.), *Dialoghi con Ugo Villani*, Bari, 2017, p. 183 ff.

PEDRAZZI M., "Lo status del personale ONU e del personale associato nelle operazioni di peacekeeping" (The Status of UN Personnel and Associate Personnel in Peacekeeping Operations), in CARACCIOLO I. and MONTUORO U. (eds.), *L'evoluzione del peacekeeping. Il ruolo dell'Italia*, Torino, 2017, p. 371 ff.

PICONE P., *Obblighi "erga omnes" e uso della forza* ("Erga Omnes" Obligations and the Use of Force), Napoli, 2017, pp. 692.

POLITI M., "*Peacekeeping*, diritti umani e sicurezza" (Peacekeeping, Human Rights and Security), in CARACCIOLO I. and MONTUORO U. (eds.), *L'evoluzione del peacekeeping. Il ruolo dell'Italia*, Torino, 2017, p. 293 ff.

PUSTORINO P., "L'intervento esterno nei conflitti armati interni a sostegno del governo al potere o degli insorti" (External Intervention in Internal Armed Conflicts in Support of either the Ruling Government or the Insurgents), in TRIGGIANI E. et al. (eds.), *Dialoghi con Ugo Villani*, Bari, 2017, p. 191 ff.

RONZITTI N., "Compagnie militari private e violazione dei diritti umani" (Private Military Companies and Human Rights Violations), in CARACCIOLO I. and MONTUORO U. (eds.), *L'evoluzione del peacekeeping. Il ruolo dell'Italia*, Torino, 2017, p. 263 ff.

RONZITTI N., "La legge italiana sulle missioni internazionali" (The Italian Statute Concerning International Missions), RDI, 2017, p. 474 ff.

SAMMARTINO L., "Protezione dei luoghi di cura in Siria: luci ed ombre del diritto internazionale" (Protection of Medical Facilities in Syria: Lights and Shadows in International Law), OIDU, 2017, p. 59 ff.

SOSSAI M., "Il mandato delle operazioni di peacekeeping e il contrasto a gruppi terroristici" (The Mandate of Peacekeeping Operations and the Fight against Terrorist Groups), in CARACCIOLO I. and MONTUORO U. (eds.), *L'evoluzione del peacekeeping. Il ruolo dell'Italia*, Torino, 2017, p. 89 ff.

VENTURINI G., "Assistenza umanitaria e diritto internazionale: alcune riflessioni" (Humanitarian Assistance and International Law: Some Reflections), in TRIGGIANI E. et al. (eds.), *Dialoghi con Ugo Villani*, Bari, 2017, p. 215 ff.

XIX. ARMED CONFLICT, NEUTRALITY, AND DISARMAMENT

AMOROSO D. and TAMBURRINI G., "The Ethical and Legal Case against Autonomy in Weapons Systems", Global Jurist (on-line), 2017, p. 1 ff.

AMOROSO D., "*Jus In Bello* and *Jus Ad Bellum* Arguments against Autonomy in Weapons Systems: A Re-Appraisal", QIL, Zoom-in 43, 2017, p. 5 ff.

BARTOLINI G., "Gli attacchi aerei in Siria, l'operazione *Inherent Resolve* e la complessa applicazione del diritto internazionale umanitario" (Air Attacks in Syria, Operation Inherent Resolve and the Complex Application of International Humanitarian Law), DUDI, 2017, p. 387 ff.

DANIELE L., "Enforcing Illegality: Israel's Military Justice in the West Bank", QIL, Zoom-in 44, 2017, p. 21 ff.

GERVASONI L., "A Contextual-Functional Approach to Investigations into Right to Life Violations in Armed Conflict", QIL, Zoom-in 36, 2017, p. 5 ff.

GUARINO G., *Il conflitto in Siria tra guerra, rivoluzione e terrorismo. Alla ricerca di una logica (...normativa?)* (The Conflict in Syria: War, Revolution and Terrorism. Looking for a Logic (...Normative?)), Napoli, 2017, pp. 196.

RONZITTI N., *Diritto internazionale dei conflitti armati* (International Law of Armed Conflict), 6th ed., Torino, 2017, pp. 448.

SILINGARDI S., "The United Kingdom's Involvement in the 2003 Iraqi War: *Jus Ad Bellum* and *Jus In Bello* Issues Before the Iraqi (Chilcot) Inquiry", IYIL, 2016, p. 347 ff.

SOSSAI M., "Come assicurare la punibilità dell'uso di armi chimiche in Siria? (Addressing Criminal Accountability for the Use of Chemical Weapons in Syria), DUDI, 2017, p. 419 ff.

TANCREDI A., "Doctrinal Alternatives to Self-Defence Against Non-State Actors", ZAÖRV, 2017, p. 69 ff.

XX. INTERNATIONAL RESPONSIBILITY

ANGIOI S., "Il *peacekeeper*: profili di responsabilità, tra norme sull'immunità e codici di condotta" (The Peacekeeper: Perspectives of Responsibility between Norms on Immunity and Codes of Conduct), in CARACCIOLO I. and MONTUORO U. (eds.), *L'evoluzione del peacekeeping. Il ruolo dell'Italia*, Torino, 2017, p. 219 ff.

ARANGIO-RUIZ G., "State Responsibility Revisited: The Factual Nature of the Attribution of Conduct to the State", RDI, 2017 (Supplement), p. 1 ff.

BUSCEMI M., "La codificazione della responsabilità delle organizzazioni internazionali alla prova dei fatti. Il caso della diffusione del colera a Haiti" (The Codification of Responsibility of International Organisations Put to the Test. The Case of the Spreading of Cholera in Haiti), RDI, 2017, p. 989 ff.

CARELLA G., "La responsabilità giuridica delle multinazionali per violazioni dei diritti umani: Fata Morgana o vaso di Pandora?" (The Legal Responsibility of Multinational Corporations for Human Rights Violations: Fata Morgana or Pandora's Box?), in TRIGGIANI E. et al. (eds.), *Dialoghi con Ugo Villani*, Bari, 2017, p. 261 ff.

CELLAMARE G., "Danni alla salute da operazioni di peacekeeping delle Nazioni Unite: profili di responsabilità e di immunità dell'organizzazione" (Damages to Health as a Result of UN Peacekeeping Operations: Issues of Responsibility and Immunity of the Organisation), in PINESCHI L. (ed.), *La tutela della salute nel diritto internazionale ed europeo tra interessi globali e interessi particolari*, Napoli, 2017, p. 421 ff.

CICIRIELLO M.C. and BORGIA F., "Deconstructing the Responsibility to Protect Doctrine: Looking for a New Legal Basis", in ACCONCI P. et al. (eds.), *International Law and the Protection of Humanity: Essays in Honour of Flavia Lattanzi*, Leiden, 2017, p. 225 ff.

FOIS P., "Violazione dei diritti umani: il problema della shared responsibility tra Stato di invio e organizzazione internazionale" (The Violation of Human Rights: The Problem of Shared Responsibility Between the Sending State and the International Organization), in CARACCIOLO I. and MONTUORO U. (eds.), *L'evoluzione del peacekeeping. Il ruolo dell'Italia*, Torino, 2017, p. 205 ff.

GIOFFREDI G., "La responsabilità di proteggere: contenuto del concetto e prassi applicativa" (Responsibility to Protect: Meaning and Practice), in TRIGGIANI E. et al. (eds.), *Dialoghi con Ugo Villani*, Bari, 2017, p. 145 ff.

LUGATO M., "Conceptualizing the Responsibility to Protect: A Short Contribution", in ACCONCI P. et al. (eds.), *International Law and the Protection of Humanity: Essays in Honour of Flavia Lattanzi*, Leiden, 2017, p. 245 ff.

PALCHETTI P., "Litigating Member State Responsibility: The Monetary Gold Principle and the Protection of Absent Organizations", in BARROS A.S. et al. (ed.), *International Organizations and Member States Responsibility: Critical Perspectives*, Leiden, 2017, p. 178 ff.

SPAGNOLO A., "Contromisure dell'Organizzazione Mondiale della Sanità come conseguenza di violazioni dei Regolamenti sanitari internazionali in contesti epidemici" (Countermeasures of the WHO for Violations of the International Health Regulations in Case of Pandemics), in PINESCHI L. (ed.), *La tutela della salute nel diritto internazionale ed europeo tra interessi globali e interessi particolari*, Napoli, 2017, p. 391 ff.

TRAMONTANA E., "Partnership pubblico-private in materia di salute globale e responsabilità internazionale per violazione dei diritti umani" (Public-Private Partnerships concerning Global Health and International Responsibility for Violations of Human Rights), in PINESCHI L. (ed.), *La tutela della salute nel diritto internazionale ed europeo tra interessi globali e interessi particolari*, Napoli, 2017, p. 359 ff.

XXI. INTERNATIONAL DISPUTE SETTLEMENT

BONAFÈ B.I., "Establishing the Existence of a Dispute before the International Court of Justice: Drawbacks and Implications", QIL, Zoom-out 45, 2017, p. 3 ff.

BONAFÈ B.I., "Maritime Delimitation in the Indian Ocean (Somalia v. Kenya): Preliminary Objections", AJIL, 2017, p. 725 ff.

CALIGIURI A., "Les conditions pour l'exercice de la fonction juridictionnelle par le cours et les tribunaux prévus dans la CNUDM", RGDIP, 2017, p. 945 ff.

CORTESI G.A., "ICSID Jurisdiction with Regard to State-Owned Enterprises – Moving Toward an Aroach Based on General International Law", The Law and Practice of International Courts and Tribunals, 2017, p. 108 ff.

CRESPI REGHIZZI Z., *L'intervento "come non parte" nel processo davanti alla Corte internazionale di giustizia* (The Intervention as "Not Party" in Proceedings before the International Court of Justice), Milano, 2017, pp. 494.

DRAETTA U., "Reflections on the Role of Arbitral Institution: Lights and Shadows", DCI, 2017, p. 471 ff.

DRAETTA U., "Truncated Tribunals: A Possible Remedy to the Misconduct of an Arbitrator", in TRIGGIANI E. et al. (eds.), *Dialoghi con Ugo Villani*, Bari, 2017, p. 855 ff.

FOIS P., "I principi della Dichiarazione sulle relazioni amichevoli del 24 ottobre 1970 e il 'nuovo ordine internazionale'" (The Principles of the Declaration on Friendly Relations of 24 October 1970 and the "New International Order"), in TRIGGIANI E. et al. (eds.), *Dialoghi con Ugo Villani*, Bari, 2017, p. 5 ff.

FONTANELLI F., "Reflections on the Indispensable Party Principle in the Wake of the Judgment on Preliminary Objections in the *Norstar* Case", RDI, 2017, p. 112 ff.

FONTANELLI F. and TANZI A., "Jurisdiction and Admissibility in Investment Arbitration. A View from the Bridge at the Practice", The Law and Practice of International Courts and Tribunals, 2017, p. 3 ff.

FORLATI S., "The Judicial Activity of the International Court of Justice in 2016", IYIL, 2016, p. 363 ff.

FORNARI M., "I cinquant'anni della Guerra dei Sei Giorni: alcune questioni poste dal ritiro dell'UNEF e dalla chiusura dello Stretto di Tiran" (Fifty Years After the Six Day War: Some Questions Posed by the Withdrawal of UNEF and the Closure of the Strait of Tiran), CI, 2017, p. 525 ff.

FUMAGALLI L., "L'incidenza sul diritto sostanziale della funzione giudiziaria nell'ordinamento internazionale" (The Impact on Substantive Law of the Judicial Function in International Law), in TRIGGIANI E. et al. (eds.), Dialoghi con Ugo Villani, Bari, 2017, p. 13 ff.

GAJA G., "Assessing Expert Evidence in the ICJ", The Law and Practice of International Courts and Tribunals, 2017, p. 409 ff.

GATTINI A., "Jurisdiction ratione temporis in International Investment Arbitration", The Law and Practice of International Courts and Tribunals, 2017, p. 139 ff.

GAZZINI T. and KOLB R., "Provisional Measures in ICSID Arbitration from 'Wonderland's Jurisprudence' to Informal Modification of Treaties", The Law and Practice of International Courts and Tribunals, 2017, p. 159 ff.

IOVANE M., "L'influence de la multiplication des jurisdictions internationales sur l'application du droit international", RCADI, Vol. 383, 2017, p. 233 ff.

MAROTTI L., "Establishing the Existence of a Dispute before the International Court of Justice': Glimpses of Flexibility within Formalism?", QIL, Zoom-out 45, 2017, p. 77 ff.

NALIN E., "Recenti tendenze nei rapporti tra peace-keeping e peace-enforcement delle Nazioni Unite: il caso della MONUSCO e della Intervention Brigade" (Recent Trends in the Relationship Between United Nations Peacekeeping and Peace-Enforcement: The Case of MONUSCO and Its Force Intervention Brigade), CI, 2017, p. 547 ff.

NIGRO R., "International Criminal Justice (2016)", IYIL, 2016, p. 425 ff.

PALCHETTI P., "Effetti giuridici e conseguenze indirette derivanti da misure cautelari della Corte internazionale di giustizia" (Legal Effects and Indirect Consequences Deriving from the Precautionary Measures Adopted by the International Court of Justice), in TRIGGIANI E. et al. (eds.), Dialoghi con Ugo Villani, Bari, 2017, p. 19 ff.

PALCHETTI P., "Responsibility for Breach of Provisional Measures of the ICJ: between Protection of the Rights of the Parties and Respect for the Judicial Function", RDI, 2017, p. 5 ff.

PALOMBELLA G., "'The Judicial Lodestar'. Funzione giudiziaria e identità del diritto internazionale" ("The Judicial Lodestar". Judicial Function and Identity of International Law), in TRIGGIANI E. et al. (eds.), Dialoghi con Ugo Villani, Bari, 2017, p. 27 ff.

PALOMBINO F.M., "I poteri del Consiglio di sicurezza in materia di esecuzione delle sentenze della Corte internazionale di giustizia" (The Powers of the Security Council relating to the Execution of the Judgments of the

International Court of Justice), in TRIGGIANI E. et al. (eds.), *Dialoghi con Ugo Villani*, Bari, 2017, p. 35 ff.

PAPA I., "*L'esecuzione delle sentenze della Corte internazionale di giustizia nel sistema dell'ONU*" (The Execution of the Judgments of the International Court of Justice in the UN System), in TRIGGIANI E. et al. (eds.), *Dialoghi con Ugo Villani*, Bari, 2017, p. 41 ff.

SACERDOTI G., "The WTO in 2016: Systemic Developments, Disputes and Review of the Appellate Body's Reports", IYIL, 2016, p. 449 ff.

SEATZU F., "The Challenge of Reforming the Pact of Bogotà", in TRIGGIANI E. et al. (eds.), *Dialoghi con Ugo Villani*, Bari, 2017, p. 49 ff.

STARITA M., "L'esecuzione delle sentenze della Corte internazionale di giustizia tra l'art. 94, par. 2, della Carta e nuovi meccanismi di pressione ed assistenza" (The Execution of the Judgments of the International Court of Justice between Article 94 paragraph 2 of the Charter and the New Mechanisms of Pressure and Assistance), in TRIGGIANI E. et al. (eds.), *Dialoghi con Ugo Villani*, Bari, 2017, p. 59 ff.

STOPPIONI E., "Decentring the ICJ: A Critical Analysis of the Marshall Islands judgments", QIL, Zoom-out 45, 2017, p. 65 ff.

TANZI A., "Remarks on Breach of State Contracts for the Purposes of Jurisdiction and Admissibility in International Investment Arbitration", in TRIGGIANI E. et al. (eds.), *Dialoghi con Ugo Villani*, Bari, 2017, p. 919 ff.

TREVES T., "The International Tribunal for the Law of the Sea and Other Law of the Sea Jurisdictions (2016)", IYIL, 2016, p. 393 ff.

VIRZO R., "La soluzione delle controversie nei contratti relativi all'Area dei fondi marini internazionali" (The Settlement of Disputes in the Contracts relating to the Area of International Deep Seabeds), in TRIGGIANI E. et al. (eds.), *Dialoghi con Ugo Villani*, Bari, 2017, p. 69 ff.

VIRZO R., "The Dispute Concerning the *Enrica Lexie* Incident and the Role of International Tribunals in Provisional Measure Proceedings Instituted Pursuant to the United Nations Convention on the Law of the Sea", in CRAWFORD J. et al. (eds.), *The International Legal Order: Current Needs and Possible Responses. Essays in Honour of Djamchid Momtaz*, Leiden/ Boston, 2017, p. 519 ff.

ZARRA G., "The Relevance of State Interests in Recent ICSID Practice", IYIL, 2016, p. 487 ff.

REVIEW OF BOOKS

(edited by *Marco Gestri*)

LARISSA VAN DEN HERIK (ed.), *Research Handbook on UN Sanctions and International Law*, Cheltenham, Edward Elgar Publishing, 2017, pp. XIV-528.

Writing Research Handbooks has become very popular nowadays, and have been written on the law of the sea, law of armed conflict, peacekeeping and even on sources of international law. The complexity and the expansion of international law have warranted a thematic and multi-voice approach instead of relying on classic manuals of international law and/or single monographs. The volume edited by Larissa van den Herik follows this trend even if it cannot be said that it fills a vacuum since several edited books on sanctions had been previously published approaching the subject from different perspectives and assessing a variety of topics.

The book under review is divided into five parts, preceded by the Editor's Introductory Chapter on The Individualization and Formalization of UN Sanctions: I. Conceptualization and Effectiveness of UN Sanctions; II. The Function of UN Sanctions; III. Design and Procedures Governing UN Sanctions; IV. Interplay with Other Regimes; and V. Regional Perspectives.

In Part I Tom Ruys tries to formulate a general theory about coercive measures, making a distinction between sanctions, retorsions and countermeasures. His conceptualisation, which follows an approach already highlighted by the best doctrinal analyses, is correct. Countermeasures have in recent times gained currency due to the fact that UN sanctions are not always a viable option, since their adoption can be precluded by the exercise of the veto power by of any one P5 member; as a consequence, the injured state may react with a countermeasure, in turn committing a further violation of international law against the wrongdoer: the countermeasure operates as a circumstance precluding wrongfulness. The alternative is resorting to armed force. However, this could be unlawful and/or not politically viable. From this point of view, countermeasures represent a useful tool of coercive diplomacy and an alternative to a much stronger reaction. Countermeasures may be taken not only by the state that suffers damages, but also by states which are not direct victims of international law violations (third-party countermeasures). The topic of third-party countermeasures against those responsible for a violation of an *erga omnes* obligation is dealt with by Ruys. He casts doubt on their legality as he believes they fall in a "grey area". "In particular" – he adds – "[...] the legality under general international law of third-party countermeasures undertaken to protect community interests remains shrouded in mystery". He concludes that it is uncertain whether state practice may provide clarity in the future.

This scepticism is based on three assumptions. (a) Third-party countermeasures are considered lawful if recommended by the Security Council (SC), by the

General Assembly (GA) or even by a regional organisation, but not when taken autonomously by the individual state/states; (b) only grave breaches of an *erga omnes* obligation can trigger third-party countermeasures; (c) procedural requirements should be observed, for instance a notification of measures which will be taken and an offer to negotiate.

Fulfilment of these conditions is rare, except sub C which is reflected in Article 52 of the ILC Draft Articles on the Responsibility of States for International Wrongful Acts dealing with procedural conditions for taking countermeasures. The Draft Articles do not prohibit countermeasures. Their limit is set out not only by Article 49 but also in specific terms by Article 50, which additionally applies to third-party countermeasures. Third-party countermeasures are clearly allowed by Article 54 even though the terminology employed is "measures" and not countermeasures – an example of constructive ambiguity. The only problem is their content, since the provision refers to "lawful measures", a compromise formula that was inserted for rendering acceptable third-party countermeasures by those opposing them. The practice of third-party countermeasures is nowadays commonplace and does not sustain the argument that third-party countermeasures are lawful only if recommended by the SC, GA or other international organisations. Moreover both the practice and the text of Article 54 do not suggest that third-party countermeasures may be taken only if a serious violation of international law is committed. A violation of an *erga omnes* or an *erga omnes partes* obligation is enough to trigger a lawful countermeasure. On this point Article 54 is at variance with Article 5 of the *Institut de Droit International* Krakow resolution on *erga omnes* obligations that allows countermeasures only if a "grave" breach of an *erga omnes* obligation has been committed.

Part I terminates with a contribution by Sue E. Eckert on "The Evolution and Effectiveness of UN Targeted Sanctions". She gives a complete picture of SC targeted sanctions, trying also to measure their effectiveness with the aid of tables and concluding that "sanctions will continue as an essential component of the UN Security Council's response to international threats".

As already stated, the second part of the Handbook deals with the function of UN Sanctions. One of the main problems is the shift from comprehensive to individual sanctions taken against terrorists and other law breakers. Their legality implies that a review against possible wrongful listing may be undertaken. The SC has made an Ombudsman mechanism available to individuals listed, which is not a court of law, but merely an administrative tool. It has been found unsatisfactory both by the European Court of Justice and by the European Court of Human Rights. Lisa Ginsborg recognises that the Office of the Ombudsperson provides a first resort guarantee to individuals listed, but the problem is more general and consists in critically assessing whether the SC is the proper forum for dealing with individual sanctions. Be that as it may, sanctions against individuals and groups for violations of human rights/humanitarian law is a current endeavour for the SC, as shown by Matthew Happold. Undoubtedly, they have a "signalling effect". The real problem is whether they are effective and address the point. Daniel H. Joyner deals with the important topic of UN sanctions and counter-proliferation. In his Chapter, economic countermeasures to curb proliferation taken by an individual state and group of states are also examined and the lawfulness of economic coercion assessed. Part II is concluded by Daniella Dam-de Jong with a thorough analysis of UN natural resources sanction regimes. A short mention of maritime interdiction to strengthen the prohibition of the shipment of natural resources would have been appropriate.

Part III is composed of four contributions dedicated to design and procedure governing UN sanctions. It is opened by Alejandro Rodiles with a Chapter that assesses the practice of restricting the financial resources of terrorists and proliferators, focusing on the interplay between the SC and the Financial Action Task Force (FATF). The following Chapter by Devika Hovel raises the issue of transparency in connection with the work of the SC that should permeate the decision making process on sanctions and their implementation. This Chapter is more tailored to general problems of SC transparency than on its application to sanctions. The contribution by Kimberly Prost on the Security Council and fair process merits being brought to the reader's attention. The author, who had a personal experience as Ombudsperson for the SC on the Al Qaeda Sanctions Committee, reviews all mechanisms aimed at rendering listing and delisting more transparent and in line with the criteria for ensuring the protection of human rights: the introduction of a Focal Point, the possibility of and limits to judiciary in reviewing legislation implementing sanctions and the introduction of the Ombudsperson mechanism. Its record should not be overlooked and the mechanisms should be ameliorated and expanded. Prost rightly points out that out of the SC "16 sanctions regimes with targeted components, only those listed under the Al Qaeda regime have access to the Ombudsperson". The Chapter by Kristen E. Boon is also of interest. She assesses the various models for terminating sanctions and argues that time-limited sanctions are more efficient than indefinite sanctions. The Chapter contains an annex with a table showing the SC resolutions and their termination clauses.

Part IV, dealing with interplay with other regimes, is the most interesting component of the Handbook and in some respect also quite new. The opening articles of this part deal with the classic topics of UN sanctions and international financial institutions (Pierre-Emmanuel Dupont) and Sanctions and the WTO (Andrew D. Mitchell).

This review concentrates on the following themes of this section: effects of sanctions on arbitration and on contracts and prosecution of sanction busters.

The topic of arbitrability of disputes and sanctions regimes is dealt with by Eric De Brabandere and David Holloway who, in reviewing the case law, assess not only UN sanctions but also countermeasures. In this connection, the main question is the following: are disputes involving sanctions arbitrable notwithstanding the public nature of international sanctions? The two authors answer in the affirmative, but with a word of caution. The other problem is whether the arbitral award is rendered unenforceable by the sanctions regime. Here again a definitive answer for all cases cannot be given and the interpreter has to find whether award enforcing would be contrary to the sanctions regime. A further problem is constituted by the arbitrators and by the arbitration institution, since targeted sanctions set out obligations for individuals and entities. An arbitrator may be held personally accountable if he/she contravenes the domestic provisions implementing international sanctions. As previously stated, this is an interesting Chapter. It lacks only a human rights law perspective under the prism of access to justice. Does the negation of arbitration because of sanctions amount to a violation of a fundamental human rights law provision?

In her Chapter, Mercédeh Azeredo da Silveira deals with the important topic of contracts and how they are affected by sanctions. Sanctions serve public interests and they prohibit the stipulation of contracts or paralyse their performance. The application of sanctions on a contract brought before a foreign court is often a question of fact which implies the nullity or the extinction of the contract. However, in certain cases a foreign court is obliged to disregard sanctions if they run against the interests of the forum state. The reviewer cannot but agree with the statement that "[d]omestic courts and arbitral tribunals may also refuse to give effect to unilateral sanctions programmes that strive to be applied extraterritorially in breach of public international law". Sanctions appear to be applied even if they are not executed into a domestic legal order by implementing legislation. This is particularly true for SC sanctions and the judge applies sanctions to contracts as a "*fait juridique*". The author finding on lifting sanctions and their impact on contracts deserves to be quoted. As a matter of principle, once sanctions have been terminated, contracts should be resumed. However sanctions can last for years and the general principle, to be applied narrowly, is that a party should not be obliged to perform its contractual obligations if the circumstances have radically changed and rendered the performance completely different from the original contractual undertakings.

Section IV terminates with an essay on prosecution of sanction busting by Ward Ferdinandusse and Pieter Rademakers. The main issue here regards the consequence of annulment of sanctions provisions on criminal proceedings carried out at national level against those who violated the sanction regime. The question is of relevance since, as practice shows, sanctions listing individuals or corporations or both are most commonly annulled on procedural grounds. The case-law of the CJEU contains numerous decisions on annulment of restrictive measures for procedural grounds. How does the annulment impact on national tribunals? The answer depends on the content of the criminal proceedings, whether only an infringement of the sanctions is raised or whether the charge concerns aid to the criminal/terrorist organisation. Even in the former case, the criminal proceedings may be retained if the violation of the law implementing sanctions occurred before the annulment of sanctions. It is open to question whether this conclusion may be reconciled with the principle of *favor rei* present in several domestic orders.

The last section on Regional Perspectives is introduced by a Chapter by Mirko Sossai, who endorses the idea that states may act through their regional organisations taking countermeasures in cases of violation of important obligations owed to the international community as a whole, provided that the SC is paralysed and unable to take action. An important Chapter has been written by

Penelope Nevill on the interpretation and review of UN sanctions by European Courts. The view of the author is rendered clear by the title since she refers to comity and conflict to describe the relationship between UN sanctions and European courts, which include the CJEU and the ECtHR as well as European domestic courts. The CJEU case law had the merit of securing the protection of human rights in scrutinising the law implementing UN sanctions. At the same time this case law had the merit of prompting SC "legislators" to improve the mechanism of focal point and Ombudsman. The author shares the opinion that the Ombudsman process should be strengthened and ameliorated. The issue of application of UN Charter Article 103 is also considered. Should UN law prevail over EU and Strasbourg law because of the supremacy of the UN Charter? The ECtHR appears to have elegantly avoided the question since a conflict between the Convention and the Charter was not found.

Section V terminates with a perusal of UN/regional sanctions in Africa and their impact on peace building in West Africa. Amelia Broodryk and Anton du Plessis offer a complete picture of the practice in Africa with a number of useful tables. The Chapter is focused on an international relations approach. UN sanctions are not very popular in Africa, a sentiment that jeopardises their implementation. The experience of UN sanctions in West Africa has not been very constructive as shown by the case-study of Jeremy I. Levitt. Also the Chapter on the Chinese and Japanese perspectives on UN sanctions, written by Machiko Kanetake and Congyan Cai, deserves to be quoted. The Chinese policy is that sanctions cannot be taken outside the SC. They should be authorised by a competent SC resolution, even though they should be applied with prudence and taken only after the exhaustion of all peaceful means. The case of North Korea is assessed and, according to the Chapter's authors, China not only did not cast a veto but also implemented all UN sanction resolutions.

In conclusion, the Handbook merits commendation for its thorough analysis of a phenomenon that is still an object of controversy and contrasting evaluations. It is made of valuable contributions, even though not of equal standing. The following are minimal critical observations which are not intended to undermine the overall value of the book. A final Chapter is lacking as well as other refinements, such as a Table of Cases (more important) and a Bibliography (less important). Also missing are a list of abbreviations as well as a preface (in part contained in the back cover). The lack of conclusions is in some way remedied by the Editor's Introductory Chapter and her final considerations, offered in paragraph 6, entitled "Outlook". Since the book deals not only with UN sanctions but also with countermeasures, an inquiry into the practice of Magnitsky-type legislation to address gross violations of human rights would have increased the relevance of the Handbook.

NATALINO RONZITTI[*]

---

[*] Of the Board of Editors

OONA A. HATHAWAY and SCOTT J. SHAPIRO, *The Internationalists. How a Radical Plan to Outlaw War Remade the World*, New York, Simon & Shuster, 2017, pp. 581; PHILIPPE SANDS, *East West Street. On the Origins of "Genocide" and "Crimes against Humanity"*, London, Orion, 2016, pp. 496.

There are at least two good reasons, based on their affinity, for reviewing together these two works, which are in many respects otherwise so different. The first reason is that both use a non-legal approach to investigate key aspects of the evolution of international law in the XX century focusing predominantly on the great figures who were instrumental in changing the law against many odds, and who opposed other politicians and lawyers who stood instead for conservation if not for denial. It is not chance that both have been published by non-academic publishers. The second reason is that the developments addressed in the two books are the key passages from the legality of recourse to war.

In the case of Philippe Sands' book, almost a non-fiction thriller of a sort, the presentation of the origins of the relevant legal developments in their historical setting is accompanied in parallel by the discovery of the author's own family involvement in those origins, previously unknown to the author himself. The setting is Lemberg (Leopolis) a typical pluri-national, pluri-language town at the eastern fringe of the Austrian-Hungarian empire until 1918, later Lvov in Poland, then again Lemberg under Nazi rule, thereafter Lviv in the Soviet Union and now in Western Ukraine. The University in which Hersch Lauterpacht and Raphael Lemkin studied in different years without knowing each other (and where their memories had been lost until Philippe Sands was invited to deliver a speech there in 2010) is in this town. We discover with the author that Sands' maternal grandfather was born there, not far from the residence of Lauterpacht's family. Two families that were completely annihilated in the Holocaust during Nazi rule, under the responsibility of two other characters of Sands' book: Hans Frank, Hitler's personal lawyer, sentenced to death in Nuremberg, and Otto von Wächter, his successor in command in Lemberg in 1942-43, who died mysteriously in 1948 while hiding in Rome with assistance from Vatican connections (but for this story we shall need to wait for Philippe's next book).

Philippe does not stop at placing the perpetrators side by side with their judges nor at describing first the might and then the demise of the "Nazi King of Poland". First we are reminded of his wife's looting of the ghettos while Frank is in command in the Wavel palace of Krakow with Leonardo's painting "the Dame with the Ermine" hanging behind him. These scenes had been already described, as Sands recalls, in the 1945 novel *Kaputt* by the Italian writer Curzio Malaparte who visited him as a journalist of *Corriere della Sera* in 1942. At the end Frank is depicted in the cell of the Nuremberg prison awaiting execution. Sands looks for the sons of the two criminals, interviews them for what has become a successful documentary available on Netflix, elicits the rejection of Frank by his son, while the son of Wächter refuses to reject his childhood memory of his father.

The second reason for examining these two works jointly is that the developments in international law and institutions at the core of the two works are basically one and the same: how war has been legally outlawed, how aggression has become a crime, how responsible individuals have been called accountable under criminal law at Nuremberg. *The Internationalists* traces the origin of this U-turn in international law and relations to the unjustly half-forgotten Kellogg-Briand Pact of 1928 to outlaw war. Notwithstanding its uneven application by the League of Nations, the Pact was the basis for the transformation of the law of neutrality in the late 1930s, inspiring the Atlantic Charter of 1942, the Nuremberg Judgment, the Charter of the United Nations and beyond.

As shown brilliantly by Professors Hathaway and Shapiro, principles that had been affirmed by Grotius, expanded by Vattel, applied for centuries in Europe, in the American War of Independence and in the Civil War until World War I, were successfully rejected by Frank Kellogg, Aristide Briand, Gustav Stresemann and their advisors. The principles of the Kellogg-Briand Pact were soon to be applied thanks to Henry Stimson's doctrine in the non-recognition of the territorial conquests of Japan in Manchuria. They became enshrined in international law thanks to figures like Hans Kelsen, Hersch Lauterpacht, René Cassin and the prosecutors and judges at Nuremberg, notably Robert Jackson. They rejected the defence of "superior orders", the denial of individual responsibility and arguments on non-retroactivity based on the belief that *jus ad bellum* had not changed. This was instead the position taken by Carl Schmitt who directly inspired some of his followers in the defence of the accused at Nuremberg. *The Internationalists* (p. 271 ff. and 285 ff.) has the full story, including the reliance on Schmitt's legal opinion to defend one of the accused by a German professor who he had called at the University of Cologne in 1933 to replace Hans Kelsen after Schmitt had ousted him. Schmitt had not been deterred by the fact that it had been Kelsen who had called him to teach there just a year before, in a gesture of superior academic objectivity notwithstanding their clearly opposed position. While these arguments did not avoid the hanging of the accused, the professor at hand went on after the war to become the Rector of the University of Cologne... (p. 297)

The many unknown anecdotal stories from the lives of the protagonists of international law and relations in the course of the centuries make reading *The Internationalists* enjoyable in the manner of reading a novel. How many internationalists know that Grotius' first appointment was that of defending the legality of the looting, seizing as a prize and auctioning of the cargo of a peaceful Portuguese galleon by a Dutch crew off the straits of Singapore in 1603? What a start for the Father of international law! And how many are aware of Grotius' adventurous escape in a case of books from the castle in Holland where he was serving life imprisonment because of a conviction of heresy in 1621 (see the reproduction of the engraving, one of the many pictures that illustrate the volume, after p. 170)?

The basic point is well illustrated. What the book covers is nothing less than the passage from the Old to the New World Order, an order no longer based on the principle that "Might Makes Right" but on the opposite: that "Might Makes No Longer Right" as the authors put it; a sort of revival of Just War theories buried by centuries of *Real Politik*. With a crucial corollary which the 1928 Pact did not contemplate: the individual responsibility for grave breaches of international law. It was Hersch Lauterpacht and, even more, Hans Kelsen in a memo of July

1945 to Jackson – one of those professors whom the latter distrusted ("God save us from the professors!") – who succeeded in convincing him to base the indictments at Nuremberg on the principles of individual responsibility and punishment, as in domestic law, a turning point compared to the previous principle of collective impersonal responsibility of states for breaches of international law (p. 268 and 282).

The authors of *The Internationalists* do not ignore the ups and downs in the application of the noble principles of the new paradigm in the post-Second World War (WWII) world, including in recent times: "Unfortunately, the growing reliance on self-defense as a justification for using force – for this and other operations against terrorist groups around the world – threatens to make self-defense the exception that swallows the rule against war". Indeed it was precisely this concern that led the authors of the Pact to omit an express exception for what they called "defensive wars" and the drafters of the UN Charter to adopt a right to self-defence only in cases of "armed attack". If states can always invoke self-defence as a justification to use force, then the prohibition on war becomes meaningless (p. 418).

The authors do not content themselves with supporting their presentation and investigation with 120 pages of historical, documentary and legal footnotes. They submit that international practice reflects the introduction of the prohibition of territorial conquest, as evidenced by a comparison of territorial conquests and forcible changes of borders in the past (from 1810), compared to post WWII practice. "Outcasting" (non-recognition) has become in their view the principal peaceful reaction of the international community to major illegalities. In their well-documented view, the new principles command effectiveness also by protecting the survival of the weakest: those small countries that in the past would not have been able to survive independently ("A World Transformed", p. 347 ff., with graphics and tables resulting from an empirical research conducted under the authors' direction by teams of their students from Yale).

In this respect, this reviewer is not convinced that all transformations of international law and relations can be explained by the outlawing of war and that the (mostly peaceful) reaction to aggression by the international community is to be principally credited for the post-WWII relative stability of states and borders. We professors should resist the temptation to stretch reality to fit our theories, beyond uncontested facts and certainty in correlation. The role of other major developments which have changed the international legal landscape cannot be ignored: such as, in chronological order, the protection of minorities, the recognition of human rights and decolonisation. Moreover, civil wars (non-international conflicts) have largely replaced wars between states as the principal source of violence and instability also thanks to systematic foreign intervention.

Going back to Sands' book, its well-deserved and world-wide success (it has been named "Non-fiction Book of the Year 2017"), including its translation to many languages, dispenses us from a *résumé*. Hersch Lauterpacht is also here a protagonist. As Kelsen supported Jackson, it was Lauterpacht, as the legal mastermind of the British team, who drafted the opening speech for the British Prosecutor at Nuremberg, Lord Shawcross. He rejected Rafael Lemkin's plea that the accused be charged also of crimes against groups. Lemkin (another international lawyer educated in the central-European legal tradition) would have to go on pleading for the recognition of the crime of genocide until it was taken up forcefully in the Genocide Convention of 1948.

Bringing changes in the law, enforcing the law and personal engagement so that the law might prevail (the *Fight for the Law* of Jehring) are at the forefront of Sands' book. A question which looms is how much this engagement owes to personal experience, and if so, from what stage of his life and under what circumstances? Thus, Lauterpacht apparently did not acknowledge that by bringing justice and sentencing at Nuremberg he was also vindicating his exterminated family in Galicia (of whose fate possibly he was not even aware). Lemkin, on the contrary, took this task upon his shoulders.

Both figures, like the group of "Internationalists" who brought about the Kellogg-Briand Pact, ultimately waged a combat for universality. Philippe Sands has added a personal contribution from the rediscovered history of his family.

GIORGIO SACERDOTI[*]

ZENO CRESPI REGHIZZI, *L'intervento "come non parte" nel processo davanti alla Corte internazionale di giustizia*, Milano, Giuffrè, 2017, pp. 494.

This timely work by the author, a professor of international law at the University of Milan, covers in depth a subject which the ICJ has had to deal with more and more frequently in recent years. It is also a subject on which the jurisprudence has shown continuous development and which is crucial for the effective and legitimate exercise of the Court's jurisdiction in our times. This is because the multilateralisation of substantive rules impinges on the consensual and bilateral underpinning of contentious jurisdiction before the Court, as evidenced by the increase in number of these interventions by non-parties in pending proceedings.

This situation has resulted in the need for solutions capable of ensuring the sound administration of justice when the subject matter of the dispute, and hence the decision of the Court, may affect interests of third states. The obstacle is that the consensual basis of jurisdiction does not allow intervention by third parties in the absence of a jurisdictional clause that admits such intervention, as narrowly provided by the Statute of the Court. The author examines in the first Part of the volume the origin of Articles 62 and 63 of the Statute on intervention and the restrictive practice of the Court that led it to reject all requests of intervention for lack of jurisdictional basis until 1990. In order to deal with this issue, the author starts appropriately with an examination of the effects of international judgments for third parties when they are not parties in the proceedings. The concept that in absence of an "indispensable" party in the proceedings the Court will not exercise its jurisdiction is an extreme, rarely used remedy that prejudices the parties

---

[*] Of the Board of Editors

to the dispute. On the other hand, the well-established fundamental doctrine of the absence of any such effects on non-parties is not adequate when the non-participating state may be factually prejudiced by the decision.

The focus of the investigation is on the "remedial" approach followed by the Court starting with the judgment of 1990 on Nicaragua's application in the Frontier dispute between El Salvador and Honduras where the legitimacy of an intervention as a non-party was admitted for the first time.

Based on the subsequent practice of the Court, the author examines critically and in-depth the basis and features of this "construction". Prof. Crespi Reghizzi does not consider it a "creation" of the Court – in view of the existence of Articles 62 and 63 of the Statute – nor a type of judicially-made procedural law, but rather an example of "law in action" developed by the Court in order to ensure the effective exercise of its jurisdiction under the Statute, responding positively to community needs.

The author points out that the contours of non-party intervention remain un-defined, the case law on its requirements being inconsistent. In light of Article 63 the author is critical of the downplaying by the Court itself of the effects of the judgment for the intervening non-party. "Indeed, if one accepts the position, set out by the Court, that the State intervening as a non-party is not bound by the future judgment, then the characterization of interpretative intervention as non-party intervention held by the most recent case-law appears irreconcilable – in the author's judgment – with Article 63, para. 2, which provides that the con-struction of the multilateral convention contained in the judgment will be binding upon the intervening State" (p. 472). The author submits rather that intervention as a non-party does fit into the scheme of Article 63, so that, though depending on the position the intervening state has taken as to the merits, the non-party will be necessarily bound by the holdings of the judgment as a consequence of hav-ing participated in the proceedings (p. 351). The author's thesis that this effect derives from general principles concerning the exercise of the judicial function appears convincingly argued to the present reviewer.

It is regrettable that since this work is in Italian most researchers and lawyers interested in the field will find it difficult to access this valuable contribution to a sensitive subject, which touches upon the jurisdiction of international courts and tribunals and not just the ICJ, where theory and practice are closely intertwined.

GIORGIO SACERDOTI*

GIOVANNI ZARRA, *Parallel Proceedings in Investment Arbitration*, Den Haag and Torino, Eleven International Publishing and Giappichelli, 2017, pp. 253.

To say that Giovanni Zarra's book is a valuable addition to the burgeoning literature on international investment law would be too conventional a way to begin a review of a book that grew out of a passionate engagement with a subject

---

* Of the Board of Editors

whose scope is not as narrow as it might seem. However much it may be hard to believe that a monograph on a seemingly dry procedural topic like parallel proceedings reads like a page-turner, Zarra's book does. How is that possible? It is not that the author avoided citing the case law chapter and verse. He does, lavishly. It is not that he minimised footnoting. Hefty footnotes are everywhere. It is not that he shunned jargon. The book is, to be sure, a page-turner for lawyers only. But why ask? My contention is that the book's core meaning is best got at by asking how the final product succeeds in being at once so typically austere and enthralling. The short answer is that Zarra's book works like a "howcatchem", a crime story where the murderer's identity is known from the start – and so is the victim's – but it is hard to guess how the detective will catch the perpetrator and bring him to justice (in a "whodunnit", by contrast, the murderer's identity remains concealed until the end).

In the book under review, parallel proceedings are the felon and international investment arbitration, whose coherence and effectiveness may be undermined by the former, the potential victim. The detective is impersonated by the "author" who, despite the small "a", buoyantly inhabits a drama swarming with "Authors". Against many of them, Zarra endeavours to show that the deadly force of parallel proceedings can be held in check: "the main goal of the author is to try to identify whether there are certain principles of general international law that may be used by arbitrators in order to preclude the continuation of duplicative proceedings" (p. XVI). Zarra defines "parallel proceedings" as encompassing "both concurrent and subsequent proceedings [...] based [...] on the same purpose, facts and interests" (p. 2). He introduces them as a well-known fact in the life of international investment law, a fact that, far from being unavoidable, could and should be done away with, if the credibility of investment arbitration "as a legitimate method of dispute settlement" is to be preserved (p. 205). As parallel proceedings are a potential cause of uncertainty and inefficiency in the settlement of international investment disputes, and even a means through which states may be "vexed and harassed" by ravenous investors (p. 45), they should be tamed and discouraged. Investors and arbitrators indulging in them imperil a flourishing dispute settlement system, against their own best interest. Zarra's indirect response to Martti Koskenniemi's clarion call – "It's not the cases, it's the system" (Journal of World Investment and Trade, 2017, p. 343 ff.) – is in essence that blame should rather be put on arbitral tribunals that allow duplicate claims to proceed in disregard of principles that are part and parcel of international investment law itself: it is the cases, not the system.

This, however, may be tantamount to admitting that a contradiction inhabits international investment law – or a tension – between the normative infrastructure that enables the filing of parallel claims and the principles that should be put to work to neutralise the very same claims. In Zarra's book, the contradiction is solved by implicitly postulating the superiority of those principles over competing rules. But what are those principles? And where do they come from?

Time to disclose the means by which "the *system*" may pull itself out of its own failings has not yet come. Readers are nonetheless advised that spoilers are just round the corner. Those in search for clues may wish to note that the italicised word above is one: the distinctive way in which Zarra frames international investment law as a legal system is indeed the key to the riddle.

The book starts with a description of how international investment law – "the system" – paves the way to parallel proceedings. Zarra pinpoints two main sources of trouble: the potential concurrence of contract and treaty claims based on the same facts and the circumstance that many bilateral investment treaties (BITs) entitle the company and all its shareholders to bring separate claims (pp. 7-13). One may of course regret that international investment law does this but, as the author rightly observes, its workings are steadily based on states' will: "the first reason leading to parallel proceedings is the same States' willingness to attract foreign investments through BITs very favourable to foreign investors" (p. 20). If, however, states are responsible for their own predicament, and if Zarra's work belongs in the positivist tradition, i.e. one in which states' *voluntas* trumps all competing normative arguments, then we would have already reached the endgame: the book would be a "negative howcatchem", one where the criminal eventually eludes the detective. But this cannot be true, as Zarra's investigation has just begun. All we know at this point is that the author will have to integrate an extra-positive ingredient in his argumentative strategy. And this is precisely what he does when he discusses the concept of a legal system and its applicability to international investment law (on the same topic see also his recent "The Issue of Incoherence on Investment Arbitration: Is There Need for a Systemic Reform?", Chinese Journal of International Law, 2018, p. 137 ff.).

In a legal environment where the exercise of judicial power remains largely uncoordinated (no general rules governing jurisdictional conflicts, no principle of *stare decisis*, etc.), parallel proceedings risk compromising the legal system's coherence and, with it, the certainty and predictability that are integral to the law's ideal. Zarra shares this point of view; he indeed makes it out eloquently and repeatedly. However, instead of using it as a springboard to jump to an all too easy conclusion, he takes a step back and asks whether international investment law, its apparent fragmentation notwithstanding, qualifies as a legal system; because if it does not, then the argument based on coherence, certainty and predictability would fall by the wayside. "Prior to talking about a lack of coherence and consistency", he writes, "one should ascertain whether, in investment arbitration, a certain degree of orderliness is required and therefore if coherence and consistency shall be ensured" (p. 27). Here we approach the book's hidden abode, on whose threshold the sentence just quoted stares us in the face. This – I submit – is the place where the book's secret lies (every good book has one). Once we have prised the lid off it, we should be able to see how Zarra's argument is produced.

The argument's anchoring point (or "*point de caption*") should be *a* concept of a legal system. Which amongst the many may one come up with? The author does not deny that his foot falls here on shifting sands: "there is no agreement even on the definition of a legal system", he wryly notes (*ibid.*). Shortly afterwards, however, he settles upon Yuval Shany's seemingly reasonable solution, according to which a system is "a purposeful arrangement or constellation of interrelated elements or components, which cannot accurately be described and understood in isolation from one another" (SHANY, *The Competing Jurisdiction of International Courts and Tribunals*, Oxford, 2003, p. 87). In Zarra's view, under this definition, international investment law clearly qualifies as a legal system. And of course he is right. No BIT could be understood in isolation from the complex web of transactions it instantiates, or from multilateral legal frameworks like that put in place by the ICSID Convention. No arbitral award would be fully intelligible without knowing the origin of the legal doctrines and arguments it deploys. But where can Zarra go from here?

In order to understand his next move, it is important to stress that Shany, in the sentence quoted above, does not define the concept of a *legal system* but, rather, a concept of *system* that he regards as useful for the purposes of legal analysis (compare GRADONI, "Systèmes juridiques internationaux: une esquisse", in RUIZ FABRI and GRADONI (eds.), *La circulation des concepts juridiques: le droit international de l'environnement entre mondialisation et fragmentation*, Paris, 2009, p. 27 ff.). Shany's definition is gnoseological, not normative: it is concerned with the things one must take account of to adequately understand a given object, whereas it says nothing about the properties a given object must possess in order to qualify as a legal system. The moment of truth in Zarra's book comes when he, almost unobtrusively, bridges the gap between gnoseology and normativity, or fact and value. He does it via the following implicit assertion: since international investment law must be studied as *a system*, as its meaning would otherwise get lost, it also must be *a legal system*, a term by which Zarra refers, not to whatever assemblage of rules and principles, but to a structure that necessarily encodes certain *normative* qualities. "Coherence, consistency and finality" – he writes, in a sentence that nicely illustrates the fact/value entanglement – "are values that cannot be ignored in a framework such as the one that has been just described" (p. 36). As if producing an effect of inexorable truth, Zarra quotes at length an opinion penned by Sir Edward Coke in 1599, on which he says: "archaic in its wording but still very up-to-date in its meaning, [it] in fact reflects the status of all legal systems, where consistency and finality are considered to be fundamental and irrevocable values" (p. 37). Like every legal system, then, international investment law embodies values that risk falling prey to, and must be mobilised against, threats like that of parallel proceedings. International investment law and arbitration is thus construed as a potential victim. How will it be rescued?

As Zarra explains in the central part of the book, in "the 'fight' against parallel proceedings" (p. 88), no legal ammunition that may be employed at the jurisdictional stage of the proceedings is up to the task of ensuring a lasting victory (Chapter 2 examines remedies like forum selection and fork-in-the-road clauses, intervention, joinder, consolidation and quasi-consolidation of proceedings, *forum non conveniens* and anti-suit injunctions). Almost halfway through the book, a feeling sets in that international investment law may not have resources of its own to muster against the dangers of parallel proceedings. As in any good crime story of the howcatchem type, however, the reader is still led to believe that there is a solution, no matter how desperate the situation appears. And if the legal system in hand, narrowly construed, is unable to provide one, it becomes "necessary to find [it] in the framework of general international law" (p. 99).

If the characterisation of international investment law as a legal system gives the detective reason for hope and, with it, the sense of longing that fuels the investigation, the connection between that body of law and the larger domain of public international law provides a trail for him to follow up. This is done in Chapter 3, where the drama reaches its denouement (a short Chapter 4 discusses the ineffectiveness of "post-award remedies", including the invocation of the public policy exception against the enforcement of "duplicative awards").

Parallel proceedings are finally ensnared – spoiler alert! – by bringing in, from general international law, a host of legal principles, maxims and related procedural notions like good faith, good administration of justice, *ne bis in idem*, abuse of process, *res judicata* and collateral estoppel (see generally Chapter 3 and p. 204). Central to the solution of the case is the idea that foreign investors may be tempted to abuse their procedural rights (there is no gainsaying that the law offers substantial inducement in this regard!) and that the legal system that generates those very same rights, insofar as it remains embedded in public international law, also possesses the antidote against their abuse (p. 130). As Zarra explains, the right moment to administer the antidote is the admissibility stage of the proceedings, where enlightened arbitrators who "realize that the continuation of (duplicative) proceedings runs against the proper administration of justice and risks undermining the judicial function that they administrate", would be called upon "to exercise their inherent powers in order to prevent these proceedings from going on", thereby "protecting the legitimacy of investment arbitration as a whole" (pp. 109). Arbitrators, the author contends, have "the power to control, *in concreto*, that all procedural rights are exercised in good faith, notwithstanding the lack of a normative basis for such power", because it is "an inherent power" that "every judge" must wield against "anti-social" uses of procedural rights (p. 131). Here, Zarra follows Hersch Lauterpacht's crisp characterisation of the abuse-of-rights doctrine: "[the] essence of the doctrine is that, as legal rights are conferred by the community, the latter cannot countenance their antisocial use by individuals" (LAUTERPACHT, *The Function of Law in the International Community*, Cambridge, 2010 [1933], p. 294). But what if no such community undergirds international investment law? What if procedural rights were conferred upon investors, not by "a community", but by single states, or pairs of states, as in countless BITs and domestic bills aimed at attracting foreign investments? Is not the community of states undone by capital's *divide et impera* strategies?

As Zarra meditatively points out at the end of his investigation, "[t]he entire analysis carried out in this book is based on a main assumption, i.e. that international investment arbitration fulfils a public function", an assumption that "justifies certain differences in the management of proceedings from international commercial arbitration, due to the fact that this last form of adjudication involves only private interests" (p. 199). He then concludes: "it is essential that phenomena like parallel proceedings, which – being perceived as an undue disadvantage for the interests of the State involved in the dispute – undermine the credibility (and, finally, the very existence) of the entire method of dispute resolution, are avoided or at least limited" (*ibid.*). Along the same lines he previously observed that, "being investment arbitration a form of dispute settlement that involves several public interests, it is of certain importance that such form of justice is not abused to the detriment of State parties" (p. 132), and that arbitral proceedings initiated "with the aim of taking an undue advantage or creating harassment to the other party" should not be tolerated (p. 130). But what if international investment law, despite its courting (and being courted by) public international law, is not at its core "public" at all? What if it ceased to be so after its decoupling from the ideology that framed foreign *direct* investments as worthy of special protection on account of their contribution to economic development worldwide? What if, in an epoch where freely roaming capital is sanctified, international investment law should rather be seen as providing "avenues through which international law can be used as an instrument of private power" (SORNARAJAH, *The International Law on Foreign Investment*, 3rd ed., Cambridge, 2010, p. 305)? But "doubt-mongering" should not stop here.

Are we sure that it is ultimately the principle of legal certainty that informs international investment law? Is not the latter warped by other "drives", perhaps not traditionally associated with the law's ideal but no less powerful, like the need to diversify and strengthen the "insurance scheme" enjoyed by investors? Is not a certain level of unpredictability useful to keep capital-unfriendly regulation at bay, as states feel encircled and about to be sued for breach of a vague standard, perhaps many times over? As David Schneiderman recently pointed out, whilst "[o]ne of the dominant rationales offered to justify investment treaty arbitration has been the uncertainty and unpredictability of host state legal orders", international legal standards have not only themselves been "vague and uncertain, even when their content has been filled in by investment tribunals, but also remain perpetually in movement" ("The Paranoid Style of Investment Lawyers and Arbitrators: Investment Law Norm Entrepreneurs and Their Critics", in LIM (ed.), *Alternative Visions of the International Law on Foreign Investment: Essays in Honour of Muthucumaraswamy Sornarajah*, Cambridge, 2016, p. 136). One may perhaps advance a similar contention with regard to procedural arrangements.

Zarra believes that international investment law "cannot allow a claimant to multiply a dispute in order to get more chances of success" (p. 45). But what if its rules are geared precisely to that purpose? What if the "substantial function" of investment arbitration is not, as the author maintains, "to finally settle investment disputes" (p. 139), but to delay or avert the investor's defeat? Although the claim that states should not be "vexed and harassed by the multiplication of proceedings" looks irresistible (p. 45), it is ultimately the states themselves – although not "the community of States" – that brought about the messy world of parallel proceedings, perhaps as an evil they inflicted upon themselves in exchange for the superior good they all nowadays beseech, the inflow of capital. What if vexing and harassing states (one may also say "disciplining") is part of the new "public" order?

If the book under review were a novel (after all, as I tried to argue, it feels and can be read like one), all the questions I have been raising in this review – I like to think – would be rumbling in Detective Zarra's mind as he stares at the culprit he just put under arrest and silently rehearses his investigation. That would be the novel's last page. But what if the crime story of international investment law does not belong in the howcatchem genre? What if it is one of those whodunnits?

In *The G File*, a crime story written by Håkan Nesser, a woman who had just hired a private detective to look into her husband's shady dealings is found dead, her body crushed against the floor of an empty swimming pool. Her husband, known as Mr. G, appears from the start as the obvious culprit so that the reader's anguish (and enjoyment) grows as Mr. G systematically outsmarts the police and is eventually acquitted of all charges for lack of evidence. *The G File* works like an anticlimactic howcatchem: the detective tries hard, and fails. Or so it seems. As the novel draws to a doleful close (or so it seems), in a masterful stroke Nesser switches the narrative frame from howcatchem to whodunnit: Mr. G and his wife, who is still alive, were actually 'partners in crime', the woman found dead at the bottom of the swimming pool was one of their victims, and Mr. G was himself a victim of his manipulative wife who, under the cover of a fictitious death, masterminded her husband's escape from justice to keep using him as her favourite piece on the chessboard of crime. What if international investment law is actually the sly Mrs G?

LORENZO GRADONI*

LAURENT MANDERIEUX and MICHELE VELLANO (eds.), *Éthique globale, bonne gouvernance et droit international économique*, Torino, Giappichelli, 2017, pp. XXIV-184.

The need to control and regulate the behaviour of legal actors – so as to make sure that law and its concrete operation are directed towards what is *ethically* right, i.e. what is good for the individual and the society – has been perceived since ancient times. In contemporary societies, "the systems of law and public justice are closely related to ethics in that they determine definite rights and duties. They also attempt to repress and punish deviations from these standards" (see "Ethics, Legal", The Free Dictionary by Farlex, available at: <https://legal-dictionary.thefreedictionary.com/Ethics%2C+Legal>). Notwithstanding the process of fragmentation of international law (see KOSKENNIEMI, Fragmentation of International Law: Difficulties Arising from the Diversification and Expansion of International Law, UN Doc. A/CN.4/L.702 (2006)), the latter remains a single and homogeneous legal order, and certain global common values – which may also be defined "common goods" (see LENZERINI and VRDOLJAK (eds.), *International Law for Common Goods. Normative Perspectives on Human Rights, Culture and Nature*, Oxford, 2014) – particularly human rights, the environment and cultural heritage, are "transversal" to all different sectorial regimes, as they inform the whole body of international law. International economic law is not immune from

---

* Senior Research Fellow, Max Planck Institute Luxembourg for International, European and Regulatory Procedural Law.

the influence of ethical considerations, which affect the processes of globalisation and liberalisation of international markets and economic affairs, with the aim of avoiding deviations from fundamental standards and ensuring proper realisation of "good governance", i.e. what is good for human beings and society. The book edited by Manderieux and Vellano has the purpose of investigating the concrete influence and impact of ethics in the regulation and operation of international economic law. The idea behind the book appears to be inspired by the experience of *Francophonie*, which – as explained by Albert Lourde in his "Préface" – may become a wide space of economic cooperation and social solidarity, with over one billion people involved, as well as a model of society regulated by law at the service of social solidarity (p. XIV). *Francophonie* also provides a defence against the economic, cultural and linguistic domination of the United States – which determines a threat of uniformity and hegemony for cultures and languages – and, *a fortiori*, a defence against the threat of an international order dominated by one language and civilisation only (pp. XIV-XV). According to Lourde, the Francophone world may participate in the determination and development of the rules of international economic law, including in the context of financing for development and international trade, therefore contributing to the achievement of the correct equilibrium between freedom of enterprise, profit and common good (pp. XVII-XVIII). This idea is reiterated at the end of the book in the "Remarques conclusives" (Conclusive Remarks) written by Denis Fadda, who emphasises that *Francophonie* offers a model of dialogue among different cultures and of understanding of others' cultures, for a more balanced globalisation based on humanity and solidarity.

The aspiration of *Francophonie* to preserve cultural diversity and contribute to the construction of a well-balanced and fair globalisation (pp. XIII-XIV) is well-reflected in the bilingualism of the book, as French is not the only language used, some chapters being written in Italian. However, the investigation carried out in the various chapters of the book is not limited to an evaluation of the Francophone world. On the contrary, the focus of the volume is more global, and a notable part of it is specifically devoted to the European Union.

The first Part of the book, entitled "Éthique globale et droit international économique" (Global Ethics and International Economic Law) is opened by a contribution written by Annamaria Monti, on "Besoins humains fondamentaux, éthique and droit des affaires: brèves remarques du point de vue historique" (Fundamental Human Needs, Ethics and Business Law: Short Remarks from a Historical Point of View). The Chapter offers a historical survey of the development of the role played by the ethical perspective in the context of international economic law, noting that ethics has come to the surface especially in the form of an attempt to limit and prevent dangerous activities of multinational enterprises, as well as of an effort to prohibit anticompetitive practices in international trade, corruption and illicit economic transactions (p. 4). Today ethical concerns have been incorporated by international organisations, and are addressed not only to states, but also to multinational enterprises and investors (p. 10). Thanks to ethics, today international trade law has been positively renovated through taking into account the fundamental rights and needs of peoples (p. 11).

The following contribution, entitled "Religione, etica e sovranità economica e finanziaria nel mondo contemporaneo" (Religion, Ethics and Economic and Financial Sovereignty in the Contemporary World), written by Michele Vellano, analyses the interesting and challenging topic of the influence of religion in establishing a global ethics of international trade. Starting from the assumption that the "soul" of the economic model dominating in contemporary times is the search for individual economic profit – through modalities which progressively cause local identities to disappear (p. 15) – Vellano notes that religion is one of the few entities which may pose some kind of resistance to such a process (p. 16). After providing a survey of (soft law) instruments relating to international economic law which incorporate references to ethical issues, Vellano undertakes a case-study of loan of money remunerated with interest, noting how it may be strongly influenced by religion. This is particularly true with respect to Jewish, Christian and Islamic religions, which traditionally do not accept unfair interest, especially compound interest (p. 21). This, however, is not reflected in the practice, especially as regards the European Union, in the context of which the prohibition of compound interest has not been accepted as a legitimate exception to the freedom of access to the market by foreign operators established by Article 49 TFEU, demonstrating how, at least in this context, economic concerns prevail over ethical ones, even of religious derivation (p. 26). Similarly, still in the framework of the European Union, religious and ethical concerns, including the idea of solidarity, have not persuaded economically stronger members to accept the reduction of the public debt of states in crisis, particularly Greece, while reduction or cancellation of interests might resolve the impasse, exactly for the reason that imposition and payment of interests is considered ethically and culturally acceptable only when certain conditions are met, i.e. that they do not impose particularly burdensome conditions for the debtor (pp. 29-30). The practice described by Vellano shows that, while it is indubitable that considerations of global ethics permeate international economic law today, their concrete translation into practice remains troublesome (p. 30).

The contribution by Vellano is followed by a Chapter written by Dominique Carreau, entitled "Le Fonds monétaire international et la gouvernance equitable" (International Monetary Fund and Equitable Governance). Carreau offers an assessment of promotion of "good governance" by the International Monetary Fund, officially inaugurated in 1996 and conceived as a form of partnership for sustainable growth, having the aim of ensuring respect for the rule of law, improving the effectiveness of responsibility of the public sector, as well as fighting against corruption (p. 35). In 2000 the concept of reference changed from "good governance" to "equitable governance", regarded as respect for law, transparency and responsibility of the public sector, eradication of corruption and combatting poverty, with the additional elements of combatting money laundering, drug trafficking and international terrorism (p. 36). In this context, the International Monetary Fund does not act in isolation, but in conjunction with other international institutions, particularly the World Bank (p. 36).

The next Chapter, written by Fabrizio Marrella and Arianna Vettorel ("Banca mondiale e diritti umani: il ruolo dell'*Inspection Panel*" – World Bank and

Human Rights: The Role of the Inspection Panel) complements the previous one in analysing how human rights are taken into consideration in the context of the activity of the World Bank, especially through its Inspection Panel (established in 1993). This Panel has the purpose of satisfying the needs of civil society, together with ensuring accountability and good governance. The main importance of the Panel – entrusted with the principal task of ascertaining whether a given activity financed by the Bank is coherent with its policies and procedures – is in promoting access to inquiry and remedies for victims of human rights violations committed in the operation of activities financed by the World Bank. The activity of the Inspection Panel, however, is not immune from problems, which notably affect its effectiveness. These problems include the procedure of nomination of the members of the Panel (elected by the Bank without involvement of the social sector), the impossibility for interested persons to dispute the determinations of the Panel, and the non-binding character of its decisions (pp. 46-47). However, in the recent past these "structural" deficiencies have been balanced by the high quality and persuasive force of the reports of the Panel, which have contributed to increase its credibility and, *a fortiori*, the level of follow-up of its recommendations (p. 47). At the same time, the activity of the Panel allows the World Bank to incorporate within its policies best practices of human rights protection, ensuing from the reports of the Panel itself (p. 55).

Another interesting perspective is offered by the contribution of Gabriele Galgani ("Regards croisés sur les conventions UNESCO et le droit international de l'économie: entre interactions pratiques et gouvernance mondiale" – Combined Considerations on UNESCO Conventions and International Economic Law: Between Practical Interactions and Global Governance), concerning the influence of UNESCO on the operation of international economic law. The author shows how it has traditionally been very difficult to ensure appropriate consideration for cultural policies of states within the context of the operation of WTO law. The strictly binding character of WTO rules and the very limited space left to exceptions to liberalisation of trade have usually prevented cultural considerations from being given effective attention in the context of international trade. Similar reflections may be developed when considering the role played by culture in the context of international investment law (although it may be noted that in the recent past a number of arbitral tribunals established under the aegis of ICSID have actually taken cultural needs into proper consideration, to the point of structuring, in whole or in part, the content of their decisions on the basis of such needs; see LENZERINI, "Property Protection and Protection of Cultural Heritage", in SCHILL (ed.), *International Investment Law and Comparative Public Law*, Oxford, 2010, p. 541 ff.). Galgani proposes a possible prospective solution for this problem, consisting in establishing a "symbiotic link" between culture and economic relations, in light of the evidence that many goods involved in economic transactions are actually the expression of identity, art and history – in a word, of "culture" (p. 70). The construction of such a symbiotic link is especially possible in light of the fact that, in international economic agreements, provisions with notable cultural implications actually exist (pp. 72-74), showing the existence of some kind of space for culture in the framework of international economic law. This argument is reinforced by the circumstance that intellectual property rights and international investment law – which are strictly linked with trade – also present notable connections with culture. Since international rules in the fields of trade, intellectual property rights and investment may play a notable influence on expressions of culture and cultural heritage, it follows that the "symbiotic link" between international economic law and culture is almost "inherent", while at the same time an overlay exists between the two. In order to valorise the link and to properly manage such an overlay, one option might consist in using instruments on international economic law for the formulation of policies in the cultural field, without establishing any hierarchy between the values at stake (p. 78). Galgani, interestingly, also proposes that the listing system adopted by UNESCO Conventions – notably the 1972 World Heritage List and the 2003 Convention on the Safeguarding of the Intangible Cultural Heritage – might be imported into the context of WTO and other economic agreements to allow the application of a preferential treatment for certain cultural goods and services in the context of the operation of international economic law (pp. 81-82).

The second part of the book, entitled "Vers une moralization et une humanization des règles du commerce international?" (Towards a Moralisation and Humanisation of Rules of International Trade?) is opened by a contribution on "Le droit international et la corruption: perspectives historiques et considerations actuelles" (International Law and Corruption: Historical Perspectives and Present Considerations), written by Claudio Dordi. The Chapter proposes some general considerations of practical character concerning the evolution of the fight against corruption in international law, in order to properly understand its main distinctive characters. Dordi concludes that, despite the existence of important international instruments in the field, some doubts remain on the application of the relevant rules at the national level, in light of the tendency of most states to consider the problem under the perspective of criminal law only, hence downsising the potentiality of the international instruments.

The following Chapter, by Fabio Bassan, deals with "Les fonds souverains et les norms éthiques pour l'investissement" (Sovereign Wealth Funds and Ethical Norms for Investment), examining the "moralising" role of sovereign wealth funds in the investment market, with specific regard to environmental protection, promotion of sustainable development and protection of human rights. The conclusions of the investigation, however, are not very encouraging, as ethical principles are applied in the context of management of the sovereign wealth funds mainly on a non-codified voluntary basis, hence only to a residual extent. The only sovereign wealth fund whose statute explicitly contemplates respect for ethical principles (controlled in practice by a specific committee) is the Norwegian fund. The hope is that the example of Norway will be imitated by other countries and serve as a spark for the development of a general practice incorporating respect for ethical principles in the management of sovereign wealth funds.

In the next contribution, entitled "Le droit à un environment salubre: quels nouveaux enjeux Nord-Nord et Nord-Sud?" (Right to a Safe Environment: What New North-North and North-South Issues?), Miriam Allena examines the level of influence played by environmental protection on international economic law in both countries of the North and of the South of the world, noting how in the two areas different responses are needed under the point of view of environmental protection (p. 114). In fact, in industrialised countries environmental protection – and, *a fortiori*, the right to a safe environment – is considered a value which must be integrated in the context of economic development, while in developing countries it is commonly seen as an obstacle to economic and social development, and, more generally, to the creation of better living conditions for people (p. 118). This reflects the fact that, in the two hemispheres of the world, environmental protection represents the tip of the iceberg of different instances of social, economic and ethical character (p. 119). As a consequence, international environmental law may become the paradigm allowing different problems to be regulated, including that of the relationships between the North and the South of the world (p. 119). For instance, the principle of sustainable development may be used as a criterion for the distribution of, respectively, advantages and responsibilities between the two hemispheres, in light of their respective realities and needs (p. 121).

The final Chapter of Part II, written by Laurent Manderieux, entitled "Accès à la culture: porquoi le droit de la culture contribute à la bonne gouvernance et à l'éthique dans la vie des affaires" (Access to Culture: Why the Right to Culture Contributes to Good Governance and to Ethics through Business), considers access to culture – conceived as a fundamental source and a guarantee of sustainable development – under the perspective of human rights at both the "universal" and regional levels. Manderieux concludes that the need to establish an equilibrium between the individual and the collective perspective of the right in point necessarily leads to the adoption of an ethical approach. In addition, if one considers the cultural elements characterising other human rights, particularly the right to property, the notable margin of manoeuvre becomes evident which allows the introduction into the business world of considerations going well beyond mere economic imperatives (p. 132).

Part III of the book (entitled "L'Union européenne et la bonne governance des nouveaux défis représentés par les affirmations identitaires à l'intérieur et à l'extérieur de ses frontières") is dedicated to the European Union, particularly to the good governance of the new challenges represented by identity claims inside and outside the Union's borders. It is introduced by a contribution by Pietro Manzini, entitled "La solidarietà tra Stati membri della Unione europea: un panorama 'costituzionale'" (Solidarity among Member States of the European Union: A "Constitutional" Survey), examining the development of the idea of solidarity in European Union law, beginning from the phase before the entry into force of the Lisbon Treaty in 2009, and highlighting the improvements brought by the latter treaty and by the subsequent evolution of EU law. In the final section of the Chapter, Manzini considers such an evolution in the face of the recent flows of immigrants claiming international protection at the borders of Mediterranean countries, concluding that the solidarity shown by European countries to Italy and Greece for the massive flows of immigrants in recent times represents a positive development, even though the behaviour by certain EU members (notably Hungary) casts some shadows on the perspectives of the development of solidarity, and shows how the concrete realisation of the latter remains difficult (pp. 152-153).

The following Chapter ("I valori religiosi nel diritto dell'Unione europea" – Religious Values in European Union Law), by Andrea Santini, explores the religious inheritance of European countries within the context of European Union law, noting that, however, the reference to the religious roots of the Union included in the preamble to the Treaty of European Union is unlikely to produce concrete legal effects (pp. 157-158). Santini then examines the fundamental rights with religious significance included in the EU Charter on Fundamental Rights, as well as the relationship between the European Union and confessional bodies, concluding that the approach of the Union is fundamentally based on a pluralistic model recognising the right of any person to choose their own religious conviction. This does not mean, however, that European Union law is insensible to religious values, the contribution of which to the process of European integration is clearly recognised by the EU treaties.

In the final Chapter of the book, entitled "L'action extérieure de l'Union européenne entre idéalisme et réalisme" (External Action of the European Union between Idealism and Realism), Fabien Terpan examines the ethical dimension of external relations of the European Union, the presence of which is clearly demonstrated by the fact that the "European project" was awarded the Nobel Prize for Peace in 2012, as it is centred on the values of peace and democracy. This ethical and idealist content of the European project is not circumscribed to the internal dimension of the Union's action, but pervades all its external relations with the rest of the world since its very first manifestations. However, the external action of the European Union is also characterised by a realist component, determining an ambiguous dichotomy with the ethical dimension, a dichotomy which has been characterised many times by the literature as problematic (p. 172). It is difficult to precisely define the equilibrium between interests and values in the context of European external action (p. 173); however, it may be concluded that European external action continues to be principally oriented towards values, as it is based on a project of peace and stability. The ethical dimension is therefore evident in the context of the European Union, while the element of interests remains preponderant at the level of member states considered individually.

In conclusion, the different chapters of the volume show how "ethicalisation" of international economic law is currently an ongoing and incomplete process, which has produced some partial results but needs to be intensified in order to ensure that the operation of this branch of international law is always consistent with the main values pursued by the international community as a whole.

Overall, the book edited by Manderieux and Vellano undoubtedly represents a useful addition to existing literature, especially for the reason that it covers a theme not extensively explored by scholars. This is all the more true with regard to some of the specific topics dealt with in the chapters making up the book. At the same time, the main apparent shortcoming of the Volume is represented by its lack of comprehensiveness, as it is far from covering all relevant issues relating to the role played by ethics and good governance in the context of the many facets subsumed within the broad area of international economic law. For example, little attention is devoted to the themes of international trade law (especially as regards the influence played by ethical considerations in determining the concrete implementation of WTO rules) and of international investment law, both triggering very interesting and challenging issues especially pertinent to the subject matter of the volume. At the same time, however, it appears quite evident that the idea underlying the Volume under review did not pursue any pretension of exhaustiveness. In the end, however, this is rather understandable, if one considers the enormous range of disciplines included in the sphere of international economic law; indeed, a volume covering all such disciplines in their numerous aspects would look more like an encyclopaedia than a book.

FEDERICO LENZERINI*

ANTHEA ROBERTS, *Is International Law International?*, Oxford, Oxford University Press, 2017, pp. 420.

This excellent volume intrigues and invites you from its title: *Is International Law International?* avoids the well-trodden debate on the normative and legal nature of international law, to investigate the international character of international law and, more specifically, of the international legal community. In this sense, the volume sits between the fields of law and sociology, equally comfortable in discussing how certain legal concepts or legal issues are tackled in different legal jurisdictions, and how national academies shape and inform the world view of their international legal community, intended as their own national community of international lawyers.

The author starts with a provocative claim: international lawyers do not belong to an *invisible college*, like Oscar Schachter said, but to a *divisible one*. One could argue that this is a banal claim, as it is obvious that international lawyers are divided by their nationality, language, legal background (common/civil law), specialisms, etc. And yet it is provocative because international law is the only discipline in law with pretensions of universality. In examining this divisible college, the author uses as a guide three crucial concepts, *difference, dominance* and *disruption.* While the first two hardly require an explanation, the role of disruption is the more intriguing, as it points to the possibility of upsetting the current order, in which difference and dominance play themselves out in the arena of international law, through technological innovation and geo-political developments. One could argue with the selection of what constitutes disruption, less so with the idea that disruptive forces can upset the current equilibrium (which is in reality dis-equilibrium predicated upon difference and domination, so eminently centripetal and unequal forces).

After staking out its claim, the central part of the volume delves into the sociological and legal implications of the central thesis: on the one hand, an examination of how students of international law are cultivated into certain world views

---

*Associate Professor of International Law, University of Siena.

and epistemic communities; on the other, an examination of the legal fall-out of this process of differentiation, both for what concerns topical legal issues, and doctrinal differences. The whole structure is underpinned by a conscious comparative exercise, in which the five permanent members of the United Nations Security Council are chosen as representatives of diverse legal background, political tradition and geographical location (with regrettable, but reasoned, exclusion of the African and South American continents). They constitute the centre of production of international law, both as a matter of state production, and of academic scholarship. The centre has its own semi-periphery (mostly Western, second-tier states) and periphery (particularly former colonies in the developing world)

Chapter Three compares international law academics, or better, academies, looking at the flow of students (from the periphery to the centre), of publications (amongst the centre and from centre to periphery) and at the relationship between academia and practice (which has country-specific characteristics).

Chapter Four tracks the production and diffusion of international law textbooks and casebooks. The pattern that emerges from the comparative exercise in these two chapters is one of hegemonic diffusion from the centre to the periphery, but according to different trajectories, with a more insistent pattern from traditional Western centres of production of international law (France and the United Kingdom) to their former colonial territories, and a more inward-looking approach from the former cold war enemies, United States and Russia. China emerges as an outlier, being both receptive to outside production and committed to a national approach. So does the United Kingdom, receptive to outside production and committed to an international approach.

In Chapters Five and Six, patterns of division, dominance and disruption are evinced from an analysis that moves beyond the world of academia and its sociological make-up to an examination of how topical issues in international law, such as the annexation of Crimea and the South China Sea arbitration, are viewed, internalised and interpreted by different international legal communities. In this Chapter, and in others where practical examples of difference are given, one can question the choices or even the framing (whether, for example, it can be said that matters of jurisdiction are *low politics* and whether there is such a thing as low politics, or whether what is meant is, simply, of low political interest) but by and large the examples given seem relevant, topical and illustrative.

In the Conclusions, the recurring themes of internationalism, globalism and nationalism are picked up again, with a rallying call to international lawyers to adopt a truly comparative, open and reflexive approach to their discipline.

There is so much to be commended about this book. It reads almost like a novel, such is its engaging style and wealth of information and insights into the collective minds of international legal communities. It opens up an overdue conversation on biases, hegemonic thought patterns and blind spots in the international legal community, of which one is superficially aware and yet one forgets all the time. It comes at a very opportune time, when the crisis of international law has opened also a period of self-reflection and investigation of the identity of the discipline and its practitioners.

The sociological approach invites the comparison, indeed pointed out by the author herself, with the influential study of the international arbitral community, *Dealing in Virtue*, by Yves Dezalay and Bryant G. Garth, who utilized Bourdieu's influential concepts of cultural capital and habitus to describe allegiances and developments in the international community of arbitrators. In fact, it might be appropriate here to quote what Bourdieu himself had to say, in his Introduction to the Dezalay and Garth study:

> The national members of this new international elite, a *noblesse de robe,* by exercising their talents in the major trans-national entities, humanitarian organizations, or even great legal multinationals, help to bring juridical forms to a higher level of universalization in and by a confrontation of different and at times opposed visions. Always at play in this confrontation, both as a weapon and as stakes, is the law (whether the rights of business, the rights of man, or the rights of businessmen) – that is, piously hypocritical reference to the universal (Pierre Bourdieu's Introduction to DEZALAY and GARTH, *Dealing in Virtue: International Commercial Arbitration and the Construction of a Transnational Legal Order,* Chicago, 1996, p. viii).

Beyond the specificities of the field examined by Dezalay and Garth and by Roberts respectively, which would attract different focus and methods, it is important not to lose sight, and Roberts never does, of the "piously hypocritical reference to the universal" that international legal communities across the world, but particularly the Western one, indulge in. At this point it seems useful to note that maybe one missing element to the otherwise impeccable analysis of this problematic universalism, and the role of comparative analysis to unpack the problematic aspects of international law, is the lack of a proper distinction between what "international", "global" and "universal" mean for the writer and the reality she describes. We should not forget that, in the classic definition by Jeremy Bentham, international law as a field signified the area where sovereign states (European, obviously) interacted as legally recognised sovereign actors and developed legal rules by which they agreed to be bound. There is very little that is universal, global or indeed coherent in this minimalist definition. States can agree a set of bilateral rules between themselves that will not be applicable outside that legal relation; interpretative strategies, scholarly attitudes and doctrinal schools should be able to differ in relation to the web of international rules that most often applies in that particular context. What is noticeable in this definition is that there is no pretense of substantive universality, but certainly of restrictive procedural universality (and of course a universality of belonging grounded in racist ideas of civilisation stages). Only certain countries can access international law, and only on those terms. It is true that, since the war especially, we have witnessed both an extension of the classic procedural universality (sovereign equality of states) and a universalisation of substantive rules of new creation, such as human rights rules. A more granular picture of the overlap and tension between these terms,

as well as the conscious decision to substitute one for the other (so that the traditional Euro-centric idea of the international is taken to signify the newer global/
universal) is crucial to understand the forces at play.

And here a second concept, clearly identified in the Volume but left untheo-
rised, is that of hegemony. This is a term that recurs at significant junctures of
this Volume, especially to identify "Western" hegemony, in a seamless overlap
with ideas of the universal. The Western international legal community constantly and iteratively operates an internationalisation of the particular because of its
hegemonic political power, which translates into cultural domination. But this
does not explain the whole phenomenon: as Roberts perceptively notes in her
comparative analysis, a country like France, which exercises a considerable hegemonic influence, through its language and its legal philosophy, does so from a
position of relative political and economic weakness. This is so because hegemonic structures deposit and calcify, surviving contingent political and economic
movements. Adopting a Gramscian approach to discussing the role of cultural
hegemony in the production and reproduction of the international in the legal
community would have yielded interesting insights, and the value of this work is
that it gives so much material to develop many strands of research (for a discussion of the concept of hegemony in Antonio Gramsci, see for example MOUFFE,
Gramsci and Marxist Theory, London, 1979, p. 186).

To my mind, another particularly useful study would be on the role of language. The Volume provides a wealth of material information, and insightful
commentary, on the role of hegemonic languages (and in international law, these
are English and French) in the universalisation of the language of international
law. I think it is important to keep the distinction between the language(s) *of* international law and international law *as* language, which are not always rigidly
separated in the Volume: for example, at p. 3, the author uses the metaphor of international law as "the world's Esperanto". This is good as far as international law
as a universal project of Western matrix is concerned, but it does not neatly map
over the predominance of English as the language of international law. In other
words, international law is not universal because it takes from all "languages"
but because it imposes, under the guise of universality, a language (English) and
with it a specific world view. This is because translations do not translate simply
words, but *worlds*. And to use English is to impose a specific outlook and world
view that is organically dependent from English. By this operation, even when
international law is translated, English, and with it the Western, Anglo-Saxon
approach to international law, remains the *measure of all things,* in the sense of
that against which all other is measured. Whether this is an argument against
having a *lingua franca* (which is inefficient and unyielding) or for multilingual-
ism in the international legal community (which is partially what happens with
the shared dominance of French and English, the old intellectual hegemon and
the new economic upstart) is contestable: the author clearly stakes her claim for
an enlightened multi-, or at least bi-, lingualism by the international legal community (I have to declare an interest here, as I co-edited a Volume in both English
and Spanish on international investment law in Latin America, where a conscious
decision was made by the editors to allow for this form of bilingualism: see

TANZI, ASTERITI, POLANCO LAZO and TURRINI (eds.), *International Investment Law in Latin America – Derecho Internacional de las Inversiones en América Latina*, Leiden, 2016).

As in other parts of the Book, it is the concept of *disruption* that introduces the possibility for a departure from the old hegemonic domination of European languages towards the chance for the outside to penetrate the old world of the traditional international community of lawyers and practitioners. This is one of the gems of the book, the repeated realisation, both in how the community is viewed and in what international law throws at us, of the existence of the *other* – be that the community of Russian international lawyers, of Chinese practitioners, or of space law or the China and Russia Joint Declaration – the Volume is filled with data, insights and points of view that rarely appear on the radar of Western international law *on their own terms*.

However, it can be said that international law has developed *dialects* jostling for hegemony, both in the sense of other languages developing their own interpretation of the language of international law (much like many European languages developed from a common Latin matrix) and in the sense that regional regimes (and here I am thinking especially of regional human rights regimes) developed their own flavour of international human rights law. This observation is germane to the realisation that the international legal regime, and the world, is undergoing both a process of increased multilateralisation and of retreat from multilateralism. These two processes, apparently inconsistent with one another, can easily be confused: so the point can be made both that the world is moving towards a multipolar model, and that the different poles are retreating from multilateralism (the author gives the example of Donald Trump's America). This is because, one wagers, a certain kind of liberal legal multilateralism is on the wane, while power multilateralism (as in, different loci of international power) is on the rise.

In agreeing with the author that international lawyers need to develop a better understanding of the other, and that international law as a project needs to be more open and more reflexive, I would add that international law by nature oscillates between cooperation and conflict and contingently, between its roles as *creating the global and mediating the national*. One can only hope that the conversation on this crucial relationship that this Volume started will be kept going.

ALESSANDRA ASTERITI*

PAOLO PALCHETTI (ed.), *L'incidenza del diritto non scritto sul diritto internazionale ed europeo*, Napoli, Editoriale Scientifica, 2016, pp. 448.

This volume edited by Paolo Palchetti collects the proceedings of the 20th Annual Conference of the Italian Society of International and European Union Law (SIDI), hosted in June 2015 by the University of Macerata and devoted to the role of unwritten law in international and EU law. The book does not at-

---

*Junior Professor of International Economic Law, Leuphana University in Lüneburg.

tempt to provide a comprehensive account of the relevance of unwritten law in contemporary international and transnational law; rather, it explores this subject through the lenses of specific topics, analysed by distinguished scholars of four fields of law: public international law, private international law, European Union law, and constitutional law. But the selectiveness in the choice of themes in no way diminishes the Book's ambitions. As the Editor explains in the Introduction, the question underlying the whole volume is a far-reaching one: that is, whether unwritten law is experiencing a period of decline or instead possesses an enduring vitality in the disciplines falling within the Society's purview (p. 11).

The book is divided into six Parts, each corresponding to one of the Conference sessions, and ends with Judge Giorgio Gaja's concise General Conclusions. The first part, dedicated to general reflections on the role of unwritten law in public international law, includes a brief introduction by Maria Laura Picchio Forlati and Chapters by Enzo Cannizzaro and Luigi Condorelli. The introduction presents some of the main reasons for the persisting relevance of unwritten sources in the international legal order and provides an overview of subject-matters that still remain primarily regulated by unwritten norms. In contrast to the approach frequently reaffirmed by the International Court of Justice (ICJ) and the stance taken by the International Law Commission in its works on the Identification of Customary International Law (on which, see the Focus in this Volume, with contributions by MILES, LA MANNA, CHIUSSI and GREEN), Cannizzaro argues against the conflation of the methods of ascertainment of customary international law with the processes leading to its formation. Citing extensively from the ICJ case law, he demonstrates that, while paying lip service to the necessity to prove the concurrent existence of state practice and *opinio juris*, the Court commonly resorts to an array of alternative techniques allowing for the assessment of customary norms by way of deduction. These techniques include: first, expanding the customary norms' originary field of operation by means of logical argumentation, so as to cover areas where state practice is lacking; second, drawing customary norms from a balance of colliding principles of international law; and third, affirming the existence of customary norms before a full consolidation of their constituent (objective and subjective) elements has taken place. Just as wide-ranging is Condorelli's analysis of the fortunes of unwritten law in contemporary international law, where written sources of law would appear to be progressively taking hold at the expense of custom. The author suggests an original reading of this ongoing process, which, in his view, would be a sign not of obsolescence of unwritten norms but of the rise of a particular category of custom, which he terms "*consuetudo scripta*" (p. 46): that is, provisions being, at the same time, engraved in treaty and customary in nature – a hypothesis which Condorelli corroborates by piling up relevant practice on the codification of custom in multiple areas of international law.

The second group of contributions deals with the role of unwritten law in international economic law. The topic is introduced by Elena Sciso. The trajectory of unwritten law in this area of international law, she contends, is descending: because states show a proclivity for treaty law in the regulation of their economic interactions, the space occupied by unwritten law is residual. Nonetheless, its role remains significant insofar as it can be used, most notably, to supplement or interpret treaty provisions and to define jurisdictional or procedural aspects in the practice of international tribunals. Giovanna Adinolfi zooms in on the practice of the World Trade Organization (WTO), where unwritten law can play both a "de-fragmenting" role, ensuring the unity between WTO law and the broader international legal environment, and a "systemic" role, allowing for an osmosis between WTO law and non-economic values that are, in origin, external to it (p. 76-77). On more technical grounds, the author describes two functions performed by unwritten law in the WTO system: it can either be resorted to for interpreting the provisions of the agreement, or be used directly as the applicable law. While the former use is undisputed (if only because the dispute settlement system is expressly empowered to do so by Article 3(2) of the Dispute Settlement Understanding) and has been emphatically taken on by the Appellate Body (according to which WTO law "is not to be read in clinical isolation from public international law": see *United States – Standards for Reformulated and Conventional Gasoline*, adopted on 29 April 1996, WT/DS2/AB/R, p. 17), the latter usage – more contested – is supported by the author as a means of filling the lacunae of WTO law. The use of unwritten law by international investment tribunals is the object of the book's only chapter in French, authored by Hervé Ascensio. Here also, general international law – regarded as a bringer of systemic coherence, although "*imparfaite*" (p. 130) – pervades the system in multiple ways: it may provide tribunals with applicable law, a possibility expressly acknowledged by, e.g., Article 42 of the ICSID Convention; it may be relevant in the interpretation of treaty provisions, as a source of "*enrichissement du tissu normatif*" (p. 124); or it may furnish principles and values guiding the future development of international investment law.

The third Part, on the role of unwritten law in international human rights law and international criminal law, consists of two Chapters, respectively exploring the jurisprudence of the European Court of Human Rights (ECtHR) and of the International Criminal Court (ICC). In the former Chapter, Massimo Starita argues that the ECtHR manages the relationship between the Convention and general international law by seeking a balance between two competing factors: the "Convention's special character as a human rights treaty", and the obligation to "take the relevant rules of international law into account" (pp. 140-141, quoting from *Cudak v. Lithuania*, Application No. 15869/02, Judgment of 23 March 2010, para. 56). He then identifies four models of interaction, reflecting as many points of balance: a model based on a broadly-framed presumption of conformity of the Convention with general international law; an antithetical model whereby the ECtHR knowingly departs, *sic et simpliciter*, from international custom; a model by which the Court considers itself bound, in principle, to ensure conformity to the unwritten norm, but in fact limits this norm's operation by carving exceptions based on the specificities of the Convention; and a model whereby general international law is but one of many factors to be weighed in the proportionality test. In the second Chapter of this Part, Beatrice Bonafè investigates the ICC's approaches against the broader backdrop of the doctrinal debate on the role of unwritten law in international criminal law. She notes that, although the Rome Statute manifests a "certain preference" for written over unwritten law (p. 165), several of its provisions allow the Court to resort to general international law, including, most notably, Article 21(1)(b) and (c), referring to "principles and rules of international law" and to "general principles of law derived from national legal systems", and Article 21(3), establishing an obligation of conformity of all applicable law to "internationally recognized human rights". Having demonstrated that unwritten law is far from marginalised in the Court's jurisprudence, the author concludes that, no statute of international criminal tribunals being a self-contained regime, all such tribunals must strike a balance between the constraints deriving from their constitutive instruments and the search for uniformity and coherence in the applicable law (p. 184).

The fourth Part, dealing with the status of unwritten norms of international law in the Italian legal system, is the book's shortest and only comprises a short introduction by Edoardo Greppi and a Chapter by Roberto Bin. Both authors – each from the perspective of his own field of scholarship – concentrate on Judgment No. 238 of 22 October 2014, in which the *Corte costituzionale* refused to conform to the judgment rendered by the International Court of Justice (ICJ) in *Jurisdictional Immunities of the State* (*Germany v. Italy: Greece Intervening, Judgment, ICJ Reports, 2012*, p. 99). Greppi outlines the key stages of the judicial saga and identifies the main issues arising from an international law viewpoint: namely, the consequences of non-compliance with an ICJ judgment, and the problematic relationship between the principle of state immunity and international human rights law. Bin, on the other hand, discusses the significance of Judgment No. 238 for Italian constitutional law. After an analysis of the legislative history of Article 10(1), of the Italian Constitution (providing for the automatic incorporation of general international law) aimed at clarifying the exact scope of this provision, the author directs a critical eye at the genesis of the doctrine of "counter-limits" and at the way the *Corte costituzionale* applied it in 2014. In particular, he focuses on the Court's method of identifying which (international) norms may be subject to its scrutiny, on the relationship between the doctrine of "counter-limits" and the balancing of rights, and on the interactions between Judgment No. 238 and the prerogatives of the Italian legislature and executive.

The fifth Part is concerned with the function unwritten law plays in EU private international law (PIL). In the introductory remarks, Angelo Davì points out that the general principles of European PIL are comprised of both principles traditionally informing PIL and principles specific to EU law. Such principles, that will remain unwritten until they are codified in a prospective "Rome 0" Regulation, bring coherence to the system and may be used to fill the gaps in the law (p. 211). In the first of the three chapters comprising this part, Rainer Hausmann aims to single out the key general principles of EU PIL by using as testing ground the practice concerning three general questions: namely, connecting factors, the problem of qualification, and the concept of universality in its interplay with the issues raised by the *renvoi*. The examination leads the author to conclude that the guiding axiom of EU PIL is not so much identifying the closest connection as it is providing European citizens with better judicial protection. This is especially evident in the strengthening of the principle of party autonomy, which Hausmann traces back to the aims of improving legal certainty and promoting mobility within the Union (p. 240). The principles of EU PIL in the field of successions are the focus of Roberta Clerici's Chapter, which analyses in detail the normative axioms underlying the EU Succession Regulation, No. 650/2012, adopted on 4 July 2012 and entered into force on 17 August 2015. She addresses, in particular, the implications of the principles of the unity of succession, of party autonomy, and of effective coordination between legal systems, as well as the restrictions that the Regulation places on each of them. This Part's last Chapter, written by Antonio Leandro, ponders the role of the principle of due process in European civil procedure law. The author defines this principle as a "vessel of rights" accorded to the parties (loosely translated from the Italian "*involucro di diritti*"), serving the cause of the promotion of substantive, and not merely procedural, rights (p. 260). He then proceeds to a more precise assessment of this principle's corollaries by evaluating, *inter alia*, the influx of ECtHR case law on this area of EU law, as well as its implications for the plaintiff's right of access to justice and the defendant's right to certainty and predictability.

The sixth and last Part of the book concerns the status of unwritten law in EU law. This part, which has no introduction, consists of three chapters respectively authored by Francesco Munari, Ornella Porchia and Chiara Amalfitano. Munari delves into the interactions between the extraterritorial application of European competition law and the customary international law norms regarding the exercise of jurisdiction. After outlining the relevant international legal framework, he moves on to an analysis of the EU practice on the extraterritorial application of competition law – either based on the theory of the "single economic entity" or on the so-called "implementation theory" – and compares it with the relevant US practice. The study leads the author to contend that states' choices in the field under consideration seem to depend exclusively on the values that that they wish to protect (p. 346). Porchia's Chapter explores the role of unwritten law in the functioning of EU institutions. While acknowledging that this theme may include two distinct aspects, i.e. the role of legal principles (such as the principle of loyal cooperation, or that of *effet utile*) and the practice of EU institutions, she chooses to focus entirely on the latter. Such category – consisting of both binding and non-binding behaviours – turns out to intertwine in a peculiar way with written law, so much so that Porchia resorts to the newly coined concepts of "law not yet written" and "quasi-written law" to describe the impact that the practices under scrutiny may exercise on the subsequent development of EU written law (p. 371). Finally, Amalfitano deals with the role played by unwritten law in the definition of fundamental rights within the post-Lisbon EU legal order. The main focus here is on the relevance retained by general principles of law – the source of unwritten law "*par excellance*" in EU law (p. 373) – concerning human rights after the enshrinement of large swathes thereof in the Nice Charter. Amalfitano demonstrates that this relevance is very much significant, the EU judiciary frequently relying on general principles of law not only in connection with the rights set forth by the Charter, but also as self-standing sources of human rights. This last scenario may occur where the Charter is not applicable *ratione temporis* or *personae*, or with regard to human rights which have been devised in the jurisprudence of the Court of Justice after the conclusion of the Charter.

As is clear from this short description, the book under review provides a wide variety of information on the role of unwritten law in international and EU law. Despite the editorial choice to focus on a limited number of specific subjects and not to aim for comprehensiveness (an understandable choice indeed, given the vastness of the Conference theme), the range of topics covered by the contributors, as well as the number of vantage points from which such topics are observed, are undoubtedly remarkable and probably cannot be matched by any other publication dealing with this subject from the perspective of just one field of law. For these reasons, this book represents a valuable resource for the scholars of public and private international law and EU law, and will certainly provide many of them with useful food for thought.

As regards the scope of the book, however, one cannot fail to notice a certain imbalance between its various Parts and Chapters – a two-fold imbalance, to be precise. Firstly, while some Parts collect Chapters that are very general in scope, the focus of other Parts tends to be quite specific (and often highly so). This causes a number of general issues not to be covered in the book, including, just to give a few examples, the role of customary international law in the EU legal order, or the relevance of general international law in the practice of the Italian courts in cases other than Judgment No. 238 of 2014 (which, after all, is only an exception, however significant, and not the rule). In the opinion of the present reviewer, the book would have benefitted considerably from a more thorough coverage of the general aspects of the use of unwritten law in the various fields of study. By contrast, the choice to focus often on specific issues does not appear to do full justice to the far-reaching question that the book aspires to answer. Secondly (but related to the first issue), the length and composition of the various Parts are also diverse. Most notably, only four Parts out of six include an introduction; moreover, the fourth Part only includes one Chapter, while the following two Parts include three each. This is probably due to the circumstance that, unfortunately, not all Conference presentations have been transformed into book chapters. This feature, too, to some extent undermines the unity of the book.

The reader will also probably miss a longer and more comprehensive final chapter. As Giorgio Gaja pointedly observes in his three-page final remarks, which confine themselves to summarising the main points raised in the book's six sections, a Conference so rich in ideas would have deserved more extensive conclusions (p. 435). In particular, one would have appreciated an attempt to reconcile on a theoretical plane the two main themes that run through the book, i.e. unwritten law as source of systemic coherence versus the latent (or patent) uncertainty in its delineation. As a matter of fact, this book seems to suggest that, depending on the observer and on how close one zooms in, unwritten law can be conceived as a source of either coherence or confusion: while specialists in specific disciplines look at it with the hope to find antidotes to fragmentation and rational guidelines for future development (in one word: order), scholars studying it from up close tend to describe it as an inherently hazy phenomenon and struggle to comprehend its constituents, contents and effects. So much so that Cannizzaro concludes the first Chapter of the book by implicitly quoting Heisenberg's uncertainty principle (p. 41), thus leaving the reader to wonder if

– notwithstanding the specialists' overall optimistic views on the defragmenting role of unwritten law – indeterminacy ultimately constitutes a fundamental feature of (unwritten) law as much as of (quantum mechanical) reality.

In conclusion, this book's ambition to give an all-round answer to the "grand question" described in the Introduction (i.e. whether or not international law and EU law are witnessing a decline of unwritten sources of law) cannot be considered unsuccessful. However, although many sectoral answers are provided, it is a matter of some regret that the task of bringing such answers to unity is left entirely to the reader. By doing so, the risk is run of having as many answers to the aforementioned "grand question" as there are readers – score one more for Heisenberg!

PIERFRANCESCO ROSSI[*]

ALEXANDER PROELSS (ed.), AMBER ROSE MAGGIO, EIKE BILTZA and OLIVER DAUM (assistant eds.), *United Nations Convention on the Law of the Sea: A Commentary*, München, Oxford and Baden-Baden, C. H. Beck/Hart/Nomos, 2017, pp. LI-2617

The Commentary on the United Nations Conventions on the Law of the Sea (UNCLOS) edited by Alexander Proelss is a valuable volume for scholars, researchers and experts interested in international law.

More particularly, it fills a gap in the academic literature. Indeed, while it is true that recent handbooks or studies on the law of the sea abound, a new article-by-article commentary on the entire Convention and its nine Protocols seemed necessary 35 years after the final session of the Third UN Conference on the Law of the Sea at Montego Bay, and 23 years after the entry into force of the Convention. There are two main reasons for this. Firstly, currently available handbooks do not devote enough attention to UNCLOS Articles that until now have been rarely applied, so an updated study appears to be useful. Secondly, a new analysis that takes account of recent developments is useful also with regard to the Articles that, on the other hand, have formed the subject-matter of decisions of international or national courts, or on which the practice of states and international organisations is based, since even the seven-volume *Commentary on the United Nations Convention on the Law of the Sea* edited by Myron H. Nordquist, Satya N. Nandan and Shabtai Rosenne, published between 1985 and 2012, is now outdated.

Another asset of the Commentary is its thoroughness. The volume has been excellently, meticulously coordinated by Professor Alexander Proelss and his collaborators and includes a table of cases (pp. XXXI-L) and a detailed index (pp. 2553-2617). The same 3-section pattern – I Purposes and Functions; II Historical Background; III Elements – has been used for every Article of the

---

[*] Ph.D., University of Napoli "Federico II".

Convention, providing: the text of the provision; a bibliography (almost exclusively in English); documents and a commentary (with footnotes).

And we should not overlook that the Commentary was prepared by some of the most distinguished scholars of the law of the sea, who were able to skilfully unravel the complexities of the Convention, which, as noted by Judge Golitsyn in the Foreword, "is a 'living instrument' and is subject to an ongoing process of change and adaption to new challenges" (p. V); a process which is still in progress, as demonstrated by the General Assembly's decision of 24 December 2017 (A/RES/72/249) to convene an intergovernmental conference to negotiate a binding international legal instrument under the UNCLOS on the conservation and sustainable use of marine biological diversity of areas beyond national jurisdiction. Besides, as emphasised by Judge Golitsyn, "progressive development of the legal regime established by the Convention is [...] not limited to the adoption of new legal instruments. It is also accomplished through interpretative implementation of the Convention" (p. V).

Thus, the authors have duly taken into account evolving practice, as well as the copious body of case law, both national and international, in this area.

So, just to give some examples, in his comment to Article 194(5), under which the measures taken by states to protect and preserve the marine environment "shall include those necessary to protect and preserve rare or fragile ecosystems as well as the habitat of depleted, threatened or endangered species, and other forms of marine life", Detlef Czybulka focuses on the 1992 Convention on Biological Diversity (CBD), on the ruling of 12 July 2016 of the arbitral tribunal in the *South China Sea case* (*Philippines* v. *China*) – "[...] An 'ecosystem' is not defined in the Convention, but internationally accepted definitions include that in article 2 of the CBD, which defines ecosystem to mean 'a dynamic complex of plant, animal and micro-organism communities and their non-living environment interacting as a functional activity'. The Tribunal has no doubt from the scientific evidence before it that the marine environments where the allegedly harmful activities took place in the present dispute constitute 'rare or fragile ecosystems' [...]" (para. 945) – and on other radical developments in this field since 1982 (pp. 1309-1315).

In his comment to Article 292, Tullio Treves examines the procedure for the prompt release of vessels and their crews in the light of the important case law of the International Tribunal for the Law of the Sea, which has had the opportunity to rule on a number of thorny issues, such as the effects of the confiscation of a foreign vessel that has been ordered by a domestic court, or the identification of any non-financial security (pp. 1881-1892).

Even from these brief remarks, it should be clear that the book is an excellent tool for legal practitioners and scholars of international law of the sea wishing to deepen their knowledge of this field. In addition, it has the great advantage of offering in-depth analyses of all provisions of the Convention and its protocols in a single, user-friendly volume.

ROBERTO VIRZO*

---

*Associate Professor of International law, University of Sannio.

INDEX*

---

* This Index has been compiled by Daniele Amoroso. The most significant judicial cases and legal instruments cited throughout the volume have also been included.